ALSO BY PETER COZZENS

The Earth Is Weeping:
The Epic Story of the Indian Wars for the American West

Shenandoah 1862:
Stonewall Jackson's Valley Campaign

The Army and the Indian,
vol. 5 of *Eyewitnesses to the Indian Wars, 1865–1890*

The Long War for the Northern Plains,
vol. 4 of *Eyewitnesses to the Indian Wars, 1865–1890*

Conquering the Southern Plains,
vol. 3 of *Eyewitnesses to the Indian Wars, 1865–1890*

The Wars for the Pacific Northwest,
vol. 2 of *Eyewitnesses to the Indian Wars, 1865–1890*

The Struggle for Apacheria,
vol. 1 of *Eyewitnesses to the Indian Wars, 1865–1890*

The New Annals of the Civil War
(editor, with Robert I. Girardi)

Battles and Leaders of the Civil War, vol. 6 (editor)

Battles and Leaders of the Civil War, vol. 5 (editor)

General John Pope: A Life for the Nation

The Military Memoirs of General John Pope
(editor, with Robert I. Girardi)

The Darkest Days of the War: The Battles of Iuka and Corinth

The Shipwreck of Their Hopes: The Battles for Chattanooga

This Terrible Sound: The Battle of Chickamauga

No Better Place to Die: The Battle of Stones River

TECUMSEH AND THE PROPHET

TECUMSEH
AND THE
PROPHET

THE SHAWNEE BROTHERS
WHO DEFIED A NATION

Peter Cozzens

ALFRED A. KNOPF · NEW YORK · 2020

THIS IS A BORZOI BOOK
PUBLISHED BY ALFRED A. KNOPF

www.aaknopf.com

Knopf, Borzoi Books, and the colophon
are registered trademarks of Penguin Random House LLC.

Library of Congress Cataloging-in-Publication Data
Names: Cozzens, Peter, [date] author.
Title: Tecumseh and the Prophet : the Shawnee brothers who defied a nation / Peter Cozzens.
Description: First edition. | New York : Alfred A. Knopf, 2020. | "This is a Borzoi book"—
Title page verso. | Includes bibliographical references and index.
Identifiers: LCCN 2019052436 (print) | LCCN 2019052437 (ebook) |
ISBN 9781524733254 (hardback) | ISBN 9781524733261 (epub)
Subjects: LCSH: Tecumseh, Shawnee Chief, 1768–1813. | Tenskwatawa, Shawnee Prophet. |
Shawnee Indians—United States—Biography. | Shawnee Indians—United States—Social
conditions—18th century. | Shawnee Indians—United States—Social conditions—19th century.
| Shawnee Indians—Wars—United States. | Indians of North America—Wars—1750–1815. |
Indians of North America—Government relations—1789–1869.
Classification: LCC E99.S35 C69 2020 (print) | LCC E99.S35 (ebook) |
DDC 977.004/9731700922 [B]—dc23
LC record available at https://lccn.loc.gov/2019052436
LC ebook record available at https://lccn.loc.gov/2019052437

Jacket images: (left) Tecumseh (detail), by Benson John Lossing after Pierre Le Dru.
Toronto Public Library; (right) *Ten-sqat-a-way, the Open Door, "Shawnee Prophet"* (detail),
by George Catlin. Gilcrease Museum, Tulsa, Oklahoma.
Jacket design by Jenny Carrow
Maps by Rob McCaleb at Mapping Specialists

Manufactured in the United States of America

First Edition

For Eric

"A wind blew west over the Atlantic, driving before it a frothy foam or scum. It blew this scum, which was evil and unclean, upon the shore of the American continent, and the scum took form. The form that it took was that of a white man—of many white people, both men and women; wherever the scum lodged on the shore of the continent, it took this form."

—TENSKWATAWA, the Shawnee Prophet, to his followers[1]

"The being within, communing with past ages, tells me that once, nor until lately, there was no white man on this continent; that it then all belonged to red men, children of the same parents, placed on it by the Great Spirit that made them, to keep it, to traverse it, to enjoy its productions, and to fill it with the same race, once a happy race, since made miserable by the white people who are never contented but always encroaching.

"The way, and the only way, to check and to stop this evil, is for all the red men to unite in claiming a common and equal right in the land, as it was at first, and should be yet; for it never was divided but belongs to all for the use of each. For no part has a right to sell, even to each other, much less to strangers—those who want all and will not do with less."

—TECUMSEH in council with Gov. William Henry Harrison[2]

Contents

Preface   xi

Maps   xvii

Prologue Dawn of the Long Knives   3

PART ONE

1 The Great Awakening   11

2 A Restless People   32

3 A Turbulent Youth   44

4 A Nation Divided   52

5 War and Wanderings   68

6 Out from the Shadows   88

7 The Making of a Chief   110

8 A Culture in Crisis   129

PART TWO

9 A Prophet Arises   149

10 Black Sun   170

11 Greenville Interlude   189

12 A Double Game   208

13 One Treaty Too Many   227

14 No Difficulties Deter Him   240

15 Southern Odyssey   262

16 The Prophet Stumbles   275

17 From the Ashes of Prophetstown   290

PART THREE

18 Into the Maelstrom   311

19 Kindred Spirits   335

20 A Man of Mercy   346

21 An Adequate Sacrifice to Indian Opinion   371

22 Death on the Thames   386

23 Twilight of the Prophet   412

APPENDIX The Indian World of the Shawnee Brothers   437

Acknowledgments   441

Notes   443

Bibliography   485

Index   509

Preface

Gov. William Henry Harrison of the Indiana Territory was amazed. In a decade on the frontier implementing a fiercely acquisitive government land policy, he had met with scores of Indian chiefs, some defiant, others malleable. Never, however, had he encountered a native leader like the Shawnee chief Tecumseh, the man he considered his principal opponent in the fight for the Northwest, as present-day Ohio, Illinois, Indiana, Michigan, and Wisconsin were then known. After a contentious council with Tecumseh in July 1811, Harrison penned a remarkable tribute to him, arguably the most effusive praise a government official ever offered an American Indian leader. Tecumseh had parried Harrison's every verbal thrust, eloquently defending his refusal to relinquish what Harrison considered "one of the fairest portions of the globe, [then] the haunt of a few wretched savages."

There was nothing remotely wretched about Tecumseh, however. As Harrison told the secretary of war, "The implicit obedience and respect which the followers of Tecumseh pay to him is really astonishing, and more than any other circumstance bespeaks him one of those uncommon geniuses which spring up occasionally to produce revolutions and overturn the established order of things. If it were not for the vicinity of the United States, he would, perhaps, be the founder of an empire that would rival in glory that of Mexico or Peru." Harrison marveled at the vigor with which the Shawnee chief pursued his dream of an Indian union. "No difficulties deter him. His activity and industry supply the want of letters. For four years he has been in constant motion. You see him today on the Wabash and in a short time you hear of him on the shores of Lake Erie or Michigan, or on the banks of the Mississippi, and wherever he goes he makes an impression favorable to his purposes."

Harrison's testimonial encapsulates the talents of this passionate and indefatigable co-architect, with his younger brother Tenskwatawa, of the greatest pan-Indian confederation the westering American Republic would ever confront. Their movement reached across nearly half of what was then the United States, from the icy upper reaches of the Mississippi River to the steamy bottomlands of the lower Alabama River. No other Indian leaders enjoyed such a broad appeal, and none would ever pose a graver threat to American expansion than Tecumseh and Tenskwatawa. At the height of their appeal, the Shawnee brothers mustered twice as many warriors as would chiefs Sitting Bull and Crazy Horse on the Little Bighorn River some three generations later.

Fables flower where facts are few or forgotten. Myths endure when people want to believe them. So it was with the Shawnee brothers. Tecumseh would come to personify for Americans all that was great and noble in the Indian character as non-Indians (whites, in the parlance of the time) perceived greatness and nobility. The reasons for this are obvious. Tecumseh advocated a political and military alliance to oppose U.S. encroachment on Indian land. This was something that whites could readily comprehend. Tecumseh, who was first and foremost a political leader, acted as *they* would have acted under similar circumstances. Tenskwatawa, on the other hand, offered a divinely inspired solution to Indian land dispossession and cultural dissolution, drawing on native tradition that was beyond white understanding. Tenskwatawa's person also repulsed whites. He was an unappealing, disfigured ex-alcoholic who as a boy had accidentally shot his right eye out with an arrow; a "man devoid of talent or merit, a brawling mischievous Indian demagogue," according to an Indian agent who knew the Shawnee brothers intimately. The same official admired Tecumseh as the exemplar of Shawnee manhood—a skilled hunter and cunning war leader, charitable, and an orator of rare eloquence. In a similar manner, history, biography, and folklore all came to deify Tecumseh and demonize his brother.

The historian Alvin M. Josephy's 1961 work *The Patriot Chiefs: A Chronicle of Indian Leadership* epitomized this tendency. Anticipating Dee Brown's seminal *Bury My Heart at Wounded Knee* by a decade, *The Patriot Chiefs* owed its considerable influence to Josephy's reputation as "the leading non-Indian writer about Native Americans," a standing that his service as an adviser on federal Indian policy to presidents Kennedy and Nixon cemented.[1] Josephy singled out Tecumseh as "the greatest of all the American Indian leaders, a majestic human who might have given all the Indians a nation of their own." He dismissed Tenskwatawa as a delusional charlatan, repeating a fabricated claim that Tecumseh tried to kill him after the Battle of Tippecanoe and advancing the equally fallacious charge that Tecumseh expelled his brother from their village to wander alone and forgotten thereafter.[2]

This unfortunate process of elevating Tecumseh at Tenskwatawa's expense continued with the 1992 release of Allan Eckert's massive and "entertaining blend of fact and fiction,"[3] *A Sorrow in Our Heart: The Life of Tecumseh*. Eckert incorporated an unconventional "hidden-dialogue"[4] technique to re-create the chief's conversations and thought. "A biography that succeeds better as fiction [and] embellishes the historical record to the point of being suspect," a reviewer observed, *A Sorrow in Our Heart* relegated Tenskwatawa to the role of a "sniveling conniver achieving renown largely through his brother's generosity."[5]

The British biographer John Sugden made enormous strides in resurrecting the historical Tecumseh with *Tecumseh: A Life*, published in 1997. Prodigiously researched, Sugden's work convincingly reconstructed Tecumseh's early years, a period that had eluded previous biographers. The comparatively scant source material for Tecumseh's life before 1805 compelled Sugden to infer certain of his activities, such as his presumed time among the Chickamauga Band of the Cherokee Indians of Tennessee. I found Sugden's chronology sufficiently persuasive that I have incorporated it into my own work. I owe an immense debt to his pioneering study, one that I cheerfully acknowledge.

While he resurrected much of the early historical Tecumseh, Sugden failed to give Tenskwatawa adequate credit for his role in creating and sustaining the Indian confederacy of the Shawnee brothers. He also neglected the nativist religious fervor that contributed to the emergence of Tenskwatawa and that he shaped into a coherent and enthralling doctrine. Nor does Sugden address the compelling evidence that Tecumseh truly believed his brother to be a divinely inspired prophet capable of communing with the Master of Life, or Great Spirit, and also embraced his creed; both are critical aspects of the Shawnee brothers' relationship that I explore in *Tecumseh and the Prophet*. The only biography of Tenskwatawa, R. David Edmunds's 1983 work *The Shawnee Prophet*, addresses something of the religious underpinnings of the Shawnee brothers' alliance. As I hope to demonstrate, Edmunds errs in contending that Tenskwatawa's influence vanished after the Battle of Tippecanoe in 1811.

I have sought to redress these and other imbalances in the historical perception of the Shawnee brothers. Simply put, without Tenskwatawa, there would have been no Tecumseh. Tenskwatawa's program, which aimed at the moral cleansing and spiritual rebirth of a united Indian people, gave rise to the alliance that Tecumseh later built upon for political and military purposes. The relationship between the brothers that emerges in my book is symbiotic in nature. During his lifetime, Tecumseh eventually dominated but never entirely replaced Tenskwatawa as leader of their pan-Indian confederacy.

Though they did not create the concept of pan-Indianism, the Shawnee brothers' achievements were prodigious. Before the Shawnee brothers, there had been prophetic movements and intertribal alliances against the French, British, and Americans in their turn. The Shawnee brothers themselves acknowledged the debt they owed the Ottawa war chief Pontiac and the Delaware mystic Neolin, who together had opposed British bullying of the Eastern Woodland tribes in the 1760s. The ad hoc confederacies of Pontiac and Neolin, and later of Chiefs Blue Jacket and Little Turtle had also blunted the white wave, but these were relatively localized movements. It was the Shawnee brothers who would emerge as truly transformative figures, able to unite adherents from more than a dozen tribes in confronting both the spiritual and physical menace the young American Republic posed to the Indian way of life. Their goal of a grand Indian alliance provides a window into the larger story of the turbulent early days of the United States, when American settlers spilled over the Appalachians and killed or intimidated Indians with a contemptuous disregard for treaty and law in their haste to exploit lands recently won from the British in the War of Independence. The violent treatment of the Indians and rampant lawlessness in the Old Northwest presaged the excesses of the American West half a century later and is the bloody bridge to that era, the story of which must be told if we are to appreciate the heritage of our nation's heartland.

Tecumseh and Tenskwatawa stepped onto the stage just as the young American Republic flexed its expansionist muscles. Indisputably, Tecumseh and Tenskwatawa were the most significant siblings in American Indian history. Giving Indians their due, it is only fair to conclude that the Shawnee brothers also were among the most influential siblings in the annals of America.

Here, presented together for the first time, are the interwoven lives of Tecumseh and the Shawnee Prophet. This book is their story, but I have tried to encompass also the events, personalities, and cultural and physical forces at play in their world. Let us begin, then, not with the birth of the elder brother Tecumseh, but with the tragic death of their father, Puckeshinwau, battling American colonists; Tecumseh was just six years old, and Tenskwatawa yet in his mother's womb. The loss of their father epitomized the disruption and disintegration of thousands of Indian families during this tragic and largely forgotten epoch in America's march westward.

List of Maps

MAP 1   The Lower Great Lakes and Upper Ohio Valley in 1768   18

MAP 2   The Shawnee Brothers' Country, 1774–1794   24

MAP 3   Eastern North America, 1792   66

MAP 4   Indian Land Cessions, 1803–1809   133

MAP 5   The United States, 1811   253

MAP 6   The Shawnee Brothers' Country, 1811   255

MAP 7   Tecumseh's Southern Odyssey, 1811   265

MAP 8   Battle of Tippecanoe, November 7, 1811   285

MAP 9   The Detroit Country, 1812   315

MAP 10   Theater of Operations, 1813   360

MAP 11   Battle of Fort Meigs, May 5, 1813   362

MAP 12   Retreat on the Thames River, October 1813   393

MAP 13   Battle of the Thames, October 5, 1813   405

TECUMSEH AND THE PROPHET

Dawn of the Long Knives

DAYBREAK, October 10, 1774. In dense forest, a column of 700 Shawnee and Mingo warriors uncoils into a ragged, mile-long line. Unlike years past, the warriors are not stalking game. Rather, they are preparing to strike 1,200 unsuspecting Virginia militiamen camped at Point Pleasant, a craggy triangle at the confluence of the Ohio and Great Kanawha rivers, approximately 150 miles southwest of modern Wheeling, West Virginia. A carpet of red and russet leaves deadens their footfalls. The warriors wear breechclouts, which are single pieces of cloth wrapped around the hips, buckskin leggings, and moccasins. A few also sport linen hunting shirts purchased from white traders. Most carry smoothbore muskets, tomahawks, scalping knives, and bow and arrows for use if their ammunition runs out. Silver rings dangle from their noses. Huge earrings hang on distended earlobes, framing faces painted in fierce patterns of red and black.

The leader of the war party, the Shawnee chief Cornstalk, would prefer to be elsewhere. Although the provocation had been immense, he had called for restraint. Virginians had flouted a royal proclamation prohibiting settlement on Indian land and instead spilled across the Kanawha River into the Kanawha Valley, part of the greater Kentucky country, all of which was prime Shawnee hunting ground. "I have with great trouble and pains prevailed on the foolish people amongst us to sit still and do no harm till we see whether it is the intention of the white people in general to fall on us," Cornstalk had told a British official, "and shall continue so to do in the hopes that matters may be settled." But the royal governor of Virginia, the Earl of Dunmore, who himself coveted Indian land for personal profit, had no expectation of a peaceful denouement. Frontier subjects, he wrote the Crown, despised treaties made with Indians, "whom they consider but little removed from the brute creation." So too did the Virginia aristocracy. With the spring thaw in 1774, surveyors representing George Washington, Patrick Henry, and other Tidewater elites staked large claims along the Ohio River. Waving away the royal edict against land grabs as a "temporary expedient to quiet the minds of the Indians," Washington told his personal surveyor not to worry.[1]

With the surveyors came settlers willing to wager their scalps on a scrap of land. For a time, Cornstalk succeeded in controlling his young warriors. They turned back white intruders with stern warnings but seldom harmed them. Then in April 1774 a gang of frontier ruffians butchered a small party of inoffensive Mingo men and women who had crossed the Ohio River to buy rum at a neighborhood grog shop. Other Mingoes who attempted to investigate were shot from their canoes. The dead included the sister and younger brother of the Mingo chief "Captain John" Logan, a longtime friend of the whites who, averred a pioneer who knew Logan well, represented "the best specimen of humanity, either white or red," that he had ever met.

The massacre shocked the colonies and the Crown. The young Virginia aristocrat Thomas Jefferson excoriated the supposed perpetrators. Hard words and hand-wringing, however, marked the extent of the white response. When the Crown's colonial justice proved empty, Logan sought revenge in the Indian fashion; he slayed just enough frontiersmen to even the score, taking care to exculpate the Shawnees from his bloody work. To the charred door of a ravaged cabin, Logan posted a succinct confession. "You killed my kin...then I thought I must kill too. The Indians is not angry [*sic*] only me."[2] Backcountry settlers saw matters otherwise. Misconstruing Chief Cornstalk's neutrality as hostile intent, Virginia militiamen destroyed a large Shawnee village in the Ohio country. They also laid waste to six Mingo towns.

The die was cast. Shawnee and Mingo war parties retaliated. Frontiersmen reciprocated. Havoc and horror rent the wilderness. As the frontier crumbled, Lord Dunmore mustered the militia to deal the Indians a two-pronged thrashing. No longer able to keep the peace, Chief Cornstalk assumed the mantle of supreme Shawnee war leader. He tried to forge a broad Indian alliance, but British threats and cajolery sidelined other tribes. And so in late September, Cornstalk sallied forth with his Shawnee and Mingo force to defend their lands. Calculating that his only chance lay in defeating Dunmore's armies before they could unite, Cornstalk turned his attention first to the command of Gen. Andrew Lewis, who was then creeping across the wilds of western Virginia toward Point Pleasant. Although outnumbered, Cornstalk had able Shawnee lieutenants, among them the rising star Puckeshinwau, already honored as both a war and a civil leader, offices the Shawnees rarely combined.[3]

The Indians hated the militiamen but respected their fighting prowess. They called the Virginians the "Long Knives" because of the butcher knives and short swords that they wielded with as much skill as the Indians did the tomahawk. Like Indian warriors, the Virginians were a colorful if undisciplined lot. A few of the officers wore regular uniforms, but most were clad in the same sort of hunting shirts, leather leggings, homemade breeches, broad-brimmed hats or animal-skin caps, and moccasins as their men. Each militiaman carried a flintlock long-rifle or English musket, a bullet pouch, and powder horn carved to individual taste. In addition to knives, many also tucked tomahawks into their belts. Well schooled in Indian warfare and raging with the Kentucky land-fever, the Virginians were impatient for the fray.[4]

This morning, however, they slumbered soundly, unaware of the approaching warriors. The night before, the Indians had slipped across the Ohio River in crude rafts beneath a cobalt sky, debouching on the rocky, timber-strewn Virginia riverbank four miles north of the militia camp. Cornstalk and his lieutenants oversaw the carefully choreographed battle preparations. Their warriors slept a few hours, leaning against trees or propped against forked poles, weapons at the ready. Hunters killed twelve deer and ritually sliced the venison under the watchful eyes of medicine men (spiritual and natural healers), who examined the roasted strips for spiritual purity before handing each warrior one piece. After eating, the men buried their blankets and shirts beneath leaves. Deploying in units of twenty, they each crammed four balls into their muskets to inflict maximum punishment at short range. They would tomahawk any survivors. Cornstalk selected the best marksmen to descend to the riverbank to pick off any Virginians desperate enough to plunge into the broad Ohio after the Indians sprang their trap.[5]

And then his plan unraveled. At dawn, October 10, 1774, two early-rising Virginians wandered into the forest to hunt deer. Instead they ran into the Indians. One militiaman crumpled, riddled with musket balls, but the other stumbled back into camp to sound the alarm. Instantly the drums beat to arms. The backwoodsmen rolled from their blankets, examined their flints and priming, and awaited orders.

Feigning composure, General Lewis lit his pipe. He blew a few puffs and then ordered two colonels to lead double columns of 150 men forward to discover the source of the commotion. Both officers fell in the first Indian volley. Concealed behind the trunks of maple and pine and in the tangled underbrush of the river bottom, the warriors dropped dozens of militiamen, screaming epithets at the "sons of bitches" and "white dogs" as they fired. Lewis pushed out reinforcements, and the combatants grappled at close quarters in the smoke-choked timber. "Hide where I would," a Virginian recalled, "the muzzle of some rifle was gaping in my face and the wild, distorted countenance of a savage was rushing towards me with uplifted tomahawk. The contest resembled more a circus of gladiators than a battle."[6]

After six hours of close combat, the two sides backed apart and traded fire from behind trees and fallen timber. Puckeshinwau and his fellow war leaders moved along the Indian line, exhorting their warriors to "lie close," "shoot well," and "fight and be strong." Near sunset, General Lewis occupied a high ridge that Cornstalk had neglected to secure. Stung by bullets from above their left flank and low on ammunition, the Indians melted back into the forest and recrossed the Ohio. The Virginians contented themselves with scalping fallen warriors and collecting souvenirs.[7]

It had been a bloody twelve hours. The Indians killed seventy-five Virginians and wounded another 140. Perhaps forty warriors died. Hoping to disguise their losses, the Indians rolled several of their dead into the river. The Virginians nevertheless collected thirty-two scalps. These they affixed to a post at Point Pleasant.[8]

The battle claimed just one prominent Indian, the Shawnee war leader Puckeshinwau. His thirteen-year-old son Cheeseekau, not yet a warrior, had accompanied him into action. After Puckeshinwau fell mortally wounded, Cheeseekau helped ease him back over the Ohio in a driftwood raft. Before dying, Puckeshinwau reputedly admonished his young son to preserve his family's honor, never reconcile with the Long Knives, and "in the future lead forth to battle his younger brothers" against them. Cheeseekau swore to obey. Puckeshinwau's warriors buried their chief deep in the forest.

Cheeseekau had accepted a heavy burden. He had three siblings, and his now-widowed mother was pregnant with triplets. Cheeseekau's favorite sibling, upon whom he would lavish most of his attention and who would best fulfill his father's last wish, was his six-year-old brother Tecumseh, the "Shooting Star."[9]

· PART ·

ONE

The Great Awakening

TECUMSEH'S FATHER had never lived in the land for which he fought and died. Nor had any Shawnee resided in the Kentucky country for nearly two decades prior to the Battle of Point Pleasant.

Puckeshinwau also had been a relative newcomer to the Ohio Valley village he had come to call home. The young war leader of a peripatetic Shawnee band, he grew to manhood in the heart of the Creek Indian confederacy, six hundred miles to the south, in what is today central Alabama. By 1759, however, the time seemed propitious for a move. White settlers were pressing the Creek country from the east, and Puckeshinwau's followers found the prospect of Shawnee unity captivating. Puckeshinwau went reluctantly, however. His first wife, since deceased, had been Creek, and he had adopted something of their ways. Methoataske, his second bride, belonged to a respected Shawnee family with ties to the Ohio bands, and she was anxious to head north.[1]

The southern Shawnees trekked hopefully toward the Ohio River Valley. So did the handful of Shawnees who lived in western Pennsylvania. All thought themselves headed for their ancestral homeland, presumably a country of peace and tribal unity beyond the reach of whites. Their destination, however, was the fault line between French and British interests, and as such was fated to become an imperial battleground.

The British had encouraged the Shawnees to assemble in the Ohio Valley, to "come home again, that you may become once more a people and not dispersed through the world." English agents claimed the French "[have] deceived you and scattered you about the woods, that they might have it in their power to keep you poor." As the brunt of mockery by other Algonquins, who derided them as "a people with nowhere a fire burning," the Shawnees found that the British beckons reinforced their own desire to return home.[2]

Then the fire engulfed them. Hoping to avoid entanglements with the whites, the Shawnees instead contributed to the onset of war when they persuaded their Miami Indian allies to settle near them and invite reputable Pennsylvania merchants to compete with French traders. The proposal made sense to the Miamis; the Ohio Valley had once been theirs, too. But France saw the Miamis and Shawnees as dangerous British surrogates who threatened its trade route between French Canada and Louisiana. Descending on the Ohio Valley from the Great Lakes, the French and their Indian allies built a fort at the site of modern Pittsburgh and in November 1755 slaughtered a large British force under Gen. Edward Braddock sent to expel them. Siding with the now-dominant French, Shawnee warriors ravaged the Pennsylvania and Virginia frontiers. Slaughtering hundreds of settlers, they made the name *Shawnee* synonymous with unbridled savagery. A French officer, horrified at their apparent cruelty, lamented that the Shawnees had become "the instrument of hatred between two powerful rivals, as also that of [their] own destruction."[3]

Which nearly occurred. When the British conquered Canada and defeated the French in 1763, Algonquin tribes like the Shawnees paid dearly for their French alliance. The Indians had hoped that the victorious British would abandon their frontier forts and, like the French before them, become a benevolent father who lavished presents on his red children. Unfortunately for the Indians, the recently ended European Seven Years' War had depleted the British treasury, and the Crown economized at their expense. The gifts of gunpowder and lead on which the Indians had come to depend for the hunt ceased; let the natives revert to bows and arrows, the British reasoned. The Indians, however, wanted the best of both worlds—European goods with no whites in their country except traders.

No sooner had the British imposed their austerity regime than a smallpox epidemic devastated Shawnee and Miami villages. Puckeshinwau and his family escaped unscathed, but scores succumbed. Compounding the Indians' despair, the British demanded they release hundreds of white captives, few of whom wanted to repatriate. Adoptive families were ripped apart. Meanwhile, as loved ones departed, unwanted whites intruded, a two-way traffic the British did not intend. Ignoring the Crown prohibition, hundreds of rural poor crossed the Alleghenies to scratch out crude homes along the upper reaches of the Ohio River.

An English missionary characterized the incoming frontier rabble as "white savages [who] subsist by hunting," an assessment with which the British military agreed. "Lamentably dissolute in their morals," these otherwise impoverished rascals had an abundant hatred of Indians and an ample supply of rum, with which they plied the Indians to rob them of their furs. Chiefs protested to no avail, and the corrosive effect of liquor rendered their warriors restive.[4]

The turmoil spared the eastern Ohio country, where the Delaware "grandfathers" of the Shawnees resided. There nevertheless lurked dangers and evil portents enough to set some Delawares to pondering. None contemplated the Delaware destiny more profoundly than did an enigmatic mystic named Neolin, who feared the white man's diseases, abhorred the niggardly and arrogant British officials who treated the Indians as infants, and understood that colonists wanted Indian land. Perhaps, he speculated, in straying from traditional ways, the Indians themselves were to blame for their misfortunes. One night, alone by his wigwam fire, Neolin beheld a man materialize from the flames to tell him that "these things he was thinking were right."[5]

The spectral visitor escorted Neolin to the gates of eternity, where the Great Spirit revealed to Neolin the path to righteousness. From that night forward, Neolin was a prophet (or an imposter, depending on the source). Clutching a hieroglyphic-painted deerskin and weeping ceaselessly, he roamed his village exhorting passersby to hear and see the Great Spirit's teachings.

Neolin offered a selective return to the old ways interwoven with promises of heavenly rewards for the faithful and damnation for skeptics. (Heaven, the Delaware Prophet assured his disciples, contained only Indians.) Within months his doctrine spread from the Ohio Valley to the Great Lakes. By early 1763, every Algonquin tribe had its devotees, awakened to a religious and cultural movement that super-seded tribal and village loyalties.

Neolin taught that Indians must abandon their sacred medicine bags, which were the playthings of evil spirits, and instead pray directly to the Great Spirit, better known to the Shawnees as the Master of Life. They must forswear rum and purify themselves by drinking and vomiting an herbal tea. The Shawnees drank and spewed the concoc-tion with such enthusiasm that their village of Wakatomica became known to white traders as "vomit town." Regurgitating herbs was one thing, but few Indians took seriously Neolin's admonition to abstain from sexual intercourse far more frequently than the Indian belief in the competing sources of male and female power dictated, nor his insistence that fire made with steel and flint was impure; flames, he said, should be started only by rubbing sticks together. Easier to accept because it entailed no immediate sacrifice was Neolin's call for the gradual abandonment of European trade goods and firearms, a seven-year transition from guns to bows and arrows.

The Indians would need their muskets in the near term because Neolin also preached a call to arms against the whites, prophesying that there would be "two or three good talks and then war." The whites would be wiped from the continent, game animals would return in abundance, earth would become an Indian paradise, and the direct route to heaven would reopen. With Neolin's appeal, pan-Indianism was born in the Old Northwest.[6]

In April 1763, near the British fort at Detroit, the Ottawa war chief Pontiac imparted a watered-down version of Neolin's moral code to a council of Indian allies. Indians could drink rum, Pontiac assured his listeners, just not to excess, and men might enjoy sexual relations, but only with their wife, and with one wife only. Finally, it was just the British colonists who were enemies of the Indians; the Great Spirit looked favorably upon the French, who after all had implicitly offered to support war against the British. Translating Neolin's call to arms into action, Pontiac laid siege to Fort Detroit. He sent black wampum belts, symbols of the call to war, to the tribes of the Ohio Valley. One British post after another fell until only three remained. It was a con-flict of unbridled violence. Drunken Ottawas tortured and ritualistically ate captives; renegade colonists slaughtered innocent Indians. The Shawnee chief Cornstalk took a huge war party deep into western Virginia, killing and seizing civilians with abandon. Nearly 2,000 British soldiers and colonial civilians perished in the opening months of Pontiac's War, but Forts Detroit, Niagara, and Pitt held out, and the Crown rushed in reinforcements. A stalemate ensued that neither side could break. Unable to defeat Pontiac, the British elevated him to the status of chief of all Algonquins, an office anathema to every Indian except Pontiac. In 1766 he made peace with the British. The war sputtered to a close, but Pontiac had forfeited his standing among the Indians. He went into exile deep in the Illinois country, and three years later an irate warrior murdered him on the fetid streets of a small French trading village. In accepting the British proffer of supreme leadership of the still fiercely independent Algonquins, Pontiac had reached too high.[7]

Tales of Neolin and Pontiac, of the prophecies of the Delaware seer and the martial talents of his Ottawa disciple, would be told around Indian campfires for years to come. They were heroes for boys to venerate, perhaps eventually to emulate.

Besides prideful stories, the Shawnees gained nothing from Pontiac's War. The British compelled them to surrender adopted white members of the tribe, and the reinvigorated Iroquois, who had sided with the British, demanded the Shawnees abandon their claim to hunting grounds south of the Ohio River, comprising most of present-day Kentucky and West Virginia. In November 1768 the Iroquois in turn ceded these lands to the British in the Treaty of Fort Stanwix. The country west and north of the Ohio, which the British lumped under the rubric "Indian Territory," was to be inviolate, the Ohio River boundary permanent. Barred from the proceedings, the Shawnees denounced the Fort Stanwix Treaty as barefaced thievery. They ceased to recognize Iroquois leadership, endeavored to build a coalition independent of the Iroquois, and forswore addressing the British as fathers. Shawnee scouting parties patrolled the Kentucky country, on the watch for white interlopers.[8]

The trespassers came through the Cumberland Gap or down the Ohio River: hardscrabble farmers in search of better land, fugitives from justice, and the congenitally restless of slack moral fiber, while from the comfort of their Virginia estates land speculators deployed surveyors to finagle title to the Indian lands.[9]

Among the first intruders was an impoverished North Carolinian named Daniel Boone and six other poor whites. Crossing the Cumberland Gap in early 1769, they slaughtered the teeming game animals wantonly without encountering a single Indian until December, when a group of Shawnees under an English-speaking war leader named Captain Will burst into their predawn winter bivouac. "The time of our sorrow was now arrived," mused Boone. Instead of meting out the expected torture and death, the Shawnees behaved "in the friendliest manner," simply confiscating his party's furs with an admonishment never to return. "Now, brothers," declared Captain Will, "go home and stay there. Don't come here anymore, for this is the Indians' hunting ground, and all the animals, skins, and furs are ours. And if you are so foolish as to venture here again, you may be sure the wasps and yellow-jackets will string you severely."

The Shawnees had shown remarkable restraint, but they were mistaken if they thought their painted faces, flashing tomahawks, and formidable war clubs would deter Boone and his companions. No sooner had the North Carolinians reached home than they made plans to return.[10]

The Iroquois betrayal at Fort Stanwix and the first wave of white emigrants left the Ohio Shawnees to navigate frightening but familiar waters—just become settled in one place, only to have it threatened. Tribal councils debated the viability of the Ohio Valley as a permanent home. Many were for pulling up stakes and relocating west of the Mississippi River. Not only were whites threatening the eastern periphery of the Ohio Valley, but the region also was fast repopulating with other Indians, stressing a game supply already depleted by overhunting for the trade in furs and skins. Relative to the British colonial population on the eastern seaboard, Indian numbers in the Ohio Valley were pitifully small, however. At the time of the Treaty of Fort Stanwix, several tribes called the region home, but disease and warfare had taken a heavy toll on all of them. The Shawnees, numbering just 1,500, claimed most of the southern half of what is today Ohio. The Delawares, 3,500 in all, occupied eastern Ohio and northern Pennsylvania nearly to the Delaware River. Unlike the Shawnees, they had no interest in Kentucky.

Immediately north of the Shawnees were the Wyandots. Remnants of the once mighty Huron confederacy, they had been reduced by warfare and disease to 1,250 members. Although their numbers were small and they were not Algonquins, their prestige was such that many Algonquins deferred to them on boundary and other intertribal questions. The northwestern border of the Shawnee country touched land claimed by the Ottawas, most of whose 5,000 members resided in what is today western Michigan. West of the Shawnees were the 1,500 Miamis. The Shawnees did not yet have much contact with other tribes of the Great Lakes region. The total Indian population of the Great Lakes and Ohio Valley in 1768 was approximately 60,000. The thirteen British colonies numbered nearly 2 million. The odds against the Indians were bad, and with high birth rates among the whites and unabated immigration to the colonies, they would only get worse.[11]

Tecumseh's father Puckeshinwau stood with those Shawnees who were opposed to leaving Ohio. And by 1768 his words carried weight. He had won considerable renown in Pontiac's War and may also have become the head chief of the Kispokos, one of five tribal divisions. His wife Methoataske belonged to the Pekowi division. Of these and the other Shawnee divisions, more will be said. Since moving to Ohio, Methoataske had given birth to the couple's first three children— a son, Cheeseekau, born about 1761; a daughter, Tecumpease, likely born the following year; and then another son, Sauwauseekau.

Puckeshinwau probably helped found Kispoko town, a new satellite Shawnee village well north of the troubled Ohio River border and some seventy miles southeast of modern Dayton. In addition to his honors from Pontiac's War, Puckeshinwau had returned from the conflict with a four-year-old white boy named Richard Sparks, seized in western Virginia.[12]

A young male addition to the family undoubtedly pleased Puckeshinwau and Methoataske. Sons were a source of pride, and a white boy taken young enough to raise as an Indian could be counted on to help fill the ranks of Shawnee warriors, which battle losses had cut to no more than four hundred. Sparks was also roughly the same age as the couple's son Sauwauseekau, making them natural playmates, once Richard's white identity was expunged.

Puckeshinwau grew quite fond of his adopted son. He renamed

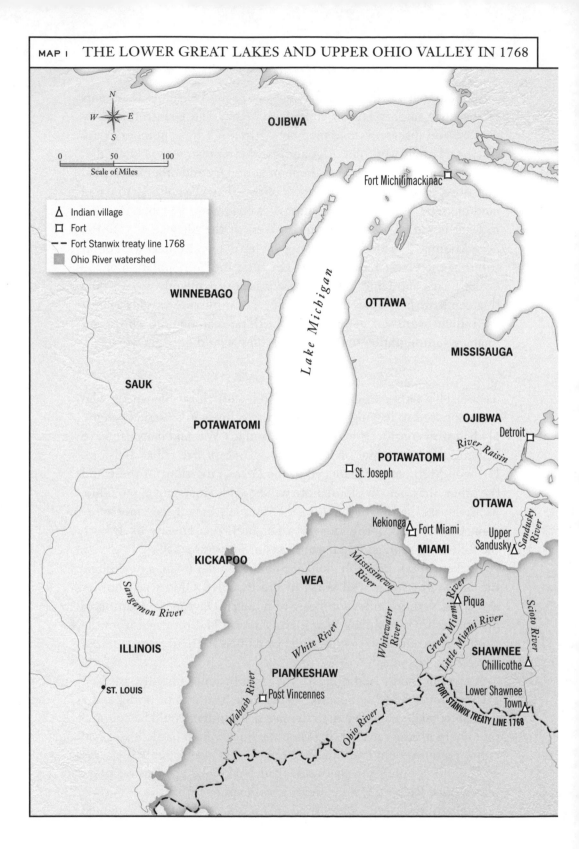

MAP I   THE LOWER GREAT LAKES AND UPPER OHIO VALLEY IN 1768

OJIBWA

Fort Michilimackinac

Lake Michigan

OTTAWA

MISSISAUGA

WINNEBAGO

SAUK

POTAWATOMI

OJIBWA

Detroit

River Raisin

POTAWATOMI

St. Joseph

OTTAWA

Kekionga Fort Miami

Upper
Sandusky

Sandusky River

MIAMI

KICKAPOO

WEA

Mississinewa River

Sangamon River

White River

Whitewater River

Great Miami River

Piqua

Little Miami River

Scioto River

ILLINOIS

PIANKESHAW

SHAWNEE

Chillicothe

•ST. LOUIS

Wabash River

Post Vincennes

Lower Shawnee
Town

Ohio River

FORT STANWIX TREATY LINE 1768

N
W   E
S

0   50   100
Scale of Miles

△ Indian village
▢ Fort
‒ ‒ Fort Stanwix treaty line 1768
▨ Ohio River watershed

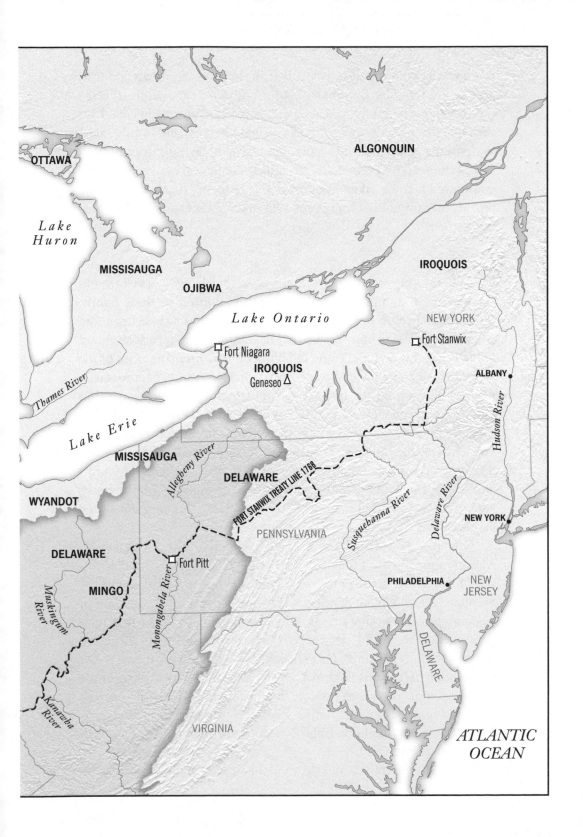

the boy Shawtunte and rejected British demands to repatriate him.
Sparks lived among the Shawnees for a dozen years before returning to white society. Late in her life, Sparks's white widow said his
adoptive parents raised him "with unusual kindness and indulgence."
Perhaps that explains why Shawtunte resisted leaving Puckeshinwau
and Methoataske. "I remember his telling me how great a calamity he
considered it to be taken away from the Indians," recalled his white
brother-in-law, "and of his schemes for making his escape and returning to them."[13]

The fateful year of the Fort Stanwix betrayal, 1768, also brought
Puckeshinwau and Methoataske a natural addition to their family.
Spring found them in Chillicothe, the principal Shawnee town and
tribal ceremonial center forty-five miles south of modern Columbus,
Ohio. Puckeshinwau had come to Chillicothe to attend another of the
interminable councils held to discuss the tribe's future. Methoataske,
meanwhile, awaited the birth of her fourth child. Indian women far
along in a pregnancy frequently traveled with their husbands, but
they customarily gave birth only in the company of female relatives
or friends. As her delivery date drew near Methoataske and her attendants retired to a secluded spot "two arrow flights" southeast of Chillicothe, near the banks of the Scioto River. One night, as Methoataske
kept to the hut and waited, the other women saw a shooting star sweep
across the sky and sink into the western horizon.

   "One passed across," the women excitedly told Methoataske.
Almost immediately, Tecumseh was born. Such is the story of Tecumseh's birth as his great-grandson Thomas Wildcat Alford related it.
Stephen D. Ruddell, an adopted white boy and youthful confidant of
Tecumseh, told a similar tale. In Ruddell's version, which he may have
gotten from Tecumseh, it was Methoataske herself who witnessed
the comet. Both accounts are plausible as to the circumstances if not
the location of Tecumseh's birth.[14] They also convey something of the
significance of Tecumseh's name, the meaning of which can only be
rendered imperfectly in English. Even the pronunciation is elusive.
Ruddell, who spoke both English and Shawnee fluently, gave it as
"Tec-cum-theth."

   While Methoataske and her infant son remained cloistered,

Puckeshinwau invited two elderly relatives or friends to the family's wigwam, calling upon them to perform the sacred naming ceremony on the tenth day after his son's birth. The name-givers were to ponder and pray until they divined two names from which the parents might choose. On the morning of the tenth day, Methoataske cleaned herself and her infant well, left her hut, and returned to the family wigwam. Her caregivers prepared the naming feast. While the extended family crowded around, the infant received a sponge-bath. Then the name-givers declaimed on the logic behind the names they offered, one of which presumably incorporated the shooting-star metaphor. They called on the Master of Life—the Shawnee creator—to protect the baby and exhorted the parents to raise him well. Having heard the name-givers out, Puckeshinwau and Methoataske made their choice.

The name they chose, *Tecumseh*, derives from *nîla-ni-tkamáthka*, meaning "I cross the path or way" of a living being. As Tecumseh was born into the Panther *umsoma* (patrilineal clan or name group), the animal whose path he crossed was a panther—no ordinary panther, but rather a miraculous creature of transcendental existence that lived in the water but periodically burst across the skies as a shooting star.[15] The panther, celestial or commonplace, was a formidable creature in the eighteenth-century Ohio Valley. A Shawnee male whose name incorporated that of the panther inspired awe because the panther's hunting skills were an object of envy. Shawnee males of the Panther clan conceived of themselves as panthers, and the birth of a boy of the clan beneath a celestial incarnation of the beast portended immense hunting prowess.[16]

The infant Tecumseh viewed the world from a *tkithoway*, or cradleboard, strapped securely onto his mother's back. The Shawnees believed the *tkithoway* helped develop good posture. To steady Tecumseh's head, Methoataske likely added a wooden hoop adorned with shells and silver ornaments. As she performed her daily chores—carrying water, gathering firewood, cooking meals, and planting the spring corn crop (Shawnee women indulged in no postpartum rest)—Tecumseh rocked gently on her back. Methoataske attended to Tecumseh's earthly needs; Puckeshinwau saw to the baby's spiritual welfare. After Tecumseh's umbilical cord fell off, Puckeshinwau tucked it into his hunting bag. He carried it with him until autumn, then buried it with the antler of a young buck. The commingling of antler and umbilical cord in the earth, blessed with the proper prayers, would help Tecumseh grow into a mighty hunter.[17]

Freed from the cradleboard after a year, Tecumseh became subject to a mild form of discipline. If he misbehaved, the toddler might feel the swat of a stick on his tiny legs or find himself tossed into a shallow stream. Shawnees generally doted on their children, however, and he would quickly discover that his parents preferred to praise good conduct rather than punish bad behavior. He would also learn to respect the elderly, whose authority over children was absolute.[18]

No sooner did Tecumseh learn to walk than he was one with nature. His feet would have glided over the cool, smooth-swept dirt surface of the family wigwam in the spring and summer and sunk into the soft and warm animal-skin rugs that covered the floor in the fall and winter months. The gratifying wintergreen scent of the birchbark walls mingled in his tiny nostrils with the pungent odor of smoke rising from the central hearth. Outdoors he waddled over a carpet of crenate leaves, learning to dodge the catkin and cones that dotted the ground. A symphony of familiar sounds—the idle chatter of women at work, the laughter of lounging warriors, the ceaseless barking and yapping of countless dogs—comforted Shawnee toddlers like Tecumseh. A thousand aromas rose from the forest floor, wafted on the wind. At night broken moonlight shivered beneath the canopy of swaying treetops. Inside the wigwam Tecumseh jostled for a spot among his parents, three siblings, adopted white brother, and the inevitable evening visitors. Most Shawnees, he would discover, abhorred solitude.

When Tecumseh was two, Methoataske gave birth to her fifth child, a son named Nehaaseemo, of whom little is known. Sometime during Tecumseh's childhood (probably when he was eight), smallpox struck Tecumseh. The vomiting, diarrhea, and excruciating headaches eventually passed, leaving in their wake a face lightly pockmarked for life.[19]

Then came the bitter autumn of 1774, when Puckeshinwau fell fighting the Long Knives at Point Pleasant, and Tecumseh's fourteen-year-old elder brother Cheeseekau assumed the role of surrogate parent. His sister Tecumpease, who had married the fine young warrior Wahsikegaboe (sometimes spelled Wasabogoa) and achieved considerable status herself among the women of the village, helped ease the pregnant Methoataske's burden. Nothing, however, could have prepared Methoataske for her delivery in spring 1775. She gave birth to triplets, a supremely rare occurrence that the Shawnees believed an ill omen and that left Methoataske shaken and ashamed. Her distress was brief, however. One of the infants, a girl, died shortly after birth. The baby boys survived, emerging from their naming ceremonies as Kumskaukau, "Cat That Flies," and Laloeshiga, a runt whose name meant, perhaps hopefully, "Panther with a Handsome Tail."[20] In addition to Cheeseekau and Tecumpease's contributions, Blackfish, a good-natured war chief of the Chillicothe division who had been a devoted friend of Puckeshinwau, did what he could as a foster father to Methoataske's younger children.[21]

Lord Dunmore's War had effectively ended with the Battle of Point Pleasant. Chief Cornstalk finally recognized the Ohio River boundary line as it had been fixed in the Fort Stanwix Treaty. Some Shawnees advocated peaceful coexistence. Others distanced themselves from the Long Knives. Several hundred Shawnees, representing the entire Thawekila division, resettled among the Creeks. And the residents of Chillicothe town, 170 families that included those of Methoataske and Blackfish, removed from the Scioto to the Little Miami River in southwestern Ohio.[22]

There was no sating the white appetite for Indian land. A memorandum to the British Secretary of State for North America urged His Majesty's Government to abrogate any agreement to abstain from exploiting the Ohio Valley because "the lands are excellent, the climate temperate, [and] the country is well-watered by several navigable rivers communicating with each other." Large boats were able to negotiate the Ohio River itself year round, making it cheaper to export goods to British West Florida and the West Indies by river (first along the Ohio, then down the Mississippi) than by sea from New York or Philadelphia.[23]

No wonder then that wealthy land speculators did a lucrative business buying up large tracts, while the less fortunate poured into the newly opened Kentucky country to grab small parcels concentrated around community forts, called stations. The more daring ventured north of the Ohio River. The deepening encroachments distressed

MAP 2 THE SHAWNEE BROTHERS' COUNTRY, 1774–1794

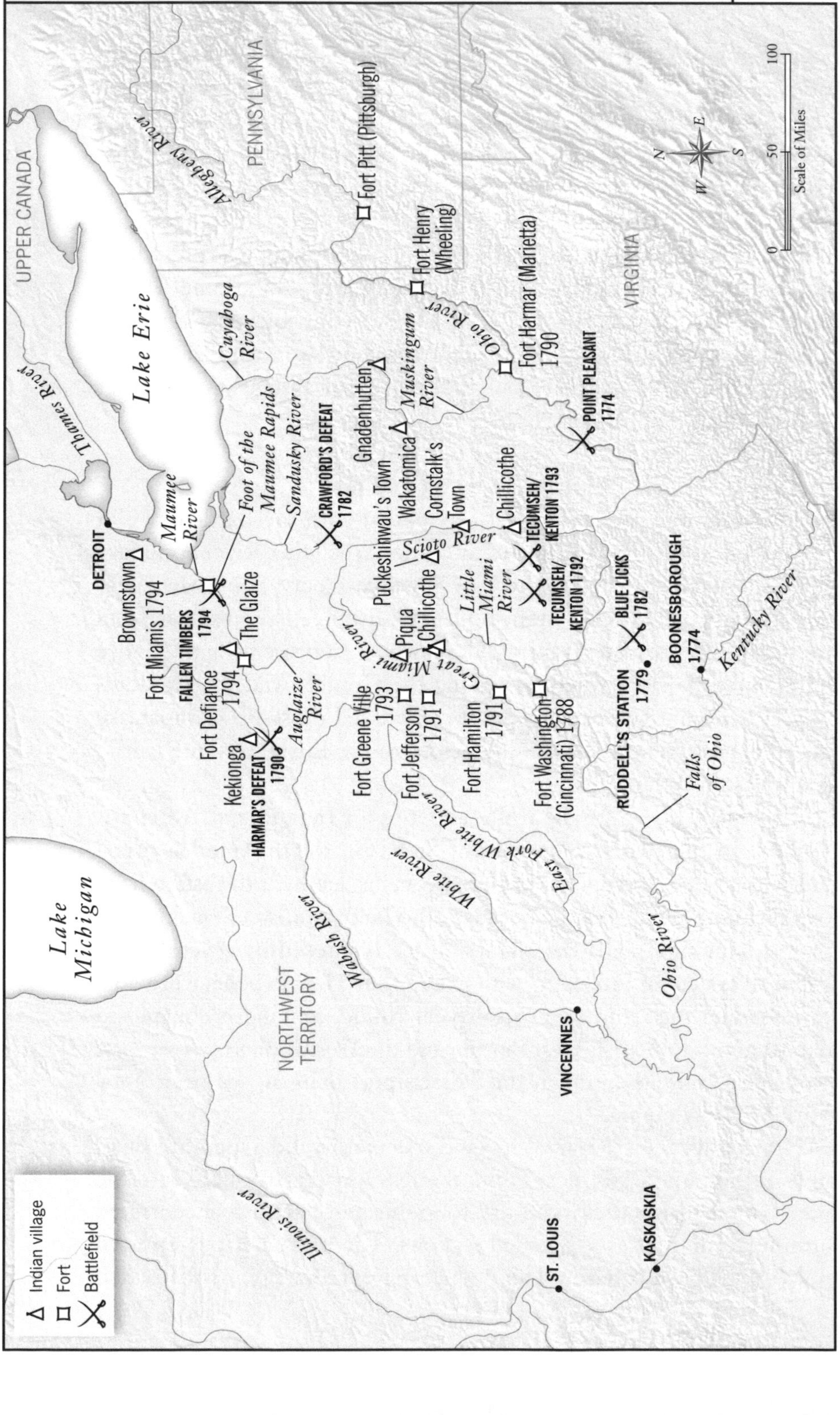

Indian village
Fort
Battlefield

Scale of Miles
0 50 100

Lake Michigan

Lake Erie

UPPER CANADA

PENNSYLVANIA

VIRGINIA

NORTHWEST TERRITORY

Illinois River

Wabash River

White River

East Fork White River

Ohio River

Kentucky River

Great Miami River

Little Miami River

Scioto River

Muskingum River

Sandusky River

Cuyahoga River

Maumee River

Thames River

Allegheny River

Ohio River

Foot of the Maumee Rapids

Falls of Ohio

ST. LOUIS

KASKASKIA

VINCENNES

DETROIT

Brownstown

Fort Miamis 1794

FALLEN TIMBERS 1794

The Glaize 1794

Fort Defiance 1794

Kekionga

HARMAR'S DEFEAT 1790

Fort Greene Ville 1793

Fort Jefferson 1791

Fort Hamilton 1791

Fort Washington (Cincinnati) 1788

Piqua

Chillicothe

Fort Pitt (Pittsburgh)

Fort Henry (Wheeling)

Fort Harmar (Marietta) 1790

POINT PLEASANT 1774

CRAWFORD'S DEFEAT 1782

Gnadenhutten

Puckeshinwau's Town

Wakatomica

Cornstalk's Town

Chillicothe

Chillicothe

TECUMSEH/ KENTON 1793

TECUMSEH/ KENTON 1792

BLUE LICKS 1782

RUDDELL'S STATION 1779

BOONESBOROUGH 1774

a missionary among the Delawares. "The whole country on the Ohio River has already drawn the attention of many persons from the neighboring colonies," he wrote. "Generally forming themselves into parties, [they] would rove through the country in search of land, and some, careless over their conduct or destitute of both honor and humanity, would join a rabble—a class of people generally met with on the frontier—who maintained that to kill an Indian was the same as killing a bear or a buffalo and would fire on Indians that came across them by the way."[24] By 1775 only Indians stood before the rabble. Unrest in the American colonies had erupted into armed conflict, forcing Great Britain to withdraw its troops from all the Indian country forts except Detroit and Niagara. The colonial empire was vanishing.

The Shawnees were uncertain what to make of the new peace emissaries who called themselves Americans. "We are often inclined to believe there is no resting place for us and that your intentions [are] to deprive us entirely of our whole country," Shawnee chiefs told a Virginia delegation in July 1775. That summer a Continental Congress emissary found the Shawnees "constantly counseling, the women very uneasy in expectation that there would be war." Shawnee tribal councils grew bitter. Representatives of the Kispoko and Mekoche divisions spoke for accommodation; the Chillicothe (among whom Methoataske's family lived) and Pekowi divisions, for war.

Cornstalk did his utmost to avoid conflict with the Americans. In October 1775 he led a Shawnee delegation to Fort Pitt, on the site of Pittsburgh. In exchange for American recognition of the Ohio River as the boundary between Indian and white lands, Cornstalk and his fellow delegates signed a peace treaty that the fledgling American government would be hard pressed to enforce. For the next two years Cornstalk maintained Shawnee neutrality in the American Revolution. As American pressure on the Shawnee border grew, however, the venerable chief slowly lost his hold over all the Shawnees but the Mekoches. While Cornstalk and his people arranged to quit the roiling frontier and withdraw north toward Lake Erie, younger Chillicothe and Pekowi leaders held their ground and accepted a British call to war against the Americans. Together with the always restive Mingoes, small Chillicothe and Pekowi war parties pricked at the frontier defenses.

In November 1777, Cornstalk returned to Fort Pitt to renew his pledge of friendship and to warn of militant Shawnee designs. It was a pointless mission. The Americans had grown distrustful of all Shawnees, and Cornstalk's words fell on deaf ears. Growing morose, he reflected, "When I was young, and went to war, I thought that each expedition might prove the last, and I would return no more. Now I am here amongst you. You may kill me if you please. I can die but once, and it is all one to me, now or another time."

The council terminated, and the officers dispersed. Suddenly a party of enraged militiamen carrying a comrade's scalped corpse burst into Cornstalk's room, crying "Let us kill the Indians in the fort." Cornstalk declared calmly, "If any Long Knife has anything against me, let him now avenge himself." In response, a volley of eight bullets riddled his body. "If we had anything to expect from [the Shawnees]," rued the American commander, "it is now vanished."[25]

Tecumseh was nine when Chief Cornstalk was murdered. He lived in the new Chillicothe town on the Little Miami River, a lovely and seemingly safe location. Wigwams interspersed with log cabins blanketed a high ridge along the river's east bank. Just northeast of the town center stood the council house, sixty feet square and built of strong, notched hickory logs. Corn, melon, and squash fields stretched far away to the south; vegetables grew abundantly in the rich, dark soil. The Little Miami teemed with fish. The wooded hills of southwestern Ohio abounded in game animals. Twelve miles northeast of the new Chillicothe lay the smaller Shawnee community of Piqua (modern Springfield, Ohio).[26]

Tecumseh was a busy youngster. Strenuous exercise consumed his days. "Running, swimming, and jumping were matters of course with us," recalled a Shawnee, "but the older men encouraged us to practice those things that developed greater strength; also, they taught us to shoot our bows and arrows with accuracy and great skill." Tecumseh would have had a scaled-down bow and small arrows, large enough to shoot small animals or to play the hoop game (in which boys tried to send arrows through a rolling grapevine hoop), but not so large as to be a danger to him.

Adult males tested Tecumseh on his marksmanship and his endurance. "When a boy got up in the morning his face was blacked with charcoal, and he was sent out to kill some game for food," Tecumseh's great-grandson wrote of the woodland practicum. "It might be a quail, a rabbit, or a squirrel, seldom larger game than that. He was given no food until he returned with what he was sent out to procure. Because his face was blacked, everyone who saw him knew why he was out, and no one gave him food or helped him in any way. He was absolutely on his own resources."

Hunting came naturally to Tecumseh. "He always killed more birds than any of his party," recalled the métis (mixed blood) Anthony Shane, who later married a cousin of Tecumseh. Shane said that Tecumseh had his own little gang, over which he exercised implicit control.

The Shawnees expected nothing less from the son of a renowned war chief, watched over by a celestial panther guardian. Emulating the animal's nobler qualities would naturally have become the adolescent Tecumseh's most ardent desire. Like the panther, he longed to be a strong and stealthy beast of prey capable of catching deer at will. He learned that the panthers who stalked the forests surrounding Chillicothe never harmed humans without provocation—neither would Tecumseh. Should an Indian draw too near the den of a female panther with cubs, however, he faced mortal danger. Surviving such an encounter required absolute self-possession. Tecumseh learned never to turn his back on a she-panther, thinking he could escape. He must stare the animal down. If he lacked the courage to shoot, he must gently but firmly walk backward until he was a safe distance away. If he shot and missed, he would almost certainly forfeit his life.[27]

Tecumseh was careful not to play with girls; Shawnee boys who did so were doomed to merciless ridicule. From the time a boy could walk, he was taught to feel superior to his sisters. Nevertheless, Tecumseh worshipped the fifteen-year-old Tecumpease, the adolescent she-panther of the family whenever Methoataske faltered. And little girls lavished affection on him. Shane said Tecumseh told the other boys that he would never tie himself to just one girl because all the pretty girls wanted him.[28]

As with childhood female attention, Tecumseh seldom wanted for nourishing food. He enjoyed a varied diet. Whites who ate Shawnee dishes usually enjoyed them, too. Favorites included venison roasted over open coals with herbs and dipped in bear oil; beaver tails, duck, or squirrel wrapped in wet corn husks and baked in hot ashes; and dried pumpkin and venison cakes. Some whites objected to the absence of salt. The Shawnees also liked salt, but it was hard to come by. Obtained from naturally occurring salt springs, or licks, it required much boiling to extract even a pinch. So the Shawnees made do with herbs, a healthy alternative. As for sweets, the Shawnees favored molasses sugar but also enjoyed chocolate acquired from traders. Corn was a dietary staple venerated as a divine gift to be harvested joyfully. The dishes made from corn ranged from a wholesome cornbread mixed with fruit to emergency hunting rations in the form of parched-corn cakes.[29]

When not visited by white men's diseases, the Shawnees were a healthy people who took great pride in their physical appearance. Their standards of hygiene were higher than those of white frontiersmen, which were frankly abysmal; a white captive boy remembered that his Shawnee father bathed regularly year round, plunging nude into frigid rivers in the dead of winter. Shawnee men thought facial and body hair unattractive and plucked it with mussel shells. Of at least medium height, slender, and well built, their skin tone varied from a light olive to a dark brown, and their eyes were generally brown. The Shawnees had jet-black hair when young, which grayed normally with age.

European trade goods comprised much of the clothing and adornments of the woodland tribes. In cold weather Shawnee men, and sometimes women, wore a cloak called a match-coat. Formerly made of deer, panther, or bearskin and worn with the fur facing inward, by the late eighteenth century, Indian match-coats more commonly were of coarse woolen cloth called stroud, usually about seven feet long, which the wearer wrapped around the upper part of the body like a toga. Match-coats also served in a pinch as blankets. Eventually ready-made European garments replaced them in the Shawnee wardrobe.

In warm weather, men dressed in a linen shirt; a breechclout, which was a long rectangular piece of tanned deerskin, cloth, or animal fur worn between the legs and tucked over a belt, so that the flaps covered the genitals; animal-skin leggings; and deerskin moccasins. Some also donned hats bought from traders or wrapped handkerchiefs around their heads. Male hairstyles also reflected a European influence. Traditionally men had shaved their heads bald to the crown, leaving only a circular handful that they adorned with a feathered plume or a colorful hair roach. Increasingly, however, warriors wore their hair long, braided, and adorned with ostrich feathers. Tattoos, never frequent among Indians north of the Ohio River to begin with, were seldom seen in Tecumseh's day. Only war paint—fashioned from iron oxide and most commonly worn as red, black, or white stripes—remained unchanged. Shawnee traditionalists found the wearing of long hair and linen shirts by men off-putting.[30]

Women's wear, on the other hand, drew general approval, even of traditionalist males. Most adult females wore calico blouses that closed at the breasts with a silver brooch and extended about six inches below the waist; a skirt of stroud terminating just below the knee; and leggings. They greased their hip-length hair with bear fat until it sheened and then braided it. Some women daubed red dots on the cheeks, but most used no facial paint. The colorful apparel and ornamentation of Shawnee females fascinated one captive white adolescent. Elderly women dressed simply, but "all of the young and middle-aged are passionately fond of finery ... having the tops of their moccasins curiously wrought with beads ribbons and porcupine quills, the borders of their leggings and the bottom and edges of their strouds tastily bound with ribbons, edged with beads, and frequently on their moccasins and leggings small tufts of deer's hair, dyed red and confined in small pieces of twine, rattling as they walked," he recalled. Jewelry was ubiquitous. "According to their ability they covered [themselves] with large and small silver brooches and wore on their wrists and arms silver bracelets from one to four inches in width."

Both sexes coveted silver baubles, the more the better. Indeed, men were more ostentatious than women. Not only did they wear silver bracelets and nose rings, they also customarily cut their ears, binding the auricle with brass wire, from which dangled silver pieces nearly to their shoulders. To white men unaccustomed to the sight, a fully decked-out woodland Indian presented an aspect variously described as colorful, bizarre, or grotesque.[31]

In these striking surroundings, the young Tecumseh passed his evenings absorbed in stories told by male elders. Like other Shawnee boys, he learned the premium their people placed on oratorical skill. Tales of the first encounter between Shawnees and whites held boys spellbound with wonder and dread. A Mekoche chief related one such story:

Our old men used to tell our people that a great serpent would come from the seas and destroy our people. When the first European vessel came in sight, the Indians saw the pennant, with its forked end darting and moving like the forked tongue of the serpent. "There," said they, "is the serpent our old men have been telling us about!" When the old men first tasted rum, tears ran down their cheeks. "This," they said, "is what will destroy our young men."

Equally fearsome were tales told of witches. As the elder of the two, Tecumseh heard them first, but they would make a deeper impression on his awkward younger brother Laloeshiga. Not that Tecumseh discounted such talk. Witchcraft cast a malevolent shadow over the Shawnees, who fervently believed that necromancers of both sexes prowled the dark-forested periphery of their existence, probing for weaknesses, ever ready to wreak pain and sow chaos. The Shawnees thought that witches derived their power from bits of the living flesh of the Great Serpent that had impeded the mythological Shawnee migration across the Atlantic Ocean. The fabled Shawnees had lured the beast ashore, where with mystical rites and menstrual blood they killed, dismembered, and then burned the creature. But malicious tribesmen had preserved a few scraps of the serpent's reanimated flesh, which they mixed with other vile substances in a medicine bag to obtain necromantic powers. Witches passed the bags secretly to succeeding generations. The Shawnees were not unique among woodland Indians in their strong belief in witchcraft or in its manifestations; other woodland tribes shared similar views.

In the perpetual struggle for eternal harmony, neglect of ritual gave witches free rein to wield their evil against fellow tribesmen, engendering earthly chaos, desolation, and anguish. Unfortunate for tribal prospects, the Shawnees believed the witches in their midst were powerless against the whites; they could, however, so weaken the Shawnees as to guarantee their subjugation.

Practitioners of the black arts were said to possess a physical characteristic, such as a red eye or an abnormal birthmark, that often betrayed them. They worked furtively and usually at night, plying their maleficent trade against neighbors and kinsmen. Envious and spiteful, witches were believed to be not entirely human, which should have made their destruction easier to stomach. As witches were a primal force of disorder and decay, everyone had a duty to eradicate them. By the time Tecumseh learned of witches, many Shawnees speculated that tribal misfortunes stemmed from neglect of the Creator's injunction that they expunge them from their midst. Few Shawnees, however, had the moral courage to undertake the task.[32]

_____

A Restless People

S HAWNEE TROUBLES, whether caused by witches, whites, or fellow Indians, predated Tecumseh's birth by more than a century. Although the mystic chords of dim memory stirred in the Shawnees a profound affection for the Ohio country, they were in doubt as to why. Later white ethnologists could offer only an educated guess. Most associated the earliest Shawnees with the Fort Ancient culture, which flourished in the Ohio River Valley until the early 1600s. The Fort Ancient Indians were hunters and farmers who lived in fixed villages surrounded by earthen and log fortifications, hence the culture's name. Whether the first Shawnees belonged to the Fort Ancient culture or lived apart in the Ohio Valley, there is no doubt of their linguistic roots. They were an Algonquian-speaking people, part of a loose amalgamation of occasionally querulous tribes with sometimes mutually unintelligible tongues that sprawled from the Atlantic seaboard, westward across the Great Lakes and Ohio Valley to the Mississippi River and northward into Canada.[1]

Surrounded by a sea of Algonquian-speaking peoples, the Iroquoian linguistic group was located in present-day New York. Comprised of five allied tribes, the Iroquois had a clear purpose—to accrue land and wealth at the expense of the Algonquins. An imperious, opportunistic, and fierce confederacy, the Iroquois prospered from the beaver fur trade, first with the Dutch, and later with the British. By the 1640s, however, the Iroquois had exhausted their own reserves, so they turned to a war of conquest, the likes of which the native peoples of

North America had never seen. Both sides counted about 12,000 warriors, but European allies had equipped the Iroquois with guns.

The Iroquois first struck west from what is today upstate New York and southern Ontario into the upper Great Lakes region, crushing the once-potent Huron nation; then they turned south into the Ohio River Valley, depopulating the region and pushing the fragments of Algonquins west toward the Mississippi River and into the arms of French explorers and traders. The Iroquois eventually overextended themselves, as invaders are wont to do. An expanding French empire, meanwhile, provided the Algonquin refugees with firearms and helped create refugee centers on the Great Lakes. The Algonquins accepted the French as leaders of a new alliance that relied heavily on the fighting prowess of the Potawatomi and Miami tribes, which had maintained their cohesion during three decades of warfare with the Iroquois. Striking back, the French and Indian combination finally repelled the Iroquois. Recurring epidemics of European diseases ravaged all Indians but seem to have struck the Iroquois hardest, and in 1701 they made peace with the French and their Algonquin allies. A new balance of power emerged, dependent on the British and French empires for its stability.[2]

Never especially cohesive, the Shawnees were arguably the principal losers in the six decades of warfare. The incessant Iroquois raids forced them from the Ohio Valley. Fleeing pell-mell, they became "a restless people, delighting in war," said an otherwise sympathetic Mahican chief who mistook their will to survive for innate belligerence. A British Indian superintendent called the Shawnees "stout, bold, cunning, and the greatest travelers in America." The fractured, migratory Shawnees trusted to the charity of other tribes or, when that failed, their ability to fight for land.

The Shawnees' precise movements are lost in the unrecorded history of native peoples. Our knowledge of their peregrinations depends on white sources. In 1683 several hundred tribesmen appeared at the French post at Starved Rock in the Illinois country and then journeyed east to join the Delawares in eastern Pennsylvania and Maryland. Other Shawnees drifted to the southeast and settled along the Savannah River in Georgia. Weary of combat with local tribes, after two decades this band split up. Some settled amid welcoming Upper Creek Indians in what is today central Alabama. The rest made their way to Pennsylvania. A few hundred Shawnees also lived for a time in western Virginia. By 1715 most tribesmen (perhaps 2,000) had reunited in Pennsylvania. The resident Delaware Indians and William Penn's benevolent Quaker administration welcomed them; a resurgent Iroquois confederacy tolerated their presence.

The Shawnees' respite proved short-lived, however. After Penn died in 1717, relations with local settlers soured. Game grew scarce. Unlicensed traders abused the fur trade upon which the Shawnees had grown dependent for European goods. They substituted addictive rum for the muskets, utensils, tools, cloth, and silver ornaments the Shawnees preferred when sober. Shawnee chiefs begged the Pennsylvania government to enforce antirum laws, but Quaker authorities were powerless to stop the enfeebling liquor trade. Compounding Shawnee woes, the pliant Delawares sold much of the land on which both peoples lived, and the Iroquois pressured them to part with the rest.[3]

The Shawnees and Delawares moved westward, settling first along the Allegheny River. Western Pennsylvania offered an uncertain sanctuary, however: it was Iroquois land, and the tribe treated them as vassals. The rum trade also followed the migratory tide. Shawnee chiefs again implored colonial authorities to rein in unregenerate rum dealers, hinting that they might switch allegiance to the French if their plea went unanswered. The Quaker assembly lent an attentive ear but took no effective action.[4]

After pillaging a few unlicensed traders, most of the Pennsylvania Shawnees moved on. As earlier related, other bands including Puckeshinwau's gradually joined them. By 1760 most of the tribe—now reduced to 1,500—had settled at a sprawling village on the Ohio River, near the mouth of the Scioto, called Lower Shawnee Town (about 110 miles east of what is now Cincinnati). For the first time in more than a century, the Shawnees were one.[5]

Tribal unity, however, had never counted for much with the Shawnees. Neither did it loom large in the Shawnee identity, unsurprising in a people so long dispersed. Shawnees owed their principal loyalty to, and derived their place in society from, membership in two types of intratribal units. The first and more formal type consisted of five patrilineal descent groups most aptly labeled divisions. They may once have been separate tribes that coalesced to form the Shawnees. Whatever their origin, the divisions had well-defined responsibilities. Coequal in power, the Chillicothe and the Thawekila divisions managed Shawnee political affairs, normally by furnishing the principal tribal chiefs. The Mekoches provided healers and saw to tribal health and medicine. The Pekowis managed matters of religion and ritual. The Kispokos took the lead in war preparations and supplied tribal war chiefs. Among a people so long dispersed, divisional duties often were more theoretical than real, and divisions remained semiautonomous even when the tribe coalesced. Shawnee villages took their names from the dominant resident division, and divisions sometimes maintained their own relations with other tribes. Each division also jealously guarded its own sacred medicine bundle, which was a secret collection of animal and natural objects believed to have divine power. Mishandling the sacred medicine bundle was believed to bring on calamity.[6]

The second Shawnee unit was the patrilineal *umsoma*, literally, "good genius society." It was less formal and more intimate than a division, which comprised multiple *umsomas*, or clans. Clan members shared names derived from the same animal or fauna, and Shawnee tradition records thirty-four original *umsomas*. By the eighteenth century they had dwindled to the following dozen: Snake, Turtle, Raccoon, Turkey, Hawk, Deer, Bear, Wolf, Elk, Buffalo, Tree, and Panther, this last of which Puckeshinwau and his children were members. Clan affiliation occasioned "strong partisanship and much pleasant rivalry." Boasting of one's own clan and deprecating others was a common form of jest.[7]

Humor came easily to the Shawnees, as it would to Tecumseh and Laloeshiga. For all their travails, the Shawnees were a remarkably resilient and optimistic people. Although they shunned vulgarity, adults enjoyed a good joke, and many a long hour was spent telling amusing stories around wigwam fires.

The Shawnees were scrupulously honest with one another. Deceit, however, was perfectly acceptable in dealings with outsiders—white men in particular. The Reverend David Jones, a Protestant missionary who visited the Ohio Valley Shawnees in 1772, gained as good an understanding of tribal character as was open to an eighteenth-century white Christian. That he converted no one to his faith did not blind him to the finer qualities of his hosts. "The Shawnees are naturally an active and sensible people [and] the most cheerful and merry people that I ever saw," said Jones. "It appears as if some kind of drollery was their chief study; consequently, both men and women in laughing exceed any nation that ever came under my notice." Jones admired their manner of discerning a white man's intentions. "This I found to be a craft among them, that when they imagine anything in their own heart about you, they would say someone told them such things, and all this cunning is to find out your thoughts about them."

A British Indian Department officer who knew the Shawnees well disagreed with Jones's claim that they had a disingenuous streak. On the contrary, he regarded them as "generally open and frank— their affability, good humor, and vivacity render them agreeable to strangers—and they always seem to derive pleasure from ... doing all in their power to make agreeable the sojourn of those who visit their villages." He particularly enjoyed the Shawnee language, which he thought "very melodious and strong, well-adapted to beautify and embellish the flowerings of natural eloquence."[8]

The opinions—be they disdainful or complimentary—that whites held of them were of little matter to the Shawnees. In common with other Eastern Woodland Indians, they considered themselves superior to whites in the sight of the Supreme Being, who the Shawnees called Waashaa Monetoo, variously translated as "Master of Life," "Great Spirit," or "Creator." The Shawnees further arrogated to themselves the place of first among the Indians while dismissing whites as a mongrel race, the offal of creation. They did concede, however, that Indians' allies, such as the British and the French, or those whites with whom Shawnee women intermarried, hovered somewhere above the eternal dung heap. Nevertheless, most Shawnees denied that the Master of Life had created the whites. Rather, when opening the heavenly door to place the first Shawnees on a great island, he had decried a naked, bald, and circumcised white man seated on the ground. The Master of Life told the Shawnees that a lesser spirit over whom he had no control had made the white man. The Master of Life warned the Shawnees that "as soon as they reached their island, this great white spirit would endeavor to thwart his designs." For a time, the Stinking Lake (Atlantic Ocean) would separate the races, but eventually the whites would alight on Indian ground.[9]

Despite their unflattering theory of the origin of whites, Shawnee racism was not absolute. Sacred rituals permitted white captives not only to be adopted into the tribe but also to be transformed into equal beings, fully entitled to the affection, respect, and rights accorded fellow tribe members. For a white captured as a child, the adoption process was relatively benign. Jonathan Alder, seized by a Shawnee and Mingo war party in Kentucky at age nine, found the most harrowing part of his experience to have been the arduous trek to the home village of his captors. Once there, a family who had lost a son to illness claimed Alder. His new Indian mother stripped him naked, rubbed him with soap and water mingled with sacred herbs, dressed him in Indian clothing, and then pronounced him family. Alder would grow to become a friend and admirer of Tecumseh.

For white adults, particularly men, adoption into Eastern Woodland tribes was fraught with pain and doubt. The Delaware captors of colonial soldier James Smith first plucked the hair from his head, except the crown; pierced his nose and ears and inserted ornaments; and finally painted him from head to toe. Next an elderly chief led him to a group of women standing waist-deep in a river. They tried to dunk him, but Smith resisted. "No hurt you," one of the women assured him. No longer struggling, Smith permitted them to plunge and scrub him thoroughly. Dried, dressed in Indian clothing, and repainted, Smith stood silently while a chief addressed him through an interpreter: "My son, you are now flesh of our flesh, and bone of our bone. By the ceremony, which was performed this day, every drop of white blood was washed out of your veins [and] you have now nothing to fear."

Smith was fortunate. Although white women chosen for adoption suffered no ritualized ordeal, most men underwent a brutal practice known as running the gauntlet in order to prove themselves worthy; those wanting in courage or stamina often were beaten to death.

A gauntlet run was great sport for all but the victim. A young white captive of Blue Jacket, the Pekowi Shawnee war chief to whom an adolescent Tecumseh would turn for a mentor in war-making, witnessed one such ordeal. Every villager capable of wielding a club or a switch turned out for the affair. The Shawnees formed two rows, seven feet apart, extending 300 yards to a cabin. A strapping white man stood before them. His goal, on which his life depended, was to reach the cabin before the blows of his tormenters felled him. Down the line he ran, kicking, head punching, and generally scattering the Indians before they could beat him. At the cabin a deputation of chiefs congratulated him on his daring and welcomed the man into the Shawnee tribe.[10]

Horrific stories of Indian captivity abounded on the frontier, but most were embellished. After the gauntlet was run and the rituals over, the reality of adopted life was far from terrifying. Whites who were adopted into a tribe, then elected to return to the white world, needed only state their desire to their Indian kinsmen, and their wish would be granted, but few availed themselves of this option. Some had been so long among the Indians that they knew no other way of life. While traveling among the Shawnees, a New York minister met a young white woman, captured when she was an infant, who spoke no English and seemed "as contented as her Indian companions." The minister also encountered a white teenager who not only recalled his precaptivity life but also spoke and wrote English fluently and knew the precise whereabouts of his relations, who he told the minister he would be happy to visit. Under no circumstances, however, would he trade the freedom of the forest for a life of frontier drudgery.[11]

Some captive whites, however, never had a chance to prove themselves worthy of adoption or to judge the relative merits of the native life. These were the unfortunates singled out for torture and execution. Like other woodland tribes, the Shawnees tortured prisoners to divine the physical and spiritual strength of an enemy or, if they prosecuted the ordeal to the victim's demise, to avenge the death of compatriots or relatives and free their spirits from the underworld. Women and children occasionally were tortured to death, but Shawnee religion forbade rape as anathema to the Master of Life. Burning with firebrands or at the stake was the favored means of torture. The adolescent Tecumseh and the younger Laloeshiga witnessed their share of grim and gory proceedings. A sampling of the horrors will suffice to convey their almost commonplace aspect in Shawnee life.

Stumbling into a Shawnee village with the war party that took her captive, a Virginia woman saw fragments of burnt bodies dangling on poles. Then she watched the war party torment a fellow white prisoner for the pleasure of it. They first made him stand while slowly shredding his ears and slicing incisions in his face. Then the warriors bound him, rolled him in the dirt, and whipped him with small rods. Their bloodlust cooled, and the Indians spared the man's life.

Two captive boys observed the gruesome fate of a white woman who had tried to escape. Warriors scalped her but did not immediately kill her. Instead, they tied her to the ground and then "laid burning splinters of wood here and there upon her body, and then cut off her ears and fingers, forcing them into her mouth so that she had to swallow them.... The woman lived from nine o'clock in the morning until toward sunset, when a French officer took compassion on her and put an end to her misery."

The torture of white prisoners peaked during the frenzied border warfare of the mid- to late-eighteenth century, well before the Shawnee brothers attained adulthood. The captive farmer Peter Williamson left a particularly gruesome account of the fate of three frontiersmen. Dragged half-starved into a Shawnee town, two of them were bound to a tree. Villagers kindled a large fire around them, and after the men were scorched, a warrior ripped them open with his scalping knife and burned their entrails. Others tore flesh from the dying prisoners' bodies. The Indians buried the third man upright in a hole that they had compelled Williamson to dig and then lit a fire. With only his head exposed above ground, the "poor creature could only cry for mercy, for his brains were boiling in his head.... They continued the fire till his eyes gushed out of the sockets." Then they lopped off his head and forced Williamson to inter the remains.

Many Shawnees abhorred torture, but they generally recognized the inviolable right of tribesmen to do as they wished with captives they had seized, particularly if they or their family had lost loved ones to their enemies. Some objected, however, and occasionally a Shawnee intervened. A son of Chief Cornstalk returned from a hunt to find the villagers assembled to watch warriors roast a white prisoner to death. Diverting to his wigwam, he grabbed a pistol, concealed it on his person, and headed for the ugly scene. He arrived to find the warriors igniting the blaze. Without a word, Cornstalk's son approached the prisoner, pulled out the pistol, and blew the man's brains out. The warriors were furious, but no one raised a hand against the young war leader.[12]

Shawnee society protected other individual rights as assiduously as it did a captor's prerogative to dispose of a victim as he saw fit. Few whites ever understood the truly democratic nature of woodland

Indian government. Chiefs possessed influence commensurate with the respect they enjoyed and their ability to provide for their people. During the best of times, noted a French observer, among the Indians there existed only "voluntary subordination. Each person is free to do as he pleases." That said, the Shawnees generally deferred to proven leaders. "Although we were absolutely democratic, believing that all men [that is, all Shawnee men] were born equal, we accorded our leaders and chiefs a deference that was spontaneous," a warrior explained. "There was no vacillating between different leaders. Once a man established his reputation for bravery, for wisdom and discretion, he became an object of admiration and confidence. Those qualities could not be assumed—they must be inborn."

The Shawnees recognized two categories of leaders: village chiefs and war chiefs. The former office was hereditary but could be forfeited for incompetence or loss of the people's confidence. War chiefs earned their titles through exploits in battle. Although no formal councils existed, village chiefs typically invited the advice of respected male elders before deciding important matters.[13]

Also acting as a brake on the chiefs' authority was the divine origin of Shawnee law, which the Master of Life had given to the people. He also populated the earth with manitous (lesser deities in animal form) to help the Shawnees adhere to them. There were laws defining marital relations (infrequent sexual intercourse, for instance, was thought conducive to good health), ceremonies to ensure a good hunt or bountiful crops, and a divinely ordained hierarchy of life. The Shawnees believed that deer possessed souls and eventually ascended to heaven together with their hunters. Wolves were intermediaries between man and the manitous. The spirits of all game animals had to be propitiated through prayer.[14]

Central to all Eastern Woodland Indian beliefs loomed the concept of power, both benevolent and pernicious. Life depended on it. Power manifested itself in every aspect of one's existence: the ability to grow crops, to hunt without diminishing the game supply, to woo lovers, to heal the sick, to converse with animals, to commune with the Master of Life, and to influence others. Rituals and the proper care of sacred medicine bundles were key to obtaining power.

Both sexes had access to power but for different purposes. Men were hunters and protectors. Women grew crops and produced offspring.

Their menstrual cycle reflected awesome forces denied to men, who avoided menstruating women. "Men with power can do anything," a Shawnee warrior explained, "but whenever they come to a woman who is not just right, they sure are afraid of her." A Shawnee myth told of a menstruating woman who discovered a malevolent horned serpent from the underworld. Warriors lost their battle with the beast, which succumbed only to the stained clothing of the menstruating woman. Menstrual blood trumped male war-medicine.[15]

Just as nature and the supernatural defined Shawnee values, so did Shawnee life and language testify to a oneness with both natural and otherworldly forces. The Shawnees expressed time in terms of the sun and the moon. Chiefs were "wise and beloved men," wisdom being synonymous with rightness. The Shawnees accorded neighboring tribes familial rank. The Wyandots were elder brothers to the Shawnees; the Delawares were their grandfathers; the Miamis, Sauks, and Ottawas their younger brothers; the Potawatomis their youngest brothers; and the Iroquois their cousins. When friendship existed among Indian nations, the intertribal council fire burned brightly, and when discord prevailed, it dimmed. Buried in peacetime, the tomahawk was taken up and sharpened for war. Peace conferences commenced with the wiping away of tears, the opening of ears, the cleansing of hearts, and the elaborate calumet (feathered peace pipe) ceremony. Treaties were recorded with belts fashioned from cylindrical shell, porcelain, or glass beads woven together with deer sinew and called wampum. White wampum denoted peace and prosperity; black with a red hatchet painted on it indicated an invitation to war.[16]

The Shawnees lived harmoniously in their village world until the mid-eighteenth century, when liquor, epidemics, and war with white interlopers disrupted their equilibrium. The land was lush and lovely, the rhythm of life regulated by the seasons. Forest of maple, oak, elm, and beech blanketed the Ohio River Valley. Closely packed treetops matted with wild grapevines vitiated sunlight. No undergrowth grew in the near-perpetual gloom. Deer bounded, wolves howled, and rattlesnakes slithered through the forest; otherwise an aching stillness prevailed. Small meadows occasionally punctuated the woodland. "But once in the space of a month, did I see more of the heavens than there was to be seen through the branches of the trees," averred a white sojourner, "and though the open space did not consist of more than twenty acres of natural meadow, I thought it a paradise." Trackless though the forest might appear to untutored whites, its Indian inhabitants gracefully negotiated the network of trails that interlaced villages and tribes.

Shawnee villages generally were located on riverbanks or near springs. Most families lived in domed oval wigwams fourteen feet in diameter. A bark partition separated the interior into a bedroom and a combination cooking and sitting room. Made of frames of bent sapling and covered with large sheets of bark in the winter and cattail mats in the warm months, or occasionally with canvas obtained from traders, wigwams could be constructed in a few days. By the latter half of the eighteenth century, the creeping white influence could be seen in the proliferation of log huts after the frontier style, as well as in the blacksmith, trading, and gunsmith shops of resident traders. Every village had its council house, which was a wooden edifice sixty to ninety feet long used for ritual and secular gatherings and for defense.

Extensive cornfields, intermingled with patches of melon and squash, blanketed the riverbank opposite or otherwise apart from the village. Horses and cattle grazed, and hogs rooted beyond the wigwams. A large and rambunctious dog population had the run of the village. Beyond the fields and dwellings stretched the endless woodlands.[17]

The annual cycle of Shawnee life commenced in the waning days of September, the Pawpaw Moon. Able-bodied Shawnees departed in small parties to make winter hunting camps in sheltered valleys, leaving behind the elderly, small children, and the infirm with ample provisions for the long winter. The hunt ended in December, after which men trapped for the fur trade. In March the Shawnees returned to their villages. It was then that most births occurred and the planting season began. Women prepared the fields, but before seeds were sown, the Shawnees held the Bread Dance, their most sacred communal ritual. Supervised by a Pekowi division chief, the Bread Dance opened with a bonfire-illuminated ball game between two teams of twelve men and twelve women. (The women were permitted to advance the ball by kicking or throwing it; the men could only kick it.) After the game a dozen men departed on a three-day hunt. When they returned, an elderly orator implored the Master of Life for a bounteous crop, the general welfare of the people, and an increase in game animals. A social dance concluded the ceremony.

The Shawnees spent the summers tending crops, fishing, hunting deer, relaxing, and copulating. They generally tried to time sexual relations to prevent pregnancies during the harsh winter months, when couples were in their crude hunting quarters. Just before the final harvest in August, the Shawnees held the Corn Dance ceremony. Originally a festive occasion, by the latter decades of the eighteenth century the proceedings had taken on something of a somber aspect. Recalled a white captive who had been with the Shawnees long enough to learn their language, "A venerable Indian arose and spoke of the 'palefaces,' whom he represented as the first murderers and oppressors; ascribed their own sad reverses to the anger of the Great Spirit for affording these murderers an asylum on their shores; of their duty to exterminate if possible these intruders on their soil, at least to drive them south of the Ohio." For a moment all were quiet. Then the natural Shawnee exuberance returned, and foot races and ball games superseded apocalyptic dread. The festival concluded, and the cycle of life recommenced with the winter sojourn into the Ohio wilderness.[18]

So it was that the Shawnees preferred to pass their days, if only the Long Knives would permit them to live in peace.

A Turbulent Youth

A s children, Tecumseh and his younger brother Laloeshiga knew only fleeting moments of real peace. Chief Cornstalk's murder in November 1777 heralded an era of upheaval. That winter Tecumseh's foster father, Chief Blackfish, led an expedition of 120 warriors to avenge Cornstalk's death. Crossing the icy Ohio River in canoes, the Shawnees filed through the Kentucky forest in a raging blizzard in search of easy victims, keeping clear of the fortified stations. They wove around a salt-boiling party of twenty-seven frontiersmen, nabbing a solitary hunter who revealed himself to be Daniel Boone, now forty-three years old. Captain Will, the Shawnee war leader who had released him a decade earlier on condition he never set foot again in Kentucky, approached Boone as though the white man were an apparition. Putting up a strong front, Boone called out, "Howdy do, Captain Will?" The Shawnee squinted at him, puzzled, then broke into a grin of recognition. "Howdy do," he replied, then chastised Boone for having ignored his warning. Speaking to Blackfish through an interpreter, Boone confessed that he belonged to the party of salt boilers. On Blackfish's promise to harm no one, Boone offered to help the Shawnees capture them. Blackfish was as good as his word. Not only were none of the men killed, but Blackfish also adopted the middle-aged Boone. After a mild gauntlet run, Boone underwent the adoption rituals. Blackfish treated him kindly, and Boone became a favorite with the children of Chillicothe, dispensing sugar cubes and hearty laughs that hid his homesickness.

Blackfish also brought home sixteen-year-old Benjamin Kelly. The younger Tecumseh—he was then nine—and Kelly grew close, and from the Kentuckian he likely learned his first words of English. One can easily imagine the two boys wandering around the village or traipsing through the forest, pointing out everyday objects and exchanging the Shawnee and English names for them. As their familiarity with each other's language grew, so too did their mutual fondness. Kelly would live with the Shawnees for five years.[1]

Nothing in Tecumseh's acquaintance with the youth Benjamin Kelly or with Daniel Boone and the other adult Kentucky salt boilers, who either reconciled themselves to a life among the Indians or eventually escaped (Boone absconded after five months), inspired bad feelings in the boy. But events soon would leave Tecumseh with an abiding distrust of Americans. In a lesser soul, they might have carved an indelible hatred.

The Shawnees condemned Blackfish's raid widely—some because he had not exacted the blood revenge necessary to permit Cornstalk's spirit to rest, others because a counterstrike by the Kentuckians seemed inevitable. Tribal factions hardened.

In 1778, the anti-American clique accepted a black-wampum war belt from the British commander at Detroit. Urged on by their British allies, then in the third year of their war with the rebellious American colonies, that September Shawnee warriors fumbled a siege of Daniel Boone's eponymous settlement Boonesborough, losing many of their best men in the process.

The Boonesborough fiasco was the last straw for the Shawnee peace faction. Availing themselves of a Spanish grant of rich farmland west of the Mississippi River near modern Cape Girardeau, Missouri, in the spring of 1779, nearly the entire Kispoko, Pekowi, and Thawekila divisions (the latter just returned from the Creek country)—perhaps twelve hundred persons in all—abandoned the Ohio Valley. The combined population of Chillicothe and Piqua dwindled to no more than eight hundred. After less than three decades of unity, the Shawnees were again splintered.[2]

It was a momentous occasion in the lives of Tecumseh and Laloesh-iga because Methoataske abandoned them to join the migration.

Tecumpease the she-panther remained; her husband Wahsikegaboe was a Chillicothe, and the Chillicothe and Mekoche divisions had elected to stay in Ohio. Tecumseh and Laloeshiga's ties were to the Pekowi and Kispoko peoples, and the two boys had little chance of gaining distinction among the Chillicothes and Mekoches. Methoataske had not only deserted her sons, but she had also sacrificed their patrimony.

Tecumpease and Wahsikegaboe welcomed the boys into their home, and Cheeseekau shared paternal obligations with his brother-in-law. The three adults clearly favored the athletic Tecumseh, whose magnetic personality had already won him a loyal band of boys, over the sickly Laloeshiga, who grew increasingly querulous with each passing year. An insecure little braggart who spoke of himself incessantly, Laloeshiga earned the uncomplimentary nickname Wannesga, or "Crazy Fellow." At some point his name was changed, perhaps by his annoyed guardians, to Lalawethika. Although similar in sound to his Panther-invoking birth name, it was far from flattering. Lalawethika loosely translated as "Rattler," connoting one who prattled. As if that were not bad enough for the boy's fragile ego, he was hopelessly inept. One day, while trying to align an arrow to his bow, Lalawethika shot out his right eye.[3]

Methoataske may have hoped that Chief Blackfish would be able to shepherd his foster sons to adulthood, but the Kentucky militia was about to erase any such possibility.

Kentucky was filling up fast. With nearly three thousand men capable of bearing arms, the settlers no longer simply cowered in fortified stations while Shawnee and Mingo war parties scoured the countryside—they retaliated. In late May 1779, Col. John Bowman set out with three hundred buckskin-and-breechclout-clothed, tomahawk-and-long-rifle-wielding militiamen to destroy that "prolific hive of mischief" Chillicothe, home to eleven-year-old Tecumseh and five-year-old Laloeshiga.

Shortly after nightfall on May 29, Bowman's unmilitary gaggle crept unseen into a clearing a stone's throw from Chillicothe. There Bowman held a hasty council of war. The officers decided on a dawn assault and passed orders that no weapons were to be fired beforehand.

The moon was in its first quarter. A dense fog hung over the village. Silence reigned until midnight, when a lone Shawnee hunter, trotting up a trail toward town, stumbled on several Kentuckians crouched behind a log. A shot rang out, the Indian crumpled, and a Kentuckian sprang forward to scalp him. "The dogs set up a great noise, and the squaws with cries and whimpering were heard to say, 'Kentuck! Kentuck!'" a militiaman remembered.

There were two hundred women and children in Chillicothe that night, but few men. Some of the Shawnee inhabitants streamed into the timber or toward the river screaming; others took refuge in the council house, where two dozen warriors and fifteen boys capable of bearing arms prepared to make a stand. Emerging from his cabin, Chief Blackfish led six warriors against the attackers in the open. A bullet crashed into his kneecap as he crouched to shoot, boring its way up the chief's leg and exiting from his thigh. Three warriors carried him back to his cabin to die. Inside the council house, a hundred-year-old medicine man chanted words of encouragement. As a promising boy with an ardent following of fellow children, Tecumseh likely was among the musket-wielding Shawnee youngsters.[4]

Outside pandemonium reigned. Instead of pressing their advantage, the Long Knives broke ranks. They burned cornfields and plundered the wigwams and cabins, stuffing their shirts with silver ornaments, furs, beadwork—anything that might fetch a profit. Others drove off the Shawnee horse herd. As his command disintegrated, Colonel Bowman became unhinged. "Make your escape! Make your escape!" he galloped about shouting. "I can bring to you no assistance!" Shortly after Bowman unraveled, a black woman claiming to be an Indian captive ran from the council house and told several Kentuckians that at least one hundred Shawnee and Mingo fighters were coming from nearby Piqua. No sooner had her story disconcerted her listeners than she vanished.

As the militiamen retreated, the outnumbered Shawnees challenged them to a stand-up fight at sunlight. Burdened with booty, the Kentuckians kept running. Warriors harassed them until they recrossed the Ohio River. The Kentuckians had lost at least a dozen dead; the Shawnees perhaps two or three. The psychological shock of Bowman's raid, however, greatly outweighed the slight loss of life. For the young Tecumseh—and for the five-year-old Laloeshiga, to

the extent he understood what had transpired—the trauma of both
the raid and Blackfish's death, coming just a few short weeks after
their mother deserted them, must have been excruciating. They could
count no home safe; no relationship secure.[5]

Then began an unbridled cycle of violence that would last for three
years. Bowman's incursion pushed wavering Ohio Shawnees into the
British camp. With the American Revolution raging inconclusively,
the English welcomed additional Indian allies. With the spring thaw,
after the harsh winter confined them, the Shawnees swept into Kentucky, their messengers regularly presenting the British at their frontier headquarters of Detroit with scalps.[6]

Normally young boys were excluded from war parties, fourteen
or fifteen being the usual ages of ascension, but these were desperate
times. At twelve, Tecumseh probably participated as a menial in what
was to prove the most successful Shawnee human-hunting foray ever
staged in Kentucky—the destruction of Ruddell's and Martin's stations in June 1780.[7]

No longer were the Shawnees and Mingoes fighting alone. Intent
on eliminating the Kentuckians and reversing the tide of war against
the Americans west of the Appalachians, the British assembled at
Detroit a mixed force of 150 British, Canadians, and American loyalists
(Tories), together with several hundred Great Lakes Indians, principally Ojibwas and Potawatomis. In canoes and bateaux, they paddled
to the Ohio River to meet the Shawnees. British commander Capt.
Henry Bird wanted to attack the westernmost American settlement
of Louisville—a small inland port founded in 1778 and consisting of a
stockade and a few cabins—and then roll eastward, hoping to induce
a panic that would cause other frontier stations to collapse. Because
falling waters on the Ohio rendered an upriver trip problematic, the
Shawnees insisted on striking stations closer to home. The nearest
"Kentuck" post was Ruddell's Station on Licking River. Bird agreed
to attack it.[8]

Ruddell's Station (thirty miles north of today's Lexington) was
a typical Kentucky pioneer bastion. Built as a parallelogram near a
spring, its perimeter consisted of twelve-foot-high logs rammed side
by side in a trench, with blockhouses built at the four corners to
prevent Indians from taking shelter beneath the walls. Crudely constructed and sparsely furnished log cabins opened inward. Comforts
were few, sanitation rudimentary. "Captain" Isaac Ruddell founded

the eponymous station, reclaiming and fortifying in 1779 a settlement that the Shawnees had forced its inhabitants to abandon three years earlier. Isaac Ruddell and his wife, Elizabeth, had an infant girl; two older daughters; and two sons—Abraham, age six, and Stephen, age twelve. Old enough to heft a musket, Stephen was assigned a stockade loophole.

Stephen never had the chance to fight. Captain Bird's Indians surrounded Ruddell's Station before the Kentuckians, huddled indoors against a raging rainstorm, knew of their approach. The stockade was impervious to rifle shots and arrows but not to artillery. When Captain Bird ordered a six-pounder cannon rolled up to the gate, Isaac Ruddell and the forty-nine defenders surrendered on the condition that neither they, their families, nor their cattle would be slaughtered. Captain Bird wanted to comply, but he faced a dilemma common among British officers west of the Appalachians. Short on regular troops, the British needed their Indian allies in order to field an adequate force. The Indians, however, had their own playbook. Matthew Elliott and Alexander McKee—two Tory leaders serving the British Indian Department who Tecumseh would come to know intimately as an adult—remonstrated with the chiefs to contain their warriors. All seemed well until the Kentuckians swung open the doors of the stockade. "Whilst Captain McKee and I were in the fort with the poor people," reported a horrified Captain Bird, "the Indians rushed in, tore the poor children from their mothers' breasts and killed a wounded man, and every one of the cattle, leaving the whole to stink." A warrior struck Elizabeth Ruddell in the face with a war club, yanked away her infant, and dashed its head against a tree, then tossed the little corpse into a roaring fire to hear it crackle. All over the fort, warriors seized Kentuckians for adoption or ransoming. Many more lives would have been lost had Bird, McKee, and Elliott not eventually succeeded in quieting the Indians. A teenaged Tecumseh had witnessed his first frenzied Indian raid.

On Captain Bird's promise of leniency, which this time the warriors respected, the next settlement on Licking River, Martin's Station, surrendered without a shot being fired. Bird was about to push on when word reached him that Gen. George Rogers Clark, the most capable American frontier commander, was marching with a thousand militiamen to intercept him. Leading 470 captive Kentuckians, Bird turned north under a ferocious thunderstorm to avoid Clark and make the miserable return trek to Detroit. Two white women drowned in the turbulent rising waters of Licking River, but the Indians valued their prisoners too highly to kill any more Kentuckians.[9]

Once across the Ohio River, the Shawnees bade farewell to Captain Bird and returned to Chillicothe with their portion of the prisoners. They included Stephen Ruddell, whom the Shawnees renamed Big Fish. The tribe had scant time to perform adoption rituals, however, as George Rogers Clark had veered toward Chillicothe. An Indian exterminator of uncommon virulence, Clark once told a British officer that "for his part he would never spare a man, woman, or child on whom he could lay his hands."

Clark's wrath consumed Chillicothe, though not with the finality that he had hoped. Apprised by scouting parties of Clark's approach, the Shawnees burned the town and the crops and retreated twelve miles north to make a stand at Piqua, on a broad plain above the Mad River. The odds against them were steep. Many Shawnee war leaders and chiefs were absent in Detroit for a council with the British. Even counting their perennial Mingo co-combatants and a smattering of Wyandots and Delawares, the total force under Black Hoof—a war chief of great wisdom, humanity, and broad experience—was unequal to the task. When Clark brought his artillery into play, the Indians fled, leaving behind at least a dozen dead, most of their possessions, and the entire corn and vegetable harvest. The Ohio Shawnees regrouped in four new villages well to the northwest. The Ohio River—which the American officials, in the Fort Pitt Treaty of 1775, had promised the late Chief Cornstalk they would recognize as the border between the Shawnees and American settlers—now lay nearly one hundred miles to the south.[10]

The Piqua fight dealt Tecumseh's self-esteem a hard blow. The massed Kentuckians, the boom of artillery, and the swirling flames of burning cabins and crops were difficult for even seasoned warriors to endure. When a bullet slammed into Cheeseekau, wounding him, Tecumseh flung aside his musket and bolted into the tall prairie grass. No one faulted him, and Tecumseh soon overcame the trauma. He vowed never again to run from a fight.[11]

Twelve-year-old Stephen Ruddell also possessed youthful courage and adaptability. Separated from parents and siblings, Ruddell was well treated by his adoptive family. He made friends easily and chose well; his closest companion was the similarly aged Tecumseh, and the two became "inseparable." With the help of Ruddell and Benjamin Kelly, Tecumseh continued to improve his English, which he came to speak fluently enough to carry on a normal conversation. It was a skill he adroitly masked when negotiating with whites later in life; as he insisted on speaking Shawnee in formal councils, officials often did not know that he understood their language.

What motivated Tecumseh to learn English? Was it a desire to know his enemy better? To deepen friendships with his adopted white "brothers"? Simple curiosity? Most likely it was some combination of these drives, the precise mix of which probably was unknown to the confused youth Tecumseh himself, who could both befriend and kill Long Knives. He had adult examples in other Shawnees, such as Daniel Boone's forgiving and good-humored captor Captain Will. Unlike most Indians who learned the Long Knives' tongue, however, Tecumseh reserved his knowledge primarily for friendly and informal encounters.

Ruddell marveled at Tecumseh's charismatic pull: "There was a certain something in his countenance and manner that always commanded respect, and at the same time made those about him love him." To Tecumseh, affable despite his early travails, leadership came naturally. Undoubtedly Cheeseekau encouraged his younger brother to assert himself; they were, after all, the sons of a great war leader. "During his boyhood," recalled Ruddell, "[Tecumseh] used to place himself at the head of all the youngsters and divided them. [Then] he would make them fight sham battles, in which he always distinguished himself by his activity, strength, and skill."

There were plenty of real battles to be fought, combat into which boys were drafted to fill the thinning ranks of Shawnee warriors. At twelve, Tecumseh was already a veteran. He had lost his father to a Long Knife's bullet and his mother to migration, fought at Chillicothe in defense of his birthplace, fled from a second fight at Piqua, and been forcibly relocated three times—ample reasons for him to hate the Americans. Nonetheless, as Ruddell discovered to his great good fortune, Tecumseh yet retained a "free-hearted" humanity. In the months to come, further tragedy and bloodshed would sound the depths of his goodwill.[12]

4

A Nation Divided

THE SHAWNEES were formidable warriors. Both their Algonquin allies and American enemies testified to the unique fury
with which they fought. All this was immensely satisfying to young
Shawnee males eager to make names for themselves. Once married, a
Shawnee man's principal duty was to provide for his family, and that
meant long and uncertain weeks searching for game, which had grown
increasingly elusive in the overhunted Ohio country.

Notwithstanding his momentary cowardice at Piqua, few doubted
Tecumseh would make a competent warrior and perhaps a solid war
leader. After all, boys subordinated themselves to him in mock battles,
a reliable sign of his potential. Tecumseh's hunting skills also matured
apace. That meant memorizing exacting rituals and cultivating a mystical empathy for the quarry. Tecumseh learned to purify his breath
with sassafras or herbs to prevent prey from smelling him; to ask the
spirits of animals he slayed for forgiveness; and to be wary of wolves,
with their knack for hexing hunters whose shots at them went astray.
Not that Tecumseh had much cause for worry on that score. "He was
a great hunter," declared Stephen Ruddell. And a peculiar one. If he
could avoid it, Tecumseh would "never hunt in parties where women
were." That was unusual because hunting parties normally were family affairs. Even as a boy, he was happiest when hunting alone.[1]

Tecumseh's love of solitude—unusual among the highly social
Shawnees—would serve him well on his vision quest, the rite of passage a Shawnee male underwent at adolescence. Practiced in seclu-

sion, it was a life-altering event calculated to prepare a boy for a man's duty of feeding his family and defending his people. As one missionary related with singular insight,

> When a boy is to be initiated, he is put under an alternate course of physic and fasting, either taking no food whatever, or swallowing the most powerful and nauseous medicines, and occasionally he is made to drink decoctions of an intoxicating nature until his mind becomes sufficiently bewildered, so that he sees or fancies that he sees visions and has extraordinary dreams, for which, of course, he has been prepared beforehand.
>
> He will fancy himself flying, walking underground, stepping from one ridge or hill to the other across the valley beneath, fighting and conquering giants and monsters and defeating whole hosts by his single arm. Then he has interviews with the spirits, who inform him of what he was before he was born and what he will be after his death. His fate in this life is laid entirely open before him; the spirits tell him what is to be his future employment, whether he will be a valiant warrior, a mighty hunter, a doctor, a conjurer, or a prophet. There are even those who learn or pretend to learn in this way the time and manner of their death.[2]

Mastering the methods and sacred underpinnings of Eastern Woodland Indian war-making was no easy endeavor even for so promising an adolescent as Tecumseh; for Lalawethika, it would prove impossible, and the humiliation would cripple him as surely as his missing eye. Like other Iroquois and Algonquin tribes, the Shawnees believed that attention to ritual was as critical in warfare as it was in hunting. Strict sacrifices were needed to gain the spiritual armor without which even the bravest warrior was reluctant to fight. He must purify himself by fasting, bathing, ingesting purgatives, and abstaining from sexual intercourse, the latter to prevent an abominable clash of male and female power. Because warriors "drink a great deal of a strong concoction of roots, which infuse a spirit of energy and strength," explained a Shawnee warrior, "if they enjoyed [sexual] connection before counteracting the effects of this medicine by some other, the consequences would be fatal to them."[3]

While living among the Shawnees, Daniel Boone carefully observed
the mystical outfitting of a war party.

One of the principal war chiefs announced the intention of a
party to commence an expedition by beating their drum and
marching their war-standard three times around the council
house. On this the council dissolved, and enough warriors supplied themselves with arms and a quantity of parched corn flour
as a supply of food for the expedition. All who had volunteered
then adjourned and drank the war-drink, a decoction of bitter
herbs and roots, for three days—preserving in other respects an
almost unbroken fast...to propitiate the Great Spirit. During
this period, they purify themselves; they were not allowed to sit
down or even lean upon a tree, however fatigued, until after sunset. If a bear or deer even passed in sight, custom forbade them
from killing it. The more punctual they are in the observance of
these rites, the more they expect success.

While the young warriors were under this probation, the aged
ones watched them to see that they did not violate any of the
religious rites, and thus bring the wrath of the Great Spirit upon
the expedition.

When the fast and purification was complete, the warriors
were compelled to set forth, prepared or unprepared, be the
weather fair or foul. Accordingly, when the time arrived, they
fired their guns, whooped, danced, and sung—and continued firing their guns before them on the commencement of their route.
The leading war chief marched first. The rest followed in Indian
file, at intervals of three of four paces behind each other, now and
then chiming the war whoop in concert.

They advanced in this order until they were out of sight and
hearing of the village. As soon as they reached the deep woods,
all became as silent as death.[4]

Warriors carried magical war bundles (medicine bags) containing
stones, bits of fur, or other items revealed during their vision quest.
They also appealed to the underworld, pausing at springs, which they
conceived of as portals to perdition, to sprinkle tobacco and pray for
victory and a safe return.[5]

Indians favored the ambush. It was a tactic requiring remark-able patience and stamina to execute, as a Kentuckian who evaded one discovered. The fortunate frontiersman habitually left his post every afternoon in order to hunt squirrels in a nearby hickory grove, unaware that Shawnees lay concealed beside his path behind a large log. For three days he passed the spot unmolested. On the fourth day the Shawnees shot and scalped two men and stole their horses. Ignor-ing the tormenting insects, relieving themselves in place, neither eat-ing nor drinking, they had remained motionless in the tall grass for thirty-six hours.[6]

Indians were pragmatic fighters. Retreat before unfavorable odds "was considered rather as a principle of tactics," said an American general with two decades of experience fighting the Shawnees. "And I think it may be fairly considered as having its source in that peculiar temperament of mind which they often manifested of not pressing fortune under sinister circumstances, but patiently waiting until the chances of a successful issue appeared to be favorable." When attack-ing a large enemy, Indians generally employed a half-moon-shaped formation. In the wilderness, the tactic seldom failed.

Indians scalped fallen enemies to obtain tangible proof of victory in single combat. They took great care of these evidentiary trophies. After "lifting" a scalp, the victorious warrior scraped the fleshy side free of fat, stretched it on a hoop, then dried it over a fire. Adorned with feathers, scalps were often strung up for exhibition. One captive recalled counting eight scalps dangling from a single pole, which its proud Shawnee owner paraded about camp.[7]

As Tecumseh entered his teen years, the opportunity to take white scalps grew commensurate with increased American infringement on Shawnee lands.

In 1782 the Ohio Valley shuddered to the drumbeat of raids and reprisals. The British surrender at Yorktown, Virginia, in 1781, while effectively ending the American Revolution east of the Appalachians, brought only greater violence to the frontier. Warfare descended into mindless brutality. On the morning of March 8, 1782, it achieved a nadir in a horrific slaughter of Indians.

The victims were ninety-six inoffensive Delawares. Their settlement of Gnadenhutten, in eastern Ohio, had prospered under the guiding hand of Moravian missionaries. Members of a small but intensely evangelical German sect, the Moravians enjoyed success among the Indians vastly disproportionate to their numbers because they dedicated themselves heart and soul to the task and respected Indians for the people they were rather than considering them merely souls to be saved. Their Delaware Indian converts were more peaceably inclined than even white Pennsylvania Quakers, but the American Revolution placed them in an untenable situation. Hoping for friendly relations with the British and their Indian allies as well as with the Americans, the residents of Gnadenhutten instead aroused the suspicions of both. Assuming the Delaware Moravians were in league with the Americans, the British commander at Fort Detroit prevailed on the Sandusky band of Wyandots under Chief Half King to confine them while he interrogated their white missionaries. With the connivance of the Delaware chief Captain Pipe, a sworn enemy of the Moravian mission, Half King uprooted the four hundred converts of Gnadenhutten and outlying communities just before the autumn corn harvest. The hungry outcasts huddled on the outskirts of the Wyandot village while the British questioned the missionaries. Satisfied of Delaware neutrality, the British commander ordered the Indians' release, and they were cast adrift in winter in a country stripped of game.

Some of the starving Christian Delawares returned home to salvage what corn they could from their forsaken fields. Their timing was terrible. Hostile Wyandots had just murdered several Pennsylvanians. Blaming the innocent Delawares, an armed Pennsylvania rabble descended on Gnadenhutten to exact revenge. They herded the Indians into two cabins—one for men, the other for women and children. The Indians knelt and prayed. Then the militiamen bludgeoned them to death with mallets. Congratulating themselves on a great triumph over a savage foe, the Pennsylvanians headed home, leaving behind the mutilated bodies of forty men, twenty-two women, and thirty-four children.[8]

That the Pennsylvanians had targeted the wrong Indians became instantly evident. Perhaps to assuage their consciences for their sorry roles in the tragedy, Half King's Wyandots and Captain Pipe's Delawares swooped down onto the western Pennsylvania frontier with a vengeance. In retaliation, in May 1782, four hundred untrained militia-men under Col. William Crawford left Pennsylvania to attack the now hostile Indian villages on the Upper Sandusky.

Crawford's expedition was a bloody fiasco. Not only were the Wyandots and Delawares ready for the Pennsylvanians, but the British also supplied troops, and outraged Shawnees from the Mekoche town of Wakatomica, one hundred miles south of modern Cleveland (neither Cheeseekau nor Tecumseh was among them), helped avenge the dead. Impossibly outnumbered, Crawford held his own for two days before ordering a retreat that degenerated into a rout when his command, a blistered shell of its former self, fragmented in the forests. Most not killed in battle stumbled to safety, but Colonel Crawford and several others fell into the hands of Captain Pipe's Delawares. They never stood a chance. Infuriated women and children beat, hacked, and clubbed to death most of the captives, kicking one man's severed head about in the dust. Colonel Crawford, however, was singled out for special treatment. Although he bore no responsibility for Gnaden-hutten, he was a high-ranking Long Knife, which made him an ideal candidate to expiate the dead. His face painted black, his body stripped naked and pinioned, Crawford endured thirteen hours of excruciating torture, prodded by flaming sticks and partially flayed, before expiring. The Delawares cut up his corpse and burned the pieces, then scattered the ashes through their village in order to free the spirits of the Delaware dead who walked among them.[9]

The ritualistic execution of Colonel Crawford outraged Americans. A respected officer, Crawford had been a close friend of George Washington, having also served as his surveyor during the illicit land speculation of the 1760s. For the moment, however, the American response was limited to outrage. The Continental Army had no resources to muster for a second assault on the Sandusky villages; nor were Pennsylvania militiamen any longer willing to fight armed Indians. With the frontier wide open, the British and their Indian allies resumed attacks on Kentucky. The Revolutionary War west of the Appalachians, a conflict characterized by lightning raids on American settlements and counterstrikes against pro-British Indian villages, had returned to the Shawnee country.

———————

Tecumseh ached for a fight. After his panic at Piqua, the fourteen-year-old had to redeem himself quickly if he were to maintain standing among his fellow adolescents. His chance came in July 1782, when the strongest Shawnee war party to assemble since his father died eight years earlier rendezvoused with 150 British Rangers and 1,100 Great Lakes Indians on the Ohio River. (Although realistic Englishmen recognized that the former colonies were lost forever at Yorktown, the Revolutionary War would drag on until 1783.) British Capt. William Caldwell commanded the July expedition. The Indians were loosely assembled under the Tories Alexander McKee and Matthew Elliott, now officially agents of the British Indian Department. All three men—Caldwell, McKee, and Elliott—were destined to loom large in Tecumseh's life. For the moment, however, Tecumseh was just a voiceless, unnoticed novice.

As so often happened when the British and Indians tried to orchestrate a campaign, far too many voices were vying to be heard. The British wanted to seize Wheeling and sever the Kentucky settlements from their river connection with the East, but the Great Lakes Indians, frightened by false rumors that George Rogers Clark was about to slip behind them with Virginia regulars, turned back. That left just two hundred Shawnees and a handful of Wyandots, who together prevailed upon the British to stage a quick attack on two exposed stations. Their botched effort cost the settlers little beyond a good deal of slaughtered livestock. As a rowdy gaggle of 182 Kentucky militiamen pursued, they found detritus along the Indian trail, which was odd. The ubiquitous Daniel Boone, now a militia lieutenant colonel, drew the only plausible conclusion: the Indians hoped to lure them into an ambush. On the morning of August 19, the Kentuckians paused on the south side of a sharp loop in Licking River near a salt deposit called the Blue Licks. Unable to see what lay on the hilly, heavily wooded north bank, Boone halted the column. A hotheaded major named Hugh McGary accused Boone of cowardice and demanded they continue. The rebuke had the intended effect. "Come on," cried Boone as he splashed across the shallow waters, "we are all slaughtered men." A war whoop and well-coordinated volley rent the air, and Kentuckians crumpled before the unseen foe. In a matter of minutes sixty-seven militiamen, including Boone's second son, lay dead. With his brother Cheeseekau beside him, Tecumseh had participated in his first ambush.[10]

The victory brought Tecumseh another white friend. Philemon Waters, a Kentucky teen, had fallen captive. The Shawnees painted his face half black and half white. Once back at Piqua, Waters watched two fellow prisoners be burned to death, but when his turn came, the warriors spared him. Tecumseh sought Waters out. Now that Benjamin Kelly had been permitted to return to his white family, Tecumseh wanted to widen his circle of white friends—at least those who had been transformed through adoption into Shawnees—and of English-language tutors. Waters would remain with the Shawnees for only a few months, but during that time he and Tecumseh became close companions.[11]

After Blue Licks a counterstroke was inevitable. The Revolutionary War in the East may have been over, but west of the Appalachians the vicious and insular cycle of violence between the Shawnees and the Kentuckians spun on, accelerated when necessary by Virginia, which maintained a proprietary interest in the district.

With so many senior Kentucky militia officers lost at Blue Licks, it fell to George Rogers Clark to lead the retaliatory expedition across the Ohio River and up the valley of the Little Miami River. The Shawnees were ill prepared to receive an attack. No sooner had they returned from mauling the Kentuckians at the Blue Licks than they learned that their British Father was negotiating a peace treaty with the Americans and thus would no longer condone or outfit forays into Kentucky. Indeed, British representatives confessed that they would be hard pressed even to supply the Indians' defensive needs, critical though an Indian buffer was to the integrity of British Canada.

The British had only just mastered the protocol of gift-giving and acknowledged the need to equip and feed their Indian allies, who when fighting could not hunt. The warriors, the governor-general of the Canadas warned the Crown, were "thunderstruck at the appearance of an accommodation so far short of their expectation and dread[ed] the idea of being forsaken by us and becoming a sacrifice to a vengeance of the Americans.... They reproach us with their ruin."

A Shawnee collapse appeared imminent. Passing the ruins of communities that he had razed two years earlier, Clark struck the new Piqua—home to Tecumseh, Cheeseekau, and Lalawethika—

and then torched it and surrounding Shawnee villages. Fewer than twenty Shawnees were killed or captured, but the material damage done was immense. "We continued our pursuit through five towns," recalled Daniel Boone, "burnt them all to ashes, entirely destroyed their corn and other fruits, and everywhere spread a scene of desolation in the country." The Shawnees were uprooted and compelled to subsist on meager British rations, the largess of neighboring tribes, and diminishing game. Shawnee war parties would continue to harass Kentucky, but relentless American assaults forced them to resettle in the northwestern quadrant of the Ohio country. For the third time in their young lives, Tecumseh and Lalawethika had lost their homes to Long Knife violence.[12]

And the pressure only mounted. On September 13, 1783, Great Britain and the United States signed the Treaty of Paris. The Revolutionary War was over. With the stroke of a pen, the British sold out their Indian allies. They transferred to the United States "sovereignty" over British claims in the Ohio Valley that the Indians had never recognized. Meanwhile the Indians refused to acknowledge defeat. "The times are very critical," the British commander at Detroit told the Shawnees. "The world wants to be at peace, and it is time [it] should be so." If the Shawnees elected to fight on, "it must be an affair of your own, as your father can take no part in it."[13]

Fearing reprisals from the tribes they had betrayed and to supply the Indians and maintain the fur trade, the British retained military posts at Detroit and Michilimackinac (the latter on an island in the Straits of Mackinac in northern Michigan, opposite the old French Fort Michilimackinac). Although the Indians clung to the British as the lesser of two evils, the days of a fighting alliance were over.

Into the breach barreled the Americans, hell-bent on settling the Ohio Valley. For the new republic, the logic of conquest was simple. Its burgeoning populace strained to break free of the Atlantic coast. The Indians had sided with the British and must give way. Besides, buying land from the Indians and then selling it to the public would help extinguish the national debt.

The federal government intended an orderly process. Instead, thousands of settlers swarmed into Shawnee country. Some 2,200 families staked claims north of the Ohio River. American officials despised the squatters as "banditti whose actions are a disgrace to the human race." The Mekoche chief Captain Johnny tried to warn them off: "You are drawing so close to us that we can almost hear the noise of your axes felling our trees and settling our country." If the settlers persisted, he promised to "take up a rod and whip them back to your side" of the Ohio.[14]

It was an empty threat. The Ohio River was the avenue of national expansion, a course of empire that was not to be denied to land-hungry American "banditti" by God, the government, or man. Some aggrieved Indians like Captain Johnny brandished verbal weapons. Others, like the Delawares, employed a fatalistic wit, comparing the British and Americans to scissor blades that "only cut what comes between them." And thus, a chief lamented, when the British and Americans go to war against each other, "It is not each other that they want to destroy, but us, poor Indians, that are between them. By this means they get our land, and when that is obtained, the scissors are closed again and laid by for further use."[15]

Some Shawnees strove to distance themselves from the strife. Others sought accommodation. And still others fought back in a desultory sort of guerrilla warfare, ambushing the flatboats laden with prospective settlers and their livestock that meandered down the Ohio River. Cheeseekau and Tecumseh stood squarely with the latter group.

Flatboats were easy targets. Exactly as the name implies, a flatboat was a rectangular, flat-bottomed craft about fifty feet long and twelve feet wide with square ends, used to transport freight and passengers on inland waterways—in a word, a sturdy tub with a hull. Intended for one-way trips, flatboats were usually dismantled for lumber when— and if—they reached their destination downstream.

The Shawnees saw to it that several never did. Likely under Cheeseekau's watchful eye, Tecumseh and Stephen Ruddell enjoyed their first flatboat ambush in the spring of 1783, when both were fifteen. Ruddell served as bait to lure the passengers and crew with a distress call. As Ruddell yelled in English and waved his arms from the shore, several boats swung near enough for the concealed warriors to climb aboard and overwhelm the passengers. All but one white man died in the initial onslaught. Tecumseh thrilled in the action—he "behaved with great bravery and even left in the background some of the oldest and bravest warriors," recalled Ruddell—but detested the aftermath. There was a lone survivor, whom the warriors slowly roasted to death at the stake. While the shrieking victim writhed, Tecumseh whispered his disgust to Ruddell. And then he did something remarkable. He verbally lashed the perpetrators, who might have included Cheeseekau, so vehemently and convincingly that the war party swore never to burn another prisoner. In taking his first stand against torture, Tecumseh baldly overstepped the bounds of Shawnee male etiquette: a fifteen-year-old fledgling warrior should never upbraid his war-tested elders. Nevertheless, he prevailed. He was a young man to be reckoned with.[16]

A year later, in 1785, Tecumseh cemented his reputation both as a rising warrior and as an accomplished hunter. His younger brother Lalawethika later said that a Shawnee was expected to "obtain his own support after the age of sixteen if he be an active hunter, or at latest after eighteen." Tecumseh exceeded this expectation. On one of the last Shawnee buffalo hunts in Kentucky, where the herds diminished commensurate with the increase in white settlers, Tecumseh, armed only with bow and arrows, killed sixteen bison, one for each year of his young life. The leader of the hunting party rewarded him with a musket.[17]

Tecumseh's youthful ascent had its rocky patches. The Pekowi war chief Blue Jacket, a protégé of Puckeshinwau, took Tecumseh and Ruddell under his wing. After a skirmish with a party of Kentuckians, Blue Jacket ordered the youngsters and the other members of his war party to stay on the enemy flanks and under no circumstances block their path. Apparently the Kentuckians moved slowly, because Blue Jacket permitted some of the men to hunt. That evening the hunters reported in. Tecumseh and another warrior had killed three bison and prepared the choicest slices of meat for packing. When Blue Jacket asked them where they had encountered the beasts, the two confessed to having made the kill on a stream that bisected the Kentuckians' path. Their disobedience infuriated Blue Jacket. Extracting the ramrod from his musket, the chief struck Tecumseh and his companion repeatedly on the back and shoulders.[18]

Blue Jacket had reasons for anger far greater than the insubordination of a talented youngster. Times were hard. White settlers slaughtered game indiscriminately. Starving Shawnees found their claim to land on which they lived precarious. In January 1785 the Wyandots and Delawares had concluded a self-serving treaty with the Americans, ceding all of Ohio except the seventy-five-mile-wide strip within which their villages rested, from the Cuyahoga River west to what is today Indiana. They had sold not only the entire Shawnee country, a disgusted Blue Jacket told a British agent, but themselves with it.

Now in his late forties, Blue Jacket was a colorful fellow, a muscular six-footer with an open and intelligent countenance who not only felt at ease unburdening himself to the British but also went considerably further than most Indian chiefs in emulating their dress and way of life. Belying his name, he customarily dressed in a scarlet frock coat, richly laced with gold and topped with gold epaulets. From his neck hung a massive silver gorget and a large medallion of His Majesty George III. Blue Jacket sent his son to Detroit for an English education. The chief and his métis wife lived in a comfortable log home, slept in a four-poster curtained bed, and dined with silver cutlery. A towering figure among the Shawnees, Blue Jacket embraced as much humanity as the brutality of border warfare would admit. Uncompromising in battle, he nonetheless opposed torture. A captive American woman attested to his kindliness, recalling that he never failed to offer her tea when she called on him. That he made an outsize impression on the youthful Tecumseh and strengthened his convictions against torture there can be no doubt.[19]

For a year the Shawnees united in disavowing the Wyandot and Delaware capitulation. In January 1786 the aging Mekoche head chief Moluntha, successor to the martyred Cornstalk, met with American commissioners at Fort Finney on the Ohio River, hoping for compassion. Instead, they browbeat him into signing the Treaty of Fort Finney, which ratified what the Wyandots and Delawares had presumed to give away the year before. In exchange for Moluntha's submission, the commissioners gave the Mekoches just six days' worth of provisions.[20]

Tecumseh was too young to have his opinion matter, but he and Cheeseekau clung to Blue Jacket, who repudiated the Fort Finney Treaty. So did the entire Chillicothe division. The Shawnee rejectionists resided in the ceded land and had no intention of moving again.

Like Cornstalk before him, Moluntha failed to maintain Shawnee unity. "The nation is divided, the people at Chillicothe will not hear reason," he confessed to the commander at Fort Finney. "They are determined not to agree to what has been done." Despite their discontent, the rejectionists took no action against the dubiously legal white settlements north of the Ohio River. Blood was shed, but not by the Shawnees. The intractable Mingoes and a contingent of Cherokees called the Chickamaugas, friends of the Shawnees recently arrived from the south, raided river homesteads. In the early autumn a Chickamauga war party dragged four female captives into a Mekoche village. The Shawnees seldom tortured females, but the Chickamaugas scalped a mother and daughter alive, severed their ears and arms, sliced their hamstrings, and tossed them into a fire.[21]

Kentuckians considered Shawnee tolerance of these outrages cause enough to attack them. In October 1786, Col. Benjamin Logan swept into the Shawnee villages along the Great Miami River with seven hundred mounted militiamen, only to discover them all but abandoned. In a rare act of frontier magnanimity, a deserter from Logan's command had tipped off the Shawnees. The Kentuckians had to make do with thirty-two prisoners, mostly women and children, ten dead Mekoche men who had offered no resistance, two hundred charred cabins, and seventeen thousand pounds of newly harvested corn. Ironically, of the seven Shawnee towns that Logan struck that day, those hardest hit were those of Moluntha and the neutral Mekoches.

Moluntha had had no cause to fear retribution. The old man had not only forbidden war parties to enter Mekoche communities but also sent runners to warn Kentuckians of the Chickamauga designs. And so when Logan's men galloped into Moluntha's own village, they encountered the chief, his three wives, and several white female captives, whom Moluntha had intended to return, huddled beside his cabin under a homemade American flag. As the Kentuckians dismounted, Moluntha greeted them with all the politeness his limited English permitted. Aware of Moluntha's good faith, the Kentuckians were inclined toward lenience. That is, until the frontier bully Hugh McGary, who had shamed Daniel Boone into stumbling into the bloody ambush at the Blue Licks, shoved his way through the throng to confront the old chief. Had he been at the Blue Licks? snarled McGary. "Yes, yes," replied Moluntha, wanting to appear obliging but not really understanding the question. "Goddamn you," McGary bellowed, "I'll give you Blue Licks play." Yanking his hatchet from his belt, McGary split Moluntha's skull and then tore off his scalp, threatening to chop down any man who tried to come between him and a damned Shawnee. McGary's defiance emboldened several sadistic comrades, who bound a Shawnee man to the stake, tied bags of gunpowder around his waist, and then had a hearty laugh blowing him to bits.[22]

The murder of Moluntha marked a watershed for the Ohio Shawnees, who closed ranks to seek retribution. They found an unlikely advocate in Joseph Brant, war leader of the Mohawks and the most prominent spokesman of the Iroquois Confederacy. The American Revolution had upended Iroquois pretensions to greatness. Losing their vast lands in upstate New York to the rebellious colonials, Brant and the Mohawks moved to Canada and cast their lot with the British. Although he preferred diplomacy to war, Brant believed the Iroquois and Algonquins should unite against American encroachment. On November 28, 1786, he presided over a grand council of the self-proclaimed United Indian Nations at Brownstown, a Wyandot settlement near Fort Detroit. To the delight of the Shawnees, and with the guarded approbation also of the Delawares and Wyandots, Brant declared that "the interests of any one nation should be the welfare of all others." He also called for abrogating the Fort Finney Treaty and restoring the Ohio River boundary. All Indians, Brant declared, must now eat from a common dish and become "one mind and one voice."[23]

The Americans made no effort to appease Brant's nascent federation. Popular sentiment for expansion was too clamorous to ignore, and on July 13, 1787, the national government promulgated the Northwest Ordinance, which created a territorial government in the Indian country from which five new states eventually would emerge. The secretary of war admonished territorial governor Arthur St. Clair to quiet the Indians peaceably—impossible instructions because an "almost incredible" white migration flooded the territory. Small war parties occasionally waylaid vulnerable travelers, but for the most part the Indians watched the fleets of flatboats descend the Ohio River and waited, hopeful that diplomacy might prevent the "unnecessary effusion of blood" that Brant warned the Americans would flow from disregarding Indian interests.[24]

At eighteen, Tecumseh was old enough to understand the impli-

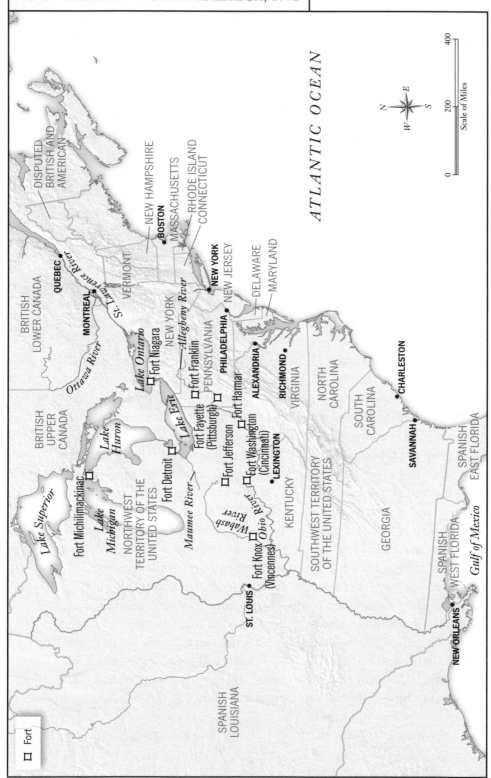

MAP 3 EASTERN NORTH AMERICA, 1792

cations of unchecked American expansion on the Shawnee way of life. As befit a younger brother, he would respond as the elder Cheeseekau deemed appropriate. And Cheeseekau deemed the appropriate response to be, first, to distance himself from the white tide, and when that failed, to make brutal and unrelenting war on the intruders.

5

War and Wanderings

Benjamin Logan's ravaging of the Great Miami River villages dispersed the Shawnees again. The tribe had enjoyed less
than thirty years of unity in the Ohio Valley. Not only the tribe but
also clans and extended families were torn asunder as the Shawnees
made their choices about where to relocate. Some journeyed south
toward the Creek country; others mingled with the Chickamaugas
along the Tennessee River. In 1788 two hundred more Shawnees relocated west of the Mississippi to the Shawnee land cession in Spanish
Louisiana, near what is today Cape Girardeau, Missouri. Most of the
Ohio Shawnees, however, drifted north and, with the permission of
the resident Miamis, concentrated near Kekionga, the center of the
fur trade at the headwaters of the Maumee River, near what was to
become Fort Wayne, Indiana. Life began again. The Shawnees built
new wigwams or cabins, cleared cornfields, put in crops, bought or
bartered for livestock, and hoped for an existence less precarious.
Tecumseh had the resilience of youth. So too did Lalawethika, in
his own insufferable fashion. As for the adults, Blue Jacket certainly
adapted readily to his new surroundings, residing in what a white captive called a "fine plantation well stocked with cattle."[1]

Fewer than one thousand Shawnees remained east of the Mississippi and north of the Ohio River. They coalesced around the leadership of Blue Jacket and the Mekoche Captain Johnny. Both men
were committed to what the Shawnees bound for Spanish Louisiana
considered a quixotic fight to drive off American interlopers and re-

establish the Ohio River boundary. Although his larger duties as a leader of tribal resistance took precedence, Blue Jacket occasionally commanded war parties against river traffic and into Kentucky. Mingo and Chickamauga warriors also accompanied Shawnee-led expeditions. Tecumseh was ever an eager volunteer.

In March 1788, Tecumseh and Ruddell joined a ninety-warrior raiding party that departed the Miami country for the Ohio River with the first spring thaw. They trekked two hundred miles through cold and leafless forest until they at last cast their hungry gaze on the broad waters of the Ohio. At twenty, Tecumseh and Ruddell were old enough to understand their duties without supervision from Cheeseekau or Blue Jacket.

Thomas Ridout, an English debt collector venturing into the backcountry, was on the second of three flatboats that shivered through the spring freshet toward the marauders, its occupants unsuspecting. As the flatboat awkwardly negotiated a river bend, Ridout contemplated the natural beauty of his surroundings—the sudden balmy turn of the weather, the gentle mist that hugged the riverbanks, the first hint of green in the trees: "Not often had I felt such delight of heart as I did [then]." The boat cleared the bend. Partly obscured by bushes, the flatboat preceding theirs lay still against the shore. Then canoes crammed with Indians "almost naked, painted and ornamented" pushed off from the pebbly bank and made straight for them.

Whether Ridout glimpsed Tecumseh amid the throng is not known. In any event, he was about to come face to face with plenty of other Indians: "About twenty leaped into our boat like so many furies, yelling and screaming horribly, brandishing their knives and tomahawks, struggling with each other for a prisoner." A young warrior painted black grabbed Ridout's arm. Then an elderly man pulled Ridout gently away: "This Indian was of a mild countenance, and he gave me immediately to understand I should not be hurt, holding me by the hand to show his property in me."

Ridout was lucky. He became the property of a good-natured Shawnee, and feelings toward him improved when it became known that he was British and not a trespassing American. At least five prisoners were burned or bludgeoned to death, however, and Ridout dreaded the worst until he met Stephen Ruddell. "Don't be afraid, sir," said Ruddell. "You are in no danger, but are given to a good man, a chief of the Shawnees, who will not hurt you; but after some time will take you to Detroit, where you may ransom yourself. Come and take your breakfast." Marveling at the transition from "apparent certain death to a renovated life," Ridout enjoyed a hearty meal of hotcakes and chocolate.

Tecumseh deeply disapproved of the murder of Ridout's companions after they had surrendered. As Ruddell later explained his friend's mindset, Tecumseh "was always averse to taking prisoners in his warfare, but when prisoners fell into his hands, he always treated them with...much humanity.... No burning—no torturing. He never tolerated the practice of killing women and children." Tecumseh would slay men in battle but not afterward.[2]

Tecumseh was growing into a strong, handsome man; Indians and whites alike found his aspect arresting. He stood five foot eleven, tall for his day, and had a larger frame than most Shawnee males. "Too heavy-built to be swift on foot," said a federal government official who knew him well, the muscular Tecumseh was "altogether formed for strength and to endure great hardships." He also had quick reflexes and excellent hand-eye coordination. His complexion was a matter of debate. Some whites thought him darker than the norm; others imagined his complexion lighter than that of most Indians. Most whites admired his high, broad forehead; slightly hawkish nose; and exceptionally fine, large white teeth. When at ease, Tecumseh was "very gay and playful" with his fellow warriors and possessed a warm and winning smile. What most struck whites about his facial features were his deep-set hazel eyes, which added a brooding intensity to his expression. In later years he would grow his hair shoulder length, eschewing the traditional scalp lock, and wear little jewelry beyond nose rings. How he adorned himself at age twenty is not known, but Ruddell said his appearance pleased young Indian women, who were as "fond of him" as the girls had been during his boyhood.

Whether he returned their affections is uncertain. John Johnston, the Indian factor (government trade representative) at Fort Wayne who later became agent to the Shawnees, swore that Tecumseh was undersexed and "never knew a woman until he was married." Ruddell agreed, saying that though polite with women, Tecumseh spurned advances and "never evinced any great regard for the female sex." On the other hand, Anthony Shane, the métis husband of his cousin, swore that as a young man Tecumseh took a bedmate whenever possible.

Most Shawnee men saw sex as something to be controlled and sublimated rather than to be indulged lightly. If one considers the numerous taboos around sexual relations, which prevented respectable men from engaging in intercourse before war or the hunt, and discouraged sex during the spring, when conception could lead to a birth in a frigid winter hunting camp, it seems likely that Tecumseh possessed the unromantic, outwardly prudish demeanor characteristic of the typical Eastern Woodland Indian male. The lack of a mother in his life may also have retarded his sexual development. A Shawnee elder revealed to a trusted white recorder both the naïveté typical of young Shawnee men and the hands-on role mothers played in their overcoming it. In accordance with laws set down by the Creator,

> When a man is twenty-five years old, at the time he is customarily married off, he doesn't know a thing about the way to have intercourse with his wife. At the time they must marry, therefore, young men are given personal instruction in the way each one should try to act when having intercourse with his wife. It seems that once a woman helped her son [learn how] he should try to act. "You must pull over your clothes like this," she said to her daughter-in-law, "and you must lie still." She then helped her son get an erection. "Crawl off," she told him. Properly she directed his penis to the woman's vaginal orifice. "Now, if you get it to go in, say 'all right' to me, and I'll turn the two of you loose."[3]

Tecumseh was about to be turned loose on an adventure far grander and enduring than momentary sexual intimacy. A new Indian confederacy was taking shape in the Ohio Valley, a union potentially more robust than the loose affiliation of bickering tribes that Pontiac and Neolin had known or the uncertain Algonquin-Iroquois combination that Joseph Brant espoused. It would mark the second serious effort at pan-Indian cooperation in the Old Northwest, an alliance with greater unity of purpose—protecting Indian land—and without the nativist religious component that had caused some Indians to shun the movement that Pontiac and Neolin had inspired but never really controlled.

Cheeseekau, however, was having none of it. Perhaps he despaired of finding a secure home in Ohio. Or simple wanderlust, so much a part of the Shawnee character, may have motivated him. Then again, he may have longed for a closer connection with his kinfolk or a reunion with his mother. Whatever the impulse, in the autumn of 1788 Cheeseekau decided to join the Shawnees in that part of Spanish Louisiana that is now eastern Missouri. He expected a hearty reception, at least from the Spanish authorities. They welcomed Shawnee and Delaware migration to bolster their flimsy defenses against rampaging Osage Indians to the west and the young and restless United States to the east. For the Shawnees, settlement in Spanish Louisiana, where the only whites were friendly French traders and accommodating Spanish officials, offered a haven from the ubiquitous Long Knives, even if it meant periodic clashes with the Osages. Although once inhabitants of the Ohio Valley themselves, the Osages had no love for the new Indian arrivals.

For Tecumseh, the decision was clear. He would accompany his elder brother, mentor, and guardian Cheeseekau. Unburdened as he was by a family of his own, it was his duty and place to stick beside his eldest sibling. He was joined by his younger brothers Nehaaseemo and Lalawethika, though the latter likely was counted a necessary burden. Frail, inept, and undoubtedly ashamed of his self-inflicted eye injury, the fourteen-year-old misfit continued the bizarre and baseless boasting that had earned him his dubious name "Rattler." Several able-bodied warriors rounded out the party.

Cheeseekau's band traveled light. Each man took no clothing but what he wore—a long hunting shirt, breechclout, leggings, and moccasins. He also carried a bundle of leather for patching, an all-purpose blanket, parched corn and jerked meat for emergency rations, a personal medicine bag, and a tomahawk pipe and hatchet tucked in his belt. Tecumseh also bore a war club. He preferred it over the hatchet because the war club had been the weapon of choice of his forefathers. On long expeditions such as this, warriors often relied on bows and arrows rather than muskets, which were bulky and hard to maintain. If needed, they could barter for or steal one along the way.[4]

The wandering Shawnees swung southwest through virgin forest, traveling leisurely and enjoying the solitude and abundant game. Skirting the small American garrison at Vincennes on the upper Wabash River, in the waning days of autumn they debouched onto the vast undulating seas of prairie grass of the Illinois country. Tecumseh and Lalawethika must have gazed awestruck at the vista. It was a land the likes of which they had never beheld. Occasional pockets of oak dimpled the endless vista. Bison in quantities unimaginable in Kentucky ambled over the open country like a moving blanket. The brothers gorged on bison meat and savored the pleasures of the hunt. With his depth perception impaired by the loss of an eye, Lalawethika was a failure as a hunter, and he may have sat out the rigorous enterprise. Not Tecumseh. In his case, enthusiasm overcame prudence. On a hunt near the junction of the Ohio and Mississippi rivers, he was thrown from his horse. Landing violently, he shattered a thighbone.

Cheeseekau's party wintered with the injured twenty-year-old in deep forests east of the Mississippi River, just fifty miles from the Shawnee villages in Spanish Louisiana. Wrapped helpless in blankets and wracked with pain, Tecumseh descended into depression. The specter of permanent disability—of lying useless in a wigwam his entire life, even more dependent than Lalawethika on the charity of others—drove him to contemplate suicide.

With the advent of spring, Tecumseh's spirits lifted. It was time to move on. Cheeseekau urged Tecumseh to stay in camp with several friends to care for him until his thigh mended, but his willful younger brother refused. Fashioning a crude pair of crutches, Tecumseh rode and walked with his companions to the Shawnee settlements. He paid the price for his bullheadedness. The stress of walking and riding too soon caused his thigh to heal imperfectly. Tecumseh was left with a slightly bowed leg, a nasty scar, and a limp—not disabling but noticeable enough that the Wyandots afterward referred to him as "Broken Thigh."[5]

Tecumseh had nearly crippled himself for nothing: Spanish Louisiana proved a grand disappointment. He had a fraught reunion with Methoataske, who had last seen her sons a decade earlier. Family ties could be mended, but what Cheeseekau and Tecumseh could not bear was the presence of Americans. A party of seventy pioneers had infiltrated the territory ahead of them and settled in the Spanish village of New Madrid in what is now southeastern Missouri, just below the mouth of the Ohio and within an easy ride of the Shawnee villages. The Americans behaved themselves, but their nearness evoked painful memories of what Cheeseekau had hoped to escape.

Tensions grew. During the summer of 1789, unfriendly American newcomers in longboats fired on Shawnee hunters, wounding one, and stole their furs. To Cheeseekau's mortification, the western Shawnees were more concerned with tending to their poultry and hogs than with confronting the offenders. It was more than Cheeseekau could bear. After a year among their assimilationist brethren, Cheeseekau and his brothers bade farewell to their mother and splashed back across the Mississippi. Some of the party, including the fourteen-year-old Lalawethika and Nehaaseemo, returned to Ohio. Cheeseekau and Tecumseh, however, were in search of a fight. They made for the secluded Tennessee River strongholds of the Chickamaugas. A splinter group of Cherokees, the Chickamaugas were then the fiercest native opponents of the United States. Tecumseh was about to gain invaluable combat experience under Dragging Canoe, a sophisticated, defiant war chief and agile intertribal diplomat, beside whom the most militant Indian leader in the Ohio country appeared merely a white man's cat's-paw.[6]

The Cherokees were an Iroquoian people. Their vast homeland had embraced portions of North and South Carolina, Tennessee, Kentucky, and Georgia. On the eve of the American Revolution, Cherokee peace chiefs sold their Kentucky and Tennessee holdings for a pittance. Only Dragging Canoe dissented. "You have bought a fair land, but there is a cloud hanging over it," he told the colonial delegates. "You will find its settlement dark and bloody." And they did. In 1776, Dragging Canoe and his warriors eradicated every trace of white settlements west of the southern Appalachians. They overreached, however, crossing the mountains to attack American communities on the eastern side. Few Cherokee leaders had any stomach for resisting the inevitable American punitive expeditions, and the Cherokee Nation signed two peace treaties yielding the land that Dragging Canoe had recovered.

Implacable in his hatred of the Americans, Dragging Canoe seceded from the Cherokee nation with five hundred warriors and their families. He taunted the peace faction as "Virginians." Obtaining arms and supplies from the British, he withdrew westward to the Tennessee River and Chickamauga Creek, near today's Chattanooga. Perhaps to

shame those who were not defiant, Dragging Canoe called his followers the Aniyuniwiya, the "Real People," which was how all Cherokees
identified themselves.[7]

A warm welcome awaited Cheeseekau and Tecumseh in the Chickamauga villages. Freedom-loving Shawnees and Cherokees had long
been firm friends and allies against American encroachment. When
Dragging Canoe assumed leadership of Cherokee resistance, he cultivated reciprocal visits between his warriors and receptive Shawnees.
Even as Cheeseekau and Tecumseh wound their way along the Tennessee River to offer their services to Dragging Canoe, a contingent of
Chickamaugas traveled to the Ohio country independent of Tecumseh's visit, one of many Chickamauga delegations that regularly paid
the Shawnees extended visits to maintain close ties between the two
peoples.[8]

Their mutual affinity is easy to understand. Although the Chickamaugas spoke an Iroquoian language, Chickamauga and Shawnee cultures were similar. Bilingual Shawnee residents presumably
interpreted for Cheeseekau and Tecumseh, elevating the brothers'
exchanges with their hosts beyond that afforded by sign language.

The Chickamauga country was a good place for two Shawnee
warriors looking to grapple with the Long Knives. Their hosts were
ensconced in five towns stretching west forty miles from Lookout
Mountain, a towering eminence that dominated the Tennessee River
opposite what is today Chattanooga. It was a rough and rugged region,
a defensive bastion of great natural grandeur from which the Chickamaugas could launch raids with near impunity. The Chickamaugas
were not all about war, however. Their villages were comfortable,
their needs supplied by Spanish West Florida and British Canada, as
well as by plunder from American frontier settlements. They lived in
solid log houses, raised corn, and kept plentiful stocks of hogs, cattle,
and poultry. Dragging Canoe's village of Running Water, with a population of four hundred, was the Chickamauga capital and home of the
principal council house. It was there that Cheeseekau, Tecumseh, and
their companions settled in late 1789, bringing the number of Shawnee
warriors in the town to about three dozen. The Chickamaugas were
then in high spirits. They had raided clear to the Cumberland River in
what is today Middle Tennessee and then repelled a counteroffensive.

What was to become the State of Tennessee was then designated the "Territory of the United States South of the River Ohio," more commonly known as the Southwest Territory. The territory was divided into three districts—two for East Tennessee and one for the Mero District (encompassing modern Nashville and environs) on the Cumberland River. Each had its own courts, militia, and officeholders, which impeded coordinated responses to the fast-moving Chickamaugas. President Washington appointed William Blount, a prominent North Carolina politician, as territorial governor. Together with Kentucky, still three years shy of statehood, the Southwest Territory represented the farthest penetration westward by the young American Republic south of the Ohio River. American settlement of the Southwest Territory was more robust than that of the Northwest Territory, which, with just over 4,000 white occupants, existed more as an aspirational abstraction than as a settled reality. By the time Cheeseekau and Tecumseh joined the Chickamaugas, nearly 36,000 whites called the Southwest Territory home.[9]

Farther south, landless Georgians were pushing at the periphery of the Creek Indian confederacy, which constituted most of Alabama and all of what would eventually become western Georgia. Border skirmishes threatened to suck the United States, with a regular army of fewer than one thousand men, into a larger conflict that it was ill prepared to wage; white settlement north of the Ohio River threatened a full-scale war with the Shawnees and its allied tribes. West of the Creeks in what is today northern Mississippi, the heretofore friendly Chickasaw Indians also had grown restive. To prevent the outbreak of simultaneous Indian wars in the Northwest and Southwest, in February 1790 President Washington dispatched thirty-six-year-old Maj. John Doughty, a veteran of the American Revolution, and a small detachment of soldiers on a peace mission to the southern tribes. Doughty descended the Ohio River and was rowing up the Tennessee on a large barge with reinforced sides to meet Chickasaw escorts. One hundred miles from the nearest Chickamauga town, several scouts—belonging to a hunting expedition of forty Chickamauga, Shawnee, and Creek warriors under the leadership of Cheeseekau— encountered them huddled on an island. It is likely but not certain that Tecumseh was with the hunting party. He would have had no leadership role; he went where his brother went, particularly when a foray offered a chance to indulge his passion for hunting in a wild and game-rich new country.

The Indians were divided over how to respond to Doughty. He seemed friendly enough and said his mission was peaceful, but Cheeseekau had heard rumors that the Americans intended to construct a fort on the Tennessee River, which Doughty's presence appeared to confirm. Indian runners from the Ohio Valley also had brought word of American aggression against the incipient Northwestern Confederacy, of which Blue Jacket was a prominent leader. Consequently, Cheeseekau was ill disposed to negotiate. Instead, he would use deception to lure the Americans into a slaughter. That he would have consulted Tecumseh, assuming his brother was present, is doubtful; Tecumseh's duty was to observe, learn, and fight. Dispersing his forty warriors in four canoes, Cheeseekau started downstream.

He discovered them at noon, Doughty and sixteen sweating soldiers at the oars of a bulky barge, toiling upstream. Cheeseekau ran up a white flag. With a few attendants he climbed aboard Doughty's craft. The remaining Indians went ashore. Would the major and his men care to join them for a meal? A wary Doughty declined the offer. Cheeseekau took his leave and paddled to shore. The soldiers set aside their muskets and grasped the oars. Then the crash of forty Indian muskets rent the afternoon stillness. Six soldiers slumped over dead; five others were wounded. Only four fought back, but their ragged fire sufficed to cause Cheeseekau to break off the contest. He had accomplished much—killing or disabling most of the Americans, disrupting whatever might have been their nefarious intent, and leaving them to limp into the nearest French settlement on the Mississippi for succor. Most important, Cheeseekau had done it all without incurring a single casualty, the mark of a truly great war leader. In societies as small as those of the Shawnees and Chickamaugas, every warrior's life was precious. Word of Cheeseekau's exploit drifted north. Northwestern Confederacy chiefs later boasted of it to the British and, painting Major Doughty as the aggressor, added the incident to their own grievances against the Americans.[10]

Cheeseekau and Tecumseh found a home among the Chickamaugas. They threw themselves wholeheartedly into the Chickamauga cause, beating back American intruders and bewailing the continued land concessions west of the Appalachians by pliant Cherokees. In April 1791 they decimated a pack of white desperados who tried to penetrate the Chickamauga stronghold in three bateaux mounting small can-nons called swivel guns. One boat ran aground. By the time the two other crews dispersed the war party, thirty-two Americans lay dead or wounded on the deck of the disabled bateaux.[11]

Tecumseh was proving to be more than simply a capable follower of his brother in battle. On at least one occasion he also asserted his own moral values. Confronting a returning war party with a white prisoner destined for death at the stake, Tecumseh urged the warriors to reconsider committing an act unworthy of brave men. When that line of appeal fell on deaf ears, Tecumseh suggested they consider the monetary loss they would incur—no ransom could be had for a dead man. The warriors again rebuffed him. Tecumseh drew a pistol from his belt. To spare the prisoner the agony of the stake, Tecumseh shot him dead and then walked away from the astonished war party unmo-lested. He had carried his point, in a manner of speaking.[12]

Around this time, Tecumseh took another bold step toward man-hood. Shedding his Shawnee reserve, he was now making love to women. Much as he had within his own tribe, the handsome young Shawnee warrior attracted the attention of Chickamauga girls. Anthony Shane said Tecumseh rejected several overtures of mar-riage because he did not wish to be "burdened" with a wife. He did keep house with a young Chickamauga woman, who reportedly bore him a daughter. Obviously, Tecumseh had had no need of his absent mother's sexual guidance in consummating the relationship, as so many young Shawnee males apparently did. Whether the Chicka-mauga girl was his first conquest is a matter of conjecture. Stephen Ruddell, who implied that Tecumseh had scant interest in the oppo-site sex, said that Tecumseh lived with his Chickamauga paramour longer than with any other woman he would ever know. Shane insisted that Tecumseh enjoyed the company of many women but jettisoned them on the smallest pretext: "Tecumseh usually had before marriage a young woman living with him. But the moment he found her negli-gent of her duty or that she failed to provide liberally for his friends, he would make her some presents and send her back to her parents, and no entreating would induce him again to receive her."[13]

In the summer of 1791, Tecumseh abandoned not only his Chick-amauga lover but also her country, to return to the Ohio Valley to join Blue Jacket's confederacy. Tecumseh also left behind Cheeseekau, who had embraced the Chickamauga cause above that of his own people. (Cheeseekau could have had no doubt that the Ohio Shawnees needed all the warriors they could muster because runners from home brought baleful reports of American belligerence.) Tecumseh's sojourn among the Chickamaugas had given him a greater appreciation for the larger Indian plight than he could have gained had he remained north of the Ohio. It exposed him to the intricacies of alliance building across vast distances. On a personal level, Tecumseh had won a woman's love and likely fathered a child at an earlier age than most Shawnee men aspired to romantic assignations. He also had earned himself a place as a minor war leader. He was ready to emerge from beneath his elder brother's shadow and, like the celestial panther, soar on his own merits. He would not be alone. When Tecumseh departed the Chickamauga country, eight warriors rode with him.[14]

Events of great moment had transpired in the Ohio Valley during Tecumseh's three-year absence. A cataclysmic clash between Indian and American arms appeared inevitable. The Mohawk war chief Joseph Brant's commitment both to pan-Indianism and the inviolability of the Ohio River boundary had proven evanescent, perhaps even false. No sooner had Brant pledged an unshakable harmony between the Iroquois and Algonquin peoples than, hoping to reassert Iroquois authority over the Ohio Indians, he exploited a rift between conciliatory Wyandots and Delawares and hard-line Shawnees and Miamis. At Fort Harmar—a formidable American stockade defiantly erected three years earlier on the north bank of the Ohio River, alongside the village of Marietta, that became a magnet for settlers—U.S. commissioners concluded a treaty with the Iroquois reaffirming American ownership of most of the Ohio country, and with Brant's help they also bullied the Wyandots and Delawares into a similar agreement.

The Treaty of Fort Harmar achieved three unintended objectives: it discredited Brant's pretensions to intertribal leadership, erasing the vestiges of Iroquois influence over the western tribes; it elevated the Shawnees and Miamis to the helm of the resistance movement; and it made them increasingly reliant on the British for aid. The Shawnee chief Blue Jacket and the Miami chief Little Turtle, both of whom disavowed the Fort Harmar agreement, emerged as the dominant Indian figures in the militant Northwestern Confederacy, which also drew disgusted Wyandots, Delawares, and Kickapoos into its ranks.[15]

To demonstrate their unyielding commitment to the Ohio River boundary, Indian war parties not only struck fledgling settlements on the north bank of the Ohio but also penetrated deeper into Virginia and Kentucky than they had in over a decade, sending scores of whites to brutish ends in lonely frontier graves. Arthur St. Clair, the governor of the Northwest Territory and a Revolutionary War hero, understood the Indians' fury. "From all accounts there is a great deal of uneasiness among [the Indians], and it is clear to me that, if it cannot be removed, a very general war will ensue," he alerted the Washington administration. "Whether that uneasiness can be removed I own, I think doubtful, for though we hear much of the injuries and depredations that are committed by the Indians upon the whites, there is too much reason to believe that at least equal if not greater injuries are done to the Indians by the frontier settlers of which we hear very little."[16]

The evidence was on the streets. In Cincinnati, Indian scalps lifted from hostile or friendly heads brought a bounty of thirty dollars apiece with no questions asked. In lieu of a cash reward, a scalp hunter might claim a good horse for a prize. Pioneer youths collected scalps as avidly as young warriors. A backcountry settler revealed how one boy submerged his humanity in the swirling struggle for land and sustenance. After a deep-woods skirmish with a war party, he and his compatriots inched through dissipating gun smoke toward a batch of high weeds in which a wounded warrior was thought to have concealed himself. Like a pack of wolves, the frontiersmen formed a circle and slowly closed the perimeter. His leg broken and chance of escape nil, the Indian sat up and, addressing a fourteen-year-old, said with a wan smile, "How do you do, brother?" To which the boy replied, "How do you do, damn you," and then cleaved his skull with a tomahawk.[17]

From the government perspective, after the recalcitrant tribes—or "banditti," as officials liked to call them—repudiated the Fort Harmar Treaty, a serious military expedition against their Maumee River towns was needed to enforce the land cession. The Washington administration blamed the Shawnees for the unrest because of Cheeseekau's attack on Major Doughty's expedition. Pro-government Wyandots, who promised to expel the militant Indian squatters from the Maumee River country, also laid blame on the Shawnees.[18]

St. Clair knew that the Wyandots lacked both the will and the means to make good on their boast to rid their land of Little Turtle and Blue Jacket's confederated militants. Realizing that only the army could prevail, he sent Bvt. Brig. Gen. Josiah Harmar with a large militia command and a regiment of regulars to subdue them. By the time Harmar reached the Maumee River country in late October 1790, the Indians had fled. With foul weather approaching, he turned back after burning Little Turtle's Miami town and its corn supply. All might have ended well for Harmar's command had not the unruly militiamen insisted on trying to ambush Indians trailing the army. Harmar reluctantly yielded, but it was the militiamen who were ambushed. Only the timely arrival of the regulars prevented a general slaughter. As it was, Harmar lost nearly two hundred killed.[19]

In March 1791 the War Department ordered the gout-ridden St. Clair to lead a second attempt to "liberate" the Ohio country. No one could accuse St. Clair of taking precipitate action. As the new commanding general of the U.S. Army, he took precautions to assemble a far larger nucleus of regulars than had been available to Harmar; in fact, nearly the entire fledgling Regular Army marched with St. Clair. Secretary of State Thomas Jefferson eagerly anticipated the coming clash of arms. "I hope we shall give the Indians a thorough drubbing this summer," he told President Washington, "and then change our tomahawk into a gold chain of friendship."

Washington likely was less sanguine. The regulars wore sharp-looking uniforms of blue coats and white trousers, as opposed to the indifferently clad militiamen, who were indistinguishable from civilians, but they were at best a marginally disciplined, untrained, poorly fed, hard-drinking lot, ignorant of Indian warfare and any other mode of fighting for that matter. And the presence of at least one hundred female camp followers (wives, laundresses, and prostitutes) was hardly conducive to good order. With this ragtag force, Knox expected St. Clair to defeat an enemy of equal strength who, in the words of a veteran Indian fighter, had been "brought up from infancy to war, and [were] perhaps superior to an equal number of the best men that could be taken against them." The Indians, moreover, had moved forty miles upriver to a new and better consolidated community at the Glaize, a natural depression in the prairie near the junction of the Maumee and Auglaize rivers (in present-day northwestern Ohio) where buffalo once wallowed. There the Indians prepared for the American approach, while scouts kept their leaders well apprised of St. Clair's activities.[20]

Jefferson expected a triumphant denouement that summer, but supply delays prevented St. Clair from setting out until October 4. Watching the rabble depart, Josiah Harmar confided to his former aide-de-camp Lt. Ebenezer Denny, who had signed up for the campaign, that he foresaw a fiasco. Soldiers who had been "purchased from prisons, wheelbarrows, and brothels at two dollars a month" would not answer for fighting Indians. Nonetheless, Harmer told Denny to look on the bright side, as "some will escape, and you may be among the number."

Pan-Indianism was about to achieve its grandest triumph in the three decades since Chief Pontiac sparked the savage war against the British that bore his name.[21]

Tecumseh was nowhere near the impending theater of conflict. Rather, the fledgling war leader was engaged in belligerent action of a more traditional Shawnee sort. That summer he had taken his small party on a roundabout route toward home from the Chickamauga country, passing leisurely through what is today eastern Tennessee into southwestern Virginia. At first the hunting was good and the journey easy. As Tecumseh neared the Ohio River in late September, difficulties arose. Evidently unknown to him, other Shawnee war parties had made their presence felt in the Little Kanawha River Valley, the avenue Tecumseh chose to take to the Ohio. Both the frontier militiamen and the citizenry were on their guard. A long dry spell had turned the thick blanket of fallen leaves in the forest so brittle that the softest moccasin tread alarmed the deer, and Tecumseh's party were unable to kill any game. Descending one of the interminable ridges that crossed their path, the Indians chanced upon a twelve-year-old slave boy named Frank, out searching for stray horses belonging to his master, James Neal. Tecumseh quietly seized him and pressed on.

Neal was a prominent pioneer whose eponymous stockade Neal's Station stood on the site of today's Parkersburg, West Virginia. Keeping clear of the garrison, Tecumseh's party edged their way cross-country toward the Ohio. For three days Tecumseh, his eight warriors, and a reluctant Frank traipsed through the forest with only a single tortoise to show for their abortive efforts at hunting. When Frank grew weary, Tecumseh cheered him with the promise of a horse of his own once they reached home—which, however, was still 275 densely timbered miles distant.

And then Frank's fortunes, and those of his Indian captors, suddenly improved. No sooner had Tecumseh given his kindhearted pledge than the famished party beheld a broad, freshly beaten track bisecting their path. Tecumseh's band followed it throughout the night. Shortly before dawn, six miles short of the Ohio River, a campfire came into view. Around it slept seven men bundled in blankets. No sentry stood watch. The prospect of plundering horses decided Tecumseh to attack. Creeping to within a few yards of the campfire, he deployed his warriors behind a fallen tree trunk. Back on the path, Frank stood silently, bound to a tree with leather straps and a warning to keep quiet.

The unsuspecting whites included Nicholas Carpenter, a "worthy, pious man, well acquainted with a forest life"; his ten-year-old son; and five cattle drovers in Carpenter's employ: Jesse Hughes, George Legit, John Paul, and two men surnamed Barnes and Ellis. They were on their way to deliver a herd of cattle and milk cows across the river.

At first light on October 4, Nicholas Carpenter awakened his crew with a call to prayer. Carpenter opened his hymnal, and a musket volley sang its greeting. A ball ripped through John Paul's hand. A better-aimed shot struck Ellis in the chest. With a terrific yell, Tecumseh and his tomahawk-wielding warriors rushed their astonished victims. Grabbing both his own musket and that of Carpenter, Jesse Hughes staggered into the woods, legs entangled in his slipped britches. Pausing to yank them off, he felt a thrown tomahawk graze his head. Hughes fired one musket at his pursuer but missed, threw away the other in fright, then lit out barelegged through the timber. He survived, his hunting shirt riven with bullet holes.

John Paul, a fast runner, escaped. Barnes, a slow, stout man, died beside the campfire. The Indians pursued George Legit two miles through the timber before overtaking and killing him. Nicholas Carpenter never stood a chance. Lame and unarmed, he huddled with his boy in a willow brake. Warriors dragged them to the tree where they had bound Frank, only to discover that he had struggled free of his restraints. From a thick patch of hazel bushes, Frank watched the warriors tomahawk Carpenter and his son. Perhaps Frank's disappearance had prompted the outrage. It certainly violated Tecumseh's credo to "kill the enemy if possible and leave none to be captured, but if prisoners fall into your hands, treat them humanely." In any event, one of Carpenter's murderers had a pang of guilt. He recognized the dead Carpenter as one who had repaired his musket the year before free of charge. The remorseful Indian wrapped Carpenter in a blanket, placed a pair of new moccasins on his feet, and forbade anyone to scalp him.

There was no time to lose. Fearing a pursuit from a local ranger unit, Tecumseh told his men to collect what plunder lay nearby and then abscond; the white men's horses, which had bolted into the forest, were too far off to be caught safely. Good fortune led Frank to a nearby settlement, where he told his baleful tale.[22]

Tecumseh hugged the south bank of the Ohio River for sixty miles to the mouth of the Scioto River. There he crossed the Ohio on crudely built rafts. Making its way northwest, Tecumseh's party met an Indian near Mad River who had been wounded in a skirmish with an army patrol. A huge American column was on the move north, he told Tecumseh; a battle was in the offing. Tecumseh hurried the pace as much as his large and limping frame permitted.[23]

At their confederated villages seventy miles distant, the Indians were well informed of the American approach. Mounted scouting parties submitted daily reports of St. Clair's lumbering, racket-inducing rabble. Bellowing oxen, creaking wagons, ringing axes, cursing soldiers, and hectoring camp followers formed a discordant wilderness choir. Riflemen occasionally glimpsed the mounted warriors. Cavalry detachments gave chase but came up empty-handed.

St. Clair made camp sixteen times during his monthlong march. At each encampment the Indians grabbed soldiers. Some were lost deserters; others were imbeciles who strayed from camp to hunt. The Indians killed or interrogated the men, whose woebegone aspect betrayed an army on the verge of collapse. Supplies ran out, cold rains and sleet tore thin uniforms to tatters, and officers quarreled. Carried on a sling between two horses, the gout-ridden St. Clair was worse than useless. He dismissed the Indians as a feckless annoyance. "The savages," he told his subordinates, "if violently attacked will always break and give way and when once broke, for the want of discipline, will never rally." Apart from his own health, St. Clair's greatest worry was that the Indians would flee before he could bring them to battle.

Flight was the furthest thing from the minds of Blue Jacket and Little Turtle. They had assembled a confident coalition of fourteen hundred warriors. On the frigid and snowy afternoon of November 3, 1791, the Indians advanced to within two and a half miles of St. Clair's camp, laid out in a rectangle beside the Wabash River, 110 miles west of today's Columbus, Ohio. That night Blue Jacket deployed the Indians in a crescent formation like that which Cornstalk had used at Point Pleasant. The Indians were within shouting distance of the outermost American picket posts. Beneath a snow-blanched cobalt sky, Blue Jacket offered up a wilderness prayer "that tomorrow [the Great Spirit] will cause the sun to shine out clear upon us, and we will take it as a token of good, and we shall conquer."[24]

Now seventeen, Lalawethika likely was among the three hundred Shawnees lying in wait "to begin the play," as one warrior later put it; to have missed the great fight would have been a disgrace from which one as roundly despised as Lalawethika could never have hoped to recover. Tecumseh, however, was elsewhere. Blue Jacket had assigned him scouting duty. Nightfall on November 3 apparently found his party on Nettle Creek, a sluggish tributary of Mad River, at least twenty miles east of St. Clair's camp. Not expecting a battle so soon, Tecumseh may have engaged in a bit of hunting far afield.

The distant boom of cannons on the morning of November 4 told Tecumseh that he had missed "the play." From the Indian perspective, it was a grand and bloody comedy. Blue Jacket's crescent engulfed St. Clair's command before the soldiers knew what they were up against. Those who resisted had not only the Indians but also the elements to contend with. "The day was severely cold," a survivor recalled. "My fingers became so benumbed at times that I had to take the bullets in my mouth and load from it." There were few clear targets. Lt. Ebenezer Denny—with whom General Harmar had shared his premonition of disaster—said the Indians darted unseen from tree to tree; even at close range the warriors were infuriatingly hard to engage. "They could skip out of reach of the bayonet and return as they pleased [and] were visible only when raised by a charge. The ground was literally covered with [our] dead.... A few minutes longer, and retreat would have been impracticable.... The only hope was that the savages would be so taken up with the camp as not to follow."

Which proved the case. After a half-hearted chase for four miles, Indian discipline gave way to the temptation of plunder, and a relieved Lieutenant Denny watched the warriors flock back to the battlefield. "How fortunate that the pursuit was discontinued. A single Indian might have followed with safety upon either flank. Such a panic had seized the men that I believe it would not have been possible to have brought any of them to engage again."

The precise number of Americans lost was never ascertained; the best estimate is 630 officers and men killed and 284 wounded out of approximately 1,700 engaged. In addition to the official casualties, most of the camp followers were butchered or captured. Indian losses were, in the British agent Alexander McKee's words, "trifling," certainly fewer than one hundred killed and wounded.[25]

The Indians ranged over the battlefield, slicing off scalps, disfiguring the dead, tomahawking the wounded, haggling over captives, and gathering spoils they never could have paid for in coin or in furs. John Brickell, adopted by the Delawares as a youth, marveled at the treasures. His adoptive father's share included two fine horses, four tents, heaps of clothing, axes, and guns—"everything to make an Indian rich," said Brickell, who carried away an army overcoat as winter wear.[26]

Tecumseh reached the slaughter grounds too late to collect much if any booty. The missed opportunity would not have troubled him. His wants were few; his generosity great. Already, at twenty-three, he displayed a liberality extreme even among the famously open-handed Eastern Woodland Indians. Lewis Cass, the future governor of Michigan Territory, later spoke admiringly of Tecumseh's munificence: "Few could boast of having intercepted so many boats on the Ohio River or plundered so many houses on the civilized shore. It goes to show the disinterested generosity always ascribed to him that, although the booty collected in the course of these adventures must have been very considerable in quantity and value, he rarely retained any portion of it for his own use. His ruling passion was the love of glory." Ruddell agreed. Tecumseh was "free-hearted and generous to excess—always ready to relieve the wants of others. When he returned from a hunting expedition, he would harangue his companions and make use of all his eloquence to instill into their minds honorable and humane sentiments."[27]

The principal Indian sentiment of the moment was celebratory, however. Little Turtle and Blue Jacket's Western Confederacy had effectively annihilated the small U.S. army. That the Americans would try to avenge their defeat could be counted a certainty. But such a prospect was too far in the future to occasion much worry, especially to a people in the thrall of a sublime, supernatural happening. On the snow-blown afternoon preceding the battle with St. Clair's Long Knives, a great sacred fire had been lit, around which the principal chiefs, war leaders, and medicine men gathered. Alongside the blaze, the entire host of warriors drew up in two lines twenty feet apart, facing inward, while the medicine men whipped the assemblage into a frenzy with their incantations and magic. When they ceased, the forest shuddered with the simultaneous cheers of hundreds of warriors. Two whites who were present—a sober-minded trader named Joseph Jackson and Stephen Ruddell's impressionable brother Abraham—both later swore to the miracle that followed. From the heart of the fire a snake twenty feet long emerged. It raised its head, red and glowing like fire, five feet into the air and then slithered with the speed of lightning between the lines of warriors and vanished into the woods. The warriors were jubilant. Truly the snake was the Great Spirit incarnate, come to show the path to victory over the Long Knives.[28]

It was within this potent milieu of faith in the fantastic—a growing sense that the Master of Life, through woodland spirits, had intervened to guide the Indians to righteous redemption and freedom from the Long Knives—that Lalawethika came of age, and Tecumseh matured as a leader, albeit a minor one. When events instead took a dark course for the Shawnees, Lalawethika would buckle under the strain of blasted hopes, and Tecumseh would grope for a greater purpose than that of a minor war leader and able hunter.

6

Out from the Shadows

THE FRONTIER RECEDED. Pioneers who dared to penetrate the
Ohio wilderness after the Treaty of Fort Harmar abandoned
their outlying settlements and huddled in the fortified communities
of Marietta and Cincinnati near two woefully understrength Ohio
River federal outposts, Forts Harmar and Washington. They were in a
state of perpetual siege. Men carried their rifles wherever they went,
strengthened their cabins, and bored loopholes into the walls for firing
on Indian attackers. Nearly all were tough New Englanders, Revolutionary War veterans, and not likely to quit the country without a
fight. Their women and children went nowhere without armed male
escorts. Rangers raised by New England owners the Ohio Company,
which sponsored the settlements, scoured the surrounding country
for hostile Indians.

Marietta, which lay across the Muskingham River from Fort Harmar, had been laid out with Yankee thoroughness as a village of wide
streets and broad squares. Now the inhabitants spent most of their
time in a strong stockade with a blockhouse at each corner. Food
shortages were common, smallpox showed itself periodically, and fear
of Indian assault was a constant. All was not gloom, however. One
resident said garrison life, having "broken up former fixed habits of
industry, led to a fondness, for sports and social meetings where drinking was practiced, and hours spent in jovial conviviality."

Founded in 1788 by twenty-seven hearty New Jersey and Pennsylvania natives, the handful of cabins that constituted Cincinnati sat

defiantly on the north bank of the Ohio near Fort Washington and a hundred miles upstream from Louisville. Its leading citizens also were no strangers to warfare; most were either Revolutionary War veterans or former members of the Kentucky militia.

Rather than attempt to dislodge the five hundred Ohio Company pioneers hunkered down in their stockades, the Indians preferred to harass them. They also availed themselves of the two hundred river-miles separating Cincinnati from Marietta and renewed raids into Kentucky.

Meanwhile in Philadelphia, the federal government fretted and temporized. President Washington implored Congress to authorize a regular army composed of something superior to St. Clair's ill-disciplined misfits and large enough to reclaim the treaty cessions in the Northwest Territory. Simultaneously he advocated fair dealing with the Indians, reasonable trading practices, and strict regulations governing the acquisition of Indian land; in short, a just treatment— from an Anglo perspective—of the Indians in all matters except the vital one: their land. For that there was no mutually agreeable solution. The rapidly growing American population hovered at just below four million. All but perhaps 150,000 resided between the Appalachians and the Atlantic Coast. Most of the population was rural, and far too many farmers faced empty prospects. They could no more be expected to ignore the rich and sparsely settled Northwest Territory than the Indians could be expected to yield the region without a struggle. Some Indians might be bought off and taught to till the earth, but there would always be a core opposition to any concessions. By slowing the pace of white settlement and playing Indian factions against one another, the government at best might lessen the magnitude of future conflicts.[1]

South of the Ohio River, the Creeks gave ground in western Georgia, with militant bands skirmishing occasionally with white interlopers, and the Cherokees ceded much of the Southwest Territory. Indian unity held in the Northwest, however, and negotiations were pointless. The Americans would have to either respect the Ohio River as the boundary between Indians and whites or accept perpetual war as the price for violating it. "After two successful engagements in which a great deal of blood has been spilt," reported the British Indian agent Alexander McKee, "the Indians will not give quietly up by negotiation what they have been contending for with their lives since the commencement of these troubles." Not even the pitiless winter of 1791–92, when game all but vanished and starvation stalked the scattered hunting camps, broke the Indian will to resist. In the spring, Blue Jacket not only reaffirmed the allegiance of those who had defeated St. Clair but, in a tribute to the vigor of Shawnee diplomacy, also sent runners deep into the Great Lakes country to invite previously uncommitted Indians to a huge autumn council. Blue Jacket himself traveled, conferring with McKee at Detroit and courting tribes along the upper Mississippi River.[2]

Although confederacy chiefs conducted intertribal diplomacy on a plane far above that on which the twenty-three-year-old Tecumseh moved, he was witness to the powerful appeal of pan-Indianism when deft practitioners, like his sometime mentor Blue Jacket and the Miami chief Little Turtle, orchestrated it. Their soul-stirring examples afforded him lessons in leadership, to be pondered and guarded, should the day arrive when he himself possessed the prestige, influence, and purpose needed to command a large multitribal following. Meanwhile, as the soft warmth of a wilderness spring caressed the Ohio Valley back to life, Tecumseh resumed his march up the Shawnee tribal ladder. Consolidating his small body of supporters and gaining a handful of new adherents, he led hunting and war parties on both banks of the Ohio River.

In December 1791 Tecumseh had an unexpected brush with the Long Knives on Loramie Creek, a placid tributary of the Great Miami River in western Ohio. It was early morning. The snow lay hard on the ground. Tecumseh, Stephen Ruddell, nine youthful warriors, and a boy attendant sat beside a fire enjoying a smoke. The low roar of long rifles shattered the gelid stillness. Thirty "Kentucks" had sneaked up on their camp unnoticed. Tecumseh emitted a war whoop. His warriors grabbed their muskets and began shooting. Waving the boy menial to the rear, Tecumseh glanced back to make sure he had left. Not only had the boy obediently dashed off, but a warrior named Black Turkey had also sprinted rearward beside him. A barked rebuke from Tecumseh froze the man in his tracks, and a second reprimand returned him to the firing line. Raising his flintlock musket at a Kentuckian just a few feet distant, Tecumseh took aim and squeezed the trigger. The flint struck the touch pan weakly. Powder fizzled, and the musket ball bounced harmlessly off his enemy's coat. Tecumseh reacted fast. Drawing his war club, he dashed forward and crushed the startled man's skull, just as the other Kentuckians retreated; the racket that Black Turkey raised in splashing back across the icy Loramie Creek had convinced them that Indian reinforcements were on the way. Tecumseh counted two enemy killed at a cost of two warriors lightly wounded. Recalling that day, Ruddell later said that Tecumseh had acted with "coolness and bravery, not rash but deliberate." Those were words Ruddell would repeat when recollecting every skirmish in which he fought under Tecumseh's leadership.[3]

It was April 1792, the season of the Half Moon. Shawnee war parties stabbed at Kentucky settlements and stole horses. So long as the Kentucks remained on their side of the river, the Shawnees largely seemed content to inflict only material loss. Nonlethal depredations, however, sat no better with the settlers than did killings. Exasperated by a horse-thieving raid below Cincinnati, Kentucky militia captain Simon Kenton mobilized thirty-five men, picked up the Indian trail, and rafted across the Ohio at the mouth of Bullskin Creek, forty-seven miles upstream from Cincinnati, to find the perpetrators. Unknown to Kenton, it was Tecumseh's band he sought.[4]

The thirty-seven-year-old Kenton was no stranger to frontier frays. Kentuckians regarded the native Virginian as second only to Daniel Boone in command presence, common sense, and courage. Kenton had absconded from Virginia at sixteen after beating to death (or so he thought) a rival for a girl's affection. Although he was not at the battle of Point Pleasant in 1774, Kenton was one of Lord Dunmore's most reliable scouts. Kenton and Boone were inseparable until Kenton left Boonesborough to stake out his own station in the Kentucky wilderness. An expert in woodcraft, Indian sign language, and tracking, Kenton imparted his skills to a group of youths known as "Kenton's boys." Their mentor, said one, was "the most natural man I ever saw or talked with." Like Boone, Kenton had been a Shawnee captive and survived the gauntlet run. Most Shawnee warriors recognized him on sight. Whether Tecumseh already knew him is not known, but he was about to.

For all Kenton's skills, his mounted foray provided an object les-

son in the painful shortcomings of the militia as then conceived. No
sooner had Kenton's party ferried across the Ohio River than one
loudmouthed tyro lost courage and demanded they turn back. That
caused the son of the man whose horses Tecumseh had stolen to whip
the recreant with his ramrod until Kenton restored order, inviting
anyone who wished to go home. A dozen men skulked off. Beneath an
intermittent rain, Kenton and the remaining twenty-three horsemen
cantered northward into the foothills of southwestern Ohio. They
made good time, tracking the Indian trail for forty miles until noon
on the second day (April 9), when the tinkle of a horse bell brought
the party to an abrupt halt. Kenton detailed two militiamen to reconnoiter but under no circumstance open fire. The rain resumed, hard
and steady.

A few moments later a single shot rang out. Kicking his horse forward, Kenton found the two men staring at a dead Shawnee. He told
the man with the smoking musket to consider himself under arrest.
"Arrest me and be damned," the militiaman retorted; had they followed Kenton's instructions, the two Kentuckians would have been
"nothing but bait for Indians."

Rolling the Indian corpse into some brush and taking hold of his
horse, which its rightful owner recognized as one of those stolen from
his farm, Kenton's surly party proceeded along the dead Shawnee's
back trail. Again, they halted. Kenton sent Alexander McIntyre, a
"small, active, resolute woodsman ... who had killed several Indians
since he settled in Kentucky," and two others ahead to reconnoiter
silently. The three dutifully discharged no weapons but returned with
a wild-eyed report. Through the pelting rain they claimed to have
counted two hundred warriors milling about an enormous Indian village composed of marquee tents scavenged from St. Clair. Why the
warriors were outdoors in the storm, McIntyre and his fellow scouts
neglected to say.[5]

Kenton called a council. He permitted each man his opinion. The
consensus was to attack, the odds be damned. They would go in dismounted in three eight-man parties, counting on darkness to disguise
their paltry numbers.

Waving his men rearward to start small fires in sheltered hollows
and dry their powder and clothing, Kenton crept forward to have a
look for himself. There were Indians, all right, although scarcely in

the numbers the imaginative scouts had concocted. Their camp of three or four small tents rested on the near bank of the East Fork of the Little Miami River in an elevated beech grove encircled by swamps and low spongy prairie. The stolen horses grazed about the bottomland. A wooded bluff overlooked the village; that would be the jump-off point for the charge. A few wet dogs sulked about the Indian camp. Occasionally an Indian emerged from a tent and hollered for the lone—and now dead—warrior who had gone off after his stray horse, but there appeared to be no sentries posted. A satisfied Kenton planned the attack for midnight on April 10. The watchword would be "Boone." Kenton wanted no deaths in the dark from friendly fire.[6]

The Indian host on the wooded rise consisted of just Tecumseh, Ruddell, nine warriors, and six women. Tecumseh had not the slightest apprehension of attack. When the rain stopped after nightfall, he wrapped himself in his blanket and lay down on a bed of damp leaves beside a campfire to sleep. A warrior and his dog settled beside a second fire nearby.

At midnight the Kentuckians filed into line along the timber's edge. The clouds parted, and the moon shone brightly. The warrior's dog darted up the bluff, baying loudly. Its owner followed cautiously. As he neared the dark trees that sheltered the Kentuckians, a dozen rifle hammers clicked in rapid succession. The tension got the better of one man, and he shot the warrior dead. With that Kenton lost what little control he had over his "boys," and they fired wildly. Pouring from their tents, Tecumseh's warriors returned an equally haphazard fire. Dogs barked, screaming women splashed across the narrow river, and whizzing bullets stripped bark from trees, but no one was hit. Muskets fouled in the dampness, and the shooting tapered off.

Tecumseh broke the impasse. Grabbing his war club, he called out, "Big Fish [Stephen Ruddell], where are you?" "Here I am," replied Ruddell. "Then you charge on that side of the tent and I will charge on this side." Rounding the tent, Ruddell bumped into Kenton. "I fired on him, but my gun having gotten a little wet, it blowed [*sic*] considerably, and at last just blowed out the ball without injuring Kenton, who took to his heels." Tecumseh, meanwhile, brained a man named Samuel Barr with his war club. The whack of club cracking skull horrified Barr's companions. "Boys!" screamed one. "It won't do for us to be here; Barr is killed, and the Indians are crossing the creek." Bellowing "Boone!" Kenton ordered a retreat, which already had begun spontaneously. The Shawnees mimicked the countersign, and soon the moonlit forest echoed with cries of "Boone! Boone!"

In the chaos the Kentuckians escaped without further loss. The next morning, however, Tecumseh and his warriors chanced upon Alexander McIntyre, who had lagged. Possessed of more hunger than good sense, McIntyre paused to cook breakfast rather than track down his companions. Raising a yell, the Indians charged him. McIntyre ran until his legs gave out, then faced about and lifted his musket, wobbling the barrel threateningly. Ducking behind trees, two warriors in advance of Tecumseh leveled their weapons at McIntyre. Before anyone fired, Tecumseh "rushed right up to McIntyre and made him prisoner," Ruddell marveled, both at Tecumseh's courage and—given his disinclination to take adult male prisoners—at his risking his life to seize the Kentuckian. Directing the other warriors to tie McIntyre to a tree, Tecumseh and Ruddell went off to gather up the party's horses. When they returned, McIntyre was slumped over dead, his skull cleaved with a tomahawk. Tecumseh could sometimes have a hair-trigger temper. This was one of those moments. Exploding with rage, he grabbed a ramrod and berated and beat the killer, reminding all present that the lives of prisoners were to be spared. No one dared to ask Tecumseh why he had taken the man alive in the first place.

It had been a poor outing for Tecumseh. He had two warriors and a woman killed; the slaying of two Kentuckians and the theft of a few horses hardly compensated for the casualties. In a war culture that measured a leader's prowess in large measure on his ability to bring his people home alive, the twenty-four-year-old Tecumseh had stumbled badly.[7]

And then a couple of months later, he left. In June 1792, Tecumseh returned to Tennessee to fight beside Cheeseekau and the Chicka-maugas. Whether he did so out of humiliation, renewed wanderlust, or longing to see his elder brother, or because time was running out for the Chickamaugas, one can only speculate.

Tecumseh's arrival brought Cheeseekau's Shawnee contingent to a respectable thirty warriors. Cheeseekau also commanded the allegiance of several dozen Creek warriors who had congregated at the

Chickamauga towns. While the Chickamaugas appreciated these accessions to their warrior strength, three events during Tecumseh's absence diluted the impact of increased numbers: Dragging Canoe had died, British aid had waned, and senior Cherokee chiefs who had made peace with the Americans threatened to betray the Chickamaugas.

Honoring Dragging Canoe's dying wish, the Chickamaugas selected the forty-year-old métis John Watts as head chief. A brilliant strategist with a gift for both diplomacy and deception, Watts met with the governor of the Southwest Territory, William Blount, to profess friendship. Blount rewarded him lavishly. No sooner had Watts beguiled Blount than the Chickamauga chief negotiated a pact with the governor of Spanish West Florida, who promised arms and ammunition enough to compensate for declining British patronage.[8]

While the wheels of duplicitous diplomacy turned, Tecumseh accompanied Cheeseekau and a war party of fifty Shawnees and Creeks on a freebooting expedition into the remote and poorly defended Mero District. Circumventing Nashville, then a rough riverside settlement of some two hundred souls, Cheeseekau's raiders set their sights on Ziegler's Station, the palisaded home of the Jacob Ziegler and Joseph Wilson families and their slaves.

On the morning of June 26, Cheeseekau and Tecumseh sprang a classic Indian ambush. They killed Michael Shaver, a farmer at work in a field near the station, then arrayed their warriors behind a bordering fence. Three neighbors hastened to retrieve Shaver. An Indian volley wounded all three, who staggered into Ziegler's Station without the body. Meanwhile the Indians vanished. That evening more neighbors arrived and helped bring in Shaver's corpse. The danger having seemingly passed, the settlers dispersed. But the Indians had only feigned retreat. After nightfall they charged the station carrying firebrands. The palisades blazed and crackled. Half-naked settlers spilled out of their cabins to find Indians swarming into the station. The elder Wilson squeezed off a harmless musket shot, then darted through the back gate, leaving behind his wife and six children. Jacob Ziegler perished in the flames that consumed his cabin. His wife escaped, but Cheeseekau and Tecumseh seized the three Ziegler girls. A Creek warrior tomahawked a young slave girl and tossed her into the burning Ziegler house. It was an unusual action for a Creek warrior. The Creeks had no fondness for blacks, but neither did they customarily kill captured slaves. Instead, they enslaved them to work their farms or sold them to white slave traders. Living north of the Ohio River, in a region where slaves were uncommon, the Shawnees, on the other hand, seem to have had no fixed tribal attitude toward slaves and slavery.

Rampaging as they withdrew, the raiders carried their captives south. The Indians rode the few available horses; their prisoners walked. Male captives fared poorly. En route to Running Water, the warriors slayed and scalped no fewer than a dozen men and boys. The killings tormented Tecumseh, but it was Cheeseekau's war party, and he evidently was of the more common Shawnee mindset that a prisoner was property of the man who seized him, his life hanging on the threaded whim of his captor. The Indians, however, were of one mind with respect to the females: they intended them no harm, and all survived the ordeal. The bruised and bleeding bare feet of the Ziegler girls even moved several warriors to fashion deer moccasins for them. Through the good offices of friendly Cherokees, Mrs. Ziegler was able to purchase her three daughters from Cheeseekau for $174, an amount equivalent to $4,600 in 2019 dollars.[9]

Cheeseekau might profit from the whites, but he was contemptuous of collaborators. When a Chickamauga subchief named Fool Charley, intent on undermining the subterfuge of James Watts, returned to Running Water from a council with Governor Blount and "friendly" Indians in Nashville, Cheeseekau thrashed him. Undeterred, Fool Charley offered to escort longboats containing treaty goods for two pro-American southern tribes, the Chickasaws and Choctaws, past the Chickamauga towns. As the boats neared Running Water, Fool Charley—who was far cleverer than his name suggested—paddled ahead to the village in a canoe laden with barrels of whiskey with which to keep the inhabitants occupied. The ruse succeeded. From that day forward, Governor Blount considered Fool Charley "one of the firmest friends the United States had."[10]

Tecumseh may have fallen victim to Fool Charley's whiskey. He had a well-earned reputation for sobriety, but he did imbibe occasionally. Ruddell swore that Tecumseh seldom drank to excess, and "when inebriated he was widely different from the other Indians—perfectly good-humored and free from those savage ideas, and always reproving them for their folly."[11]

Bigger things were in the wind than punishing collaborationist

Chickamaugas. Returning from Spanish West Florida in late August with swords, saddles, and other equipment enough for two hundred armed horsemen, John Watts called a grand council to coincide with the Chickamaugas' green corn dance, a celebration the Shawnees found reminiscent of their own autumn festivities. The issue at hand was compromise or total war with the settlers of the Southwest Territory.

One can imagine Tecumseh transfixed by the power of Watts's oratory as the Chickamauga head chief measured the merits of war. A half-Cherokee informer later told Governor Blount that Watts's argument to the assembled chiefs and warriors unfolded along the following lines:

> The [Spanish] governor had received him with open arms; asked him if he had seen any Spanish settlers before he arrived at Pensacola [in West Florida]; assured him that the Spaniards never wanted a back country; wherever they had landed, they sat down; even such a sandbank as [Pensacola] is enough for them. They are not like the Americans, who first take your land and then treat with you and give you little or nothing for it. This is the way they have always served you, and, from time to time, killed some of your people. In the late war with Great Britain and the United States, the Spaniards assisted them, and lent them money, and they owe the Spaniards a great deal, and instead of paying them what they owe, they take our lands, as well as yours. That the King, his master, had sent in powder, lead, and arms for the Southern [Indian] nations in plenty; and that then was the time for them to join quickly in war against the United States ... while they were engaged in a war with the Northern tribes.[12]

Scarcely had Tecumseh digested Watts's call to war than Cheeseekau rose to exclaim, "With these hands I have taken the life of 300 men, and now is the time to come when they shall take the life of 300 more. Then I will be satisfied and sit down in peace. I will now drink my fill of blood." A Cherokee peace chief made a half-hearted effort to rebut Cheeseekau before Watts closed the council. Everyone was to reunite beneath the jagged summit of Lookout Mountain the next morning, ready to march. Before then, custom demanded a war dance.

The men dispersed to prepare themselves or dodge the war call, as their consciences dictated. Ninety minutes later fully six hundred returned, stripped to their breechclouts, painted black from head to foot, and wielding tomahawks and muskets. The Indians danced until nightfall, occasionally shooting holes in an American flag that lay in the dirt.[13]

The next morning the Creek, Chickamauga, and Shawnee fighting men reassembled. Word that a chief had just returned from Knoxville, the forted capital of the Southwest Territory, with several barrels of whiskey interrupted Watts's final preparations. The war party got roaring drunk, Cheeseekau and Tecumseh doubtlessly partaking as well. Then the war leaders and Watts bickered over tactics, before finally settling on a multipronged push to clear the Cumberland River Valley of settlers, the principal objective being Nashville. It was September 15 before the Indians paddled their canoes and rafts across the broad Tennessee River and headed north.[14]

Watts had put the delay to good use. Learning that informants had tipped off Governor Blount, who in turn had called out the militia, Watts coerced two pro-American Cherokee chiefs into writing Blount that war rumors were merely the harmless talk of restless young men; the peace-loving Watts, they added, had sent the warriors home to hunt. Blount took the bait and discharged the militia, reopening the road to invasion.[15]

Watts gave Cheeseekau an outsize role in the strike against Nashville, a reliable measure of the esteem Tecumseh's elder brother had come to enjoy among the southern tribes. Although Cheeseekau's personal following was comparatively small, Watts assigned him one of two contingents of two hundred dismounted warriors, retaining for himself the command of the second foot-unit. Watts equipped a third, mounted two-hundred-man unit with the cavalry gear obtained from the Spaniards. Two other contingents swung east to cut off the roads from Nashville to Knoxville.[16]

As the Indians trod three-abreast over the vast Cumberland Plateau, Cheeseekau grew insubordinate. He quarreled with Watts over the planned attack on Nashville, insisting that the war party first assault Buchanan's Station, an inconsequential stockade four miles south of the Cumberland River town, before taking on the principal target. The expedition ground to a halt. Precious days were lost while the Indian leadership wrestled with the issue. At heart a weak commander, Watts acceded to Cheeseekau's demand. Its fulfillment would erase the element of surprise against Nashville.

Perhaps Cheeseekau regretted his defiance. He was restless by night, morose by day. Shortly before the war party reached Buchanan's Station, Cheeseekau revealed to Tecumseh and the other Shawnees a disturbing dream that had seeped into his sleep from the spirit world. He, Cheeseekau, would fall in the coming attack at precisely noon with a bullet through the center of his forehead. His followers were not to weep for him. If the Indians persevered, as they had in his dream, they would carry the fort. Besides, Cheeseekau considered it an honor to fall in battle. It was how his father had died, and he desired the same for himself. Cheeseekau "did not wish to be buried at home like an old squaw," Tecumseh later told Ruddell, "[but] preferred that the fowls of the air should pick his bones." Noble sentiments, but Tecumseh implored Cheeseekau to turn back. He refused. Perhaps, however, he could cheat death by altering the time of the attack from dawn to midnight, when Indians normally were loath to give battle. Cheeseekau suggested the change, and Watts again deferred to him.[17]

Buchanan's Station appeared an easy mark for six hundred warriors. It consisted of a few log cabins encircled by a picket stockade and a single blockhouse. Mill Creek, a sinuous stream, babbled past the place through pastures of lowing cows in its course to the Cumberland River. Thirty-three-year-old John Buchanan, a co-founder of Nashville, commanded the station. Fifteen armed men and several families huddled in the stockade for protection against the small war parties that often prowled the country after dark.

September 30, 1792, the last day of the Pawpaw Moon, was a Sunday. The moon rose full in a clear night sky, casting glimmering beams over meadows and forests. At midnight Watts's horsemen dismounted a mile south of Buchanan's Station. Together with the foot soldiers, they trod lightly across the pastures and through the intermittent woods between themselves and the stockade. Their stealth served well until they approached a herd of cattle grazing near the gate. The cattle bellowed, the garrison awoke, and the warriors rushed the palisades. The blockhouse sentry dropped an Indian at ten yards, sending the painted swarm scurrying for cover. Several dozen warriors clustered in the open cellar of an unfinished cabin outside the wall; others crouched beside stumps or dropped behind felled trees. They returned fire rapidly, aiming for the portholes through which the defenders poked their muskets. Splinters rained down on the station, slightly wounding one defender. Thirty Indian musket balls lodged in the blockhouse roof within a hat-sized circumference, but Indian fire struck not a single defender during the sixty-minute contest.

Seldom was the Indian aversion to pressing an attack against a fort more evident than at Buchanan's Station. A young Chickamauga métis renowned for his athletic prowess grabbed a burning brand and scaled the blockhouse wall, only to tumble from the roof wounded. He struggled to set fire to the lower logs until a second ball killed him. No one took up the brand, nor did anyone else dare to climb the walls. John Watts crumpled with bullets through both thighs. Dragging Canoe's younger brother was hit, and a Creek was killed. Five other warriors were wounded before the Indians broke off the assault, shooting as they melted back into the night.

Although the Indian retreat was orderly enough, the invasion was over. The district militia was alert and prepared to defend Nashville. A few small war parties waylaid incautious travelers or killed the unfortunate occupants of isolated cabins. Tecumseh also roamed the countryside, raging with grief. Cheeseekau's premonition had been fulfilled. Early in the attack on Buchanan's Station, a single ball had struck him square in the forehead, killing the famed Shawnee warrior instantly.

Tecumseh now walked in no shadow save his own. He would return home with word of Cheeseekau's death, but not until "he had done something to show his good conduct." With his usual following of eight to ten Shawnee warriors, Tecumseh crossed to the north bank of the Cumberland River. Six miles outside Nashville he took revenge on a man named William Stuart, killing and scalping him, then burned a nearby distillery for good measure. Cheeseekau's spirit could now rest in peace.[18]

Perhaps Cheeseekau's erratic conduct on his final campaign and Watts's vacillation taught Tecumseh the need for unity of purpose and rock-hard resolution on the eve of battle. Musing over the fiasco that had befallen the Indians, Governor Blount divined its cause. "Fourteen days elapsed from the passing of the Tennessee to the attack upon Buchanan's Station, when the distance between could have been marched in from four to six days," he informed the secretary of war.

"Difference in opinion, as to the mode and place of attack, at the rendezvous after they passed the Tennessee, probably was the cause of the delay; I have no other way to account for it; and it is a rock on which large parties of Indians have generally split especially when consisting of more than one nation."[19]

From his late brother, Tecumseh had learned much about making hit-and-run raids on flatboats, skirmishing with settlers and poorly trained frontier militia, and deceiving a small party of unsuspecting regulars. What value Tecumseh's experience would have in the future was uncertain. After their stunning victory over St. Clair, the confederated chiefs were too confident to concede anything in negotiations. During the coming months, the American would send peace missions meant more to divide the Indians and lessen their attacks than to achieve a peaceful settlement. The Washington administration also played at peace in order to convince the eastern citizenry that everything possible was being done to avoid war. In fact, the government was reconstituting the Regular Army, building a force capable of beating the Indians decisively in large-scale open combat.

On September 30, 1792, while Cheeseekau followed his fevered premonition of death to Buchanan's Station, the chiefs of the Ohio tribes met in a council of spiritual renewal and sacred unity from which the tormented Cheeseekau, the timorous John Watts, and the spiritually torn Tecumseh might have learned much.

The great council occurred at the Glaize, the old buffalo wallow on the Maumee River that had become home to the seven Shawnee, Miami, Delaware, and Mingo villages that constituted the core of pan-Indianism north of the Ohio River. There were also Chickamauga and Nanticoke Indians, the latter pushed west a century earlier from the Chesapeake Bay, and enough English and French traders to constitute a separate village. Métis, adopted whites, and runaway black slaves also mingled freely in what was essentially a community of two thousand refugees with two common interests—to yield not one further inch of land to the Americans and to reclaim what they had lost by dint of unjust treaties.

The council at the Glaize represented the most profound step toward pan-Indian singleness of purpose among the natives of the Northwest since Pontiac introduced the concept three decades earlier. It was also a tribute to Blue Jacket's vigorous diplomacy. He had traveled far and wide to drum up support. Chiefs of thirty tribes attended. By common consent of the Glaize Indians, the Mekoche Shawnee civil chief Red Pole, half-brother of Blue Jacket, presided. Sac, Three Fires (Potawatomi, Ottawa, and Ojibwa), and Wyandot allies also deferred to Red Pole. Canadian tribes dispatched representatives as sympathetic observers. The Iroquois nation sent Seneca delegates with the unenviable task of presenting the U.S. perspective.

The Senecas counseled compromise. The Ohio tribes had been "fortunate that the Great Spirit above was so kind as to assist you to throw the Americans twice on their back when they came against your villages," but they had best not press their luck. Iroquois chiefs had visited Philadelphia and spoken with President Washington, who promised to compensate the "real owners" of land ceded in the Fort Harmar Treaty.

Red Pole rebuked the Senecas sharply: "We know very well what the Americans are about and what their designs are. Last fall when the Great Spirit was good enough to assist us, to throw them on their back, we got St. Clair's papers and instructions.... If the Americans had been successful, they were to ... afterwards drive all the Indians entirely out of the country, to clear the lakes of them.... You say Washington will make us a compensation if our land was not purchased of the right owner. We do not want compensation; we want restitution of our country which they hold under false pretenses."

The Delaware chief Buckongahelas, who had led the tribe's contingent in St. Clair's defeat, also reproved the Senecas. "Don't think because the Shawnees only have spoken to you that it was their sentiments alone, they have spoken the sentiments of all the Nations. When we met four years ago you told us, and all Nations agreed to it, that if any one of us was struck, we should consider it as if the whole of the Nations had received a blow and that the whole should join in revenging it: Think well of this Uncles of the [Iroquois]. All of us are animated by one mind, one head, and one heart, and we were resolved to stick close by each other and defend ourselves to the last."[20]

The Northwestern Confederacy was determined not to be duped by the Americans again.

Having seen his elder brother shot dead and endured the humiliating reversal at Buchanan's Station, Tecumseh must have found a welcome tonic in the military might and sense of spiritual right that permeated the towns at the Glaize, when he returned early in the winter of 1792 to rejoin his remaining siblings in Blue Jacket's town. A pleasant community of forty bark cabins and three hundred Shawnee and métis residents on the north bank of the Maumee, it rested four miles downriver from Little Turtle's Miami town and five miles northeast of the Delawares' Auglaize River enclave.

Blue Jacket's lavish lifestyle was on open display. Outside his immaculately maintained cabin, which his métis wife provided with European furniture, he maintained a huge collection of muskets, war clubs, bows and arrows, and animal skins. His light-complexioned daughters were famously beautiful, his two sons well-educated and bilingual. For all Blue Jacket's hostility toward the Americans, he and his family epitomized the mingling of native and European influences in the Old Northwest.

Little Turtle also lived astride two cultures. The military hero of the Miamis took a captive American woman as his second wife, and he adopted William Wells, the scion of a prominent Kentucky family, who had been captured at age thirteen. Wells had fought with the Indians against St. Clair; now he worked for the American army, carrying messages from the fort at Vincennes to the chiefs at the Glaize. Multilingual and loyal to Little Turtle, Wells married the chief's daughter. A brave and decent man, Wells walked a perilous tightrope between clashing societies. He and Tecumseh might mingle on friendly terms at the Glaize, but their relationship was destined to be fraught.[21]

The Glaize possessed a bucolic beauty. Cornfields dotted with melon and squash patches stretched for fifteen miles along the south bank of the Maumee. Cattle and horses lined low, grassy ridges. John Brickell, a young captive of the Delawares, left an engaging description of the home life he shared with his "very kindly" Indian family. They lived in an amalgam of wigwam and white man's cabin, a modest structure typical of the Glaize. Recalled Brickell,

Our cabin was of round logs, like those of the first settlers, except the roof was of bark and it had no floor. It consisted of a single room with a French-made chimney of [straw and] clay. The door was made of hewed puncheons. We had nothing more like bedsteads than forks driven in the earth, from which there were cross-pieces to holes in the walls, and lengthwise on these was laid bark in large slips; upon these we laid skins, which completed the sleeping accommodations.

On going to bed the men pulled off all but their breeching, and the women all but their shrouds, and the clothes thus pulled off were put under the head and served as pillows.

The [Indians] are not very regular about going to bed, but in general are very early risers. They almost uniformly sleep singly on their bunks, even small children. The men and their wives, and mothers with their infants, making the only exception.[22]

Tecumseh may have shared a similar sort of home with Tecumpease, her husband, and a brood that included Lalawethika, now seventeen. More likely he lived in the small, simple bark wigwam typical of bachelors.

At the Glaize, Tecumseh mixed with many whites on friendly terms. Equidistant from the communities of Blue Jacket, Little Turtle, and the Delawares stood the palisaded Traders' Town, an all-purpose shopping and repair center consisting of clapboard cabins, pinewood sheds, and stalls of unhewn timber. Residents included a French baker; a British silversmith married to a Shawnee; a British gunsmith; an American couple captured at St. Clair's defeat and now working off their ransom, she by sewing and taking in laundry, he as a boatman between the Glaize and a British supply depot downriver; and the British agents Matthew Elliott and Alexander McKee, whose unenviable task it was to foster Indian loyalty to the Crown without provoking hostilities that might drag Great Britain into war with the United States. Both had Shawnee wives. Presiding over the Traders' Town was George Ironside, a Scotsman who had attended King's College before coming to America to enter the Indian trade. A convivial character, Ironside spoke Shawnee and was fond of the Indians.

The spiritual heart of the Glaize lay on the north bank of the Maumee. There, between the towns of Little Turtle and Blue Jacket, stood the solitary cabin of the "Mohawk Woman" Coocoochee, the widow of a Mohawk warrior who had migrated from their Canadian homeland to live among the Shawnees in Ohio. Her two eldest sons were prominent warriors in Blue Jacket's town; her daughter had married

George Ironside. Coocoochee lived alone but seldom lacked for company. Expert in the use of herbal medicines, she was also believed to possess divine power. Blue Jacket and other war leaders consulted Coocoochee before undertaking important expeditions, and she shared the spoils of their victories.

Of medium height, stout, and possessed of a pleasant demeanor, Coocoochee went about in a long calico shirt fastened with a silver brooch, a blue cloth skirt belted with a striped sash, blue leggings, and deerskin moccasins. Young people gathered to hear her tell stories handed down by her eastern ancestors about the first appearance, on the shores of the Stinking Lake, of avaricious pale-faced people in giant canoes topped with broad white wings. Coocoochee preached that whites would be satisfied only after they had killed or pushed the Indians into the Great Western Sea, where the survivors would drown. But there was a distant land, ten times larger than the American continent, where the seasons were always pleasant, the aged never became infirm or died, and vegetables sprang spontaneously from the earth. The Great Spirit would make the path to this earthly paradise clear to the Indians only if they restored themselves to his favor.[23]

Although he never spoke of the Mohawk Woman, Lalawethika undoubtedly listened to her sermons and enjoyed her hospitality, for she hosted lavish meals and spirited games during the festival seasons. And the one-eyed youth was not one to deny himself pleasure. He fell victim to the darker side of the cultural smorgasbord of the Glaize: liquor. At eighteen, Lalawethika was already an alcoholic, sponging off Tecumpease and Tecumseh, both of whom were of too generous a nature to deny their ne'er-do-well brother.

While Lalawethika lolled about the Glaize, Tecumseh ranged far afield, hunting and raiding. In the early spring of 1793, he and Stephen Ruddell led six or seven Indians and the white warrior John Ward, who had been seized as a boy nearly three decades earlier, through the old Shawnee lands into Kentucky, where they made off with a half-dozen horses. Only one Kentuckian died in Tecumseh's foray, ironically shot by Ruddell.

Other war parties, emboldened by the victory over Arthur St. Clair's army in November 1791 and the bracing rhetoric of unity at the Glaize council, already were in the bluegrass country, renewing their feud with the Kentucks. Their depredations sent the settlers scurrying. "To see the country all in forts, breaking up, leaving their farms, their houses, and corn burnt up, is truly distressing," lamented a frontiersman. "At this time nearly half the country is in forts."[24]

For the second time in as many years, Kentuckians looked to Simon Kenton to repel the raiders. Few, however, showed enthusiasm for service as mere enlisted men. Where one captain would have sufficed, seven of the thirty-four members of Kenton's "company" held that rank. In late March the rank-heavy gaggle crossed the Ohio River and followed a fresh Indian trail forty miles north through deep undulating forest to a tributary of the Scioto River called Paint Creek, just west of old Chillicothe. At dusk on their third day out, the Kentuckians heard laughter rising from the far side of a ridge. Kenton edged through the timber to reconnoiter. Espying a knot of unwary Indians gathered around a campfire on the far bank of Paint Creek, Kenton returned to his men with a plan. At daybreak they would attack, dismounted, in three groups of ten. Capts. Joshua Baker and Charles Ward would each lead a contingent; Kenton the third. No one was to shoot until Kenton gave the signal.

Tecumseh had let his guard down again. Only militia indiscipline and watchful Indian dogs saved him. As Ward and Kenton edged their men into place, someone in Captain Baker's command fired at a snarling canine. Startled by the shot, Kenton's men stumbled into Baker's detachment. Tecumseh responded well. By the time the Kentuckians sorted themselves out, he had his warriors posted behind trees. As a hard rain began to fall, Kenton's intended surprise assault degenerated into a desultory exchange that cost Tecumseh one man—the white warrior John Ward, brother of Kentucky captain Charles Ward, an example of the frequent blurring of racial lines and loyalties on the Kentucky frontier.

During the skirmish, Tecumseh had the presence of mind to detach two or three warriors to search for the Kentuckians' horses. They made off with about half the mounts, which more than compensated for a quantity of powder, musket balls, and blankets that the Kentuckians grabbed from Tecumseh's camp. With no prospect of overwhelming Tecumseh's outnumbered but stubborn warriors, Kenton called off the contest. He later said he retreated because he had learned of a large—and nonexistent—Shawnee camp five miles from that of Tecumseh. How he came to that conclusion, Kenton never said.[25]

Tecumseh's second scrape with Kenton could be counted a draw. As with the first, the Kentuckians had gotten the drop on him. To give up without undertaking a revenge raid would cost Tecumseh mightily in prestige, a war leader's greatest asset, especially as he had lost a man. With the Kentucky stations on high alert, Tecumseh elected to take his war party deep into the Virginia frontier settlements, a move in keeping with his growing reputation as "one of the boldest and most terrible" young war leaders.[26]

Tecumseh prowled the tranquil farms that lined Hacker's Creek, a meandering watercourse one hundred miles east of the Ohio River, searching for a suitable target. On May 7 he settled on the homestead of forty-year-old Revolutionary War veteran John Waggoner. Twilight had descended, and Waggoner sat on a log near his cabin, resting from a day of plowing and clearing logs. His wife and seven children milled about the cabin and yard. Secreting his warriors in a ravine close to the Waggoner place, Tecumseh crept through the tall grass to within thirty paces of Waggoner. Rising slowly, he fired at the large man silhouetted in the gloam—and missed. Tecumseh dropped his musket, grasped his war club, and sprang after Waggoner, who made for the cabin, easily outrunning the limping Tecumseh but not his warriors, who swept into the yard ahead of Waggoner.

Realizing he could do nothing for his family unarmed, Waggoner sprinted through the fields toward a neighbor's place as the ululations of his unfortunate family grew fainter. By the time Waggoner returned with a handful of avenging friends, a sickly hush hung over the cabin. Tecumseh had sacked the place. In the yard lay Waggoner's youngest son, tomahawked and scalped. A mile from the cabin, the searchers found another dead child with its brains beaten out. A short distance deeper into the timber, they encountered the mangled bodies of Waggoner's wife and two more children. Tecumseh absconded with the remaining two daughters and a son. All survived, the boy growing up to replenish the ranks of Shawnee warriors.[27]

Jonathan Alder, a longtime captive of the Shawnee, said he once heard Tecumseh reproach a warrior for boasting about the great numbers of scalps he had taken, calling him a "low, mean Indian" who preyed mainly on women and children. "I have killed forty men with my own hand in single combat," Tecumseh purportedly said, "but never yet have I taken the life of a woman or child." Perhaps not, but his warriors had. That he could have prevented the butchery is doubtful, but it is unclear whether Tecumseh even wished to spare the Waggoners' lives; everyone at one time or another falls short of their noblest intentions, and though nearly a year had passed, the loss of Cheeseekau may have yet dulled his compassion.

Tecumseh's single raid sufficed to frighten the Virginia frontier. "From the reports of scouts, I am in constant expectation that a severe stroke will be made somewhere on the frontier," a local official wrote the Virginia governor just days after the Waggoner massacre. "Where it will fall is uncertain, as the last attack [Waggoner] was made where least expected, and where the people thought themselves in perfect safety. The people in this county are greatly alarmed, and numbers of them seem determined to abandon the settlements."[28]

Other Shawnee war parties marauded the frontier well into the summer. Not Tecumseh. He returned to the Glaize in June and spent the remaining six months of 1793 hunting. Perhaps he found solace in the solitude of the forest.[29]

In the great council at the Glaize in September 1792, the confederated tribes had shown no inclination to compromise. If the Americans wanted peace, they must dismantle the Ohio River forts and accept the river as the boundary between themselves and the Indians. Nevertheless, the Shawnee chief Red Pole consented to meet with American commissioners in the spring.

Neither President Washington nor Secretary of War Henry Knox expected much to come of the council, which they orchestrated in part to give the reconstituted U.S. Army time to train for combat. Even before Red Pole articulated Indian terms, Knox told the commanding general, Anthony Wayne, to prepare to invade the Northwest Territory because the Indians undoubtedly would demand "more than we can grant consistently with any sort of dignity."[30]

And so it proved. For two weeks in October 1792 the American commissioners and the Indian representatives sparred rhetorically. A Wyandot chief framed the impasse clearly: "We regard this side of the Ohio as our property. You say you cannot remove your people, and we cannot give up our lands. We are sorry we cannot come to an agreement." In a half-hearted attempt to salvage the talks, the Indians suggested the government pay its citizens to relocate south of the Ohio River as a cheaper alternative to war. The commissioners rejected the proposal, an outcome that pleased Secretary of State Thomas Jefferson. "Our negotiations with the northwestern Indians have completely failed, so that war must settle our difference," he wrote confidentially. "We expected nothing else and had gone into the negotiations only to prove to all our citizens that peace was unattainable on terms which any of them would admit." Secretary Knox gave Wayne the green light to go to war.[31]

During the American Revolution, Wayne's impetuosity had earned him the sobriquet of "Mad Anthony." His preparations to strike the Indian confederacy at the Glaize were anything but rash, however. While Tecumseh passed the early spring hunting, Wayne readied his eighteen hundred regulars for battle through a regime of hard training and draconian discipline. The fifteen hundred mounted Kentucky volunteers who joined Wayne's Legion of the United States made up in ferocity what they lacked in training. The regulars were colorfully uniformed, nearly as splendid as the kaleidoscopically festooned Indian warriors. Infantrymen wore blue short coats with red facings, white vests and trousers, and black cocked hats with a bearskin crest and colored plume. The Kentucky horsemen were garbed in long white hunting shirts and leather pants. All possessed a confidence that St. Clair's ragtag command had sorely wanted.

Wayne moved methodically. Following St. Clair's route north from Fort Washington on the Ohio River, he wintered at a sprawling wooden stockade called Fort Green Ville, which he constructed ninety miles south of the Glaize. From there in late 1793, he sent a detachment twenty miles deeper into Indian country to build a small fort on the site of St. Clair's defeat. After sweeping the ground clear of human and horse bones, in March 1794 the troops completed a strong fortification of four log blockhouses connected by a wooden palisade. They dug up ten cannons the Indians had buried and then cleared fields of fire for 250 yards in every direction. Wayne defiantly named the post on recaptured soil Fort Recovery.[32]

As an emerging war leader, Tecumseh participated in the heated, recriminatory Shawnee councils that debated the proper response to Wayne's provocations. Tecumseh's was one of many voices in the council house, and a minor one at that. But the lessons he was to learn of the instability of intertribal alliances and the evanescence of English support would remain with him forever. And at twenty-six, he was about to be tested in his first great battle with the Long Knives, an encounter on the scale of the clash that had killed his father two decades earlier.

7

The Making of a Chief

IN 1794 THE ARCHITECTS of the Northwestern Confederacy
remained the Shawnee war chief Blue Jacket and the Miami war
chief Little Turtle, who cordially detested each other. The tall, muscular, and much-esteemed Delaware chief Buckongahelas played a
strong if erratic supporting role. And then there was the governor-
general of the Canadas, Guy Carleton, who appeared to want the
Indians to go to war and implied the British would participate. His
stance was unaccountable because Great Britain and the United States
were at peace, and His Majesty's forces were embroiled in a costly
European struggle with France. Nevertheless, Carleton ordered a fort
built at the rapids of the Maumee River in the Ohio country, ten miles
southwest of present-day Toledo, with an easy line of communication
to the Indian towns at the Glaize. The move contravened imperial
policy—the British government even then was negotiating the evacu-
ation of Forts Detroit, Niagara, and Michilimackinac—but was welcomed by the aggressive lieutenant governor of Upper Canada, John
Simcoe, who was the ranking official in the young wilderness province, and by Indian Department officials McKee and Elliott, whose
Shawnee family ties bound them to the Indian confederacy. By early
summer the new post, named Fort Miamis, was nearly complete, and
a British garrison settled in.[1]

Blue Jacket, meanwhile, had not been idle. With the spring thaw he
began the exhausting task of marshaling the confederacy's far-flung
warriors. Traveling the intricate web of paths that threaded through

the Great Lakes wilderness, he visited one village after another, cajoling the northern tribes to return to the Ohio country. By mid-June fifteen hundred fighting men had assembled sixty miles south of the Glaize. Warriors of the Three Fires—Potawatomis, Ojibwas, and Ottawas—mingled with the Miamis, Wyandots, Shawnees, and Mingoes of the Glaize. Buckongahelas's Delawares, delayed by a rum bacchanal, were soon expected. Lalawethika and Sauwauseekau stood with their brother Tecumseh; so did seventeen more of the two hundred Shawnee warriors present. Counting himself, Tecumseh was responsible for one-tenth of the Shawnee fighting force. It was not an inconsequential contingent for a twenty-six-year-old to command, and perhaps the anticipated battle with the Long Knives would give him a chance to add to his reputation and his following.

The portents were mixed. As the warriors gathered from near and far, the first fissures appeared in the Indian alliance. Ojibwa late arrivals pilfered dwellings at the Glaize and raped defenseless women, prompting Blue Jacket to quarantine the towns. The Shawnees simmered with anger against the freebooting northerners; when the moment was right, they would avenge their ravaged women.

And what of the British? They provided powder and lead, but the Indians were skeptical of their commitment. "War or peace depended on the conduct of the British," a Shawnee warrior from Tecumseh's band, seized by American scouts, told his captors. "If they would help, it would probably be war, but if they would not, it would be peace— the Indians would no longer be set on like dogs by the British."[2]

Blue Jacket tried to force the issue. He shoved a black wampum belt into Matthew Elliott's hands, insisting that he and all British traders and officials in the Indian camp fight with them. Togging up in Indian dress and war paint, Elliott and his compatriots reluctantly agreed. What the garrison at Fort Miamis would do remained to be seen.

Distrust of the British paled beside the internal strife that threatened to rend the Northwestern Confederacy before the American invaders fired a single shot. Little Turtle preferred peace, but if they must fight, he believed the Indians should sever Wayne's long supply lines rather than risk a direct attack. Blue Jacket was all for war but agreed with Little Turtle's indirect approach. Buckongahelas likely would have supported them in council, but he had not yet shown up. The tribes of the Three Fires offered an alternative plan that promised immediate gratification in scalps and plunder and ran minimal risk: strike one of the periodic supply convoys between Fort Recovery and Wayne's legion at Fort Green Ville and, if that succeeded, attack the exposed post itself. The Shawnees and Miamis reluctantly acquiesced.[3]

On June 29 the vast Indian war party converged on Fort Recovery. Clad only in their breechclouts and moccasins and painted red and black, the warriors stalked through the tall timber in twelve long noiseless columns spaced fifty yards apart. Scouts reported that a supply convoy had entered the fort at sunset; it likely would depart the next morning. Accordingly, at nightfall the Indians settled into ambush positions. Some overeager Three Fires warriors took spots in the trees just beyond the fort itself. Most of the Indians, however, lined the wooded road over which the train must pass on its return to Fort Green Ville.

Tecumseh and Stephen Ruddell were with the main body. So too was the adopted Shawnee warrior Jonathan Alder. He had been under no obligation to fight. "The [Shawnees] never insisted on my taking up arms against the whites," he recalled, "but always left that to my own choice." The prospect of easy plunder, however, overcame Alder's scruples about shooting other Americans, and he crouched expectantly in the brush beside the road.

At seven a.m. on June 30 the gates of Fort Recovery swung open. Three hundred packhorses and sixty oxen spilled onto the open ground between the palisades and the wooded road, eased along by the horse masters and oxen drivers. Not a soldier was in sight. The ninety riflemen and fifty dragoons responsible for convoy security were still gathering their gear or readying their mounts while the major in charge enjoyed a leisurely breakfast. Blue Jacket held his twelve hundred warriors in check until the drovers and their animals turned onto the road. Then he sprang the ambush.

It was almost too easy. The Indians made off with the convoy horses, tomahawked the stunned drovers, and shot the oxen. Bareheaded and frantic, the detachment commander sallied forth with the derelict members of the convey escort. He was shot in an instant, and his men slaughtered. Survivors staggered into the fort under the covering fire of the two-hundred-man garrison.[4]

Jonathan Alder could hardly make sense of it all. "The first thing I heard was exciting. I heard the whites hallooing, 'Indians! Indians!' We had come onto about [fifty dragoons], and the Indians on horseback made for them. Now, there was a mighty rush by all the American horsemen and footmen toward the fort and the Indians run them so close that there was, I reckon, as many as fifty horses that the whites sprung off and got into the fort the best they could. These horses were left running at large outside the fort and was finely equipped with saddles, bridles, and horse pistols. The fort was soon surrounded, and a furious fire kept up." There the battle should have ended, but the Three Fires warriors rushed the fort. A blaze of musket fire from the palisade loopholes drove some to ground behind tree stumps. Others retreated into the timber, hurling war cries lost in the din of the booming cannons.

Alder had intended to grab one of the dragoon mounts, but not at the cost of his life. Crouched in the woods, he watched "several other Indians who would go up within fifty yards of the fort and then take a circle round and out again," unable to snag a bridle. A nearby Shawnee asked Alder why he held his fire. Because, replied Alder, he saw no targets. "Shoot those holes in the fort," the warrior suggested, "you might kill a man." Alder declined. "Well," the warrior sighed, "if you ain't going to shoot, you had better fall back out of reach before you are shot." No sooner had the warrior warned Alder than a musket ball tore into the man's chin. Alder watched the Shawnee run off while he stood frozen behind his own tree until a cannon blast sent Alder scurrying deeper into the forest.[5]

Alder's wounded compatriot had neglected to tell him of a richer, easier target—the hundreds of Three Fires warriors milling in the cleared space between them and the fort. Discreetly, as the opportunity arose, Shawnee and Miami warriors shot Three Fires warriors in the back—retribution for the Ojibwa crimes against their women and homes.

That night the Indians feasted on army oxen. The next morning a few Three Fires combatants half-heartedly harassed the garrison with a desultory fire lost in the lingering fog. At noon the Indians withdrew. They had killed twenty-two soldiers and wounded thirty, most in the opening moments of the melee. Three Fires casualties are uncertain, but Blue Jacket counted seventeen of his own warriors killed, all but three while supporting the reckless rush on Fort Recovery by Three

Fires warriors. Reporting on the Fort Recovery fiasco, a British officer who was present lamented, "I must observe with grief that the Indians never had it in their power to do more—and have done so little."[6]

Returning to the Glaize, the Indians conducted a heated postmortem that shattered what remained of the fragile alliance. The Ottawas stood fast, but the Potawatomi and Ojibwa leaders, aware their warriors had been the victims of vengeful sniping, declared that the white scalps they had taken at Fort Recovery fulfilled the obligation they owed the Ohio Valley tribes under the black wampum protocol, then headed home. Blue Jacket prepared his force, now reduced by nearly half, to meet Wayne's inevitable advance. Little Turtle traveled to Fort Detroit to take the pulse of the British and plead for more meaningful assistance. The Miami war chief verbally grappled for three days with the post commander, insisting that the Indians needed two cannons and twenty British regulars (redcoats) in order to continue the conflict with Wayne with any hope of success. The English colonel found Little Turtle "the most decent, modest, sensible Indian" with whom he had ever conversed. Nevertheless, he gave Little Turtle neither troops nor artillery.[7]

Little Turtle had had enough of war. When Wayne's legion advanced on the Glaize in August, he advocated opening negotiations with the relentless American commander. In council Little Turtle counseled his fellow chiefs not to press their luck. "The Americans are now led by a chief who never sleeps: the night and day are alike to him. And during all the time that he has been marching upon our villages, notwithstanding the watchfulness of our young men, we have never been able to surprise him. Think well of it. There is something whispers to me [that] it would be prudent to listen to his offers of peace." Instead the chiefs reproached Little Turtle for cowardice. The proud Miami relinquished his leadership role in the confederacy but was prevailed upon to assume command of the Miami contingent. His rival Blue Jacket stepped forward as the preeminent leader of the confederacy, and a recrudescent militant faction rejoiced. Tecumseh stood squarely in the ranks of hard-liners.[8]

Events proved Little Turtle a truer prophet than his accusers. On August 8 the Indians abandoned the Glaize just ahead of Wayne's advancing soldiers. "We scattered like a flock of partridges, leaving our breakfast cooking on the fire," recalled an adopted Delaware. For four years the sprawling complex of towns, trading centers, and cornfields had served as the nerve center of the Northwestern Confederacy. Now women, children, and the elderly salvaged a few kettles and blankets and then paddled their canoes nearly fifty miles northeast to find refuge on the lower Maumee River. Blue Jacket assembled his warriors for a stand near the foot of the Maumee Rapids, four miles upriver from Fort Miamis.[9]

Gen. "Mad Anthony" Wayne moved deliberately downriver from the Glaize. Everything about his campaign had been so methodical that Little Turtle had concluded the 3,300-man American leviathan was unstoppable. On the morning of August 18, Blue Jacket deployed his 1,100 warriors on the north bank of the broad Maumee River. The ground was dark and gloomy, tinged with a supernatural foreboding. A broad floodplain of six-foot-high prairie grass extended several hundred yards northward from the river, obscuring anyone wading through it. Beyond the floodplain, above the waving grass and sparkling prairie flowers, ran a low, intermittent wooded ridge dappled by ravines and combed with large trees that a recent tornado had toppled. The Americans called the place Fallen Timbers.

Blue Jacket employed the same linear, crescent formation that had carried the day against St. Clair. The right wing consisted of two companies of Canadian volunteers, 250 Wyandots under Chief Tarhe, and a sprinkling of Mingoes. The left wing, a portion of which drew duty on the floodplain, comprised mostly Ottawas, with a handful of Potawatomis and Ojibwas. The soul of the Ohio country alliance held the center: two hundred Delaware warriors under Chief Buckongahelas, one hundred Miamis assembled by the reluctant Little Turtle, and two hundred fiercely determined Shawnees under the immediate command of Blue Jacket himself, aided by the aging chief Black Hoof.[10]

Carrying a musket, a brace of pistols in his belt, and his indispensable war club, Tecumseh was ready for the fight. Blue Jacket had assigned him the advance post, a great but hazardous honor that meant Tecumseh's small contingent would be the first to meet the Americans in that sector of the three-quarter-mile Indian line. Stephen Ruddell stood beside Tecumseh. So did Tecumseh's brothers Sauwauseekau and Kumskaukau. Sufficiently sober to wield a weapon in what would be his first trial of arms, the dissolute loudmouth Lalawethika wobbled and worried.[11]

He would have a long wait, painfully prolonged by the absence of rum or whiskey with which to brace himself, because the day passed with no sign of the Americans. The next day elapsed in a like fashion, and even the stoutest warriors grew restless. When August 20 opened to a downpour, warriors peeled away to camp to cook breakfast. The chiefs offered no objections. Observed Jonathan Alder, "If an Indian expects to go into battle, he will eat nothing that morning, as they claim that if a man is wounded in the bowels when he is empty, his internals is not so likely to be cut as when they are full." A sound practice, but not one to be endured three mornings running.[12]

Neither Tecumseh, his brothers, nor Stephen Ruddell left the line that morning, however. And so all were on hand when several small detachments of Kentuckian horsemen appeared at 9:45 a.m., leading their mounts through the tangled swath of fallen timber. The rain had stopped. In the storm's wake came heat and stifling humidity. Wearing only their breechclouts and moccasins, the Indians shone with sweat. The dismounted Kentucky horsemen picked their way nearer. Tecumseh raised his musket and fired one of the first shots of the Battle of Fallen Timbers. Ruddell squeezed the trigger of his musket to a dull clack; he had neglected to keep the flint and the pan dry. Whether or not Lalawethika discharged his weapon is unknown, but enough of the nine hundred warriors then in the main Indian line of battle got off shots to send the despised Kentucks fleeing. In their place came soldiers in the blue coats, white trousers, and cocked black hats of Wayne's regular infantry. The battle grew general, as each side tried to outflank the other. Outnumbered more than three to one, Blue Jacket found the tactics employed against St. Clair worse than useless. After an hour, Wayne outflanked him.

Of the larger ebb and flow of the fight, Tecumseh knew nothing. He and his followers were locked in their own smoke-obscured struggle among the uprooted trees, holding fast until the uncertain glint of bayonets grew brighter. In the rear of the approaching infantry, a twenty-one-year-old aide watched over the commanding general. "General Wayne," said Lt. William Henry Harrison, his hands ready to grab the reins of the general's horse, "I am afraid you will go into the fight yourself and forget to give me the necessary field orders." "Perhaps I may," replied Wayne, "and if I do, recollect that the standing order for the day is 'Charge the damned rascals with bayonet.'"[13]

Tecumseh had never seen the business end of a bayonet, and the long blue-coated line bristling with them briefly unnerved him. Loading his musket while watching the regulars draw nearer, Tecumseh inserted the ball before the gunpowder, rendering his weapon useless. He was unarmed and probably alone. Ruddell had fled. Lalawethika "ran away and never halted until he reached Detroit." Their brother Sauwauseekau already was dead.

Tecumseh discarded his musket and bounded through the brush onto the trail to the Indian camp as fast as his heavy frame and bad thigh could carry him. Meeting a group of Delawares who had lingered over breakfast, Tecumseh urged them to hold their ground and asked for a weapon in order to "show them how to do it." Someone handed him a fowling piece. Tecumseh steadied the Delawares until the distinct notes of army bugles sounded from beyond both ends of what had been the Indian line, which meant that they faced a large army. "The horns way over there," remembered a Delaware warrior, "go toot, toot; then way over here it goes toot, toot; then way over on the other side go toot, toot."

The Delawares scattered in the face of the American attack, and Tecumseh continued rearward in search of men to rally. Eventually he chanced upon a party of Shawnees. Through the timber the battalion standards of the Long Knives were plainly visible, lightly flapping under the summer sun. Beneath clearing skies and amid stifling heat, Tecumseh steadied the men in a dense thicket. They peppered the approaching soldiers until the enemy paused and poured a volley into the brush. Like scattered quail, Tecumseh and his party joined a general Indian flight toward the presumed safety of Fort Miamis.[14]

Beneath its sturdy, cannon-lined palisades, the Indians met with a shock more profound than that induced by the overwhelming assault of Wayne's Legion. British redcoats stood at the gate, bayonets fixed and muskets at the ready, forbidding any Indian to enter. Blue Jacket barked at the post commander for an explanation. Looking down at the stripped and painted warriors packed tightly beneath the wall, the officer called out, "I cannot let you in! You are painted too much, my children." With the Long Knives closing fast, Blue Jacket's disintegrating force continued its course downriver past the rapids to join their families near the mouth of the Maumee. Recalled a furious

Blue Jacket, "It was then that we saw the British dealt treacherously with us."[15]

The British commander had never intended to help the Indians. Unknown to Blue Jacket, American diplomats in London led by John Jay were concluding a treaty by which the British would surrender the western posts they had retained in contravention of the 1783 Peace of Paris, together with Fort Miamis. This was only the beginning of British duplicity. Alexander McKee and Matthew Elliott lamented the cruel hand dealt the Indians. Neither did they take kindly to the desecration of Indian dead by Wayne's Kentucky contingent. "The American army have left evident marks of their boasted humanity behind them," reported McKee. "Besides scalping and mutilating the Indians who were killed in action, they have opened the peaceful graves in different parts of the country, exposed the bones of the consumed and consuming bodies, and horrid to relate, they have with unparalleled barbarity driven stakes through them and left them objects calling for more than human vengeance."[16]

General Wayne, under orders to avoid conflict with the British while Jay negotiated his treaty, returned to Fort Green Ville, content to permit disunity, hunger, and hardship to bring the Indians to heel.

Wayne calculated well. After Fallen Timbers, Blue Jacket's dispirited followers dispersed. The remaining Three Fires warriors went home. The Wyandots, who had lost three of their four principal chiefs in the battle, rallied around Tarhe, the most moderate of all, at their village on the lower Sandusky River. Little Turtle and the Miamis withdrew to their tribal homeland in today's northeastern Indiana. The Delawares stuck by Buckongahelas, who at the barred gate of Fort Miamis had spit words of eternal contempt for the British. His 1,216 people, together with Blue Jacket's 949 followers and 83 Mingoes, loitered about the fort during the winter of 1794–95, their survival contingent on woefully inadequate British handouts. "Our crops and every means of support being cut off, we had to winter where Toledo now stands," a captive American remembered. "We were entirely dependent on the British, and they did not half supply us, and to make matters worse, the shrub which causes the staggers in cattle [milkweed] grew abundantly in that neighborhood.... Cattle began to die one after another, next the dogs.... Starving conditions made the Indians very exasperated at the British. They concluded ... to make a treaty with the Americans."[17]

Tecumseh would have none of British charity. Nor would he associate with the tribesmen who seemed willing to treat with the American victors. He had turned his back on the Ohio country Shawnees before, first to follow Cheeseekau to Spanish Louisiana, then to fight with the Chickamaugas. Now he would go it nearly alone with Lalawethika, Tecumpease and her husband, and a handful of ardent cohorts. Together they passed the winter at the headwaters of the Great Miami and Scioto rivers, in a game-rich country emptied of Indians but not yet occupied by white settlers. There for a season Tecumseh roamed content.[18]

The Northwestern Confederacy formally died on August 3, 1795, when ninety-nine chiefs signed the Treaty of Greenville, by the terms of which they relinquished all but the northwestern corner of present-day Ohio. The treaty represented nothing less than a cataclysmic upheaval of Indian society. The U.S. government became both usurper and benefactor, its influence within tribal governments secured through an annuity system that granted signatories annual payments ranging from $500 to $2,000.

The Treaty of Greenville also proclaimed an American commitment to culturally transform the Indians by encouraging them to abandon the hunt and take up exclusively agricultural pursuits—whether they liked it or not. Other treaty articles permitted the U.S. government to construct forts and trading posts on Indian land; abjured further American claims to land between the Ohio and Mississippi rivers (a promise that would prove meaningful only while George Washington and his successor, John Adams, held the office of president); permitted only federal purchase of Indian land; bound the government to protect remaining Indian lands from white squatters and to provide licensed traders to the Indians; and granted the Indians peaceful hunting privileges in the ceded country so long as no legal white occupants objected. The once proudly independent tribes of the Ohio country, who for more than a century had played European powers and the United States against one another, were now inextricably bound to their conquerors. As the Indians became increasingly dependent on annuity goods and cash to survive, so did their chiefs, whose influence derived from their authority to distribute annuities within their tribes as they saw fit, a disquieting dynamic that mitigated against future unified resistance. Peace had come, but at a cost no Indian could have contemplated before Fallen Timbers.[19]

The immediate impact of the Treaty of Greenville varied from tribe to tribe. The Miamis fared well. Little Turtle's son-in-law William Wells finagled $2,500 in annuities for the tribe, while other confederacy tribes received just $1,000. The Miamis also retained the heart of their homeland. The Potawatomis, an opportunistic people who even their Indian allies conceded were "deceitful and treacherous," had long since moved elsewhere. Yet they appeared at the council in droves and pocketed a share equal to that of the Shawnees, who found themselves defeated and landless, beholden to the Wyandots and Miamis for a home.[20]

And what of the chiefs of the defunct Northwestern Confederacy? Each adapted to the new reality according to his nature. Little Turtle, who expressed himself as "perfectly acquainted with every article of the treaty," asked only that William Wells be appointed resident interpreter to the Miami villages that sprang up near newly constructed Fort Wayne in what would become the Indiana Territory. Tarhe retired to his town in north-central Ohio, assuring Wayne "that we [Wyandots] do now and will henceforth acknowledge the fifteen United States of America." Buckongahelas likewise buried the hatchet.

The Greenville proceedings cost Blue Jacket dearly. The treaty not only negated his lifetime of resistance to Anglo domination, but now that the wars were ended, Shawnee tradition compelled him to surrender his authority to the Mekoche peace chief Black Hoof, an aged but alert leader content to meander along the white man's road. He did manage to protect his comfortable lifestyle, however. In a private conference with General Wayne, Blue Jacket spurned the inconstant British and repeated his "assurances of the sincerity of my sentiments and resolution, to be, for the future, a steady friend to the United States." The promise of a house and an audience with the president helped mollify Blue Jacket, and he moved his fine furniture, gun and fur collection, métis wife, English-educated sons, and gorgeous daughters to a new settlement on the Detroit River.

There Blue Jacket set to work to demonstrate his good feelings for his American father. He convinced seventy "refractory" Shawnee warriors under the minor war leader Puckeshaw to return four prisoners to General Wayne. "I now surrender them up to you, my Father, and promise sincerely that we will do no more mischief," groveled Pucke-shaw. "I hope that we shall be permitted to live and hunt in peace and quietness. We were poor, ignorant children, astray in the woods, who knew not that our nation, and all the other tribes of Indians, had come in and made peace with you. I thank the Great Spirit for at length opening our eyes."[21]

A lone Shawnee warrior stood on the north bank of the great river of his childhood, which the Long Knives called the Ohio, and gazed upon the distant Kentucky shore. He knew he would never again hunt in the bluegrass country. The barrier had fallen. The Long Knives, Spawn of the Great Serpent, now occupied the center of the universe. The earth was in chaos. The Shawnees had lost their homeland.[22]

Yet Tecumseh would truckle to no one. Although he ultimately accepted the treaty, he refused to come within a day's ride of Green-ville. Erecting a village on Deer Creek, a broad tributary of the upper Scioto, Tecumseh passed the long summer weeks of the Greenville council deep in the forest, hunting. These were no longer solitary forays. Fallen Timbers had been Tecumseh's first stand-up fight with soldiers. He had conducted himself so well that his entourage grew in proportion to the courage he demonstrated during the retreat, when most had lost their heads. The warriors who gravitated to Tecumseh were angry and baffled young men, fellow Kispoko Shawnees mostly, and their families, alienated from Blue Jacket, Black Hoof, and the other chiefs who had capitulated to the Long Knives. These "mili-tants," as wary Americans styled them, did not necessarily want war, but they abhorred the thought of abandoning the traditional life. They wanted commerce on fair terms with the Americans, of whom more than ten thousand were now congregated in settlements in southern Ohio; otherwise they wished to be left alone. Tecumseh's surviving brothers were among them, as was his elder sister Tecumpease and her husband Wahsikegaboe. Ruddell, however, was absent. After Fallen Timbers, Ruddell returned to his white relations in Kentucky. As he was a proven warrior, Shawnee culture prohibited anyone from inter-fering with his decision. No doubt his leave-taking from Tecumseh was an emotional one. Neither could then know that their paths would cross again.

Tecumseh did not look for trouble. It found him. In June 1795 he and thirty followers collided with fifty Kentuckians near their Deer Creek village. A spontaneous fight erupted in which the Shawnees killed one Kentuckian but lost some of their supplies—an even exchange by frontier standards. Tecumseh did not retaliate.

Indian leadership had to be earned and reconfirmed. One afternoon after the skirmish, Lalawethika and some of the young warriors wagered with Tecumseh that they could kill as many deer as he in three days. The bets were made, and the men dispersed. When they reconvened at the hunting camp, Tecumseh had nearly forty skins. No one else had slain more than one or two deer. "After that," attested Anthony Shane, "he was universally held to be the greatest hunter in the Shawnee nation."[23]

At twenty-seven, Tecumseh presided over a village of one hundred people, representing about 10 percent of those Shawnees still residing in the Ohio country. The venerable civil chief Black Hoof, rather than summon Tecumseh to his own town of Wakatomica on the Auglaize River, where the Mekoche Shawnees had congregated—a summons Tecumseh might decline—journeyed to Deer Creek himself to convey to the Pekowi upstart news of the Greenville Treaty.[24]

Tecumseh had arrived as a power—albeit a minor one—in Shawnee politics. Henceforth he would consolidate his position through political means and not, as had been the case to date, through warfare. He would prove adept at the art. His greatest ally would not be his talent for winning over people on his own merits but rather a mystical catalyst from a most unlikely source.

Before parting, Tecumseh and Stephen Ruddell discussed the Greenville Treaty. Although Tecumseh had stood aloof from the council, Ruddell claimed his friend was not hostile to the peace of Greenville: "He said that now he was happy that he could pursue his hunting without danger." Availing himself of the provision that permitted the Indians to hunt on the ceded lands, for several months Tecumseh wandered widely across central Ohio.[25]

In the spring of 1796, Tecumseh's band made a final pilgrimage to the site of old Piqua, with its mixed memories of tradition and tragedy. There they planted a corn crop. And there too Tecumseh took his first

Shawnee wife, Mamata, at the behest of his friends, who thought it proper that their leader should have female companionship. Several years older than Tecumseh, she was, as Lalawethika later observed, "perhaps not the handsomest or most agreeable lady in the world." But she bore him a son, whom the elder name-givers called Paukeesa, or Crouching Panther. Tecumseh felt no great attachment to either his spouse or his child. He and Mamata kept separate beds, and his son's light skin put him off. "He is too fair and like a white man," Tecumseh later told a British confidant. Tecumseh had no wish to be encumbered with a wife, but Mamata died shortly after giving birth to Paukeesa. Tecumpease, ever the she-panther, took the boy into her den to raise as her own.[26]

Freed of familial duties, Tecumseh scouted a new home for his band. In the winter of 1796–97 they relocated to the Whitewater River, a roiling tributary of the Great Miami in what is today eastern Indiana. There Tecumseh and his people passed a peaceable year, hunting and growing corn in a country free of whites. He thrived in his role as a village chief, giving of himself fully and freely. Whatever his shortcomings as a parent or spouse, Tecumseh was solicitous of his villagers' needs. He looked after the aged and infirm, repairing their frail wigwams when winter approached, giving them skins for moccasins and clothing, and sharing with them the choicest game that forests and the seasons afforded. Quietly he sought out what an admirer called the "humblest objects of charity and in quick unostentatious manner, relieved their wants."[27]

Tecumseh's reputation for goodness grew. In the spring of 1798 he accepted the suggestion of a Delaware band that their villages consolidate on the White River. Tecumseh's peregrinations became less frequent. He gained new adherents and married again. Although young and beautiful, the new wife also failed to win Tecumseh's heart. As had been the case with his first Shawnee wife, Mamata, he insisted they sleep apart in their shared wigwam—each wrapped nude in their respective animal skins in a space not more than fourteen feet in diameter, his wife's body evidently unappealing to him. They separated abruptly after only a brief cohabitation. Privy to the details of the domestic rupture, Anthony Shane said that Tecumseh had returned from hunting one day with a fine turkey for his wife to dress, in expectation of a dinner with friends. When his wife presented the cooked bird, Tecumseh discovered a few small feathers still stuck to it. After his friends left, he handed his wife her clothing and told her to leave. The astonished woman asked Tecumseh why he was banishing her. Because of the turkey feathers, he replied. Her entreaties to stay met with a cold rebuke. "No, you must go. I am ashamed of you. We must separate forever." And he drove her out.

Tecumseh emerges from Shane's account as a persnickety and fickle spouse with either a lesser or a better-controlled sex drive than that of other Shawnee men, all of whom had similarly learned the virtues, both spiritual and mundane, of sexual frugality. Tecumseh's dismissal of his spouse was entirely permissible, however. An early Protestant missionary observed that Shawnee couples often parted "on the smallest offense." A Moravian missionary explained that Woodland Indian marriages were contracted on a trial basis: "The husband may put away his wife whenever he pleases, and the wife may in like manner abandon her husband." Theoretically at least, no shame attached to a jilted spouse.[28]

At thirty, Tecumseh once again was single and apparently happy to be unattached. He was convivial with the frontiersmen he came to know while living on the White River. He displayed a keen sense of humor and a sharp business acumen, and he made white friends easily. So long as the Americans adhered to the treaty and did not overpopulate the Ohio country, Tecumseh gave them the benefit of the doubt—a remarkable concession from a man who had suffered so much personal tragedy at the hands of the Long Knives. Withal, Tecumseh at heart was a sincere proponent of peace as long as he was permitted to live the hunting life he loved. Once a loss was avenged, as after Cheeseekau's death, hatred for its own sake had no place in his constitution.

Jonathan Alder, who exchanged the life of a Shawnee warrior for that of a settler after Greenville, had the advantage over white newcomers of having fought against the Long Knives. His prior residence with the Indians also made Alder an easier object of jest. One day Tecumseh approached Alder with an offer: he would swap him a horse for a keg of rum. Alder accepted, only to have the animal die on him. The annoyed Alder asked Tecumseh for another horse. Tecumseh grinned in refusal, employing a witty logic that Alder was hard pressed to challenge: "He said he had drunk the rum up and it was all gone, and he supposed I was about as well off as he was. He said the rum was of no use to either of us; that he had suffered all the bad consequences of drinking it. He reasoned that the horse had done me as much good as the rum had done him, and perhaps more, but as it was, if I was satisfied, we would 'quit square,' as so we did."[29]

Tecumseh's conversational English enabled him to mingle readily with those Americans open to a friendship with Indians. Although a Kentuckian, James Galloway was such a man. An early pioneer and participant in the 1782 attack on Chillicothe, the home of Tecumseh's youth, Galloway came to the Ohio country in 1797 because he detested slavery, which had taken a firm hold in Kentucky. Ironically, he settled with his family near the site of old Chillicothe in a two-story, white-oak log house. Elegant by frontier standards, the Galloway residence boasted glass windowpanes, two large fireplaces, and a carefully tended herb garden.

Tecumseh paid frequent visits that Galloway, a kind and generous man, encouraged. Tecumseh grew found of Galloway's prepubescent blond daughter Rebecca. In their first calls, her father's exotically bedecked friends frightened Rebecca, and she made a habit of hiding under the bed or in the cabin loft when Tecumseh and other Shawnees dropped by. The late Chief Cornstalk's son Peter often accompanied Tecumseh, as did the murdered Chief Logan's son Jim. All three spoke English. Occasionally they camped beside the house and shared a bottle of frontier whiskey with Galloway. Tecumseh also wrestled with tall and strong Jim Logan for the benefit of white onlookers. As Tecumseh's visits become more frequent, and Rebecca's father showed his affection for the Shawnee leader by offering him the family's "guest chair" whenever he dropped by, the young girl's shyness evaporated, and she delighted in coaching him in the finer points of English grammar.

Tecumseh expressed his appreciation of the Galloway hospitality and sealed their friendship in a manner that honored the family. Filling his ceremonial tomahawk pipe with kinnikinick (herbal tobacco), Tecumseh took the first puff, then passed it to his host. Then each member of the family touched the handle. After the ceremony, Tecumseh gave Galloway the pipe "as a token of their inviolable agreement." It became a cherished family heirloom.[30]

Galloway's amiable neighbor Abner Barrett also counted Tecumseh among occasional visitors. One impromptu call was the source of considerable amusement. A big Kentucky greenhorn happened to be at Barrett's, hoping to buy land on the Mad River. When a few of Barrett's friends mentioned that Indians were in the area, the Kentuckian grew alarmed. Then the door of Barrett's house burst open. In strode Tecumseh "with his usual stately air." The Kentuckian's fear was palpable. Pointing to the man, Tecumseh exclaimed, "A big baby!" Slapping the Kentuckian on the shoulder, he repeated, "A big baby." The stranger's alarm rose in proportion to the laughter of his hosts.[31]

Genuine cordiality notwithstanding, Tecumseh had personal boundaries. The Indian factor John Johnston called him a "perfect stoic," one of the few Indian men to dress entirely in traditional buckskin: "He disdained to wear white men's manufacture, and when Indian agents offered him clothing, he would receive it on a stick and pass it to someone else, remarking that such things were fit only for women." When dining with Johnston at least, he would eat nothing but potatoes, presumably because they were the least adulterated item on the menu.[32]

Evident in Tecumseh's dealings with his white neighbors was a growing political acumen. His first foray in cross-cultural diplomacy came in 1799, the year he gave the Galloways his ceremonial pipe. Settlers in the Mad River Valley, near the Galloway homestead, had worked themselves into a war scare after the Shawnees began to act oddly. First a small Shawnee band evacuated the area with their corn crop still standing. Then Tecumseh's warriors stood armed watch around their own village. Black Hoof's warriors at Wakatomica readied themselves as well. Some even sent their wives and children to American forts for protection. Frightened settlers, meanwhile, fled to Cincinnati; those who remained behind erected blockhouses against an expected Indian attack.

"Colonel" William Ward, a leader of the Mad River settlements, and Simon Kenton were skeptical of the alarm. (Like Tecumseh, Kenton possessed a certain wanderlust. Sometime after his last skirmish with the Shawnees, he moved from Kentucky to Ohio. Now he too was an amateur diplomat.) To sort the matter out, Ward, Kenton, and James Galloway invited the Shawnee chiefs to a council near today's Urbana, Ohio, at the home of a Shawnee-speaking French-Canadian trader named François Duchouquet.

On August 13, after Kenton and Tecumseh amicably buried the

hatchet, the council convened. Seven more Shawnee leaders attended, and they selected Tecumseh to speak on their behalf. Although Duchouquet confessed difficulty translating Tecumseh's "lofty flights of eloquence," Galloway said his friend's talk was "much admired for its force." Ward recorded Tecumseh's words, which found their way into the *Cincinnati Western Spy*. They read in part as follows:

> Brothers. You know very well that we were the last that made the treaty at Greenville with our father General Wayne. We have intended all along that we would be the last that would break the peace as we have our headmen to direct us; without their orders we never will.
>
> Brothers. We are sorry to find that you have received a false alarm by some bad person, which has caused you to send your families away and leave their homes. It was not our intention to cause you the least trouble or put you or your families to the least inconvenience.
>
> Brothers. Should you see the Chickasaws, we have now to beg of you to advise them plainly to go home and do no mischief to us the Shawnee nation, as we do not mean to do them any harm.[33]

Unlike Galloway and Duchouquet, the whiskey-guzzling Lala-wethika was unimpressed with his brother's maiden speech or, for that matter, with Tecumseh's oratorical abilities in general. Shawnee custom provided that speeches not be composed and delivered by the same person, which, Lalawethika later implied, was a good thing, as Tecumseh "was not an able composer of speeches." Neither did he always deliver them well, being "sometimes confused and generally tedious and circumlocutory."[34]

Lalawethika's barbs hint at jealousy. Whether they had merit or not, Tecumseh's speech on this occasion assuaged the concerns of Ward and Kenton. As Tecumseh explained it, the cause of the apparent Shawnee war preparations was fear that a Chickasaw war party up from the South intended to attack their towns in retaliation for the death of Chickasaw scouts who had served with General Wayne. The Chickasaw threat evaporated, and the skittish settlers drifted back to their farms.

Although perhaps lacking in magniloquence, Tecumseh's speech

preserved the peace. At thirty-one, he had become a chief of considerable political promise. With the war scare passed, Tecumseh could
dedicate himself to his people. Or so he thought. Fate was about to
hand him two foes: one, an ambitious transplanted Virginia aristocrat
with almost unlimited power to cause trouble; the other, a liquid poison for which the Indians had no antidote.[35]

A Culture in Crisis

WILLIAM HENRY HARRISON was a young man in a hurry. He had to be, if he was going to make something of himself. Born on February 9, 1773, the third son of Benjamin Harrison V, a signer of the Declaration of Independence and wartime governor of Virginia, William Henry grew up in a time of turmoil, experiencing personal upheaval akin to that which Tecumseh endured as a boy. In January 1781 a British expedition under the turncoat Maj. Gen. Benedict Arnold laid waste to the Harrison family plantation of Berkeley, pilfering silverware and jewelry, burning clothing and family portraits, slaughtering cattle, and carrying off slaves and horses—a devastating loss from which Governor Harrison never recovered and that instilled in William Henry Harrison a lifelong hatred of all things British.

Benjamin Harrison's family sank into genteel poverty. Only their status as an Old Dominion first family kept them from utter ruin. Primogeniture, however, doomed William Henry to inherit little of what remained to his father. And so in 1791 he left the family estate to make his own way, intending to obtain a degree from the Medical College of Pennsylvania. Then his father died suddenly, leaving him a paltry inheritance of three thousand acres of undeveloped timber and scrub and no funds for school. At eighteen, William Henry Harrison had neither prospects nor money.

The young Harrison's cousin, Virginia governor Richard Henry Lee, had a suggestion: Why not apply for an army commission? The time was ripe. Congress had authorized an increase in the standing army to enable St. Clair to wage his war in the Northwest Territory. Harrison applied, and President Washington approved the application. "In twenty-four hours," Harrison recalled, "I was an ensign in the First United States Regiment of Infantry."

He hardly looked the part. Slightly built, he stood five foot eight (three inches shorter than Tecumseh) and was handsome in a delicate way and bookish by nature. Unlike most young officers, Harrison was both abstemious and of distinguished lineage. His first duty was to lead three hundred recruits across the Pennsylvania frontier to Pittsburgh. From there, they would travel by flatboat down the Ohio River to Fort Washington, near the remote settlement of Cincinnati. Packing a copy of Cicero and a book on rhetoric, Harrison headed into the hinterland with enough self-awareness to understand that the prospects were "certainly not encouraging to a youth not yet nineteen who had been tenderly brought up, and of a frame of body and constitution apparently but ill-suited to sustain the fatigues and hardships incident to a military life in a country where the first traces of civilization were yet to be made."

Prospects appeared even more dismal when Ensign Harrison and his recruits landed on the riverbank below Fort Washington on a bleak November afternoon in 1791. The garrison was in chaos. Stunned and bedraggled survivors of St. Clair's wretched and broken army sprawled about the post, most of them drunk. Harrison kept sober, and after seven months of distasteful garrison duty, the slender and aloof young Virginian received his lieutenant's commission. In October 1792, Mad Anthony Wayne appointed Harrison to succeed an alcoholic, whoremongering captain as commander of a company in his Legion of the United States. Harrison went to work with a will, executing deserters, lashing malcontents, and suggesting that notorious cowards be branded on the forehead, a proposal that Secretary of War Knox disapproved, not as a punishment too brutal but as one of doubtful legality. Good soldiers appreciated Harrison's hard but fair brand of discipline. Fellow officers, who initially resented him as a haughty pretender, warmed to him.

In February 1793, shortly after his twentieth birthday, Harrison obtained a leave of absence. During his nearly eighteen months of wilderness duty, much had changed at home. Harrison's mother had died, and his brother Benjamin presided at Berkeley unchallenged.

While home, William Henry sold Benjamin the dubious acreage his father had willed him and then turned his back forever on the Tidewater. Plunging into his military duties, Harrison earned further notice from Mad Anthony Wayne, who appointed him aide-de-camp. A prominent settler who met Harrison shortly after his elevation to the commanding general's staff liked what he saw: "Lieutenant Harrison was a young man of popular manners and very prepossessing appearance, a great favorite with the soldiers and the army. He had the character of a peacemaker, and from the relation in which he stood to the commander-in-chief exercised much influence."

Most important, Harrison demonstrated courage and calmness under fire. At Fallen Timbers he not only delivered Wayne's orders but also assisted in forming the legion's left wing in thick woods. On another occasion, after conveying the decisive order for the dragoons to charge the Indian line, Harrison found himself "between two fires," one of which may have been delivered by Tecumseh's advance guard. The lieutenant had hopefully named his horse Fearnaught, and the animal proved true to its name. "My gallant steed bore me along so rapidly as to prevent a direct aim from the Indians, and I was fortunate enough to escape the balls of my friends." Harrison also came away from Fallen Timbers with the approbation of General Wayne, who officially commended him for "conduct and bravery exciting the troops to press for victory."[1]

Peace presented Harrison with a dilemma. He could stay in the army on a slow road to obscurity. Or he could embrace the Northwest Territory and the vast opportunities it dangled before men who were swift and sure enough to grasp them. Harrison counted himself one such man, and he scripted his future artfully. In 1798 he resigned his commission, then married the delicate, well-educated Anna Tuthill Symmes, youngest daughter of John Cleves Symmes, a Revolutionary War hero and one of the largest landholders in the territory. Next, he parlayed his army reputation into an appointment as register of the Land Office in Cincinnati. Shortly thereafter President John Adams commissioned him as secretary to the governor of the Northwest Territory, a post with few responsibilities and a comfortable annual salary.

Allying himself with his influential father-in-law and other critics of Governor St. Clair, in 1799 Harrison won election as the territory's delegate to Congress. His singular contribution during his brief tenure was to introduce a change in public land sales that would flood the western country with new settlers faster than the government, or the Indians, possibly could have expected. Formerly purchasers were required to buy at least four thousand acres, a law that favored speculators at the expense of actual settlers, who seldom were able to raise the capital for even a fraction of that amount. Harrison introduced a bill that permitted the sale of lands in a half section of 320 acres west of the Muskingham River or a full section of 640 acres east of the river at two dollars an acre, with one-quarter down and the remaining payments spread over four years.

Speculators may have resented Harrison's initiative, but residents of the Northwest Territory applauded the Public Land Law and rewarded its author. In early 1800, when Congress divided the Northwest Territory into the Ohio and Indiana territories, John Symmes and his cronies secured Harrison's appointment as governor and superintendent of Indian affairs of the Indiana Territory. An enormous tract of land, the Indiana Territory comprised what is today Indiana, Illinois, and Wisconsin, together with bits of Minnesota and Michigan. Harrison accepted the appointment only after receiving assurances that incoming president Thomas Jefferson would retain him.[2]

Harrison's powers were vast. He appointed the territorial legislature and filled the judgeships, exercising near-absolute authority over a nonnative population of 4,875 (including 135 black slaves) that was concentrated in the southwestern fringe of modern Indiana. The neighboring Ohio Territory was more robust, and its 45,000 inhabitants were more dispersed, including a disturbing number who squatted north of the Greenville Treaty line.

Early pioneer life in both territories was bleak. A fledgling frontiersman entered the region down the Ohio River by flatboat with a rifle, an ax, an ox-drawn cart, his family, and little else. First he built a lean-to of limbs and branches. Then he felled trees to fashion a cabin, drove away or killed prowling panthers and bears, and yanked out tree stumps to clear enough soil to scratch out a meager living. His wife's lot was superficially lighter, largely because the ordinary comforts of everyday life were wanting. Furniture was minimal, mostly homemade benches, tables, and three-legged stools. Bearskins took the place of mattresses and blankets. There were no windows to wash; greased paper did the duty of glass. But deprivation made life hard.

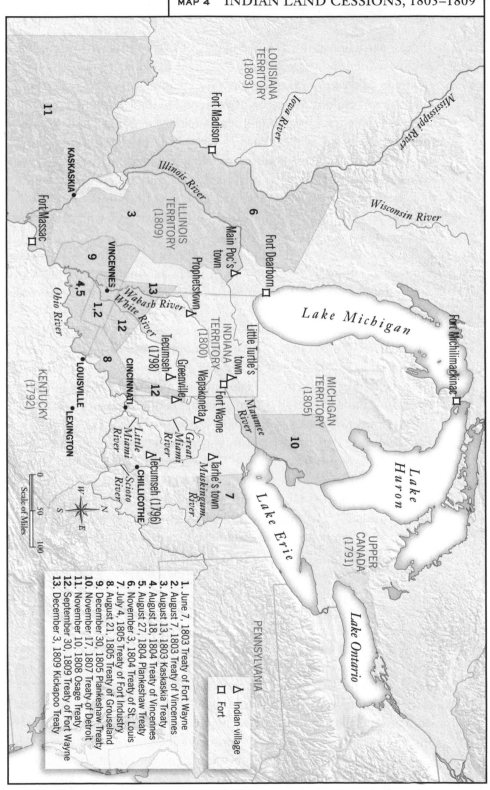

MAP 4   INDIAN LAND CESSIONS, 1803–1809

LOUISIANA
TERRITORY
(1803)

Iowa River

Mississippi River

Fort Madison ☐

11

KASKASKIA •

Illinois River

6

Fort Massac ☐

ILLINOIS
TERRITORY
(1809)

3

Main Poc's △
town

Fort Dearborn ☐

Wisconsin River

Lake Michigan

Fort Michilimackinac ☐

9

VINCENNES ☐

13

Prophetstown △

△ Little Turtle's
town

MICHIGAN
TERRITORY
(1805)

4,5

1,2

Wabash River

White River

△ Tecumseh
(1798)

INDIANA
TERRITORY
(1800)

Fort Wayne ☐

Maumee River

Lake
Huron

12

8

12

△ Greenville

△ Wapakoneta

△ Tarhe's town

10

Ohio River

CINCINNATI •

*Great
Miami
River*

Muskingum River

7

Lake Erie

Lake Ontario

LOUISVILLE •

KENTUCKY
(1792)

LEXINGTON •

*Little
Miami
River*

△ Tecumseh (1796)
CHILLICOTHE •

*Scioto
River*

0
50
100
Scale of Miles

W

N
S
E

PENNSYLVANIA

UPPER
CANADA
(1791)

△ Indian village
☐ Fort

1. June 7, 1803 Treaty of Fort Wayne
2. August 7, 1803 Treaty of Vincennes
3. August 13, 1803 Kaskaskia Treaty
4. August 18, 1804 Treaty of Vincennes
5. August 27, 1804 Plankeshaw Treaty
6. November 3, 1804 Treaty of St. Louis
7. July 4, 1805 Treaty of Fort Industry
8. August 21, 1805 Treaty of Grouseland
9. December 30, 1805 Plankeshaw Treaty
10. November 17, 1807 Treaty of Detroit
11. November 10, 1808 Osage Treaty
12. September 30, 1809 Treaty of Fort Wayne
13. December 3, 1809 Kickapoo Treaty

Illness, particularly the dreaded ague (malaria), was ever present, the seldom-varied diet of pork and cornmeal weakened constitutions, a common cold could transform itself into pneumonia in an instant, and the rigors of childbirth prematurely aged or killed women. Trapping, shooting matches, log rolling, corn shucking, weddings, and whiskey relieved the strain of the pioneers' contracted lives. Rare indeed was the cabin that lacked a generous stock of jugs filled with corn or rye whiskey distilled at local copper distilleries, and the pioneer who did not cheer a passing traveler with drink, often to the point of insensibility, was reckoned inhospitable. Such were the settlers who called the Indians savages.

Vincennes, the capital of the Indiana Territory, offered backwoodsmen little in the way of diversions. A mean and muddy settlement of four hundred cabins on the lower Wabash River, Vincennes reeled with knife-wielding drunks and ill-tempered Indians. Withal Harrison made the best of it. "I am much pleased with this country," he wrote a friend in late 1801. "I have purchased a farm of about 300 acres adjoining the town which is all cleared. I am now fencing it and shall begin to build next spring if I can find the means." Harrison not only found the means to build a farm, but he also began work on one of the grandest residences in the Old Northwest, an elegant Georgian-Federal brick structure with stunning Doric columns that when finished in 1804 would have done a Tidewater plantation owner proud. A monument of frontier magnificence, the Harrison estate, which the governor named Grouseland, became the center of government for the Indiana Territory. It would also serve as a fortress in times of unrest. Such moments were to come sooner than Governor Harrison expected.[3]

Tecumseh could joke with Jonathan Alder about the relative merits of a keg of rum and a sick horse or confess to an occasional bender because his moments of insobriety were few. Lalawethika, on the other hand, was a debauched rogue. Thin and weakened by drink, his depth perception impaired by the loss of his right eye, Lalawethika rattled around the village, boasting of phantom virtues and living on handouts. Drink, however, seems not to have clouded his natural shrewdness, nor diminished Tecumseh's affection for him. Tecumseh had already lost his father, two brothers, and for all intents and purposes his mother. Perhaps their absence caused him to cling closer to Lalawethika than he might otherwise have.[4] In any event, as a village chief, Tecumseh faced a problem far greater than his brother's insobriety. He was at war with a foe that threatened to engulf the entire White River Indian population, both Shawnee and Delaware, as it had Lalawethika—an enemy more pernicious and harder to bring to heel than the cleverest Kentucky backwoods fighter: liquor.

Two Moravian missionaries who settled with a dozen Delaware converts fifteen miles downriver from Tecumseh's village witnessed the horrible ravages alcohol wrought on the Shawnees and their "heathen" Delaware neighbors, and how easily their own small flock succumbed to it. "They screamed all night in the woods and acted like madmen," the Moravians wrote of the congregation's first bacchanalia. "No one who has not seen an Indian drunk can possibly have any conception of it. It is as if they had all been changed into evil spirits." Although contrite after every indulgence, the Christian Delawares nonetheless kept on drinking. Most tragically, an elderly survivor of the Gnadenhutten massacre perished from alcohol poisoning. She sold her corn crop and all her belongings to buy whiskey and then "sat down and drank so long that she gave up the ghost and fell over dead."

Indian villages sank into squalor. Scarcely a day went by without a drunken murder or a maiming. Brother attacked brother. Inebriated Indians slaughtered their own livestock and horses in drunken fits. Neglected children fell victim to dysentery and died. Women, and sometimes children, imbibed as heavily as men. Elders lamented the loss of their young but often succumbed to drink themselves.

A death in Tecumseh's village particularly horrified the Moravians as surely as it did Tecumseh. "We heard that the Shawnees had murdered, in pitiful fashion, in their town, an Indian of their own nation, while drinking whiskey. First, they chopped three holes in his head with their tomahawk, and as he did not fall dead at once, one of them jumped on him with a knife and ran it into his body, while another cut his stomach open. Thus, also lately a Delaware murdered a Shawnee woman." Generalizing on the paralytic ubiquity of liquor along the White River, the missionaries concluded, "This drinking never passes without the shedding of blood. Most of them looked as if they had passed through some great sickness. In this way they destroy themselves."

American miscreants dealt in whiskey wholesale. Indian middle-

men, and women, retailed the rotgut concoction in their villages, usually in lots of one hundred or more gallons, which the Indians drained
dry. The traders dared not deliver the whiskey themselves "because
their lives are not safe during the drunkenness of the Indians."[5]

The strain broke Tecumseh. Turning away from the death,
debauchery, his dissolute brother, and his chieftainship for a season,
in 1801 Tecumseh journeyed five hundred miles west across the Mississippi River (more than a month's trip each way) to visit his mother
and western kinsmen and to regain his equilibrium. The western
Shawnees might lack the urge to repel American intruders, but they
were a sober and industrious lot. Hunting parties roamed a country
still rich in game, and women planted fields naturally fertile. Resident
French traders dealt squarely with them, and Creek delegations paid
frequent friendly visits. Occasional clashes with neighboring Osages
kept warrior skills sharp. All told, the western Shawnees were a satisfied people. But theirs was not Tecumseh's world, and he could not
long absent himself from the White River whiskey maelstrom.[6]

Meanwhile, at his town near Fort Wayne, the Miami chief Little
Turtle also confronted a people awash in alcohol. Little Turtle drank
moderately, as did his son-in-law and political ally William Wells,
but as a tribe, the Miamis were rolling down the road to perdition
in a whiskey barrel. Little Turtle and Wells earnestly wished for the
Miamis to become more reliant on agriculture and livestock raising
but thought the transition impossible until the federal government
shut down the whiskey trade. They pleaded their case directly to the
newly elected president, Thomas Jefferson. "Father," Little Turtle
said, "your children are not wanting in industry, but it is the introduction of this fatal poison which keeps them poor. Your children have
not the command over themselves that you have, therefore before
anything can be done to advantage this evil must be remedied."

Little Turtle made the same case to the Baltimore annual meeting
of the Society of Friends (Quakers), whose help he solicited:

> Brothers! When our young men have been out hunting and are
> returning home loaded with skins and furs; on their way, if it
> happens that they come where some whiskey is deposited, the
> white man who sells it tells them to take a little drink. Some of
> them will say No, I do not want it. They go on till they come to

another house, where they find more of the same kind of drink. It is there offered again; they refuse; and again, a third time; but finally, the fourth or fifth time, one accepts of it, and takes a drink, and getting one, he wants another; and then a third, and fourth, till his senses have left him. After his reason comes back again to him, then he gets up and finds where he is and asks for his peltry. The answer is, "You have drunk them." "Where is my gun?" "It is gone." "Where is my shirt?" "You have sold it for whiskey!"

Now, brothers, figure to yourselves what condition this man must be in. He has a family at home; a wife and children who stand in need of the profits of his hunting. What must be *their* wants, when he himself is even without a shirt?

Little Turtle was one of three figures at Fort Wayne with whom Tecumseh, and later Lalawethika, would wrestle. The second was William Wells, recently appointed Indian agent to the Miamis; the third, John Johnston, the government factor. For obscure reasons, Johnston became an inveterate enemy of Wells and a sometimes admirer of Tecumseh.[7]

As an Indian agent, William Wells theoretically was subordinate to territorial governor William Henry Harrison. The lines of authority between the secretary of war, who had overall supervision of Indian affairs; the governors, who were the "organs of all negotiations and communications between the Indians and the government" within their respective territories; and the agents to individual tribes were often opaque in the early days of the republic, a tendency that secretaries of war exacerbated by communicating directly with agents.

Notwithstanding this uncertainty, it was the Indian agent who dealt directly with the Indians on a day-to-day basis, informing them of government policy and enforcing it, distributing annuities, adjudicating Indian-related disputes to keep the peace, and often acting as interpreter or aiding at treaty negotiations. In his capacity as distributor of annuities, the Indian agent also had authority to use part of the annuity money, at Indian request, to buy agricultural implements and domestic animals, and to hire laborers such as carpenters and blacksmiths to work for the Indians.

The job of the Indian factor was to manage Indian trading stations, known as factories, which the federal government had instituted during the Washington administration to receive and dispense goods that the Indians needed or desired. The larger purpose of the factory system, as expressed by President Jefferson, was to "undersell private traders, foreign and domestic; drive them from the competition; and thus, with the goodwill of the Indians, rid ourselves of a description of men who are constantly endeavoring to excite in the Indian mind suspicions, fears, and irritations to us."[8]

His prejudice against Wells notwithstanding, Johnston proved an excellent factor. The Fort Wayne Indian factory shipped pelts and deerskins to Detroit every fall and spring for transport east. In exchange, the Indians obtained goods as varied as tea, vinegar, coffee, soaps, coats, nails, needles, tobacco, china, and cloth, or they ran up dangerously high balances when they lacked the skins to pay for the white man's goods that had become indispensable to them. While they incurred debts with Johnston, they also kept trading with licensed private traders, one of whom raked in eight hundred deerskins in three days from Indians in exchange for whiskey. Poverty, anguish, and alcoholism appeared to be the Indians' fate.[9]

For William Henry Harrison, there was no escaping the reality of Indian decline. Drunken Indians—mostly Weas or Piankeshaws, whose villages stood nearby—staggered along the rutted dirt streets of Vincennes. They posed a grave danger not only to anyone who chanced across their wobbly paths but also to themselves. No more than six hundred warriors inhabited the lower Wabash Valley, yet Indian traders in Vincennes annually trafficked in six thousand gallons of alcohol. A French tourist who visited Vincennes in 1797 observed with mixed awe and disgust the indigenous peoples who assembled at the territorial capital to barter pelts and skins. What he saw differed in no way from what Harrison would encounter three years later. In the first flush of discovery, the Frenchman found the Indians a "new and most whimsical sight." The women reminded him of European gypsies. He wondered at the tanned, nearly naked bodies of the warriors, glittering with grease and soot, faces smeared with red, black, and blue paint, ears and nostrils supporting rings of silver and copper, wrists adorned with wide metal bands, and loins draped in "little square aprons." He supposed the Indians delighted in their dress because they carried small mirrors with which "they examine [themselves] with as much attention and complacency as any European coquet." And then the Indians began to drink. Men and women bartered all they owned, "never ceasing to drink till they had lost their senses." They lay by the dozens in the streets, wallowing in filth with hogs. A liquor-inflamed warrior stabbed his wife four times within a few paces of the Frenchman, who had planned to spend a few months among the Indians. Being "satisfied with this sample," however, he opted against it.[10]

The suffering on his doorstep distressed Governor Harrison. He did what he could to ameliorate the Indians' misery, removing squatters from Indian land and employing the militia to block would-be trespassers who violated the Greenville Treaty Line. He forbade traders to supply Indians with liquor in Vincennes or within a mile of the town (at least the noxious trade would no longer be carried out beneath his office window), then ordered the peddlers to confine themselves to Indian villages rather than follow warriors on the hunt so that the men would be sober enough to provide for their families.

On July 15, 1801, Harrison penned his first official letter. It was a long, thoughtful, and sympathetic missive on the Indian plight. Over the course of twelve weeks, the chiefs of most of the villages near Vincennes had presented their grievances to the governor. All professed friendship for the United States. Harrison found them sincere and their complaints of trespassing, wanton destruction of game, whiskey peddling, and unpunished homicides credible. "A great many of the inhabitants of the frontier consider the murdering of Indians in the highest degree meritorious," Harrison informed the secretary of war. Illicit hunting on Indian land had become "a monstrous abuse." These and other injuries "the Indians have borne with astonishing patience."

Harrison detested the liquor traffic. "Liquor not only incapacitates [Indians] from hunting but leads to the most atrocious crimes—killing each other has become so customary among them that it is no longer a crime to murder those whom they have been most accustomed to esteem and regard." That is to say, the chiefs who dared disrupt the trafficking. The degradation that liquor induced was apparent. "I can tell at once by looking at an Indian whether he belongs to a neighboring or more distant tribe. The latter are generally well-clothed, healthy, and vigorous; the former half-naked, filthy, and enfeebled with intoxication."[11]

In his otherwise incisive appraisal of the cultural crisis confronting the Indians, Harrison failed to connect the dots fully. The existential threat to the tribes stemmed not only from the liquor trade and the white man's depletion of game animals but also from the Indians' own overkilling of bear, elk, deer, and—on the prairie of the Illinois country—buffalo. Skin hunting—the killing of large animals critical to subsistence simply to have something to barter for liquor—became commonplace. Previously an Indian hunter might kill for food anywhere from fifty to 150 deer during the autumn hunt; now hunting became a year-round endeavor, giving herds no chance to replenish their numbers. What animals remained also roamed over increasingly constricted grounds because the farms of white settlers stripped away their habitats.[12]

Harrison neglected to mention another disorienting element in the Indian communities. The land concessions made at the Treaty of Greenville had intensified the Shawnee and Delaware migration from modern Ohio to Indiana, which in turn accelerated a trend evident since the first days of the old French alliance. Indian villages were becoming increasingly mixed, often composed of people of disparate tribal loyalties. Tecumseh's White River village was reasonably unified, but the fabric of larger Indian society was descending into a nightmarish dystopia in which traditions teetered on the lip of a whiskey jug, and the forests, stripped of game animals, brooded dark and silent.

When it came to Indian land, Governor Harrison flailed about in contradictory musings. On February 19, 1802, he wrote to Secretary of War Henry Dearborn that the chiefs with whom he had conferred "had heard we resolved to destroy them that we might take possession of their lands," a notion Harrison believed had been "infused by British agents or traders, which enjoy every opportunity to prejudice the Indians against us." Yet just a week later Harrison told Dearborn that he believed the Treaty of Greenville in fact entitled the United States to more land than was generally assumed, and he wanted to call a council of tribes later in the year to fix permanent boundaries. It would be a hard slog, getting them to come to terms on anything, cautioned Harrison, as "there appears to be an agreement among them that no proposition which relates to their lands can be acceded to without the consent of all the tribes, and they are extremely watchful and jealous of each other lest some advantage should be obtained in which they do not all participate." Accordingly, the governor summoned area tribes to a September 1802 council in Vincennes. No invitation was extended to Tecumseh's small Kispoko Shawnee settlement or to the White River Delawares because both the governor and the other tribes agreed that neither the Shawnees nor the Delawares had a proprietary claim to land in the Indiana Territory.[13]

There was no objection from Tecumseh, who may not have even been aware of the impending council. Not that it would have mattered to Harrison or to the Jefferson administration. Tecumseh was unknown beyond the Shawnee world except to Stephen Ruddell, Jonathan Alder, James Galloway, and a few other former white captives and local settlers. With Tecumseh's former mentor Blue Jacket in retirement, the Mekoche Black Hoof, who disdained Tecumseh as a troublesome upstart, emerged as the Shawnee spokesman to the government, and he was firmly committed to peace, seemingly at any price. Despite his age and diminutive size—Black Hoof stood just above five feet—he continued to command his people's respect both as a great orator and as a near legendary former war leader.

The elderly Black Hoof's sunset gambit was part intratribal power play, part exercise in tribal survival. As refugees on Miami and Wyandot lands, the Shawnees were liable to have their homes sold out from under them, the more so as they had scattered after the Greenville Treaty. Not only had Blue Jacket, Black Hoof, and Tecumseh gone their separate ways, but small bands of Shawnees had also begun to trickle west to join those already living beyond the Mississippi. Hoping to reverse the centrifugal trend, Black Hoof received Wyandot permission to build the town of Wapakoneta on the Auglaize River in western Ohio, just above the Greenville Treaty line and fifty-five miles north of modern Dayton. Here Black Hoof's Mekoches raised cabins, acquired cattle and hogs, and tilled the soil with quiet earnestness. The young men went on periodic drunks but generally behaved themselves well enough to win the grudging respect of their white neighbors.[14]

The Wapakoneta Mekoches adopted a new strategy for bolstering Shawnee land rights in the Great Lakes region. First, they invited scattered tribesmen to relocate to their village under Mekoche leadership with a promise that "all we can get here will do well for themselves, their women, and children." Then Black Hoof visited the Great Father, Thomas Jefferson, to request he grant the Shawnees title to Wapakoneta, which lay on land that belonged to the Miamis, so that "nobody shall take any advantage of us," meaning not only whites but also other Indians.

It was a remarkable request, asking the government to give the Shawnees land on the *Indian* side of the Greenville line—the antithesis of the pan-Indian alliance for which Black Hoof had fought less than a decade earlier. But the collapse of the Northwestern Confederacy had left the Shawnees again vulnerable to diaspora. Apart from the trans-Mississippi country and perhaps the upper Great Lakes, they had nowhere left to roam. The Jefferson administration, however, turned Black Hoof down. Secretary of War Dearborn told the Shawnee chief that the Great Father "does not consider himself authorized to divide the lands of his red children." All Black Hoof had to show for his visit were a few hoes and plows and a vague offer to consider future assistance to his Wapakoneta Shawnees.[15]

Dearborn had spoken truthfully. The government had no authority to partition that which belonged to the Indians. But a larger consideration underpinned Jefferson's refusal. He wanted to acquire every inch of Indian land between the Ohio and Mississippi rivers that could possibly be gotten peaceably. His reasons were twofold. First, he needed Indian land to facilitate the expanding Jeffersonian "Empire of Liberty." Only by moving westward, Jefferson believed, could Americans maintain the republican society of independent yeoman farmers that he idealized and not descend into the black swirl of urban misery that blighted much of the Old World. Second, at least until the 1803 Louisiana Purchase rendered the point moot, he wanted to seed the region with American settlements to counter Napoleonic France, the potentially belligerent successor to the vast Spanish claims west of the Mississippi.

Shorn of flowery public professions of benevolence and eternal amity, Jefferson's plan for dispossessing the Indians of much of their land may be summarized as follows. Peace would be maintained through a small number of forts garrisoned by regular troops to discourage white trespassing and trafficking in liquor, either one of which might ignite border warfare. The system of nonprofit, whiskey-free government factories would be made more robust to counter the influence of British traders and to drive the Indians so deeply into debt that they would willingly part with their lands to liquidate their obligations. Jefferson's policy would compress the Eastern Woodland Indians into a shrinking enclave between the Mississippi and Ohio rivers. As game in the enclave diminished, the government would offer the Indians the capital goods and the training needed to become farmers in exchange for yet more land. Those who rejected "civilization" would be removed west of the Mississippi, where they could hunt to their hearts' delight until the day came when whites wanted to settle the country that Jefferson would obtain in the Louisiana Purchase. Then the cycle would presumably repeat itself: the Indians would either assimilate or lose their land.

With characteristic moral dualism, Jefferson combined a genuine if myopic concern for Indian welfare with a voracious appetite for their land. Despite all evidence to the contrary, most notably the cultural prescriptions to men tilling the soil, Jefferson rationalized that Indians would be happier and healthier as small yeoman farmers. And being small farmers, they would need far less land. Everyone except those Indians who refused to assimilate would benefit.[16]

Jefferson had no doubt that his plan would ultimately succeed. Two years earlier he had written Gov. James Monroe of Virginia of the joyous future of his Empire of Liberty (this while the United States was yet hemmed in by British Canada to the north, the Spaniards on its southern frontier, and the Indians to the west). "It [is] impossible," said Jefferson, "not to look forward to distant times, when our rapid multiplication will expand itself beyond those limits, and cover the whole northern, if not the southern continent with a people by similar laws."[17]

To facilitate this grandiose eventuality, Jefferson must first deal with the Indians. In a confidential letter to Harrison on February 27, 1803, Jefferson laid bare exactly what he expected of his young territorial governor,

> We wish to draw [the Indians] to agriculture.... When they withdraw themselves to the culture of a small piece of land, they will perceive how useless to them are their extensive forests, and be willing to pare them off in exchange for necessaries for their

farms and families. To promote this disposition to exchange lands...we shall push our trading houses and be glad to see them run [up] debt because when these debts get beyond what the Indians can pay, they will become willing to lop them off by a cession of lands.... In this way our settlements will gradually circumscribe and approach the Indians, and they will either incorporate with us as citizens of the United States or remove beyond the Mississippi.... Should any tribe be foolhardy enough to take up the hatchet, the seizing the whole country of that tribe and drive them across the Mississippi as the only condition of peace would be an example to others and a furtherance of our final consolidation.[18]

Harrison had his instructions, and he went to work to dispossess the Indians of their country. His preferred tactic was to negotiate with tribes or bands whose claim to an area was weak or nonexistent; they would be more inclined to trade land for annuities than would those with stronger rights to a region. (The notion of common Indian land ownership—what Blue Jacket had called the "bowl with a single spoon"—had faded after Fallen Timbers.) Chiefs might occasionally protest such cessions as fraudulent, but they could not outright oppose them because their chieftainships depended on treaty annuities. The most influential chiefs—Little Turtle, Buckongahelas, Blue Jacket, and Tarhe—all objected to treaties in which their voices were muted, but they were complicit in concluding others that added to their wealth and influence. In one instance, Harrison resorted to outright bribery to secure Little Turtle's cooperation, adding fifty dollars to his annual pension and buying him a slave from Kentucky. In every case, Harrison used his power to withhold annuities to buy off chiefs.

Thus Harrison carved up the Old Northwest for eventual white settlement. In two treaties signed in the summer of 1803, he obtained over 1 million acres around Vincennes. In three treaties concluded over the course of the following two years, Harrison purchased residual Indian lands in southern Indiana. Most spectacularly, in the Treaty of Fort Wayne (1803) he obtained from the nearly extinct Kaskaskias practically all of Illinois east of the Illinois River. In the Treaty of St. Louis (1804), he swindled the powerful Sauks and Foxes out of 51 million acres, planting the seeds of deep hostility toward the Americans. After adding one final tract in southern Illinois in December

1805, Harrison halted his treaty-making to permit white settlement to catch up with the land acquired and to keep Indian rancor from boiling over—some of the Indians recognized the real monetary value of the land they had parted with for a pittance. The cost of Harrison's purchases was less than $100,000, often as little as a penny an acre for land worth six hundred times that amount.[19]

The swirl of swindles left Tecumseh's White River village untouched. Lalawethika continued his career as an irredeemable drunkard, although in sober moments he dabbled in traditional medicine. At the insistence of friends, Tecumseh married again in 1802 at age thirty-four. His third Shawnee wife, Wabelegunequa (White Wing), was several years older than him and homely. Tecumseh apparently did not then place a premium on physical beauty. Their marriage lasted longer than his previous liaisons, but Tecumseh felt no greater attachment to her than he had to his former wives.[20]

As a village chief in trying times, Tecumseh sublimated his ambivalence toward his white neighbors. Settlers like the Galloways were friends; others were painful reminders of past injustices who must be tolerated and sometimes respected. In the latter category was a white man with whom Tecumseh traded a worn-out saddle for a better one. The settler repaired the saddle until it looked newer than the one Tecumseh had obtained in the trade. When Tecumseh next met the man and saw the saddle, he tried to claim it as his own. The saddle owner challenged Tecumseh to settle the question of ownership by personal combat. Tecumseh declined; chiefs did not wrangle violently over mere possessions. Neither did they yield to unwarranted impulses toward war.

Tecumseh's restraint was tested in April 1803, when an Ohio militia officer was shot twice, tomahawked, and scalped while working his field sixteen miles west of the state capital, Chillicothe, which was located on the very spot and retained the Shawnee name of Tecumseh's childhood village. Rumor had it that forty Shawnee warriors were lurking in the area, and a company of volunteers hastily organized itself in Chillicothe. After a second settler and a Shawnee warrior were found dead, Gov. Edward Tiffin, a fair-minded frontier statesman, rode out with the volunteers to investigate. Tiffin's responsibilities were more circumscribed than those of Harrison; the burgeoning white population of Ohio had elevated the former territory to statehood the previous month, meaning that the federal government was now the ultimate arbiter of Indian matters within the state's boundaries.

Tiffin hoped to avoid any such escalation of tensions. He met Tecumseh and his warriors hunting in their old Ohio haunts. Tecumseh claimed to know nothing of the murders, assuring Tiffin that his intentions were peaceable and his commitment to the treaty genuine. He was guilty of nothing more than nostalgia for his old home. Tiffin took Tecumseh at his word. He attributed the killings to "private quarrels" between "individuals who have suffered, and without the knowledge of their chiefs, who are sincerely disposed to cultivate peace and harmony with the white people." Reflecting further, Tiffin added, "We have imprudent men settled on our frontiers, and the Indians have inconsiderate young warriors amongst them. It requires much prudence to keep both sides in order."[21]

Notwithstanding the pacific words of Black Hoof and Tecumseh, the Shawnees simmered with discontent. Harrison had excluded the tribe from most of his treaty councils, though he did invite them to the Fort Wayne proceedings, where the Shawnee delegates educated Harrison on the correct cosmic pecking order. "The Master of Life, who was himself an Indian, made the Shawnees before any other of the human race, and they sprang from his brain," said their leader, an emissary from Black Hoof. All other Indians were descended from the Shawnees, he continued. Perhaps for diplomatic purposes, the old chief gave an apparently sanitized version of the creation of white men. The Master of Life fashioned them as well, he conceded, just from lesser parts of his body—the French and British from his breast, the Dutch from his feet, and the Long Knives from his hands. "These inferior races of men he made white, and placed them beyond the Stinking Lake." For many ages the Shawnees reigned as masters of the American continent. But eventually they became corrupt. An angry Master of Life gave their knowledge to the white men, to be restored to the Shawnees only when they "returned to good principles."

The old chief told Harrison to tread carefully. The day of Shawnee redemption was near at hand. "The Master of Life is about to restore to the Shawnees their knowledge and their rights," he proclaimed, "and He will trample the Long Knives under his feet."[22]

· PART ·

TWO

A Prophet Arises

T HE WINTER OF 1804–5 struck the White River villages with hellish fury. Coruscated cornfields glittered frozen through long icy nights. An eerie hush engulfed the brief but dreary daylight hours. Huddled in their council houses, chiefs and headmen contemplated their misery and struggled to divine its causes. Whiskey was an obvious culprit, but the chiefs could hardly condemn the Indians who consumed it because village leaders often peddled it themselves and because liquor had infiltrated the rituals and ceremonies central to Indian lives.

The Great Father's insistence that Indian men take up the emasculating work of farming, as well as the insatiable white hunger for Indian land, also came under scrutiny in the council houses. So too did the white man's diseases, especially influenza, which ravaged Miami, Delaware, and Shawnee villages into the spring of 1805, striking down children, the infirm, and the elderly. Even the relatively prosperous Wyandots, with their neatly tilled fields and snug cabins, succumbed by the score.[1]

Other tribulations blossomed with the spring. Melting snows brought severe flooding. The White River inundated barren Shawnee and Delaware cornfields. Game animals grew scarcer; white settlers drew nearer. The spiritual pan-Indianism of Neolin and Pontiac, dormant since Pontiac had betrayed the cause and Neolin reluctantly had told the Indians to lay down their arms two generations earlier, appeared ripe for renewal amid the soul-crushing suffering. Into the shadows of death and dissipation came dreams and visions. To comprehend their misfortune, Indians plumbed the depths of their conscious and subconscious minds. A Delaware warrior told the venerable Chief Buckongahelas of a vision he experienced while hunting. A spectral Indian calling himself the warrior's grandfather had blocked his path, warning that young Indian men were to blame for the scarcity of game. Their only hope rested in redemption. "This is all your own fault. You should not listen to the white people nor seek to imitate them by keeping horses, cows, and pigs, and by clothing yourselves in the cloth which the whites bring you," enjoined the phantom. "You must live as you did before the white people came to this country. Everything that you have from the white [men] must be put away. If you do this, you will have wild game in plenty, and the deer will once more come in front of your doors." It was as if a reanimated Neolin were speaking, and Buckongahelas listened attentively. Buckongahelas was an old man now, of some eighty snows. And he was complicit in questionable land sales that had contributed to the tribe's decline. But as the "George Washington of the Delawares," his opinions still carried great weight among his people. He believed the warrior's tale.

An old Delaware Moravian apostate named Beata propagated a similar vision. She claimed that one evening, while she was sitting outside her cabin, two invisible Indians had told her that the Great Spirit was angry with the Indians for abandoning the old ways. "You must love one another," the spirits had said. "If you fail to do so, a terrible storm will arise, tear down all the trees and every Indian shall be killed." Another Delaware crone seconded her sister in faith, claiming that a benevolent demon had begged the Delawares to heed the words of Beata's celestial visitors.

Buckongahelas opened the Wapicomekoke council house to the mystics. Rattling pebble-filled turtle shells, singing, dancing, and gesticulating, the old women circled a totem pole, giving thanks to the Great Spirit for having opened their eyes. A few days later Buckongahelas, their most prominent convert, died of influenza. The Delawares gave way to a spasm of grieving violence. Surely, they said, Buckongahelas had been poisoned, and the terrible scourge that had killed him and so many other tribesmen must be the fruit of witchcraft, which the Delawares dreaded as profoundly as did the Shawnees, and to which many reflexively ascribed their misfortunes. Reasoning that witches must have targeted Buckongahelas for having endorsed Beata and her sister seer, a horde of drunken Delaware warriors, their faces painted black, accused three visiting Wyandots of sorcery and hacked them to death.

At the nearby Moravian village, the missionaries and their converts trembled. "Never since we are here, have the Indians been in such a state of revolution as they are now," recorded a Moravian brother. "They spend days and nights in sacrificing, dancing, and drinking whiskey [and] live in a constant state of fear because the old woman [Beata] tells them that they will be destroyed if they do not give perfect heed to [what] she tells them."[2]

Terror of divine displeasure roiled Indian inhabitants of the White River, including those of Tecumseh's village, where disease and dissolution danced unfettered. Tecumseh was helpless to restore his people to health and prosperity. Like their Delaware cousins, the Shawnees longed for otherworldly direction, something that Tecumseh, for all his prowess in battling mortal enemies, could not offer.

While Tecumseh struggled to hold together his village, Lalawethika lolled away his days drinking and dabbling in medicine. He was thirty years old but had accomplished little beyond alienating most of those around him. Notwithstanding his unappealing aspect, alcohol-ravaged body, and blind eye, he had managed to marry two women and father four children. Selfish and morose, still given to bluster despite his meager accomplishments, Lalawethika nevertheless possessed latent abilities that awaited the proper catalyst. Two decades later Gov. Lewis Cass of the Michigan Territory would come to regard Lalawethika as an "able coadjutor" whose character had been always poorly understood: "He is shrewd, sagacious, and well qualified to acquire an influence over those about him." Some Indians thought that in his sober moments Lalawethika possessed an eloquence superior to that of Tecumseh. Perhaps Tecumseh also understood his dissolute brother's potential because he often subordinated himself to Lalawethika's will. Some whites also liked him. Although he spoke little English, Lalawethika counted several friends among the neighboring pioneers. He befriended John Conner, who had been captured as a boy twenty years earlier and then ransomed to the Moravians. Conner found him "in every way truthful and reliable" and always spoke highly of him. Be that as it may, Lalawethika himself later affirmed that he had been "a very wicked man" the better part of his life, a mean drunk who stole from villagers to buy liquor and a wanton adulterer who intimidated women into having sex with him. In terms of their sex drives, he had Tecumseh beaten hands down.[3]

Evidently the elderly Shawnee medicine man Penagashea, esteemed both as a healer and as a seer, discerned worthy qualities in the boastful and wanton wastrel because Penagashea and Lalawethika became close when the latter was in his late twenties. Although Lalawethika had not yet been blessed with a vision, which normally was expected of those admitted to the ranks of healers, Penagashea accepted him as an apprentice. He acquainted Lalawethika with the symptoms of the principal ailments afflicting the Shawnees—malaria, influenza, venereal diseases, headaches, toothaches, rheumatism, smallpox, tuberculosis, and asthma—and the appropriate root and herbal remedies.[4]

Under Penagashea's tutelage, Lalawethika earned enough in healing fees to ease the burden Tecumseh and Tecumpease bore in helping to keep their dissipated brother's family of six fed and sheltered. Then in 1804 Penagashea died, leaving Lalawethika the sole medicine man in Tecumseh's village. An influenza epidemic in early 1805 proved too much for the aspiring healer, however. As his herbs and incantations withered before the burning winds of disease, Lalawethika retreated to drink and to his wigwam to contemplate his failings and the destiny of his diminished people. Tribesmen grumbled and wondered if such a reprobate could ever truly wear the mantle of healer, much less seer.

It happened late one afternoon during the *poosh kwitha*, or Half Moon (April). The sun had sunk below the horizon, and a chill settled over the darkening village. Inside his wigwam, Lalawethika sat cross-legged before the hearth, a blanket wrapped around his drooping shoulders. The blaze crackled with scorching reminders of Lalawethika's sins, each of which "struck him with a deep and awful sense" of a life ill spent. Had he not been destined to misfortune, a triplet among a people to whom multiple births were inauspicious? A sorry excuse for an adolescent, who, unable properly to string a bow, had shot his eye out with an arrow? The butt of warriors' jokes for ineptitude at Fallen Timbers, his sole serious foray into battle? Cloaked with an adult name that induced scorn—Lalawethika, "Loudmouth," "Rattler," "Noisemaker"? A mediocre medicine man who lost more patients than he saved? A lecher and henpecked husband whose eldest wife, Gimewane, ran roughshod over him?

Not that Gimewane was any bargain. Stephen Ruddell thought her a "low, heavy set, and sour woman." Others referred to her as the "Queen," evidently a disparaging sobriquet meant to imply dominance over her husband. Being saddled with, and unwilling to divorce, such a woman may have contributed to Lalawethika's one certain skill—the ability to drink himself into swaddling stupors that temporarily erased his failures.[5]

But Lalawethika was cold sober now. He "cried mightily to the Great Spirit to show him some way of escape." The entire history of Eastern Woodland Indian religion suddenly lay before him. A rich tradition of prophecies told by countless seers, stretching from first contact with the French to the present, opened itself to his penitent spirit. The rigid and demanding syncretic creed revealed by the Master of Life to the Delaware prophet Neolin, and propagated in a milder form by the war leader Pontiac a decade before Lalawethika's birth, stirred his imagination. Memories of the displaced Mohawk prophetess Coocoochee washed over him; her eldritch tales of the first "palefaces" to appear on the shore of the Great Waters, their insatiable avarice, the Master of Life's rage at the Indians for permitting the desecration of the land, then his promise of a sweeter life for them in a country beyond a second sea far to the west.

Swirling around Lalawethika were the spirits of a multitude of Delaware and Shawnee visionaries whose mystical insights also had informed his boyhood education. After Fallen Timbers, the dissolute, self-absorbed Lalawethika had likely dismissed their spiritual and physical pan-Indianism as obsolete. But three generations earlier, in the 1740s, they had been the bearers of a nativist response to British colonial bullying and to the wrenching French and English competition for Indian allegiance that culminated in the French and Indian War. In the Susquehanna Valley, briefly home to migrating Shawnees, believers had spoken to the Quakers of a "vision of God" of one of their seers, who taught that the Master of Life had "driven the wild animals out of the country" as punishment for the Indians having slaughtered deer to trade their skins for English rum. The Master of Life had also told a young Delaware prophetess, while she was in a trance, that the Delawares and Shawnees should "destroy the poison from among them"—that is, the corrupted sacred bundles that their "old and principal" men employed to sicken and to kill their people. In the 1750s a recovered Delaware alcoholic had preached against liquor and the deerskin trade, urging followers to overcome their reliance on European manufactured goods and instead adhere "to the ancient customs and manners of their forefathers." A decade later, after Neolin passed from the scene, another Delaware prophet, Wangomend, spoke of separate paths to heaven for Indians and whites. While Wangomend was hunting deer, a manitou had warned him that the Indians should "not have so much to do with the whites but cherish their own customs and not to imitate the manner of the whites, else it would not go well with them." Wangomend also called for witch hunts to purge his people of evil. All these teachings may have coalesced in Lalawethika's troubled subconscious.[6]

In his tortured state, Lalawethika also pondered recent spiritual upheavals among the whites. In 1801 a raucous religious fervor had gripped the frontier communities in Kentucky and Ohio. Thousands of pioneers congregated in open-air meetings that lasted days and even weeks. The whites wept and trembled, screamed in soul-wrenching agony, swooned and sank into trances, stretched deathlike upon the ground, then miraculously arose, some to cry for mercy, others to laugh with joy or bark like beasts. Believers called this "outpouring of the spirit of God in the western states" the Kentucky Revival; detractors labeled the converts "Shakers." The Indians of the White River knew only that whites along the Miami and Ohio rivers were collapsing and "lay as if dead for two or three hours" before regaining consciousness and repenting of their sins.

Not to be outdone by the strangely possessed whites, the Delaware female mystic Beata reanimated an abbreviated form of Neolin prophecies. Council houses downriver from Lalawethika's village shook with the antics of adherents and aspiring clairvoyants. Otherworldly beings peopled the fevered imaginings of the drunk and the desperate. Truly, observed a frightened Moravian missionary, "this was a time of visions."[7]

Lalawethika reached into the fire to pluck out a brand to light his long-stem pipe and still, if only momentarily, the nausea of spiritual malaise. He raised the pipe to his lips, gasped, dropped both brand and pipe, then toppled over, cataleptic. Neighbors and family gathered around his prostrate form. His wives spoke to him. No answer came. Nor could they detect breathing. Neighbors led the grieving widows from the wigwam. Liquor, they assumed, had claimed another Indian victim. As was the custom, Shawnee men from outside the Kispoko division washed the body, dressed Lalawethika's corpse in new clothing, and painted his face, all in anticipation of the prescribed two-day interval between death and burial.

The night passed with no sign of life. Next morning Lalawethika's attendants began digging a grave and splitting rough planks with their tomahawks to fashion a coffin.[8]

Suddenly Lalawethika stirred. A moment later he awakened. Regaining his senses, he told the amazed onlookers—Tecumseh among them—a startling story of death, the afterlife, and resurrection.

Two phantoms had led Lalawethika along a spectral road until it forked. The right fork, the ghosts told him, led to heaven, the left to hell. Those who took the right fork shed "all evil and wicked ways and became good." Those who persisted in their waywardness were fated to follow the left fork, which led into the country of Motshee Manitou, the Evil Spirit. Propelled with the sinful down the left fork, Lalawethika came to three houses. From the first and second houses, paths led across the evil country to the right fork, offering the hope of redemption for those who eventually accepted "The Light." But Lalawethika discerned no pathway from the third and last house. This place he called eternity. Its occupants clung obstinately to their mischief. Their crimes included drinking liquor, beating their wives, committing murder, and practicing witchcraft, which Lalawethika described as the "art of hurting or torturing one another with poison." Vast crowds flocked to each dwelling. To Lalawethika's amazement, many literally ran to the horrific third house. From all three abodes he saw masses of people—Indians and whites—"under awful torments," and he heard them "roaring like the falls of a river."

Lalawethika witnessed the punishments meted out to each type of transgressor. The fate of drunkards like himself most horrified him. A cadaverous attendant handed them cups of molten lead. An awful burning seized the bowels of those who imbibed. An attendant rebuked those who refused, thundering, "Come, drink, you used to love liquor. Now you must drink it." Inhabitants of the third house all suffered the same fate: They were tossed into a great fire and reduced to ashes.

Lalawethika proceeded no farther along the left fork; nor was he permitted to take the right fork. The Master of Life (Great Spirit) thundered at him to return to earth, reveal what he had seen, and warn the Indians of their danger. Although Lalawethika expressed sympathy for doomed whites, they must fend for themselves. While describing his vision, Lalawethika wept and trembled. He expressed a distress for the welfare of others previously foreign to him. The power and conviction with which he spoke won him disciples on the spot.[9]

Convinced that Lalawethika not only had a direct channel to the Master of Life but also possessed supernatural powers of his own, Tecumseh embraced his brother's revelation. Whether he truly believed him a prophet can never be known with certainty, but he must have wondered at what had transformed his formerly worthless sibling. As Tecumseh "stood the brunt of any disbelievers," others in the village converted apace. For many new adherents, Lalawethika's abrupt change in behavior from self-centered alcoholic to empathetic teetotaler, whose latent eloquence now flowed movingly in the profound tale he told of eternity, was proof positive of his divine gifts. As one Delaware devotee told the Moravians, "This new Indian teacher had been a very bad person, but now he spoke only good things, for which reason the Indians believed what he said."[10]

Stephen Ruddell, in a better position to know than most, thought Tecumseh had become a true disciple. Ruddell was on the White River in the early days of Lalawethika's rise. He was now a Baptist minister preaching to the Shawnees and Delawares, who listened politely to their old friend but were unmoved. When competition from the rehabilitated Lalawethika proved unbeatable, Ruddell tried to convince Tecumseh that Lalawethika possessed no supernatural powers and that divine revelations no longer occurred. The white man might be barred from receiving new revelations, countered Tecumseh, but not the Indian, and Lalawethika was the chosen vessel for these new divine teachings. Ruddell concluded sadly that the spiritually reborn Lalawethika possessed "unbounded influence" over Tecumseh. Tecumseh's principal weakness, Ruddell said, was the "implicit confidence he placed in his brother's conjuring." When the Kentuckian persevered, Tecumseh merely shrugged; his friend had become a well-intentioned but misguided nuisance.[11]

Soon Lalawethika had a second vision in which spirits conducted him along the right fork of the ethereal road to the realm of the Master of Life. There the souls of the good thrived in a "rich, fertile country, abounding in game, fish, pleasant hunting grounds, and fine cornfields.... They plant, they hunt, play at their usual games, and in all things are unchanged."[12]

Lalawethika's visions continued into the summer months. From pure jeremiad, they rapidly metamorphosed into a religious and social program aimed at delivering the Indians from their sins and rebuilding a robust society capable of resisting the onrushing white frontier. To many, it must have seemed as if the legendary Neolin had been reborn. The mystical light of nativist, pan-Indian splendor glowed warmly in the breasts of believers.

The ease with which he won over White River Shawnees and Delawares emboldened Lalawethika. He denounced the treaty chiefs, accusing them of bewitching their people into walking the white man's road and of poisoning those who resisted. Implicit in his assault on the accommodationists was a rebuke of American authority. The Master of Life had chosen Lalawethika to separate the "wicked chiefs" from their people. Converts must join him in a pilgrimage from the White River to establish a new and sacred town ten miles over the American side of the treaty line. If that proved a provocation, no matter. Lalawethika scorned treaty boundaries, for the Master of Life had told him where he must settle. That place was Greenville, well removed from the baleful influence of "bad" Indians. There Lalawethika would receive "all of the different [Indian] nations that would become good." Greenville was to become a benevolent Babylon of native peoples built to last one hundred years.

Lalawethika hoped first to unite the Shawnees at Greenville in spiritual and cultural renewal. He dissuaded a small Shawnee band that was then encamped on the Auglaize from moving to Wapakoneta, convincing them instead to partake in the sacred exercise at Greenville. He and Tecumseh, united in mutual respect and a common purpose, superintended construction of the holy town. Work began

on wigwams and cabins to house the faithful on the south bank of
Greenville Creek, a stone's throw from the palisaded remains of the
abandoned Fort Green Ville and approximately two hundred miles
southwest of modern Cleveland. Cornfields were laid out beyond the
dwelling sites. For the time being, both the state of Ohio and the federal government tolerated Lalawethika's violation of the Greenville
Treaty, keeping alert, however, for any signs of hostility on the part of
the Indians who gathered at the site of his proposed village.

Construction consequently proceeded unimpeded. The greatest
possible care went into building the council house, where the Master
of Life would reside in spirit and communal feasts would be held
in his honor. An immense, single-story whitewashed structure comprised of hand-hewn posts, planks, rafters, and clapboard, the council
house when finished stood 150 feet long and 34 feet wide and fronted
the rising sun. There were four doors, one at each end and one in the
middle of each side. No floor was laid; instead, the ground was beaten
hard and level. Hewn logs served as seats. A long line of cooking tri-
pods supporting trammel hooks stretched across the center of the
lodge. Firewood was stacked in the corners. A white visitor thought
"everything neat and clean and in good order."[13]

So too did Lalawethika, both morally and materially. Lalawethika
incorporated his visions, or epiphanies, into a sweeping syncretic
doctrine that integrated facets of Shawnee culture, Christianity as he
understood it, and the doctrines of Neolin, Pontiac, and other Indian
prophets. Lalawethika both created new religious tenets and synthe-
sized the teachings of the past. All this, for Lalawethika, was the mental labor of a single summer. Work on Greenville was scarcely under
way in late autumn 1805 when he took to the trails with his program
for Indian renewal. Declaring himself "particularly appointed by the
Great Spirit," Lalawethika traveled to Black Hoof's town "to reclaim
the Indians from bad habits and to cause them to live in peace with
all mankind."

Black Hoof's immediate reaction to the rogue's redemption is not
known, but in late November 1805 he permitted the new Shawnee
holy man to meet with delegations of Ottawas, Wyandots, Senecas,
and his own Mekoche Shawnees at Wapakoneta. Tecumseh accompanied Lalawethika. His younger brother was about to find his place
in the sun.[14]

Lalawethika cut a colorful figure in the Wapakoneta council house. Around his head he wrapped a solid red or patterned turban extruding ostrich feathers. A silver-plated hair tube enclosed his scalp lock. Large, intricately patterned, silver-plated circular medallion earrings dangled from each of his ears. He thrust two arrows and a feather through his pierced earlobes. Around his neck Lalawethika wore a broad, half-moon-shaped silver-plated gorget. Broad silver-plated armbands encircled his biceps. Lalawethika rounded out his lustrous look with wide silver-plated wristbands. Because it was cold, he completed his wardrobe with a fringed buckskin coat and leggings.

Lalawethika's outerwear might vary depending on the season, but he had shed forever his opprobrious verbal skin of "Rattler." Henceforth he would be called Tenskwatawa, meaning "He who opened the sky for red men to go up to the Master of Life," or "Open Door" for short. The whites would come to call him the Shawnee Prophet, some derisively, others genuinely mystified by him.[15]

Having opened the door, Tenskwatawa revealed the doctrine that would revitalize Indian culture on earth and ultimately lead the Indians along the road to paradise. The "Master of Life had taken pity on his red children and wished to save them from destruction," Tenskwatawa proclaimed, but only on the condition that they adhere to laws that the Master of Life had revealed to him and that Tenskwatawa articulated passionately in the Wapakoneta council house.

First and foremost, the Indians were no longer to drink frontier whiskey, which was "poisoned and accursed." He had witnessed the tortures awaiting unrepentant drunkards; their chilling cries of agony and the flames shooting from their mouths, and it had cured him.

Condemning the violence and disorder endemic to tribal society, Tenskwatawa enumerated precepts designed to promote harmony and love. He admonished tribes against fighting one another and urged warriors to treat one another as brothers because all Indians who followed his creed were equal in the eyes of the Master of Life. A return to communal living also was essential. Indians who accumulated "wealth and ornaments" would "crumble into dust," but those who shared their possessions with fellow believers would die happy: "When they arrived in the land of the dead, [they] would find their wigwam furnished with everything they had on earth." Communal virtues also dictated that the "young should always cherish and support the elderly and infirm."

Women held a special place in Tenskwatawa's teachings. They must adhere to tradition and "rise with the sun, wish themselves happy, and mind their duty as women." Men also must be mindful of their obligations to women. None were to take more than one wife; those who had multiple wives might keep them—perhaps Tenskwatawa dreaded domestic unrest if he tried to dismiss either of his spouses—but the Master of Life would be better pleased if men had only one. Casual liaisons were discouraged. "No Indian was to be running after the women," declared the reformed lecher. "If a man was single, let him take a wife." He should refrain from striking his children under any circumstances and should strike his wife only when she neglected her work or shamed him. Once the requisite strokes of the rod had been applied, "both husband and wife were to look each other in the face, laugh, and bear no ill will to each other for what has passed."

The Master of Life demanded the Indians shun the Americans. He had revealed their true aspect to Tenskwatawa. Although they appeared to be so many thousands of individual beings, they were in fact one creature—a great crab with claws draped in seaweed and caked with mud. "Look," the Master of Life had told Tenskwatawa. "This crab is from Boston [in Indian imagination, the source of much wickedness] and has brought with it something of the land there." Before they coalesced into a hideous crab, the Americans were an unsightly froth. "A wind blew west over the [Atlantic], driving before it a foam or scum," revealed the Master of Life. "It blew this scum, which was evil and unclean, upon the shore of the American continent, and the scum took form. The form that it took was that of a white man—of many white people, both men and women; wherever the scum lodged on the shore of the continent, it took this form." And then it seeped inland, evidently with the crab. "The Americans are numerous, but I hate them," said the Master of Life. "They are unjust. They have taken your lands, which were not made for them."

Not all whites were evil, however. Indians were to treat the French, English, and Spaniards as "their fathers or friends, and to give them their hand, but they were not to know the Americans on any account, but to keep them at a distance." Should an Indian encounter an American in the forest, he might greet him but never shake his hand. If the American was starving, the Indian might give him a small quantity of native food. To scrape the American scum from their society, Indians must heed the following injunctions:

All Indian women living with white men must return to their Indian relatives without their métis children. Sexual relations between the races was forbidden.

Indians were to give all items of white dress they owned to the first white person they encountered. Dogs and cats obtained from the whites also were to be returned. Indians indebted to American traders should only reimburse "half their credits because they have cheated you."

The Indians were permitted to keep their guns for defensive purposes but must return to bows and arrows for the hunt. The trade in hides must cease. Indians were to kill no more animals than necessary to feed and clothe their families.

Indians were to eat no foods that whites cooked, nor any that were not native to their culture. They must relinquish their cattle, sheep, and hogs and shun mutton, beef, and pork as unclean. It was permissible, however, to keep horses. The Master of Life had given the Indians "the deer, the bear, and all wild animals, and the fish that swim in the water." These species, together with corn, beans, and other native crops, were enough for Indian needs. Maple sugar was a favorite of the Master of Life (as it was of Tenskwatawa).

Eternal bliss was desirable, but what of the earthly reward for adhering to the divine commandments? Tenskwatawa reassured listeners that the recompense would be grand. The Master of Life had shown him that deer, now so scarce in the forests, were merely "half a tree's length" underground and would reappear in abundance if the Indians followed Tenskwatawa's teachings. Not only that: if the Indians obeyed, then the Master of Life also would cause a cataclysmic upheaval and bury the Americans beneath the earth forever.

There was one further obstacle to the creation of an Indian Eden, however. While the Americans were children of the Motshee Manitou, or Evil Spirit, they were not its most active or insidious agents on earth. That distinction belonged to Indian witches, who would labor ceaselessly to thwart the Master of Life's will and to spread chaos among the Indians. Because the Master of Life had chosen Tenskwatawa to return the Indians to righteousness, those who opposed him—chiefs included—necessarily were witches. If they did not repent, then they must be killed.

Less nefarious than witches, but still a threat to the new order, were medicine men. Those who opposed Tenskwatawa's doctrine must be cast aside as fools or false prophets. To remove any vestige of the corrupt old ways that the medicine men advocated, Tenskwatawa ordered his followers to discard their sacred medicine bags and cease all traditional dances and songs. Medicine and rituals that once were beneficial had lost their efficacy and had "become vitiated through age." As the healing and strength-enhancing properties of bags faded, the malignant substances they contained would grow more powerful. In the hands of witches and evil-minded medicine men, these bags could kill. Tenskwatawa believed the destruction of medicine bags was necessary to restore health and harmony to Indian communities.

The malignant contents of medicine bags were pieces of the Great Serpent, which the ancestors of the Shawnees had slain during their migration to their homeland. Or so they thought. As Tenskwatawa explained, the hideous beast in fact had endured,

> His body was like that of a snake, and he had the head, horns, and neck of a large buck. His body was cut into small pieces, and everything connected with it, even to the excrement, was carefully preserved. The head, horns, and flesh were mixed with the heart and flesh of [a lesser dead serpent] found upon the seashore and forms the medicine which the witches use. It is still preserved and the flesh, though many thousand years old, is as fresh as if it had just been killed.
>
> By means of this medicine they can take a piece [of] stick, of dirt, a hair, or anything else and transform it into a worm, which they depute and send to any distance to accomplish their designs against the victims of their power.[16]

Tenskwatawa's spiritual program was more radical than any of his divinely inspired predecessors. In place of medicine bags and the old rituals, he proposed new dances that would please both the Master of Life and the dancers. He also enjoined believers to pray morning and night and provided them with intricately inscribed prayer sticks to facilitate their worship. And they must confess "in a loud voice all of the bad deeds they had committed during their lifetime and beg for forgiveness," which the Master of Life was "too good to refuse." Finally, they were to light a fire in their home, kindled without using the white man's flint and steel. The blaze, which symbolized rebirth in the new faith, must burn constantly. "Summer and winter, day and night, in the storm or when it is calm, you must remember that the life in your body and the fire in your lodge are the same."

Tenskwatawa had presented his listeners with a syncretic creed of spiritual and cultural renewal that he had developed in a matter of weeks from a combination of his own visions and the prophecies of Neolin and other seers of days past. Like Neolin, Tenskwatawa blamed the Indians for their decline. To propagate the new faith beyond his immediate audience, Tenskwatawa appointed messengers to the Indian nations of the Great Lakes region and the Illinois country to enlist converts to come to Greenville for further instruction. Those unable to make the journey would be taught the tenets in their home villages. These prospective converts in the outlying nations must first confess their sins. Then they would enter a lodge in which Tenskwatawa's envoys had assembled holy items, to include an effigy of the Prophet hidden beneath a blanket, with four strings of beans representing Tenskwatawa's limbs extending outward. The neophytes were to take hold of each string and draw it gently through their hands, a ceremony called "shaking hands with the Prophet." By this act they committed themselves to obey Tenskwatawa's injunctions and accept his mission as divinely ordained.

New disciples were sworn to secrecy and admonished at a minimum to dispatch one or two men from each village to Greenville to be personally instructed by Tenskwatawa in order to propagate the new faith further. "Those villages which do not listen to this talk and send me two deputies," he warned, "will be cut off from the face of the Earth."[17]

The Wapakoneta council ended in mid-December 1805. How Tenskwatawa's faith would fare among outlying tribes remained to be seen. But Black Hoof and the tribal council at Wapakoneta left no doubt where they stood. The Wapakoneta chiefs wanted nothing to do with Tenskwatawa, Tecumseh, or the dogma they peddled, and few if any of the Mekoches broke ranks with their leaders.

It was an inauspicious start for a sacred doctrine that Tenskwatawa had expected would unite the Shawnees under his divinely endowed leadership. But the sun had not set on his new creed—of that Tenskwatawa was certain.

Greenville was still more of a holy concept than a habitable town when Tenskwatawa and Tecumseh returned from Wapakoneta during the waning days of the Eccentric Moon (December). So the Shawnee brothers and their two hundred followers squatted the winter along nearby Stoney Creek, at the headwaters of the Great Miami River, on the American side of the Greenville Treaty line in the young state of Ohio. There they passed the long, severe winter nights in loud prayers and noisy rituals.

The raucousness frightened white neighbors. Huddled in their White River congregation with a handful of Delawares, Moravian brothers John Kluge and Abraham Luckenbach believed the Devil was at work on Stoney Creek. "The wicked enemy is very busy again among the savages," Brother Kluge scribbled in the congregation diary in late December 1805. "His instrument, the heathen teachers, have come to the front with might again and say that they have again had visions from God. The Shawnees sacrifice day and night at the direction of their teacher.... Oh, that the Savior might have mercy on these slaves of sin and Satan and open their eyes."[18]

The female Delaware mystic Beata not only met Tenskwatawa on his own terms but also did him one better. Tenskwatawa had described the Master of Life as having a head half gray and half white, with his body the hue of an Indian. Beata said he had white hands but otherwise was entirely Indian. She knew this because the Master of Life had given her a small luminescent white object—a "good spirit"—to ingest. She had done so and now spoke only the word of the Master of Life.[19]

While Brother Kluge saw Tenskwatawa as an emissary of Satan bent on corrupting Indians whom the Moravians labored to turn to Christianity, settlers on Mad River perceived the strange Shawnee celebrations as a prelude to war. Rumors of black wampum belts, war dances, tomahawks painted and feathered, and a pending Indian war council at Greenville flew through forests and farms to Chillicothe.

Governor Tiffin responded with characteristic prudence. In February 1806 he asked Simon Kenton to deliver a white wampum belt and conciliatory letter to the Shawnees. "Our people are likely to be misled," Tiffin wrote the Shawnee Prophet, "and I wish to quiet their fear. . . . If you have any cause of complaint against our people, make it known to me. I hope the Great Spirit will still incline your hearts and ours to keep the chain of peace shining bright."[20]

War with the whites was the furthest thing from Tenskwatawa's mind. Endorsed by Tecumseh, the Prophet's reply sparkled with peace and goodwill. "Never was a speech received with more joy than yours," Tenskwatawa assured the governor. "We are very much pleased with your saying that you didn't believe that we wished to cause any disturbance with the white people. No, be well assured it was never our intention, nor will it ever be on our part. . . . We pray that we may love one another like two brothers ought to do." The Prophet's answer satisfied Governor Tiffin. It likewise mollified the Mad River settlers, and the militiamen stood down.[21]

Tenskwatawa could ill afford strife with the Americans. The Mad River settlers correctly adduced that the Shawnees had been locked in a war council but were mistaken as to the motive. Discussion centered not on neighboring pioneers but on turbulence among their "grandfathers," the Delawares. Uprooted and shoved west repeatedly since the early eighteenth century, decimated by disease and permanently scarred by the Gnadenhutten massacre, belittled by the Miamis, on whose land they squatted, and suffering yet another smallpox epidemic, the White River Delawares felt themselves a poisoned people on a downward slide that Buckongahelas's death accelerated. Several years before Tenskwatawa unveiled his divinely bestowed doctrine in 1805, the Delawares had suspected sorcery to be the cause of their misfortune. In the autumn of 1802, when the annual round of malaria took a larger toll than usual at Wapicomekoke, Delaware witch-hunters bribed a visiting Shawnee warrior to hack to death two women living at the margin of their society—a Mingo and a Nanticoke—to counteract the scourge. Thus far they had spared their own people, but after Tenskwatawa roiled the leaderless tribe with his admonitions against witchcraft, the Delawares turned inward, probing their own ranks for servants of the Evil Spirit. Guided by the white light that she had ingested, Beata named several suspects. The Delaware appointed her judge, but Beata lacked the wherewithal to prosecute witches. Within a month she relinquished the judgeship on the grounds that "it was too hard for her, being after all a woman."[22]

Beata's withdrawal created a leadership vacuum that angry young Delaware warriors exploited. In February 1806 the young bloods cordoned off the village, rounded up elderly chiefs tainted by their complicity in land sales and other alleged witches, and invited Tenskwatawa—who had assured attendees at the Wapakoneta council that he was able to determine guilt or innocence simply by looking into the face and heart of an accused sorcerer—to come to Wapicomekoke and pass judgment. The Shawnees deliberated the invitation in council. Tecumseh argued against death sentences for witches, but Tenskwatawa carried the day. In early March he set out for Wapicomekoke to face his first test as a seer.[23]

The Delaware usurpers grew impatient for Tenskwatawa's arrival. Tribesmen were falling sick daily. Atonement could not long be postponed. What followed was to the whites bizarre and horrific, but it was wholly in keeping with the Indian dread of witches.

The first victim of the witch-hunting young warriors was Tetapachsit, the eldest chief in the tribe. In the view of Eastern Woodland Indians, great age was either a reward for a life well lived or the consequence of siphoning off the lives of others through witchcraft. Tetapachsit's recent record suggested the latter. Although he lamented the evils of liquor, Tetapachsit also sold whiskey by the barrel. At a feast five years earlier for the young warriors who now turned on him, Tetapachsit had anticipated Tenskwatawa's condemnation of wastrel chiefs when he confessed, "My children, you see how old I am, how gray my hair is. I am still not on the right road as God desires it of us. We have also often admonished you not to drink, nor to commit any evil, but nothing came of it. We remained as we were. We chiefs have now discovered why you have not changed either, because we ourselves do not do what we tell you to do." As the gathering broke up, Tetapachsit remarked to a Moravian brother that the chiefs had agreed to stave in the barrels of anyone who brought whiskey into Wapicomekoke, all the while patting his horse, to which were lashed two barrels of whiskey.[24]

By 1805 Tetapachsit's chieftainship had grown precarious. He signed Governor Harrison's noxious land treaties and infuriated his adult children by abandoning their mother for a younger wife. Buckongahelas's death robbed him of his best advocate. Now was the moment for the young to overthrow their elders, a break with cultural norms that would have been unthinkable in better days. The warriors accused Tetapachsit of possessing poison with which he had killed many Delawares. Denial availed the old man nothing; the warriors bound him to a stake and tipped him over a fire until he confessed to having stored his toxin at the home of Joshua, a dissipated, womanizing Delaware Christian who resided at the Moravian mission. Joshua's fluency in German and English and his mastery of the white man's music also rendered him suspect. On the afternoon of March 13, seven warriors with blackened faces galloped into the Moravian mission and dragged him away.[25]

Two days later Tenskwatawa arrived at Wapicomekoke. After briefly conferring with the Delaware inquisitors, he went to work. Joshua and others whom the Delawares suspected of witchcraft were brought before him, and Tenskwatawa asked that they be seated in a circle facing one another. After performing a multitude of ceremonies, he examined the captives, staring in their eyes and pronouncing their guilt or innocence of the high crime of witchcraft. The Delawares proved eager executioners of the ones found culpable.

The first guilty party to die was a seventy-year-old woman known as Ann Charity, who had been raised by a Moravian family, spoke fluent English, dressed and kept a neat house in the manner of the whites, and apparently had run afoul of Beata. Her captors stripped her naked, then for four days scrubbed her with the burning concoction of water and lye that she used to clean her home, demanding that she deliver up her evil charms and potions. Rubbed raw and caked in blood, a dying Ann implicated her grandson. He had her witch's bundle but was away hunting. Delaware inquisitors tracked him down and dragged him to Wapicomekoke. The frightened youth readily confessed to having used his grandmother's bundle once. With its power, he had been able to fly from the White River to the Mississippi River and back in a matter of hours, after which he returned the bundle to Ann Charity. The boy's audacious testimony surprised Tenskwatawa, and without saying why, he ordered him released.[26]

The gory chaos continued. Chief Tetapachsit's fate was never in doubt. Tenskwatawa instantly affirmed his guilt. Later that day, March 17,

Brother Kluge espied "ten of the wildest Indians, with their faces painted black, partly on foot and partly on horseback, coming with the poor old Chief Tetapachsit into our village." Near Kluge's home, the warriors built a huge fire. Tetapachsit's son willingly sank a tomahawk into his father's head and then heaved him stunned and bloodied into the blaze. "The savages stood around the fire and amused themselves with the pitiful cries and contortions of the unfortunate one," said Kluge. Sparks drifted into the adjacent woods, setting them ablaze. As smoke settled over the mission, Tetapachsit's slayers busted into the Kluge cabin, demanding tobacco and food. When Kluge meekly inquired about Joshua, the intruders promised no harm would come to the prodigal Delaware convert.[27]

They lied. Joshua had been dispatched with three tomahawk blows to the head and tossed into a fire in Wapicomekoke earlier that day. He had gone to his death reciting prayers in German; the incomprehensible tongue seemingly confirmed that the Evil Spirit possessed him.

After sentencing seven others to death, including a chief whose guilt rested solely in having participated in land cession councils, Tenskwatawa took his leave of the Delawares. Brother Kluge alleged that prosperous tribesmen had purchased their acquittal from Tenskwatawa with "several hundred strings of wampum, silver, and cattle." Kluge's unsubstantiated charge rings false; it's unlikely that Tenskwatawa, raised to dread witches and convinced of the righteousness of his mission, would have risked all with an act so banal.

The execution of Delaware witches ground on. Next to perish was Tetapachsit's half-white nephew Billy Patterson, a devout Christian, skilled gunsmith, and literate spokesman for the Delaware who had corresponded with Thomas Jefferson and William Wells on behalf of tribal land rights. Patterson's alleged crime was unclear. But a few days after Tenskwatawa departed, his Delaware acolytes led Patterson and Tetapachsit's young widow into the Wapicomekoke council house, where two tall stakes surrounded with firewood awaited them. Patterson died well. Taunting his captors, he refused to confess himself guilty of sorcery and, vowing to die as a "Christian and a warrior," endured the flames with fortitude.

Tetapachsit's widow suffered a kinder fate. As the executioners dragged her to the stake, her twenty-year-old brother stepped forward, took her hand, and to everyone's amazement led her out of the council house. He then returned and declared the killings at an end. Tenskwatawa's allies withdrew, and the executioners consoled the families of victims with gifts and wampum.

The end of the purge did not presage better days for the White River Delawares. Famine and disease returned, and the Delawares relapsed into drunkenness and despair. Some blamed Tenskwatawa for what now appeared to have been pointless killings. "I heard the Shawnee teacher three times but could in no wise detect anything in what he taught to convince me of the truth of his teaching," a prominent Delaware told Kluge. "Much less could I believe that his words came from God."[28]

Despite the doubting Delawares, Tenskwatawa had cause for optimism. His first foray into witch-hunting represented no real setback. He had answered a call from Delawares in need of spiritual cleansing. Their own prophetess had identified tribesmen likely to blame for Delaware misfortunes; Tenskwatawa had simply affirmed their guilt. Although the White River Delawares had veered from apathetic torpor to hysterical fanaticism and back again, they might yet return to Tenskwatawa's teachings. In any event, his ministry was young, and the country Tenskwatawa's acolytes trod, vast. By the late spring of 1806, Greenville was ready to receive new believers. Its new whitewashed council house stood as testimony to Tenskwatawa's vision, a forest beacon to the multitude that the Master of Life would direct his way.

10

Black Sun

Tenskwatawa had little time to reflect on his foray among the Delawares. In May 1806, Wyandot warriors appealed to him to cleanse their villages of sorcery. From his perspective, evil undoubtedly abounded among the Wyandots, who lived principally in three places: a village near Amherstburg, Upper Canada; the farming community of Brownstown, south of Detroit; and a network of villages on the Sandusky River known collectively as Tarhe's town. Christianity had made considerable inroads among the Wyandots. Many were Roman Catholics; others, like Chief Tarhe, were receptive to Protestantism. In 1805, Tarhe invited Presbyterian missionaries to evangelize in his communities.

The Reverend Joseph Badger joined the Presbyterian mission to the Wyandots in July. His first sermon was on the "injurious effects of ardent spirits." Tarhe took no umbrage at a young white man lecturing on so volatile a topic, and he provided Badger with both an interpreter and use of the council house. From a makeshift pulpit, Badger implored his listeners to embrace sobriety. "In the first place, after drinking a little, you get drunk and lose your reason, and then you quarrel and abuse one another; sometimes one friend kills another, and you often abuse your women. This is one reason why you are wasting away and have few children that grow to be men," he began. "But when you are sober, there are no people friendlier."

"*Entooh, entooh* [True, true]," the crowd responded.

"Secondly, when you get drunk, you often lie out in [the] wet and cold and contract wasting disease, which renders you unable to hunt or hoe corn, or do anything for your support." Thrusting forward an accusatory arm, Badger bellowed, "Look at that man, a son of the head chief; he is shaking all over and can scarcely walk with a staff. This he has contracted by drinking to excess: He must soon die, although a young man."

"*Entooh, entooh!*"

"Thirdly, by reason of your drinking, the traders impose upon you and cheat you and get away [with] your property for almost nothing. When you have been out and made a good hunt or a good quantity of [maple] sugar, the traders will often visit you on your hunting ground with kegs a whiskey and a few goods, and get you drinking, and get away from you all your winter's hunt for a mere trifle, and you come home and have nothing to make your families comfortable."

"*Entooh, entooh!*"

Badger concluded his sermon, an old headman spoke a few words in Wyandot, and then the council house quieted. Thirty minutes later the elderly Wyandot approached Badger. "Father, you have told us the truth," he said. "We thank you, Father. We have all agreed to use no more ardent spirits." Sobriety did not suddenly return to wayward Sandusky Wyandots, but Badger's admonition frightened away whiskey peddlers, and Tarhe's people welcomed his ministry.

The wheels of assimilation grinded painfully, but Badger persevered—and faced down Tenskwatawa. Returning to Tarhe's town on the afternoon of May 14, 1806, from a visit to the Brownstown Wyandots, Badger came upon a group of warriors seated before the Shawnee Prophet. Several terrified Wyandot women huddled nearby; they were to be burned as witches at sunset. Badger said they were among the "best" women in the community, which meant that they were probably the most acculturated. Their accusers were disaffected young men bent on bringing down Tarhe and the government chiefs. Tenskwatawa chose the executioners, but one Wyandot warrior objected to the duty and told Badger what was about to transpire. Badger got hold of Tarhe and an interpreter. A passionate debate ensued, with Tarhe intervening decisively on behalf of Badger. Also outspoken against Tenskwatawa was a subchief named Leather Lips, who that day won for himself Tenskwatawa's abiding enmity. But the women were spared, and the authority of the chiefs restored. Humiliated, Tenskwatawa returned to Greenville, having suffered a second setback in his war for the Indian soul.[1]

So long as Tenskwatawa confined his activities to Ohio and to the Indian country falling under its jurisdiction, he was the responsibility of Governor Tiffin. But the Prophet's White River Delaware witch hunt had occurred in Gov. William Henry Harrison's jurisdiction. Unaware that the crisis had passed, Harrison urged the Delawares to "regain the straight road which you have abandoned" and to demand Tenskwatawa prove himself God's messenger. "If he is really a prophet, ask of him to cause the sun to stand still—the moon to alter its course—the rivers to cease to flow or the dead to rise from their graves. If he does these things, you may then believe that he has been sent from God." The Delaware chiefs shrugged. Tenskwatawa's followers forwarded the missive to Greenville and hoped him capable of answering the governor's challenge.[2]

Tenskwatawa was delighted to oblige. Harrison had unwittingly played into his hands. The governor evidently had forgotten that astronomers expected a total eclipse of the sun on June 16, which would last eight minutes. Tenskwatawa had not. How he learned of the impending phenomenon is uncertain, but the source was hardly otherworldly. Although most of the Indians of the Ohio Valley were unaware of the upcoming celestial drama, the secretary of the recently formed Michigan Territory had spoken openly about it to the Indians at Detroit. A messenger from the northern tribes might have then conveyed the information to Tenskwatawa. Or Frederick Fisher, the Indian trader at Greenville, might have told him. At first blush, the presence of a white trader in the holy town appears incongruous with Tenskwatawa's rejection of the white man's way of life. But Fisher was no opportunist out to cheat Indians. Neither did Tenskwatawa advocate a rejection of all white goods; rifles, for instance, must be retained in case of war. In Fisher's favor also was his long and friendly association with the Eastern Woodland tribes. A British citizen, he had been a trader for three decades and an interpreter for the British Indian Department since the 1790s. He also functioned as an agent in disguise, ready to do the Crown's bidding should relations with the United States deteriorate. Whomever his source, Tenskwatawa knew both the predicted onset of the eclipse and its duration.[3]

Battle Ready by Doug Hall. A Shawnee warrior of the late eighteenth century.

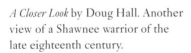

A Closer Look by Doug Hall. Another view of a Shawnee warrior of the late eighteenth century.

A flatboat negotiating the Tennessee River. As a young warrior, Tecumseh cut his teeth storming these unwieldy pioneer river conveyances.

ABOVE A reconstructed Shawnee village. Tecumseh and Lalawethika spent their childhood years in wigwams like these.

LEFT *Red Coat—Shawnee Chief Tecumseh* by Doug Hall. Tecumseh as he may have appeared as a young war leader.

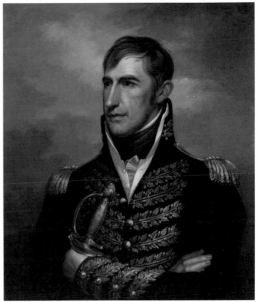

Simon Kenton. A tough and capable Kentucky frontiersman and militia officer, he met the young Tecumseh twice in sharp skirmishes that severely tested the fledgling Shawnee war leader's mettle.

William Henry Harrison, the Shawnee brothers' eternal nemesis, as painted by Rembrandt Peale.

The charge of the dragoons at Fallen Timbers. Tecumseh stood his ground; Lalawethika fled incontinently.

ABOVE Edward Tiffin, first governor of Ohio. Prudent and patient, Tiffin worked with the young chief Tecumseh to defuse potential crises between settlers and Indians.

LEFT Ragged and inebriated Indians impoverished by white avarice and liquor sales.

BELOW The Chillicothe, Ohio Territory, courthouse as it appeared in 1801. Here in August 1806 Tecumseh gave a memorable public oration to a rapt white audience.

There are no paintings of Tenskwatawa as a young man; his portrait was first painted in 1824. This image of Tenskwatawa dates from that decade.

Chief Black Hoof's assimilationist tendencies won over far more Shawnee adherents than did the traditionalist doctrines of Tecumseh and Tenskwatawa.

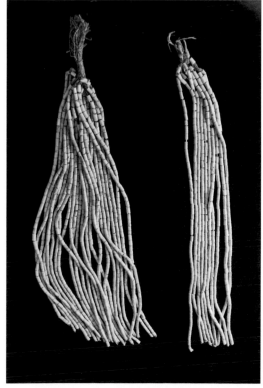

White wampum strings owned by Tecumseh.

Tecumseh from a furtive sketch done from life by a French trader. This sketch formed the basis for most subsequent renditions of the Shawnee war chief.

Old Fort Wayne. A faithful reconstruction of the military post and Indian factory on site. Tecumseh paused at Fort Wayne while on the way to visit British authorities in Upper Canada in June 1812.

Grouseland, William Henry Harrison's stately residence at Vincennes, Indiana Territory. In its shadow, Harrison and Tecumseh held two crucial councils.

Tecumseh and Harrison squared off at Vincennes in August 1811, as shown in this early stylized rendition.

Fort Harrison in 1812. Gen. William Henry Harrison built the eponymous post on the bank of the Wabash River during his march to Prophetstown in October 1811. Indians under Tenskwatawa attacked the post unsuccessfully in September 1812.

The Battle of Tippecanoe. An early stylized depiction of the American counterattack.

Gen. William Hull, the superannuated and timid commander who led the U.S. expedition to defend Fort Detroit and invade Upper Canada.

Col. (later Maj. Gen.) Henry Procter, the much-maligned and poorly supported British commander of the Military District of Amherstburg. Tecumseh traduced him as "a fat animal that carries its tail on its back."

RUINS OF OLD ELLIOTT HOMESTEAD NEAR AMHERSTBURG, CANADA.

British Indian Department official Matthew Elliott's homestead outside Amherstburg, Upper Canada. When allied with the British, Tecumseh regularly made the small brick shed in the rear his headquarters.

Maj. Gen. Sir Isaac Brock. On learning of
Brock's intention to attack Fort Detroit,
Tecumseh exclaimed, "This is a man!"

The first meeting of General Brock
and Tecumseh.

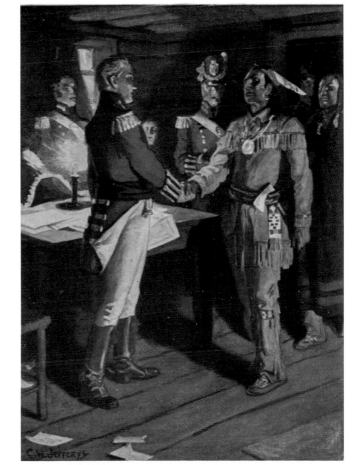

Tecumseh by Keith Rocco, as the Shawnee chief likely appeared in the winter of 1812–13.

View of Amherstburg, 1813. Tecumseh appears in the foreground, second from right. Gen. Henry Procter appears in the middle ground wearing a British officer's longcoat.

The Battle of Fort Meigs. Tecumseh wearied of fighting American "groundhogs" who refused to leave their fortifications and give battle like warriors.

"Remember the River Raisin!" At the Battle of the Thames, Col. Richard M. Johnson's Kentucky Mounted Riflemen crash through the thin British line on Tecumseh's left, sealing the Indians' fate.

ABOVE An early popular, fanciful depiction of Colonel Johnson's alleged killing of Tecumseh.

RIGHT Tecumseh at the Battle of the Thames, a somewhat less stylized depiction that would have been more authentic had the charging Kentuckians been depicted on foot.

Life into legend: After nearly twenty years of intermittent work, the German sculptor Ferdinand Pettrich completed a larger-than-life, heroically proportioned statue called *The Dying Tecumseh*. It resides at the Smithsonian American Art Museum. The statue was entirely imaginary in its composition—any resemblance to the mortal Shawnee leader is coincidental. In 1866 museum-goers were enjoined to keep their hands off it.

A portion of the Indian delegation that visited Governor-Gen. George Prévost Drummond in 1814. Tecumseh's sister Tecumpease is believed to be the second woman from the left.

Lewis Cass. As governor of the Michigan Territory, he collaborated with Tenskwatawa, during the Prophet's declining days, to resettle Shawnees west of the Mississippi.

TENS-QUA-TA-WA
or THE ONE THAT OPENS THE DOOR

Tenskwatawa, as painted by J. O. Lewis during a visit to Detroit in 1824.

ABOVE Tenskwatawa by George Catlin. This may be the most faithful representation of the Shawnee holy man ever painted.

RIGHT *Tenskwatawa,* by Henry Inman, oil on canvas, c. 1830–33.

BELOW Catlin's formal portrait of Tenskwatawa holding the sacred symbols of his bygone days as prophet and seer.

A solar eclipse was an event of great moment to the Indians. Some saw it as a manifestation of divine wrath; others—including the Shawnees—believed a Black Sun, or Mukutaaweethee Keesohtoa, to be a portent of war. Not understanding its cause, Indians dreaded that an eclipse might prove perpetual.[4]

Tenskwatawa was delighted. If his visions did not suffice to win converts, he would gain them through chicanery—it was all done in the Indians' best interest and at Harrison's expense in any event. And so in early June he assembled the people of Greenville to deliver on a promise that astonished even his most ardent believers. To prove Tenskwatawa's holiness, the Master of Life intended to alter the heavens. Tenskwatawa bade the people of Greenville to spread the word of the pending miracle and reassemble before June 16. On that date the Master of Life would send a Black Sun to reaffirm Tenskwatawa's divine authority. Roundhead, the gifted chief of a small Wyandot village on the upper Scioto River and an early ally, helped gather spectators from the northern tribes. Whether Tenskwatawa shared his foreknowledge of the eclipse with Tecumseh cannot be known.

Scores of devotees and doubters assembled at Greenville. Tenskwatawa communed nightly with the Master of Life about the coming miracle. The appointed day dawned clear and still. To enhance the sense of drama, Tenskwatawa kept to his wigwam. As the noon sun faded into twilight, the Prophet burst forth, declaring, "Behold! Did I not speak the truth? See, darkness is coming." Consternation and awe rippled through the crowd until Tenskwatawa assured his audience that, just as he had caused the sun to fade, so he would soon return it to its former radiance. The assembly waited and hoped.[5]

Elsewhere in the Indian country, the eclipse elicited reactions ranging from mild interest among Tarhe's Wyandots, whom the Reverend Badger had prepared for the occurrence, to abject horror. A white traveler in Tennessee watched Cherokee warriors gather to "shoot away the eclipse." Nearly a thousand muskets cracked at the bedimmed heavens. Meanwhile in the Michigan Territory, "some villagers appeared impressed that the darkness would be equal to that of the darkest night and would continue for months, and that vegetables and game animals would perish," recalled the territorial secretary, whose assurances had fallen largely on deaf ears. "Others ran up and down with agitation, while a few wrapped themselves in their blankets and prepared to die."[6]

In Greenville the tension was palpable but brief. The sun reemerged precisely when Tenskwatawa commanded. (Perhaps Fisher stood beside him with a pocket watch.) Grumbling doubters became ardent apostles and—steering clear of Tarhe's town—departed to spread the word that the Master of Life indeed favored the Shawnee Prophet.

Despite the "miracle" Tenskwatawa had wrought, only a trickle of pilgrims straggled to Greenville, very few of whom were Shawnees. Chief Black Hoof and the Wapakoneta Mekoches still considered Tenskwatawa a charlatan. They also regarded Tecumseh as an able but minor war leader floundering about in a time of peace, with pretensions to civil leadership inappropriate for a Kispoko. Relations between the two Shawnee factions were strained at best, and the Mekoches were confident that they had the upper hand.

Then Black Hoof heard disturbing news. Blue Jacket, his old rival and the most famous man in the Shawnee nation, had thrown in with the parvenu brothers. It seemed a startling turn of events. Blue Jacket represented much that Tenskwatawa rejected. A heavy drinker who lived in luxury in his Detroit River village, he not only fraternized with whites but also had married a white woman and educated his sons in Detroit schools. Likely Blue Jacket saw in the Prophet's crusade a means to challenge Black Hoof and other old Mekoche rivals. For their part, both Tecumseh and Tenskwatawa recognized early on that compromise was necessary if the movement was to flourish.[7]

In Greenville, Blue Jacket assumed the mantle of elder statesman. He recommended that the Shawnee brothers reassure neighboring whites of their peaceable intentions, advice they wisely heeded. The Wapakoneta chiefs had warned Indian agent William Wells at Fort Wayne that Tenskwatawa's settlement on ceded land was bound to provoke a conflict, and the resultant rumors rekindled old fears among the Mad River settlers. In mid-August, Blue Jacket and Tecumseh, with Blue Jacket's son George as interpreter, traveled to Chillicothe to offer Acting Gov. Thomas Kirker their assurances of perpetual amity. "We desire that you will pay no attention to any bad reports," the chiefs told Kirker on August 11. "We [also] desire that you will let all the white people on the frontier know that we have [come] to renew our friendship with you, and that you will give us a few lines to show both our people and yours when we go home, that we have been to see you, and the peace and friendship is renewed, to be broke again no more forever." Three days later Chillicothe newspapers reported the happy conclusion of the meeting.[8]

Blue Jacket's initiative reassured Ohioans and at least temporarily blunted the intrigues of the Wapakoneta Shawnees. For their part, the Shawnee brothers kept a low profile, consolidating their community and awaiting evidence that their missions to the tribes of the upper Great Lakes and the Illinois country had found a receptive audience.

Winter passed pleasantly enough. The snows receded. The muddy, milder mornings of March, the Sap Moon, heralded the coming of the spring of 1807. Tenskwatawa looked hopefully to the forests beyond Greenville for the influx of pilgrims for which he had preached so fervently. The first religiously motivated visitors indeed arrived that month, but they were scarcely the young Indian recruits that Tenskwatawa had expected. Rather they were three white men—outriders of the Ohio branch of the United Society of Believers in Christ's Second Appearing, more commonly known as the Shakers, whose faith had emerged from the so-called Kentucky Revival of 1800–1. Celibate, pacifist, egalitarian, and ecstatic in their worship, the Shakers were looked on with suspicion by their white neighbors, both for their unconventional faith and for their prophecies, which revealed to them that the Indians were on the verge of "coming into the Gospel."

Vague reports had reached the rustic Shaker village of Turtle Creek, sixty miles southeast of Greenville, that a prophet had arisen among the Indians "who told of great things at hand." The Shakers were hopeful: "Sometimes we heard one thing and sometimes another, but we fully believed the spirit of God was at work among them." Convinced that God had touched Greenville, three Shaker men— David Darrow, Benjamin Young, and Richard McNemar—went to meet the Shawnee Prophet.

On March 23 they rode unchallenged into Greenville. The Shakers admired the whitewashed council house standing amid sixty tidy clapboard cabins. (Apparently Tenskwatawa did not insist that the Indians abjure cabins in favor of traditional wigwams.) Smoke curled placidly from chimneys. All appeared tranquil. Nervous nonetheless, the Shakers asked the first English-speaking Indian they met if their feelings toward the whites were friendly. "Yes, we are brothers," replied Peter

Cornstalk, son of the great chief treacherously murdered by the Long Knives. The relieved Shakers fell into genial conversation with the young Shawnee.

"What is that big house for?" they inquired.

"To worship the Great Spirit," Peter Cornstalk answered.

"How do you worship?

"Mostly in speaking."

"Who is your chief speaker?"

"Our Prophet. He converses with the Great Spirit and tells us how to be good."

"Do all that live here believe in him?"

"Yes; we all believe—he can dream to God."

As the men conversed, villagers gathered around the Shakers, who divined a deep devotion envelop them. "All seemed to be moved, and some appeared very solemn in tears and could scarce take their eyes off us," recalled Benjamin Young. Tecumseh stepped forward with papers from Governor Tiffin attesting to the village's friendly disposition. Mounting his horse, he led the Shakers along a wooded trail four miles to the Greenville sugar camp, where the early spring tradition of maple sugar making was in full swing. The ride passed largely in silence, Tecumseh feigning not to understand English. At the camp, he handed the Shakers over to George Bluejacket, who greeted them with a cheerful skepticism and laughed at their desire to speak to the Prophet—white ministers counted his faith foolish; therefore Tenskwatawa would not entertain the thought. Besides, the Prophet had a bad headache.

McNemar insisted they were genuine seekers of truth whom white clergymen despised, to which the highly literate George Bluejacket responded, "Do you believe a person can have true knowledge of the Great Spirit, in the heart, without going to school and learning to read?"

"We believe they can," McNemar intoned. "And that is the best kind of knowledge."

Seemingly satisfied, George Bluejacket left to join Tecumseh in the Prophet's tent. An hour later Tenskwatawa emerged smoking a large tomahawk pipe. He seated himself before a circle of twenty-five expectant Indian acolytes. The blaze of a large campfire tinctured the coming twilight. Benjamin Young studied the Prophet intently:

He was divested of all his tinkling ornaments but a round [gorget] on his breast that fastened his garment. His dress [was] plain and decent, his countenance grave and solemn. His person [was] of a common size, rather slender and of no great appearance.

All was silent for some time. He began to speak, and with his eyes closed continued his speech about half an hour in a very eloquent and emphatical manner. He sensibly spake by the power of God—his solemn voice, grave countenance, with every motion of his hand and gesture of his body, were expressive of a deep sense and solemn feeling of eternal things.... At every remarkable pause or sentence, a solemn assent sounded.

Tenskwatawa spoke of his doctrine and the substance of his visions, which George Ironside interpreted carefully. Nonetheless, averred Benjamin Young, the "weighty and spiritual concern, and that solemn sense, love, and simplicity that we felt in the assembly cannot be put into words." Dinner was then served—one turkey and a tin kettle with eight quarts of broth to feed the entire gathering. Moved by the meager repast—for many of the Indians, it was their only meal of the day—the Shakers handed George Bluejacket ten dollars, which the Prophet in turn gratefully acknowledged. The Shakers, he concluded, were no ordinary Americans. Their gift, given with a pure heart, was therefore acceptable.

The Shakers returned to Greenville for the night. Contemplating the full moon as it rose above the forested horizon, Benjamin Young said he felt as did the biblical Jacob when he awakened from a dream wailing, "Surely God is in this place, and the world know it not!" The "heathenish" aspect of the male villagers—their shaved heads, painted faces, tinkling silver ornaments, and prominent ear and nose rings—in no way dissuaded the Shakers from believing God was with them.

The next morning Blue Jacket summoned the Shakers to his tent. With his son George interpreting, Blue Jacket, Tecumseh, and other "notable persons" engaged the three Shakers in a frank and spirited exchange. Above all, they wished to know if Shakers drank whiskey. When told they did not, the Indians expressed "great joy to find any among the whites so far reformed from wicked ways." From the Indians, the Shakers learned a curious element of Tenskwatawa's teaching—his gift for discerning the sins of those as young as seven years old, and his insistence that they confess them. The Prophet had integrated the practice into his creed courtesy of the Wyandots. "A great many Wyandots have belonged to the Roman Catholics at Detroit," explained the British Indian Department official and trusted Indian trader George Ironside, "but they have left them and now believe in our Prophet," adding, "The Roman Catholics would confess their sins but would still go on and be wicked, but our people forsake their evil ways when they have confessed."

No longer reticent, Tecumseh spoke passionately to the three Shakers about his brother's faith. They figuratively shook with delight when he told them that it was his most ardent desire that Shawnee nonbelievers—Black Hoof's people—enter the fold and find salvation. It is doubtful that Tecumseh dissembled or tried to manipulate the visitors. The Shakers were good, sincere white men, the sort Tecumseh respected and with whom he would speak truthfully.

Before departing, the Shaker trio addressed a letter to Tenskwatawa, expressing their love of the "good spirit" at work among his converts and encouraging them to come to Turtle Creek whenever they wished.

It was a gratifying visit for Tenskwatawa. There were good and godly white men whom he could win over with his words. But where were the Indian truth seekers to whom he had sent his emissaries? They were his real concern. Most of his fellow Shawnees had spurned him categorically, and the Delawares, Miamis, and Ohio Wyandots were doubtful future converts at best. Without a massive influx of wayfaring northern Indians, Tenskwatawa would have opened his spiritual door for naught.

He would not have long to wait for his answer.[9]

The Shaker emissaries had visited Tenskwatawa a month too soon. Had they come in April instead, they would have witnessed a spectacle far more marvelous than that which convinced them that God was at work in Greenville. At long last, Indian pilgrims from the Great Lakes were descending on the holy town in numbers large enough to worry officials and settlers. The northern Indians had been restive even before Tenskwatawa's message reached them. In 1806 a delegation of Great Lakes tribes had traveled to Fort Malden at Amherstburg,

Upper Canada, to reaffirm their fealty to the British and rail against the "White Devil with his mouth wide open ready to take possession of our lands by any means." They needed look no farther than across the Detroit River from Fort Malden for confirmation of their fears. The once predominantly French-Canadian town of Detroit, opposite Amherstburg, was now sprinkled with the advance guard of Jefferson's Empire of Liberty. While the population shift occurred gradually, the physical aspect of Detroit had changed instantly. In June 1805 a fire ravaged the town. The century-old thatched cottages flamed and flashed and vanished. Of the nearly two hundred structures that had defined Detroit, only one remained standing; stone chimneys alone marked the sites of the others. Wealthy residents of mutable loyalty moved across the river to Amherstburg or Sandwich, making way for the pro-American entrepreneurs who rebuilt Detroit with solid stone, lime, brick, and firm timber. Sturdy, cedar-shingled houses coated with plaster sprang up. New and wider streets were laid out, and a brick Indian factory and council house were constructed.

The old British fort overlooking the community survived. Its ramparts frowned with American cannons, and a small garrison of Long Knives occupied the barracks. Tiny American settlements sprang up on the outskirts of Detroit. Their presence troubled the local Indians. Some, like the Michigan Wyandots, sought accommodation. A few responded by relocating. Others prepared for trouble. The Potawatomis who lived nearest the Americans placed tribal affairs in the hands of their war chiefs. The British exhorted them against bloodshed, but the Indians had fastened a fuse that could easily be lit.[10]

The Indian agent William Wells sounded the alarm first. In April 1807 nearly four hundred Ottawa, Potawatomi, and Ojibwa warriors passed Fort Wayne on their way to Greenville. Although confident their intentions were pacific, Wells feared that the mere appearance of so many strange Indians would stampede Ohio settlers. Wells also believed that the Shawnee Prophet intended to manipulate the outsiders into toppling Black Hoof so that he might become "first chief" of the Shawnee people. That, Wells speculated, could spark a wider conflagration. "There are men . . . that are dissatisfied with the conduct of their chiefs and appear anxious to follow the example of this Shawnee [Prophet]," Wells told the secretary of war. "Where this business will end time must determine."[11]

For the moment, Tenskwatawa was content to revel in the presence of a multitude of potential disciples, one well-informed white official estimated their number at 800, who had come to him from as far away as Lake Superior. Their spiritual ardor was real; they had suffered from hunger and exposure on the long journey, and many had died.[12] Those who completed the pilgrimage, however, did not want for attention from the Prophet, who welcomed tribal delegations warmly. Occasionally language barriers blunted the full impact of Tenskwatawa's creed, as when the Prophet entertained a dozen Winnebagos—a Siouan-speaking people on friendly terms with the Algonquin tribes—who had walked to Greenville from their villages in what is today Wisconsin.

"It is good, my younger brothers. There are many tribes here, but I wanted to see you here especially," Tenskwatawa greeted the sojourners. "It is good you have come. I want to talk to you, but it is impossible because I cannot speak your language."

A wizened Winnebago who spoke some Shawnee stepped forward. "I can understand what you are saying, but I am afraid to talk to you because I don't know whether I could make myself clear to you."

Tenskwatawa thanked the old man and then proceeded. "Younger brothers, we are not doing the right thing, and that is why we are not getting along very well in life," he began. The old Winnebago missed the subtleties of Tenskwatawa's doctrine, but he understood fragments pertaining to the Prophet's shameful days as Lalawethika:

He said ... the devil had told him that he would go to heaven and that he could not be killed. He had told him that he had given him a holy belt. He was a bad person. Whenever he got angry, he would throw his belt on the ground and it would change into a yellow rattlesnake and rattle. When he did this the rest of the people were afraid of him.

He was very mean when drunk.... He was unkind to the women. They would go with him not because they liked him but because they were afraid of him. It was a dangerous thing to say anything about him. Whenever he wished to drink, he would take some person's valuables and buy drink with it.

The Creator had sent him on a mission to the earth, but the devil had misled him.

Tenskwatawa's Faustian life tale was destined to end in truth and glory for all Indians, if only the Winnebagos and others would heed his holy admonitions—such as the interpreter understood them.[13]

One Indian from afar who had no difficulty in comprehending the Prophet's creed was a charismatic Ottawa warrior named Le Maigouis (the Trout), a brother of the principal chief of L'Arbre Croche, a large Ottawa and Ojibwa community near Michilimackinac in the upper Michigan Territory. Because these were precisely the Indians that Tenskwatawa longed to reach, he shrewdly singled out the influential and highly intelligent young Ottawa for special attention, telling him he was to become "the Herald of this new religion" to both his people and the Ojibwas. An ardent apostle, Le Maigouis drank deeply of Tenskwatawa's creed. And Tenskwatawa embellished it lavishly for his Ottawa apostle. No longer was he merely a transformed incarnation of the sinful Lalawethika, atoning for his transgressions and sharing the revealed word of the Master of Life. Rather, Tenskwatawa told Le Maigouis, he was the first man created on Earth, awakened from the dead in order to offer his wise counsel to the Great Spirit, who had "closed [his] book of accounts" with mankind and decided to destroy the world. The resurrected Tenskwatawa preached that the Indians had degenerated. They were "scattered and miserable," but he had convinced the Master of Life to spare his red children long enough for him to try to redeem them. "I requested the Great Spirit to grant [this] in case they should listen to my voice, that the world might yet subsist for the period of three full lives, and my request was granted," claimed Tenskwatawa. Those who hearkened his words, and their progeny, would in effect receive a stay of execution.

Tenskwatawa instructed Le Maigouis to close his addresses to the northern tribes with a request, an apology, and a warning from the Prophet, who was "now on the Earth sent by the Great Spirit to instruct" the Indians. Each village must dispatch two or more principal chiefs to Greenville to be taught; Le Maigouis would show them the road to the Prophet. Tenskwatawa was sorry that he could not come himself to L'Arbre Croche, but if he left Greenville, the world would end. "It is broken and leans down, and as it declines the Ojibwas, Ottawas, and all beyond will fall off and die" unless their chiefs heeded the Prophet's summons. Those villages that failed to send delegates to learn from Tenskwatawa would be "cut off from the face of the Earth."[14]

If William Wells had his way, Greenville would fall from the face of the Earth first. Goaded by an opportunistic Chief Black Hoof and by uneasy pioneers, but lacking higher authority, Wells convinced the métis Anthony Shane to invite Tenskwatawa and Tecumseh to Fort Wayne to receive a (nonexistent) letter from the Great Father President Jefferson imploring them to abandon Greenville.

Tecumseh had a low opinion of Shane, and he dismissed both the message and the messenger. It was a signal moment in Tecumseh's unfolding relations with the Americans. Without consulting Tenskwatawa or Blue Jacket, he rejected Wells's summons out of hand. "Return to Fort Wayne and tell Captain Wells that my fire is kindled on the spot appointed by the Great Spirit above, and if he has anything to communicate to me, he must come here," Tecumseh told Shane. If Wells agreed, Tecumseh would invite two of his most "respectable" white friends to attend the council on behalf of their settlements. Tecumseh said he expected to hear from Wells within six days. Tecumseh's unilateral action is not hard to understand. He, not Tenskwatawa or their distinguished elder guest Blue Jacket, was the village chief. Although yet uncertain in what direction they lay, Tecumseh clearly had political ambitions of his own that he was unwilling to sublimate. He would loyally support Tenskwatawa but not lose himself in the process.

Tecumseh's indifference to American demands flummoxed Wells. It also boxed him into a corner. Visiting Greenville ran the risk of legitimizing its existence. Consequently, on April 22, 1807, Wells drafted a speech for Shane to deliver to the Greenville leadership in Jefferson's name, although there is no evidence that the president ever authorized the approach or the ultimatum it contained.

Shane dutifully delivered the demand. While entirely reasonable under the terms of the Greenville Treaty, in the spiritually charged atmosphere of the Prophet's community, it was an order such as would have caused many a man to fear for his scalp. Tenskwatawa, Tecumseh, the Shawnee subchiefs, and Blue Jacket were on hand to receive it. Reminding his "Shawnee brothers" that the Great Father brooked no trespassing on either side of the Greenville line, Wells insisted that the Indian presence south of it not only was illegal but also had frightened the settlers. The Indians therefore must vacate Greenville at once. Concluding in a manner certain to infuriate Tenskwatawa, Wells wrote, "I now take you all by the hand and commit you to the care of the Great Spirit and hope that he may lead you from under the dark clouds that appear to be hanging over you at this time and show you the path that will lead you to happiness."[15]

Tecumseh rose to speak. Since Tenskwatawa had begun his quest to unite the Indians spiritually, he had done much thinking of his own. Should there not be something sacred to the Indian beyond his soul? Tecumseh believed he had found the answer. Now he would share it. He was about to utter the most profoundly important words of his thirty-nine years. And he would spare no one whose actions had contravened that which he was about to declare most dear to him—the sanctity of what land remained to the Indians.

Turning not to Shane but rather to his fellow Shawnee leaders, Tecumseh lectured them at length—"harangued them," as Shane put it—on the unending white encroachment. "These lands are ours, and no one has the right to remove us, because we were the first proprietors. The Great Spirit above has appointed this place for us to light our fires, and here we shall remain. As to boundaries, the Great Spirit above knows no boundary, nor will his people acknowledge any." Tecumseh told Shane that if President Jefferson had anything to say, he must send "a man of note." He would deal no further with Wells, either directly or through an intermediary.

Tecumseh's pronouncement marked a stunning and indisputable departure from his previous acquiescence to the Greenville Treaty boundary. His emphasis on Greenville as a sacred exception to the lands surrendered suggests that his convictions arose at least in part from a belief that his brother's mission was indeed divinely inspired. There also was no mistaking the line he had drawn between himself and the treaty chiefs, for such an insult to Wells also constituted an insult to Little Turtle and Black Hoof. Little Turtle might fatten at the government pap in his fine house, attended by his black slave. The spiritually bankrupt Black Hoof might debase himself for annuities. But the Shawnee brothers would go their own way, answering only to the Master of Life.

Although still only a village chief, Tecumseh had announced himself a political force to be reckoned with in the Indian country. Henceforth he would be the primary spokesman for the Prophet's pan-Indian religious movement, both to whites and to potentially hostile Indians. Increasingly, Tenskwatawa would concern himself largely—but not exclusively—with sustaining the spiritual flame and attracting new adherents to his faith. William Wells's antagonistic gambit served simply to deepen the Shawnee brothers' interdependence.

Shane was left speechless. Not so the Prophet, who endorsed Tecumseh's address with a few vicarious insults leveled at Thomas Jefferson. "Why did not the government send the greatest man they have to us? I can talk to [the president]. I can bring darkness between him and me. Nay, more. I can bring the sun under my feet, and what white man can do this?" With that, the council adjourned.[16]

Wells had lost the first round to the Shawnee brothers. The defeat cost him in the capital as well. Denying the magnitude of a problem that he lacked the gumption to confront, or to trouble the president with, the oleaginous secretary of war, Henry Dearborn, blamed Wells for the "improper collection" of Indians at Greenville. An apoplectic Wells in turn advised Dearborn that another two thousand pilgrims were expected to visit the Prophet in the late summer. "No time should be lost in sending this villain and his insolent band off U.S. land," he sputtered; it was a task that mere words could not accomplish. Dearborn pigeonholed Wells's note and pondered whether the time had come to find a new Indian agent.[17]

William Wells genuinely feared for the safety of settlers on the fringe of the Indian country. But in the late spring of 1807 the likelihood of war between Black Hoof and Tecumseh was greater than that between Indians and Ohioans. The trouble began when the scalped corpse of one John Boyer was discovered face down in a creek bed near Mad River. Two Indian rattles, a bow and arrows, hair, and feathers rested on Boyer's back. At least one local newspaper suggested Boyer may have been murdered in a private quarrel, with the scene staged to appear as though Indians had killed him. But others suspected that Tecumseh's band had slain Boyer to provoke a conflict between the Mad River settlers and Black Hoof's people.

As always, Governor Tiffin acted judiciously. He activated two militia companies, but rather than deploy them, he sent Simon Kenton and the militia general Benjamin Whiteman to hold a council with Tecumseh in a glade outside Greenville.

Kenton and Whiteman found Tecumseh brimming with sardonic humor. Before the council opened, Whiteman strolled off for a moment. After swapping yarns, Tecumseh asked Kenton the identity of the solitary man. Kenton told him, adding that Whiteman had been among his band of Kentuckians that Tecumseh had bested on the Great Miami River in 1793. Excusing himself, Tecumseh sneaked up behind Whiteman. Slapping him on the shoulder, he bellowed in English, "Are you a big man?"

"Yes," Whiteman calmly replied, "I am."

"I am a bigger man than you," said Tecumseh with a sneer.

"That is yet to be tried."

"Oh no." Tecumseh laughed. "I whipped you when we were boys, and maybe I can do it again."

The pleasantries over, the council was brief. Tecumseh blamed Boyer's murder on Black Hoof, and the participants agreed to a second council in the nearby village of Springfield in June to give Black Hoof a chance to refute Tecumseh's accusation.[18]

Not content to let the matter rest until the Springfield council, Whiteman sounded out Chief Roundhead on the Boyer murder. If the general had expected an answer different from that which Tecumseh had given him, he was sorely disappointed. A prominent Wyandot war chief in the great confederacy of the 1790s, the forty-seven-year-old Roundhead had established an independent village on the upper Scioto River after the Treaty of Greenville. He shared many of Tecumseh's personal traits. Fair-minded and good-natured, he was a hard fighter, spoke English, and cut a fine figure. Mediating many disputes between Indians and whites in his neighborhood, Roundhead earned a reputation for honesty and integrity. As an early convert to the Prophet's faith, he moved his band to Greenville and became a devoted friend and ally of the Shawnee brothers.[19]

Roundhead's loyalty to Tecumseh may have caused him to shade the truth. "We people at Greenville is [*sic*] thinking no evil," he told General Williams. "We employ ourselves in trying to make peace with our maker [and] lay the murder of that white man to a Shawnee that professes friendship to [the] white people ... Black Hoof."[20]

On June 24 the disputants descended on Springfield, a small but growing community consisting of perhaps two dozen clapboard cabins—including that of Simon Kenton—and the inevitable tavern. Each of the two Shawnee factions turned out some sixty heavily armed warriors prepared to defend their chief if words turned to blows. A few Wyandot warriors escorted Roundhead.

The armed retinues got no farther than a gunsmith's cabin a mile or two north of town. There Col. William Ward, who represented Governor Tiffin, insisted they stack their arms—tomahawks and hunting knives included. Knowing who he was up against, Tecumseh ordered his warriors to comply. His family and the Wards had a long and violent history going back to the Battle of Point Pleasant, where Ward had fought as a teenager. Colonel Ward's brother John, a captive of the Shawnees and an early follower of Tecumseh, had been killed in Tecumseh's first skirmish with Kenton, in which the colonel's brother James had fought with the Kentuckian. Tall, arrogant, and robust at fifty-five, William Ward made it clear to the three chiefs that he was in charge—and he had 120 armed militiamen to back him up.

The militia formed a hollow square around the council ground, and the Indians filed in. Tecumseh cradled his splendid silver-mounted tomahawk-pipe openly in his left arm. As militia officers stepped forward to disarm him, Tecumseh recoiled. A chief, he declared, was entitled to smoke his pipe in council. The officers stood firm. Ward intervened on their behalf. Tecumseh fumed but reluctantly handed him his bladed badge of rank. The altercation caught the eye of a kindly old Methodist preacher who stood nearby puffing his stubby corncob pipe. He offered it to Tecumseh. Perhaps now was the moment for a bit of levity. Tecumseh took the pipe gingerly between his thumb and forefinger, sniffed it, turned up his nose, then heaved it far over his shoulder. Laughter rippled through the militia ranks. Tecumseh assumed his place in the semicircle of Indians seated before Colonel Ward, and the council opened.[21]

Ward spoke first. He was blunt. The Indians were charged with killing a white man. If they valued their lives and those of their wives and children—indeed the very survival of their nations—they had better surrender the perpetrator of the crime or reveal his identity.

The chiefs wilted before Ward's ultimatum. Black Hoof, who had accused Roundhead of the crime, now suggested that wandering Ojibwas were to blame. Roundhead rose next. A Wapakoneta Shawnee clutched a tomahawk hidden under a blanket. If Roundhead besmirched Black Hoof again, he would kill the Wyandot. But Roundhead meekly apologized for having disparaged him.

Now came Tecumseh's turn to talk. He was a disaffected man, a secessionist from the legitimate authority of the Shawnee nation who, like his brother the Prophet, trod a path that promised ruin for any Shawnee foolish enough to follow him. At least that was how the Wapakoneta warriors saw him, and they readied themselves to defend their chief. But Tecumseh wanted no quarrel with Black Hoof. Perhaps he recalled for a moment the teachings of his youth. "The aged," Tecumseh had been instructed, "have lived through the whole period of our lives, and long before we were born; they have not only all the knowledge we possess, but a great deal more. We, therefore, must submit our limited views to their experience."[22]

Tecumseh spoke rapidly in Shawnee, and with such obvious energy and fluency that one white observer would later compare him to the great Kentucky senator and orator Henry Clay. Articulating the motives of the Greenville believers, he disavowed any hostile intent or knowledge of the Boyer murder. Tecumseh gave no affront to Black Hoof and reaffirmed his friendship for the settlers, saying that he "well knew that it was repugnant to the will of the Great Spirit to break friendship with the white people, and that if he knew the guilty, he would give information."

Ward was not amused. He told the chiefs that if they did not come up with something more tangible than good intentions—and soon— then a "general war would ensue and their whole people would be exterminated." On that lovely note, the irascible colonel terminated the assembly.

Clearly shaken by Ward's threat, that evening Black Hoof and Tecumseh literally hurled a tomahawk over their shoulders to eradicate evil spirits and obtain everlasting peace between their factions. Always conscious that strife between Indians was counterproductive, Tecumseh publicly disavowed his brother's call to execute the Wapakoneta chiefs as sorcerers. Then the Shawnee chiefs did what they could to placate the Americans. Black Hoof hurried home to Wapakoneta to investigate the Boyer murder further. He eventually informed General Whiteman truthfully that a Potawatomi war party had slain Boyer in retaliation for the killing of one of their number by white residents four years earlier. That ended the uproar. Tecumseh, meanwhile, lingered in Springfield for a few days, mixing with villagers and competing with men in wrestling, rifle shooting, tomahawk throwing, and other frontier amusements. He lodged with the family of William Renick, who were quite fond of the charismatic Shawnee. Tecumseh's popularity was general in Springfield, recalled Renick's son. Villagers appreciated his open-handed honesty and warm humor and always wished him well. So long as the Americans claimed no more Indian land, Tecumseh was content to reciprocate their goodwill, Tenskwatawa's admonitions against fraternizing with them notwithstanding.[23]

But the burgeoning white presence in Ohio could not forever be contained behind a line drawn more than a decade earlier. Since the Greenville Treaty, the nonnative population of Ohio had grown nearly tenfold to some 150,000, while Indian numbers had remained constant or declined to no more than six thousand. The Prophet's sacred town strode the boundary as tenuously as a pebble in a tidal pool awaiting an onrushing wave. Two days before the Springfield council, a naval battle occurred off the distant coast of Virginia that would roil the waters far beyond the Shawnee brothers' capacity to contain them.

Greenville Interlude

T ENSKWATAWA CHOSE WELL when he selected Le Maigouis to be
his herald to the upper Great Lakes tribes. Returning to L'Arbre
Croche in April 1807, the Ottawa warrior crisscrossed the north country, converting most of the Ottawa, Ojibwa, and Winnebago peoples
with his impassioned preaching of the Prophet's gospel. Le Maigouis
created such a stir that Capt. Josiah Dunham, the commanding officer
at Fort Michilimackinac, feared an Indian uprising. "There appears
to be an extensive movement among the savages of this quarter which
seems to carry with it a good deal of the dark and mysterious," Dunham told Secretary Dearborn. "Belts of wampum are rapidly circulating from one tribe to another, and a spirit is prevailing by no means
pacific.... I cannot say that I apprehend an immediate attack, [but]
I have thought it no more than a dictate of prudence to watch their
motions and be in constant readiness."

Fort Michilimackinac (later renamed Fort Mackinac) was a formidable work, but Dunham had few resources with which to defend
it—some four dozen officers and men, a few cannons, and no provisions except those obtained from the Indians. From his island post
in the Straits of Mackinac, Dunham was responsible for the security
of most of a territory that existed largely as an abstraction. Carved
from Indiana in 1805, the Michigan Territory was overwhelmingly
Indian country. Forts Michilimackinac and Detroit represented the
only American military presence, and outside Detroit the civilian
population of three thousand consisted principally of former French-

Canadians of dubious loyalty to the United States. It was the far frontier of Jefferson's Empire of Liberty, fated to remain so if the Regular
Army did not grow apace with the president's territorial aspirations.

Le Maigouis did not preach war with the whites and remained
faithful to the essence of Tenskwatawa's doctrine. Nevertheless, he
frightened the few American inhabitants of the upper country, many
of whom had lived with the Indians long enough to sense impending
trouble. In Green Bay, a small trading settlement in a sea of Indians, they prepared for the worst. The "savages are very badly disposed toward the Americans [and] seem determined to make war on
them," the justice of the peace advised Dunham in early June, "and
have appointed a place of rendezvous whence they may be able to
attack several posts at the same time." They "have a parable, in which
a prophet is sent to them from above to instruct them and to teach
them the true method of living," which he presumed included killing
Americans.

He was wrong about that. What Le Maigouis did preach was the
innate superiority of the Indians and the need for unity against any
future American encroachment. The Master of Life spoke through Le
Maigouis as he had Tenskwatawa. "My Children. You are to have very
little intercourse with the whites," he preached. "They are not your
Fathers, as you call them, but your brethren—I [the Master of Life]
am your Father. When you call me so, you do well—I am the Father
of the English, of the French, of the Spaniards, and of the Indians....
But the Americans I did not make. They are not my children, but the
children of the Evil Spirit. They grew from the scum of the Great
Water, when it was troubled by the Evil Spirit and the froth was driven
into the woods by a strong east wind. They are numerous, but I hate
them. They are unjust. They have taken away your lands, which were
not made for them."

Captain Dunham could have precipitated the war he hoped to avert
by detaining Le Maigouis. The "looks and deportment" of the Ojibwa
and Ottawa chiefs unnerved him. They no longer addressed him as
"Father." And they could be downright insolent, as when they refused
to attend a treaty council at Detroit that the territorial governor William Hull hoped to convene. "Our brethren below are forgetting their
children," the principal Ottawa chief told Dunham. "If they are fools
enough to throw away their hunting ground, let them do it. We how-

ever in this quarter will do no such thing, and we hope you will not think of taking one hand's breadth of our land, for we have not much to spare." It was when the chiefs told him they had more important business than meeting with the governor that he arrested Le Maigouis. "Brothers," Dunham declared, "I believe that your prophet is a great imposter.... The Great Spirit would never tell you that the Americans were not his children."

The chiefs took the captain's ill-advised tirade in stride. They convinced him that neither they nor Le Maigouis meant any harm. Dunham backpedaled and released the irksome Ottawa on a pledge that he would tone down his rhetoric. Lest there be any misunderstanding on the land question, however, the chiefs advised Governor Hull to keep away. Hull prudently let the matter rest. He still hoped to conclude an "advantageous treaty" but advised Secretary Dearborn that "this Shawnee Prophet is certainly gaining influence, and what the consequences may be, it is difficult to determine."[1]

The truth is that the Prophet's northern adherents expressed a militancy that the Shawnee brothers had not yet evinced. After dressing down Anthony Shane, Tecumseh and Tenskwatawa had trod lightly about further land cessions and labored to maintain good relations with their American neighbors. Not that Tecumseh's proclamation to Shane had been insincere. Rather, there had been no cause for him to match his words with action because neither governor, Harrison or Tiffin, had expressed any desire to obtain more Indian land. But William Wells nevertheless saw trouble on the horizon. He knew the Ojibwas, Ottawas, and Potawatomis planned to make a second pilgrimage to the Prophet in August. "It is absolutely necessary that the Shawnees at Greenville should be sent from that place as soon as possible," Wells told Secretary Dearborn. "I am afraid the Shawnee Prophet will stimulate the Indians to do something against the Indians or white people unless he is handled pretty rough." But no one in Washington listened.[2]

That is, until June 22, 1807, when the British warship HMS *Leopard* fired on the frigate USS *Chesapeake* off the Virginia coast. Tensions between Great Britain and the United were already high. Locked in a costly war with Napoleon Bonaparte in Europe, Britain had sent a squadron to blockade French ships in Chesapeake Bay that were attempting to purchase American supplies. Several Royal Navy seamen jumped ship, and local American authorities granted them sanctuary. One of the deserters joined the crew of the USS *Chesapeake*, which provoked the captain of the *Leopard* to blast away at the *Chesapeake* until the outgunned American frigate struck her colors and surrendered not only a British-born deserter but also three Royal Navy deserters of American birth. The American public was outraged. War fever gripped the land. Rather than risk a conflict for which the United States was unprepared, President Jefferson imposed an embargo on British goods, a response that satisfied few and brought economic hardship to much of the nation.

On the American frontier, the *Leopard-Chesapeake* affair not only released latent anti-British sentiment exacerbated by numerous cases of the Royal Navy "impressing" American sailors into its service, but it also raised the specter of a British-instigated Indian uprising should the United States and Great Britain go to war. Finding Tenskwatawa's doctrine incomprehensible or worse, most American officials assumed him to be a British puppet waiting for his master to pull the strings of war. Sensing an opportunity, Black Hoof also warned the Americans that the British were stirring up trouble at Greenville.

In truth, the British were not abetting Tenskwatawa; in fact, they had no idea what to make of the Prophet's faith. Between 1795 and 1807, British interest in the Indians had declined. Only the bellicose American reaction to the *Leopold-Chesapeake* affair caused them to take a renewed interest in their old allies. Even then, it fell far short of material support.

Reality, however, often played no part in the fevered imaginings of many frontiersmen, Gov. William Henry Harrison included. Many pioneers were Revolutionary War veterans and shared the governor's visceral distrust, if not his outright hatred, of all things British. That so many Tories (American colonists who had supported the British side during the American Revolution) now lived just across the border in Canada was also cause for continued mistrust.

After the eclipse debacle of the year before, Harrison had had nothing further to say about the Shawnee Prophet or Greenville, which after all lay outside his jurisdiction. But the *Leopold-Chesapeake* affair rekindled his near-paranoid hatred of the British and their imagined intrigues. "The blood rises to my cheeks when I reflect on the humiliating, disgraceful scene aboard the *Chesapeake*," he told the Indiana legislature. "We are indeed, from our situation, peculiarly interested in the contest which is about to ensue; for who does not know that the tomahawk and the scalping knife of the savages are always employed as the instruments of British vengeance. At this moment, fellow citizens, as I sincerely believe, their agents are organizing a combination amongst the Indians for the purposes of assassination and murder."[3]

Overstepping his jurisdiction, Harrison sent John Conner, a long-time Indian trader and former captive of the Shawnees, to Wapakoneta to rebuke Black Hoof, of all people, for abetting the Prophet. "My children, it must be stopped," scolded Harrison. "I will no longer suffer it. You have called in a number of men from the most distant tribes to listen to a fool who speaks not the words of the Great Spirit but those of the Devil and the British agents."

Black Hoof, who may have thought Harrison a fool, chose not to respond. Conner then made his way to Greenville. Tenskwatawa gave him a brief reply to take to the governor in which he truthfully claimed never to have "had a word with the British" and enjoined the governor not to listen to "bad birds" who fluttered about chirping false rumors. Tecumseh had no message for Harrison. But he did unburden himself to his old friend Conner. Lamenting the government's "lax performance" in meeting its treaty obligations, Tecumseh foresaw a day when the Indians would be pushed farther west or else exterminated through the "bitterness and hate of the white man who coveted his land." Perhaps a new alliance with Great Britain might postpone the inevitable day. Conner evidently held Tecumseh's musings in confidence because Harrison had nothing yet to say about him, if he even was aware of his existence. But the governor growled on about the Shawnee Prophet, calling him a "vile instrument" of the British whose sole purpose was to seduce the Indians into fighting for the Crown.[4]

William Wells shared Harrison's absurd opinion of the Prophet. Estimating that Tenskwatawa commanded the allegiance of three hundred warriors, he urged the War Department to expel him from Greenville, where "there is great reason to believe some mischief will be done." He directed similar appeals to Harrison and to Gov. Thomas Kirker of Ohio. (Edward Tiffin had resigned to take a seat in the Senate.)[5]

The only evidence Wells had to back up his assertion was the testimony of Frederick Fisher, who claimed that the Prophet had told him that he cared no more for the Americans than for the dust at his feet. Thereupon, he said, Tenskwatawa had risen to his feet, farted loudly, slapped his ass, and threatened to yank down the moon and stamp it and the Americans underfoot.[6]

Stephen Ruddell added his voice to the accusatory choir. Although not predicting war, he blamed his soul-saving rivals the Shakers for what unrest did exist at Greenville, accusing them of funneling to the Prophet the money and foodstuffs needed to maintain a large transient population of Indian pilgrims. Wells echoed the charge, and frontiersmen added baseless accusations that the Shakers were also providing Tenskwatawa with ammunition. In fact, the Shakers had helped feed the Prophet's people, but they stopped after angry Ohioans threatened to run them out of the state.[7]

Ultimately cooler heads prevailed. In late August, Simon Kenton, William Ward, and two other seasoned frontiersmen took the pulse of Greenville themselves. They found the Indian pilgrims peaceable, drawn there only to learn the Prophet's religious creed. A well-placed Quaker at Wapakoneta agreed. He thought the Indian sojourners at Greenville "sober and friendly disposed...without any intention of molesting our people." Governor Kirker proved as prudent as his predecessor. In early September he asked former senator Thomas Worthington and militia colonel Duncan McArthur to travel to Greenville to "ascertain the number and disposition of the Indians."

Worthington and McArthur departed Chillicothe on September 8. Stephen Ruddell joined them on the road as interpreter. On September 13 the trio rode tentatively into Greenville, unsure what to expect. All three well understood how rapidly the mood of a crowd might shift. But Blue Jacket and Tecumseh met them "in a friendly way and gave us a kind reception." They had been "much agitated and anxious about their safety," the chiefs told Worthington and McArthur, having learned that the settlers on Mad River were marshaling a force to march against their village. They were about to hold their own council to determine how to respond and invited the governor's commissioners to join them.

At two p.m. on September 13, the Shawnee chiefs ushered Worthington, McArthur, and Ruddell into the whitewashed council house.

Worthington and McArthur carefully counted the number of Indians present. One hundred seventy-three chiefs and warriors sat expectantly in a semicircle on the immaculately swept dirt floor; another twenty-five men crowded about the doors. Council attendees included Shawnees, Potawatomis, Ojibwas, Ottawas, Menominees, Winnebagos, Sauks, and Wyandots.

In keeping with Indian protocol, the chiefs bade Worthington and McArthur to speak first. The Americans read a letter from Governor Kirker reminding them how flimsy British friendship had always proven, particularly after Fallen Timbers, when the redcoats had "shut their gates against you and driven you away like dogs." War between the United States and Great Britain appeared in the offing. But the Indians had best stay out lest they be thrashed by a (fictious) one-hundred-thousand-man army that the Great Father had assembled to invade Canada. Worthington and McArthur also asked why the Prophet had built his town on the American side of the Greenville Treaty line, which had frightened the settlers and compelled the governor to call out fifteen hundred militiamen.

The militia call-up startled Blue Jacket and Tecumseh. They invited their guests to remain overnight; a formal reply would be forthcoming on the morrow. As the council dispersed, Blue Jacket buttonholed Ruddell. He handed him an Ohio newspaper and asked him to translate a speech attributed to the Prophet. Ruddell obliged. Blue Jacket insisted it was bogus; Tenskwatawa himself resented it as slanderous, adding that people constantly misinterpreted or told lies about him and his doctrine. Frederick Fisher's fart-and-ass-slap anecdote especially incensed him, or so the Shawnee Prophet pretended. The truth of the matter cannot be known, but it would have been consistent with Tenskwatawa's nature to have leveled such an insult as Fisher alleged.[8]

Tecumseh deferred to his elder mentor Blue Jacket, who stood in council the next morning to deliver the official Indian reply. He pronounced the residents of Greenville unafraid of the Americans but peaceable. "If our white brethren are going to war," Blue Jacket said, "their red brethren have formed a determined resolution to interfere in no way, but to sit still and mind their own concerns." Then Blue Jacket surprised the commissioners, calling Indian agent William Wells a bad man and "disturber of our peace" who ought to be dismissed. The commissioners rebutted Blue Jacket, suggesting that

Black Hoof and the Wapakoneta chiefs had induced Wells to suspect the motives of the Greenville Shawnees.

Tenskwatawa rose next. He had violated the treaty line to build Greenville not because the site was attractive or valuable—it was neither—but because the Master of Life had revealed the place to him as best suited to teach His sacred doctrines. And then Tenskwatawa pleasantly surprised the commissioners. The Great Spirit's revelations were not immutable: The Indians intended to abandon Greenville the following spring and settle somewhere along the Wabash River on Indian land. (Tenskwatawa and the chiefs may have concluded there simply were too many jittery whites nearby to make Greenville viable.) They hoped to establish a large village in the Wabash country and begged the commissioners to use their influence to have Stephen Ruddell appointed both their agent and the keeper of the store that they hoped the government would establish in their new town. The latter request was rather incongruent given Tenskwatawa's professed antipathy to American goods, but pragmatism, it seems, was slowly undermining the Prophet's absolutist dogma.

As a final expression of good faith, Tenskwatawa offered to have Tecumseh, Blue Jacket, Roundhead, and a fourth chief accompany the commissioners to Chillicothe, where they could personally apprise the governor and the public of their benign intent. Tecumseh had yielded to Blue Jacket during the council with the governor's emissaries, but in Chillicothe he would have a large audience. And he would be heard.

On September 15 the chiefs and commissioners set out for Chillicothe. Before leaving, Worthington and McArthur completed their surreptitious count of Greenville's population. They calculated the resident community at 305, of whom 80 were men, and the total number then in town at 505, of whom 240 were men. Worthington thought their mission had been a monumental waste of time. Nothing about the place had struck them as warlike. "After the strictest enquiry, we could hear of nothing which left a doubt in our minds as to their sincerity," the commissioners told Kirker. "There was no hostile appearance— their women and children were engaged generally in their ordinary labor. We were treated with great hospitality and kindness from all."

Both commissioners were impressed with Tenskwatawa. McArthur styled him "an orator of the first class." Worthington marveled at the Prophet's "astonishing influence among his red brethren." So far as Worthington was able to see, "his life was in harmony with his doctrines," his adherents inoffensive and sober-minded.[9]

The good impression was mutual. On one occasion while the party lodged at the Worthington farm outside of Chillicothe, Tecumseh pulled aside Ruddell and, pointing to Worthington, who walked a few paces ahead of them, whispered, "That man is a good man and has treated us so kindly that I could not lift my tomahawk against him in battle."[10]

Senator Worthington's son James watched Tecumseh intently during his weeklong stay at the family farm. The chief spoke little and dressed simply in a fringed buckskin suit without gorgets, bracelets, or earrings. Blue Jacket and Roundhead gave him a wide berth. Tecumseh paced daily around Adena, the ample, two-story, freestone-constructed Worthington estate. Tucked into a range of high hills west of Chillicothe, near a huge prehistoric Indian burial mound of the same name, Adena overlooked the Scioto Valley. The summer had receded, yielding to a cornucopia of flaming leaves that certainly stirred in Tecumseh boyhood memories both pleasant and grim. His birthplace on the outskirts of the old Shawnee village of Chillicothe, now plowed over by pioneers, lay a scant sixty miles away. The wooded spring beside which Methoataske had given birth to him remained unchanged, no more than a leisurely hour's horseback ride from the Worthington place. With childhood remembrances tugging at him and his forthcoming speech taking shape in his mind, it is no wonder that Tecumseh struck the Worthington boy as perpetually lost in thought, "grave and reserved in manner," and so inward focused that he never uttered a word in English. Blue Jacket and Roundhead, on the other hand, conversed politely with Mrs. Worthington.[11]

James Worthington might have caught Tecumseh silently rehearsing the speech he intended to give at the Chillicothe courthouse. There, on the morning of September 19, 1807, the governor, state and local officials, and an edgy public gathered to hear the Greenville notables. The four chiefs took their places in the courtroom, a snug, two-story brick structure that also served as the statehouse. Several taverns, stores, and artisan shops, ranging from the tidy to the rough-hewn, stood nearby. Although the town had fewer than fifteen hundred people, it was the largest white community Tecumseh had ever visited. Nevertheless, he appeared at ease. His manners and those of his companions were "familiar, unassuming, and engaging." Governor Kirker, whom one observer thought "a weak and rather blundering speaker," opened the proceedings. Then anxious heads turned toward Blue Jacket. The Ohioans instantly warmed to the old man of "extremely dignified [and] of calm persuasive eloquence." Reviewing six decades of conflict in which the Indians had been passed about as pawns of the French and British, only to lose their lands, Blue Jacket concluded sadly, "We have deluged the country with blood to satiate our revenge, and all to no purpose—we have been the sufferers. The Great Spirit has shown us the vanity of these things. We have laid down the tomahawk never to take it up again."[12]

The courtroom breathed a collective sigh of relief. The question remained, however, as to the comings and goings of distant Indians to Greenville. And what of the purported Prophet? The Indians came to pray, not to fight; the Prophet instilled in them moral principles to ensure their welfare and future happiness, Blue Jacket assured his listeners, his voice faltering with authentic emotion that Governor Kirker appreciated.

Then Tecumseh stood and cast his gaze over the crowd. The first impression he made was raw and powerful. "He appeared one of the most dignified men I ever beheld," recalled a newspaperman. Tecumseh addressed the courtroom, slowly at first, then with a swift eloquence that so captivated listeners that no one thought to transcribe his speech. For nearly three hours Tecumseh held forth, the audience "preserving the most profound silence" while he orated in Shawnee and Ruddell interpreted. Tecumseh echoed Blue Jacket's pledge of peace. But he also declaimed against the Treaty of Greenville, which had hemmed his people into a small quadrant of northwestern Ohio. And Tecumseh railed against Governor Harrison's questionable treaties. Occasionally his composure deserted him. A future mayor of Chillicothe detected the anger and grief that Tecumseh fought hard to contain: "His utterance was vehement, his manner and bearing bold and commanding, his gestures differing from his ordinary manner remarkably quick... as if something within was struggling for utterance more than he deemed prudent to allow escape." Although bitter about the past, Tecumseh reiterated his resolve to adhere to the terms of the Greenville Treaty and respect existing cessions. But there he drew the line. Tecumseh vowed to contest any further land sales—not alone but with a confederation of like-minded Indians drawn from many tribes—by inference, the warriors who comprised the heart and soul of his brother's revitalization movement.[13]

Not only did Tecumseh say he would abide by the Greenville Treaty, but he surprised listeners by announcing that the Greenville Indians were about to pull up stakes and set out for an as-yet-to-be determined location on the Wabash River in the Indiana Territory. Practicality had trumped the sacred. Apparently the followers of Tenskwatawa were not yet sufficiently pure of heart, because the multitude of deer that the Master of Life had promised to bring forth from the earth to feed the faithful had not materialized. Faced with the real prospect of starvation if they remained longer with their growing numbers in a country nearly depleted of game animals, the Shawnee brothers had decided to look to the unspoiled Wabash country for a new home.

While he was fond of Ohioans, Tecumseh reviled Black Hoof and William Wells. The year before at Springfield, Tecumseh had buried the hatchet with Black Hoof, but now he condemned the Mekoche chief as an enemy who spread vicious lies about Tenskwatawa. And then Tecumseh prevaricated. Black Hoof, he declared, was "a king without subjects" who had lost most of his people to the Prophet. As for Wells, he had aligned himself with Black Hoof to prejudice the Americans against Tenskwatawa. Wells also "set doors" to prevent northern Indians from coming to hear him preach. The courtroom reverberated with Tecumseh's rage. "Congress has a great many good men," he thundered. "Let them take away Wells and put one of them there—we hate him. If *they* will not remove him, *we will*."

Tecumseh concluded late in the afternoon. Governor Kirker wanted to hear more about his threat to remove Wells. Tecumseh backtracked; he meant to say that the Greenville Shawnees would simply ignore Wells. With that, Kirker adjourned the meeting. It was a grand success for the chiefs. The citizenry went home, their fears allayed. Kirker discharged the militiamen and wrote President Jefferson that the Indians had given "every satisfaction I could ask," adding that the Prophet's doctrines were "such as will do them honor." He even forwarded Tecumseh's request that Wells be replaced. Like his constituents, Kirker was pleased that the Prophet intended to vacate Greenville and asked Jefferson to do all he could to facilitate their move to the Wabash. The local newspaper rhapsodized about the "manly, firm, and majestic deportment" of Blue Jacket and Tecumseh and their repeated invocations of the Great Spirit to witness the "rectitude of their intentions and truth of what they advanced."[14]

The Chillicothe council marked the public debut of Tecumseh's earthly vision. Few if any seem to have appreciated the enormity of Tecumseh's allusions to a possible future pan-Indian alliance to resist American encroachment. Although the state population was growing briskly, Ohioans had more land than they could use profitably. They were satisfied knowing themselves safe from Indian attack on their side of the Greenville Treaty line.

On the eve of the chiefs' departure, Thomas Worthington held an elaborate banquet in their honor. Beforehand he enjoined his children to take no notice of any "eccentricities" the Indians might display, nor get upset over any contretemps of etiquette that might occur. It was not with his children that Worthington needed concern himself, however, but rather his friends and neighbors. In serving coffee, a waiter overlooked one of the chiefs. From the Indian viewpoint, such an omission at a friendly feast opened a fine field for banter at the expense of the "coffeeless" chief. As the jesting grew boisterous, the white guests became tense and not a little fearful that the Indians were angry. Tecumseh intervened. He drew Mrs. Worthington's attention to the oversight, and the grateful hostess poured the neglected chief "gospel measures of coffee" for the remainder of the reception. When not exercising his good offices, Tecumseh ate heartily despite Tenskwatawa's injunctions against consuming white foodstuffs. Before the chiefs departed, Stephen Ruddell assured the Worthington family that the entertainment had delighted them. In the waning days of September 1807, goodwill was the watchword of Indians and Ohioans.[15]

Chief Black Hoof was scarcely the king without subjects that Tecumseh alleged. To be sure, the Prophet had won over eighty of the best warriors in the Shawnee nation—or at least that portion still residing east of the Mississippi River. That angered the Wapakoneta chiefs, but their town was far from deserted. A vibrant community, it achieved small victories on the bumpy road to peaceable assimilation and suffered anguishing setbacks occasioned by erratic government policy. It endured with a permanent population of approximately eight hundred Mekoche and Chillicothe Shawnees—nearly four times the number of Shawnees resident at Greenville. To most Shawnees, Wapakoneta represented the best hope of survival short of migrating westward. For Tecumseh and Tenskwatawa, it was the road not taken—unmanly acquiescence rather than principled defiance; unacceptable acculturation over a vigorous revitalization of the traditional ways as they had evolved during the century-long alliance with the French. And it was a bitter irony that while the Shawnee brothers commanded followers from distant tribes, they proved unable to unite their own.

In February 1807, Black Hoof again asked President Jefferson to grant the residents of Wapakoneta title to their land. He also conceded the virtues of Jefferson's "civilizing" mission. "You express a wish to have your lands laid off separately to yourselves," the president summarized in a reply, "that you may know what is your own, may have a fixed place to live on of which you may not be deprived after you shall have built on it and improved it." In a word, Black Hoof said the Shawnees wanted to pursue the settler's dream—even if that meant Shawnee men would eventually have to work the fields, and the women take up white domestic-arts. He presented Jefferson with a singular opportunity to make good on his civilizing promise.

But the president declined to grant Black Hoof's principal request. Wapakoneta lay on Indian land, and the government did not "intermeddle as to the lines dividing" one tribe from another. The chief had also asked for carpenters, blacksmiths, and others capable of teaching his people the white manner of living. Here Jefferson was more accommodating, dispatching the zealous, hardworking Quaker missionary and farmer William Kirk to instruct them. Kirk originally had been destined for Little Turtle and Five Medals' Miami and Potawatomi villages near Fort Wayne, but he had run afoul of both chiefs and of Wells, largely because he was too eager—Little Turtle had not yet been able to persuade his young warriors to take up farming, preordaining the project's failure. The Wapakoneta Shawnees, on the other hand, were grateful for Kirk's guidance and worked hard. The indefatigable Kirk arrived at Wapakoneta in August 1807. Before the end of autumn, the Shawnees—men and women pooling their sacred powers in an unprecedented cultural shift—had cleared five hundred acres of farmland. They built rail fences, planted apple trees, bought hogs and cattle, and supplemented their traditional corn and bean crops with potatoes, cabbage, and turnips. "Comfortable houses of hewn logs and chimneys" began to replace wigwams, and work commenced on a gristmill. Visiting Ohioans returned home full of praise for the sober and industrious Shawnees.[16]

Word of Kirk's early success infuriated the Prophet. He and Tecumseh also were winning over their white neighbors in Ohio—to whom they would soon bid farewell—but they were losing the epochal war for the Shawnee soul. And then in November 1807 came word that Michigan Territory governor William Hull had cajoled thirty northern chiefs into signing the Treaty of Detroit, by which the Indians ceded to the United States nearly all of what became southeastern Michigan together with a desirable sliver of Indian land in northwestern Ohio that included the Fallen Timbers battlefield. The Americans paid two cents an acre for land that would have been worth $2.50 per acre at auction. Outrage greeted the treaty signatories. Grumbling that "their chiefs would sell all their land and ruin them," young warriors throughout the Northwest clamored to be heard in the council houses. But no one yet contemplated open resistance to the Americans. At Chillicothe two months earlier, Tecumseh had harangued his white listeners with the prospect of a mighty pan-Indian confederation determined to oppose further land cessions. Despite this latest provocation, for the moment such an alliance existed only in Tecumseh's mind.[17]

Two and a half years had passed since Lalawethika glimpsed the spirit world and became Tenskwatawa. His fame as a holy man had spread from the Ohio River to the Canadian border. But permanent disciples were few. Hundreds of pilgrims had visited him, and another thousand, Winnebagos and Menominees mostly, were traveling the forest trails from the distant Green Bay country to hear the Prophet's creed. But with their own country intact, they had little incentive to commit themselves to an alliance that might bring war. The Potawatomis, Ojibwas, Ottawas, and Wyandots were divided, with many potential recruits reluctant to accept the Prophet's strict code of conduct. Pilgrims to Greenville also drifted home after a few weeks' stay simply to avoid starving. With game scarce and crops inadequate, returning Indians frequently begged rations from William Wells, who fed them to prevent their plundering of frontier settlements.

By year's end the three principal chiefs of the Ohio and Indiana territories—Black Hoof, Little Turtle, and Tarhe—were aligned against the Shawnee brothers. Tarhe had sent his trusted subordinate Chief Between-the-Logs to Greenville to study the Prophet's doctrine. Between-the-Logs spent a year with the Shawnee brothers and returned home convinced that the Prophet was a delusionary fraud.[18] Only two chiefs of consequence—the great Blue Jacket and the lesser Roundhead—had allied themselves with the Prophet, and their personal followings were small. Parlaying his fame into lasting influence over large numbers of Indians had proven elusive for Tenskwatawa. But then in late October 1807 one of the most powerful and fearsome Indian leaders of his day rode into Greenville to confer with the Shawnee brothers. If Tenskwatawa and Tecumseh could persuade him to make common cause with them, they would acquire an ally capable of shifting the balance of intertribal politics.

Main Poc was a human whirlwind, striking terror and awe into friends and foes alike. The mere thought of him made William Wells tremble. Main Poc was the "greatest warrior in the West," Wells told his superiors, a "dangerous man" and "pivot on which the minds of all the Western Indians turned."[19]

Like Tecumseh, Main Poc was fortyish (his precise birth year is unknown) and the son of a prominent war leader. There the resemblance ended. Unlike Tecumseh, he also was a holy man, the foremost *wabeno* (sorcerer) of the Illinois River Potawatomis. The Three Fires (Potawatomis, Ottawas, and Ojibwas) tribes believed that *wabenos* possessed magical powers that could be channeled for great good or deep evil. They were capable of transforming themselves into living fireballs to incinerate enemies, or into animals that prowled their own villages after dark sniffing out dissenters. Well-schooled in pharmacognosy, *wabenos* were able to cure diseases and reputedly could control the weather, speak with spirits, and prognosticate. Potawatomis blamed personal misfortunes—illness, accidents, battle wounds, loss of property or lovers, and so forth—on the machinations of evil medicine. Tribesmen attached themselves to a *wabeno* in order to obtain protection against malevolent conjurers, for which they compensated their protector with gifts of tobacco, liquor, or trade goods.

Main Poc owed his power partially to a deformity. He had been born without fingers or a thumb on his left hand, hence his name, which meant "Withered Hand." Main Poc turned this liability into a virtue, claiming that his birth defect was a divine gift that enabled the Great Spirit to differentiate him from other Indians, and to compensate for which the Great Spirit also gave him powers far beyond those of an ordinary *wabeno*. Not only could Main Poc communicate with spirits, but unlike the Shawnee Prophet, who relied on random visions for his celestial messages, he also professed to speak directly with the Great Spirit at will. Main Poc could also protect his warriors in battle—he himself being immune to bullets, as he had the power to see them in flight—and defeat enemies handily.

Despite his deformity, Main Poc was imposing. A huge, muscular man with long black hair, he had a "surly and brooding countenance" and dark eyes that bored into a subject's soul. A stirring orator, Main Poc also was something of a showman. He girdled his waist with a belt of human scalps and wore strings of bear claws and hawk beaks around his ankles. He regularly retreated deep into the forest to a solitary lodge, where he would commune with the Great Spirit. Once back in his village, Main Poc would maintain a silence fraught with anticipation. He waited until the fortunate soul he wished to address was present; to him, Main Poc would impart the Great Spirit's message, together with whatever Main Poc himself might have in mind. Main Poc preempted those who might question why he did not employ his immense power against the Americans, whom he despised. Americans, Main Poc lamented, ate too much salt for his medicine to have any effect on them; otherwise he long since would have destroyed them.

Main Poc's hatred of the Americans dated from at least 1802, when the U.S. government had established a military presence in the Illinois country. That autumn a company of troops garrisoned the old French bastion of Kaskaskia. The following summer a detachment marched from Detroit to establish a fort at the mouth of the Chicago River. The new post, Fort Dearborn, was raised on a small parcel of the Potawatomi heartland ceded in the Greenville Treaty. In the years to come, the fort would prove a casus belli for the Illinois River Potawatomis.

Main Poc's people embraced him as divine. The western Potawatomis told Indian agent Thomas Forsyth that Main Poc "was not born of a woman but that he was got by the Great Spirit and sprang out of the ground, and that the Great Spirit marked him in consequence without fingers on his left hand." So great was their veneration of Main Poc and fear of his power that his partisans tolerated monstrous outbursts that would have cost any other Indian man his life. A notorious alcoholic, when drunk he brutalized both kinsmen and friends and raped any female to whom he took a fancy (this despite having no fewer than three wives—all sisters—and often as many as six). Even sober he was a dangerous adversary. Main Poc obtained a good supply of arsenic from British traders, with which he eliminated rival *wabenos*.[20]

Main Poc's talents transcended the realm of the *wabeno*. He also was an accomplished war leader who led immense parties of Potawatomis, Sauks, Foxes, and Kickapoos against their mutual tribal enemy, the Osages. When not striking at their native foes, Main Poc's war parties often cut wide swaths of destruction through fledgling American settlements in the southern Illinois country and attacked the Miamis on contested ground along the Wabash River.

Main Poc likely learned of Tenskwatawa from the Kickapoos, who were among the Prophet's earliest disciples. Fortunately for Tenskwatawa, the truculent Potawatomi regarded him not as a rival but as a potential ally against the Americans. At Greenville they conferred through interpreters for two months. The Prophet failed to prevail in their doctrinal disputes. Saying that the Great Spirit told him if he ever stopped drinking or fighting, he would sink to the level of a commoner, Main Poc rejected both Tenskwatawa's temperance program and his strictures against warring on other Indians. He also feared losing face with the Illinois tribes if he yielded too much to the Shawnee. Main Poc agreed that the Americans were spawn of the Great Serpent, however, and offered to help propagate portions of the Prophet's creed when he returned home. And Main Poc made a providential suggestion. The Shawnee brothers wanted to move to the Wabash country but had no precise destination. Main Poc offered them a spot near the junction of the Tippecanoe and Wabash rivers in country the Potawatomis had wrested from the Miamis. Well removed from the white frontier, the place was plentiful in game and far less vulnerable to American attack than Greenville, or so said Main Poc.

The Shawnee brothers held a council to consider the offer, to which they invited their Potawatomi friends. Somehow Tenskwatawa convinced his believers that Greenville was no longer the sole sacred place of the Master of Life's choosing. The only one present who spoke out against the move was Zachariah Cicot, the son of a Canadian trapper and a Potawatomi mother. A well-educated horse breeder who served the Potawatomis and the Kickapoos, Cicot disliked the Shawnee brothers. A few Potawatomis voted with him, but they were a hopeless minority. And so the deal was struck. Come the spring of 1808, the Shawnee brothers and their adherents would abandon Greenville and reestablish themselves deep in the unceded portion of the Indiana Territory. His business concluded, Main Poc departed Greenville in December with twenty warriors.[21]

Despite Tenskwatawa's plan to relocate, William Wells saw an opportunity to score a win over him—or so he imagined. Wells's alarmist drumbeat had continued into December 1807, becoming more lurid with each letter. The Prophet was a British pawn with a huge cache of English arms supplied from Fort Malden, the principal British post in Upper Canada, Wells warned Secretary Dearborn. If not thwarted, he intended to decimate the frontier settlements in the spring. Nor was Wells alone in his wrongheaded assessment. Indian factor John Johnston—apparently unaware that the Shawnee brothers intended to move—similarly advocated a preemptive strike against Greenville, saying, "The sooner they are dispersed the better, and in my humble opinion, if nothing else will do, force ought to be used."[22]

The treaty chiefs were playing Wells and Johnston, feeding them rumors or telling them outright lies in the hope that the government would neutralize the threat the Prophet posed to their leadership. Tecumseh had yet to appear in dispatches from Wells, Johnston, or any other government officer in the Northwest—all eyes were squarely on Tenskwatawa. That is, until Main Poc and his men paused at Fort Wayne on their way home to the Illinois country. The Potawatomi *wabeno* let drop that he had left his best warriors at Greenville to help Tenskwatawa launch a spring offensive against the settlements. It was a self-serving lie—the Prophet had no hostile intentions—but it caused Wells to dote on the Potawatomi during the long, lean winter months to "prevent his ever listening to the Prophet again." Housed and fed for the winter at government expense, Main Poc acted suitably contrite. He said Wells had hobbled him like a wild horse caught in a salt lick and he should now have a bell on his neck so that the agent would always know his whereabouts. But Wells pressed his luck. He also urged Main Poc to make peace with the Osages, who by the terms of the Louisiana Purchase lived under American protection. The Potawatomi treaty chief Winamac had buried the hatchet—why could not Main Poc? The *wabeno* snickered; Winamac was a dog, not fit to mend his moccasins. Hoping a talk with the Great Father might convince him, Wells offered to arrange for Main Poc to visit the capital. Main Poc agreed and then headed home with a full stomach, horseloads of provisions and trade goods, and a deeper contempt for the easily manipulated Americans.

No sooner had Wells bade farewell to Main Poc than he bored into Tenskwatawa. The Shawnee Prophet, Tecumseh, their brother-in-law Wahsikegaboe, and seventy-nine warriors were slogging through the spring muck toward the Wabash River southwest of Fort Wayne to break ground for a new village; the women and children would follow once the men had staked their claim. "It is not yet known where the chiefs of this agency will suffer him to settle," Wells reported. If the pugnacious agent could marshal enough support from Little Turtle and his chiefs, he hoped to suffer the Prophet to settle in hell.[23]

A Double Game

TECUMSEH TRAVELED LIGHT. He divorced his third wife Wabelegunequa in 1807 because she was unhealthy and unable to conceive. Tecumseh's son Paukeesa lived with Tecumpease, removing another burden. Freed physically and emotionally, Tecumseh was increasingly his own man with ambitions distinct from those of Tenskwatawa. At the public meeting in Chillicothe he had articulated an outline for Indian resistance that gave earthly muscle to his brother's divine creed. Tenskwatawa embraced Tecumseh's sentiments. Henceforth he would espouse them as vigorously as did Tecumseh. Tenskwatawa remained the leader of the nascent Indian confederation. Tecumseh accepted the subordinate role as spokesman and chief messenger for the Prophet. But their relationship had become truly reciprocal. Neither stood much chance of success without the other. If their public pronouncements are any indication, both seemed satisfied with the arrangement.

In the spring of 1808 the obstacles to their mutual objective of a spiritually purified, pan-Indian alliance appeared formidable. Blue Jacket had fallen ill and died, robbing the Shawnee brothers of a thoughtful adviser and senior statesman. Game had all but vanished from the Greenville area. Starvation stalked the town, and the winter witnessed a steady decrease in the Prophet's ranks until just eighty warriors and their families—perhaps two hundred people in all—remained to make the long and muddy journey to the Wabash.[1]

Plenty of Indians were intent on preventing them from reaching their new home. Miami and Delaware chiefs whose villages stood astride the Prophet's path assembled with Wapakoneta Shawnee leaders on the banks of the Mississinewa River, a sluggish tributary of the Wabash, to plot a course of action. For ten days they talked. Finally, as Chief Little Turtle phrased it, they had "sufficient evidence before them that the Shawnee Prophet had determined to settle low down on the Wabash and draw all the western Indians together and commence war against those Indians that would not listen to him," after which he would attack the Americans. That was patently false, but it suited the council's purpose, and they elected Little Turtle and nine other chiefs to tell the Prophet to turn back. (Regardless of Main Poc's representations to the contrary, Tenskwatawa knew that the land on which he intended to settle rightfully belonged to the Miamis.) If the Prophet refused, Little Turtle was to tell him that the Miamis and Delawares must "cut him off," in other words, kill Tenskwatawa and slaughter his adherents.

Little Turtle, the nine chiefs, and a small retinue of Delaware warriors met the Prophet's party farther down the Mississinewa, where they were building canoes and rafts to descend the Wabash. Little Turtle delivered the council's decree. The Prophet set aside his tools and approached the chiefs. Potawatomi warriors loyal to Main Poc quit their work to undertake "religious duties," which consisted of firing arrows and hurling their tomahawks at targets. The tension mounted, and the Delawares grew wary.

Tenskwatawa spoke. No earthly council could prevent him from fulfilling the Master of Life's command that he erect a new town near the Tippecanoe River. (Tenskwatawa elevated Main Poc's invitation to the level of divine mandate.) There they "would be able to watch the boundary line between the Indians and the white people, and if a white man put his foot over it the warriors could easily put him back." Tenskwatawa declaimed against war but would tolerate no further treaties with the "three evil white men"—William Wells, Governor Hull, and Governor Harrison. The Prophet also took a swipe at Black Hoof, whose Quaker "master" William Kirk was reshaping the Wapakoneta warriors into women. "But," added Tenskwatawa, "when the Indians were all united, they would be respected by the president as men." Warming to the subject, the Prophet claimed to be in regular contact with the Illinois tribes and with the British. He relied on

Main Poc to make good his promise to meet him on the Wabash with hundreds of Potawatomi, Sauk, Fox, and Kickapoo warriors "when the corn was ripe." In the meantime, the Prophet's famished people would requisition provisions from Indiana settlers, who dared not refuse him. The Prophet had only to look at a white man, and the man would "give him anything he wanted." Tenskwatawa's bluster left Little Turtle unmoved. He considered the Prophet desperate and on the decline. But his fellow chiefs decided to let the intruders alone for the moment.[2]

Ten days elapsed. The Miami and Delaware delegation returned with an ultimatum: Tenskwatawa must turn back or die. The Prophet refused to meet with them. Instead he sent Tecumseh and the tomahawk-tossing Potawatomis, who together so overawed the Delaware contingent that Little Turtle and the Miami chiefs, isolated and outnumbered, permitted the Prophet to proceed downriver.[3]

Wells reported the proceedings to the War Department, together with Little Turtle's assessment that Tenskwatawa's influence was on the wane. Harrison, on the other hand, overstated the Prophet's standing, writing in May 1808, "The Shawnee Imposter has acquired such an ascendency over the minds of the Indians that there can be little doubt of their pursuing any course which he might dictate to them and that his views are decidedly hostile to the United State is but too evident." While Harrison fretted and fumed about these new Indian troublemakers in his backyard, Tenskwatawa and his followers paddled down the Wabash River unmolested toward the home Main Poc had promised them.

Tenskwatawa's speech on the Mississinewa confirmed his acceptance of the shift from a purely spiritual solution to white encroachment toward the muscular response that Tecumseh had warned of at Chillicothe. The food shortages at Greenville had shaken the Prophet's confidence in divine intervention and righteous living as the panacea to Indian problems. Tenskwatawa's talk of hard and fast boundaries between Indian and white lands, and of large numbers of warriors from multiple tribes "united" in a common cause, also reflected Tecumseh's emerging influence. Although it was Tenskwatawa's mystical authority that attracted adherents from the northern and western tribes, a growing practicality leavened his movement. The Shawnee brothers worked in concert, each drawing on the other's talents, to meet to the dual challenge of white aggression and accommodationist chiefs.

They called their new village Prophetstown. The site stood on the northwest bank of the wide and winding Wabash River eight miles northeast of today's Lafayette, Indiana. Two miles upstream the gentle Tippecanoe River enters the Wabash from the north. Prophetstown, when completed, would occupy a strategic position in the Indiana Territory, standing between the Indian agency at Fort Wayne (roughly one hundred miles to the northeast) and the territorial capital of Vincennes (150 miles to the southwest). It would command navigation of both the Wabash and the Tippecanoe rivers. And as Main Poc had promised, a reasonable population at Prophetstown would not lack for food. The soil was fertile, and game abundant. The nearest neighbors were the Potawatomis of Winamac's town, located on the northeastern side of the Tippecanoe. A slavishly loyal government chief, Winamac wanted nothing to do with the Shawnee brothers.

Tenskwatawa superintended much of the construction of Prophetstown. Wigwams and cabins were laid out in neat rows, with lanes between them, on a forty-acre elevation above the Wabash bottomland. A large welcoming wigwam known as the House of the Stranger rose at the foot of the hill nearest the river. A council house equal in grandeur to that of Greenville commanded the landscape. The Shawnee brothers built their own dwellings near each other on the southwestern edge of Prophetstown, with an unimpeded view of the river and the abutting prairie.[4]

Tecumseh did not lack for creature comforts—or for female companionship. He erected a neat and clean cabin and had a full-time sentry to screen visitors, turning away far more than he admitted. As his Kickapoo neighbors in Prophetstown recalled, Tecumseh "kept himself aloof from the people of his village and did not participate in their sports and amusements but evinced in his whole conduct a gravity of deportment calculated to induce respect and obedience from all around him." Young men paid their respects but rarely stayed long; nor did they trouble him in large numbers. Women, however, were always welcome. Having rid himself of his older and unattractive third Shawnee wife, Tecumseh indulged his hitherto sublimated sexuality to the fullest. "Unable to withstand the temptations held out to him by the opposite sex," the Kickapoos remembered, Tecumseh became "engaged in a good deal of illicit intercourse with the females of his village."[5]

Not only did he enjoy the women, he also was pleased with his new surroundings. After a life of upheavals, he was determined to make Prophetstown his permanent home. "We must not leave this place," he would say regularly. "We must remain steadfast here, to keep those people who wear hats in check." Tecumseh was growing into middle age. He installed himself in his cabin, cossetted by willing young women and admired by aspiring warriors who wished for a war that he would prefer to avoid. He had seen another springtime under, and in 1808 he was forty years old.[6]

After their near brushes with angry militiamen at Greenville, the Shawnee brothers understood that resisting American intrusion on Indian lands depended on more than native allies alone. They must make common cause with the British. Tecumseh held no illusions about a new partnership with the capricious redcoats. "No white man who walks on the earth loves an Indian," he cautioned in council. "The white people are made up with such materials that they will always deceive us, even the British who say they love us, [it] is because they may want our services, and as we yet want their goods, we must show them some kind of friendship."[7] That Tecumseh really held such a low opinion of all whites is doubtful; his many seemingly genuine friendships with Ohioans belie the sentiment, which he may have uttered to steel his warriors against capitulation. Or perhaps he had misled the whites for whom he professed affection.

In any event, Great Britain was receptive to Indian overtures. After a decade of benign neglect, the *Chesapeake-Leopold* affair had shocked the Crown into resurrecting its Indian alliances. With the British Army stretched thin fighting Napoleon, Indian warriors—properly led and restrained by British agents and the limited number of regulars that could be spared from the Continent—appeared the best guarantor of Canadian security.

In December 1807, Sir James Craig, the governor-general of the Canadas, sent a secret letter to Francis Gore, the lieutenant governor for Upper Canada, outlining the policy that would guide the British Indian Department for the next three years. Should war with the United States occur, the Indians "would not remain idle," reasoned Craig. "If we do not employ them, there cannot exist a moment's doubt that they will be employed against us." Craig had "no hesitation in saying that we must employ them if they can be brought to act with us." But Gore must act with discretion, conciliating the chiefs with the promise of British aid, if the Americans declared war, while convincing them to refrain from precipitating a conflict. Gore in turn tasked William Claus, the deputy superintendent of Indian affairs, to assemble as many Indian leaders from the American side of the border as possible and privately remind them of the "obvious intention" of the United States ultimately to seize all their land. Claus, however, was also to dissuade tribes from taking up arms independently of Great Britain; in other words, he must persuade the chiefs to subordinate their interests to those of the Crown Matthew Elliott, the old friend of the Shawnee brothers who was about to be reappointed as Indian agent at Amherstburg, accompanied Claus to interpret and do what he could to make the message more palatable.[8]

The appointed council place was the village of Amherstburg, at the mouth of the Detroit River opposite the Michigan Territory. On the western edge of town stood Fort Malden, a ramshackle redoubt with a garrison of four dozen British regulars. Twenty miles upstream on the American side, Fort Detroit overlooked the capital of the Michigan Territory. Both Detroit and Amherstburg had their fair share of French-Canadian residents of elastic loyalty.

Tenskwatawa opened negotiations with the Crown informally. At the onset of winter, he asked the British for a small supply of clothing, a request they promptly granted. In April 1808, Tenskwatawa dispatched the Indian trader and sometime British agent Frederick Fisher to assure His Majesty's representatives in Upper Canada of his friendship and say that he would be glad to visit Amherstburg whenever the British desired.

Tenskwatawa's overture delighted Lieutenant Governor Gore, who had been unsure what to make of him. He had read Tenskwatawa's disparaging remarks about the U.S. government in American newspapers, particularly his assertion that he "could throw over the Americans as easily as a basin of water," but he had little else to go on apart from the memories of Matthew Elliott, who had last known the Prophet as the drunkard Lalawethika. Gore believed Tenskwatawa needed the British more than they needed him. Nevertheless, his "considerable influence," Gore told the governor-general, made him a man well worth cultivating.[9]

In mid-May, William Claus invited the Shawnee Prophet to Amherstburg. "I will be very glad to take you by the hand," said the deputy Indian superintendent. "And as there will be several nations with you, I will be glad to take some of their young men by the hand also." Claus's invitation put Tenskwatawa in a quandary. For the good of the Shawnee brothers' pan-Indian movement, he must accept. But with large parties of western Indians arriving at Prophetstown, Tenskwatawa hesitated to absent himself. And so he asked Tecumseh to represent him.

Tecumseh agreed to forsake his comfortable cabin and eager female bedmates. Accompanied by five warriors, he departed Prophetstown at the end of May. William Wells's Miami scouts detected him as he skirted Fort Wayne. On June 8, Tecumseh set foot for the first time on British soil. It was good to see his old friend Matthew Elliott, who lived on the outskirts of Amherstburg. The town itself was pleasant, with its tidy cottages, half-dozen two-story brick houses, and busy wharf. And the residents were friendly; they were on good terms not only with the local Wyandots and Ottawas but also with the tribes that came from distant parts to draw provisions or make representations before the British Great Father's representative—who happened to be absent. Tecumseh drew some provisions from the tumbledown warehouse that stored Indian Department supplies; then, promising to return in three days when Superintendent Claus was expected back in Amherstburg, he paddled to the west bank of the Detroit River with his retinue to retrieve their horses and explore the countryside.

Steering clear of Detroit, Tecumseh enjoyed the hospitality of the farmers whose well-tended acreage lined the riverbank from the River Rouge to Detroit. The Michigan settlers, especially those of French descent, were well disposed toward the Indians—a rational approach because their security depended on the sufferance of the neighboring Wyandots and Ottawas. Three days stretched to five before Tecumseh presented himself to Claus as his brother's envoy. Masking his disappointment that the Prophet had not come himself, Claus engaged

Tecumseh in a three-hour council at Fort Malden. Elliott interpreted. Four of Tecumseh's warriors also attended.

What precisely Claus and Tecumseh discussed is not known. Claus said notes were taken, but they have not been found. Claus did brief Lieutenant Governor Gore, however, who in turn encapsulated Tecumseh's remarks in a report to the governor-general. As Tecumseh apparently told it, the Shawnee brothers were "endeavoring to collect the different nations to form one settlement on the Wabash . . . in order to preserve their country from all encroachment." They intended to steer clear of the white man's quarrels, but "if the Americans encroach on them, they are resolved to strike." And if "their Father the King should be in earnest and appeared in sufficient force they would hold fast by him." Tecumseh, in a word, wanted to see troops, not merely supplies and pledges of support, before he would commit militarily to the British. While Tecumseh appeared "decidedly hostile to the United States," he also scolded the British for bad faith at Fallen Timbers, lamenting the many fine warriors who died because the gates of Fort Miamis had been closed. But in the main it was an amicable encounter. Claus gave Tecumseh a "handsome present" and asked him to remain until mid-July, when Lieutenant Governor Gore was expected. Tecumseh "cheerfully agreed" to the proposal and repaired to the Michigan Wyandot settlements of Manguaga and Brownstown. There he engaged in another first for him—intertribal diplomacy on ground other than that of the Shawnee brothers' choosing.[10]

He faced a tough challenge. As descendants of the formerly great Huron nation, the Wyandots enjoyed a prestige among their fellow Indians far in excess of their numbers. Mustering just 250 warriors, the Wyandots were trifurcated into Chief Tarhe's pro-American Sandusky band; the Michigan (Detroit River) Wyandots, whose sympathies rested with the British but whose location dictated neutrality; and a small Canadian band openly loyal to the Crown. Mostly, however, the Michigan Wyandots and their chief, the cautious and grave Walk-in-the-Water, wanted peace. Many clung to Catholicism, and even those who resisted Christianity had embraced white farming methods—adopting the plow, fencing their fields, and raising sheep and hogs in addition to horses and cattle. They had begun to replace their bark wigwams with clapboard-sided, oiled-cloth windowed, and bark-shingled or thatched-roof houses hardly distinguishable from those of their white neighbors. Some Michigan Wyandots had even adopted the white man's wardrobe in its entirety.[11]

Accommodations with the Americans notwithstanding, the Michigan Wyandots possessed the white, eight-inch-wide Great Wampum Belt that before Fallen Timbers had symbolized the British alliance with the Northwest tribes. The Indians called their side of the alliance the Council Fire, and its seat was now Brownstown. There representatives of the constituent tribes would assemble when necessary to discuss matters of war and peace.

On July 11, in near-hundred-degree heat, Tecumseh sat in the crammed council house outside the gates of Fort Malden with one hundred chiefs and one thousand warriors to hear Gore. Unlike Tecumseh, most of the Indians present were either pro-American, neutral, or only guardedly receptive to the British. It was a splendid if sweat-soaked affair, with all the pomp and ceremony Indians expected on such an august occasion. The lieutenant governor's carriage rolled onto the parade ground. The fort's guns boomed in salute, and then Gore addressed the assemblage. His public comments were anodyne and vague, in keeping with his instructions from Governor-General Craig to conduct himself with a "cautious circumspection." Tecumseh listened approvingly as Gore introduced Matthew Elliott as the new Indian superintendent at Amherstburg, and, with perhaps less enthusiasm, to the lieutenant governor's confession that he had come not to invite them to take up the hatchet but rather to be on their guard and to help the British keep the peace. After the public council, Gore invited twenty-eight chiefs to dine with him, Tecumseh included. The Prophet's brother made quite an impression on him—a "very shrewd, intelligent man" was how Gore described the stocky, buckskin-clad Shawnee to the governor-general.

In late July, Tecumseh returned to Prophetstown. His mission had been successful. Impressed by the treatment the British accorded him, the Michigan Wyandots entrusted him with the Great Wampum Belt, the symbol of the British alliance with the Indians before Fallen Timbers. It was a singular honor for a Shawnee, particularly one who was only recently known to them. Claus and Gore liked and respected Tecumseh. Governor-General Craig was moved to urge an expansion of the Indian Department. British indifference, Craig complained, had "driven the Indians into the arms of the Americans," and "though they would be of little use as friends, it [was] an object of infinite consequence to prevent them from being enemies." Craig might scoff at the natives, but Tecumseh would one day show the British the value of Indian friendship.[12]

Tecumseh found Prophetstown overflowing with warriors from the northern and western tribes—good for the cause, although less so for his nocturnal dalliances. More than seventy Winnebago and Three Fires men had augmented Tenskwatawa's following during Tecumseh's absence. Another 110 warrior-filled canoes were expected soon.

Tecumpease and the other women of Prophetstown planted as much corn as they were able, but food was so short that most of the villagers and their guests were reduced to a diet of roots and game meat. John Conner, in Prophetstown at William Wells's behest searching for stolen horses, thought the Indians were starving. Famished followers would not long remain acolytes, and so Tenskwatawa compromised his principles. He would solicit food from the spawn of the Great Serpent, the Americans. And he would dissemble to feed his people, beginning a double game that would infuriate Wells, who saw through the bluff, but that seduced Governor Harrison into embracing the Shawnee Prophet as a potential American ally. For a former drunkard and village laughingstock who had never led a single warrior in battle, Tenskwatawa was proving an able and dexterous diplomat. John Conner's brother William, a friend of the Shawnee brothers, considered Tecumseh and Tenskwatawa to be equal in oratorical and diplomatic skills at this juncture in their careers.[13]

Tenskwatawa took center stage in the unfolding diplomatic dance. He initiated contact with Harrison, sending a delegation to Vincennes in late June with a formal reply to the governor's bitter missive of the previous autumn, in which Harrison had accused the Prophet of being an instrument "of the Devil and the British agents." Through his emissaries, Tenskwatawa assured Harrison that he intended no harm to anyone. On the contrary, the Master of Life had advised him to live in peace with the Americans because "we are all His children . . . although we differ a little in color." After that egregious bit of heresy, Tenskwatawa asked Harrison for food. The move to Prophetstown had left his people in "great distress." Could the governor "assist our women and children with a little corn?"

Harrison capitulated. He accepted the Prophet's "solemn assurance" of goodwill, as well as his offer to visit Vincennes, but warned that if the Indians ever again dared to "lift up the tomahawk" against the United States, the Americans would not rest until they all were dead or driven beyond the Great Lakes. Laden with corn, hoes, and a plow, Tenskwatawa's delegation hastened back to Prophetstown. Harrison smugly informed Secretary Dearborn that the Prophet might be manipulated to effect a "radical and salutary" change in the Indians, insofar as his followers were abstemious and "no longer ashamed to cultivate the earth." Harrison had repeatedly tempted Tenskwatawa's delegates with free whiskey, which they had refused. Somehow Harrison also became convinced that the men were willing to till the soil.[14]

Tenskwatawa was elated. Not only had Tecumseh returned from Amherstburg with a promise of British assistance, but he himself had also hoodwinked Harrison. Hungry and wavering supporters heaped adulations on Tenskwatawa. Flush with his coup, Tenskwatawa departed for Vincennes. To impress the Americans with the strength of his following and further alleviate the chronic food shortage at Prophetstown, he rode with a retinue of several hundred chiefs and warriors, which the Long Knives would be forced to feed. Tecumseh remained in Prophetstown.

The Indians entered Vincennes in mid-August. For two weeks the Shawnee Prophet met intermittently with Harrison while the entourage ate heartily but abstained from whiskey, impressing both the governor and the community. Tenskwatawa had excellent intelligence on the Americans, of which he made commendable use in council. Aware that Harrison loathed William Wells, he chided the governor, saying, "Father, I was told that you intended to hang me," but then confessed that Wells had been the source of that information. Perhaps the agent lied?

Having deepened the divide between Wells and Harrison, Tenskwatawa swore that the Master of Life had directed him to teach the Indians to coexist with their American brothers, to drink no whiskey, and to "never take up the tomahawk" on behalf of either the British or the Long Knives. The Indians at Prophetstown wanted merely to mind their own business. Tenskwatawa implored Harrison to curtail the whiskey trade. He also publicly harangued his proselytes daily on the evils of alcohol and of war. Once again Harrison attempted but failed to entice the Indians to imbibe. Tenskwatawa returned to

Prophetstown with the governor's good wishes and a generous supply of corn, hoes, needles, flint, powder, and ball. He had proved a cunning if duplicitous diplomat. And he had impressed Harrison. "The celebrated Shawnee Prophet...is rather possessed of considerable talents, and the art and address with which he manages the Indians is really astonishing," Harrison told Dearborn. Tenskwatawa might even prove a useful tool. "Upon the whole, Sir, I am inclined to think that the influence which the Prophet has acquired will prove rather advantageous than otherwise to the United States."[15]

Ironically, Tenskwatawa's very success threatened to undo him. His people had struck Harrison as "the most miserable set of starved wretches" he had ever beheld. The corn rations the governor granted Tenskwatawa scarcely sufficed to feed the residents of Prophetstown, much less the hundreds of Indians who streamed into the village from the Illinois, Wisconsin, and Michigan countries throughout the summer and fall of 1808. Tenskwatawa's religious revelations and Tecumseh's calls for political unity and opposition to land cessions fed their souls, but their physical hunger grew more acute with each new arrival. Main Poc had not lied in claiming that the area teemed with game enough to support a reasonable population, but Prophetstown had become overpopulated. To make matters worse, the corn harvest came up short because the religious frenzy had caused women to neglect the crops. The men were equally remiss. Ignoring Tenskwatawa's injunction against killing for skins, they slaughtered deer for the fur trade. By late autumn, overhunting had hushed the surrounding forests. The Shawnee brothers also received their first lesson in Main Poc's fickleness. The fearsome Potawatomi had promised to help provision Prophetstown from his tribe's plentiful Illinois country caches. Instead, he left his pledge unfulfilled and went to Washington with William Wells and Little Turtle to meet the Great Father. And then winter came, early and harsh. In the Long Moon (November), three feet of snow blanketed the prairie and forests. Food gave out. During the Eccentric Moon (December) the Indians began slaughtering their dogs and horses to survive. Another wave of the white man's "coughing sickness," as the Indians called influenza, and whooping cough cut down scores of them.[16]

The Master of Life struck the visiting Indians as ominously selective in his choice of victims. During the winter 160 Ottawas and Ojibwas succumbed, including several chiefs. But only five Shawnees died of disease, and relatively few Kickapoos and Wyandots were taken ill. Some northerners suspected the Prophet had poisoned their fellow tribesmen. Nearly all came to doubt his divinity. With the spring thaw, they fled Prophetstown muttering vows of vengeance.

While Tenskwatawa reckoned with the ravages of winter, in January 1809 Tecumseh left Prophetstown for northern Ohio on a quixotic recruiting mission, perhaps as much to escape the insalubrious village as to gain new adherents. At Tarhe's town he met in council with the Sandusky Wyandots and the small bands of Senecas and Munsees who resided in the neighborhood. Tecumseh told the chiefs that the country around the Tippecanoe was "better than that which they inhabited—that it was removed from the whites, and they could live happily there." It seems he was learning how to lie like his brother in the interest of their alliance.

The interpreter John Conner's son said that his father often remarked that Tecumseh's persuasive powers were so great that he "never failed to move his hearers, red or white, nor failed to rally the Indians." In Tarhe's town, however, he failed miserably. After Tecumseh finished his roseate recital of Prophetstown's virtues, Tarhe administered a stinging and imperious rebuke on behalf of the gathered chiefs. Plainly Tecumseh was "working for no good." The Sandusky Indians would "wait a few years, and if they perceived that their red brethren lived so happy, they might possibly join them." Tecumseh turned his face into the bitter winter wind and headed home to pestilential Prophetstown.[17]

He rode past the wooded trail to Wapakoneta without pausing. There was no point to a visit there. The Wapakoneta Shawnees were beyond his reach. Chief Black Hoof had written President Jefferson that his people were "hearty and strong" and had awakened to the "advantage of minding our work to raise plenty for our women and children." Their white neighbors concurred. From objects of pity or disdain, who often begged for food or burgled cabins, the Wapakoneta Shawnees had become "sober and civil" neighbors whose gardens, houses, and livestock were as good as their own. Their progress would suffer a setback when the War Department dismissed the Quaker William Kirk in April 1809 because he had been lax in his bookkeeping, but Wapakoneta was nevertheless solidly situated on the white man's road. Tecumseh headed home.[18]

Prospects for Prophetstown blackened. William Wells speculated that the Shawnee Prophet might retreat west of the Mississippi to avoid wrathful northern Indians. Tenskwatawa had no intention of abandoning Prophetstown, but in April 1809 a small war party of Ojibwas and Ottawas put the Prophet's authority to a gruesome test. He had preached that the Master of Life would punish any perpetrators of violence in Prophetstown. Slipping into the village at night, the heretics tomahawked a Shawnee woman and her child to death. Absconding to a temporary camp thirty miles away, they waited for the Master of Life to wreak vengeance. Nothing happened. Once home, the war party gloated over the Prophet's fallibility. That roused other warriors not merely to attempt to replicate the selective killings but also to contemplate slaying the Prophet himself.[19]

Tenskwatawa lied creatively when his life depended on it. Enemies had not slain the woman and her child, he declared; they had died from a white man's disease. The war party had tomahawked corpses. Prophetstown remained inviolate. Tenskwatawa, however, was not content to trust to his powers of dissimulation. He dispatched messengers to the Illinois country begging Main Poc to marshal Sauk, Fox, and Potawatomi warriors to defend the town against attack by the aggrieved northerners.[20]

But Main Poc was not at home. He hadn't breathed a sober breath since November, when he left for Washington with Wells, Little Turtle, and two other Potawatomis and their wives. Not the least intimidated by the Great Father, a snarling Main Poc, clad in buckskin, his face painted red and black, told Thomas Jefferson that Potawatomi obligations to the Great Father did not include making peace with the Osages or tilling the soil. He would remain neutral in any war between the United States and Great Britain, and that was all. Repairing to his hotel room, Main Poc went on a bender, terrifying the hotel staff and anyone else who dared approach him. "Main Poc exceeds everything I ever saw," an exasperated Wells complained to Secretary Dearborn. "His conduct is insufferable." It hardly improved after Main Poc's return to the Northwest. In the spring, when Tenskwatawa needed him most, Main Poc was at Fort Wayne meeting with a delegation of Quakers he had snubbed while inebriated in Baltimore. The council proved a fiasco. In a drunken rage, Main Poc ranted and brandished his war club at the inoffensive Friends, who beat a hasty retreat to Baltimore.[21]

Paradoxically, it was not Main Poc but an "evil white man" who saved Tenskwatawa from wrathful Ottawas and Ojibwas. Learning of their plans, Governor Hull of the Michigan Territory forbade them to attack the Shawnees. In keeping with government policy to discourage intertribal squabbles, Hull warned the ringleaders that he would construe any hostilities against the Shawnee Prophet as an act of war against the United States. The befuddled northern war chiefs scrapped their plans to raze Prophetstown and murder its leader.[22]

While not in direct mortal danger himself, Tecumseh suffered a significant humiliation that spring when the Michigan Wyandots, evidently adjudging Prophetstown an unsafe repository for the Great Wampum Belt, demanded its return. Tecumseh obliged them, and forty warriors saw it safely back to Brownstown.[23]

Again, Tecumseh took to the trails. This time he rode west to the newly constituted Illinois Territory in the name of the Prophet. His purpose was to recruit the Fox and Sauk Indians of the Mississippi and Rock River valleys because Main Poc had reneged on doing so. The Foxes and Sauks were Algonquian-speaking tribes so closely allied that the U.S. government often treated them as a single unit. The Shawnees called them their younger brothers, but the Foxes and Sauks rejected the lesser status; they considered themselves on an equal footing with the Shawnees.

Fox and Sauk hostility toward the United States had originated with Harrison's extortionate 1804 Treaty of St. Louis, which deprived them of most of their land, on paper at least. The government then built Fort Madison on the Mississippi River, in the heart of Sauk country. The Americans posed no immediate threat—the population of the Illinois Territory consisted of twelve thousand souls huddled along a hundred-mile stretch of the Mississippi well south of the Indians, but Fort Madison infuriated the warriors like an inflamed boil begging to be lanced.

When Tecumseh arrived in western Illinois in June 1809, the Sauks, Foxes, and Winnebagos were conspiring to attack both Fort Madison and Fort Dearborn. In council Tecumseh convinced them to abandon their plan as contrary to the interests of a larger Indian confederation. "With great ceremony," the Illinois tribes buried the hatchet. Hoping popular opinion had shifted to him, Tecumseh appealed to the Sauks and Foxes to come to Prophetstown and embrace Tenskwatawa's cause. "If you do not join your friends on the Wabash, the Americans will take this very village from you!" proclaimed the Shawnee. And he told them to discard their medicine bags for good measure.

A cool and palpable silence descended over the council house. Tecumseh had misread his audience. Among the skeptics was the rising Sauk warrior Black Hawk, who would one day lead a war of his own against the Americans in which a lanky Illinois volunteer captain named Abraham Lincoln would participate. Rejecting Tecumseh's call, he reasoned, "I little thought then that his words would come true, supposing that he used these arguments merely to encourage us to join him, which we concluded not to do." Tecumseh's insistence that the Sauks throw away their medicine bags because they supposedly had become vitiated with age appalled the young Sauk warrior Wennebea. He scolded Tecumseh for trying to impose his ludicrous beliefs on the Sauks, whose medicine bags were both virtuous and efficacious. Tecumseh exploded at the affront. He reached for his war club and started for Wennebea. In the ensuing commotion, Tecumseh's Shawnee retinue restrained him. After order was restored, the Sauk chiefs, largely to console their honored guest, ordered four of their warriors to accompany him to Prophetstown to meet Tenskwatawa and learn his doctrine firsthand. The Foxes, however, wanted no part of the program.[24]

While Tecumseh stumbled in Illinois, Tenskwatawa struggled to maintain his grasp on the home front, a task made more difficult because he was battling a chimera of William Henry Harrison's creation. Its constituent parts were fantastic. Harrison somehow interpreted distant Sauk and Fox discontent with his shifty 1804 treaty—as well as more recent Ojibwa and Ottawa anger at Tenskwatawa, which Harrison thought feigned—as actually elements of a byzantine British-engineered intrigue aimed at employing the Shawnee Prophet to smash the Indiana Territory. French traders, whose business suffered because of the Prophet's ban on alcohol and most other trade goods, whispered lies and half-truths that fed Harrison's predilection to see a nefarious British purpose in anything for which he had no ready explanation. Harrison employed as spies two particularly mendacious Frenchmen, Peter Lafontaine and Toussaint Dubois, who would resurface repeatedly as sources for accusations Harrison leveled against the Prophet in his dispatches to Washington. In reporting Tenskwatawa's strength, for instance, the spies included the Potawatomi villages of Winamac and Five Medals, both of which were decidedly pro-American, as well as Miami communities equally inimical to the Shawnees. Trusting in his unreliable informants, Harrison, who a few months earlier had seen the Shawnee Prophet as a potential ally, now perceived him as the Crown's cat's-paw. Ironically, Harrison came to this conclusion without knowing of Tecumseh's visit to Fort Malden.[25]

"I can no longer doubt of the hostile disposition of the tribes of the Mississippi and Illinois River and those on the Wabash who adhere to the Shawnee Prophet," Harrison assured the secretary of war. "I also fear that the story which has been circulated for some time of the determination of the Chippewas [Ojibwas] and Ottawas of Lake Michigan to fall upon the Prophet is a mere pretense suggested by the British to cover the reason design of the former, and then when they reach the Wabash they will join the Prophet and the Winnebagoes to fall upon our settlements." Harrison called out the militia to meet the phantom threat and hunkered down in Vincennes.

In April 1809, then, Tenskwatawa faced not only the real prospect of assassination at the hands of vengeful northern Indians but also the sudden hostility of the territorial governor. His promising double game with the British and Americans, intended as a defensive measure, now threatened to extinguish his foundering movement. With no more than eighty loyal warriors on hand at Prophetstown, he had to act fast to allay American suspicions. Fortunately for Tenskwatawa, William Wells had just been ousted as Indian agent at Fort Wayne.

Wells's dismissal was a metaphor for the futility of attempted coexistence between Indians and whites on the northwestern frontier. He had tried to be an honest broker between the government that employed him, the Miamis whom he loved as family, and other Indians who tried to balance accommodation with cultural integrity. Wells was the first to construe the Shawnee Prophet's movement not only as threatening to the "civilization" policy the government paid him to implement but also as likely to provoke an apocalyptic war. Government officials, however, distrusted Wells because he alerted the Indians to the dubious aspects of treaties. And so Harrison and Tenskwatawa—characters at polar extremes—were equally pleased to see Wells go.

John Johnston, the Fort Wayne factor who had ceaselessly disparaged Wells to the War Department, usually without cause, angled himself into the agent's job. Johnston reserved his petulance for Wells; for the Indians, he had nothing but good feelings, the Shawnee Prophet included. Saluting Tenskwatawa with three strings of white wampum, the new agent invited the Prophet to visit Fort Wayne. He promised to take Tenskwatawa "by the hand in my own house ... use you well when you are here and send you back safe when you wish to return home."[26]

The Shawnee Prophet arrived on May 25 in fine feather. He brought with him eleven leading men—seven more than Johnston had invited—representing the five tribes residing at Prophetstown. An ingratiating Tenskwatawa also returned two horses that his warriors had stolen from Ohio settlers. He dominated the four-day council that followed. Employing his uncanny ability to play government officials against one another, he flattered and beguiled Johnston just as he earlier had Harrison. All the accusations against him and his movement, which he assured Johnston was purely religious, arose from the "personal and private motives" of Wells and Little Turtle. "The Prophet related to me all that passed between them, and put the right construction on Wells's motives," reported a delighted Johnston. He also contradicted Governor Harrison's claim that Tenskwatawa harbored hostile intent: "I have also taken much pains and have not been able to find that there existed any grounds for the alarm." Nor had discerning private observers. A Kentuckian recently arrived in Vincennes in late May had expected to find war commenced and the first campaign against the Prophet under way. Condemning the "pompous and alarming orders of the [Indiana] governor," he instead assured the home folk that reports of Indian troubles were "false and unfounded." Confronted with contrary reports, Harrison backtracked. He dismissed the militia with the assurance that there existed "not the smallest probability of hostilities with any of the neighboring tribes."[27]

In fairness to Harrison, it must be said that Governor Hull also assumed Tenskwatawa to be the instrument of a British government intent on war with the United States, or as Hull put it, "the powerful influence of the British has been exerted in a way alluring to the savage character."[28] With the two governors predisposed to see war clouds whenever an Indian visited Amherstburg, the Shawnee brothers would have to tread carefully when it came to future contacts with representatives of the Crown.

Tenskwatawa left Fort Wayne on May 29, having won over Agent Johnston. A month later he called on Governor Harrison. Again, he expressed his friendship for the United States. Harrison, however, was not about to be duped a second time—even when Tenskwatawa spoke the truth. Denying any intention to fall upon Indiana settlements, the Shawnee Prophet told Harrison that war preparations had been limited to the western Illinois tribes, and that he had interceded to stop them. Tenskwatawa spent ten days in Vincennes. Each encounter with Harrison served only to deepen the governor's suspicions of him. Harrison now believed Tenskwatawa to be a "great scoundrel" but concluded that the Prophet's star was on the wane.[29]

Harrison's assessment appeared sound. Tecumseh's early-summer recruiting efforts in western Illinois yielded little; nor could Main Poc be relied upon to muster the Illinois Potawatomis. Winning back the northern tribes would be difficult at best. The four hundred warriors then at Prophetstown posed a threat only to the village's limited food supply.

But an event was about to occur that would reinvigorate the Shawnee brothers' cause, recapturing former adherents and bringing new allies. It would also stimulate Tecumseh to espouse more forcefully, and independently of his brother, his deep-seated suspicions of American intentions toward the Indians. The catalyst for the Shawnee brothers' resurgence: an arrogant and ill-conceived power play by Governor Harrison.

One Treaty Too Many

WILLIAM HENRY HARRISON had grown frustrated with his office. The creation of the Illinois Territory (which also included the future state of Wisconsin) from the Indiana Territory had left him as governor of a greatly diminished realm that embraced only the southern third of what is today Indiana. All the rest was unceded Indian country. Small though the American tract was in relative terms, it met the needs of the nonnative population, which in 1809 consisted of no more than 23,000 whites and 600 slaves and black freedmen. But it was insufficient for Harrison's political ambitions. The slicing away of the Illinois Territory also slowed the Indiana Territory's march to statehood. That irked Harrison immensely. After nine years Harrison was tired of administering a territory, especially one that had shrunk. He wanted to govern a full-fledged state in the Union. Finally, Harrison was also serving a new administration. He could not be certain that the incoming president, James Madison, would share Jefferson's views on Indian affairs or support the aggressive land acquisitions Harrison had undertaken at his predecessor's behest.

In the hope of attracting new pioneers to push the population over the threshold needed for statehood, in May 1809 Harrison lobbied Washington for permission to purchase additional lands east of the Wabash River with outright lies about settlers being "much cramped by the vicinity of Indian lands." Only a "further extinguishment of [Indian] title," he assured the new secretary of war, William Eustis, would permit the "feeble" Indiana Territory to flourish.

Harrison had tested the waters in Washington and found them frigid. President Madison shared Jefferson's general notions of Indian affairs, but he wanted no trouble on the frontier. "Your Excellency will be satisfied that a proposal of this kind," Eustis admonished Harrison, "will excite no disagreeable apprehension and produce no undesirable effects before it shall be made." Furthermore, Harrison was to ensure that any tribe that had, or pretended to have, a right to the land Harrison sought was represented at treaty negotiations.[1]

Remarkably, Harrison ignored Eustis's instructions. He went after pliant chiefs, rendering them more malleable with copious amounts of whiskey; played tribes against one another; and threatened to withhold annuities from those who disputed his terms.

Harrison arrived at Fort Wayne on September 19 to open negotiations with the Delawares, Miamis, and Potawatomis. He wheeled along several wagons of alcohol to lubricate the proceedings. Indian sobriety and industry no longer interested Harrison. Land he wanted, and land he would have, even if it meant reducing all 1,396 Indians in attendance to abject inebriation. Only nine Shawnees showed up. Having no claims to the country in question that either the government or other Indians recognized, they were merely mute observers.

Harrison lectured the chiefs on the benefits of ceding land for annuities, after which he granted a Miami request for two gallons of liquor. While the Miamis imbibed, Chief Winamac assured Harrison that the 660 Potawatomis present would accept the treaty—Harrison cleverly had invited only friendly tribesmen; Main Poc's western Potawatomis were excluded.

To Harrison's chagrin, the whiskey did not render the Miamis more malleable; on the contrary, they refused to sell unless the government paid them fair market value, which was two dollars an acre, not the two cents an acre Harrison offered. They also insisted that the governor lacked presidential authority to negotiate. A cornered Harrison accused the Miamis of playing the part of British pawns. In refusing to sell, he suggested they ran the risk of war with the United States. Little Turtle asked for an adjournment, whereupon the Miamis and Potawatomis fell to quarreling over the value of the land. Harrison persuaded William Wells—whom he had rehired as an interpreter—to support him, and the warriors were plied with whiskey and their chiefs bribed with annuities until they agreed to the two-cent-per-acre price.

On September 30, Harrison concluded a treaty with the marginally sober Miamis, Potawatomis, and Delawares (they had consumed 218 gallons of whiskey), purchasing 2.6 million acres of what Fort Wayne Indian agent John Johnston called "some of the finest land in the United States" and pushing the American frontier to within sixty miles of Prophetstown. By rewarding the Potawatomis and Delawares with $500 annual annuities for land that belonged to the Miamis, Harrison also marginalized Little Turtle. Fearful that the Kickapoos, "very much under of the influence of the Prophet," would resist any cession, he excluded them from the Fort Wayne council. Waiting until their neighbors had signed the treaty, Harrison bypassed militant Kickapoo leaders and presented the treaty as a fait accompli to a handful of minor chiefs, whom he badgered into ceding their sole remaining tract in the Illinois Territory. Most Kickapoos vehemently objected to both cessions.

Harrison was confident that the divisive and devious negotiating tactics he had employed to secure the Fort Wayne treaty would not stand in the way of a lasting peace with the Indians. "The arrangement which has been made is just to all," he assured the secretary of war, "and is therefore, I believe, satisfactory to all." William Wells begged to differ. "Notwithstanding the cruel treatment I had just received"—a reference to Harrison's role in Wells's dismissal as Indian agent—"I stepped forward and effected what the governor desired, though much against the will of the Indians, and nothing but my influence with them could induce them to sell their land." But Wells had had enough. "After this transaction I did not concern myself with the Indians, and the purchase made by the United States immediately became unpopular with them, and as no effort was made to keep down the spirit of discontent among them, they threw themselves into the arms of the Shawnee Prophet."[2]

Time would soon tell whether Harrison's or Wells's version of the treaty council better reflected reality in the further diminished Indian country.

The winter of 1810 came, as hard as the year before. Snow lay deep, trodden mostly by ravening hunters; deer tracks were as infrequent as a full meal at an Indian fireside. Hungry Indians devoured their horses and dogs. Traders packed up and left them without ammunition or powder. The whimpering of famished children and the hacking of influenza victims blended in a nightly symphony of suffering. Witchcraft was afoot, said Wyandot and Delaware villagers formerly impervious to the Shawnee Prophet's preaching. And the very same Three Fires chiefs who had threatened to murder Tenskwatawa now reconsidered their relationship with him and with their former British father. They began work on an elaborate wampum belt to be delivered to Amherstburg in the spring, the purport of which, reported the British Indian agent Matthew Elliott, "is to say that the United States is making rapid encroachment on their lands and making them poor indeed; that their wants are daily increasing; and that they are alarmed for the fate of their children, who will no doubt be reduced to a state of slavery."[3]

No Indian would be further debased so long as the Shawnee brothers had a say in the matter. With the spring thaw, an angry Tecumseh took to the spongy trail from Prophetstown to Wapakoneta. Perhaps Governor Harrison's treacherous Fort Wayne Treaty would render Black Hoof's people more amenable to the Shawnee brothers' doctrine, which incorporated a strident rejection of the transaction. For Tecumseh and Tenskwatawa, it had been one treaty too many. Beginning with the assimilationist Ohio bands, Tecumseh would make the case not only that the time for a united front against the insatiably expansionist Americans was at hand, but also that any delay might be the death knell of the Indian people.

Riding into Wapakoneta, Tecumseh could not have been pleased with its air of relative prosperity, or with what that boded for his recruiting drive. John Norton, a prominent British Indian Department official and the adopted nephew of the Iroquois chief Joseph Brant, visited the town just after Tecumseh left. He found the surroundings delightful: "The place had a cheerful appearance; the houses were near each other in a clearing covered with grass." Norton also marveled at the "many cornfields in view, tolerably extensive and under a very good fence." Herds of cattle and passels of hogs grazed outside the village; two decades earlier, mused Norton, the Shawnees had had only dogs and a few stolen horses.[4]

Black Hoof and the leading men of the village refused to meet with Tecumseh. Not so the young warriors. They flocked to the council house to hear Tecumseh's recruiting pitch, knowing it would not pass unchallenged because Stephen Ruddell happened to be in Wapako-neta on a recruiting drive for the Lord. With Bible in hand, the Baptist missionary faced off with his old friend.

Speaking first, Tecumseh denounced the Fort Wayne Treaty as an affront to the Master of Life, who had given the Indians the land for their exclusive use. They in turn had an eternal obligation to defend it with their lives. Glancing at Ruddell, Tecumseh acknowledged that the "Lord of All had greatly favored the European Americans at the expense of the Native tribes, but that the day might come when he would smile upon their exertions in defense of their independence and territory against the hitherto fortunate intruders, unless they bridle their ambition and content themselves within the boundaries already established."

Ruddell interrupted. Black Hoof's people had no intention of quitting Wapakoneta. Waving a recent letter from Governor Harri-son, Ruddell said that the Ohio Shawnees were loyal to the Seven-teen Fires (United States) and considered the Prophet a charlatan. Tecumseh's sometimes hair-trigger temper betrayed him. He yanked the letter from Ruddell, tore it to shreds, and tossed the scraps into the fire, saying that American promises were as worthless as ashes. If Gov-ernor Harrison were present, he would tell him as much. Tecumseh's histrionics won him his first supporters from among the Wapakoneta Shawnees. Ruddell's influence probably prevented a stampede to him, but several warriors did accompany Tecumseh to his next destination, Tarhe's Wyandot town on the Sandusky.[5]

Bloodshed trailed Tecumseh. Most of the Wyandots rebuffed him, and one elderly chief lost his life, probably on orders from Tenskwa-tawa. The victim was Leather Lips, the sixty-three-year-old Wyan-dot peace chief who had reproached the Prophet three years earlier. Leather Lips's small village rested on the Scioto River near Chief Roundhead's town. Jonathan Alder, who lived near him, esteemed Leather Lips as an intelligent, pious, and inoffensive old man. Still a strong voice in Wyandot affairs, Leather Lips continued to oppose the Prophet. That likely would have sufficed for Chief Roundhead and five of his warriors to condemn him for witchcraft, but they also charged Leather Lips with helping spread an influenza virus that had killed several Wyandots, a crime for which fellow villagers already had executed a Wyandot "witch."

Roundhead's party found the old chief at home with American

friends. Leather Lips pleaded his innocence to no avail. Granted permission to eat a last meal, Leather Lips retired to his wigwam, dined on jerked venison, arrayed himself in his finest clothes, painted his face, and then accompanied his executioners to a wooded spot eighty yards from camp. All the while, he intoned his death song. They halted before a shallow grave that Roundhead and his cohorts had dug secretly. Horrified at what was about to occur, Leather Lips's American friends offered up a fine horse in exchange for his life. Roundhead refused. "You have laws to punish your bad men and the Indians do not interfere," he said. "This old man is a bad man, and we have our mode of punishing bad men, and the white man must not interfere."

Kneeling at the gravesite, Leather Lips prayed fervently to the Great Spirit. When he was finished, he buried his face in his hands and said he was prepared to die. Drawing a glittering new tomahawk from under his cloak, Roundhead smashed in his skull. "He is in Hell now," remarked one of the Wyandots. Roundhead delivered several more blows for good measure, after which the warriors rolled Leather Lips's corpse into the grave. Also marked for death, Chief Tarhe managed to dodge Roundhead and his henchmen.[6]

While Tecumseh sojourned in Ohio, Tenskwatawa called a conference to consider the Fort Wayne Treaty. Several hundred western Indians attended. In May 1810 the Michigan Wyandots, keepers of the Great Wampum Belt, agreed to assist him. They were "tired of their situation [and] had nothing nearer their hearts than to see all the various tribes united again as one man" to halt American encroachment. Displaying the Great Wampum Belt that had signified the previous British-Indian alliance, the Wyandots reproached the Miamis for collaborating with the Long Knives. The thoroughly shamed Miamis consented to send a delegation to Tenskwatawa's council.[7]

Tenskwatawa and Tecumseh found themselves in the suddenly awkward position of trying to tamp down war fever. Both were loath to promote a conflict with the United States without the promise of British troops, a commitment that they knew would not be forthcoming. They also lacked enough ammunition for the seven hundred warriors who were then arrayed under their banner. With difficulty they reined in more extreme elements, which ironically included the same Three Fires chiefs who had vowed to smite the Prophet a year earlier. Working in tandem, the Shawnee brothers ensured that nothing came of the Prophetstown gathering except a great deal of angry talk.

At Amherstburg, the local British Indian agent Matthew Elliott lent a hand in dissuading the Three Fires tribes from dragging Great Britain into war with the United States. "The great concourse of Indians to this post at such an early period of the year has truly astonished me," he informed William Claus on June 10. "From the present disposition of the Indians it appears evident that the least encouragement from our government would raise them all in arms, and tribes who formerly with reluctance and others who never sent warriors against [the Americans] would now with joy accept the invitation."[8]

The roiled tribes did not include the signatories to the Fort Wayne Treaty, who stood to forfeit their annuities should the United States lose its grip on the region. Winamac and Five Medals of the eastern Potawatomis, together with the Miami and Delaware treaty chiefs, exerted their diminished but still considerable influence against the Prophet, apparently unaware that he was pressing for continued peace. They also spread inflammatory rumors intended to stoke the hostility of Governors Hull and Harrison toward him.[9]

Main Poc had been conspicuously absent at the Prophetstown gathering, having gone west to raid the Osages. The Potawatomi *wabeno's* summer entertainment came largely at his own expense, however. After the Osages repulsed his war party, Main Poc took revenge against an American settlement in the Louisiana Territory (as the vast lands west of the Mississippi River that constituted the Louisiana Purchase north of the state of Louisiana were called), killing four innocent men. A pro-American Potawatomi chief helped the governor evict him, after which Main Poc terrorized American traders in southern Illinois. In September he attacked the Osages again. This time a bullet found him. His followers were shocked. Had the Osages discovered a medicine more potent than that of their heretofore bulletproof *wabeno?* Up the Illinois River they fled, hauling the grievously wounded Main Poc in a canoe. But the peevish Potawatomi refused to die. As his wound healed, he reassured his warriors that his medicine was undiminished. He had seen the bullet that struck him but had jumped in its path to save one of his wives, who rode beside him, from otherwise certain death. Main Poc's hold on his warriors remained firm. They believed the violent womanizer had risked his life to save a spouse.[10]

Their role in undermining their own Prophetstown council took a hard toll on Tenskwatawa and Tecumseh. Neither relished the thought of being perceived as weak. Tenskwatawa periodically reverted to the braggadocio and loose talk that had earned him the unflattering moniker of Lalawethika. When the "Rattler" in him reemerged, Tenskwatawa would speak of challenging Harrison to single combat, reducing Vincennes to ashes, or of traveling to Washington, D.C., to demand that the Great Father remove the governor.

While Tenskwatawa chattered menacingly, Tecumseh occasionally yielded to physical outbursts of fury. In early June a boat loaded with salt for Tenskwatawa's Kickapoo allies, whose village lay nearby, docked at Prophetstown. Uncertain whether to accept the shipment (the salt comprised part of the Kickapoo annuity goods), the Prophet prevailed on the Kickapoos to await Tecumseh, who was away, and to abide his decision. Accordingly, the Prophet asked the boatmen to leave the salt on the riverbank and call again in a few days. When the boat returned, Tecumseh directed John Gamlin, the master, to reload the barrels; the Indians would have nothing to do with annuity goods. As the boat hands rolled the barrels on deck, Tecumseh climbed aboard and began violently shaking Gamlin's hair and that of his crewmen, asking each if he was an American. Only when he learned that they were all Frenchmen did Tecumseh calm down. The Prophet also leveled a threat, telling Gamlin that if any attempt was made to survey the boundary of the treaty tract, the "surveyors should survey no more." Tecumseh's rage was infectious. A young Potawatomi ally and his warriors plundered the nearby house of Michel Brouillette, a presumed Indian trader who kept just enough trade goods to disguise his true role as spy for Governor Harrison. Tecumseh looked on approvingly. Then he expelled Brouillette—a well-merited and mild enough outcome.

Despite his fluctuating temperament, Tecumseh held constant to four earthly purposes that he had injected into the Prophet's divinely inspired alliance: forestall further inroads on Indian land, resist any attempt to survey or settle the 2.6 million-acre tract Harrison had swindled from the Indians at Fort Wayne, prevent the Americans from continuing their efforts to divide and conquer the Ohio Valley and

Great Lakes tribes, and continue recruitment of western Indians. War was not yet the answer, but the battle lines were hardening.[11]

It was scarcely an ideal moment for the Shawnee brothers to challenge the Americans. The Indians south of the Ohio River had been relatively quiet for nearly a decade. After the defeat of the Chickamaugas, no other Indian opponents to federal authority had risen up, and white population pressure against the boundaries of the tribes in the Deep South, while real, for the moment did not threaten to erupt into violence. If there were to be an Indian conflict anytime soon, it would be in the Northwest, with the full force of the United States available to combat any uprising.

In Vincennes, Governor Harrison sputtered and fumed. Unable to accept that the unrest at Prophetstown, which he exaggerated, stemmed from his own deceitful treaty, he defaulted to his standard object of blame—the British. "I have no doubt that the present hostile disposition of the Prophet and his votaries has been produced by British interference," he told Secretary Eustis. Harrison's solution? The "rascally prophet" must be driven from his town—which happened to be in Indian country—or else a fort must be built on the Wabash at the upper boundary of the Fort Wayne Treaty lands to hold him in check. When Eustis appeared skeptical, Harrison evoked lurid images of the "artful scoundrel" Tenskwatawa reaping "a rich harvest of blood and plunder from our defenseless frontier."[12]

There were those in Vincennes who found Harrison's deflection of blame darkly comical. No one was more mordantly amused than John Badollet, the scrupulously honest but, if Harrison is to be believed, somewhat "peevish and easily duped" registrar at the territorial land office, who led a growing anti-Harrison clique that objected to the governor's near-proconsular powers and to his advocacy of slavery in the territory. Badollet admired the Shawnee Prophet for encouraging sobriety and industry among his people. He dismissed Harrison's talk of British intrigue as self-serving twaddle and told his close friend, Secretary of the Treasury Albert Gallatin, that the governor traduced the Prophet to "stifle the murmurs of the Wabash Indians in relation to the late treaties and the unwarrantable means employed to affect them."

On June 18, 1810, Harrison suffered a meltdown. Calling together territorial officials and prominent citizens, he announced that the Prophet and his warriors were about to descend on Vincennes in overwhelming numbers, intending to tomahawk him and then slaughter the citizenry. "[Harrison] painted his fears in lively colors," recollected Badollet, "and said that if it was not for fear of spreading too great an alarm, he would immediately send his family to Kentucky and convert his house into a fort." At a minimum, Harrison declared he must call out the two local militia companies to defend the town, understrength and poorly trained as they were. Badollet and the lieutenant governor suggested that Harrison instead send the French trader Toussaint Dubois to Prophetstown to take the pulse of the Indians. After equivocating, Harrison acquiesced.

That the threat was a figment of Harrison's imagination became evident a week later when a reliable settler just in from Prophetstown told Badollet that the Prophet's people were peaceable and courteous to their American neighbors. Far from sharpening tomahawks and readying muskets, the men were building fences, communing with the Great Spirit, and generally lounging about while their women cultivated two hundred acres of corn. "This business may end unpleasantly," Badollet's correspondent added, but only because the Indians believed that Harrison intended to make war on them.[13]

In addition to sizing up Prophetstown, Toussaint Dubois greased the neglected wheels of diplomacy. Perhaps to Harrison's surprise, and certainly to Dubois's relief, Tenskwatawa greeted the Frenchman warmly. He denied any intention of going to war, suggesting that the Delawares and other Indians unfriendly to his cause had been bribed with whiskey to accuse him. When Dubois pressed the Prophet on his feelings toward Harrison personally, Tenskwatawa answered as if scripted by Tecumseh. "The Indians," he said, "had been cheated of their lands and no sale was good unless made by all the tribes." Tenskwatawa dismissed Dubois's suggestion that he go to Vincennes and confer again with the governor; he had been ill treated the time before. Or so reported Harrison, who hastened to assure Secretary Eustis that the Prophet's complaint about the land sales was a "mere pretense" that British emissaries had planted in his mind. Harrison's talent for dissembling to superiors seemingly was exceeded only by his gift for self-deception.

Harrison decided to try a different tack with the Prophet. He would send his interpreter Joseph Barron, a friend of the Shawnee brothers, to Prophetstown to give a menacing speech, tempered by an invitation for Tenskwatawa to address his complaints directly to the Great Father, the theory being that a journey to Washington would impress the Prophet with the vast power of the United States. At the very least, Harrison told Secretary Eustis, the trip would better acquaint the government with him—that is, if Barron lived long enough to deliver Harrison's address. The interpreter arrived at Prophetstown in the last week of July to an icy reception. Someone had told Tenskwatawa that Dubois, like Michel Brouillette, had been a spy, which did the amateur diplomat Dubois a disservice. In any event, the Prophet was neither amused nor prepared to entertain another snooping envoy from the governor.

Warriors conducted Barron with great ceremony to Tenskwatawa. They seated him facing the Prophet from a distance of twelve feet. Chiefs from each tribe with a presence in the village surrounded the visitor. The slender, sallow-complexioned Barron sweated. Time seemed to stand still. Tenskwatawa stared silently at Barron for several minutes, offering no hint of recognition. Unknown to Barron, Tenskwatawa's domineering wife Gimewane, the "Queen," had assembled the women of the village to decide Barron's fate—and their judgment was that he should die. Under Shawnee custom, it was their prerogative to decide a prisoner's fate. But Barron was an emissary. The Shawnee brothers were in a quandary. Could they orchestrate a face-saving exit?[14]

At last Tenskwatawa spoke. Anger—perhaps exaggerated for effect—blackened his every word. "For what purpose do you come here?" He permitted no reply, but continued, "Brouillette was here; he was a spy. Dubois was here; he was a spy. Now you have come. You, too, are a spy." Pointing to a spot near which Barron stood, the Prophet declared, "There is your grave! Look on it." At that instant Tecumseh stepped forward and addressed Barron in cold and formal Shawnee. His life was in no danger, but he must forthwith state the true purpose of his appearance in Prophetstown.

A shaken but markedly relieved Barron translated Harrison's speech. "There is yet, but very little harm done but what may easily be repaired," he began haltingly. "The chain of friendship which unites the whites with the Indians may be [made] as strong as ever." The choice rested with Tenskwatawa. Then the tone of Harrison's address turned harsh. He told the Prophet to entertain no hope of resisting the force of the Seventeen Fires, as the Indians called the United States, even "for a Moon." Harrison complimented the Prophet's men, but all their war-making skill would prove of no avail. "I know your warriors are brave; ours are not less so, but what can a few brave warriors do against the innumerable warriors of the Seventeen Fires? Our blue-coats are more numerous than you can count, and our hunting shirts [militia] are like the leaves of the forests or the grains of sands on the Wabash." Tenskwatawa well understood the truth of Harrison's metaphor. Already warriors from the more distant tribes were drifting away from Prophetstown, heading to their home villages for the autumn hunt, a natural occurrence that American officials wrongly assumed represented a loss of influence on the Prophet's part. Harrison mockingly denied the Shawnee brothers' core principle of common Indian ownership of the land but offered to facilitate a safe visit to Washington if the Prophet wished to carry his complaints to the Great Father.[15]

Tenskwatawa offered no immediate reply to Harrison's letter. He and Tecumseh evidently consulted as to the best stratagem to pursue, because when Tecumseh invited Barron to lodge with him that night—in part to ensure the interpreter's safety—he had plenty to say about the governor's missive, among other wide-ranging topics. Tenskwatawa had the greater challenge that night: to explain to Gimewane why he had not killed Barron.

Tecumseh and Barron conversed deep into the summer's night. Tecumseh assured Barron that he had no intention of starting a war. But he saw no way for the Indians to "remain friends" with the United States unless the Americans stopped demanding more land and accepted the principle that all remaining Indian country was held in common, no tract to be sold without the consent of all. "The Great Spirit said he gave this great island to his red children," Tecumseh lectured Barron. "He placed the whites on the other side of the big water. They were not contented with their own but came to take ours from us. They have driven us from the sea to the lakes, we can go no further." Moderating his tone, Tecumseh said Harrison's letter did not annoy him. He recalled glimpsing the governor as a young subaltern mounted alongside General Wayne at Fallen Timbers. Tecumseh told

Barron he had "not troubled white people much," nor did he intend to, but he, and not the Prophet, would go to Vincennes to see the governor.[16]

For the first time since the Battle of Fallen Timbers, Tecumseh and William Henry Harrison were about to come face to face.

No Difficulties Deter Him

C APT. GEORGE FLOYD and the small army garrison at a post
called Fort Knox above Vincennes kept a keen lookout for Indian
canoes descending the Wabash. It was Sunday, August 12, 1810, and
Harrison had ordered Floyd to watch for Tecumseh, who might bring
as many as thirty principal men and one hundred warriors—not to
threaten, but to partake of the free food and festive atmosphere of
grand councils. At last, eight canoes brightly painted in multiple hues
came into view. Paddling gracefully, the Indians turned them onto the
riverbank. Captain Floyd inspected the canoes for weapons, of which
there were many. And then he met Tecumseh. The Shawnee looked
firmly at Floyd, and the instant burned itself in the captain's memory.
"The brother of the Prophet," he later wrote, "is perhaps one of the
finest looking men I ever saw—about six feet high, straight, with large,
fine features, and altogether a daring, bold-looking fellow." After the
inspection, Tecumseh and his men paddled to the outskirts of Vincennes, where they disembarked and made camp. The council was to
begin the next morning.

Joseph Barron had briefed Governor Harrison fully on his
Prophetstown adventure. One can glean from Harrison's report that
Tecumseh with his sober commentary had impressed the interpreter
far more favorably than had Tenskwatawa with his menacing theatrics. "The brother of the Prophet will be here in a few days," Harrison
informed Secretary Eustis on August 6. "[He] is really the efficient
man—the Moses of the family ... a bold, active, sensible man, daring

in the extreme and capable of any undertaking." Barron also trumpeted Tecumseh's virtues to the editor of the *Vincennes Western Sun*, saying that the "Prophet's brother" was the most "efficient character" among the Indians at Prophetstown. The *Western Sun* article marked Tecumseh's third appearance in print, albeit in the guise of an unnamed if gifted second fiddle to Tenskwatawa.[1]

Before hearing from Barron, Harrison had written off the Prophet's plan for a general confederacy against American encroachment as "blasted." Now he realized that, in Tecumseh, he would be squaring off not with a British stooge but with an exceptional man who knew his own mind and meant to adhere to its musings.[2]

Harrison was justly proud of his estate, Grouseland. For sheer size and splendor, no other home in the Indiana Territory approached it. Eighteen large shuttered windows graced the two-story, redbrick Federal-style residence. The roof shined with new copper flashing. The bright white portico, accentuated with four massive colonnades that supported an equally exquisite balcony, had been fitted out with chairs for the council with Tecumseh. Judges of the territorial supreme court; several interpreters, including Joseph Barron and Stephen Ruddell; a cluster of army officers; and a thirteen-man detail from Fort Knox awaited his arrival. Three hundred townspeople crowded the well-manicured periphery of Grouseland, hoping for a look at the Shawnee chief and his retinue.

At the appointed hour on the morning of August 13, Tecumseh approached the portico with forty warriors. One of Harrison's military guards appraised him as five feet eleven, with long features, a high, broad forehead, and "the appearance of nobleness and dignity." Thirty yards short of the steps, Tecumseh halted. Joseph Barron invited the Indians to be seated on the portico. Tecumseh demurred; he thought the setting inappropriate. He preferred a nearby grove of shade trees. Harrison consented. The chairs and benches were moved from the portico to the grove. Motioning toward a chair, Barron said to Tecumseh, "Your father, General Harrison, offers you a seat." The Shawnee feigned indignation. He understood white customs but intended the council to proceed in the Indian fashion, adding a gentle rebuke in the bargain. "My father invites me to a seat? The sun is my father, and the Earth is my mother, and I will repose on her bosom." (That was no mere rhetorical device on Tecumseh's part; the Shawnees did perceive the sun as the essence of the fatherly Master of Life, and the earth as the mother of life.) Harrison let pass what most whites would regard as a slight. Tecumseh and his men then sat down cross-legged in the grass together, facing Harrison and the American crowd. The Potawatomi treaty chief Winamac squatted beside Harrison, cradling a brace of pistols that the governor had given him a few days earlier. Winamac needed them, he told Harrison, to guard against assassination by Tecumseh's warriors. Several Wea chiefs also were on hand, ostensibly to lend Harrison rhetorical support; in fact, Tecumseh's mere presence cowed them.[3]

Tecumseh opened the council. He passionately recited past American wrongs toward his people, warned of the consequences of future misdeeds, and bluntly stated his and the Prophet's purpose. He gestured frequently, punctuating his words with sign language for the benefit of non-Shawnee-speaking Indians like the timorous Winamac, and with seeming ferocity. Uneasy white eyewitnesses—unaware of the gestures' meaning—called Tecumseh's address a "harangue." Continuing to speak rapidly and gesticulate sharply, Tecumseh iterated the expected: that it was his and Tenskwatawa's intention to unite the Indians to stop American encroachment. The policy of divide and conquer must cease. "You want by your distinctions of Indian tribes in allotting to each a particular tract of land to make them [go] to war with each other," grumbled Tecumseh. "You are continually driving the red people, when at last you will drive them into the Great Lakes where they can't either stand or work."

Tecumseh had much to say about the Fort Wayne Treaty. He believed Harrison had acted over the opposition of half the American residents of Indiana. Many whites had told Tecumseh's informants that they had plenty of land already. This he knew to be true because he also had sent some of his warriors to reconnoiter the settlements and found much of the country near the Ohio River empty.

Tecumseh's anger grew as he enumerated the wrongs done the Indians, from the Gnadenhutten massacre and the assassination of Cornstalk to the present. He grimaced and gesticulated at Harrison, Winamac, and everyone else who had done wrong by him and his people. It was for Tecumseh a moment of catharsis. No longer did he pretend to be the Prophet's mouthpiece. With this speech, Tecumseh spoke his heart—and it got the better of him. He proclaimed a degree of authority over the Indians that would have caused even the overreaching Pontiac to quake. Tecumseh wanted no war with the Americans but would avenge himself on the peace chiefs if necessary. "I now wish you to listen to me," he told Harrison. "If you do not, it will appear as if you wished me to kill all the chiefs that sold you this land. I tell you so because I am authorized by all the tribes to do so. I am at the head of them all. I am a warrior and all the warriors will meet in two or three moons from this. Then I will call for those chiefs that sold you the land and shall know what to do with them. If you do not restore the land you will have a hand in killing them." The warriors had toppled the chiefs; the tradition of respecting elders was upended. A new order was emerging. It was pragmatic and political. Tenskwatawa's divinely defined moral order would take a back seat. Tecumseh spoke on. His threats against the treaty chiefs was bluster, but his contempt for Winamac was boundless. Tecumseh ridiculed him mercilessly—"a torrent of abuse," Harrison called it. Winamac shakily charged his pistols.[4]

The governor rose. He spat contempt back at Tecumseh. Why, he asked, if the Indians were all one people, did they not speak the same language? More to the point, the Americans knew the Miamis to be the rightful owners of the Wabash country; the Shawnees were mere interlopers. Harrison sat down. Ruddell began to interpret. Suddenly Tecumseh interrupted him; he understood English well enough to capture the essence of Harrison's rebuke, if not every word of it. Ruddell froze as Tecumseh, still seated, erupted. In Shawnee he called Harrison a liar and a land swindler. Lt. Gov. John Gibson, who understood Shawnee, yelled to a militia officer, "Those fellows intend mischief; you had better bring up the guard."[5]

At that instant Tecumseh sprang to his feet. Then his warriors stood as one. All drew their pipe tomahawks and war clubs and glared at the governor. Harrison tried to stand but caught his scabbard in the armrest of his chair. Disentangling himself, he drew his sword. Captain Floyd brandished a dirk. Winamac cocked his pistols. Civilians yanked posts from a rickety fence. A Methodist minister grabbed a musket and ran to the front door of Grouseland to defend the governor's family. The guard filed into line and leveled their muskets. After that, no one uttered a word or moved. Slowly, Harrison raised his left arm and waved the soldiers away. Tecumseh and his warriors sat back down. Harrison resumed his oration. Tecumseh had shown himself to be a "bad man," and so Harrison must extinguish the council fire. As Tecumseh had come to Vincennes under the protection of the council fire, so he might leave in safety; Harrison, however, was finished with him. Tecumseh and the Indians paraded away and paddled their canoes back to camp. After dark, Harrison mobilized the Vincennes militia and ordered up two additional companies of militia from the countryside.

Harrison's performance disgusted John Badollet. That night he wrote Secretary Gallatin urging the Madison administration to inquire more closely into the Fort Wayne Treaty and "rather cherish than exasperate [Tecumseh], that the Indians want nothing but good treatment to become well-disposed to the United States."[6]

Tecumseh's throat tasted of blood and bile. Near the Indian camp stood the lone home of a pioneer couple. The man was away. Stepping from their canoes, Tecumseh and several warriors stalked toward the frail clapboard cabin. Seeing them, the absent settler's terrified wife slammed and locked the door. Tecumseh shook it, exclaiming, "If you were not a woman..." By morning, Tecumseh had calmed enough to send Harrison an apology, asking that he reconvene the council.[7]

Tecumseh was subdued but firm when the public council resumed, and he politely received Harrison and Barron at his camp the following day for a private parley. In both instances, his message was the same—that he would make war only if the United States declined to abrogate the Fort Wayne Treaty. Harrison promised to forward Tecumseh's terms to the Great Father but advised the Shawnee to hold out no great hope that Madison would accede to them. "Well," replied Tecumseh, "as the Great [Father] is to determine the matter, I hope the Great Spirit will put sense enough in his head to induce him to direct you to give up this land. It is true, he is so far off, he will not be injured by the war; he may still sit in his town and drink his wine, whilst you and I will have to fight it out."

Harrison asked Tecumseh a pointed question. In the event of war, would he refrain from butchering women and children and slaughtering wounded or captured soldiers? Tecumseh agreed; he would abide by the white man's rules of war. That impressed Harrison. "Tecumseh," he concluded, "possesses more integrity than any other of the chiefs who [has] attained so much distinction."[8]

The fiery words of the council flew no farther than Grouseland. No trouble came from Prophetstown. Nor did Governor Harrison expect any. Too many warriors from distant tribes had gone home for the autumn hunt. Tecumseh also knew he lacked the force necessary to back up his threats. Particularly troubling was the wounding of Main Poc in battle against the Osages. Without his leadership, Illinois Potawatomi warriors wavered in their support for the Shawnee brothers' cause, which increasingly bore Tecumseh's imprimatur.

In late August, Tecumseh left Prophetstown to shore up the western alliance and perhaps recruit new adherents before the winter snows drew a blustery curtain on intertribal diplomacy. To what extent Tenskwatawa had a part in his brother's designs remains uncertain. But Tenskwatawa was fixed to the village. Perhaps his strong-willed wife Gimewane kept him at home. More likely Tenskwatawa believed he must remain in Prophetstown to keep the sacred fires burning and the followers faithful. Tecumseh, however, was unencumbered. It would be he who would carry the message farthest afield, a call to unity that was now as political as it was spiritual.

The Illinois Territory ached with beauty sure to stir an itinerant Indian's soul. Here the deep and dark deciduous forests of Tecumseh's country gave way to vast grasslands interlaced with a spidery network of broad rivers. Bison herds roamed widely. Indian corn grew tall and strong. The wide, well-timbered river valleys abounded with deer. North of the Sangamon River, the Indians held sway. The only American presence was John Kinzie's trading post and Fort Dearborn on the Chicago River, around which huddled a handful of settlers.

Shabbona, a burly, thirty-five-year-old Ottawa, found life in northern Illinois eminently satisfying. He had married well; his wife was the daughter of a Potawatomi village chief. When his father-in-law died, Shabbona succeeded him. He moved the band up the Fox River to a spot a day or two's ride west of Fort Dearborn. On a warm and sunny afternoon in September 1810, while Shabbona and several friends kicked a leather ball around the village's dirt playing-field, Tecumseh and three of his leading warriors rode into the village on fine black ponies lightly dulled with dust. A gregarious and accommodating host, Shabbona ordered a dog killed and served at a feast in Tecumseh's honor. Tecumseh took care not to rush his message. He sang and danced the night away with his host. When he addressed the village council the next day, he won over Shabbona. Together they journeyed to Potawatomi villages on the Illinois River. But Shabbona's enthusiasm for the pan-Indian brothers' alliance was not contagious, and Tecumseh's appeal fell flat with Potawatomis who were not already loyal to Main Poc.

Swinging far north into what is today Wisconsin, Tecumseh, his retinue of three warriors, and Shabbona visited Menominee villages near Green Bay. Again, Tecumseh stumbled. In council with the powerful Chief Tometah and his warriors, Tecumseh spoke fervently of certain victory if the Americans provoked a war, citing as omens his own personal triumphs—the enemies he had slain, the scalps he had taken, and his besting of Kenton's Kentuckians. Tometah politely acknowledged Tecumseh's exploits. Then, lifting his arms, he exclaimed, "But it is my boast that these hands are unstained with human blood!" That broke the spell Tecumseh had cast over the young warriors. Tometah continued, calmly now. Although he appreciated the injustice of American intrusion on Indian lands, he saw nothing to be gained from a conflict. If his young men wished to leave their own untrammeled hunting grounds on a hopeless quest with Tecumseh, they were free to do so; none did. Shabbona parted company with Tecumseh on the Rock River in northwestern Illinois, where the Shawnee met with a lukewarm reception from the Sauks, and Shabbona returned to his village with a promise to visit Prophetstown come spring.[9]

His recruiting drive in shambles, Tecumseh decided to journey on to the western Shawnees. Perhaps he might win some of them over. At a minimum, he would renew kinship ties. Nearly two decades had elapsed since he ventured across the Mississippi with Cheeseekau and contemplated making a home among the transplanted Shawnees. Tecumseh's mother may have died; there is no reliable record of her later life. In any event, Tecumseh found the Missouri Shawnees in turmoil. Their villages boasted comfortable log houses, well-made barns and granaries, and an admirable quantity of livestock. Relations with a nearby American settlement were friendly. But there were ominous portents. Game had grown scarce. Frontier ruffians filtered onto their land, hawking whiskey and stealing horses. American officials were sympathetic only to a point. "In truth," reported one government agent, the Shawnees were "said to be the wealthiest [Indians] in the country, but they are greatly debauched and debilitated by . . . ardent spirits." And, the official might have added, they were hysterical over a witchcraft scare, which was inspired not by Tenskwatawa but by the traditional Shawnee fear of witches and roiled by a prospective war with the Osages. Already the Shawnees had hacked to death three tribesmen accused of having transformed themselves into beasts to torment their people. Tecumseh was appalled. He threw his considerable influence into ending the witch hunts. But arguments against fighting the Osages fell on deaf ears, and he convinced no warriors to return east with him.

Tecumseh went home empty-handed. Alliance building was at best a halting endeavor.[10]

In the autumn of 1810 the Wabash Valley basked in a tranquility that Tenskwatawa had no desire to disturb. The Winnebagos and Kickapoos had departed for the autumn hunt, their loyalty intact. The women of Prophetstown harvested enough corn and pumpkins to last the three hundred villagers until spring. Michel Brouillette benefited from Tenskwatawa's good spirits when he came to Prophetstown in mid-October with a conciliatory letter from Harrison. Just four months earlier, Tecumseh had expelled Brouillette as a spy. Now Tenskwatawa embraced him as an old friend. The Prophet expressed himself pleased with Harrison's message but also made clear that he would resist surveys of the Fort Wayne Treaty land. With typical bravado, Tenskwatawa boasted about the great number of warriors he commanded, even if only from afar.[11]

The diplomatic maneuvering of the Shawnee brothers versus the territorial governors ground on. At Brownstown in September, Gov. William Hull of the Michigan Territory called an intertribal council to bestow gifts and assess loyalties. The task appeared easy enough. At least two thousand Indians attended. The chiefs—Tarhe, Little Turtle, and Black Hoof being the most notable—opposed the Shawnee brothers, though their young warriors were ambivalent. To win them over, Hull invited the Iroquois chief and renowned orator Red

Jacket to declaim for a day on the beneficence of the American Great Father and the contrasting evils attendant to walking Tenskwatawa's crooked road.

Not only the Indians present but also the people of the United States were listening—such was both Red Jacket's prominence and the growing American unease over the Shawnee Prophet. Red Jacket spoke as if the Great Father had scripted him, and newspapers nationwide reproduced his speech. Red Jacket did not consider that Tecumseh merited a mention, but he went to great lengths to discredit Tenskwatawa. The Shawnee Prophet, asserted Red Jacket, had "no object except his own interest and the gratification of his ambition; that he was endeavoring to destroy the authority of the old chiefs, assume the power himself, and depend upon the inconsiderate young warriors for support." The young men, however, should "all unite against him and listen to the advice of their old chiefs" and help them "prevent [the Prophet's] interference with other nations and his pernicious influence."

At Governor Hull's behest, the gathered chiefs warned Tenskwatawa against subverting their authority. If the Prophet wished to live apart from other Indians, they had no objection but declared, "You must invite no other nations. We are willing to forget what is past, provided the same thing does not take place in the future."[12]

Their words were written on the wind. Not only did Tenskwatawa ignore them, but so did the young warriors. At least that was the conclusion of Matthew Elliott, who had crossed the Detroit River from Amherstburg to interview Indian informants, including many of the very chiefs whom Hull feted. From them, Elliott concluded that the warriors indeed were ascendant. They "now see that their interests are trampled upon by their neighbors [and] publicly say so."[13]

Meanwhile, at Fort Wayne, the American Indian agent John Johnston was having troubles of his own with the heretofore pliant treaty tribes. In early October he met with 1,779 Potawatomis, Delawares, Shawnees, and Miamis to distribute annuity payments, much of which was compensation for the 1809 Fort Wayne Treaty. Black Hoof's Shawnees and the eastern Potawatomis, who together comprised more than half the total present, were eager to be paid. But a large portion of the Miamis, who had fallen under the sway of a radical chief named Pacan, spurned the annuities. They claimed they had signed the Fort Wayne Treaty with "the tomahawk hung over their necks." If the Long Knives

attempted to occupy the region, the Miamis would fight. Johnston was
up against the wall. He had so antagonized Little Turtle and William
Wells that they would have nothing to do with him. Consequently, his
only recourse was to threaten to use soldiers to enforce compliance
with the treaty. Sputtering with frustration, Johnston accused Pacan
of being a pawn of the Shawnee Prophet, whose "insolence" had
exhausted the Great Father's patience. After the dissidents stalked off,
Johnston distributed annuities to the eastern Potawatomis and Black
Hoof's Shawnees. He then covered his tracks with official Washington.
Papering over the possibility that the Miamis might fall in with the
Prophet, Johnston termed the conference "highly satisfactory." Neither Tenskwatawa nor Tecumseh had dared to attend, but they sent
two emissaries to encourage the malcontents.[14]

Dissension in the Miami ranks represented a diplomatic victory for
the Shawnee brothers. They did more than vicariously upend Johnston's council, however. After Tecumseh returned from the Illinois
Territory, they collaborated to blunt American initiatives and shore
up British support. Tenskwatawa sent the Great Wampum Belt—
which the Michigan Wyandots, perhaps fearful that the Fort Wayne
Treaty portended similar machinations by Governor Hull, had loaned
to the Shawnee brothers—to Illinois tribes that had been unrecep-
tive to Tecumseh's overtures. The sacred object had the desired effect.
Troubled Indian agents reported that the Sauks and Winnebagos not
only welcomed the Prophet's envoys but also "breathed nothing but
war against the United States." The Fort Wayne Treaty cast a sinister
shadow far deeper into the Indian country than Harrison had imagined possible when he contemplated his land grab.[15]

Having made progress in winning over new Indian adherents, in
November 1810, Tecumseh and a contingent of Prophetstown warriors
traveled to Amherstburg to take the measure of the redcoats. The first
order of business was somber. The Indian trader and part-time British
agent Frederick Fisher had died unexpectedly on November 12. Three
days later, at a gathering of two thousand northern and western chiefs
and warriors, some of whom had attended Hull's conference, Tecumseh took center stage. He had his grandest audience to date, and he
made the most of it.

First, Tecumseh offered Matthew Elliott prodigious quantities of
white wampum to express his grief over Fisher's passing. Then he

wept. Next, Tecumseh unwrapped the Great Wampum Belt, with its depiction of a British hand at one end, an Indian hand at the other, and a heart in the center, for all to see. He pronounced the Prophet's confederacy strong enough to defend itself. He also declared an end to the influence of the treaty chiefs, many of whom were present. "We the warriors now manage the affairs of our nation," Tecumseh avowed, "and we sit at or near the borders where the contest will begin." The Indians had no need of British troops, just powder, ball, arms, and provisions. And then Tecumseh dropped a diplomatic bombshell. He intended to expand the alliance with a visit to the "Mid Day"—the land of the four powerful tribes south of the Ohio River, the Choctaws, Cherokees, Chickasaws, and Creeks—that he would undertake in 1811.

After the stir from Tecumseh's announcement subsided, Elliott lavished gifts on the Shawnee chief's party. He promised arms and ammunition but "out of regards to [the] safety, comfort, and happiness of the Indian people" cautioned Tecumseh against making war. In other words, Great Britain did not want to be sucked into a confrontation with the United States. Three months later Governor-General Craig confirmed Elliott's advice as official policy. Indian agents were to dissuade the Indians from hostilities but also to confirm British regard for their interests.[16]

The Shawnee brothers apparently took Elliott's cautionary, if inconsonant, words to heart because the winter of 1810–11 passed without incident, as did the early spring of 1811. Runners from the Prophet resumed their proselytizing among the northern tribes, particularly the Menominees, who continued to resist his appeal. Governor Harrison, meanwhile, made plans to survey the Fort Wayne Treaty lands when the snow melted and the trails dried, despite a warning from the normally pacific Weas to keep away. The man who saw the British bogeyman lurking behind all Indian actions inimical to American interests was about to test the sincerity of the Shawnee brothers and the Miami chief Pacan's stated intention to repel survey crews. Harrison was simply too wedded to his hatred of all things British and too certain that they controlled the Shawnee brothers to consider that American land hunger alone might suffice to provoke war with the Indians.[17]

More ominous to the Indians' future that winter than Harrison's posturing was the unrelenting white population growth in the Northwest. In January 1811 white inhabitants of the Indiana Territory topped 25,000, and those of the state of Ohio numbered 227,843. Ohioans were delighted. "It is almost sufficient to astonish the person who would reflect on this whole country being a perfect wilderness twelve or fifteen years ago, and now to pass through our state and attentively observe the farms, the buildings in the country, [and] the populous and flourishing towns," boasted a state official. "Well it may be said that 'the forest blossoms like the rose.'"

In 1811, in the shadow of the white man's "forest," the Shawnee brothers' doctrine also blossomed like a rose, with steel-tipped thorns ready to repel intruders.[18]

The Weas administered the first thorn prick. In early June, Wea warriors briefly detained two surveyors who had begun to mark the Fort Wayne Treaty boundary, so frightening the head surveyor that he and his crew lit out for the town of Cincinnati, the only community of real consequence north of the Ohio River and west of Pittsburgh. Harrison thought the entire incident overblown, a case of surveyors not wanting to work rather than any hostility on the part of the Weas. Despite his suspicions of the Prophet, Harrison's measured response showed he was still capable of perceiving the Indians as fellow human beings. "I wish I could say the Indians were treated with justice and propriety on all occasions by our citizens, but it is far otherwise," he wrote Secretary Eustis in June 1811. "They are often abused and maltreated, and it is very rare that they obtain any satisfaction for the most unprovoked wrongs." Harrison had no use, however, for Main Poc's Potawatomi band. Nor did the Shawnee brothers care for the convalescing chief's inconstancy. Despite their insistence he behave, at least until Tenskwatawa consolidated support among the Great Lakes and western Illinois tribes and Tecumseh undertook his planned southern trip, Main Poc sent war parties to strike isolated settlements. Several civilians in the Illinois Territory perished, and rumors of a general Indian uprising flew across the frontier. Friendly Indians advised Gov. William Clark of the Louisiana Territory (and of Lewis and Clark fame) that the Prophet had declared that "the time is drawing near when the murder is to begin, and all the Indians who will not join are to die with the whites."

That was pure nonsense, and Harrison treated it as such. But he had no doubt that "a crisis with this fellow [Tenskwatawa] is approaching." Seemingly reliable sources reported that the Prophet intended to march against Vincennes should the Americans not abrogate the Fort Wayne Treaty, a bit of pure bluster on the Prophet's part. Tecumseh measured his words more carefully. He told William Wells that he would resist American encroachment but would not launch an offensive war. That the Long Knives would attempt further inroads, Tecumseh had no doubt.

Unquestionably, by the summer of 1811 the Shawnee brothers believed war with the United States to be inevitable because neither expected the Americans to renounce the Fort Wayne Treaty. Tenskwatawa promised the warriors who arrived at Prophetstown on their annual armed pilgrimage a "rich harvest of plunder of scalps." The British, he assured them, would supply the arms, ammunition, and provisions necessary to fight. But the Shawnee brothers urged the warriors to wait until they determined the most propitious time because only a well-coordinated attack would defeat the Long Knives. For Tecumseh, that meant bringing the southern tribes (Creeks, Cherokees, Choctaws, and Chickasaws) into the alliance.[19]

The Shawnee brothers differed markedly in their tactics. Tecumseh acted the part of diplomat, and Harrison's respect for him grew commensurately. Tenskwatawa, on the other hand, put up an antagonistic and boastful front, taunting Harrison with provocative words and gestures. In June 1811 he nearly went too far.

It was delivery time for the annual salt annuity, which Tecumseh had turned back the year before. Up the Wabash went a pirogue laden with salt destined for the Weas, the Wapakoneta Shawnees, the Kickapoos, the eastern Potawatomis, and the Miamis. The Weas received their allotment without incident. But when the boat reached Prophetstown, Tenskwatawa confiscated the remaining cargo. Evidently enjoying himself, Tenskwatawa told the crewmen to beg the governor "not to be angry at his seizing the salt, as he had got none the last year and had more than 2,000 men to feed."

Tecumseh was not on hand to muzzle his mendacious younger brother (Tenskwatawa had no more than one hundred warriors present, which the boat captain noted) because he had undertaken a visit first to Wapakoneta, where he was again rebuffed, and then to the

MAP 5 THE UNITED STATES, 1811

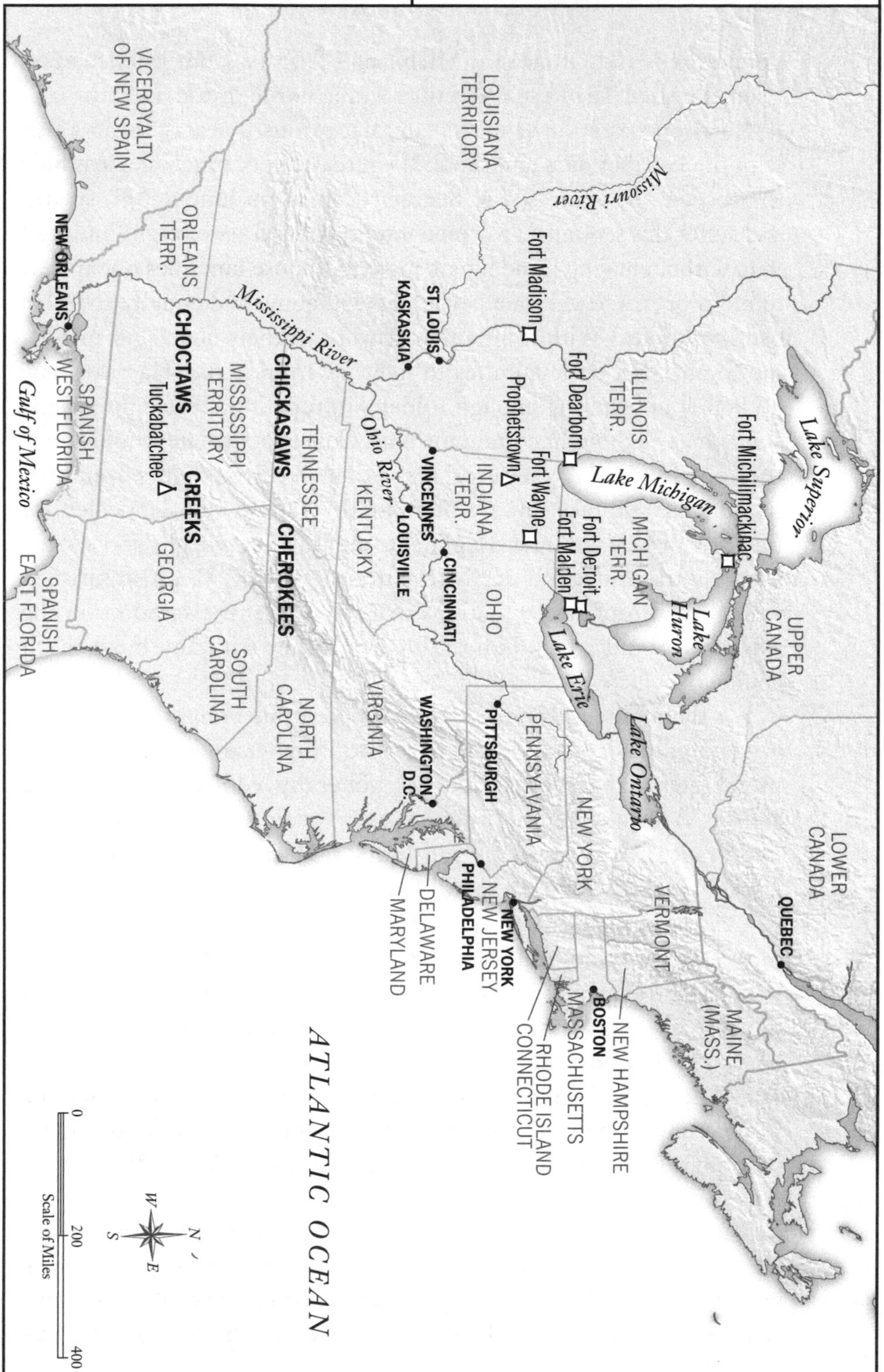

VICEROYALTY
OF NEW SPAIN

LOUISIANA
TERRITORY

Missouri River

ORLEANS
TERR.

NEW ORLEANS

SPANISH
WEST FLORIDA

Gulf of Mexico

SPANISH
EAST FLORIDA

Mississippi River

KASKASKIA

ST. LOUIS

Fort Madison

CHOCTAWS
Choctaws

CHICKASAWS

MISSISSIPPI
TERRITORY

Tuckabatchee △

CREEKS

GEORGIA

TENNESSEE

CHEROKEES

Ohio River

VINCENNES

Fort Dearborn

Prophetstown △

INDIANA
TERR.

Fort Wayne

LOUISVILLE

KENTUCKY

CINCINNATI

OHIO

ILLINOIS
TERR.

Fort Detroit

Fort Malden

MICHIGAN
TERR.

Fort Michilimackinac

Lake Superior

Lake Michigan

Lake Huron

Lake Erie

Lake Ontario

UPPER
CANADA

LOWER
CANADA

QUEBEC

SOUTH
CAROLINA

NORTH
CAROLINA

VIRGINIA

WASHINGTON,
D.C.

PITTSBURGH

PENNSYLVANIA

NEW YORK

VERMONT

NEW HAMPSHIRE

MAINE
(MASS.)

PHILADELPHIA

DELAWARE

MARYLAND

NEW JERSEY

NEW YORK

BOSTON

MASSACHUSETTS

RHODE ISLAND

CONNECTICUT

ATLANTIC OCEAN

0

200

400

Scale of Miles

N
S
E
W

Potawatomis and Ottawas in Michigan Territory, from whence Harrison expected Tecumseh to return with a horde of warriors.

Harrison was at loose ends—and dangerously near starting a war with the Prophet then and there. "I am really very much at a loss how to proceed," he confessed to Secretary Eustis on June 19. "To sit still and suffer this scoundrel to come into town with six or eight hundred men without having an adequate force to oppose him does not appear to me proper, and yet I am certain he will come and equally so of his bad intentions." With militiamen at work in their fields and unwilling to abandon their families to fight far from home, Harrison saw no hope of mustering enough soldiers to repel the onslaught against Vincennes he thought certain to come. Consequently, he would "temporize" with the Shawnee brothers until he received orders from Eustis, which could take upward of a month. Harrison also appealed for the Fourth U.S. Infantry Regiment, then at Pittsburgh, and closed with a stark confession of his true desire, writing, "I am so satisfied of his [the Prophet's] intentions that if I had any discretion on the subject, I would attack him on his way hither with any force that I could collect."[20]

For the moment, however, Harrison kept his temper. On June 24 he sent militia captain Walter Wilson to Prophetstown with an interpreter and a sharply worded but generally conciliatory message addressed to the Shawnee Prophet and Tecumseh "about matters of importance" to both whites and Indians. Harrison demanded satisfaction for the Prophet's theft of the salt annuities. "Brothers," the governor cautioned. "I am myself of the Long Knife fire; as soon as they hear my voice, you will see them pouring forth their swarms of hunting shirt men, as numerous as the mosquitos on the shores of the Wabash. Brothers, take care of their stings." But, Harrison added, he would issue no such call because he preferred to live in peace with "brave men" such as the Shawnee brothers. If they wished, he would convey their grievances over land purchases to the president or arrange for their travel to Washington for a personal audience with the Great Father.

Tecumseh was back in Prophetstown when Captain Wilson arrived. His words were brief but conciliatory, with none of the maundering characteristic of Tenskwatawa's saccharine pronouncements. Tecumseh was sorry that the settlements were alarmed by the "bad stories"

MAP 6 THE SHAWNEE BROTHERS' COUNTRY, 1811

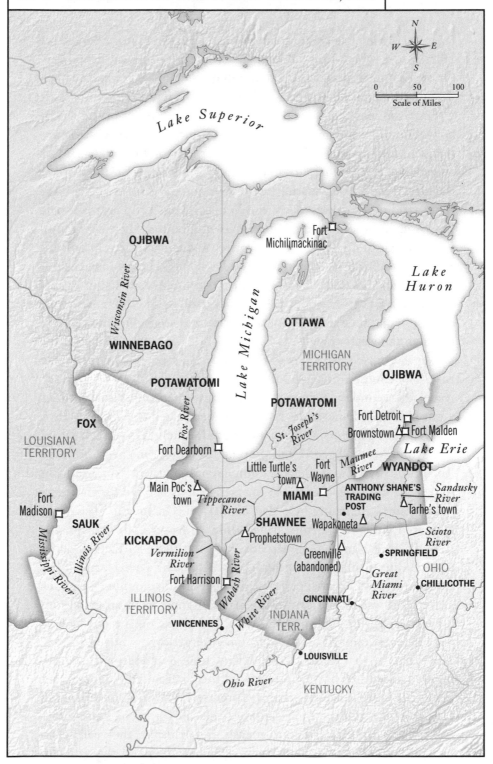

N
W E
S

0   50   100
Scale of Miles

Lake Superior

OJIBWA

Fort Michilimackinac

Lake Huron

OTTAWA

WINNEBAGO

Wisconsin River

Lake Michigan

MICHIGAN TERRITORY

POTAWATOMI

POTAWATOMI

OJIBWA

FOX

Fox River

St. Joseph's River

Fort Detroit

Brownstown   Fort Malden

LOUISIANA TERRITORY

Fort Dearborn

Lake Erie

WYANDOT

Little Turtle's town   Fort Wayne

Maumee River

Main Poc's town   *Tippecanoe River*

MIAMI

ANTHONY SHANE'S TRADING POST

Sandusky River

Fort Madison

SAUK

SHAWNEE   Wapakoneta

Tarhe's town

KICKAPOO

Vermilion River

Prophetstown

Scioto River

Illinois River

Greenville (abandoned)

SPRINGFIELD

OHIO

Mississippi River

Wabash River

Fort Harrison

Great Miami River

CHILLICOTHE

ILLINOIS TERRITORY

White River

CINCINNATI

VINCENNES

INDIANA TERR.

LOUISVILLE

Ohio River

KENTUCKY

then circulating. He would come to Vincennes in eighteen days to see Harrison, at which time "all will be settled in peace and happiness." Or at least until he had forged an alliance with the southern tribes, Tecumseh might have added, had he been entirely candid.[21]

Harrison awaited Tecumseh's arrival with admiration tinged by apprehension. "Tecumseh has taken for his model the celebrated Pontiac, and I am persuaded that he will bear a favorable comparison in every respect with that far-famed warrior," he wrote Eustis. Word of the fifty-three canoes, bearing from two to ten warriors each, that were then winding their way down the Wabash from Prophetstown held Harrison and the people of Vincennes spellbound. "If it is [Tecumseh's] object to begin with the surprise of this place, it is impossible that a more favorable situation could have been chosen than the one he occupies," fretted Harrison after Tecumseh made camp twenty miles short of the capital. "It is just so far off as to be removed from our immediate observation and yet so near as to enable him to strike us when the water is high."[22]

But Tecumseh had come to talk. And because he had not come to raze Vincennes, he paddled downriver slowly, taking two weeks to travel just 130 miles. He brought with him women and children, which a war party would never do. Finally, he apologized to Captain Wilson for the many warriors who had attached themselves to his delegation.

Beyond treading gently and keeping his temper in check, however, Tecumseh would not yield his chiefly prerogatives. Nor would he grovel before the governor. He rejected Harrison's call for an immediate council, delaying by a day his arrival. On July 30, Tecumseh appeared with 180 warriors armed only with war clubs, knives, and tomahawks. By mutual agreement, they left their muskets in camp, a significant display of good faith on Tecumseh's part. Harrison had erected a grand arbor for the event. Seventy dismounted dragoons, armed with sabers and two pistols stuck in their belts, attended him. Nearly eight hundred militiamen milled about on the outskirts of Vincennes, nominally prepared for an emergency.

Tecumseh took such a conciliatory tone that Harrison complimented himself on having intimidated the chief into diffidence, when in fact an uneventful encounter was precisely what Tecumseh wanted. He apologized for the confiscation of the salt shipment, adding ruefully that it was impossible to please the governor; the year before he had been angry because Tecumseh had declined the salt, this year because Tenskwatawa had seized it. Thunderclaps punctuated Tecumseh's remarks, and a violent downpour adjourned the council until the next afternoon.

When the council reconvened, Tecumseh declaimed on both his devotion to peace as well as his great strength; he had, after much difficulty, united the northern tribes under his leadership. But there was no cause for concern. The Indians were only following the example of the United States in "forming a strict union amongst all the fires that compose their confederacy." Tecumseh readily confessed his plans to expand the alliance to include the southern tribes and to also visit the western Shawnees and the Osages, having brokered a peace between the former enemies. Once he was able to convince all Indians to "speak with one heart and with one mouth," Tecumseh would accept Harrison's offer to arrange a visit to the president. He hoped the governor would permit no survey or settlement of the Fort Wayne Treaty tract while he traveled. For his part, Tecumseh pledged to prevent his northern followers from misbehaving in his absence.

Harrison took a hard line. He reproached Tecumseh for Main Poc's murder of Illinois settlers, actions that were beyond Tecumseh's control and that he too regretted. As for the Fort Wayne Treaty lands, the "President would put his warriors in petticoats sooner than he would give up a country which he had fairly acquired from the rightful owners."[23]

Tecumseh held his tongue with Harrison; he needed the governor's goodwill while he expanded his pan-Indian alliance. But when a treaty chief, Deaf Chief, dared to rebuke him, Tecumseh marked the man for death. After the council, Deaf Chief, an eastern Potawatomi who was indeed hard of hearing, repaired to Grouseland to expose Tecumseh as a liar. Deaf Chief told Harrison that he had been in Prophetstown when Tenskwatawa received a British call to hold his people in readiness for war (but to precipitate no conflict, Deaf Chief might have added had he been wholly truthful). In the presence of other Indians, the handicapped Potawatomi assured the governor that he would have exposed Tecumseh had he heard him correctly. A Tecumseh supporter slipped off to the Shawnee's camp with word of Deaf Chief's betrayal. That was more than Tecumseh could bear. Flying into a rage, he dispatched a runner to Tenskwatawa with a death warrant for the Potawatomi.

The intrigue deepened. An Indian who overheard Tecumseh's outburst hastened to warn the Potawatomi. Much like Leather Lips, Deaf Chief accepted the news with dignity. Unlike the Wyandot, however, he fought back. Donning his finest war dress and carefully painting his face, Deaf Chief gathered up his musket, tomahawk, war club, and scalping knife and paddled his canoe across the Wabash to Tecumseh's camp.

Tecumseh was lounging outdoors with interpreter Joseph Barron when Deaf Chief strode up and challenged the Shawanee chief to single combat. Tecumseh ignored him. Undeterred, Deaf Chief denounced Tecumseh as a coward for ordering his assassination. "But here I am now," barked Deaf Chief. "Come and kill me." Still Tecumseh disregarded him. Deaf Chief went for the verbal jugular. "You and your men can kill white people's hogs and call them bears, but you dare not face a warrior." When that drew no response, Deaf Chief directed an arsenal of Indian obloquies at the Shawnee. He reproached him for being a slave of the redcoats, more a woman than a warrior. Tecumseh kept conversing with Barron. Weary of trying to draw out Tecumseh, Deaf Chief gave a parting war whoop and then paddled off in his canoe. He was never seen again.[24]

Tecumseh might have lost face for not having challenged Deaf Chief to open combat, but he had had to sublimate whatever anger he felt in the interest of the larger objective of bringing the southern tribes into the Shawnee brothers' cause. Nevertheless, Deaf Chief had rattled Tecumseh. No sooner had he brushed the noisome chief off with apparent nonchalance than the Shawnee begged Harrison for a private meeting to reassure the governor that his forthcoming travels were not a prelude to war. Then, accompanied by twenty warriors, Tecumseh rode out of Vincennes to what fate might await him south of the Ohio River.

The Vincennes land office registrar and anti-Harrison clique leader John Badollet found Harrison's performance at the council with Tecumseh sadly wanting. Badollet not only took Tecumseh at his word but also suspected that Harrison was trying to manufacture an Indian war to bolster his flagging political fortunes. Losing the Illinois country in 1809 when Congress divided the Indiana Territory had strengthened anti-Harrison elements in the Indiana electorate.

Despite an explicit prohibition against slavery in the Northwest Ordinance, in his early days as governor Harrison, representing the slave-holding interests, had advocated its legalization. He narrowly lost the legislative fight, and in the intervening years, antislavery sentiment had grown greatly as most of the new settlers in Indiana hailed from New England or the mid-Atlantic seaboard. In 1809 the New Jersey-born populist Jonathan Jennings, who campaigned as the common man, defeated Harrison's choice for territorial delegate to Congress. From Washington, he hounded and besmirched Harrison at every opportunity. Utterly nonplussed, Harrison was reduced to slandering Jennings as that "poor animal who represents us." Harrison may have reckoned that a military victory over the Indians could restore his tarnished leadership. Certainly, Badollet saw nothing that would objectively call for a resort to arms. "We were in perfect peace and in full hope that the alarms of the last two years would not be renewed," Badollet apprised Secretary Gallatin, "when rumors of hostile designs suddenly broke upon us, although travelers daily passed the Prophet's station not only undisturbed but well treated."

Badollet also penned a heartfelt defense of the Shawnee brothers. Concluding that the "present apparent panic" was calculated to convince President Madison that the Shawnee Prophet was "a chief of banditti" bent on destruction, Badollet offered Gallatin an alternative perspective,

> Whether or not [Tenskwatawa] is a chief of banditti, you will be able to judge yourself. He has settled on the banks of the Wabash with the consent of the adjoining tribes, numbers of whom have joined him, where he and his followers have cleared, fenced in, and planted corn in a space not less than three miles in length. He has built comfortable houses; they drink no ardent sprits and go regularly to work every morning and their hands become callous[ed]—indubitable evidence of their being in earnest. They appear to be governed by a regular kind of institutions, and rise, go to their meals, and to their rest at stated hours with as much regularity as monks. They seem to taste the comforts of a civilized life.
>
> Nothing can be more interesting to a reflecting and philanthropic mind than the accounts given of them by travelers, and

the sundry heralds whom the governor has been sending to their village. How that can indicate hostile intentions I with many others am at a loss to discover. The more I think of that man and the measures he pursues, the more I am convinced that his superior mind (I mean Tecumseh) has seen the impending destruction of the Indians in their present mode of life, he has seen with sorrow the fatal effects of spirituous liquor amongst them, [and] their criminal imprudence in destroying the game to supply the avarice of traders.

As for Shawnee brothers' warriors, they impressed him "with the look of sobriety, thoughtfulness, and decency by which they were distinguished."[25]

The governor and land registrar's offices stood just a few hundred feet apart, but they may have been on different continents for the disparity in their assessments of Indian intentions. While Badollet wrote Secretary Gallatin praising the Shawnee brothers' peaceable mien, Harrison advised Secretary Eustis that Tecumseh had set forth to "excite the Southern Indians to war against us." On one point, however, Harrison and Badollet agreed: Tecumseh was a remarkable man. Indeed, Harrison's esteem for his putative enemy exceeded the praise that Badollet lavished on the Shawnee.

No American official ever paid a greater tribute to an Indian adversary than that which Harrison addressed to Secretary of War Eustis on August 7, 1811:

The implicit obedience and respect which the followers of Tecumseh pay him is really astonishing and more than any other circumstance bespeaks him one of those uncommon geniuses, which spring up occasionally to produce revolutions and overturn the established order of things. If it were not for the vicinity of the United States, he would perhaps be the founder of an empire that would rival in glory that of Mexico or Peru.

No difficulties deter him. His activity and industry supply the want of letters. For four years he has been in constant motion. You see him today on the Wabash and in a short time you hear of him on the shores of Lake Erie or Lake Michigan, or on the banks of the Mississippi and wherever he goes he makes an impression favorable to his purposes.

Harrison's encomium to Tecumseh was the last thing the Shawnee brothers needed. For underlying his tribute was the governor's contention—whether he really believed it or was trying to stir the pot for political motives as Badollet maintained—that Tecumseh was hostile and that only his own show of force during the council had prevented the Shawnee from sacking Vincennes. Dismissing Tecumseh's peaceable protestations, Harrison reckoned the Shawnee chief had gone south to put "a finishing stroke to his work," which Harrison concluded was to drive the Americans from the Northwest with British aid and encouragement. But with reinforcements of his own and free rein from the War Department, Harrison hoped to demolish Prophetstown and uproot the foundations on which the Shawnee brothers' alliance rested before Tecumseh returned from his travels.[26]

Mail traveled slowly between Washington and the Indiana Territory. Not until mid-August did Harrison get an inkling of the Madison administration's thinking on the Prophetstown problem. But the wait was worth it. Secretary Eustis had ordered the Fourth U.S. Infantry Regiment and an additional rifle company to Vincennes. Although the president desired that peace be maintained with the Indians, that sentiment did not extend to "the banditti under the Prophet." Harrison, however, should attack them only "provided such a measure should be rendered absolutely necessary."[27]

Harrison went to work with a will to make the measure mandatory.

Southern Odyssey

I T WAS AN ECUMENICAL ENTOURAGE that filed south through the forests of western Kentucky and Tennessee during the dog days of the summer of 1811. There were seven Shawnees, including Tecumseh and Jim Bluejacket, who was a grandson of the late chief Blue Jacket; six Kickapoos; six Winnebagos; and two Creeks. Apart from Tecumseh, the key member of the party was the forty-year-old Creek warrior Seekaboo. A gifted orator and agile interpreter dedicated to propagating the Shawnee brothers' creed, Seekaboo spoke English, Shawnee, Choctaw, Muskogee (Creek), and the trade jargon of the southern tribes, Mobilian. Nothing, however, physically distinguished Seekaboo from the others. Tecumseh erased all outward tribal distinctions among the men, insisting they dress alike to convey their core message: We are all one Indian people.

And so they rode as one. The southern tribes appreciated fine costuming, and Tecumseh was going to indulge their tastes. He and his men wore buckskin hunting shirts, leggings gartered beneath the knees, breechclouts, and multicolored beaded moccasins. They shaved their heads until just three flowing braids remained. These they garnished with hawk feathers. Around their heads they wrapped red flannel bands. On each arm they wore silver bands—one above and one below the elbow, and a third around the wrist. Around their necks hung silver gorgets, and heavy silver rings dangled from their ears. Semicircular streaks of war paint ran from eye to cheekbone. Their temples bore a small red dot; their chests, a large red circle.

They carried new .60-caliber British Indian-trade flintlock muskets, tomahawks, and scalping knives. Tecumseh's attire varied from the others in only one respect; instead of wearing hawk feathers in his braids, he crowned his head with two crane-feathers: one the bird's natural white color, symbolizing peace, and the other painted red, connoting both council and conflict. As befitted the somber purpose of their expedition, Tecumseh and his men rode black ponies.[1]

As they journeyed, Tecumseh must have marveled at the night sky because he and his party had a celestial companion—a comet of astounding size, length, and longevity. Discovered in March, the Great Comet of 1811 maintained a low altitude for five months, making it difficult to see until August. But with each passing day the comet grew clearer and rose higher and brighter until in early October it conquered the heavens with a coma 50 percent larger than the sun and a tail stretching 100 million miles. Indians and some whites believed that comets portended cataclysmic events. What better omen could one who had been named for a shooting star have to watch over his most ambitious enterprise to date?[2]

But the charismatic Shawnee chief would need more than human or heavenly brilliance to bring the tribes south of the Ohio River into a political alliance and to convince them of the merits of Tenskwatawa's moral doctrine. The odds against him were enormous. The four Indian nations that were the object of his appeal—Chickasaws, Choctaws, Cherokees, and Creeks—were further down the road to acculturation than Indians north of the Ohio River. "Our plan of civilization is progressive and has taken such a strong hold of the Indian mind that it is not in the power of our enemies to render it abortive," wrote the Creek Indian agent Benjamin Hawkins, with a complacency that events would demonstrate to be unwarranted. Nevertheless, the American grip on the Indians of the Old Southwest (the region bounded by the Ohio River to the north, the Gulf of Mexico to the south, the Red River to the west, and the western boundaries of Virginia, North Carolina, and Georgia to the east) was far firmer than its tenuous influence in the Northwest. Partly this was a consequence of population pressure. The four Indian nations occupied a large but sparsely populated island consisting of modern Alabama, northern and central Mississippi, and western Georgia in a surging sea of white settlement. Nearly 260,000 persons inhabited Tennessee, which had achieved statehood in 1796. Just over 31,000 persons resided in the Mississippi Territory, as the southern portion of modern Mississippi was known. And the slave population alone of Georgia—nearly 70,000—equaled the total Indian population of the Old Southwest.[3]

Another impediment to Indian resistance was the absence of a powerful foreign patron. The southern tribes had no Great Britain at their doorstep, only an enfeebled Spain, with a precarious hold over its Gulf Coast possessions of East and West Florida. Spain traded with the Indians but was careful to do nothing to provoke the Madison administration. Like President Jefferson before him, Madison regarded the Spanish holdings as rightfully American. Tribal politics also worked against Tecumseh. Métis chiefs exercised disproportionate power in the Southwest. Although committed to preserving what remained of Indian lands, many of them had taken up American ways, including a commitment to individual land ownership and accumulation of wealth, over traditional Indian egalitarianism. Only among the Choctaws did full-blooded chiefs predominate, but government pensions compromised them. The four southern tribes frequently were at odds, and the Creeks had particularly frosty relations with the other three tribes. To combat these formidable obstacles, Tecumseh could draw on more than personal magnetism and celestial majesty. By 1811 land cessions had fed a rising anti-Americanism and a nascent nativist spiritual movement in the southern tribes, especially among the Creeks. Exploiting these sentiments offered Tecumseh his best hope for success.

Apart from the sultry climate, Tecumseh would have found little that was foreign to him during his southern sojourn. He still counted several Shawnee relations living with the Creeks, and Creeks frequently visited the Shawnees north of the Ohio. From his time with the Chickamaugas, and his romantic involvement with one of their women, Tecumseh certainly knew the Cherokee culture intimately. The Choctaw and Chickasaw way of life was fundamentally the same as that of the Cherokees and Creeks. In all four cultures, as in the tribes of the Northwest, women worked the land and men hunted—great care was taken to keep male and female powers separate. Deer constituted the principal game meat, and corn in the form of cracked hominy was the agricultural staple. The same fear of witches that possessed the northwestern tribes ran deep among the Indians of the Old

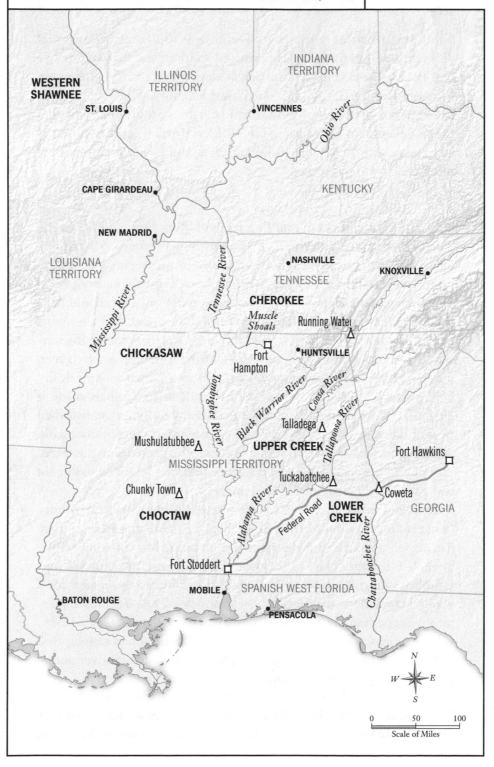

MAP 7 TECUMSEH'S SOUTHERN ODYSSEY, 1811

WESTERN
SHAWNEE

ILLINOIS
TERRITORY

INDIANA
TERRITORY

ST. LOUIS

VINCENNES

Ohio River

CAPE GIRARDEAU

KENTUCKY

NEW MADRID

LOUISIANA
TERRITORY

Mississippi River

Tennessee River

NASHVILLE

KNOXVILLE

TENNESSEE

CHEROKEE

Muscle
Shoals

Running Water

CHICKASAW

Fort
Hampton

HUNTSVILLE

Tombigbee River

Black Warrior River

Coosa River

Talladega

Tallapoosa River

Mushulatubbee

UPPER CREEK

Fort Hawkins

MISSISSIPPI TERRITORY

Tuckabatchee

Chunky Town

Coweta

GEORGIA

CHOCTAW

Alabama River

Federal Road

LOWER
CREEK

Chattahoochee River

Fort Stoddert

BATON ROUGE

MOBILE

SPANISH WEST FLORIDA

PENSACOLA

N
W   E
S

0   50   100

Scale of Miles

Southwest. For the purposes of Tecumseh's diplomacy, the crucial difference between the tribes north and south of the Ohio River was that the southern tribes traced clan affiliation and tribal membership through the mother's family. Matrilineal kinship enabled white traders who took up with Indian women to obtain for their male offspring the same opportunity to ascend the ladder of tribal leadership as the sons of full-blooded Indians. Tecumseh would have to win over the métis if he were to succeed.

Tecumseh's travels took him first to the Chickasaw country in the Tombigbee River watershed of present-day northern Mississippi. His stay there was short. White ruffians were rampaging the eastern periphery of Chickasaw land, stealing horses, cattle, and hogs and plundering and burning down houses, depredations that should have rendered the tribe amenable to Tecumseh's appeal. But the métis chief George Colbert, who owned the ferry concession that Tecumseh used to cross the Tennessee River, ordered the Shawnee to keep moving. The Chickasaw nation was at peace with the Americans, Colbert told Tecumseh, and wished to remain so. Colbert made it clear that he would pit his influence against any designs that disturbed the equilibrium—an indifference that white interlopers undoubtedly appreciated. Colbert even reported Tecumseh's presence to the secretary of war and speculated that the Shawnee chief intended to foment war against southern frontier settlements.[4]

Rebuffed by Colbert, Tecumseh hastened to the Choctaw country (what is today central Mississippi). Prospects there appeared brighter. Tecumseh spent several nights at the home of Mushulatubbee, the amiable but crafty chief of the tribe's northeastern division. Mushulatubbee entertained Tecumseh while the Choctaws prepared for a general council to hear the Shawnee's message. Then Tecumseh journeyed deeper into the Choctaw country to the village of Chief Hoentubbee, where the council was to be held. Tecumseh got along well with Hoentubbee. He gave his host a fine English-made silver gorget that became a treasured Hoentubbee family heirloom.

Tecumseh tried to expand on the rapport he had built with Mushulatubbee and Hoentubbee. Before the council convened, he and his six Shawnee followers performed a traditional tribal dance. Afterward the attendees repaired to a thatched-roof, open-air pavilion that ran alongside a pleasant spring. Dressed only in a breechclout, with a red flannel band wrapped round his head, Tecumseh arose amid a swirling host of gnats and mosquitoes. Through the interpreter Seekaboo, he spoke passionately and at great length. It was vintage Tecumseh. He declaimed on the American perfidy and greed that had impoverished the Indians and left them morally bankrupt, and he implored the Choctaws to join him in taking the British hand in the inevitable conflict to come with the Long Knives. Tecumseh also begged the Choctaws, who were then at war with the Osages and on poor terms with the Creeks, to live harmoniously with all tribes. He called on the Choctaws to renounce the Indian custom of slaughtering women and children in war. And he gave the tribal elders an out. If the Choctaw nation was reluctant to confront the Americans openly, could the chiefs not at least permit those of their young warriors who wished to return north with him do so covertly?[5]

Tecumseh sat down. A murmuring of mixed sentiments rippled through the Choctaw ranks. Most concurred with the Shawnee's call to end intertribal strife, as well as the killing of noncombatants. But few trusted the British, and fewer still wanted to sever their ties with the United States. Nearly all resented his meddling in tribal policy.

The next day a stout, moon-faced, hard-drinking, and hard-fighting chief of the southeastern division of the Choctaw nation who also enjoyed a generous government pension put an end to Tecumseh's aspirations among the Choctaws. With Seekaboo interpreting each piercing sentence, Chief Pushmataha verbally eviscerated Tecumseh. "The Choctaws have never shed the blood of white men in war, and they do not intend to begin it now," he asserted. "Our people cannot go to war against them without a cause, and we have no cause. And if any Choctaw warrior should join you in your war, Tecumseh, and he is not slain in battle, he shall be put to death on his return home." Pushmataha's rebuttal held the Choctaw warriors in check. Tecumseh exited the council snarling. The Choctaws, he told his cohorts, "were cowards [with] the hearts of women." Saddling their black ponies, Tecumseh's cavalcade cantered on to Mokalusha, one of the most populous Choctaw towns, hoping for a better outcome before a new audience.[6]

But Pushmataha stalked his path. The council convened, the Shawnees danced their dance, and Tecumseh orated as he had in Hoentub-bee's town. Pushmataha then rebutted him as he had before, and the Mokalusha Choctaws rejected the Shawnee's appeal. Tecumseh was at his wit's end. After the council he confronted Pushmataha; if the irksome Choctaw did not desist from speaking against him, Tecumseh would slay him.

Both men changed tactics accordingly. Continuing southward to the next Choctaw community, called Chunky Town, Tecumseh and Seekaboo called on an influential French Indian trader married to Pushmataha's niece and asked him to try to persuade the Choctaws to join the northern alliance. The Frenchman was furious; he was an honest trader whose principal concerns were his Choctaw family and his abundant apple orchards. He not only spurned Tecumseh, but he also alerted a fiery nephew of Pushmataha to Tecumseh's gambit. Pushmataha's nephew, in turn, enjoined his warriors to "mold bullets and [give] battle" to Tecumseh and his men. Pushmataha, meanwhile, worked quietly to prevent a council in Chunky Town. Tecumseh lit-erally slunk away in the night from Chunky Town beneath the disap-proving light cast by the panther in the sky.[7]

Thanks to Mushulatubbee, who called a grand council of the entire nation at his second home near the Tombigbee River, Tecumseh had one last chance to sway the Choctaws. Three weeks passed while run-ners crisscrossed central Mississippi, summoning the leading chiefs and warriors to hear him. Unfortunately for Tecumseh, the govern-ment interpreter for the Choctaws and the prominent pro-American well-educated métis David Folsom were also invited. Both labored to undermine him.

The council was held on a prominent hill beneath a massive red oak tree on Mushulatubbee's property. The Shawnees danced, and then Tecumseh gave his standard speech. The next day Pushmataha presented his standard refutation. Other Choctaw chiefs stepped for-ward, likewise threatening to kill any warrior who joined Tecumseh. After the public council, the principal chiefs deliberated privately. Their decision stunned Tecumseh: he was to leave the Choctaw nation immediately, on pain of execution should he tarry. The Choc-taw nation would have no part in the schemes of the Shawnee broth-ers. David Folsom, Hoentubbee, and a band of Choctaw warriors and neighboring Americans would see Tecumseh safely across the Tombigbee River to Creek country. Tecumseh yielded to the injunction with respectful alacrity.[8]

Hard as the Choctaw rejection must have been to bear, the largest prize still lay before Tecumseh—the sprawling Creek confederacy, which encompassed much of western Georgia and most of modern Alabama. Counting at least six thousand warriors, the Creeks would have represented a powerful accretion to the Shawnee brothers' alliance, had they been unified. But the Creeks were a schismatic people, divided into two factions with ways of life increasingly at odds. On one side were what the Americans called the old chiefs, principally Lower Creeks who had benefited most from government annuities and the proselytizing of Benjamin Hawkins, agent to the southern tribes and a zealous advocate of assimilation. On the other side were the traditionalist chiefs, primarily Upper Creeks who resented American intrusion. Most of the leaders of both factions were métis. The two factions not only had differing views of the Americans, but by 1811 they had also come to distrust each other.[9]

Tecumseh intended no town-to-town peregrination through the Creek confederacy such as he had done among the Choctaws. He would instead aim straight for the town of Tuckabatchee on the Tallapoosa River in eastern Alabama. There the Creeks were about to hold the most important national council in their history, one freighted with great danger for their sovereignty. If Tecumseh succeeded in rallying only the disaffected Upper Creeks to his cause, his eight-hundred-mile sojourn would have been worth the effort.

But first Tecumseh had to cross the Tombigbee River border between the Choctaw and Creek nations, and that seemingly simple step nearly proved fatal. Escorted by David Folsom's party, Tecumseh arrived on the soft sandy west bank one evening in early September. The next morning everyone set to work building rafts to cross the gentle, four-hundred-foot-wide watercourse, tying logs together with grapevines. By sunset, Tecumseh and his men had launched their craft. Some paddled, while others clutched the bridles of swimming horses. Folsom remained on the west bank. Everyone passed a quiet night.

Everyone, that is, but renegade Creek horse thieves who slipped into Folsom's camp, stole several animals, then withdrew deep into a swamp. To prevent pursuit, after securing the horses the raiders doubled back on their trail and assumed ambush positions in a cane-brake two miles from Folsom's bivouac. The next morning the victims started in search of their horses with more eagerness than good sense. No sooner had they discovered the marauders' trail than they stumbled into the Creek trap. The first volley killed or wounded several and sent the rest reeling with the Creeks in pursuit.

The gunfire echoed across the river. Tecumseh and his party pushed off in their rafts to join the Choctaws in repelling the Creeks. Both sides traded gunshots until sunset—the Creeks huddled on a wooded rise, the Choctaws and Tecumseh's warriors hidden in the canebrake. Folsom fell wounded with a musket ball through his right shoulder. Chief Hoentubbee took a spent ball in the chest. "*Sallishke!* I am dead!*"* he bellowed, only to discover, to the amusement of his warriors, that his death wound was just a scratch. Assuming command, Tecumseh charged uphill with his mixed force, the first and only time he led Americans in battle. The Creeks broke. Choctaws scalped and plundered several Creek dead with vengeful abandon. Tecumseh restrained his own men; he had not come south to desecrate dead Indians. At dawn, he started for Tuckabatchee.[10] The incident on the Tombigbee marked Tecumseh's first fight since the Greenville Treaty sixteen years earlier. A cruel irony had pitted him against fellow Indians during a mission dedicated to native unity.

Tecumseh's party arrived at Tuckabatchee, approximately thirty miles northeast of modern Montgomery, Alabama, on September 19, 1811, the most highly anticipated of several outside delegations scattered among the five thousand Creeks who crowded the town. On hand also was a motley collection of American and British traders, free blacks and slaves, Spaniards, and spies of varying loyalties. The council had begun two days earlier, called by Benjamin Hawkins ostensibly to obtain formal, public Creek acquiescence to widen a federal road through the heart of their land. Currently a rough trail for mail carriers and for civilians emigrating to the young Mississippi Territory, the United States intended to broaden it to accommodate soldiers and heavy wagons in case of war with Great Britain. The debate over the road was both heated and bogus; Hawkins had coopted the Lower Creeks and enough Upper Creek chiefs to render any objections to the proposal irrelevant. Moreover, construction had already begun. Hawkins, in fact, had come to Tuckabatchee to present a fait accompli.

Through the good offices of friends and family among the Creeks, Tecumseh was permitted to attend a gathering in which he had no legitimate interest. He kept silent, taking the pulse of the Creeks for a day or two. When asked to speak, he demurred on account of the lateness of the hour. Finally, on the third day—in a bit of theatrics that Tecumseh undoubtedly orchestrated—his warriors interrupted the council with whoops and yells, brandishing a sacred war pipe brought from the banks of the mighty Mississippi, or so they said. They urged Creek warriors to smoke from the pipe and join their crusade. The chiefs angrily intervened, unanimously rejecting the pipe and its symbolism.

Order was restored, and Tecumseh addressed the council. His brother the Prophet had sent him to the Creek country to spread word of his faith, avowed Tecumseh. Smoothly dissembling, he assured Hawkins and the chiefs that he rejected any hint of war with the United States. Rather, the Indians should "unite in peace and friendship among themselves and cultivate the same with their white neighbors." More than that Tecumseh would not say publicly until Hawkins left town. At the end of each day's council, he continued to excuse his reticence to a crowd eager to hear him speak, on the grounds that it was too late for him to have enough time to reveal all that his heart held. At night in the town square, Tecumseh and his men delighted the Creeks with what he called the sacred Dance of the Lakes, taught the Shawnees by the Master of Life. The dancers jerked, twitched, grimaced, and fell into trances but gave no further hint of their true purpose. Weary of endless Creek bickering, Hawkins announced that he had come not to seek Creek approval of a wider road but to inform the tribe that construction was under way. Opponents seethed but at length ratified a suitable agreement, and on September 29, Hawkins headed for home.[11]

Even after Hawkins's departure, Tecumseh took care to keep his message from hostile ears. No white men were admitted to the brightly painted, thatched-roof town rotunda when he at last delivered his speech. "Brothers, there are two paths," Tecumseh told the gathered chiefs. "One is light and clean. The other is covered with clouds. If you take the dark path you may lose your lands. Perhaps the United States may wish to exchange lands with you. We advise you to keep your lands. The lands we now have are not [as] good as we had formerly. Brothers, the Indians often suffer by taking bad talks; do not listen to bad talks."

Tecumseh took care not to advocate outright hostility to the United States. Rather, he groped for a commitment to the Shawnee brothers' alliance, with war a last resort to defend remaining lands and then only with British aid. Two prominent Upper Creek métis chiefs rejected Tecumseh's address as "bad talk" and suggested he leave the Creek nation posthaste. The Americans were too strong for the Indians, and the notion of meaningful British help was laughable, the métis skeptics argued, because a quarter century earlier, when the Americans were far weaker, they had defeated the British. In the event of war, the Creeks should either remain neutral or side with the Americans. A visiting Cherokee chief also rejected Tecumseh's overture, and the Lower Creeks unanimously denounced the Shawnee.[12]

Tecumseh had been dealt a hard blow. Neither his eloquence nor the refulgent Great Comet, which he told the Creeks heralded his coming, had sufficed for Tecumseh to prevail. Although nothing remotely like a formal alliance emerged, Tecumseh did gather about him some thirty warriors and a chief who agreed to accompany him back to Prophetstown to learn more about the Shawnee brothers' program. Others among the Upper Creeks were just discovering the seductive appeal of native spiritualism. To instruct them and other potential converts in the Shawnee Prophet's creed, Tecumseh prevailed upon Seekaboo, his Creek protégé and travel companion from the Indiana Territory, to remain behind.

In convincing Seekaboo to proselytize among disaffected Upper Creeks, Tecumseh had made a decision that was to have shattering consequences for the entire Creek nation. Seekaboo's acolytes would provoke first a Creek civil war, then in autumn 1813 drive the Upper Creeks into a brutal conflict with the United States that would begin with the worst massacre of white and métis men, women, and children in American history and that would rage for nearly a year. Ultimately the war would cost the Creek confederacy much of its western Georgia and more than half of its Alabama domains. Although these events were well in the future and certainly were not intended by Tecumseh, it would have been far better for the Creeks had the Shawnee chief never entered their country.[13]

In early October Tecumseh and his enlarged entourage left the Creeks and headed north in time to see the riotous colors of changing leaves and partake of the crisp mountain air that characterized autumn in the Cherokee country. Nature wore the same face she had during Tecumseh's residence among the Chickamaugas nearly two decades earlier. But Cherokee politics and culture had undergone upheavals that boded ill for his mission. Slavery had proved to be the most significant driver of cultural change. Among slaveholding Cherokees, Indian agents found the "desire for individual property very prevalent." A curious irony of their long years of war with white interlopers made the Chickamaugas the leading slaveholders in the Cherokee nation; they had amassed large numbers of slaves during their many raids on American settlements. Far from a majority of Chickamaugas owned slaves, but those who did constituted the political elite. They, together with Cherokee leaders who benefited from government bribes and control of annuity payments to tribesmen, consolidated authority over their people.

Opposition emerged to the land cessions and to the government chiefs, as it had in the North, but Cherokee militants faced geographical constraints unknown to their spiritual brethren in the Shawnee brothers' alliance. The Indiana Territory was sparsely settled, and Tenskwatawa and Tecumseh always had the option, if necessary, of retiring northwest into a Great Lakes region largely uninhabited by whites to regroup. The 12,400 members of the Cherokee nation, however, were wedged between the populous states of Tennessee and Georgia. They had no place to go except far, far to the west, and permanently. Beginning in 1808, that was what the government tried to convince the Cherokees to do—to "remove" themselves west of the Mississippi River. The ill-conceived initiative had two consequences, both of which were favorable to Cherokee unity. Some one thousand of the most militant tribe members voluntarily emigrated, while the heretofore accommodationist Cherokee national leadership stood firmly against forced removal. The government backed down, and the Cherokee chiefs' strong stand on behalf of tribal rights enabled them to diffuse opposition.[14]

For Tecumseh, the Cherokee nation was a country turned upside down. In every town he met with a frigid reception. The newfound support enjoyed by the Cherokee national leadership made it difficult for Tecumseh to find anyone willing to follow him. After lingering for two months, he reluctantly turned away from the allies of his youth and headed for the Mississippi River. Perhaps he would find a receptive audience among the western Shawnees and Osages.

The Prophet Stumbles

Tenskwatawa stood at a crossroads. Before Tecumseh left, the Shawnee brothers had agreed not to provoke Harrison. But Tenskwatawa soon had second thoughts. Tecumseh's increasingly pragmatic brand of pan-Indianism was eclipsing Tenskwatawa's leadership of the movement he had begun. And now Tecumseh was proposing a primarily political alliance with the southern tribes that would marginalize Tenskwatawa's medicine. Although he endorsed Tecumseh's mission, and Tecumseh did fervently preach his younger brother's doctrine to the southern tribes, Tenskwatawa could not find it in himself to remain idle while Tecumseh sought support in the South. And so he encouraged actions that were bound to alarm Governor Harrison, who was itching for an excuse to make war on him. In mid-September Tenskwatawa sent runners to the Kickapoos, Potawatomis, and Miamis, enjoining their warriors to return to Prophetstown. Other envoys from Prophetstown met with British agents at Amherstburg to arrange additional supplies of arms, ammunition, clothing, and blankets.

Tenskwatawa's actions were partly defensive—the Long Knives had done their share of saber-rattling—but were ultimately counterproductive. In the porous communities of Indians, métis, and white traders, there was no concealing his machinations from Harrison and little hope that they would be conveyed to the governor honestly. Harrison's principal informants, a French interpreter and a Delaware Indian, cautioned the governor that despite British calls for restraint,

Indians across the Northwest were preparing to raise their tomahawks against the United States at the Prophet's instigation.[1]

It was not only whites of questionable intent and self-serving Indian spies who cast Tenskwatawa's actions as belligerent. Seeing an opportunity to rid himself of the Shawnee brothers, Chief Black Hoof blamed Tenskwatawa for Main Poc's depredations in Illinois, casting him as the agent of Indian evils—past, present, and future. "Since [Tenskwatawa] situated himself on the Wabash, it has been [his] usual practice to gather the Indians about him for bad purposes, and I believe he will continue to do so," Black Hoof told American officials in late August. "It is him that has been the principal cause of all the mischief that has been done." While less absolute in their condemnation of the Prophet, Little Turtle and the other Miami chiefs promised to remain neutral in any conflict between Tenskwatawa and Harrison. The Wyandots also pledged neutrality and offered to provide the Americans with "early information if we know of any mischief coming your way."[2]

Both the easily frightened governor Ninian Edwards of Illinois and the recently installed governor Benjamin Howard of the Louisiana Territory advocated military action against the Shawnee Prophet before Tecumseh returned from the South, presumably with reinforcements to initiate a war himself. "Whether the Prophet intends to make war or not, partial war must continue to be the consequence," reasoned Edwards. "The hostility which he excites against the United States is the cement of union among his confederates, and such is the nature of Indians that they cannot be collected and kept together under such circumstances without having their minds prepared for war; and in that situation, it is almost impossible to restrain them from premature acts of hostility. Were this the only danger," he cautioned the War Department, "it would be sufficient to justify the dispersion of the Prophet's party."[3]

Harrison heartily concurred in the need to dismantle Prophetstown or, at a minimum, to prevent more warriors from congregating there. Tecumseh's uncharacteristic diffidence after the altercation on the first day of their August council deepened Harrison's conviction that recalcitrant Indians respected only brute force or the threat of its use. He peppered the secretary of war with requests for permission to march against Prophetstown. "Heedless of futurity, it is only by placing the danger before his eyes that a savage is to be controlled," averred Harrison. "Even the gallant Tecumseh is not insensible to an argument of this kind." The Shawnee chief had been as complaisant as a courtier on his last visit, a "wonderful metamorphosis in manner entirely produced by the gleaming and clanging of arms."[4]

There were discordant notes in the overwhelming drumbeat for war. John Badollet continued to attribute the clamor to Harrison's personal animus toward the Shawnee brothers, as well as his desire to "stifle the murmurs of the Wabash Indians in relation to the late treaties and the unwarrantable means employed to affect them." And then too, Badollet might have added, Harrison's political fortunes were flagging. The tranquility at Prophetstown proved to Badollet that Tenskwatawa contemplated only a "defensive war to protect his infant settlement." So too, at least to Badollet, did the mid-September visit to Vincennes of a delegation from Tenskwatawa proclaiming that "his heart was warm" toward the United States. The governor, however, had heard such protestations before. Seizing on a recent string of horse thefts by parties unknown as evidence of Tenskwatawa's hostility, on September 26, Harrison started up the east bank of the Wabash River with 1,020 officers and men to disperse the warriors concentrated at Prophetstown before Tecumseh was able to bring the southern tribes into the confederacy. Instructions from Washington, D.C., were minimal: Secretary of War Eustis asked only that Harrison try to preserve the peace if possible.[5]

Harrison led a colorful procession northward. The 404 regulars of the Fourth Infantry wore high black-visored caps, blue coatees, white pantaloons, and black gaiters and shoes. With their wide-brimmed black hats, fringed hunting shirts, linen or buckskin Kentucky jeans, and moccasins, the 616 militiamen were indistinguishable from frontier settlers. Harrison himself inclined toward western informality. An officer's wife who saw him leave said the lankly, dark-eyed, sallow-complexioned governor had on a hunting shirt "made of calico and trimmed with fringe, the fashion of it [resembling] a woman's short gown...tied in a hard knot. On his head he wore a round beaver hat ornamented with a large ostrich feather."[6]

At Prophetstown, the colors Tenskwatawa wore were consternation and confusion. He had on hand approximately five hundred warriors. Indian agent John Johnston placed the number at 350, Harrison at between 450 and 600, and a resident French trader at 700. Most were militant Kickapoos, Potawatomis, and Winnebagos. There were no

Miamis, only a scattering of Delawares and Ottawas, perhaps a dozen Creeks, Chief Roundhead's small contingent of Wyandots, and fewer than fifty Shawnee warriors. Although outnumbered two to one, the Indians were well armed with British muskets. Having learned from Wayne the devastating impact of a bayonet charge at Fallen Timbers, many also carried spears to deter the Long Knives from fighting at close quarters.

Tenskwatawa had expected an enthusiastic response to his summons to the Illinois tribes, but just 125 Potawatomis answered the call. Although his gunshot wound had healed, the erratic Main Poc elected to go to the Michigan Territory early for the winter rather than join Tenskwatawa. The Sauks and Foxes also held back. Tenskwatawa was furious. He made clear his anger in the speech and the black wampum belt he entrusted to loyal Potawatomi couriers to carry to their absent western allies. "Brothers," the speech ran, "you promised me last year that you would be ready in the spring. The spring came but no person was ready. The fall has come, and I look towards the sun setting, and I cannot discern anything. You have not been true!" No longer banking on reinforcements, Tenskwatawa prudently erected a strong line of log breastworks around Prophetstown.[7]

While Tecumseh argued his case at Tuckabatchee six hundred miles to the south, Harrison marched up the east bank of the Wabash. On October 2 he paused at the edge of vast grasslands seventy miles southwest of Prophetstown. There he erected an elaborate fortification, which his officers insisted he name Fort Harrison, and dispatched Delaware emissaries to Tenskwatawa with harsh terms: surrender warriors who had attacked American settlements (none from Prophetstown had), return stolen horses (his people had taken none), and appear immediately at a council on ground of the governor's choosing.

An uneasy interregnum obtained. Dark clouds rolled over the prairie. Heavy rains alternated with light snowfalls, churning the ground around Fort Harrison into a pasty ooze. Food ran short. The Delawares did not return. While awaiting resupply and a reply from the Prophet, Harrison received a letter from Secretary Eustis granting him wide latitude to act as circumstances dictated so long as he committed no acts that might threaten British interests. As for the Shawnee Prophet, Eustis suggested Harrison order him to dismantle Prophetstown. Should Tenskwatawa decline, Harrison was free to attack him.

With the prospect of war with Great Britain ever present, the Madison administration might have calculated it would be better to eradicate the presumably belligerent Indians before a conflict did break out.[8]

If Harrison found himself unfettered, Tenskwatawa, by contrast, felt increasingly constrained. His own turbulent followers, as well as his previous success in beguiling the governor, choked off the Shawnee Prophet's options as effectively as did the approaching Long Knives. Small war parties slipped out of Prophetstown, intent on winning laurels without regard for the larger consequences. Lurking Indians nightly prowled Harrison's encampment, keeping the sentries on edge. Finally, one young warrior went too far. Creeping through the soggy brush near Harrison's camp on the cold and cloudy night of October 10, he shot an unsuspecting sentry through the thighs and then scampered off. Another guard aimed at the musket flash, but his weapon misfired twice. Pandemonium ensued. Nervous sentries fired on mounted militiamen. Dragoons combed the woods in vain for signs of Indians. Foot soldiers struggled in the deep darkness to find their assigned posts. Governor Harrison rode the lines till dawn, "animating the troops to do their duty in case we were attacked."[9]

The lone Indian warrior had not only thrown a scare into Harrison's army, but he also had doomed Prophetstown to retribution. Harrison assumed Tenskwatawa had ordered the harassment that culminated in the sentry's wounding. His attempt at righteous indignation boomed as a hyperbolic expression of delight. "The powers given me in your last letter and circumstances which have occurred here at the very moment on which it was received call for measures of a more energetic kind," he told Secretary Eustis, adding, "I had always supposed that the Prophet was a rash and presumptuous man, but he has exceeded expectations. He has not contented himself with throwing the gauntlet but has absolutely commenced the war."[10]

It is preposterous to think that Tenskwatawa would have jeopardized Prophetstown and his six years of labor gaining converts simply to score a few casualties in Harrison's camp. But he was unable to control the wild young warriors from the western tribes. They spoiled for a fight and, as the Ottawa chief Shabbona later confessed, sorely underestimated the Long Knives. "If they cross the Wabash, we will take their scalps and drive them into the river," boasted the warriors. "They cannot swim. Their powder will be wet. The fish will eat their bodies. The bones of the white men will lie upon every sandbar. Their flesh will fatten the buzzards. These white soldiers are not warriors. Their hands are soft. Their faces are white. One half of them are calico peddlers. The other half can only shoot squirrels. They cannot stand before men."[11]

Into this belligerent milieu rode Governor Harrison's Delaware emissaries. Never long on self-restraint, Tenskwatawa at last succumbed to the war fever, evidently with renewed confidence in the inviolability of his own medicine. After all, he had hoodwinked Harrison and served up the Black Sun when the governor challenged him to produce a miracle. And later Harrison had naïvely provided him with food for his hungry followers. Perhaps the Master of Life would again favor Tenskwatawa at Harrison's expense. And so, while the young men gave themselves over to war dances, Tenskwatawa communed with the Master of Life—not, however, before declaring that he would burn the first American prisoner taken. For good measure, Tenskwatawa's disciples roughed up the Delaware emissaries.

Tecumseh's injunction against provoking war was lost in the blustery bravado that pervaded Prophetstown.[12]

Tenskwatawa's abuse of the Delaware envoys exasperated Harrison. "I cannot account for the conduct of the Prophet upon any rational principle," he wrote Eustis. "Nothing now remains but to chastise him, and he shall certainly get it." On October 29, Harrison marched cautiously north from Fort Harrison. Rather than follow the old Indian trail up the southeast bank of the Wabash, he forded the river and took a roundabout route to Prophetstown through trackless prairie. On a cold and rainy November 1, Harrison's army splashed across the Little Vermillion River and entered Indian land, on which, by the terms of every treaty negotiated to date, Indians were free to congregate as they pleased, subject only to the acquiescence of neighboring tribes, on the condition that they commit no violence against legally settled white neighbors.

Disallowing the doubtful claim that the Prophet was behind the recent raids in the Illinois and Indiana territories, Harrison was clearly the aggressor. Perhaps mindful that political opponents would raise objections, he made a final attempt to avert bloodshed. Before crossing the Wabash River, he prevailed on the Delaware chiefs to send three or four men with another message to the Prophet, a mission that the Miamis endorsed and to which they also contributed two dozen chiefs and warriors. Harrison's terms were tantamount to a surrender of all for which the Shawnee brothers had strived. The Winnebagos, Potawatomis, and Kickapoos, who constituted three-quarters of the Prophetstown warrior population, were to return to their respective tribes. The Prophet was to deliver up the stolen horses Harrison assumed he had and turn over the "murderers of our citizens" or offer "satisfactory proofs that they were not under his control."[13]

The Delaware and Miami troop entered an Indian community roiled by internal conflict. The Potawatomis were divided between Shabbona's small moderate faction and a larger contingent under Chief Wabaunsee, who had demonstrated his desire to kill white men by swimming out to an army keelboat on the Wabash two days earlier and tomahawking and scalping a crew member. The Winnebagos clamored for a fight, the Kickapoos were ready to take up arms if necessary, and Chief Roundhead's contingent of Wyandots likely deferred to the Shawnee Prophet.

Confronted with factious followers, Tenskwatawa temporized. He expected Harrison to approach along the southeast side of the Wabash opposite the village. With the river as a barrier, Tenskwatawa hoped to stall him until Wyandot and Ojibwa warriors who were expected from the Michigan Territory arrived. He also agreed to a council. Unfortunately for him, however, the Delawares and Miamis were unaware that Harrison had crossed the Wabash. Less several Miamis who elected to cast their lot with the Prophet, the emissaries forded the churning Wabash beneath a hard, cold rain and started up the wrong bank. Harrison would next see them several months later.[14]

Whatever powers the Master of Life may have granted Tenskwatawa, they clearly did not include the gift of omniscience. On the bleak and chill afternoon of November 6, Tenskwatawa was as startled as his most myopic follower when Indian scouts stumbled into Prophetstown to warn that the Long Knives were groping through the patchwork of leaf-choked ravines, soggy prairie, and barren autumnal forests southwest of the village. Warriors ran to occupy the log breastworks surrounding the town or spread out in the marshy pasture beyond to confront the enemy in the open. Women, children, and the elderly spilled across the Wabash to safety in canoes and rafts. To the approaching Long Knives, the moment appeared ripe for an assault.[15]

To save his village, Tenskwatawa resorted to subterfuge. Certainly, he saw nothing immoral in deceit; to his way of thinking, the Americans had precipitated the conflict. "Who began the war?" he later asked a government official rhetorically. "Did not General Harrison come to my village? If we had come to you, then you might have blamed us, but you came to my village; for this you are angry at me."[16]

Out from Prophetstown at Tenskwatawa's behest, several chiefs galloped toward Harrison's army as it deployed in line of battle in tall prairie grass just 150 yards beyond the Indian fortifications. While the troops clutched their muskets and awaited the expected order to rush the village, Harrison held an impromptu council with the Prophet's representatives. The Indians expressed surprise at Harrison's rapid advance because the Delawares and Miamis had assured Tenskwatawa that Harrison would remain in place until he had the Prophet's reply. The chiefs assured Harrison that Tenskwatawa wanted to avert bloodshed. Would the governor agree to meet with the Prophet the following day? Much to the army's dismay, Harrison accepted not only the offer of a council but also an Indian suggestion that he camp for the night on an oak-covered ridge three-quarters of a mile northwest of, and clearly visible from, Prophetstown. The interpreter Joseph Barron foresaw trouble. "I was mistrustful of the Indians from the moment of our arrival and told [Harrison] that their professions could hardly be depended on. I was averse to the place selected for encampment. I saw from appearances, and I knew from my long acquaintances with the Indians that they consider stratagems honorable in war."[17]

While Barron fretted and the Long Knives bedded down on the horizon, Tenskwatawa and the war chiefs faced off amid the lengthening shadows of what promised to be an exceedingly dark, cold, windy, and rainy November night. The issue at hand was whether to launch a surprise night attack or to confer with Harrison in the morning. Tenskwatawa had deceived the governor, not with respect to his own predilection, which in the actual face of the enemy leaned toward the pacific, but with respect to his failure to mention the belligerence of the war chiefs. Now their differences were made manifest. The Winnebagos demanded immediate action, and the war chiefs expected Tenskwatawa to provide the divine protection essential to victory. Tenskwatawa's earlier bluster before the Delaware envoys had backed him into a corner. The Prophet reluctantly retired to commune with the Master of Life. After a suitable interval, he emerged from his wigwam, wearing a necklace of deer hooves and grasping a string of his sacred beans to announce a bevy of miracles and a plan of action.[18]

The battle must be fought that night, he announced. The Master of Life had conferred upon Tenskwatawa the power to sow chaos in the American lines. An impenetrable darkness would shield the Indians from the Long Knives, but Tenskwatawa would provide light "like the noontime sun" to guide the warriors and illuminate the stupefied Americans. His medicine also would disable American muskets. The Indian triumph would be as complete as had been the slaughter of Arthur St. Clair's army two decades earlier. Tenskwatawa "promised us a horse-load of scalps, and a gun for every warrior, and many horses," recalled Shabbona. Every woman, moreover, "should have one of the white warriors to use as her slave, or to treat as she pleased." Victory, however, was contingent on the warriors killing Governor Harrison. The Master of Life demanded his death. When he fell, the surviving soldiers "would run and hide in the grass like young quails," insisted Tenskwatawa. "You will then have possession of their camp and all its equipage, and you can shoot the men with their own guns from every tree. But above all else, you must kill the great chief."[19]

Shabbona said that one hundred Kickapoo warriors were chosen to find and kill Harrison. They would know him by the white horse he customarily rode. Tenskwatawa retired with these men to the great council house to instruct them on their crucial mission. They were to crawl like snakes through the prairie grass, subdue the American sentries, then infiltrate the army camp until they reached Harrison's tent. If American sentries spotted the warriors, they must "rush forward boldly and kill the great war chief of the whites." If the Kickapoos failed to slay Harrison, the battle would be lost. This the Master of Life had told Tenskwatawa, and this, said Shabbona, "the Indians all believed." Tenskwatawa retired to a low knoll near Prophetstown to pray—possibly for himself—and watch the forthcoming contest, leaving the execution of his plan to the war chiefs.[20]

The Indian commanders led their warriors across the sodden prairie after midnight. A sharp wind whipped over the open ground. Rain fell cold and hard. The going was slow, gaps in the twisting files of warriors frequent. After making allowances for Tenskwatawa's proposed rush on Harrison's tent, the war chiefs agreed to attack in the usual fashion. The horns of an approaching Indian crescent would encircle the American camp. The Kickapoos, who led the march, would form the right horn, and the Winnebagos, who brought up the rear, would form the left. The Potawatomis and other Indian contingents would comprise the base of the crescent. After the Kickapoo infiltrators killed Harrison, the general assault would commence. The Indians would communicate across the battlefield with bone whistles and dried deer hoof rattles.[21]

The Long Knives occupied a hollow, compact trapezoid on the oak ridge where the Indians had recommended Harrison bivouac. Rising just ten feet above a grassy marsh, the ground was too low to offer any real defensive advantage. But it was hard, and a creek running behind the ridge provided the soldiers with an ample supply of fresh water. Harrison's front line, facing Prophetstown, ran 150 yards, as did the rear line, which faced the creek. The left flank was about seventy yards long, the right flank, fifty. Harrison's tent stood among leafless oak trees in the left center of the American position. The militiamen slept beneath the open sky or under lean-tos in a single rank, their muskets primed and loaded, and bayonets fixed. The regulars huddled in tents erected on the firing line. Huge bonfires roared behind them. Troops took turns warming themselves and drying their weapons. Sentries surrounded the encampment. That they would be able to spot an approaching foe was doubtful, however. "The night was one of the darkest I ever saw," recalled a Regular Army lieutenant. "The wind blew, it was cold, and the rain poured down in torrents."[22]

Five hundred warriors neared the oak ridge, their medicine seemingly strong. The black rainclouds fulfilled one of the Prophet's predictions, the American bonfires another. The flames would impede the Long Knives' visibility and silhouette them to the oncoming warriors. But the Indians squandered their advantage. Overeager Kickapoos outpaced the other Indians. Coming up opposite Harrison's southern flank at four-thirty a.m., they approached the American line while the Potawatomi, Winnebago, and mixed-tribal files were still struggling across the prairie. A disgusted Shabbona described the opening moments of the fight:

The men that were to crawl upon their bellies into camp were seen in the grass by a white man who had eyes like an owl, and

MAP 8   BATTLE OF TIPPECANOE, NOVEMBER 7, 1811

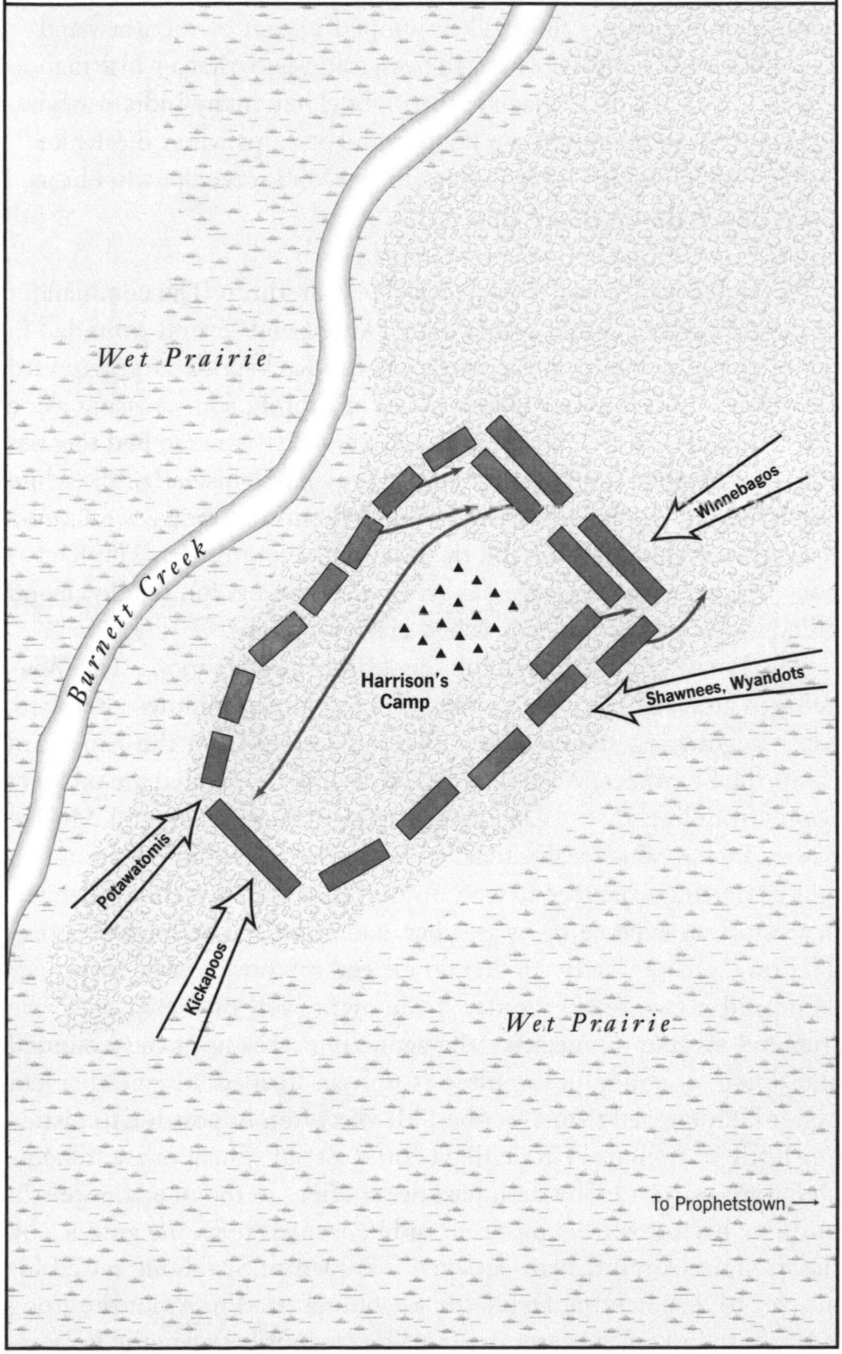

Wet Prairie

Burnett Creek

Winnebagos

Harrison's
Camp

Shawnees, Wyandots

Potawatomis

Kickapoos

Wet Prairie

To Prophetstown →

he fired and hit his mark. The Indian was not brave. He cried out. He should have lain still and died. Then the other men fired. The other Indians were fools. They jumped up out of the grass and yelled. They believed what had been told them, that a white man would run at a noise made in the night. Then many Indians who had crept very close to be ready to take scalps when the white men ran all yelled like wolves, wild cats, and screech owls; but it did not make the white men run.[23]

Shabbona was too hard on his Kickapoo brethren. The commander of the American sentries lost two men killed and several wounded in the opening moments of the battle. As the Kickapoos surged toward Harrison's tent, the surviving sentries scattered, some tossing aside their muskets. Two companies of regulars nearly succumbed too, but Harrison escaped death by mounting a gray horse instead of the white horse the Indians expected him to ride. He shifted troops to blunt the Kickapoo assault and ordered the bonfires extinguished. The Kickapoos withdrew behind large oak trees, and soldiers hunted down and killed the warriors who had rushed Harrison's tent.[24]

The Potawatomis came up on the left of the Kickapoos. The Winnebagos attacked Harrison's northern flank fifteen minutes afterward. After negotiating stampeding cattle and horses from the American camp, the Shawnees, Wyandots, and other Indians opened fire on Harrison's front line. By five a.m. the fighting had become general. Musket flashes lit the rain-streaked darkness, briefly revealing furtive Indian figures darting from tree to tree. Soldiers crumpled without the men nearest them even being aware they had fallen. "The horrors attendant on this sanguinary conflict far exceed my power of description," confessed a frightened regular. "The awful yell of the savages, the tremendous roar of musketry, the agonizing screams of the wounded and dying, mingling in tumultuous uproar, formed a scene that can better be imagined than described." It was often impossible to distinguish friend from foe. Crouching behind an oak, Shabbona watched a Delaware warrior easily dash past the soldiers to the one bonfire still burning; his musket had misfired, and he wanted to fix the gunlock by the firelight. A militiaman personally known to Shabbona raised his musket to dispatch the Delaware. Shabbona tried to shoot the Long Knife first, but a flag bearer unfurled his banner between the Potawatomi and his intended victim, blocking his shot. Then Shabbona heard the militiaman's musket and saw the Delaware fall. "I thought he was dead. The white man thought so too and ran to him with a knife. He wanted a Delaware scalp. Just as he got to him the Delaware jumped up and ran away. He had only lost an ear." Shabbona, who wanted neither scalps nor glory, declined to rush the American lines. The Potawatomis were more determined. An army lieutenant opposing them recollected the difficulty of dislodging them: "The manner the Indians fought was desperate; they would rush with horrid yells in bodies upon the lines. Being driven back, they would remain in perfect silence for a few seconds, then would whistle on an instrument and commence the rush again, while others would creep up close to the lines on their hands and knees and get behind trees for their support."

Joseph Barron understood the significance of the brief pauses between onrushes: every time a warrior fell, the whooping leaders nearest him would cease their clamor. As the darkness melted into a gray gunpowder-tinged twilight and Harrison's lines held, the hiatuses grew more frequent. At seven a.m. sunrise put shadows to flight, and Indian morale weakened. "Our warriors saw that the Prophet's grand plan had failed—that the great white chief was riding fearlessly among his troops in spite of bullets, and their hearts melted," remembered Shabbona. "After that...our men all scattered and tried to get away."

Shabbona perhaps overstated the impact of Governor Harrison's survival on Indian resolve. Unlike the Ottawa Shabbona, many Potawatomis believed themselves on the verge of victory notwithstanding Harrison's escape and instead blamed their failure to rout the American army on a lack of powder and lead. Most were down to their last rounds. In any event, counterattacking infantrymen drove the Indians from the field at bayonet point. Saber-wielding dragoons pursued them into the marshes beyond the ridge. Slow runners among the warriors suffered a hard fate. An Indiana militiaman saw a wounded Indian stand up in the middle of the flooded prairie and stagger toward the timber bordering Prophetstown. A moment later a member of his company rushed down the ridge and shot the man dead. Then four brutal Kentucky volunteers crossed the prairie to claim the spoils of war. They divided the warrior's scalp into four pieces, "each one cutting a hole in a piece, putting his ramrod through the hole and placing his part of the scalp just behind the first thimble of his gun near its muzzle. Such was the fate of nearly all of the Indians found dead on the battleground, and such was the disposition of their scalps."[25]

Tenskwatawa took no part in the Battle of Tippecanoe. On a hill well beyond the range of American bullets, he passed the early morning in incantations, enjoining the Master of Life to fulfill his promise of victory. As the warriors broke, Tenskwatawa fled into Prophetstown, where furious warriors denounced his impotent medicine. The Winnebagos, long his most devoted followers, had suffered disproportionately high losses, including their war chief. Seizing Tenskwatawa, they brandished war clubs over his head and demanded to know why he had misled them into believing "that the white people were dead or crazy when they were all in their senses and fought like the Devil."

Tenskwatawa thought fast. The blame for defeat, he said, rested not with him but with one of his wives, who had neglected to tell him that she was menstruating. All warriors understood that menstrual blood could nullify the strongest medicine of men; consequently, menstruating women were forbidden to handle sacred objects. But the foolish woman had not told Tenskwatawa, who permitted her to assist him in his prayers and manipulate his sacred strings of beans. If the Winnebagos and other warriors would only rally, Tenskwatawa would clean his sacraments and again make medicine guaranteeing victory over the Long Knives. Spurning him but sparing his life for fear that killing the Prophet would bring divinely wrought death on themselves, the Winnebagos joined the general exodus from Prophetstown. Tenskwatawa also abandoned his sacred village, his reputation tarnished but not forfeited.[26]

Harrison was content to allow the Indians to depart. He had been hurt badly, losing 62 dead and 126 wounded, or nearly 20 percent of his force. On November 8 his hungry troops entered Prophetstown. After stuffing themselves and their knapsacks with abandoned Indian food supplies, they burned the village and the five thousand bushels of corn that the Indians had laid up for the winter. The next afternoon Harrison began the march home. The temperature plummeted. Wagons jostled the wounded over a prairie slick with ice. Muddied and weary soldiers stumbled along in ragged files. Vincennes would see no victory parade.

Indian casualties at Tippecanoe are difficult to calculate. They likely ranged from twenty-five to thirty-six dead and perhaps twice that number wounded. Harrison hastened to paint the battle as a stunning triumph, but dissenting voices emerged before the ink had dried on his report. From Indian accounts of Tippecanoe, the Indian agent John Johnston concluded that "the governor has been outgeneraled by them, which is the more extraordinary when we consider his long acquaintance with their history and character." Meeting with a Kickapoo chief who had seen action at Tippecanoe, Matthew Elliott, the venerable Indian superintendent at Amherstburg, reported that the "Prophet and his people do not appear as a vanquished enemy." Elliott's upbeat appraisal notwithstanding, difficult days lay ahead for Tenskwatawa.[27]

From the Ashes of Prophetstown

Tecumseh's tour of the Old Southwest was over. As he departed, so did the comet that had illuminated his ill-starred odyssey. The skies quieted. The moon cycle continued the predictable path by which the Indians measured the passage of time. The Long Moon yielded to the Eccentric Moon; the Severe Moon waited its turn. And then the earth exploded.

It was 2:20 a.m. on Monday, December 16, 1811, by the white man's reckoning. A sound like massed cannon fire, or the sudden blast of huge stores of gunpowder, rent the stillness of a Louisiana Territory night. An instant later the earth's surface trembled, rolled, and burst open. Horizontal undulations resembling huge ocean waves traveled for miles, growing higher until they fractured, spurting sand, coal, and hot water as high as treetops. Flashes of light danced across the land. A dark, sulfurous vapor arose. Trees bent earthward, their boughs interlocking. Gaping fissures, landslides, and floodwaters reshaped the landscape. At the village of New Madrid, the epicenter of the earthquake, cabins collapsed, and the cemetery slid into the churning Mississippi River. Residents staggered, vomiting and disoriented, about the dirt streets, awaiting the Final Judgment.

Fewer than a dozen whites died in the cataclysmic five-minute-long shock, and the earth swallowed up seven Indians. One who escaped death told of being sucked into the ground to a depth of two tall trees before upward-roaring water disgorged him. The warrior waded or swam four miles before reaching dry land. His explanation of the hor-

rifying occurrence: the Shawnee Prophet had summoned the earthquake to wipe away the white man.

The first shock of the New Madrid earthquake, together with the
strongest of the nearly three thousand aftershocks that lasted until
March 1812, was felt across the entire nation. In Vincennes, an army
wife's first impression was that Indians were trying to break into the
house. A Louisville man was certain that witches were trying to topple
his brick home. In the Kentucky backcountry a preacher darted outdoors in his nightclothes screaming, "My Jesus is coming!" When his
wife begged him not to abandon her, the ecstatic clergyman yelled
back, "When the Lord comes, I wait for nobody."

The prolonged tremors gave rise to a raucous frontier millennial
literature, which claimed that the end of "the wickedness of the world
was at hand." Plenty subscribed to the notion. "We have had a great
number of earthquakes in this place," a sober-minded resident of central Ohio wrote his senator in late February 1812. "The credulous and
superstitious think that the time is nearly arrived when the last trum-
pet will sound."[1]

Indians interpreted the violence done their earth mother as a display of godly wrath. The presumed cause and chosen response varied greatly. The shocks advanced Tecumseh's cause with the Upper
Creeks, many of whom believed the Master of Life's rage was a consequence of their rejection of the Shawnee brothers. Among the Cherokees, a clamor arose for a restoration of old traditions independent of
Tecumseh's preaching. Closer to home, the ongoing tremors hastened
a return of frightened and furious warriors to Tenskwatawa's fold. As
a friendly Indian chief explained to an Ohioan, "the late earthquakes
took place because the Great Spirit was not pleased that the white
people had taken possession of so much of the Indian country and
lately had killed so many Indians on the Wabash."

Tecumseh likely had crossed the Mississippi River and entered the
western Shawnee and Osage country when the first shocks of the New
Madrid earthquake convulsed the land. A white man living with the
Osages averred that the quake filled those proud and predatory people
"with great terror.... Most thought that the Great Spirit, angry with
humanity, was about to destroy the world." The western Shawnees
were also fearful. Availing himself of their alarm, Tecumseh appealed
to his fellow tribesmen to return east and embrace the confederacy

and Tenskwatawa's religion. But they had no use for the Shawnee brothers—celestial fury or not. Although times had grown harder for them, they at least lived in solid log houses and owned hogs, chickens, and horses. And most neighboring Americans continued to like them. "I have always admired the Shawnees," said a journalist who traveled through their Missouri villages in early 1811. "They possess a generosity, refinement, and courage that would do honor to any people on earth, [and] their white neighbors speak favorably of their sobriety and correct deportment."

After the earthquake, the western Shawnees revived an obsolete rite to propitiate the Master of Life that left no place for Tecumseh. Erecting a small sacrificial hut, they dispersed into the forest on a deer hunt. Returning with their kill, the warriors ritually cleansed themselves, skinned the deer, then suspended the carcasses by the forefeet, so that the heads might be directed skyward as an offering to the Great Spirit. Three days of fasting followed. Men rigorously abstained from sexual intercourse lest the female power cause their immediate deaths. They prayed for absolution of their sins and the welfare of their families. Believing themselves forgiven, the Shawnees joyfully consumed the sacrificial deer and then fornicated.[2]

Disappointed by his fellow Shawnees, Tecumseh endeavored to recruit followers from Delawares who had resettled nearby. They too rebuffed him. That left only the Osages. Prospects for gaining an audience with the traditionally hostile tribe appeared good. Although the Osages and western Shawnees would not make peace formally until May 1812, they at least were able to meet without taking one another's scalps, as the naturalist John James Audubon, who made winter camp in their country, attested. Audubon, who had moved with his family west of the Mississippi, was doing field research among the Indians, for whom he evinced a genuine affinity. Although no evidence suggests that he and Tecumseh crossed paths, Audubon hosted both Osage and western Shawnee visitors simultaneously. He formed a higher regard for the Osages, who he found "athletic, well-formed men, of a nobler aspect than the [Shawnees], from whom they kept apart." In Audubon's opinion, too much contact with whites had "reduced" the western Shawnees, who "condescended to kill opossums and even wild turkeys for their subsistence" and who, in contrast to the "robust" Osages, bore the cold poorly and were less adept with bows and arrows.[3]

The Osages unquestionably would make a fine addition to the Shawnee brothers' cause. Winning them over, however, would not be easy. The Osages granted Tecumseh a hearing, probably in late December 1811, but their mood was hard to gauge. While the Osages had warmed to the western Shawnees, their relationship with the Americans was unsettled. Three years earlier the Osages had signed a treaty ceding a large tract in exchange for the usual small sum of cash and annuities. Now sellers' remorse threatened to tear the tribe asunder. As a government factor observed in late 1811, the Osages were "very much distracted by the jealousies and intrigues of the principal warriors, and for want of energy and decision in the chiefs." Such circumstances favored Tecumseh because his rallying cry appealed to warriors eager to win reputations. To succeed, he must separate them from the moderate elder chiefs, some of whom were compromised by too close an association with the American government.

Tecumseh addressed a council that the longtime American captive John D. Hunter claimed was more heavily attended than any Osage assembly he had ever before witnessed. The Shawnee chief purged himself of his disappointments and focused on the task at hand. If Hunter is to be credited—and the weight of evidence, however circumstantial, is in his favor— then Tecumseh put on the performance of a lifetime. He spoke in "long, eloquent, and pathetic strains" that apparently lost a little in translation. "I wish it was in my power to do justice to the eloquence of this distinguished man, but it is utterly impossible," confessed Hunter. Tecumseh's discourse made an indelible impression on him, and a decade later he reproduced the Shawnee's oratory as faithfully as memory permitted.

Tecumseh surveyed his audience with a look of sympathy in his dark and piercing eyes. A pregnant pause of several minutes settled over the council. Then he began. He talked first of the basic oneness of all Indians—a concept foreign to tribes west of the Mississippi— and the need to unite against the Americans. "Nothing," Tecumseh insisted, "will pacify them but the destruction of all the red men." Taking care to differentiate between the British, their "Great Father over the great waters" who stood ready to help the Indians, and the avaricious Long Knives, who sought only their annihilation, Tecumseh offered the Osages a brief history of the rise of the Americans at the Indians' expense.

Brothers! When the white men [Americans] first set foot on our grounds, they were hungry; they had no place on which to spread their blankets, or to kindle their fires. They were feeble; they could do nothing for themselves. Our fathers commiserated their distress and shared freely with them whatever the Great Spirit had given his red children. They gave them food when hungry, medicine when sick, spread skins for them to sleep on, and gave them grounds that they might hunt and raise corn.

Brothers! The white people are like poisonous serpents: when chilled, they are feeble and harmless, but invigorate them with warmth, and they sting their benefactors to death. The white people came among us feeble; and now we have made them strong, they wish to kill us, or drive us back, as they would wolves and panthers.

Every effort at an amicable settlement had failed because the Americans despised, cheated, and abused the Indians. "My people wish for peace; the red men all wish for peace," emphasized Tecumseh. "But where the white people are, there is no peace for them except it be on the bosom of our mother." Construing the earthquake as a hopeful sign, Tecumseh continued, "Brothers! The Great Spirit is angry with our enemies; he speaks in thunder, and the earth swallows up villages and drinks up the Mississippi. The great waters will cover their lowlands; their corn cannot grow; and the Great Spirit will sweep those who escape to the hills from the earth with his terrible breath."

Now was the time to resist as one. The Osages were mistaken if they thought the American threat distant and manageable. "If you do not unite with us, they will first destroy us, and then you will fall an easy prey to them," predicted Tecumseh, who closed with an impassioned call for solidarity. "Brothers! We must be united; we must smoke the same pipe; we must fight each other's battles; and more than all, we must love the Great Spirit; he is for us; he will destroy our enemies and make all his red children happy."

Tecumseh's oratory impressed the Osage chiefs, and they retired for several days to consider his proposal. When the council reconvened, they gave him their decision—a thundering rejection of his plea. The authority of the elder chiefs held; no Osage warriors accompanied Tecumseh when he departed the Osage country.[4]

It was a hard blow, but Tecumseh persevered. He swung north and then east through what is today southern Wisconsin and northern Illinois to visit vacillating allies in a country where the British influence was more immediately felt. It was likely then that Tecumseh first learned of Tippecanoe. The news marked a dismal end to a remarkable but largely unavailing six-month, three-thousand-mile recruiting drive. No Indian leader had ever before undertaken such a rigorous and extended journey in the interest of pan-Indianism; nor would anyone again attempt such a canvas. Apart from sowing deep seeds of dissent among the Creeks that eventually erupted into a bloody internecine conflict, then war with the United States, and attracting a handful of Creek followers for the remainder of his travels, Tecumseh had accomplished nothing in the Old Southwest. Neither did he succeed with the western Shawnees, transplanted Delawares, or Osages. As he crossed the Illinois Territory on the homeward leg of his trek, he enjoyed a warmer reception among tribes already committed to the Shawnee brothers, but that was cold comfort in view of the humiliation and disappointments he had endured. And now he faced an existential challenge. Much hard work lay ahead to regain, at a minimum, what had been lost on the banks of the Wabash.[5]

Winter came early to the Indiana Territory. Bitter cold numbed and harsh winds lashed at Indian hunters struggling to feed their families off a deer population decimated by white poaching and their own overhunting. The corn stocks that Tenskwatawa's people had counted on to help sustain them through the lean winter months had gone up in flames after Tippecanoe, together with their homes. A winter of misery was a certainty, and starvation a real danger. After their initial anger at defeat subsided, most of Tenskwatawa's followers accepted his explanation for the failure of his medicine at Tippecanoe. And they had only to look too at their nearly empty ammunition pouches to know that even the most adroit conjuring could not compensate for a lack of powder and ball. With food scarce and a need to attend to their families, many of the western warriors headed home. Far from judging themselves vanquished, they were eager to renew the fight against the Long Knives under the Shawnee brothers' leadership.

Some warriors drifted into Forts Harrison and Wayne to beg food for their women and children, offering as collateral false pledges of peace and friendship, which credulous officials like John Johnston readily accepted. "Our late meeting with the Indians at this post was as friendly as I had ever witnessed," the Indian agent wrote a friend in early December. "Lest any uneasiness might prevail in the minds of our fellow citizens, I feel it necessary to observe that all the accounts which had reached us agree that the war is at an end [and] that the Indians were exceedingly incensed against the Prophet and bent on his destruction." Chiefs Tarhe, Black Hoof, and Little Turtle all despised Tenskwatawa, to be sure—they even hatched a plan for assassinating the Prophet, which Johnston nixed as unnecessary—but their people were hungry, and the loyalty of hungry Indians could not be assumed.

William Henry Harrison rang in 1812 with a boastful report trumpeting resounding victory over the Prophet. Territorial newspapers friendly to the governor assured readers that "the late formidable combination of Indians is entirely dissolved, and the severed chastisement which they have received has so humbled them that they are ready to submit to any terms which the government may think proper to impose." President Madison took the hopeful commentary at face value. In December he told Congress that the "critical defeat and dispersion of a combination of savages" at Tippecanoe could "reasonably be expected" to bring a lasting peace on the frontier.[6]

Madison was guilty of wishful thinking. He expected peace with the Indians because the government needed it. Relations with Great Britain had tumbled to their lowest point since the *Chesapeake-Leonard* affair five years earlier. Still at war with Napoleon, Great Britain had imposed a naval embargo on goods destined for France that crippled American shipping. To man the blockade and fight the French fleet, Great Britain impressed American sailors of British birth into the Royal Navy. In addition to maritime grievances, Madison believed not only that Britain's support of hostile Indians impeded American expansion but that Canada also threatened national growth. A small but vocal group of recently seated congressmen espoused the violent annexation of the British possession and the outright extirpation of intransigent Indians like the Shawnee brothers.

Pushing back against the so-called "War Hawks," the Madison

administration urged Harrison to bury the hatchet with the Indians he reputedly had vanquished at Tippecanoe. That included extending an invitation to Tecumseh and Tenskwatawa to visit the White House and experience the Great Father's "sincere regard for his red children" firsthand—or feel his wrath if they refused to mend their ways. Harrison raised no formal objection to the president's proposal, but privately he must have scoffed at its absurdity.[7]

Unaware of the Great Father's sudden solicitude, Tenskwatawa ushered in the New Year eking out a meager existence with fifty warriors and their families in a small Wyandot village twelve miles from the charred remains of Prophetstown. At one point the brutal prairie winter drove them in search of game to within thirty-five miles of Greenville, Ohio. Some of his warriors boasted to other Indians that they would kill any whites they came across. But until Tecumseh returned from his six-month hegira, Tenskwatawa wanted no trouble with anyone.[8]

Tecumseh rode into Tenskwatawa's temporary village in late January 1812. The temperature might have been below freezing, but inwardly Tecumseh simmered. Whatever pleasure the brothers took in their reunion was secondary to Tecumseh's rage over the Battle of Tippecanoe. Certain that he could have prevented the clash with disingenuous reassurances to Harrison, Tecumseh upbraided Tenskwatawa for fighting before their plans had "sufficiently matured."

Opponents of Tenskwatawa would spread tales of Tecumseh "seizing him by the hair and shaking him violently," of deriding his "false prophecies and cowardice," and even threatening to kill him. There is no reliable evidence, however, to suggest that Tecumseh contemplated apostasy, much less his brother's assassination. He appears only to have faulted Tenskwatawa for not reining in the malcontents. "Had I been at home and heard of the advance of the American troops towards our village," Tecumseh later told the British, "I should have gone to meet them and, shaking them by the hand, have asked them the reason of their appearance in such hostile guise." If that had failed to pacify Harrison, then he would have retreated rather than risk battle before the Indian alliance had achieved its full potential. "But those I left at home were, I cannot call them men, a poor set of people, and their scuffle with the [Long] Knives I compare to a struggle between little children who only scratch each other's faces." Tippecanoe, then, was but a temporary setback, to be overcome by the Shawnee brothers working in concert, as they had done before, to animate the Indians to a shared quest for power, both sacred and profane, with which to preserve their remaining land from American inroads.[9]

After Tecumseh returned, the Shawnee brothers relocated with their followers to a temporary village on Wildcat Creek thirty miles east of the ruins of Prophetstown, which they intended to rebuild with Tecumseh, by mutual agreement, as chief. Tenskwatawa would superintend reconstruction, attend to the spiritual and moral needs of the alliance, and summon their dispersed followers. As the brothers always intended, political and military matters were to rest primarily in Tecumseh's hands. Having established himself as the more nimble diplomat of the two, despite his disappointing southern mission, Tecumseh would assume three delicate and critical tasks: appease the Americans sufficiently to prevent a renewal of hostilities while the Indians were weak and scattered, rebuild and if possible expand their alliance farther westward, and obtain desperately needed military assistance and other supplies from the British before the inevitable showdown with the land-hungry Long Knives.

The Madison administration's conciliatory Indian policy helped Tecumseh keep the Americans at bay. Although neither Tecumseh nor Tenskwatawa had any intention of joining a delegation to Washington packed with American minions like Little Turtle and Black Hoof, Tecumseh tried to disarm Harrison with a reassuring if dishonest profession of goodwill. Not only would the Shawnee brothers visit the Great Father, but to demonstrate their peaceful intentions, Tecumseh told Harrison that he would send a delegation of his own to Vincennes as soon as the winter storms abated.[10]

Tecumseh's emissaries strode amiably into Vincennes in early March. They told Harrison that the Shawnee brothers wanted peace but that they must decline the governor's demand that Prophetstown, which Tenskwatawa was well on the way to rebuilding, be abandoned. Harrison did not press the matter, and the Vincennes council went off precisely as Tecumseh had hoped. "We are happy to have it in our power to state that the council between the governor and the Indians who came in as representatives of the Prophet has resulted in the establishment of peace," crowed the pro-Harrison Vincennes *Western Sun.* "The tomahawk has been buried."

Before leaving Vincennes, the Indians serenaded the townspeople, dancing before each house and banging out "direful humdrum noise" on their kettledrums. They struck resident Lydia Bacon as a colorful if bizarre-looking assemblage, "painted and ornamented no doubt to their own admiring eyes very beautifully." One warrior cavorted with his face tinted half red and half green, jewelry dangling from his nose and ears. Another wore a pair of cow horns on his head. Silver gorgets and medals abounded. Despite the cold, the men danced in their breechclouts. Their friendly manner notwithstanding, Bacon was eager for the Indians to depart, particularly after they offered her a puff from a calumet that had touched the lips of "so many red brethren."[11]

Just as Madison's conciliatory shift enabled Tecumseh's placatory smokescreen, so did Indian outrage over Harrison's Tippecanoe expedition facilitate his confederation rebuilding and recruitment. In making war on the Prophet, Harrison had succeeded only in kicking the hornets' nest. No sooner had Tenskwatawa's warriors scattered to their home villages after Tippecanoe than Kickapoo, Winnebago, and Potawatomi war parties began slogging through deep winter snows from the banks of the Mississippi to the Chicago River in search of scalps to avenge their dead. Reports from the field offered a gloomy assessment of long-term Indian intentions. In January 1812 friendly Fox Indians told their Indian agent that the Winnebagos "were determined to perish or revenge themselves on the Americans for what Governor Harrison had done to their nation at the time they went to see the Prophet." The commander at Fort Dearborn learned from a Frenchman intimate with the Illinois River Potawatomis that they considered the "war between the Indians and the white people to have just commenced." Such reports led Illinois territorial governor Ninian Edwards, who never believed that the Battle of Tippecanoe would yield a permanent peace, to conclude that "our Northwestern frontier at least will be greatly annoyed as soon as the weather moderates." Louisiana territorial governor Benjamin Howard agreed that "our difficulties with the Indians are not at an end, and that so soon as the winter is over, we have much danger to apprehend from them." Even some heretofore friendly Indians appeared doubtful. The Michigan (Detroit River) Wyandots, for instance, complained that Tippecanoe "had been entirely the fault of the white people," who had invaded Indian land, where the Indians "were their own masters and would go where they pleased."[12]

A wild card in the calculations of government officials, and likely of the Shawnee brothers as well, was the Potawatomi firebrand mystic and war leader Main Poc. Having recovered from his embarrassing bullet wound and with his medicine largely intact, Main Poc had kept a low profile near a Wyandot settlement in Michigan Territory since autumn 1811, making only periodic visits to Fort Malden to replenish his stores. With him already were 120 of his best warriors, and Potawatomi veterans of Tippecanoe gravitated to his camp daily. Main Poc was expected to reemerge in the spring. As an American spy put it, "He no doubt will turn the scale of affairs either for better or worse."[13]

As the American threat abated, Tecumseh ramped up his efforts to expand the pan-Indian confederacy. Emissaries from Prophetstown carried wampum belts far and wide. Tecumseh's appeal even reached the Dakotas (Sioux) in what is today Minnesota. Although intrigued, they were noncommittal. Most of the Sauk, Fox, and Iowa Indians showed no interest. But the Shawnee brothers made marked gains nonetheless. First there was Prophetstown itself, where forty Shawnee cabins and 160 Kickapoo wigwams, the latter containing more than one hundred warriors, were raised on the ashes of Harrison's burning. Several dozen Creek radicals also resided in the resurrected holy town. Five miles distant, Winnebago allies built forty longhouses and numerous huts. Potawatomi and Wyandot supporters drifted back. Significantly, some two hundred Miami warriors broke free of Little Turtle, whose grip slipped as his gout—a by-product of the chief's taste for rich American foods and easy living—worsened. The Miami renegades drifted into Prophetstown, bringing its warrior population to eight hundred.

In the Illinois Territory another 650 Potawatomi, Ottawa, and Ojibwa warriors congregated near Lake Peoria. Although they were not yet committed to the Shawnee brothers' confederacy, Tippecanoe had hardened their suspicions of the Americans, and they were in constant contact with the Shawnee brothers. At the Indian settlement of Milwaukee, five hundred Winnebago, Ojibwa, and Ottawa warriors hosted war dances for Tecumseh's emissaries. Another hundred Ottawa warriors residing in northern Ohio had also grown hostile to the United States. Add the mercurial Main Poc to the mix, and the Shawnee brothers' confederacy already was broader than that of Pontiac and comparable to that of Little Turtle and Blue Jacket. More than two thousand warriors stood ready to oppose further American inroads.[14]

The Shawnee brothers must have been optimistic. At last the tide of Indian opinion was turning in their favor. But food was short, and therein lay the rub. To prevent another round of near starvation, Tecumseh turned to the British. He sent two dozen envoys bearing white wampum and tobacco to Amherstburg to make his needs known to Indian superintendent Matthew Elliott. On March 13, the deputation delivered Tecumseh's appeal:

> Father—When last here I told you that I would soon go to the southward. Before I went, I desired my young men to remain quiet and attempt nothing until my return. My young men did so as far as in their power, but on my return lately I found great destruction and havoc—the homes of our followers destroyed, the bodies of my friends lying in the dust around our village, burnt to the ground and all our kettles carried off.
>
> Father—All your children are truly poor, in want of the common necessities of life both for us and our women and children, everything being destroyed by the Big Knives.
>
> Father—Let me find that my young men of the different nations return with joy in their countenances; serve them alike in ammunition to enable them to provide for their families and give them enough clothing.
>
> Father—The first whiff of this tobacco from your pipe will bring to your recollection past of our discourses in our last interview, and the second will still more bring into your recollection, and the third will make everything that then passed between us clear that you must recollect the whole.

After delivering Tecumseh's speech, the warriors then demanded muskets, flints, knives, and a keg of gunpowder for each Indian nation represented at Prophetstown, with thirteen more to be laid over "for the arrival of others that they might support their families." Elliott complied. Although mindful of instructions not to precipitate a rupture with the United States, both the British commanding general in Upper Canada, Maj. Gen. Sir Isaac Brock, and the Indian Department had to prepare the Indians for the growing likelihood of war. They hoped to do so secretly, but news of Tecumseh's delegation circulated rapidly on the permeable frontier.[15]

Tecumseh's peculiar difficulty was to invigorate resistance on the one hand and to counsel restraint on the other. As the spring of 1812 flowered, he appeared to have stabilized the situation, steadied the confederacy, restarted the flow of material from Fort Malden, and stayed the hand of the Long Knives. But Governor Harrison was suspicious. He had learned of the Amherstburg council. Tecumseh also refused to discuss a visit to Washington any longer. Although the proposed trip never materialized for other reasons—Little Turtle begged off because of his gout, and Black Hoof declined because his warriors were out hunting—Tecumseh's change of heart irked Harrison. Nevertheless, the uneasy peace held.

That is, until Main Poc made his presence felt. In the early spring of 1812 he sent a subordinate to Potawatomi villages in the Indiana Territory, advising them to prepare for war. That was all the vengeful young Potawatomi warriors needed to hear. Actual attacks were few but horrific. On April 11 a settler named Hutton left his wife and four small children in the care of a hired man and visited a nearby mill. When he returned home, he found only smoldering ruins and the charred and mangled corpses of his family and employee. That same day a war party murdered and scalped another man in the same neighborhood, tossing his body in the Wabash. About a week later a family was ambushed while seeking the relative safety of Vincennes. Warriors shot the husband through the head and then ripped out his bowels. They shot and tomahawked the wife and hacked to death the five small children. All the family were scalped.[16]

The raids stunned Wabash settlers. Many were new arrivals who had come after Tippecanoe, thinking the Indians subdued. Now they clustered in rough, rapidly raised blockhouses or flocked to Vincennes. John Badollet believed the raids, however loathsome, vindicated his aversion to war with the Shawnee brothers. "The expedition of last fall up the Wabash can be considered in no other light than that of an outrageous aggression against an unoffending and peaceable neighbor, and a wanton waste of treasure and blood," he wrote his friend Secretary Gallatin in late April. "But whatever opinion may be entertained in relation to it, the consequences are at this moment as disastrous as real. The bloody tomahawk is now *in fact* raised; the work of murder has begun.... The terror is inexpressible, the country hitherto flourishing is fast returning to a state of wilderness." Harder to stomach than the fugitive families crowding Vincennes was the "consummate panic" of Governor Harrison, who "has laid down all his heroical airs and is in a state of inertia, unable to devise a single step for the common defense."[17]

Badollet's accusation was no mere partisan hyperbole. After calling out the militia, Harrison confessed to the secretary of war that he was "perfectly at a loss as to the orders proper to be given in the present state of the country." Harrison was certain, however, as to the cause of the sudden violence. Neither his corrupt 1809 land treaty nor the sacking of Prophetstown played any part in Harrison's assignment of blame. British instigation and the inherently warlike natures of the Shawnee brothers were to him the sole reasons for the unrest. Main Poc escaped both Harrison's and the public's notice; rumors were rife and speculation plentiful that the Potawatomi depredations were merely the precursor to a general war that Tecumseh and the Prophet had conceived to drive the whites from the entire Indiana Territory. Word spread throughout Vincennes that Tecumseh had told Harrison, "You have destroyed my town in my absence; I shall, when the corn is two inches high, destroy yours before your face." In far-off St. Louis, a government Indian agent wrote that his white informants in the Wabash country warned that there was "everything to fear from the Prophet," whose numbers were greater than before Tippecanoe and continued to grow daily.[18]

In fact, the Shawnee brothers were suddenly in trouble, and they knew it. Once again fractious followers, in this case Main Poc's loyalists, threatened to derail their plans. The Wyandots, perennial arbiters of internecine Indian strife, appeared to offer them a way out, though it involved a byzantine bit of deception engineered by the British commander in Upper Canada, Maj. Gen. Isaac Brock, that exceeded any ruse that either Tecumseh or Tenskwatawa had ever practiced on the Americans.

Neither Great Britain nor President Madison wanted war, but the Republican War Hawks in the U.S. Congress were implacable. Nothing that the Crown did appeared likely to appease the truculent American faction, which conceived of war as necessary to restore the nation's honor, tarnished by years of British embargoes and impressment of American sailors, and rid the frontier of the scourge of Indian warfare. In January 1812 the new Congress added 25,000 troops to the small Regular Army and charged the individual states with raising another 50,000 one-year volunteers. With fewer than 5,000 redcoats in Canada, and the war with Napoleon draining British manpower, the Crown's prospects against the United States appeared doubtful.

As the risk of war with the United States grew, the British sought a way to warn the Shawnee brothers to ready themselves but, as in the past, to avoid precipitating a conflict that Britain yet hoped to avoid. In January—concerned that the Americans, who were on high alert for British spies among the Indians, might intercept any emissary to Prophetstown—General Brock devised a scheme by which the messages could be delivered, pro-American chiefs deceived, and American fears of the Shawnee brothers assuaged.

Matthew Elliott at Amherstburg would be Brock's intermediary; the métis Isadore Chaine, the confidential messenger. Chaine was an ideal choice. Born of a Wyandot mother and a French-Canadian father, he was a respected chief of the neutral Michigan Wyandots. Elliott instructed Chaine to play the part of peacemaker publicly but to inform the Shawnee brothers privately to prepare for possible war. Stuffing his saddlebags with both a white wampum belt signifying peace and a black one signifying war, Chaine called first on the American governor of the Michigan Territory, William Hull, to suggest that some of the "most respectable young [Wyandot] men" should visit the Shawnee brothers and "forbid them to make any further depredations on the Americans." Hull was absent, but his unwitting secretary not only endorsed Chaine's proposal, he also furnished him with provisions and letters of introduction.[19]

Next Chaine and his "respectable young men" traveled on to Fort Wayne. There they ingratiated themselves with the gout-ridden Little Turtle and with Five Medals, the latter a staunchly pro-government Potawatomi leader. It was natural for the Wyandots, as keepers of the Great Council Fire, to propose multitribal councils, and so the two chiefs cheerfully helped Chaine arrange what they believed would be a peace conference on the Mississinewa River, sixty miles west of Fort Wayne. For the Shawnee brothers, it would mark their first council appearance together outside their home village since Tenskwatawa premiered his doctrine at Wapakoneta six years earlier.

The Mississinewa council opened on May 15. Nearly six hundred Indians representing twelve tribes were present. As interpreter and government agent, William Wells kept a watchful eye on Tenskwatawa and Tecumseh. Superficially, all appeared to go in the Americans' favor. Chaine publicly reproved the Shawnee brothers for having incited the Battle of Tippecanoe. Sorry to see their "path filled with thorns and briars, and [their] land covered with blood," he said the Wyandots had intervened after Tippecanoe to "put an entire stop to the effusion of blood," a measure that met with "the approbation of our fathers, the British, who have advised all the red people to be quiet and not meddle in quarrels that may take place between the white people."

Tecumseh seethed. He could not bring himself to accept Chaine's rebuke, even if he understood that Chaine was dissembling. Pride—and the simple truth—prevented him from accepting responsibility for Tippecanoe. "Our hearts are good; they never were bad. Governor Harrison made war on my people in my absence. We hope it will please God that the white people may let us live in peace; we will not disturb them, neither have we done it, except when they come to our village with the intention of destroying us.... Had I been home," Tecumseh added, likely causing Tenskwatawa to cringe, "there would have been no blood shed at that time." Tecumseh accused the Potawatomis of committing the recent depredations. "We are not accountable for the conduct of those whom we have no control; let the chiefs of that nation cause their warriors to behave themselves."

The Potawatomi peace chiefs Five Medals and Winamac churned at Tecumseh's challenge. Everyone present knew that Potawatomi warriors had committed the Wabash River atrocities; all also knew, however, that they were "vagabonds" loyal to Main Poc, over whom the treaty chiefs had no control. Such was their fear of Main Poc, however, that the Potawatomi chiefs instead fixed an accusatory gaze on

Tenskwatawa. "Some of the foolish young men of our tribe...killed some of our white brothers this spring," conceded Five Medals. They had, however, "been encouraged in this mischief by this pretended prophet...He has been the cause of setting those people on our white brother."

Tecumseh delivered a stinging rebuttal on his brother's behalf. "We defy a living creature to say we ever advised anyone, directly or indirectly, to make war on our white brothers," he thundered. The only "pretenders" present were the Potawatomis. "It has constantly been our misfortune to have our views misrepresented to our white brethren...by the pretended chiefs of the Potawatomis and others that have been in the habit of selling land to the white people that did not belong to them."

The Delaware chiefs interrupted Tecumseh. They were solidly in the U.S. camp, and it showed: "We have not met at this place to listen to such words. The red people have been killing the whites, the just resentment of the latter is raised against the former." All present should "join hearts and hands together and proclaim peace through the land of the red people." Little Turtle endorsed the Delaware motion, as did the Kickapoo representatives, who also absolved Tenskwatawa of blame for Tippecanoe. Tecumseh also reaffirmed his commitment to peace.[20]

With that the grand council closed. After the hoodwinked treaty chiefs and William Wells, who had no reasonable grounds for complaint, cleared out, Isadore Chaine got down to the business that had brought him to Mississinewa. Secreting himself with the Shawnee brothers, Chaine instructed them to gather their allies but otherwise keep quiet. He also invited Tecumseh to visit Matthew Elliott, who would further relate British plans and dispense generous quantities of guns, ammunition, clothing, and foodstuffs.

Tecumseh gave Chaine a speech to deliver both to Elliott and to the Michigan and Canadian Wyandots. He wanted there to be no doubt that he and his brother were no one's pawns. "Father and Brothers! We will now in a few words declare to you our whole hearts," declared Tecumseh. "If we hear of the [Long] Knives coming toward our villages to speak peace, we will receive them; but if we hear of any of our people being hurt by them, or if they unprovokedly [sic] advance against us in a hostile manner, be assured we will defend ourselves like men. And if we hear of any of our people having been killed, we will immediately send all the nations on or towards the Mississippi, and all this island will rise as one man—Then Father and Brothers it will be impossible for either of you to restore peace between us."[21] That said, the promise of lead and powder greatly relieved the Shawnee brothers, whose stores were so reduced that their warriors had laid aside their muskets in favor of bows and arrows. Food too was so scarce that Tecumseh had sent thirty men to Fort Harrison to treat for corn from the Americans. The post commander turned them away empty-handed.

In early June the Shawnee brothers bade each other farewell for what both undoubtedly assumed would be a brief period. Their spirits were good. Harrison, on the other hand, churned impotently. Tecumseh's conciliatory speech at Mississinewa, coupled with the end of the Potawatomi raids, robbed him of any excuse for belligerence. The women of Prophetstown could tend their corn crops without fear. Trusting Tenskwatawa to prevent a repeat of Tippecanoe, Tecumseh set off for Canada with ten warriors. His purpose was threefold: to make another effort to win over the uncommitted Michigan Wyandots, Ojibwas, and Ottawas; to reaffirm his pact with Main Poc; and to continue to Amherstburg to draw the promised supplies.[22]

Nearly nine months would pass before Tecumseh again set foot in Prophetstown.

· PART ·

THREE

18

Into the Maelstrom

Tecumseh left Prophetstown unaware that war clouds loomed just beyond the horizon, or that Congress had him and Tenskwatawa in mind as it contemplated a formal declaration of war on Great Britain. Kentuckians led the clamor. No longer a sparsely populated fringe of the United States, Kentucky in 1812 was a rough and restless state of nearly half a million people. Relentless expansion was the watchword; wiping the region clean of obdurate Indians like the Shawnee brothers and seizing Canada, or at least administering the British there a sound drubbing, were the necessary first steps. When Kentuckian Henry Clay became Speaker of the U.S. House of Representatives in late 1811, the ascendancy of the War Hawks was complete. For them, Tippecanoe was unfinished business. "The conquest of Canada is in your power," Clay told his fellow congressmen. "Is it nothing to extinguish the torch that lights up savage warfare?"[1]

Clay found plenty of support from the public, the press, and other Republican-dominated states. Tippecanoe and the subsequent Indian depredations, few though they were, had intensified American hatred of Great Britain, an outcome that delighted Harrison. Republican newspapers had carried accounts of Tippecanoe under headings such as "Anglo-Savage War" and "Anglo-Indian War." Calls for retribution came loud and shrill. "The war on the Wabash is purely British," said a typical editorial. "The scalping knife and tomahawk of British savages is now, again devastating our frontiers [and] the blood of our fellow citizens calls aloud for vengeance."[2]

For six months, Madison had delayed the day of reckoning. But with Clay and his allies continuing their bellicose drumbeat unabated, a reluctant President Madison finally submitted a war message to Congress on June 1, 1812, which enumerated hostile acts that Britain had committed against the "independent and neutral" United States. All had occurred on the high seas, in British or European ports, or along the American coastline except one, which Madison blamed on the Shawnee brothers and their supposed British abettors. "In reviewing the conduct of Great Britain toward the United States our attention is necessarily drawn to the warfare just renewed by the savages on one of our extensive frontiers, a warfare which is known to spare neither age nor sex and to be distinguished by features peculiarly shocking to humanity," said Madison of the Battle of Tippecanoe and the subsequent Indian revenge raids. He directed not even a nod at American lust for Indian land as a cause of hostilities; they could be accounted for only by British "interpositions." On June 18, Congress returned a declaration of war against Great Britain.[3]

Although the Madison administration had taken no real steps to prepare for war beyond a halting and badly managed mobilization, it could not neglect one vital point—Detroit. The "key to the northern country," the remote settlement of twelve hundred residents lay within cannon shot of British territory. Fort Malden, just twenty miles downstream from Detroit on the east bank of the Detroit River, was the hive around which hundreds of hostile Indians buzzed. By contrast, only ninety-four American soldiers garrisoned at Fort Detroit. The entire white population of the Michigan Territory was less than five thousand, of whom four-fifths were French-Canadians of questionable allegiance. Outside Detroit, warned loyal residents, "every individual house is a frontier; no one farm is covered by another farm in the rear of it." In other words, they would be easy prey for warring Indians.[4]

Concern that the British would unleash the Shawnee brothers had brought the sedate, snow-white-haired governor of the Michigan Territory, William Hull, to Washington in February 1812 to discuss how to hold the Indians in check. Hull urged Secretary of War Eustis to build a fleet to control Lake Erie and to send to Detroit an army that, in the event of war, could seize Upper Canada. President Madison vetoed the naval plan but endorsed a troop buildup at Detroit. After declaring war, he prevailed on a reluctant Hull to command the expedition.

A minor Revolutionary War hero, Hull was fifty-eight but felt much older. "Although too far advanced in years, I am again entering a military life," he confided to a friend before setting out for Ohio to organize his army. "It inspires me with great confidence, and it is a source of great satisfaction to me to witness the spirit of my country-men nearest the scene where I shall probably be called to act." Hull's praise went unreciprocated. Indian agent John Johnston condemned his appointment. "The people of the country where he was to operate had no confidence in him; he was too old, broken down in body and mind to conduct the multifarious operations of such a command." Hull's lieutenants agreed. "He won't do," an Ohio militia colonel con-fided to a subordinate. "He is not the kind of man we want, and I fear the result of our campaign will be disastrous."[5]

But the Ohio militiamen, who comprised the majority of Hull's 2,075-man army, were stuck with him. The contrast between the ele-gantly uniformed, "corpulent, good-natured old gent" and the vigor-ous frontiersmen he commanded could not have been more striking. The Ohioans, officers and enlisted men alike, dressed in homespun linen hunting shirts and trousers. Around the waist, each man sported a stout leather belt, from which dangled a large tomahawk and a butcher knife. The only concession to army regulations were the standard-issue muskets that most of the men carried. Expert marks-men, more comfortable in loose ranks behind trees than in close order, the Ohioans could be expected to give Indian opponents a hard fight. But Hull hoped that would not be necessary. Chiefs Black Hoof and Tarhe acquiesced to the army's passing through their country, roundly denouncing the Shawnee brothers in the bargain. Before starting for Detroit, Hull called for another Indian council at Brownstown, Michigan Territory, this time in late July. There he would endeavor to conquer Tecumseh by "justice and humanity." The alternative, Hull assured Eustis, lest the secretary of war think him naïve, was unremit-ting war against the Shawnee brothers.[6]

Tecumseh rode into Fort Wayne on June 17, unaware of the army chopping its way through the wilderness 120 miles to the southeast, or of Hull's overture to him. His reasons for pausing at the Indian agency en route to Fort Malden are obscure, but if he thought he could deceive the new Indian agent, Benjamin Stickney, who had replaced John Johnston, he was mistaken. From Indian informants, Stickney learned of Isadore Chaine's private meeting with Tecumseh and the black wampum the Wyandot had carried on behalf of the British. Stickney would talk with Tecumseh, but he would not be fooled.

Tecumseh arrived relaxed and jovial. Content to linger at the agency for three days, he dined regularly with the post commandant and Stickney. At one meal he teased an attractive fifteen-year-old white girl raised by Indians, asking why she had not yet married. Because she intended to wed an Indian, she said. A delighted Tecumseh related to her the relative merits of the warriors of each tribe.[7]

When his formal councils with Stickney grew suddenly tense, Tecumseh's good humor deserted him. On June 19 he spoke for three hours. Unknown to him or Stickney, Congress had declared war on Great Britain the day before. After condemning Harrison's attack on Prophetstown, he took "a general view of all the difficulties since several months before the battle" before finally confessing to Stickney that he intended to go to Fort Malden to receive twelve horse-loads of powder and lead. The agent answered the next day. Stickney told Tecumseh he knew of the chief's "schemes" with Chaine and that under the present circumstances the government would regard his trip to Fort Malden as an "act of enmity" for which he would have to answer. Evidently startled, Tecumseh dissembled when the two next met. He "urged very strongly" his need to travel to Michigan to advise the Wyandots, Ojibwas, and Ottawas to reaffirm their commitment to peace with the United States. Tecumseh's pretending left Stickney unmoved. Other tribes had no need of Tecumseh's counsel; if the Shawnee chief wanted peace, Stickney said, he could make it with General Hull, whose command he likely would meet at the falls of the Maumee River. Tecumseh accepted the startling news that an American army was on the march to Detroit "very patiently." Not so his warriors. "One of his party became sick and determined to return home immediately after our conference," recorded Stickney, who thought it "quite possible that others of the party will be taken with the same kind of sickness."

Tecumseh afforded them no time to waver. With his nine remaining men, he departed abruptly that night. He swung clear of Hull's army but detached several warriors to track American movements. The time for diplomatic feints and deceit was over. In exchange for pledging himself to the Crown, he would learn what beyond supplies the British were prepared to offer.[8]

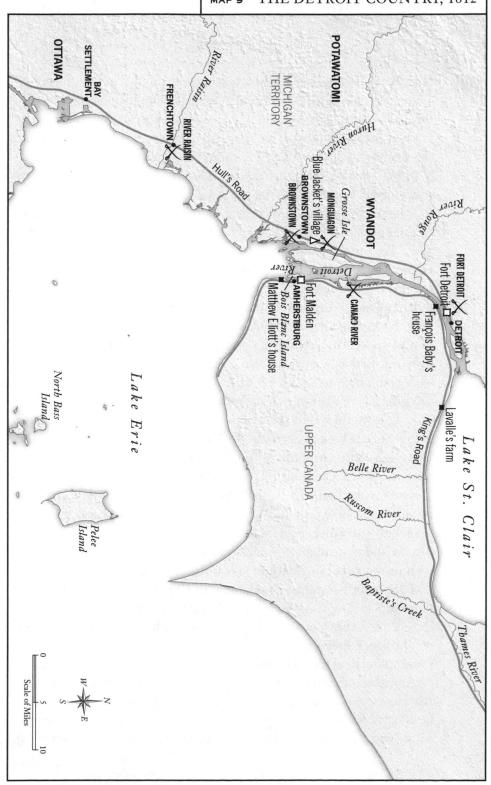

MAP 9 · THE DETROIT COUNTRY, 1812

OTTAWA

BAY SETTLEMENT

POTAWATOMI

MICHIGAN TERRITORY

River Raisin

FRENCHTOWN

RIVER RAISIN

Hull's Road

Huron River

WYANDOT

River Rouge

Blue Jacket's village

MONGUAGON

BROWNSTOWN

Grosse Isle

FORT DETROIT
Fort Detroit

Detroit River

CANARD RIVER

DETROIT

François Baby's house

Fort Malden

AMHERSTBURG

Bois Blanc Island

Matthew Eliott's house

Lavalle's farm

King's Road

UPPER CANADA

Lake St. Clair

Belle River

Ruscom River

Lake Erie

North Bass Island

Pelee Island

Baptiste's Creek

Thames River

W · N · S · E

0 · Scale of Miles · 5 · 10

Had Tecumseh been permitted a glimpse behind the veil of Isadore Chaine and Matthew Elliott's enticements, he might well have reconsidered his trip to Fort Malden. He was no one's cat's-paw—he had made that clear enough. The Shawnee chief intended to fight, not for the British, but rather alongside them. He expected British troops to help the Shawnee brothers defend what remained of their country, and together they would deal the Americans the hard blows needed to forestall any further loss of land. Perhaps they might even roll the frontier back to the Ohio River; a chief could dream the same as any man. Tecumseh would commit the Indian confederacy to defend Upper Canada only as a necessary prelude to a combined British and Indian counteroffensive that would secure Indian freedom.

Unknown to Tecumseh, the commander in chief in Canada, Lt. Gen. Sir George Prévost, had neither the resources nor the inclination to undertake anything so grandiose. At the outbreak of the war, Prévost commanded just 4,500 regular troops, only a quarter of whom were committed to Upper Canada. By contrast, the United States was recruiting a regular force of 36,000, together with militia and volunteer units that would weigh the manpower imbalance even more heavily in favor of the United States. With Great Britain locked in war on the European continent, Prévost could expect supplies from home but no reinforcements. Cautious by nature, he regarded the preservation of Quebec as the "principal consideration to which all others must be subordinate." In other words, British Canada was like a tree; the outer branches—of which Fort Malden and Amherstburg were the most distant and expendable—could be lopped off so long as the trunk, with its roots reaching back to Great Britain, was secure.

The recently installed commander of Upper Canada, Maj. Gen. Sir Isaac Brock, disagreed. He reckoned the perimeter to be of real strategic value. After touring the District of Amherstburg in December 1811, he urged Prévost to reconsider his posture. Bolstering the British presence on the Detroit frontier would offer the best deterrent against an American offensive, as it would compel the United States to "secure their western position from the inroads of the Indians, and this cannot be effected without a very considerable force." The Indians, moreover, were "eager for an opportunity to avenge the numerous injuries of which they complain." To guarantee Indian allegiance, however, the British must demonstrate that they contemplated no repeat of 1794, when the doors of Fort Miamis had been slammed in the face of Blue Jacket and his warriors and their interests sacrificed. That ultimately meant seizing Fort Detroit. But first, Brock would augment the garrison at Fort Malden with two hundred troops from the 41st Regiment of Foot—a veteran unit well trained and disciplined—under the command of his inspector general, Lt. Col. Thomas St. George, whose initial task would be to make the repairs needed to restore the sadly neglected post.[9]

Prévost tolerated Brock's aggressive posture—to a point. While agreeing it was "highly proper" to employ the Indians, he cautioned Brock to "restrain and control them as much as you can." The British must "maintain our ascendancy over the Indians and feed with proper food their predilection for us," but not at the expense of prudence. As he cautioned Brock in early July 1812, "Our numbers would not justify offensive operations being undertaken, unless they were solely calculated to strengthen a defensive attitude." In other words, the ranking British officer in Canada would not help the Shawnee brothers reverse American encroachment.[10]

Absent a change in British intentions, Tecumseh was chasing a chimera.

General Hull had problems of his own. Although he had no ocean between him and potential reinforcements, for the foreseeable future the chances of his receiving any accretion to his ranks, should the need arise, were minimal. Congress had created an imposing army on paper, but the individual states had done next to nothing to meet their quotas of volunteers. Regular enlistments had hardly begun either. The Regular Army on the eve of war numbered just 6,744 men, occupying twenty-three forts, from which troops could not safely be withdrawn for field duty. The ten Regular Army regiments, with half-filled ranks scattered across the nation, were commanded by even older officers. The senior general of the army, sixty-two-year-old Henry Dearborn, had seen no combat duty in the Revolutionary War. The only officer above the rank of major possessing an ounce of aggressiveness was the brilliant twenty-six-year-old lieutenant colonel Winfield Scott. And he knew it. As he aptly put it, his fellow officers were "swaggerers, dependents, [and] decayed gentlemen ... utterly unfit for any military purpose whatever."

If the army was dispersed and led by incompetent relics, the navy was all but nonexistent. Perhaps because the War Hawks were frontiersmen, Congress had decided that the United States did not actually need a navy to fight the impending war. It voted down a proposal to build a fleet, which for Tecumseh's purposes meant that all-important Lake Erie, over which British supplies traveled, would be undefended by the Long Knives. Provided the British and Indians could rally to defeat General Hull, their odds of rolling back the American presence in the Northwest, should the British be so inclined, would be better than even, at least for the remainder of 1812.[11]

Tecumseh knew nothing of American vulnerabilities. As he cantered up the west bank of the Detroit to the Wyandot settlement of Brownstown, opposite Amherstburg, he was aware only that Hull and his army were coming close behind him. On the American side of the river, the signs nonetheless looked deceptively favorable for his cause. There Tecumseh and his entourage rode into a vortex of confusion and consternation. Few whites observed his approach, and none offered any resistance. The French-Canadians withdrew behind the gates of their small farms, uninterested in the outcome of the coming struggle. Loyal Americans absconded to Detroit, where the garrison huddled uncertainly behind the wooden walls of their one-acre fort. The acting governor was paralyzed, the militia unaccounted for. The territory, reported an advance scout for Hull, was "like a body without a head."

The Indians also flailed about "at a loss how to act," noted the same American scout, who believed their allegiance was up for grabs. Canoes crisscrossed the two-mile-wide Detroit River between Brownstown and Fort Malden. They bore Canadian Wyandots hoping to convince their fellow tribesmen in Michigan to come over to the redcoats, Main Poc's Potawatomis relocating from the west bank to the thickly wooded Bois Blanc Island under the guns of Fort Malden, and Ottawas paddling with all speed to reach British lines.[12]

Tecumseh approached the shoreline on July 1. As was his wont, he dressed plainly. A Michigander watched him come briefly ashore on the American side clad in a simple waist-long buckskin shirt, fringed buckskin leggings, and buckskin moccasins, with a red and blue handkerchief wrapped around his head. At forty-four, Tecumseh still possessed a physique that impressed white observers. After glimpsing the chief bringing his canoe to rest on the shore at Amherstburg, a captured American officer scribbled in his journal, "I have seen the great Tecumseh. He is a very plain man, rather above middle size, stoutly built, a noble set of features, and an admirable eye." Six of his best warriors accompanied him.

Tecumseh would need them simply to clear a path to Fort Malden. Indians had overrun the dirt streets of Amherstburg. Most were good-natured. Some sang and danced from door to door, begging food and whiskey from residents who watched the entertainment from their cottage windows. Other Indians performed war dances on the wharf, which were answered with applause and cannon shots from a docked British warship. One drunken warrior, however, emerged from a tavern and tomahawked an American prisoner who chanced to walk past in the company of a British officer. What if any punishment the warrior suffered is unknown.

Nearly two years had passed since Tecumseh last gazed on Fort Malden. Despite Colonel St. George's recent efforts to repair the dilapidated works, the post was hardly in a state to inspire confidence in British readiness. Tecumseh saw before him a square field work with four decrepit artillery bastions connected by a thin, rickety palisade perforated with loopholes for muskets. A stone magazine topped with a pine-shingle roof highly pervious to exploding shells housed the fort's ammunition; in other words, one well-aimed or chance shot could send the entire garrison sky high. Indian Department supplies were kept in the same rotting Amherstburg warehouse as before; it was now in even greater danger of collapsing. Just outside the fort the British Indian Department had constructed a wooden council house. There the business of winning over the Indians would be conducted.[13]

Provided Colonel St. George showed up. The harried commander was then sixteen miles upriver at Sandwich, a small settlement opposite Detroit, trying to steady five hundred fidgety Canadian militiamen who were more interested in tending their crops than in defending an exposed outpost. While waiting for St. George, Tecumseh made camp beside Matthew Elliott's house, using his brick barn as a makeshift headquarters. With the elderly Elliott weakened by lumbago, it fell to Tecumseh to bring order to the Indians congregating in crude shelters across a narrow channel on Bois Blanc Island.

It was no easy task. No more than 350 warriors, many traveling with their families, had answered the Great Father's call. They included Tecumseh's old comrade Chief Roundhead and his Ohio Wyandots; Chief Warrow and his small band of Canadian Wyandots; Main Poc and his unruly Potawatomis; several dozen Ottawas, Kickapoos, and Ojibwas; and—perhaps most satisfying of all to Tecumseh—fifty enthusiastic Sauk warriors who had traveled from the western reaches of the Illinois Territory to fight under the Shawnee chief; hardly the grand assemblage of warrior nations toward which Tecumseh aspired, but all that could be expected in view of the weak British position.[14]

This position descended to gravely precarious on July 6, when Hull's army entered Detroit. American artillerymen trained their cannons on Sandwich, and an invasion of Upper Canada appeared inevitable. On July 7, Colonel St. George hastened back to Amherstburg to meet with the Indians, whose allegiance was now critical. Some two hundred chiefs and warriors paddled over from Bois Blanc Island to attend the grand council. They pledged to fight with the redcoats, to refrain from taking scalps, and to spare prisoners. Main Poc's sincerity on the latter two scores may have been doubtful, but Tecumseh's probity was unquestionable. Much impressed, St. George wrote General Brock that Tecumseh "acted a conspicuous part on the occasion."[15]

That same day General Hull held his own gathering at Brownstown. The crafty, pragmatic Wyandot chief Walk-in-the-Water nominally presided over the council, but it was Hull's military might that guaranteed a robust turnout. Chiefs Tarhe and Black Hoof attended. So did several other treaty chiefs. The only notable pro-American Indian leader absent was Little Turtle, who lay at his son-in-law William Wells's home in the last agonies of gout. He would die on July 14 and be buried "with the honors of war" by Indian agent Benjamin Stickney, a gesture that the Miamis appreciated. All present at Brownstown, meanwhile, pledged to stay out of the forthcoming struggle. Hull had no other demand of the Indians; with their neutrality apparently assured, the general took no actions to protect his vulnerable supply line back to Ohio. It was an oversight for which Tecumseh would make him pay dearly.[16]

The Brownstown council chiefs had no love for Tecumseh, but neither did they want to see Indian blood spilled in a white man's war. So they sent the Wapakoneta Shawnee war leader James Logan, a trusted scout in Hull's army, across the Detroit River to invite Tecumseh to their council. Roughly the same age, the two men were boyhood friends who had remained close despite having chosen divergent paths. But the chiefs underestimated Tecumseh's resolve. Indignant, he dismissed his old friend. "I have taken sides with the King my father," Tecumseh told Logan, "and I will suffer my bones to bleach upon this shore before I re-cross to join any council of neutrality."

Evidently regretting his curt dismissal of Logan, if not his reply to the message he carried, Tecumseh asked him back for a final talk as friends. Walking into the woods near Fort Malden, they sat on the forest floor and spoke kindly until dawn, each trying to convince the other of the correctness of his chosen course. Tecumseh admonished Logan to oppose the Americans because they had desecrated ancestral Indian burial sites, spread apocalyptic diseases, and seized nearly all Indian land from the Atlantic Ocean to where they then sat. Logan answered that the Americans occupying the country were not the ones who had crossed the Great Water and inflicted such catastrophic losses on the Indians. They were long dead and gone. These were their progeny, and Logan found them to be good friends and neighbors. If vengeance must be visited on anyone, it had best be on the British because it was British colonial policy that had first driven the Indians westward; the Americans had merely followed that example. Tecumseh conceded the point but said he had "pledged his honor" to the redcoats.[17]

Tecumseh had come to Canada a week earlier for the express purpose of drawing British supplies, gauging the Crown's intentions toward the Indians, then returning to Prophetstown to continue rebuilding the Shawnee brothers' confederacy. What accounted for his sudden and seemingly unconditional commitment to British interests, particularly when the odds appeared stacked against the redcoats? Beyond the little that he confided to Logan, he never articulated his reasons. But they can be fairly assumed from circumstances and the testimony of others. Matthew Elliott clearly played a large role in Tecumseh's decision. Increasingly infirm, he retained a burning loyalty to his Shawnee wife's people and to Indians in general, sentiments that had often led him to exceed Indian Department instructions. Consequently the old man told Tecumseh precisely what the Shawnee chief hoped to hear at such a dire time. From his Shawnee friends, Stephen Ruddell later learned that the British (read Elliott) had vowed to fight until they had won for their Indian allies the permanent possession of lands not relinquished to the United States in the Treaty of Greenville, reversing the Treaty of 1809 and all that had come in between. "With this guarantee," Ruddell learned, "Tecumseh again took up the sword."[18]

Not that Tecumseh necessarily expected to win or even to survive the upcoming struggle. Shortly after he declared his allegiance to the British, he sent a messenger through the lines to Tenskwatawa. Stealing a horse from an American farm, the man rode night and day until the animal gave out near Fort Wayne. William Wells intercepted the courier, who confessed Tecumseh's instructions to his brother. They rang with desperation. The man was to have told the Shawnee Prophet to "unite the Indians immediately and send their women and children towards the Mississippi, while the warriors should strike a heavy blow at the inhabitants of Vincennes; that he, Tecumseh, if he lived, would join him in [the] land of the Winnebagos."[19]

The first shots of the war on the Detroit River suggested that Tecumseh might never leave Canada alive. On July 8, Hull cannonaded the outpost at Sandwich, scattering the Canadian militia. Four days later the American army crossed the Detroit River and occupied the town. A few militiamen regrouped with fifty redcoats under Capt. Adam Muir on the south bank of the Canard River, a narrow but swift stream six miles north of Amherstburg. Along its marshy banks, St. George hoped at the very least to "annoy" the Americans. Despite the loss of Sandwich and the "totally inefficient" state of the militia, St. George was reluctant to commit the Indians to combat. But Tecumseh broke the colonel's restraints. "As to the Indians, I wished those here to act when I could support them," St. George wrote Brock. "But as they are so anxious, I must let them on and sustain them as I see occasion, to the utmost of my power."[20]

If not for Tecumseh, Colonel St. George likely would have had few Indians to draw on. "The Indians with us have resisted every allurement which General Hull laid before them. Tecumseh has kept them faithful," testified Matthew Elliott. "He has shown himself to be a determined character and a great friend to our government."[21]

Powder and ball were in short supply at Fort Malden, but Tecumseh made good use of what the British issued him. Blackening his face for war, he hastened to the Canard River line with Main Poc and fifty warriors to bolster the flagging defenses. He was an easy man to spot. The Potawatomis went about in their breechclouts and moccasins only. Tecumseh, on the other hand, retained his buckskin frock and leggings. Together he and Main Poc reinforced the small command of redcoats and militiamen holding the sole bridge over the river. They fought several spirited skirmishes with American detachments probing the flat and lightly forested country along the riverbank—the first time Tecumseh had raised his flintlock musket to fire a shot in anger against Americans since Fallen Timbers, eighteen years earlier. Despite his recent lack of combat experience, after an otherwise inconclusive skirmish on July 19, Tecumseh supplanted Main Poc in the high esteem of their fellow Indians, the British, and the Ohio militia against whom they fought.

The contest occurred in a small pocket of marshy prairie on the north side of the Canard River. As the Ohioans approached, Main Poc and two or three other Indians, hoping for a kill and a scalp, darted across the bridge and discharged their muskets. The Ohioans returned the fire. A musket ball struck Main Poc in the neck. He crumpled to the ground, apparently dead. After several minutes he rose and staggered rearward, supported by a fellow Potawatomi who guided him to the safety of a British battery. Mortified that his medicine had again failed to guard him against bullets, the lightly wounded but deeply chagrined Main Poc surreptitiously scalped a dead, redheaded British soldier, intending to pass his hair off as that of an Ohioan. But when he waved his trophy about in camp that night, the dead man's friends— tough Welshmen of the 41st Regiment—recognized the auburn scalp. The angry redcoats pummeled Main Poc while the Potawatomi howled his innocence. After the beating, he became the laughingstock of the encampment.[22]

Meanwhile Tecumseh shined. As Main Poc staggered from the field, Tecumseh led thirty warriors across the river and into a thicket on the Ohioans' flank. Their commander halted his attack on the bridge and turned to face the Indians. The Ohioans squeezed off a volley. All the Indians ducked to the ground except Tecumseh who, in the words of one admiring enemy soldier, "stood firm on his limbs, without any apparent concern." After trading fire until sunset, the Ohioans withdrew, their ammunition exhausted.

On July 25 he engaged another Ohio detachment. Numbering 150 men under Maj. James Denny, the Ohioans were out to "waylay and cut off" a band of Indians reported to be ranging in the woods near the Canard River. Unknown to Denny, Tecumseh had planned the action several days in advance. Intending to ambush the next Americans to show themselves near the Canard River, Tecumseh had even dropped in on a local trader whose fighting skills he admired and invited him to join in the sport. Denny marched and countermarched his men until midafternoon without detecting a single Indian. Yielding to fatigue, the Ohioans paused to rest in a grove of timber. Within minutes most were asleep. As they slumbered in the sun, a small party of Indian decoys advanced to within fifteen yards of the camp. Major Denny, who happened to be awake, bellowed, "Rush like Hell, boys, and fire well!" A few dozen drowsy soldiers obeyed the order, chasing the Indians for half a mile before Denny recalled them to meet a greater threat—Tecumseh and nearly 150 warriors, some mounted, making for the Turkey Creek bridge, which lay between the Ohioans and the safety of their camp. Discipline dissolved, and the militiamen staggered through wheat fields and swampy thickets for five miles to escape encirclement. When Denny and his officers threatened to shoot the men if they did not stop and fight, the Ohioans responded, "It's better to be killed by [officers] than those damned Indians."

Tecumseh's drubbing of the Ohio militia ended American efforts against the British and Indian defenses along the Canard River. None had been particularly robust or well coordinated. Several days before his defeat, Major Denny had complained of an odd lethargy that gripped General Hull after the army entered Canada. "We had big swelling hopes of having our names handed down to posterity with a distinguished name of the heroes of Canada, but these flattering hopes begin to languish. We have no stimulus to urge us on.... Several plans have been laid down for attacks on the British forces, but all are dropped." With Hull paralyzed, the Americans waited uneasily for the next British and Indian move.[23]

Tecumseh had to have felt proud of his actions on July 25. Never had he led such a large warrior contingent in action against American soldiers. Notwithstanding Hull's apparent languor, the Ohioans had fought hard; Tecumseh had simply fought harder and smarter. Like the celestial panther, he had sprung with irresistible force against a bewildered enemy. And he had won more than glory. The Shawnee chief had stopped an army, blunting Hull's half-hearted Canadian offensive. And he had done it largely on his own initiative. While Tecumseh gave battle, Colonel St. George floundered, uncommunicative and irresolute. That sat poorly with General Brock, who in any case longed to confront Hull himself. But his civil responsibilities—the Upper Canada legislature was then in session—held him back, and so he ordered Col. Henry Procter, the commanding officer of the 41st Regiment of Foot, who was then watching the Americans on the Niagara frontier, to replace St. George at Amherstburg.

It was a momentous decision, not only for British fortunes on the Detroit frontier but also for Tecumseh personally. No white man apart from William Henry Harrison would play a greater role in the Shawnee chief's adult life than Henry Procter. Five years Tecumseh's senior, the forty-nine-year-old Procter was a career soldier of thirty-one years' service, nearly half of it with the 41st Regiment in Canada. With "indefatigable energy," he converted what had been a dispirited amalgam of garrison troops, most of whom had not seen their families since the regiment disembarked in Canada in 1799, into a well-disciplined unit capable of sustained field operations. As General Brock reported shortly before the war broke out, "Colonel Procter may justly claim the merit of having brought the [regiment] to its present high state of discipline."

Battered about by the choppy waters of Lake Erie in an open long-boat for five days, Procter stepped unsteadily ashore at the Amherstburg wharf on July 26. A French-Canadian youth thought Procter more amusing than martial. "As I remember, he was a very stout man, so stout that he did not like to ride on horseback. I guess the horse not like it pretty well neither [*sic*]. His face was very full and very red like the moon when she come up in the fog. He had a big bush of brown whiskers." Procter, the youth added, ascended the steep wharf in a horse-drawn cart.[24]

Despite his ungainly appearance, Procter marshaled his resources to further Brock's objective of seizing Detroit. He halted militia desertions and, in Indian parlance, took Tecumseh firmly by the hand. Not only did Procter recognize the Shawnee's great "ardor in the cause" and ability to "sway the whole Indian body," but the British colonel also liked Tecumseh. "His habits and deportment were perfectly free from whatever could give offense to the most delicate female. He readily and cheerfully accommodated himself to all novelties of his situation and seemed amused without being embarrassed by them." Procter thought Tecumseh looked the warrior. "He was above the middle stature, the general expressions of his features pleasing and eyes full of fire and intelligence."[25]

Procter brought Tecumseh news that fed the Shawnee's inner flame. Fort Michilimackinac, the conquest of which General Brock deemed second only to Detroit as essential to maintaining Indian allegiance, had fallen without a shot to a small force of British regulars and militiamen and more than seven hundred warriors, mostly northern Ojibwas, Ottawas, and Dakotas united under the charismatic Indian trader and British agent Robert Dickson. Already Dickson and his Indians were making for Fort Malden from the upper reaches of Lake Huron.

After acquainting himself with Tecumseh, Colonel Procter sought a council with the Michigan Wyandots to apprise them of the shifting winds of war. Hull had expended considerable capital, much of it in the form of gold, to keep them neutral. Their prosperous farming villages of Brownstown and Monguagon (or Maguaga) rested on the road to the Indiana Territory and Ohio. Should the Wyandots in his rear defect, Hull would not only find his supply line in jeopardy but also face the prospect that wavering western Indians would follow the influential kindlers of the Great Council Fire into the British camp.

Chief Walk-in-the-Water and his subchiefs convened at the council house alongside Fort Malden to hear what the new redcoat commander had to say. Procter, who knew better than to expect an easy sell, recognized the unique merits of the Wyandots, who "have all the energy of the savage warrior, with the intelligence and docility of civilized troops. They are Christians and remarkable for orderly and inoffensive conduct; but as enemies, they were among the most dreadful of their race . . . all mounted; fearless, active, and enterprising; to contend with them in the forest was hopeless, to avoid their pursuit impossible."[26]

Opening the council, Procter reaffirmed Great Britain's commitment to Indian independence and announced the capitulation of

Michilimackinac. Walk-in-the-Water was unmoved. Reproaching the British for their betrayal after Fallen Timbers, he refused to contemplate war against the Long Knives. "Fight your own battles, but let us, your red children, enjoy peace," he told Procter. Chief Roundhead urged his friend to reconsider but to no avail. And then Tecumseh stood to speak. Indians who had been drowsing or lazily smoking their pipes gave the Shawnee their rapt attention. First Tecumseh demolished the notion of neutrality as an option for a people living on a road over which American armies would continually pass. He asked Walk-in-the-Water who would protect the Wyandots from the Sauks and Foxes, their hereditary enemies, when the Long Knives were fighting the British. "Moreover," added Tecumseh, "if you take the neutral ground in this war you will be looked upon by other nations as cowards." A day of rancorous exchanges ensued, after which, to wipe away residual ill will, the Michigan Wyandots offered Tecumseh the customary peace pipe. He studied the red stone bowl and three-foot wooden stem, adorned with multicolored, braided porcupine quills, then snapped the stem, threw the pieces into the fire, and stormed from the council house. That night, as if to underscore the Wyandots' vulnerability to attack from behind, and perhaps at Tecumseh's instigation, his Sauk allies engaged in a boisterous war dance near Walk-in-the-Water's camp.

The next day Tecumseh escalated his rhetoric. After again equating neutrality with cowardice, he appealed to the Wyandots' long-term interests as he saw them. "For my own part, I have more confidence in the word of a British than of a Long Knife," he declared before expounding on his vision for the Indians.

> Here is a chance presented to us such as will never occur again, for us Indians of North America to form ourselves into one great combination and cast our lot with the British in this war; and should they conquer and again get the mastery of the whole of North America, our rights, at least to a portion of the land of our fathers, would be respected by the King. Otherwise, we see it plainly, that if the whole country was to pass into the hands of the Long Knives, it will not be many years before our last place of abode and hunting ground will be taken from us and the remnants of the different tribes, between the Mississippi and the

lakes and to the Ohio River, will all be driven towards the setting sun. Or, if after the close of this war, we find the British dominion still extended over the country west of the lakes and the vast regions of the northwest, the British would give us a home for ourselves and for our children's children hereafter.[27]

Again, Tecumseh broke the proffered peace pipe. After a fourth session, during which Tecumseh reiterated his unconditional support for the British, most of Walk-in-the-Water's subordinates deserted their chief. The Michigan Wyandots, they declared, would come to Canada and cast their fortunes with the redcoats. Tecumseh had carried the day.

Six months earlier Tecumseh had scarcely merited a passing mention in British dispatches except as the Prophet's brother or, in General Brock's words, as a "Shawnese of no particular note." But with his diplomatic triumph over those consummate diplomats the Wyandots, he assumed a place of prominence in Crown correspondence. "We are indebted to Chief Tecumseh for our Indian arm," reported Procter. "He convinced the Indians that our cause was theirs, and his influence by example determined and fixed the Wyandots, whose selection determined every tribe." Like Harrison, Procter also recognized Tecumseh's inner gifts. "Tecumseh raised himself to the situation of a chief by his tried hardihood, and that natural superiority of genius which, sometimes in civilized communities and almost always in a rude society, challenges deference from common minds."[28]

To prevent the Michigan Wyandots from reconsidering their decision, Procter acted fast. He asked Tecumseh to remove them, forcibly if necessary, to Canada. To augment Tecumseh's two hundred warriors, Procter detached the reliable Captain Muir with one hundred regulars and the young Capt. Billy Caldwell, a métis admirer of Tecumseh, with a similar number of militiamen for the duty.

On August 3 the Wyandots quietly crossed the Detroit River to Fort Malden. Word of their defection, coming on the heels of the loss of Fort Michilimackinac and the absence of a meaningful American offensive on the Niagara frontier, which would have taken pressure off Hull, further depressed the general's already flagging spirits. "You will perceive that the situation of this army is critical," he wrote the secretary of war. "I can promise nothing but my best."[29]

Tecumseh worked to render Hull's pledge empty. After seeing off the last of the Wyandots, he and Matthew Elliott remained in Browns-town with forty warriors. They stood astride Hull's logistical lifeline, the only road between Ohio and Detroit, and their presence was per-fectly timed. Wary of encountering hostile Indians, a column of green Ohio militiamen escorting supply-laden packhorses and a huge drove of beef cattle bound for Hull's army from Ohio had halted behind the River Raisin, a mere five miles south of Brownstown. On August 4, eager to augment his rapidly depleting food stocks, General Hull dis-patched two hundred Ohio volunteers under Maj. Thomas Van Horne with orders to escort the militiamen to Detroit.

Tecumseh knew Van Horne's every move. On the night of August 4, while the American detachment slept near the abandoned Wyandot village of Monguagon, Tecumseh's scouts stole about the perimeter of their camp, counting the recumbent soldiers. At daybreak, masked by a dense fog, the Indians paddled off to report their findings.

The odds against Tecumseh were nearly five to one, but he hoped a well-chosen ambush site would compensate for his lack of numbers. He found it three miles north of Brownstown, where the trail followed a narrow ford across the muddy Brownstown Creek. Indian cornfields interspersed with thick brush lined the approach. In the seven-foot-high cornstalks and behind bushes on both sides of the trail, Tecumseh deployed his warriors with orders to fire on mounted men first. Like the warriors, he had painted his face and stripped to his breechclout for combat. The day was clear and warm, the wait tolerable.

Having sent forward no scouts, Van Horne suspected nothing. At the ford, officers permitted their horses to pause and drink. Riflemen adjusted their gear or lounged in column behind the cavalrymen. Men grew sleepy in the muggy heat; officers dropped their guard. A sudden volley of musketry shattered the stillness. Wounded and terrified horses reared and plunged, pitching their riders and throw-ing the column into abject confusion. Whooping and yelling, war-riors dashed out of the bushes to draw a better aim. Scarcely a soldier discharged his weapon. Even the few veterans in the ranks thought themselves hopelessly overwhelmed. Oblivious to orders to re-form their ranks, the terrified Ohioans stumbled three miles back up the road with Tecumseh in pursuit. Once they were safely behind a river, Van Horne sent his wounded by boat to Detroit. American casualties were considerable. Eighteen were killed, of whom ten were officers; a dozen were wounded; and seventy were missing. Tecumseh lost two wounded, and Logan Blue Jacket, the chief of a Shawnee band living near Monguagon, was killed by a cavalryman's sword.[30]

Logan Blue Jacket's death presented Tecumseh with a grim reminder of the limits of his authority. As much as he abhorred the killing of captives, the warrior ethic demanded that the young Blue Jacket's death be avenged. A wounded American prisoner was brought before Tecumseh. Reluctantly he selected two dozen warriors to exact retribution on the unfortunate soldier. The ritual proceeded with grim solemnity. The warriors carried Logan Blue Jacket's blood-drenched corpse, the head nearly severed from the body, into a log council house in Brownstown and then arrayed themselves in a circle. The prisoner was given a place among them, and a bowl of food was set before the American to distract him. While the man ate, a young warrior rose and, coming around behind him, struck the American a single blow to the head with his tomahawk. The cracking of the prisoner's skull was the only sound heard. Silently, the executioner slid his weapon inside his belt and resumed his seat in the circle. After a few minutes, the war party withdrew, leaving behind a select few to bury the victim. Tecumseh had approved the tribunal but absented himself from its sentence.[31]

Tecumseh's victory at Brownstown stunned General Hull. "This little discomfiture ... divested him of all self-possession or control over his fears," wrote an army staff officer.[32] And those fears centered on so-called savage hordes—Robert Dickson's loyal following descending from the north, Tecumseh's stealthy warriors severing the army supply line from the south, and the Wyandot turncoats striking from across the Detroit River. Hull had just enough fight left in him to try a second time to reach the supply train stranded on the River Raisin. He chose for the duty his best unit, the Fourth U.S. Infantry, which had borne the brunt of the fighting at Tippecanoe, and a mixed force of Ohio and Michigan volunteers, a total of six hundred troops under the command of Lt. Col. James Miller. A no-nonsense regular officer, Miller marched carefully, taking care to deploy mounted scouts well ahead of his main body.

Miller departed Detroit on August 8. At sunset he reached the River Rouge, six miles south of town. But there was no bridge over the deep waters. By the time two commandeered scows ferried his troops across, night had settled over the forests. Rain fell sporadically. With nothing to be gained from marching farther in the pitch-black and muck, Miller ordered the men to rest on their arms until dawn.

Tecumseh, meanwhile, had remained at Brownstown after routing Van Horne, hopeful that the American convoy might venture forth from the River Raisin. Wyandots under Walk-in-the-Water and Main Poc's Potawatomis, together with small contingents of Winnebagos and Ottawas, swelled the Indian force to four hundred warriors. Captain Muir lacked Tecumseh's patience. On the morning of August 9, he began to embark his ninety redcoats and two small Canadian militia companies for the river crossing to Amherstburg. Suddenly Tecumseh's scouts streamed toward the riverbank, yelling and gesticulating that American soldiers were approaching "as thick as mosquitos in a swamp." Captain Muir halted the boats.

Tecumseh and Muir conferred. The Shawnee's blood was up. He urged Muir to march with him to Monguagon and ambush the Americans. Tecumseh knew the terrain, and Muir deferred to him. The Shawnee chief outlined his plan. A quarter-mile north of the deserted Wyandot village a wooded ravine bisected the road. Tecumseh said the British should form a battle line in the sheltering fold. Beyond the ravine, the ground rose to a low, open ridge that the Americans would have to ascend, and in doing so would offer the British a neatly silhouetted target. The Indians would melt into the cornfields and tall prairie grass slightly in advance of the British flanks, hidden from view and facing inward toward the road. After the enemy deployed, Tecumseh wanted the British to launch a bayonet charge while the Indians closed in behind the Americans. Muir liked the scheme. He sent a messenger by canoe to Fort Malden for reinforcements, and then the mixed procession of painted warriors, panting redcoats, and motley militiamen started up the road to waylay the Americans.

The ankle-deep mud and encroaching forest were no obstacles to Tecumseh's warriors. An admiring British regular watched them glide past noiselessly, painted in a multitude of colors, all with hair plastered like the "bristling quills of the porcupine." The Indians wore only breechclouts, belts, and moccasins, but despite their near nakedness they managed to carry muskets, tomahawks, war clubs, spears, scalping knives, and bow and arrows.

The stink of decomposing horseflesh and human corpses hung over the dark and hushed site of the Brownstown fight. Indian warriors had stripped, scalped, and driven stakes into the American dead, who lay gnawed and mangled by crows and wolves. "The stench from these rotting bodies is impossible to describe," wrote a nauseated Canadian. "And the same fate might soon be ours, marching to war with consequences no one could predict."

Nearing Monguagon, the forest thinned into open oak woods. Tecumseh directed the British and Canadians into the shallow ravine. After dragging together a few fallen trees and logs to serve as makeshift breastworks, the troops sprawled on the earth for a brief rest. While they waited, sixty more soldiers of the 41st Regiment arrived from Fort Malden. Muir placed the reinforcements in the center of the line. Tecumseh, meanwhile, guided three hundred Shawnee, Wyandot, and Winnebago warriors into tall cornrows slightly in advance of the British left flank, then waved forward a small party into a small wood to watch for the enemy. Main Poc and Billy Caldwell positioned a hundred Potawatomis and Ottawas beyond the British right. All appeared ready for a classic Indian-style ambuscade.

Colonel Miller's column advanced to the beat of the drum. At four p.m., Tecumseh's scouts opened fire on the American advance guard. "Shortly the report of a single shot echoed throughout the wood," recalled a redcoat. "The instant afterwards the loud and terrific yells of the Indians, followed by a heavy and desultory fire, apprised us that they were engaged." Miller advanced in a long line of battle, and the combat became general. Within minutes a sulfurous blue cloud of gun smoke settled over the field, obscuring targets beyond twenty feet.

Captain Muir gave his drummers the signal for a bayonet charge. And then disaster struck. Flushed from their cover by bayonet-wielding American riflemen, Main Poc's warriors tumbled toward the British right flank. Mistaking the Indians for Americans, the British shot at them. The warriors shot back, and the right of Muir's line wavered. At the same instant, Muir's center collapsed; not being briefed on the plan of battle, the reinforcements mistook the drumbeat for an order to retreat. As the British fire waned, the smoke thinned. Discerning the disorder in the British ranks, Colonel Miller ordered a general bayonet charge. Muir's line collapsed. The captain, incapacitated with a bullet wound in the leg, was unable either to halt his men or to communicate with Tecumseh, who fought on unaware that the British, Canadians, and Main Poc's Indians had fled to their boats.

Tecumseh's stand caused the American line to splinter, enabling his retreating allies to escape. Half the Americans accompanied Colonel Miller after the absconding enemy, while the right units remained on the field to tangle with Tecumseh. The Shawnee war chief tried to work his way into their rear, but American bayonets drove his warriors back into the cornfield. A buckshot caught Tecumseh in the shoulder, leaving a nasty flesh wound. Withdrawing sullenly, Tecumseh's warriors fired as they fell back westward into the forest. The Americans followed. When he learned that his command had split, Miller halted his pursuit, and the wounded Muir and the shamed Main Poc crossed the Detroit River unmolested. The road from Detroit to the River Raisin was now open, but the price paid had been high. Eighteen American soldiers lay dead—most of them members of the mounted advance guard that Tecumseh had engaged—and another sixty-three were wounded. British and Indian losses were considerably less. One redcoat and two Indians were killed in the Battle of Monguagon (Maguaga), and fifteen redcoats and eight Indians, including Tecumseh, were wounded. Tecumseh dressed his wound, reassembled his warriors, and with them glided over the river in canoes to Amherstburg after dark.[33]

Some British officers grumbled over Tecumseh's choice of the ambush site, believing they should have fought in the thick forest nearer Brownstown. But responsibility for the defeat rested with Muir, who had neglected to apprise the reinforcements of the battle plan, and with Main Poc, who had lost control of his warriors. Colonel Procter apportioned blame lightly. "In this affair, we have not entirely succeeded," he reported. "The ground on which the Americans had been so roughly treated on the fifth [Brownstown] was not as it ought to have been, occupied, and some mistake was made." No matter. What should have been a grave setback ended up being a victory of sorts. Rather than permit Miller to accomplish his mission of securing the army supply line, Hull recalled him. The abandoned convoy and its escort dug in on the River Raisin, and Hull's enraged army hunkered down with its mentally enfeebled commander inside Fort Detroit.[34]

General Brock was pleased with the turn of events on the Detroit frontier. "The judicious arrangement which had been adopted immediately upon the arrival of Colonel Procter had compelled the enemy to retreat and take shelter under the guns of his fort," he told General Prévost. "That officer commenced operations by sending strong detachments across the river with a view of cutting off the enemy's communications with his resources. This produced two smart skirmishes... in both of which the enemy's loss was very considerable."[35]

Procter had indeed performed well. But unlike Brock, to whom Tecumseh was yet a "Shawnese of little note," the colonel knew much of the praise rightly belonged to the Shawnee war chief.

19

Kindred Spirits

M AJ. GEN. SIR ISAAC BROCK, aged forty-two, epitomized the very best of the British gentleman officer. He was gallant, charismatic, devoted to his men, boyishly handsome, and—at a large-boned, muscular six-feet-three inches tall—physically imposing. Brock was firmly convinced not only that Indian allies were essential to victory, but also that common decency demanded the Crown reward their service with a homeland carved out of territory that he hoped to conquer in the Old Northwest.

Brock believed in leading from the front, and at that moment, the only active front in the War of 1812 was the Amherstburg district. Maj. Gen. Henry Dearborn was supposed to have launched an offensive across the Niagara River simultaneous with Hull's operation. Instead, the timorous Dearborn negotiated a local cease-fire with the British. Relieved of any threat on the Niagara frontier, and after proroguing the provincial legislature, on August 5 Brock boarded a schooner and sailed over the roiled and rain-swept waters of Lake Erie to assume command at Amherstburg. Along the way he gathered up 350 Canadian volunteers, 100 more men from the 41st Regiment, and a small war party of Mohawk Indians. Shortly before midnight on August 13, Brock's flotilla reached the village.

On Bois Blanc Island, opposite Amherstburg, Tecumseh and the chiefs and warriors of seven tribes awaited Brock's landing. Tecumseh expected a great deal from Brock. "When the war was declared," he later remarked, "our father stood up and gave us the tomahawk and told us he would certainly get us our lands back which the Americans had taken from us." Tecumseh had much to offer in return. Great Lakes warriors eager to fight for Tecumseh had swelled his force to nearly a thousand men. Roundhead, Main Poc, Walk-in-the-Water, and numerous other prominent Indian leaders readily subordinated themselves to the Shawnee. Tecumseh was dealing from a position of strength, and he knew it. But he also knew that without the British, his fragile alliance stood no chance against the Americans. Matthew Elliott readied Tecumseh for Brock's arrival with assurances that the general held Indian interests dear and could be trusted. Tecumseh waited anxiously.[1]

As the boats docked, a straggling fire of musketry rattled from the island and then rose to a steady thunder. Elliott told Brock that the shooting represented Indian "joy at the arrival of reinforcements under their great father." Aware that munitions were scarce, Brock sent the old man to Bois Blanc to ask the Indians politely to stop wasting powder. Elliott departed, and the musketry soon ceased. Repairing to Elliott's house on the outskirts of town, Brock learned from Colonel Procter not only that Hull's invasion had collapsed but also that his army had withdrawn to Fort Detroit. Not long afterward Elliott escorted Tecumseh into Brock's presence. The general sat at a desk by candlelight, poring over correspondence captured from the Americans, dispatches that spoke to Hull's despondency and his army's discontent. The door opened. Tecumseh entered, clad in a plain buckskin jacket and leggings, his large silver King George III medallion glinting in the dim light. The Shawnee's bright hazel eyes beamed cheerfully. Resolution and energy were written on his light-copper countenance. Tecumseh's "very prepossessing" appearance and "finely proportioned" figure impressed Brock's aide-de-camp, who thought the forty-four-year-old Tecumseh looked nearly a decade younger.

Tecumseh and Brock shook hands warmly, and the general alluded to the recent musket firing. Tecumseh apologized for the waste of powder. As the hour was late, Brock and Tecumseh agreed to reconvene at a public council the next morning. Before Tecumseh departed, General Brock removed his red army sash and presented it to the chief as a token of esteem.

The next morning hundreds of chiefs and warriors assembled on Elliott's lawn to hear the Great Father's war chief speak. Brock did not disappoint. He announced that the Crown had sent him to recapture

Detroit and then drive the Americans to the Ohio River, restoring the Indians' rightful hunting grounds. War whoops rent the air. The chiefs unanimously called upon Tecumseh to reply, further proof that he had achieved the place of first among equals, the most to which any rational Indian leader could aspire. Tecumseh's pulse quickened. He expressed joy that the "Great Father beyond the Great Salt Lake" (the King of England) had awakened from his long sleep and permitted his warriors to assist their red children, who had never wavered in their friendship and were now ready to shed their last drop of blood in his service. The warriors whooped and shook their rifles in agreement.[2]

Roundhead, Walk-in-the-Water, and several other chiefs also made speeches, but it was Tecumseh who truly impressed Brock. In a letter to London, he enthusiastically acquainted the prime minister with the Shawnee's virtues. "Among the Indians whom I found at Amherstburg [were] some extraordinary characters. He who most attracted my attention was a Shawnee chief, Tecumseh.... A more sagacious or a more gallant warrior does not I believe exist. He was the admiration of everyone who conversed with him."[3]

Preferring to reveal his specific plans only to Tecumseh and a select few elder chiefs, Brock repaired with them to Elliott's home. A bit taken aback that Tecumseh had appeared that morning without the sash Brock had gifted him, the general asked Elliott to inquire as to the reason. Because the Wyandot chief Roundhead, who Tecumseh said was an abler warrior than he, was present, Tecumseh had transferred it to him—an adroit bit of intertribal diplomacy that Brock admired. The talk then turned to war. Brock declared his intention to move immediately against Fort Detroit, but he needed the help and guidance of his Indian allies. He had grappled with the Great Father's foes across the ocean and never shown his back. Addressing Tecumseh, Brock said he was there "to fight his enemies on this side of the Great Salt Lake, and now desire with my soldiers to take lessons from you and your warriors that we may learn how to make war in these great forests." Brock's humility touched Tecumseh. Turning to the chiefs but pointing to Brock, he declared loudly in Shawnee, "This is a man!" Shifting briefly to English, something he rarely did in council, Tecumseh remarked that, while previous British commanders had said, "Tecumseh, go fight Yankee," General Brock instead said, "Tecumseh, come fight Yankee."

Tecumseh and the chiefs vowed to cooperate fully in Brock's planned attack. The grateful general had just one question for Tecumseh: could he induce his warriors to refrain from drinking liquor before the battle? Speaking for the fighting men from Prophetstown, of whom comparatively few were present, Tecumseh replied that they had sworn off alcohol until they humbled the Long Knives. "If this resolution be persevered in," Brock responded, "you must conquer."[4]

Brock and Tecumseh had taken an instant liking to each other, and their mutual admiration was genuine. But Brock well understood that Tecumseh's loyalty, like that of the chiefs he represented and the warriors he led, was conditional and necessarily self-serving. Neither Tecumseh nor those old enough to remember the British betrayal at Fort Miamis had overcome their deep suspicion of the redcoats. "But the violent wrongs committed by the Americans on their territory have rendered it an act of policy with them to disguise their sentiments," Brock told General Prévost. Either Britain would press the contest until the Indians reclaimed the "extensive tract of country fraudulently usurped from them," averred Brock, or it must lose their support and even endure their hostility. So long as Brock lived, he intended to do everything within his power to help Tecumseh realize his vision of an Indian nation free from American encroachment.[5]

Tecumseh now had a powerful champion among the redcoats. His dream of an untrammeled Indian homeland appeared within reach. But first Fort Detroit must be taken, a formidable challenge that General Brock hoped to accomplish without bloodshed. From Hull's intercepted dispatches he learned that his enemy's deepest fear was of the Indians, unbridled and brutal. True, the Indians had taken no lives at Fort Michilimackinac, but there had been no resistance. "It was a fortunate circumstance that the fort capitulated without firing a gun," declared a British official who had helped control the Indians there. "For had they [Americans] done so, I firmly believe not a soul of them would have been saved." If fighting occurred at Detroit and the Indians lost men, Tecumseh could not be expected to restrain his warriors from seeking vengeance; the Logan Blue Jacket episode showed the limits of both his humanity and his influence. And so Brock played a daring bluff. On August 15, as his small command of 750 regulars and

marginally reliable militiamen marched to a staging area near Sandwich, Brock sent Hull an ultimatum: surrender his garrison of sixteen
hundred men at once, or fall victim to angry Indians. Hull chose to
fight it out.[6]

British cannons roared from two batteries at Sandwich and two
warships on the Detroit River. The American guns answered. It was a
noisy but harmless cannonade. Far more frightening were the sounds
emanating from Bois Blanc Island. There Tecumseh and his warriors
staged raucous war dances to prepare themselves physically and spiritually for the upcoming battle. A French-Canadian trader friendly
with the Indians circulated among the dancers. Although he had seen
many war dances, they never ceased to horrify and amaze him. The
warriors stripped to their breechclouts and painted themselves vermilion and blue, or black and white. Like flickering phantoms in the
tenebrous forest, they circled about the campfires to the discordant
beat of drum and gourd rattles, scalp locks swinging madly. "A European witnessing this strange spectacle for the first time would have
thought, I truly believe, that he was standing at the entrance to hell,
with the gates thrown open to let the damned out for an hour's recreation on earth."[7]

The dance was no mere recreation. A deadly serious method of
battle preparation, it continued until near daybreak on August 16,
when the Indians pushed off in canoes to rendezvous with the redcoats under the protective guns of British warships anchored above
Sandwich. At five a.m. the British batteries opened fire, answered at
long intervals by the American artillery. The cannonade ended, and
the day dawned, mild and still. As a soft sun rose over the placid waters
of the Detroit River, General Brock stepped into the first boat to shove
off. An admiring Tecumseh apostrophized him as the warrior "standing erect in the bow of his canoe, [who] led the way to battle." Utter-
ing what an appreciative redcoat styled "yells of mingled defiance of
their foes and encouragement of the soldiery," the Indians glided in
their canoes beside the boats and scows carrying Brock's troops. All
landed together beneath Detroit.

Tecumseh went to work to deceive the Americans. He shepherded
his warriors into a forest west of the palisaded town and then marched
them three times through an opening in the timber in full view of
the garrison, leading an astonished Hull to conclude that more than

two thousand Indians confronted him. As the warriors melted back into the trees behind the fort, British regulars and Canadian militiamen advanced in a single column over open, gently rolling meadows directly toward the front gate. Two heavy cannons planted on a hillock commanded the approach. Their gunners stood with fuses burning. "At each moment we expected that they would fire," recalled a redcoat. "Yet although it was evident the discharge must literally have swept our small but dense column, there was neither halt nor indecision perceptible." But the American cannons stood hushed while the British troops wheeled from column into line of battle just two hundred yards distant. Not so the British artillery, which hurled shrapnel at the fort with growing accuracy.

General Hull had more to consider than the best interests of the garrison. Hundreds of civilians, including his own daughter, huddled in the fort, terrified of the cannonade and a potential Indian massacre in about equal measure. The strain told on Hull. His orders grew erratic. When a projectile sailed through an embrasure and burst in the mess hall, splattering the blood and brains of four officers over the walls, the general buckled. His lips quivered; tobacco juice ran from his mouth down his shirt. "The fort was filled with women, children, and the old and decrepit people of the town and the country," Hull later wrote. "They were unsafe in the town, as it was entirely open and exposed to the enemy's batteries. And nowhere were they safe from the Indians."[8]

Always with Hull it was the Indians. What of the "hive" of hostile warriors who had seized Fort Michilimackinac? Hull had no way of knowing that most were far off, "drunk as ten thousand devils." What few warriors had emerged from the timber hardly acted in a manner to inspire confidence in their restraint. Before Tecumseh drove them back into line, they plundered a house, chased down some stray horses, and slaughtered a few sheep.[9]

Hull hoisted the white flag. After a brief parley with Brock, he surrendered Fort Detroit. The garrison—looking ragged and ill-fed but angry and combative nonetheless—filed out, and the British marched in. While the Americans surrendered their arms, Brock sought out Tecumseh to secure his promise that his warriors would not abuse the prisoners. "No," Tecumseh promptly replied. "I despise them too much to meddle with them."[10]

With the help of McKee and the Wyandot chiefs, Tecumseh kept the Indians—including Main Poc and his Potawatomis—in check. Not "a drop of blood [was] shed by the hand of the Indians," Brock reported. "The instant the enemy submitted, his life became sacred." An American prisoner acknowledged it "no more than an act of justice to the Indians to state that they conducted themselves better than could be expected of savages" and took only what they needed to eat.[11]

From another prisoner came a vivid snapshot of Tecumseh after the surrender. Captured quartermaster officer William Hatch had met Tecumseh six years earlier at a council with Simon Kenton. On August 17, 1812, the day after the surrender, Hatch ran into him again on the streets of Detroit, dressed in his customary buckskin and walking as briskly and vigorously as his limp allowed. Hatch admired his weapons, which included an "elegant, silver-mounted" tomahawk, a knife sheathed in a strong leather case, and a British flintlock Indian-trade musket, with its thirty-six-inch barrel and potent twenty-gauge bore. Tecumseh's features remained unchanged—nose "handsome and straight"; mouth "beautifully formed"; eyes a "clear, transparent hazel"; teeth "beautifully white"; expression "mild [and] pleasant when in repose or conversation." As the men passed, Tecumseh exchanged a few words of recognition with Hatch in English, then moved on to superintend the recrossing of his warriors to Amherstburg to learn what Brock had next in mind.[12]

In council, Tecumseh complimented Brock on the capture of Fort Detroit. "The Americans endeavor to give us a mean opinion of British generals, but we have [witnessed] your valor," he declaimed in Shawnee as Elliott interpreted. "In crossing the river to attack the enemy, we observed you from a distance standing the whole time in an erect posture, and when the boats reached the shore, you were among the first who jumped on land. Your bold and sudden movements frightened the enemy, and you compelled them to surrender to half their force."[13]

The American defeat in the Old Northwest was more complete than either Brock or Tecumseh realized. The day before Hull surrendered Detroit, the garrison of Fort Dearborn, the linchpin of northern Illinois territorial defenses, had capitulated to the Potawatomis at Hull's orders. The post commander destroyed the ammunition and liquor stocks before abandoning the fort, which so infuriated the warriors that they butchered most of the soldiers and many of their dependents. Among the dead was William Wells, who had led a small party of Miami warriors from Fort Wayne to guide the column to safety.

Tecumseh bore no responsibility for the massacre, but he had created the warlike conditions in which it occurred. He had encouraged an attack on Fort Dearborn. Since arriving at Amherstburg, Tecumseh had sent a steady stream of couriers bearing black wampum belts and "carrots of tobacco painted red"—incontrovertible emblems of war— over the wooded trails and prairie paths to his brother at Prophets-town and to allies in Illinois. Word of his victory at Brownstown also emboldened the Illinois warriors.[14]

Back in Detroit, Brock and Tecumseh acted swiftly to sweep the last vestiges of the American presence from the Michigan Territory and the strategic Maumee River rapids. It would be largely an Indian operation, with Matthew Elliott and his son Alexander, old Alexan-der McKee's son Thomas, now an Indian agent, and two army officers, Maj. Peter Chambers of the 41st Foot, and Canadian militia captain Charles Askin also taking part. No soldiers would go with them to prevent Indian atrocities. Evidently trusting Tecumseh and Chief Roundhead to restrain the warriors, Brock saw the raiding party off on August 19.

It was a signal moment for Tecumseh. Achieving a Michigan Terri-tory emptied of Americans and placed firmly in the hands of the Brit-ish and Tecumseh's Indian allies was the necessary and consequential first step toward the creation of the independent native domain to which he and his brother had given their all. Tecumseh accepted his mission with alacrity.

Tecumseh's first target was Frenchtown on the River Raisin, where the forlorn supply train escort had built a stockade to defend them-selves. The Indians arrived to find the Ohioans gone; a dejected set of disarmed Michigan militiamen gathered under the watchful eye of Alexander Elliott, who had arrived first, while the defenseless resi-dents of Frenchtown milled about nervously. The warriors had a field day ransacking houses and stealing horses. "We found the Indians were taking everything they could get hold of," recalled the Canadian captain Charles Askin. "They paid no attention to us when we tried to make them desist." Tecumseh raged and rode about, trying vainly to restore order. Askin admired the chief's efforts: "Tecumseh I must say behaved remarkably well. He assisted us very much in trying to prevent the Indians from pillaging." Major Chambers, who persuaded some of the Indians to return plundered goods, agreed with Askin. Although Frenchtown presented "one universal scene of desolation," Tecumseh and Roundhead bore no blame. "It affords me great pleasure to say that the conduct of Tecumseh and Roundhead was such as to reflect on them the highest honor," reported Chambers.[15]

Tecumseh went further than Matthew Elliott—who had gone along ostensibly to help keep order—in respecting the property of townspeople. One story that sounds apocryphal but for which sufficient witnesses existed to give it credibility has Tecumseh wrangling with Elliott over whether to pay a poor, elderly man named Rivard for two oxen that the Shawnee chief felt compelled to requisition to feed his warriors.

Tecumseh had encountered Rivard's son on the road outside Frenchtown trying to hide the beasts from scavenging warriors. Drawing on his conversational English, the Shawnee conveyed to him that his men were hungry and must have the oxen. When the young Rivard resisted, telling the chief that his father's livelihood depended on the beasts, Tecumseh promised to pay him one hundred dollars for them. The youth yielded. Tecumseh got a white man to write an order on Elliott for the money, and Indians killed and roasted the oxen. But Elliott refused to pay, telling Rivard the rules of war entitled the Indians to live off the land. An angry Tecumseh sought out Elliott. Tecumseh demanded and received one hundred dollars in coin—he wanted no "rag money," only "hard money" would do. As Elliott counted out the coins, Tecumseh demanded an extra dollar. "Take it," he told the young Rivard while also giving him the rest. "It will pay for the time you have lost in getting your money."[16]

Reembarking in their canoes at the mouth of the River Raisin, on August 21 Tecumseh's raiding party paddled to their next target, an American blockhouse at the rapids of the Maumee that controlled river traffic to Fort Wayne. The post commander, Capt. David Hull (the general's nephew), and his men had decamped ahead of the Indians, leaving behind a few sick soldiers, a backwoods settlement of thirty frightened families, and a stock of goods that included seventy-seven barrels of pork and seven barrels of whiskey. By the time the British brought up boats to haul away the supplies, the warriors had helped themselves to the liquor with predictable results. The inebriated Indians plundered the pork barrels and killed and scalped a Canadian boatman who tried to stop them. Others defaced and toppled the gravestone of the deceased wife of an unfortunate settler, who wrote to Procter of the matter. News of the incident found its way to the American press, which embellished it to incite sentiment against the Indians. A single damaged headstone became wanton despoliation of the dead. "Even the tomb was not held sacred; dead bodies were unearthed and stripped of their scalps by the Indians, who after robbing the dead, cheated their employers by selling these trophies the same as if torn from the living!" Tecumseh and Roundhead had intervened to restrain the tribesmen as best they were able.[17]

Tecumseh's troubles followed him back to Detroit and Amherstburg, where unruly warriors carried away most of the horses and cattle seized when Hull surrendered, robbed houses on both sides of the Detroit River, got drunk on liquor supplied by British enlisted men, and confiscated several British boats.

British officers disparaged Indian conduct, which Procter's quartermaster complained "becomes outrageous in proportion to the impunity with which they offend." Therein lay the root of the problem. There were too few redcoats to control the Indians, and Tecumseh and Roundhead faced cultural obstacles to keeping optimal order. An American prisoner thought the British refrained from interfering for fear the Indians might turn on them.

Yet the wrongs the warriors committed were against property, not persons, and for that Tecumseh and Roundhead deserve great credit. The Indians neither killed nor wounded any American prisoners or Michigan residents. And in fairness to the Indians, they had rallied to His Majesty's colors to fight for a homeland, not to lay about the Detroit frontier as part of an occupying force. As had Tecumseh. The Shawnee war chief made known his expectations to all within earshot. Even prisoners heard his avowals. "Tecumseh has been boasting for some weeks past that the Ohio River is to be the Indian boundary," wrote one American. "The same has been repeated to me by several of the British officers at Detroit—they no doubt feed him up with this vain expectation."[18]

Brock had promised Tecumseh more than the conquest of the Michigan Territory, significant though it was to Tecumseh's vision. The Indiana and Ohio frontiers beckoned, with the closest American forces resting beyond the Great Black Swamp of northwestern Ohio. The Wabash and Maumee rivers now constituted the military boundary of the United States in the Northwest, with the integrity of even that line doubtful. But the general with whom Tecumseh enjoyed a unique rapport was gone. On August 19, the day Tecumseh left for the River Raisin and Maumee River raids, Brock departed Amherstburg for the Niagara frontier, intent on "sweeping it of the American garrisons." Colonel Procter took command in his absence.

Despite Procter's admirable service to date, he lacked the charismatic touch that had drawn Tecumseh to Brock. The general's departure clearly disappointed the Shawnee chief. But having pledged himself and his honor to the British alliance, he was bound to the redcoats, come what might. He hoped for a homeland and then peace. Should the Long Knives somehow prevail instead, the Shawnee chief would at best be a fugitive, a man without a country or a future worth living.[19]

20

A Man of Mercy

T ENSKWATAWA POSSESSED a remarkable talent for prevarication. At Fort Wayne in mid-July 1812, he put on his most patently dishonest performance since wangling corn from William Henry Harrison to feed the people of Prophetstown. Before leaving for Fort Malden, Tecumseh had asked Tenskwatawa to keep Prophetstown safe—the same request he had made before his southern sojourn the year before. Neither brother, of course, wanted a second Tippecanoe. To prevent it, on July 12 the Shawnee Prophet and an entourage of ninety-four disciples visited Fort Wayne.

In a string of councils with Agent Benjamin Stickney, Tenskwatawa disavowed any hostile intent, either on his part or that of Tecumseh. The agent should ignore the contrary whispers of bad birds who looked to "interrupt his great and good intentions to maintain peace." It was true that the British had appealed to the Shawnee brothers to take up arms against the Long Knives, but they had rejected the summons. The British "considered them as dogs who would run at their call and bite anything, they directed them to [but] they were determined not to listen to them."

As proof of his sincerity, Tenskwatawa presented Stickney with a large white wampum belt spotted with purple at the center. The purple wampum represented Prophetstown, the white ends, Vincennes and Fort Wayne respectively. For the sake of peace Tenskwatawa would relinquish any claim to land ceded in the 1809 Fort Wayne Treaty and place himself under the protection of Agent Stickney. All he asked in return was food for his famished women and children and powder and lead to enable his men to hunt.[1]

Tenskwatawa had woven numerous wampum belts, however. In June he had sent a Kickapoo runner to the western tribes bearing a belt that conveyed a diametrically opposed message: they were to journey to Prophetstown "when the corn is made" (in August) to plan when and where to attack the Americans, who were "a bad people and never will tell you the truth. They will also cheat you out of your lands and keep you and your families in poverty."[2]

At Fort Wayne, William Wells, a month away from death at Fort Dearborn, seethed over both the Prophet's double-dealing and Stickney's gullibility. "It is now evident," Wells wrote Secretary of War Eustis in one of his last official letters, "that [Tenskwatawa] has completely duped the agent, who has suffered him to take the lead in all his councils with the Indians, giving him ammunition to support his followers until they can receive a supply from Tecumseh." Although unaware of the Prophet's approach to Stickney, Governor Edwards of the Illinois Territory, who heard rumblings among local Potawatomis and Kickapoos not already with the Shawnee brothers, concluded like Wells that the Indian plan "is to amuse and deceive us till they are prepared to strike a decisive blow."[3]

It was then that Tenskwatawa received Tecumseh's grim appraisal of affairs on the Detroit frontier and his call for him to send the women and children of Prophetstown west to safety, strike a blow against Vincennes with all available warriors, then withdraw to western Illinois, where Tecumseh hoped to join him if he lived. Tenskwatawa hastened to comply. Stealing Wells's best riding horses, two trusted Kickapoo confederates hurried westward on July 20 at the rate of one hundred miles a day to effect Tecumseh's plan. Early the following morning Tenskwatawa called on Stickney to report that two of his "bad young men" were missing; he feared they had stolen some horses. Wells was beside himself: "The agent found no difficulty in swallowing the bait offered him and applauded the Prophet for his honesty."[4]

On July 22, having achieved what he came for, Tenskwatawa returned to Prophetstown to await the outcome of his petitions to the western tribes. Before setting out for Fort Dearborn, Wells, tired of wasting his breath on Agent Stickney, warned Governors Harrison and Edwards that the Prophet planned to "strike a heavy blow in Indiana Territory" if he had enough manpower; otherwise he would go on professing peace. Musing over the Shawnee brothers, Edwards concluded that Tecumseh was the one who bore closest scrutiny. "Tecumseh is the real officer and man of the Prophet's party," he advised the secretary of war in early August. "The Prophet will not be our friend while Tecumseh is our enemy." By then, Eustis could have discerned as much from the newspapers.[5]

But apart from condoning horse theft, Tenskwatawa had yet to offer any serious provocation. While the Detroit frontier roiled uncertainly, and with no troops but Hull's embattled army available for field duty in the Northwest, Harrison and Edwards could only keep a watchful eye on Prophetstown and hope for the best.

Summer lengthened, and the Prophetstown corn crop rose. Women harvested the fields while western warriors flocked to the village in answer to Tenskwatawa's call. With Tecumseh in Upper Canada, it fell to the Prophet to take the first steps to roll back the American frontier. Not everyone in the loosely constituted Indian alliance cooperated, however. The Potawatomis elected to fight alone rather than as part of a coordinated effort. Invigorated by the victories at Detroit and Fort Dearborn, they gathered to attack Fort Wayne, while on the Tippecanoe the Prophet and his mostly Kickapoo and Winnebago followers plotted against Fort Harrison, the outpost standing on the east bank of the Wabash River between Prophetstown and Vincennes that William Henry Harrison had built during the Tippecanoe campaign. Although not orchestrated in tandem, both the Potawatomi and Tenskwatawa's efforts were critical to the Indian cause. If Forts Wayne and Harrison both fell, the entire Wabash Valley as far south as Vincennes would be open to an Indian onslaught, and the land lost to the Long Knives in the Treaty of 1809 would be recovered. Perhaps the Master of Life would accord the military misfit Tenskwatawa, and not his elder brother, the honor of conquering the Indiana Territory. The notion surely crossed Tenskwatawa's mind. Neither war nor the grand cause of Indian liberty could wholly subdue natural sibling rivalry.

Little stood between the Prophet and an easy capture of Fort Harrison, a necessary prelude to Tecumseh's desired attack on Vincennes. With Indiana militiamen more interested in protecting their families than in organizing, an exasperated Governor Harrison went to Kentucky to petition for a commission as major general of the Bluegrass State militia, which he knew was eager to take the war to the Indians. In the meantime only the seventy-man garrison at Fort Wayne and the fifty-man company at Fort Harrison remained to defend the Indiana frontier. Indians friendly to the Americans recognized the threat; the warriors of Tarhe and Black Hoof huddled in their villages while the chiefs pleaded with the War Department to build them blockhouses to fend off attacks by the Shawnee brothers. Closer to Fort Harrison, the Prophet's advance scouts browbeat resident Weas into joining the assault. With their accession, Tenskwatawa's war party swelled to five hundred warriors.

A few Weas remained faithful to the Americans, however. They warned Capt. (and future U.S. president) Zachary Taylor, the twenty-seven-year-old commander of Fort Harrison, to expect an onslaught from Prophetstown, though the foreknowledge would not do Taylor much good. Fever had prostrated him and all but fifteen of his officers and men, and while a dozen frontiersmen had brought their families into the fort and stood ready to reinforce the haggard garrison, Fort Harrison itself left much to be desired. Single rows of wobbly pickets formed three sides, and the fourth consisted of a range of log barracks flanked at each corner by a primitive blockhouse. Taylor was a born fighter from a Virginia family of military stock, however, and would grapple with the Indians to the last man.[6]

Tenskwatawa—whom few would follow into battle under the best of circumstances—delegated both the planning of the assault and the actual command of the war party to the senior Kickapoo war chief Pakoisheecan, a longtime follower, who opted for a surprise attack. Overeager young scouts upset Pakoisheecan's calculations. At sunset on September 3, they ambushed two civilians gathering hay. The shots alerted the garrison. Rousing himself from his cot, Taylor gathered the eight healthy soldiers and a dozen nervous civilian men to defend the fort.

The night passed quietly. Having lost the element of surprise, Pakoisheecan resorted to a transparent charade to inspect the fort for weaknesses. On the afternoon of September 4 forty Indians—among whom were ten women to give the group a peaceable veneer—emerged from the forest bearing a white flag and begging provisions.

While Taylor exchanged words with an English-speaking Shawnee, the other warriors milled about the walls in feigned indifference. Taylor turned away the Indians at dusk, unaware that the warriors had discovered the vulnerability they had sought—bits of chinking had dropped away from logs at the base of the outer wall of one of the blockhouses.

Night fell, and dark clouds blanketed the moon. Warriors assembled at the forest's edge. Pakoisheecan, with a butcher knife in each hand and a blanket full of kindling and dry grass tied to his back, snaked toward the weakened wall. He paused as sentries approached the spot, resuming his approach after they turned away. Reaching the blockhouse, he unfastened the blanket and stuffed the combustibles through the cracks. Striking a fire with his flint, he fanned the flames with his blanket until a steady blaze burned. At the appointed signal, hundreds of warriors whooped, yelled, and opened fire at the opposite side of the stockade. By the time Taylor and his soldiers realized the ruse, the blockhouse was a raging inferno, the flames fueled by the barreled whiskey inside.

Sick and convalescing soldiers spilled from the barracks. Two men leaped over the wall and scampered panic-stricken toward the timber, where warriors dispatched one and shredded the arm of the other before he escaped back to the fort. After firing a shot, a soldier boasted, "I killed an Indian." Forgetting to duck, he fell dead himself from a warrior's bullet.

Taylor despaired but kept his wits. Ordering several men to douse the barracks roof, he detailed others to build a temporary breastwork behind the burning blockhouse, which prevented Pakoisheecan and his warriors from entering the fort. The Indians maintained a steady fire of musketry and arrows for nearly seven hours, but Taylor had checked the attackers. Even with overwhelmingly superior numbers, Indians were loath to assault fortifications, however rickety. Before melting into the forest after daybreak, aggravated warriors slaughtered all the hogs, oxen, and cattle they could find. A few men lingered in the area for several days, burning abandoned cabins and killing more animals. Others ranged far to the southeast, massacring two dozen settlers, mostly women and children.

Although Pakoisheecan orchestrated the assault on Fort Harrison, the Prophet had blessed it. For the second time in less than a year, his medicine had proved deficient. Few of Tenskwatawa's warriors returned to Prophetstown. Disgusted Winnebagos dispersed for the autumn hunt. Many of the Kickapoos also scattered. With too small a force to defend Prophetstown against an American counterthrust— six hundred mounted rangers had already assembled at Vincennes hell-bent on retribution—Tenskwatawa withdrew up the Tippecanoe River to await word from Tecumseh. The Prophet was hopeful withal. A Potawatomi victory at Fort Wayne would ease the shame of the Fort Harrison fiasco, stymie the Long Knives, and end the fighting season with the Shawnee brothers well positioned to reassert Indian control over lands lost to fraudulent treaties and shameful defeats.[7]

At Amherstburg, Tecumseh was restless. In late August, Indian runners brought news that the Potawatomis had started their siege of Fort Wayne by hacking to death the brother of Indian agent John Johnston outside the gates and slaughtering neighborhood livestock. The Potawatomis asked for British help to reduce the stockade, an appeal that Tecumseh and Roundhead endorsed. Procter wanted to oblige them, but he was bound by an armistice that commanding general Sir George Prévost had negotiated with Henry Dearborn in the naïve hope that London's belated agreement to stop impressing American sailors would end the war. Prévost also remained committed to defensive offensive operations only.

That was an easy posture to espouse from the safety of Quebec. But for Procter, who stood face to face with an increasingly suspicious Tecumseh, denying the Potawatomis was strategic suicide. When the armistice ended, Procter authorized a combined British and Indian expedition against Fort Wayne under the pretext of preventing a second Fort Dearborn massacre. General Brock endorsed Procter's initiative. Urging support for their native allies, he told Prévost that the armistice had infuriated the Indians and that refusing to join them in attacking Fort Wayne would doom the alliance and Upper Canada with it. Brock also reminded his myopic superior of Tecumseh's expectations, saying, "I have already been asked to pledge my word that England would enter no negotiations in which their interests were not consulted, and could they be brought to imagine that we should desert them, the consequences must be fatal."[8]

Tecumseh's patience with the redcoats indeed had grown thin, more so as the strain of campaigning and an unspecified illness brought on by his wounding at Maguaga had depleted his famously robust health. On September 14 he left Amherstburg by canoe for the rapids of the Maumee River at the head of six hundred warriors, mostly Wyandots. Matthew Elliott and Alexander McKee, both aged and ailing, went with him, as did Chiefs Roundhead and Main Poc. Two hundred Ottawas and Ojibwas from the north country, the sober vanguard of Robert Dickson's rowdy Indians, most of whom still reveled uproariously over the fall of Fort Michilimackinac, also traveled downriver with Tecumseh.

The Shawnee chief was now the United States' principal Indian foe. Newspapers claimed incorrectly that he held a commission as a brigadier general in the British service, commanding both warriors and redcoats and capable of bringing "the greatest distress" to the Northwest frontier. He might be ill, but he was far from sidelined.

Behind the Indians came three hundred redcoats under Capt. Adam Muir, artillery to breach the walls of Fort Wayne, and one hundred handpicked Canadian militiamen led by the thirty-six-year-old captain Billy Caldwell. Gentlemanly and pleasant, Caldwell was the well-educated son of an Irish colonel in the British service and a Potawatomi mother. The six-foot-two-inch-tall métis also was an emerging confidant of Tecumseh.

Tecumseh elected to announce his approach with a bit of his brother's brand of bluster. Hoping to intimidate Indians allied with the Long Knives, runners from the Shawnee chief proclaimed that Tecumseh was coming to the Wabash country with an army of seven thousand Indians and a great force of redcoats, and that "he should put his foot on Fort Wayne as he came along and crush it." The Miamis must step aside, "for his feet were very large and required much room." If they remained, "he might step upon them."[9]

The Miamis probably laughed at Tecumseh's threat. Unknown to the Shawnee chief, the vanguard of a reconstituted Northwest Army (to replace that which Hull surrendered) had already raised the siege of Fort Wayne. Apart from butchering cattle, burning outbuildings and farms, and killing two or three men, the Potawatomis had skulked away having done little real damage. On September 25, Tecumseh's scouts blundered into an estimated three thousand Long Knives on the Maumee River. Captain Muir was in a precarious position, his expedition in jeopardy. A council of war resolved nothing. Elliott, Roundhead, and Main Poc advocated giving battle. Muir was for a hasty retreat, as were the Ojibwas and Ottawas, who registered their views with their feet, simply heading home. Their defection decided the matter for Muir, who at once turned back. The remaining Indians trailed behind him because their only source of food was the British provisions at Amherstburg. Both Muir and Procter blamed the expedition's failure on the delay that Prévost's armistice had caused.[10]

Tecumseh missed the painful deliberations with Captain Muir. No sooner had he learned of the Potawatomis' defeat at Fort Wayne than he quit the expedition and went in search of Tenskwatawa's makeshift village to convalesce and consider the Shawnee brothers' options. In fact, they had just one: fight it out with every available warrior. William Henry Harrison, who had leveraged his Kentucky commission into command of the Northwest Army and the rank of major general of volunteers, had raised a formidable force of regulars, militia, and volunteers from across the region. Despite logistical problems, he hoped to recapture Detroit and Michilimackinac before the year's end and then seize Fort Malden, with search-and-destroy operations against native villages in northern Indiana and Ohio preceding the offensive. The complete annihilation of the Crown's Indian allies would come apace. With winter approaching and the Shawnee brothers having temporarily removed themselves from the scene, it fell to Roundhead to muster what Indians he could to aid the British in defending Upper Canada.

Writing Procter from the Niagara frontier, General Brock was hopeful so long as Tecumseh returned to the fold. "An active, interesting scene is going to commence with you. I am perfectly at ease with the result, provided we can manage the Indians and keep them attached to our cause, which in fact is theirs.... If the Indians act as they did under Tecumseh, who probably might be induced to return to Amherstburg, [the Northwest Army] will very soon dwindle to nothing.... Harass [Harrison] continually. May every possible success attend you."[11]

Those were Brock's last words to his subordinate. On October 13 he fell mortally wounded leading a charge against invading Americans at the Battle of Queenston Heights, on the Niagara frontier. Brock's vision survived after a fashion, however. General Prévost at last understood the need to guarantee the Indians an independent homeland as part of any peace with the United States, as much a barrier to future American aggression against Upper Canada as a reward for Indian service to the Crown.[12]

Tecumseh would not learn of Brock's death for several months, though it would have had little impact on his immediate concern, which was to keep clear of Indian-hating American volunteers who wrought swift and indiscriminate retribution. They burned twenty-one Indian villages, most of them evacuated; destroyed crops and stores; desecrated graves to strip Indian corpses of silver trinkets; and turned Indian country into a wasteland. Not even the Miamis were spared. The Potawatomis had railroaded enough of them into taking part in the attack on Fort Wayne that the government declared the entire tribe "unquestionably hostile" with no claim to government protection. The unsuspecting Miamis were in their villages on the Mississinewa River when the Americans struck. They killed or captured fifty-two villagers before a bold Miami counterattack drove them away. In another egregious act of bad faith, a soldier shot Black Hoof while the chief was paying a friendly visit to one of Harrison's generals. The officer posted a substantial reward for the culprit, but he escaped justice. Black Hoof survived, his loyalty to the United States remarkably undiminished.[13]

Prophetstown itself became the object of a large and raucous American incursion. Although vacant, the village's symbolic value as the hotbed of Indian extremism rankled Harrison no less than it had a year earlier, when he stumbled into the Battle of Tippecanoe. On November 19, Maj. Gen. Samuel Hopkins of the Kentucky militia led one thousand ill-disciplined horsemen to the Shawnee brothers' sanctuary. It took four days, but Hopkins razed the village and all the standing and stored corn.

It was a hard but not a mortal blow to the Indian alliance, for which the warriors exacted a measure of revenge. Tecumseh and Tenskwatawa were farther up the Wabash—the former recuperating. Both appealed to scattered warriors to rejoin them, but their brother Kumskaukau, a well-liked and capable warrior in his own right, helped punish the raiders. On September 22, from atop craggy bluffs overlooking the Wabash, Kumskaukau's war party ambushed a mounted scouting party, toppling eighteen riders from their saddles. Hopkins prepared to counterattack, but a sudden and violent snowstorm quelled further combat.[14]

Kumskaukau traipsed back to his brothers' camp with his fellow victors. The triumphant war party included several Kickapoos leading a Kentuckian marked for death. Custom prohibited the Shawnee brothers from intervening on the condemned man's behalf. The Kickapoos confined him overnight, then led the prisoner, bound and stripped, to the place of execution, an oak grove three miles from the village. They thrust a green sapling into the snow-covered ground, to which they attached a grapevine. In deathly silence, the Kickapoos bound his arms to the vine. Then they took firebrands and began to jab the Kentuckian. He endured the torture from sunrise until early afternoon. After he died, the Kickapoos skinned and quartered him and boiled his limbs for a feast. Tenskwatawa witnessed the Kentuckian's grim end and later spoke of the killing with genuine regret.[15]

More bloodshed lay ahead before snow, ice, and frigid cold drew a curtain on the year's campaigning. Harrison's scorched-earth tactics had made the hostile Indians dependent on British provisions. Rations were short in the Amherstburg stores, compelling Procter to approve an expedition to the Maumee River rapids in northwestern Ohio, a region rich in corn and livestock and a critical staging area for operations against Detroit. In late October, in Tecumseh's absence, Matthew Elliott and Chief Roundhead mustered five hundred at Amherstburg to gather foodstuffs at the foot of the rapids. All went well until a ragged American column interrupted their work. A brief skirmish ensued, from which many of the hungry Americans defected to scrounge food themselves, but in the end the Indians retreated to Amherstburg, their wants only partially supplied.[16]

Somehow in that bitter, blighted winter of 1813, the Shawnee brothers managed to feed the three hundred warriors who assembled in their Wabash River camp in expectation of renewing the war against the Long Knives come spring. They also sent runners bearing gifts to their Illinois allies, most of whom wintered with Main Poc on the Fox River, where game abounded and Long Knives were scarce. Main Poc chose the site also to prevent "those troubles of the earth, the Americans," from reoccupying Fort Dearborn.[17]

Many of "those troubles of the earth" were buried on the frigid morning of January 22, 1813, in a victory that must have sent the spirits of the convalescent Tecumseh soaring. General Harrison had hoped to gather four thousand men at the rapids of the Maumee River and cross the iced-over Detroit River to attack Fort Malden. But Maj. Gen. James Winchester, a willful and bungling subordinate, advanced from the Maumee rapids to the small River Raisin settlement of French-town, without informing Harrison. Seizing the opportunity to deal a blow to Winchester's exposed command, Colonel Procter and Round-head attacked. With the Americans more interested in gathering fire-wood than keeping watch, and their senior leaders lodged comfortably in the rear, the allies made short work of Winchester's command. In the most decisive victory either side had achieved to date, the British and Indians killed 290 Americans and captured 600 others. Two days after the battle the triumph was tarnished, however, when drunken Indians massacred sixty prisoners. Frenchtown nevertheless ended Harrison's planned invasion and returned the momentum of war in the Northwest to Procter.

Both the victory and a later promotion to brigadier general cheered Procter. But one disturbing uncertainty plagued him: would Tecum-seh return? During the winter, he reported that the Shawnee chief was "aloof" and still incapacitated. Rumors placed him on death's door. John Johnston heard that one leg had so "entirely withered" that he would "never recover the use of it." Possessing more reliable sources than Johnston, Procter told Maj. Gen. Roger Sheaffe, Brock's suc-cessor in Upper Canada, that Tecumseh had "scarcely recovered his health."[18]

A British triumph in the Northwest without Tecumseh to unite the Indians was beyond Procter's imagining. Should the Shawnee recover, however, Procter could offer him greater inducement to continue the struggle. Events in Europe had warmed the British government to the late General Brock's arguments for an inviolable Indian homeland under English protection. In November 1812, Napoleon abandoned Russia, his Grande Armée demolished. The French emperor's over-throw being now a real possibility, the new English minister for war and the colonies, Lord Bathurst, committed Great Britain to Tecum-seh's cause, albeit for an Indian domain short of the Ohio River line of which the Shawnee brothers dreamed.

But would Tecumseh recuperate from whatever ailed him?

Tecumseh had become a celebrity to Americans comfortably removed from the turbulent frontier. No blame attached to him for the massacre of Winchester's Kentuckians on the River Raisin. By late February 1813 his reputation was well established. American newspapers introduced the Shawnee chief to their readers as a brutal but brilliant Indian Robin Hood,

> about forty-five years of age, of the Chawonoe [*sic*] tribe, six-feet high, well-proportioned for his height, of erect and lofty deportment penetrating eye, stern in his visage; artful; industrious in preparing enterprises and bold in their execution. His eloquence is nervous, concise, and impressive.
>
> In his youth, and before the treaty of Greenville, he was of the boldest warriors who infested the Ohio River—seizing boats, killing emigrants, loading the horses with the most valuable plunder—and returned to the Wabash where, careless of wealth himself, he soon lavished the treasures of his rapine upon his followers, which when exhausted, [were] replenished by fresh depredations.
>
> Among the Indians, Tecumseh is esteemed the boldest warrior of the west.[19]

Of far greater import to the pan-Indian cause than good press from the Americans, Tecumseh's health was restored, and Tenskwatawa regained much of his influence. A longtime agent on intimate terms with the western tribes assured territorial governors that "many Indians still follow the dictates of the Prophet in a great measure." Despite his doctrinal differences with Tenskwatawa, Main Poc invoked the Prophet's image to rally warriors, sending his son to enjoin the Illinois tribes to "go on immediately to Detroit; that the Americans were tired of fighting with the Prophet [and] were obliged to acknowledge [his] superiority."[20]

In March 1813 a revitalized Tecumseh returned to Amherstburg with a promise that vast Indian reinforcements were on the way. General Procter could scarcely hide his delight: "Among the Indians that joined [me] from the Wabash was the highly gifted and celebrated Chief Tecumseh, who united in his person all those heroic qualities which romance has ever delighted to attribute to the 'children of the forest,' and with them, intelligence and feelings that belonged not to the savage. He possessed such influence among his brethren that his presence was of the utmost importance."

Procter often invited Tecumseh and Matthew Elliott, at whose home the Shawnee chief again settled, to dine at his quarters. Tecumseh spoke freely around the general, too much so where Tenskwatawa was concerned. On one occasion he disparaged the Prophet's teachings and laughingly spoke of him as his "foolish brother."

Never had Tecumseh expressed anything short of absolute fidelity to Tenskwatawa's doctrine. Only he knew what prompted his remarks to Procter. Perhaps, exulting in the royal treatment the general gave him, he merely wished to elevate himself at his brother's expense—a very human display of sibling rivalry. Or, in the wake of Tippecanoe and the Fort Harrison debacle, he might genuinely have come to doubt the Prophet's medicine. Whatever his convictions, Tecumseh would not abandon their partnership. After a brief stay in Amherstburg, he returned to the Wabash. Before leaving, he swore to use his influence—what Procter marveled as his secret gift for swaying the Indians to his purpose without "any formal authority"—to persuade the gathered warriors to bring their families to the Michigan Territory to strengthen their alliance with the British, not as difficult a proposition as might appear because most of the Indians were hungry.

By mid-March the Shawnee brothers were on the trail to Detroit, having pulled up stakes as Procter had asked. On April 16, Tecumseh and a small entourage rode into Fort Malden, with Tenskwatawa and more than twelve hundred fighting men and at least as many dependents close behind. Providentially for Tecumseh, Procter talked about offensive operations with a forcefulness reminiscent of Brock. And like his late superior, Procter was willing to exceed General Prévost's orders. Rather than exploit the British victory on the River Raisin, the timid commanding general wanted Procter to hold fast while Tecumseh did no more than harass Harrison's lines of supply and reinforcements.[21]

Procter contemplated a larger purpose for his redcoats and Tecumseh's warriors, one that would take them back into Ohio. In February 1813, Harrison had broken ground on an expansive nine-acre stockade called Fort Meigs, atop a gentle bluff at the foot of the Maumee rapids (eleven miles southwest of modern Toledo), on the south bank of the river and directly opposite the ground where Anthony Wayne had shattered the Northwestern Confederacy in 1794. Situated astride the road from Detroit deep into Ohio, Fort Meigs fulfilled two critical American needs—blocking a British and Indian invasion of the Ohio settlements and serving as a springboard and supply depot for an American thrust against Detroit and Upper Canada.

For the moment, however, General Harrison's posture was strictly defensive. Having finally recognized that control of Lake Erie was necessary to retake and hold Detroit, as well as to invade the Western District of Upper Canada, the War Department ordered Harrison to hold fast while workmen built a fleet offshore. Harrison offered no objections. The Kentucky and Ohio militias had disbanded at the end of their enlistments in February. Harrison could expect no new volunteers until May, leaving him only three understrength regular regiments to garrison Fort Meigs. With a "frontier so extensive to protect and a [fort] so sacred to guard against the attempts of an enemy as subtle and formidable as Indians and British when united certainly are," Harrison doubted he could protect either the navy shipbuilders or the Ohio settlements.[22]

Procter decided to attack Fort Meigs to exploit Harrison's predicament. Tecumseh endorsed Procter's plan, and he assembled his Indian allies ahead of the late April timetable. Tenskwatawa accompanied the Indian force as intermediary to the Master of Life. For the first time since Fallen Timbers, the Shawnee siblings would fight together, their partnership solid despite Tecumseh's snide remarks about his "foolish brother."

General Harrison acknowledged Tenskwatawa's continued role in the alliance, ranking him above Tecumseh, at least in his official correspondence. "The Prophet and his brother [have] arrived at the River Raisin with a reinforcement of Indian warriors," he wrote the secretary of war on April 21. "Their [British] employers stimulate them by every means possible. To the Prophet and his followers, assurances were given that the Michigan Territory should be theirs."[23]

First they and the British had to defeat the Americans holed up in Fort Meigs. As General Procter sailed from Fort Malden on April 24 with

MAP 10 THEATER OF OPERATIONS, 1813

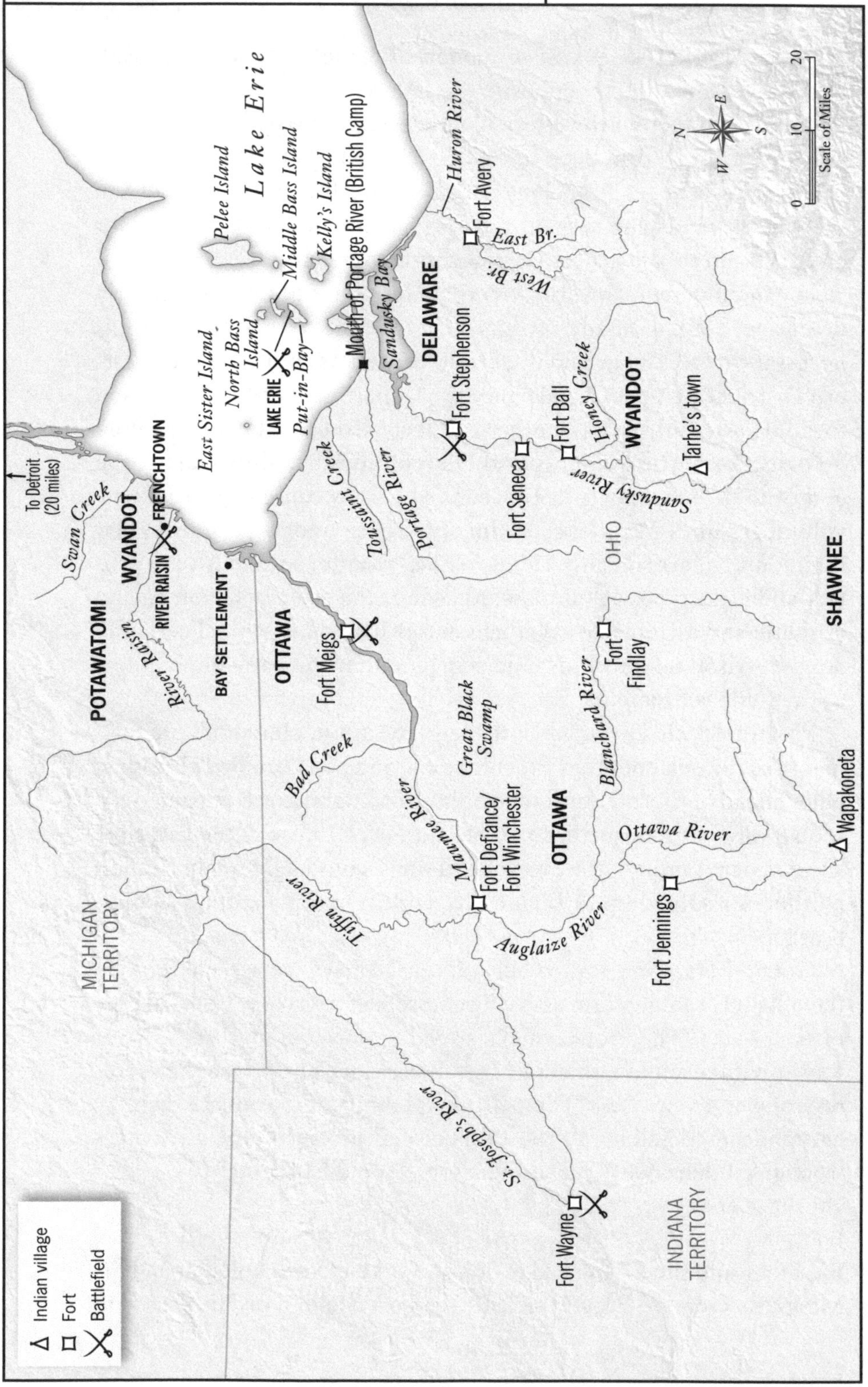

Lake Erie

Pelee Island

Middle Bass Island

Kelly's Island

North Bass Island

East Sister Island

LAKE ERIE
Put-in-Bay

Mouth of Portage River (British Camp)

Sandusky Bay

Huron River

Fort Avery

East Br.

West Br.

DELAWARE

Fort Stephenson

Fort Ball

Honey Creek

Tarhe's town

WYANDOT

Fort Seneca

Sandusky River

Portage River

Toussaint Creek

OHIO

Swan Creek

To Detroit
(20 miles)

WYANDOT

FRENCHTOWN

RIVER RAISIN

River Raisin

POTAWATOMI

BAY SETTLEMENT

OTTAWA

Fort Meigs

Bad Creek

Maumee River

Great Black
Swamp

Fort Findlay

Blanchard River

Fort Defiance/
Fort Winchester

OTTAWA

Ottawa River

Tiffin River

Auglaize River

Fort Jennings

Wapakoneta

SHAWNEE

MICHIGAN
TERRITORY

St. Joseph's River

Fort Wayne

INDIANA
TERRITORY

N
E
W
S
Scale of Miles
0   10   20

△ Indian village
□ Fort
✕ Battlefield

522 British regulars, 462 Canadian militiamen, and a formidable artillery train to rendezvous with the Indians at the foot of the Maumee rapids, torrential rains lashed Lake Erie and pounded the shores. Two days later Procter met Tecumseh and Tenskwatawa near the ruins of old Fort Miamis, the long-abandoned British post that had barred its gates to them after the Indian retreat from Fallen Timbers nineteen years earlier. The physical reminders of such painful times could not have been pleasant for the Shawnee brothers, but they had the satisfaction of commanding the allegiance of nearly as many warriors as Blue Jacket had commanded on that fateful day in 1794, and from a wider range of tribes.

While the infantry made camp near the rotting and tumbled down palisades of Fort Miamis two and a half miles downriver from Fort Meigs, British engineers mapped out artillery positions on the north bank of the Maumee River directly opposite the American post. Plodding through knee-deep mire, rain-soaked redcoats labored three days to haul four artillery batteries into place. Meanwhile Indian skirmishers harassed the American garrison, edging near enough to slaughter pigs and oxen outside the walls and to kill or wound a dozen defenders. Hiding behind felled beech and oak trees, often for a day or more without moving, the warriors came to be "very impudent," said an American officer, "and it became necessary for us to keep an eye on them, and occasionally give them a few shells and grape."[24]

Tenskwatawa withdrew to communicate with the Master of Life, leaving Tecumseh to exercise his prerogatives as war chief. Scrutinizing Fort Meigs through rainfall from the far bank of the Maumee, Tecumseh must have been impressed. Standing sixty feet above the river, Fort Meigs described a misshapen ellipse 2,500 yards in circumference. Its exterior bristled with abatis (breastworks of stakes). Deep ditches traced the perimeter. The walls were fifteen-foot-long timber pickets driven three feet into the ground. Seven two-story log blockhouses, each boasting a cannon, frowned at irregular intervals. Two batteries of five to six guns each enhanced the defenses. While the British struggled with their own artillery, the Americans built two enormous mounds of earth twenty feet wide and twelve feet high that ran the length of the interior. They also dug squalid and muddy recesses into the reverse sides to shelter themselves from British bombardment.[25]

MAP II   BATTLE OF FORT MEIGS, MAY 5, 1813

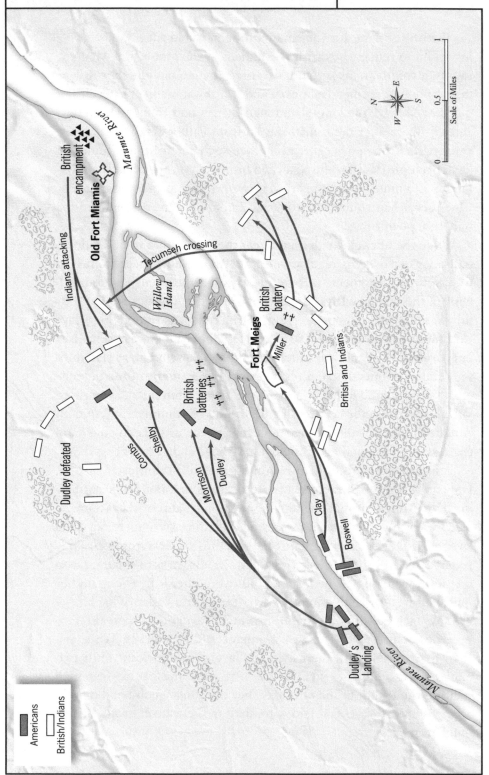

Scale of Miles

N
E
W
S

Maumee River

British encampment

Indians attacking

Old Fort Miamis

Tecumseh crossing

Willow Island

British battery
++

Miller

Fort Meigs

British and Indians

Dudley defeated

Combs

Shelby

British batteries ++
++
++

Morrison

Dudley

Clay

Boswell

Dudley's Landing

Maumee River

Americans

British/Indians

As no Indian in his right mind would dare storm a fort, particularly one so well constructed as Fort Meigs, Tecumseh and the chiefs counted on the British artillery to level the place and force the Americans into the open. Procter miscalculated badly, however, opening his bombardment at two a.m. from the far bank and from two gunboats downriver. The American colonel Alexander Bourne thought him either cowardly or of unsound judgment for having placed his guns on lower ground across the river rather than on the south bank, where the British might have approached to within 250 yards of the fort and "knocked all our defenses down in a short time." As the first guns roared, Harrison ordered all lights extinguished. "It was extremely dark, wet, and muddy," recalled Colonel Bourne. "We often fell down in the ditches, sometimes one or two on top of another." The cannonade, however, proved a bust. Projectiles sank harmlessly into the sodden earth, hissing and smoking. Shells eviscerated a few soldiers and collapsed some blockhouse roofs, but the fort was in no real danger. Although Tecumseh's Indian snipers inflicted more casualties than did two days of British shelling, the warriors enjoyed the pyrotechnics show just the same. "It was extremely diverting to see with what pleasure and delight the Indians would yell, whenever in their opinion damage was done by the bursting of a shell," another American officer remembered. "Their hanging about the [fort], and occasionally coming pretty near, kept our lines almost constantly in a blaze of fire."

After three days of the feckless cannonade, Tecumseh, Tenskwatawa, and Roundhead approached Procter with a better location for the British cannons. It was a bushy elevation three hundred yards east of Fort Meigs that Indian riflemen had been using to harass the defenders. He obliged them. A three-cannon artillery company went to the spot—then negated the potential terrain advantage by building gun emplacements below instead of on "Indian Hill," as the Americans called the knoll. Shells fired from beneath Indian Hill landed outside the walls of Fort Meigs, prompting defenders to assume the battery commander "must be a friend and felt for our situation."[26]

On the morning of May 5, the stalemate broke. Beneath a beating rain, eighteen large flat-bottomed boats bearing twelve hundred Kentucky militiamen under Brig. Gen. Green Clay crashed down the rapids above Fort Meigs. The reinforcements Harrison hoped for had arrived. Their appearance caught Procter and Tecumseh unawares,

but not Harrison. A small advance party riding a raft had negotiated the rapids and passed through the Indian lines into the fort the
night before, and Harrison had a plan for the Kentuckians. Clay was
to divide his force. Four hundred men were to land on the American
(south) side of the Maumee and fight their way into the fort. A guide
from Harrison would lead the remaining eight hundred men under
Lt. Col. William Dudley to the north bank, where they would attack
the British batteries opposite the fort, spike the guns, return to their
boats, cross the rushing river, and retreat to Fort Meigs. Meanwhile
Harrison would send a sortie from the stockade to attack the battery
beneath Indian Hill.

The plan would have been complicated even for the best-trained
troops to execute, and Clay's brigade was little better than an armed
rabble. After inspecting the recruits, the governor of Kentucky had told
Harrison not to expect much from them. The "greater part appeared
to [be] men undersize and in other respects hardly Kentuckians, the
better kind of people" having paid for substitutes to serve in their
stead. Despite much talk about avenging the River Raisin massacre,
Kentucky war fever had ebbed.

That morning Tecumseh was on the south bank with five hundred
warriors, harassing Fort Meigs under cover of the continuing British bombardment, when the Kentucky flatboats disgorged their sub-
standard soldiers. Many stumbled ashore drunk, sick, or enfeebled by
measles. They were also confused, as neither Clay nor Dudley had
informed them of their missions. Tecumseh responded well to Clay's
sudden appearance, fighting the wobbly Kentuckians to a standstill
in deep timber between the riverbank and Fort Meigs. Not until two
hundred dragoons thundered out of the gates to their rescue—the
Indians had a deep dread of saber-wielding horsemen—were they
able to enter the stockade, regroup, and counterattack. Tecumseh's
warriors withdrew into the forest, having killed twenty Kentuckians
and wounded forty-five—nearly one in six of those who disembarked
on the south bank.[27]

No sooner had Tecumseh withdrawn than a new American threat
presented itself. A detachment of 350 well-disciplined regulars swept
out of Fort Meigs toward Indian Hill employing clubbed muskets and

bayonets to bloody effect. The Americans overran the gun emplacements, spiked the cannons, and took forty-four redcoats prisoner. But they had a hard fight back to Fort Meigs. Tecumseh counterattacked, recovering the cannons and nearly encircling an American company. Before the regulars regained the fort, they lost thirty dead and ninety wounded, a third of those engaged. As the gates of Fort Meigs swung shut and American artillery raked the open ground beyond the walls, Tecumseh again regrouped in timber northeast of the stockade.[28]

It was 10:45 a.m. Tecumseh had led his warriors brilliantly, but Harrison nevertheless had silenced the irksome battery east of Fort Meigs. All attention now turned to the north bank of the Maumee, where Colonel Dudley and his eight hundred Kentuckians belatedly appeared. Before coming aground two miles southwest of the British batteries, their boats had taken fire from Indians lurking on the shore. Forming his ragtag regiment into three columns, Dudley marched the men through muck and mire under the drumming rain toward the roar of the British cannons opposite Fort Meigs. Only Dudley understood the mission, and the burden of command paralyzed him. "What we were to do in case of success or defeat was never explained," recalled one befuddled officer. Evoking the memory of the River Raisin, another officer urged his men stand fast at all hazards.

The results were predictable. At first the battle went Dudley's way. Startled by the wildly yelling Kentuckians bearing down on them from behind, the British gunners fled. Dudley captured the batteries without losing a man. Then his luck changed. No one had brought the spikes needed to disable the cannons. Nor had anyone thought to roll the guns into the river. Dudley babbled while his men mingled aimlessly around the artillery emplacements. From Fort Meigs, Harrison signaled frantically for them to return to their boats.

A sudden staccato of musketry diverted the Kentuckians' attention to their left and rear. Their scout company, which included friendly Shawnees, had run into Indians hidden in timber a half-mile from the batteries. With no orders to retreat, the scouts held their ground. Forgetting his instructions, Dudley led his regiment in a confused and impetuous dash to support them. It was precisely the response for which the Indians, likely under Chief Roundhead's command, had hoped. For the next three hours they teased the Kentuckians deeper into the forest—forming a line, firing a volley, then falling back in the center while unseen warriors held fast on the flanks—until Dudley's command found itself more than a mile from the river. Behind them the bodies of fifty dead Long Knives littered the swampy forest floor.[29]

Tecumseh was annoying the Fort Meigs garrison with desultory firing from woods northeast of the fort when the racket of the battle raging on the north bank of the Maumee attracted his attention. Gathering his warriors, he crossed the river below the rapids. Once on the north bank, he shook out a loose line of whooping and painted followers and swept toward Dudley's rear, "completely hemming us in upon every side," said a frightened sixteen-year-old militiaman. "Our case was then hopeless."

Coincidental with Tecumseh's appearance behind the Kentuckians, the Indians to Dudley's front and flanks sprang a grand ambush. Colonel Dudley crumpled to the ground with a bullet wound. Exultant warriors tomahawked and hacked him to death. A bullet passed through both temples of a company commander, expelling his eyeballs from their sockets. Waving his sword above his head, Dudley's second-in-command stuck the point in a tree. While drawing out the sword, he inadvertently sliced open his neck. Badly wounded, he hid in a hazel thicket and left his men to their fate. A wild rout ensued through ankle-deep mud. The Kentuckians strove to reach the presumed safety of the artillery emplacement, where a company had remained behind to guard the captured cannons. "Those who were strong and most able to, ran," confessed a frightened lieutenant, "leaving the weaker and wounded far behind [to be] overtaken and tomahawked by the Indians." A young British soldier saw one such death. He came upon a scalped Kentuckian begging for water and covering his raw and bloody head from the sun with tree branches. Before the Redcoat was able to minister to the man, a party of Indians pushed the Redcoat aside and tomahawked the Kentuckian. Some Kentuckians were too frightened to even try to escape. Said the Shawnee scouts, "The men stood as if they could not help themselves and got shot down very fast."[30]

Those who managed to elude Tecumseh's rapidly encircling warriors found no refuge in the artillery emplacements. Redcoats had driven off the Kentucky company charged with holding them. With the Indians close on their heels, the dazed and exhausted survivors of Dudley's foray grounded their arms and surrendered to the British. A small detachment of redcoats herded the prisoners toward decrepit Fort Miamis. Furious warriors buzzed about grabbing captives to plunder, or worse. "Almost all lost their hats and coats, and some their pantaloons also," remembered a Kentucky officer. "He who did not instantaneously give up his clothes frequently paid his life for it."

Approaching the fort, the prisoners saw two fifty-foot-long parallel lines of warriors arrayed on either side of the entrance. Powerless to intervene, their captors could only warn the Kentuckians of what awaited them. "We were told by the British soldiers that the Indians intended to make us 'run the gauntlet' just before we entered [the fort], and while we were running, they would whip and kill us as they pleased, but when we got in, we would be molested no more," Lt. Joseph Underwood recalled. That, at least, was the Indian custom. As Underwood awaited his turn, he watched warriors throw war clubs and tomahawks at those ahead of him, shooting down the slow of foot. Underwood passed the gauntlet having endured only blows to the head and shoulders with whipping sticks. Inside the earthwork, British sentries ordered Underwood to sit down with those who had preceded him. Many bled from untreated wounds; all hoped the worst had passed.

"And now it was my time," sixteen-year-old Thomas Christian remembered. Clutching a mudda coat his mother had made him, he darted forward through the blood-drenched mud, winding his way around corpses of fellow Kentuckians. "With a strength and speed that astonished me I made a bolt, but ere I had reached the prized entry, I felt a sudden jerk at the back of my head, saw a button strike the ground some feet in front, my arms were forcibly jerked back, and the precious gift of my mother was lost forever." A few more bounds landed Christian among his fellow survivors.

An eerie silence, broken only by the groans of the wounded, fell over the rain-soaked ruins. Then a band of Ojibwas led by Split Log, a war leader whom one British officer labeled a "bloodthirsty villain and sneaking ruffian," appeared. Having missed the battle, Split Log and his cohorts were in search of easy scalps. Painted black and scowling, Split Log mounted the fort's low earthen embankment. Other Ojibwas clambered over the fallen walls onto the parade ground where the Kentuckians sat huddled. Sensing what was about to transpire, some of the redcoats cried, *"Oh! Nichee wah!"* (Oh! Brother, desist!) But the warriors were in an ugly mood. Raising his musket, Split Log fired, and a prisoner fell dead. He calmly reloaded and shot another Kentuckian. Then, laying aside his musket, he leaped among the prisoners with a tomahawk in hand and began cleaving skulls and ripping off scalps. Raising a war whoop, his followers waded in. When a British sentry leveled his bayonet to protect a Kentuckian, an Indian drew his pistol and shot him, exclaiming "You damned Yankee too!" With that, the rest of the redcoats stepped aside. A group of angry Potawatomis joined in the killing.

Young Thomas Christian never forgot the horror. With "unearthly yells" the warriors descended on the Kentuckians, "killing and scalping as fast as their own crowded ranks would admit, while we, like terror-stricken sheep hemmed in by dogs, or a parcel of hogs in a butcher's pen, were piled one upon another in one corner. Those at the bottom were being smothered, while those upon the top were being drenched with blood and brains." Christian prepared himself to die. "Suddenly as a lightning flash, the yelling ceased, the uplifted war clubs descended harmlessly by the side of the now shamed warriors, and above the groans of the dying, and the prayers of the living, is heard the brave Tecumseh putting a stop to the massacre, shaming his warriors for behaving like squaws." The Shawnee chief who had been the bane of Kentuckians was now their deliverer.[31]

Tecumseh had been lingering on the battlefield with Matthew Elliott when a breathless courier from Procter pulled rein, urging him to help prevent a massacre at Fort Miamis. "Never did Tecumseh shine more truly than on this occasion," an admiring redcoat later wrote. "Ever merciful and magnanimous as he was ardent and courageous, the voice of supplication seldom reached him in vain."[32] Tecumseh's humanity was real. But another concern also likely impelled him down the path to the crumbling fort: the Indians had to keep the respect of the British and rise above the opprobrious label "savages."

Into the fort rode Tecumseh on a dapple-gray horse. Dismounting, he strode through the throng of warriors and climbed atop a high point on the nearest tumbledown wall. Then he delivered with words and sign language what Kentucky lieutenant Leslie Combs styled a "brief but emphatic address" that ended the killing. "I could not understand his language," wrote Combs, who was near Tecumseh, "but his gestures and manner satisfied me that he was on the side of mercy." Warriors lowered their weapons and grunted their assent to Tecumseh's entreaties. Split Log argued with Tecumseh, then stormed off. Old white-haired Matthew Elliott, meanwhile, brandished his saber and spoke sharply in support of Tecumseh. Gradually the remaining warriors dispersed. As the terror subsided, Lieutenant Underwood sized up the Shawnee: "Tecumseh was an admirable-formed man with an intelligent look and dignified demeanor." Writing of Tecumseh's intercession but unaware of his identity, another prisoner also noted the chief's "very masterful appearance. Some said it was Tecumseh, but who he was I knew not, but he was the only man that acted like a gentleman, as an officer."[33]

General Procter's whereabouts during the massacre are unrecorded. It is unthinkable that he would have condoned such an outrage; he likely had no more power to stop it than he had had to halt the atrocities at the River Raisin. There were simply too many riled Indians and too few redcoats for a British officer of any rank to quiet them. Only a chief of Tecumseh's prestige could have mastered the moment. Where Tecumseh dared not intervene, however, was in preventing Indian families from adopting prisoners to replace warriors killed in battle. Within a matter of days, several Kentuckians found themselves shorn of their facial hair, scrubbed clean, and adopted into Indian households.

Despite Tecumseh's magnanimity, Dudley's disobedience of Harrison's orders had cost his command dearly. Of the 800 volunteers who disembarked on the north bank of the Maumee, at least 70 died and 580 fell captive. Only 150 made their way safely to Fort Meigs.[34]

The day after the battle Tecumseh again intervened on behalf of prisoners, this time Wapakoneta Shawnees from Dudley's scout company whom the Wyandots held in their camp. Tecumseh found them tied fast to poles and badly bruised from repeated whippings. Chief Walk-in-the-Water himself had taken a turn beating the warriors about the head with a ramrod—a war chief's equivalent of a hickory switch—to which they responded with defiant whoops as befitted young fighting men unwilling to show fear. "Tecumseh came to us and shook hands with us," recalled one. "He told the Wyandots to let us alone." In high spirits, Tecumseh boasted to the Wapakoneta warriors that the current conflict was the culmination of eight years of careful planning on his part; "that he had everything accomplished and that all nations from the North were standing at his word [to] come as a great army ... from different parts." At Tecumseh's request the Wyandots released the Shawnees; they would return to Wapakoneta in a prisoner exchange a few days later.[35]

Tecumseh's boasting likely was a bluff to conceal the truly ephemeral nature of the pan-Indian alliance, as well as the limits of his authority. In fact, the Indians nominally under his command were deserting in droves. As was customary after a victory, they drifted off with their wounded, their prisoners, and their booty, a considerable quantity of which they had taken from the Kentucky boats. Forty-eight hours after Dudley's defeat, only Tecumseh, Tenskwatawa, and twenty chiefs and warriors remained with the British. "Under present circumstances at least," lamented Procter to General Prévost, "our Indian force is not a disposable one, or permanent, though occasionally a most powerful aid."[36]

The Indians were not alone in abandoning the expedition. Half of the Canadian militiamen went home to plant spring crops; dictates of raw survival surpassed their military duty. Deprived of three-quarters of his command, Procter found himself in the untenable position of encircling an enemy force larger than his own. Although Procter had lost fewer than one hundred soldiers in combat (Indian losses were unrecorded but trifling), his remaining redcoats were in sorry shape. "The absence of tents, the privations of the campaign, and the unhealthiness of the camp—a very hotbed of ague, fever, and dysentery—gradually told on the small regular force of the command," summarized the historian of the 41st Regiment. Under such circumstances, Procter had no alternative but to raise the siege and return to Fort Malden before Harrison exploited the British weakness. After a parting bombardment, Procter sailed away down the Maumee River.[37]

From aboard a British vessel, Tecumseh and Tenskwatawa watched Fort Meigs recede in the distance, and with it seemingly their best hope for expelling the Long Knives from northern Ohio. At an end too, it appeared, was their larger quest to disgorge the state of its 235,000 white inhabitants and restore the Ohio River as the boundary between themselves and the relentlessly expansive United States. But as General Procter was about to learn, Tecumseh was not yet prepared to abandon his dream, however quixotic it might strike others.

An Adequate Sacrifice
to Indian Opinion

THE SHAWNEE BROTHERS RETURNED to Fort Malden to find their Indian allies settling into villages along the Detroit River with the prisoners and plunder they had taken from Dudley's decimated Kentucky command. Procter was happy to accommodate them in their new surroundings. However much the commanding general in Canada, Sir George Prévost, might temporize, General Procter himself intended to remake the Michigan Territory into an Indian buffer state. His first act to that effect, upon returning from Fort Meigs, was to transfer the Indian Department staff and supplies from Amherstburg to Detroit.

While Procter courted Indian goodwill, Tecumseh and Tenskwatawa raised a village of bark wigwams for their Shawnee adherents, who numbered no more than eighty warriors and their families, on the Huron River, twenty miles south of Detroit. There the Shawnee brothers' paths diverged. The words that passed between them are lost to time, but the basic disagreement was simple: Tenskwatawa had had enough of fighting, Tecumseh had not. Not that Tenskwatawa had ventured much during the siege of Fort Meigs. As befitted a holy man whose life was sacred, the Prophet had clung to camp safely beyond the range of American artillery. Henceforth he intended to leave politics and war-making entirely to his elder brother.

Tecumseh was determined to attack Fort Meigs again. He could not reconcile himself to sanctuary in a British-administered Michigan Territory without trying again to reclaim the Ohio of his childhood.

So now he shuttled between his headquarters at Matthew Elliott's house and Fort Malden, importuning Procter at every opportunity to make a second push against Fort Meigs.[1]

In principle, Procter supported Tecumseh, but only insofar as Fort Meigs was concerned. If anything, his reasons for wanting to destroy the sprawling stockade had grown more urgent. General Harrison had publicly declared himself committed to retaking Detroit and invading Upper Canada, once the fleet under construction on Presque Isle wrested control of Lake Erie from the British. Should the American navy prevail, it would sever Procter's fragile supply line across Upper Canada and make his entire position untenable. Despite his worries about Fort Meigs, however, Procter was unable to accommodate the Shawnee chief. He needed more soldiers, more seamen for the Lake Erie flotilla, and more supplies both for his own troops and for Tecumseh's Indians. General Prévost had promised to send him the remaining half of the 41st Regiment once Great Britain reinforced Canada. When nine new regiments arrived in Canada, together with an admonition from His Majesty's Government that Prévost pay more attention to Procter's plight, Prévost declined to send Procter even the rest of the 41st Regiment. Instead, Prévost reverted to his old trope about the Amherstburg district being the most distant branch of the expendable Upper Canadian limb of the Canadian tree and Lower Canada the trunk that must be defended at all costs.

Procter's petitions grew desperate. Indians judged the British commitment by the strength of its forces at Fort Malden. Without a reliable core of redcoats around which the Indians and the Canadian militiamen might rally, Procter saw "very little chance here at the end of the line." Not only did his soldiers lack essentials, but the fifteen hundred warriors and their families then encamped across the Detroit River were "not half fed and would leave us if they were not warm in our cause." To a friend on Prévost's staff, Procter confided that the Indians seldom received any food except bread and smoked whitefish; additionally, Indian Department storerooms were dangerously short of muskets and gunpowder. In despair, Procter lied to the chiefs, telling them that four hundred redcoats were on the march to Fort Malden. "I can assure you," Procter confessed to the commanding officer of the absent portion of the 41st Regiment, perhaps hopeful his mendacity might prod reinforcements from Prévost, "that it might have the worst effect were they to conceive I was deceiving or amusing them." Tecumseh and Roundhead might stand fast, but Walk-in-the-Water, always one to hedge his bets, would reingratiate himself with the Americans. Main Poc's probable reaction to British deceit was too horrible to contemplate.[2]

Things would get worse for Procter. On a fine, bright late-June morning, fifteen hundred Indian warriors glided down the Detroit River in birch canoes flying British flags, singing war songs, and firing their muskets. On the Canadian shore a detail of troops and the 41st Regimental band awaited their arrival. Wheeling their canoes to land in perfect order, one after the other, the Indians disembarked and formed fifty-man squads, each distinguished by its members' unique pattern of body paint. Escorted by the redcoats, they marched to General Procter's quarters, where their chiefs spoke earnestly of their desire to fight the Long Knives at Fort Meigs.[3]

The new arrivals were western Indians whom Tecumseh had been unable to reach or, having met in council during his sojourns, to win over. Menominees, Winnebagos, Ojibwas, Ottawas, Sauks, Foxes, and even Dakotas made up the colorful horde, who to a man were loyal to the Scottish métis fur trader and Indian agent Robert Dickson. Such was Tecumseh's reputation that they agreed to subordinate themselves to his leadership, as Roundhead and Main Poc continued to do, so long as he brought them victory. Procter approached the evolving alliance—the largest gathering of Indian warriors in the history of the Old Northwest—with something akin to dread. "I had the mortification to find instead of the Indian force being a disposable one, or under my direction, our movements should be subject to the caprices and prejudices of the Indian body, to the degree in which my regular force was disproportionate to their numbers." Because Prévost had failed to send him the promised few hundred redcoats, the Indians, not the British, were calling the shots. Worse yet, Procter somehow had to feed the new arrivals and their families.[4]

At a fraught war council, the Indians demanded action. Tecumseh was their spokesman. In vain Procter argued against attacking Fort Meigs. His twenty-four-pounder cannons had made no impression on the stockade, with its defenders burrowed behind earthen traverses.

The only British warships capable of transporting the heavier guns needed to breach the fort walls were deployed to watch the rapid progress of the American shipbuilders at Presque Isle. And Prévost had given him no troops. Having exhausted his arguments, Procter sat down. With each excuse Tecumseh had grown angrier, but he hid it well. Now he arose, "calm, cool, deliberate, thinking in look, very hard in what he said," a Canadian volunteer recalled. Matthew Elliott interpreted. "Our father has brought us here to take [Fort Meigs], why don't we take it? If his children can't do it, give us spades, and we will work like beavers; we'll eat a way in for him." Turning to his true intent, Tecumseh suggested a ploy purely Indian in nature—stage a *ruse de guerre* to decoy the garrison deep into the woods, then storm the open fort.

Procter found the plan preposterous. His composure shattered, the general accused Tecumseh of treason. Procter and Elliott gripped their sword hilts. Tecumseh, who after speaking had sat down to fill his tomahawk pipe, rose slowly and, dumping out the tobacco, asked Elliott, perhaps rhetorically, "What does he say?" "Sit down," replied Elliott, placing a hand on Tecumseh's arm. "Never mind what he says." Other officers interceded to restore calm, and Procter yielded to Tecumseh's proposition.[5]

News of the proposed invasion passed through the Indian encampments and via spies to General Harrison, who reported that Tecumseh had "pressed General Procter to make another attack upon Fort Meigs and [was] much dissatisfied with his putting [him] off," and to Green Clay, now in command of the two thousand well-fed and confident defenders of Fort Meigs. Hardened by their first brush with the British and Indians, the Kentuckians were eager for a second encounter.[6]

On July 20 a reluctant Procter and a hopeful Tecumseh laid anchor at the mouth of the Maumee River. The next morning Tecumseh began quietly to surround Fort Meigs with part of the Indian force. Warriors captured the nine-man picket guard as it marched out of the fort before the garrison realized the danger. The British, meanwhile, returned to their old campsite near the skeletal Fort Miamis. For the next three days, the Indians contented themselves with harmless potshots at the garrison. And then Tecumseh set in motion his stratagem, which at least some of Procter's subordinates, if not the general himself, believed "gave every fair promise of success."

Tecumseh's scheme drew upon reports from his scouts that Harrison had encamped with the Northwest Army about forty miles southeast of Fort Meigs, and had arranged to reinforce General Clay should the latter come under attack. The only road available to an American relief force ran north to Fort Stephenson, an outpost below Sandusky Bay eighty-five miles west of modern Cleveland, then west thirty miles to Fort Meigs. On July 25, Procter evacuated his camp and crossed the Maumee River with his redcoats, taking position south of Fort Meigs. Tecumseh, meanwhile, dispatched three hundred mounted warriors on an ostentatious feint north of the stockade. Pounding across a bridge in plain sight, they milled about on the near bank. The ruse roiled the Kentucky defenders. "We expect to have warm work this night," an anxious captain scribbled in his pocket diary.

The night passed without incident, and on July 26 Tecumseh moved the bulk of his warriors, together with a detachment of redcoats and Canadian militiamen, through dark forests north of Fort Meigs, unobserved by the garrison, and into position alongside the Sandusky road, where the allied forces hid in timber on the north side opposite Fort Meigs. Tecumseh planned to begin a sham battle at four p.m. a mile up the road, gradually drawing nearer the fort. The Indians would fire blank cartridges at will, while the British and Canadians were to fire by platoon. This shooting pattern would suggest the approach of a relief column under attack and in need of succor. If the garrison took the bait and sallied forth, Tecumseh would attack it from the rear with part of his Indians and with the rest rush into the fort. British troops would join in the attack from the south. "The whole thing was executed with admirable precision and consummate finesse characteristic of the great Shawnee chief," remembered an American, "well calculated to deceive the unwary and draw out such a force from the fort into ambuscade as would fatally weaken the garrison."[7]

At four p.m. the sudden rattle of musketry, swiftly cresting in a rolling thunder, aroused the Kentuckians. The whoops and yells of more than a thousand warriors deepened the forest cacophony. Crowding the blockhouses, the Kentuckians strained to see the cause and begged their officers for permission to sally forth. Redcoats privy to the charade watched intently for the gates to creak open and the tan-coated

Kentuckians to pour out. "But they gave not the slightest indication of a design to leave the fort, even when the musketry had become so animated and heavy that we were half in doubt ourselves whether the battle was a sham one or real," an exasperated British soldier recalled. For an hour the mock battle raged unanswered. Tecumseh seethed. Not a single Long Knife showed himself. Suddenly the skies opened with a brief but thunderous downpour. Tecumseh called for a cease-fire and, as a redcoat wrote, "we had the mortification to find ourselves utterly foiled in the grand design of the expedition." The forest fell silent. Only a trace of blue-white gunpowder smoke lingered to mark the place where Tecumseh had staked so much.

General Clay, who had had a hard time restraining his men, was wise to Tecumseh's ploy. That morning two messengers from Harrison had snaked through the Indian lines with word that reinforcements were still two days away, meaning that there were no friendly troops near enough to have fallen into an Indian ambush.

The daylight hours of July 27 passed quietly. At nightfall the Indian camp erupted in a war dance. Hideous shrieks knifed through the war whoops. Sharing Tecumseh's rage at their discovered deception, warriors tortured and burned to death the prisoners taken six days earlier. Precipitously the next morning, the British packed up and sailed away, and the Indians rode or stalked away toward the lakeshore. "Whether they have actually abandoned all idea of attack this post," Clay wrote Harrison that evening, "or what are their views I can form no conjecture."[8]

If Procter had had his way, the expedition would have ridden the waves of Lake Erie back to the safety of Amherstburg harbor. But Tecumseh insisted on continuing the fight for Ohio. Without a victory somewhere on American soil, he knew that irreparable fissures would open in the Indian alliance. Already some of Dickson's western warriors, having found it hard to "fight against men who lived like ground-hogs" (in other words, soldiers who would not budge from behind their entrenchments), were deserting. Tecumseh too found himself in the awkward posture of demanding a victory but being unable to contribute to it because his warriors refused to put Fort Meigs and its two-thousand-man garrison between themselves and their defenseless families in Michigan. As an Indian war leader, Tecumseh was stymied. Warriors could set their own priorities, and in this instance, it was their families.

Tecumseh struck a compromise that satisfied no one. While Procter, with his five hundred regulars and seven hundred Indians under Dickson and Elliott, attacked Fort Stephenson, the inconsequential American outpost below Sandusky Bay, he would occupy the forested swamps between the Maumee and Sandusky rivers. From there he could intercept General Clay if he marched east to reinforce the post or fall on his rear if he started for Michigan instead. Procter grumbled but conceded the argument, his confidence in his native allies fast declining. "You will perceive that the Indian force is seldom a disposable one, never to be relied on in hour of need, and only to be found useful in proportion as we are independent of it," he later complained to General Prévost.[9]

On August 1, Procter sailed into Sandusky Bay and disembarked his troops for the brief march to Fort Stephenson. Dickson's Indians joined the redcoats in deep timber beyond a 150-yard-wide plain surrounding the fort. Although merely an outpost, Fort Stephenson looked formidable. It stood on rising ground. Sixteen-foot-high palisades overlooked a seven-foot-deep and twelve-foot-wide ditch. A glacis earthwork sloped downward from the ditch to the plain. The garrison consisted of 160 regulars commanded by Maj. George Croghan, the pugnacious twenty-one-year-old nephew of George Rogers Clark. Harrison's army encamped ten miles south of the fort.

Reluctant to assault the place, Procter tried to invoke the Indian bogeyman, as General Brock had with Hull at Detroit. Under a flag of truce, Dickson, Elliott, and a British major implored the American to surrender to "prevent the dreadful massacre that will be caused by your resistance." Croghan's representative declined: "When the fort shall be taken, there will be none to massacre. It will not be given up while a man is able to resist." Returning in disgust to the British lines, Dickson paused to speak with the Sauk war chief Black Hawk. "You will see tomorrow," he snarled, "how easily we will take that fort." Procter, however, was beset with doubt. The general wanted to quit without shedding British blood in what he feared would be a futile assault, but Elliott and Dickson dissuaded him. It was their "decided opinion that unless the fort was stormed, we should never bring an Indian warrior into the field with us." The Indians, they added, pledged to assault one corner of the fort if the British stormed another.

Grudgingly Procter concurred. On the morning of August 2, the British dragged three cannons to the timber's edge and shelled the fort without making a dent in its defenses. As the day deepened, the Indians grew uneasy. Procter's own subordinates urged him to approve an assault. At four p.m. he agreed to hurl a storming party against the blockhouse at the northwestern angle and send another column to feint against the fort's southern face while the Indians swarmed the southwestern corner.

Smoke from British cannons blanketed the plain. The storming party closed to within fifty yards of the palisades before the defenders spotted the redcoats. A musket volley momentarily staggered them. Rallying, most of the British spilled over the glacis and leaped into the ditch. Instantly a masked American cannon rolled forward to the blockhouse window and raked the milling redcoats with grapeshot, nails, broken pottery—anything that would fit in the cannon barrel. The ditch became a gory abattoir. After thirty minutes not a man in it remained upright. The few British who had wisely taken cover behind the glacis streamed back to the woods, leaving behind eighty-four casualties. Procter was heartsick. "Where are all the rest of the men?" he cried as survivors stumbled past. A private halted to reply, "I don't think there are any more to come; they are all killed or wounded." Weeping, Procter added, "Good God, what shall I do about the men?"[10]

Rage replaced anguish when Procter learned that the Indians, after making a token approach toward the fort, had melted back into the woods without losing a warrior. Most kept on running. "I was disappointed. The British advanced and commenced the attack, fighting like true braves, but were defeated by the braves in the fort," remembered Chief Black Hawk. Expressing a common concern among the Indians, he added, "The British army was [preparing] to retreat. I was now tired of being with them, our success being bad and having got no plunder. I determined on leaving them to see what had become of my wife and children, as I had not heard from them since I left home." Procter set sail for Amherstburg. "A more than adequate sacrifice having been made to Indian opinion," he told Prévost, "I drew off the brave assailants."[11]

On learning of Procter's imbroglio, Tecumseh shepherded his two thousand warriors back to their families in Michigan. The Shawnee chief had nothing about which to boast. In addition to his own inaction during Procter's foray against Fort Stephenson, one of his war parties was decimated attempting to ambush a column of Kentucky mounted infantry on the Sandusky road. Appearing from behind scattered trees, the Indians had fired confidently into the six-man advance guard, unaware of the several score Kentuckians cantering along the trail fifty yards behind until they charged. "The Indians did not have time to seek shelter. We killed them as fast as we came up to them," said a thrilled Kentuckian. "The Indians were all killed in less than ten minutes, and I suppose fifty swords made red with their blood." Seventeen warriors died. No Kentuckian was so much as scratched. "The Indians were surprised...and cut to pieces," Procter reported, adding, "the Indians have always had a dread of cavalry, of which the enemy have a considerable number." That number would only grow as Harrison marshaled reinforcements for an offensive of his own.[12]

Tecumseh's return to the Detroit country brought only despair. He had marshaled under his leadership more Indians than any other chief in history, but it was proving an empty feat. His returning warriors found their families hungry and frightened, their days spent crowded about the British Indian Department headquarters begging for scarce food and clothing. The British had no intention of starving their allies, but Procter lacked the means to support not only twelve thousand Indians but also his own eleven hundred soldiers and the Lake Erie flotilla, which lay idle in Amherstburg harbor for lack of guns and sailors. General Prévost made light of Procter's appeals for aid. He suggested that the careworn commander of the Right Division look to his own devices and to the legendary gallantry of the British soldier and sailor to bolster his prospects. Fixated on the Niagara frontier and Lower Canada, Prévost remained unmoved even after the American commodore Oliver H. Perry employed his newly launched fleet to disrupt the British supply route across Lake Erie, leaving the miserable forest trail along the Thames River across what is today southwestern Ontario as Procter's principal lifeline.

Prévost erred in thinking that Procter's recent elevation to major general would placate his hectoring subordinate. "The probable consequences of any further delay in sending an adequate supply of Indian stores to this district are of so serious a nature that I cannot refrain from urging the necessity of their being pushed forward by every possible means," Procter warned headquarters. "The long-expected supplies cannot any longer be delayed without the most frightful consequences. The Indian and his family, suffering from cold, will no longer be amused with promises; his wants he will attribute to our neglect at least, and defection is the least of [the] evils we may expect from him."[13]

Tecumseh could not have expressed Indian sentiments better himself. It was the Plum Moon (August), traditionally a season of plenty and the time when the Eastern Woodland tribes looked to stockpile foodstuffs for the winter. Tecumseh and most of his followers were far from home, however. Local crop yields were short, and the displaced Indian women had no land on which to harvest corn of their own. The men combed the forests for phantom game. With nothing to hunt, they sank into the ennui of a sedentary camp. Part of the food shortage was the fault of Dickson's Indians, who Matthew Elliott was happy to see leave. "All those who came on with Dickson," he opined, "who have nearly ruined the country by killing the cattle and robbing the inhabitants have returned home. Indeed, had they never rejoined us it would have been a most fortunate circumstance." As the food crisis deepened, Tecumseh's warriors roused themselves enough to slaughter the farm animals and even the dogs of the local populace. When rations declined from beef and bread to just whitefish, an Indian delegation threatened to take Procter's quartermaster hostage and starve him.[14]

Tecumseh, for his part, grew churlish and peremptory in his dealings with Procter. He was understandably annoyed that the general had removed his headquarters from Fort Malden upriver to Sandwich, where he was harder to reach. When he learned that Procter had arrested an American friend of his and secreted him on a vessel in Amherstburg harbor, Tecumseh not only demanded his friend's release but also castigated the general for denying knowledge of the man's whereabouts. "If I ever detect you in a falsehood, I with my Indians will immediately abandon you," snapped Tecumseh. Procter scribbled the release order, adding sardonically that the "king of the woods" wished it.

To his fellow chiefs, Tecumseh meditated aloud on the merits of abandoning the redcoats. Even after the defection of most of Dickson's rabble, he led—albeit loosely, in the Indian fashion—thirty-five hundred warriors, far more than Pontiac, Blue Jacket, or Little Turtle ever commanded. But British numbers had calcified—a sure sign, to his mind, of a want of commitment on Procter's part. When the British "took up the tomahawk" on behalf of the Great Father, argued Tecumseh, they had promised that plenty of redcoats would fight with them. "But the number is not now greater than at the commencement of the war, and we are treated by them like the dogs of snipe hunters—we are always sent ahead to start the game," he grumbled in open council. "It is better that we should return to our country and let the Americans come on and fight the British." Tecumseh's motion almost carried the day, until a delegation of Ojibwa and Dakota stay-behinds from Dickson's horde privately urged Tecumseh not to quit the British, and he reversed himself. For the time being at least, the British-Indian alliance would endure.[15]

Tenskwatawa had even greater reason to lose hope than did his elder brother. Little of his native revival movement, beyond temperance, endured. How could it, when the Indians were dependent on their British Father for the necessities of life? His influence on the wane, Tenskwatawa contemplated repairing deep into the forests of Upper Canada, where game was plentiful and war but a distant rumor. Separated physically in times of battle, the Shawnee brothers were growing apart spiritually as well.[16]

Spies carried news of the Shawnee brothers' misfortunes to General Harrison, whose large army of invasion methodically assembled along the Sandusky River. Already the shifting tide of Indian opinion had helped him. Eager to embrace a force whom the Great Spirit appeared to favor, four hundred northern Ohio Indians signed on as scouts and auxiliaries for the Americans' upcoming campaign. In addition to contributing his warriors, the Sandusky Wyandot chief Tarhe also proposed to undermine Tecumseh's confederacy diplomatically. He would send a formal embassy to the Michigan and Canadian Wyandots—and incidentally to all Indian adherents to the British cause—recommending they "consult their true interest" and switch sides before it was too late. Harrison bade him proceed.[17]

Tarhe appointed his principal subchief Between-the-Logs as

ambassador, bearing the proper white wampum belt. As Between-the-Logs was an emissary of the principal diplomats of the Northwest, custom guaranteed his personal safety. But times were uncertain, and so an escort of eight warriors accompanied him. Tarhe's envoy also bore two speeches, one for the council, the other for the Wyandots only.

The council convened at Brownstown on August 23. Tecumseh and Tenskwatawa attended. Each harbored his own growing spiritual angst, but publicly they presented a united front against the pro-American chiefs. To the visitors' chagrin, British Indian Department officials, as well as a splendidly uniformed British major, were also present. Amid a host of enemies, Between-the-Logs delivered Tarhe's speech. Clutching the white wampum belt, he proclaimed that their American father was about to march against the British with a huge army but wished to spare his red children. They needed only bury the hatchet, and take hold of the wampum belt that Between-the-Logs thrust toward them, and General Harrison would allow them to return to their lands and live as before. Not a hand moved to accept the symbolic badge of peace. Instead Chief Roundhead rose to reply. With Tecumseh moody and introspective after the last Ohio imbroglio, and as the council was a Wyandot affair, Roundhead—assuming he remained true to the cause—was the logical choice to reproach Between-the-Logs.

Roundhead was up to the task. His words were few but forceful. The council would neither forsake the British standard nor lay down the war hatchet. On the contrary, they looked forward to fighting the Americans. On behalf of all present, Roundhead enjoined Between-the-Logs to tell Harrison that it was their "wish he would send more men against us, for all that has passed between us, I do not call fighting. We are not satisfied with the number of men he sends to contend against us. We want to fight in good earnest." Matthew Elliott added a few choice insults of his own. Calling the American father his "wife," Elliott wanted Harrison to fight fairly. "If she wishes to fight with me and my children, she must not burrow in the earth like a groundhog, where she is inaccessible."

Elliott's taunt neither amused nor daunted Between-the-Logs. "Brothers," he said to the chiefs, "I am directed by my American father to inform you that if you reject the advice given you he will march here with a large army, and if he should find any of the red people opposing him in his passage through this country, he will trample them under his feet. You cannot stand before him." Addressing Elliott, Between-the-Logs turned the old man's taunt on its head. The Americans were indeed groundhogs: "I must confess, that a groundhog is a very difficult animal to contend with. He has such sharp teeth, such an inflexible temper, and such an unconquerable spirit, that he is truly a dangerous enemy." And he would grant Elliott's wish: "Before many days, you will see the groundhog come floating on [Lake Erie], paddling his canoe towards your hole; and then you will have an opportunity of attacking your formidable enemy in any way you may think best."

Between-the-Logs moved to close the council. Before dispersing, the pro-British chiefs, Tecumseh included, consulted among themselves and then responded with more resolve than they felt, saying, "We are happy to learn your father is coming out of his hole.... [It] will save us much trouble in walking to meet him." And so long as their British Father's navy "swam on the lake," they would never take the Americans by the hand.[18]

The Shawnee brothers returned to their village, seemingly the victors in the council thanks to the redoubtable Roundhead. Their diplomatic success was illusory. Unknown to them, Between-the-Logs met secretly with the Wyandot chief Walk-in-the-Water. Ever the opportunist, Walk-in-the-Water swore that he and his people were in fact prisoners. Taking hold of the tendered white wampum belt, Walk-in-the-Water pledged that on the advance of the American army, he and his band would quit both the British and Tecumseh's confederacy. He asked only that Harrison show them mercy.[19]

Walk-in-the-Water had no need to worry that Roundhead would learn of his duplicity. Within a week of the Brownstown council, Tecumseh's fifty-year-old Wyandot lieutenant lay dead of natural causes. Not since Long Knives gunned down his brother Cheeseekau two decades earlier had Tecumseh suffered so severe a personal blow. With Tenskwatawa folding into a figurehead, Roundhead's counsel had become indispensable to Tecumseh, his combat talent equal to the Shawnee's. The Ottawa chief Naiwash, a loyal lieutenant and an accomplished war chief, ascended to the second spot but could not fill Roundhead's moccasins. Roundhead's demise also disturbed Procter deeply. As he informed the new commander of Upper Canada, Maj. Gen. Francis de Rottenburg, "the Indian cause and ours [has] experienced a serious loss in the death of Roundhead."[20]

The appearance of American sails flapping in the hard breeze at the mouth of Lake Erie on September 1 abbreviated Tecumseh's grief. Commodore Perry's nine-ship fleet had set up a base at Put-In-Bay, a natural harbor created by a ring of islands off the Ohio shore. Now he challenged his opponent, the acting commander Robert Barclay, to fight. Tecumseh was on Bois Blanc Island when the enemy warships heaved into view. Disturbed to see the five-ship British squadron cling to its anchorage at Amherstburg harbor, Tecumseh paddled his canoe across the narrow channel to Fort Malden and demanded Procter tell him why "our father with one arm," as he called Barclay, who had lost a limb fighting the French, did not give battle to Perry. "A few days since, you were boasting that you commanded the waters—why do you not go out and meet the Americans? They are waiting for you and daring you to meet them; you must and shall send out your fleet to fight them." Procter explained that Barclay's flagship was then being equipped with cannons cannibalized from Fort Malden, and the 250 redcoats from the 41st Regiment and 85 Canadians that made up nearly half of Barclay's crews—his naval superior had sent him only a handful of sailors—were acquainting themselves with basic shipboard duties. A subdued Tecumseh returned to Bois Blanc. "The big canoes of the Great Father are not yet ready," he told the Indians. "The destruction of the Americans must be delayed for a few days."[21]

These were sad and anxious days. Tecumseh struggled to keep up a strong front. While waiting for Barclay to meet the American fleet on Lake Erie, he and Procter dined one evening at the home of the commander of the Canadian militia. At the banquet too was the merchant Thomas Verchères de Boucherville, who had fought under Tecumseh in the opening skirmishes against General Hull the year before. Time had not lessened Verchères's admiration of the chief. "Tecumseh was seated on my left with his pistols on either side of his plate and his big hunting knife in front of him. He wore a red cloak, trousers of deer skin, and a printed calico shirt, the whole outfit a present from the English. His bearing was irreproachable for a man of the woods as he was, much better than that of some so-called gentlemen."[22]

While Procter and Tecumseh dined, the commissary at Fort Malden issued its last barrel of flour. That forced the matter. Procter and Barclay must either defeat the American fleet and reopen their water-borne supply line or blow up Fort Malden and abandon the entire District of Amherstburg. On the afternoon of September 9, the British ships slipped their moorings and floated down the Detroit River into Lake Erie. Two audacious warriors went with the squadron as crew members.[23]

At noon the next day the muted thunder of distant cannonading rolled across Lake Erie. Great clouds of cannon smoke churned on the horizon. Spectators on the Canadian shore strained to make sense of the shifting gray billows. After three hours the roar ceased, and the clouds dissolved. Most felt that Barclay had prevailed, and on the night of September 10 a muted hopefulness prevailed in Amherstburg.

But the tenth melted into the eleventh, the eleventh into the twelfth. No word came from Barclay; nor did the two Indian sailors return to their villages. The conclusion was inescapable. "Circumstances have since placed it beyond a doubt that the whole of our fleet has been taken or destroyed," Procter wrote General de Rottenburg on September 12. That same day Commodore Perry told General Harrison, "We have met the enemy and they are ours." Lake Erie was now undisputedly in American hands. The Battle of Lake Erie was a defining moment of the War of 1812. The way was clear for Perry to bear Harrison's five-thousand-man army across Lake Erie. Throughout the American Republic, the 1812 cry of "On to Canada!" again echoed. Tecumseh's dream of a prosperous Indian homeland was about to become a nightmare of sheer survival.[24]

Death on the Thames

G ENERAL P ROCTER saw no alternative to retreat. With the Americans in control of Lake Erie, he had no prospect of restocking
his empty storerooms. He had stripped Fort Malden of most of its
heavy artillery and ammunition to arm Barclay's squadron, leaving
himself with only a few cannons to oppose American gunboats or
Harrison's army, which could land anywhere at will. Although Procter
commanded over eight hundred redcoats, they were in sorry shape—
underfed, unpaid for six months, lacking blankets and heavy coats, and
buckling under a malaria epidemic. The only route east across Upper
Canada toward reinforcements and resupply—the so-called King's
Road along the Thames River—was a miserable forest track littered
with rotted trees, protruding stumps, and long stretches of oozy clay
that autumn rains already had rendered a brutal obstacle course for
infantrymen weighted down with weapons and sixty pounds of gear;
with the onset of winter, the trail would become impassable. In a word,
Procter had no strategy beyond simple survival.[1]

Although Procter ached to evacuate the Amherstburg District
posthaste, he quailed before the probable reaction of Tecumseh to
what the Shawnee chief undoubtedly would see as a betrayal of the
solemn alliance between the Great Father and his red children. Procter told Rottenburg, "The abandonment of the district [without them]
would render them our most inveterate enemies," jeopardizing both
Procter's small command and the local population.

Procter's intentions toward Tecumseh were admirable, but the execution of his designs, for which he bore the blame, was execrable. By shifting his headquarters from Fort Malden to Sandwich after the Ohio expedition, he had removed himself from ready communication with both Indian Department officials and the chiefs, all of whom were either on the Michigan side of the Detroit River in widely scattered villages or on the islands opposite Amherstburg. Getting word to them would take time, which for Procter was at a premium. Aware of the urgency, on September 12 he sent senior staff officer Capt. John Hall to track down Elliott and Tecumseh and ask them to call the Indians together for a general council as soon as possible. Procter assumed they would need three days to gather the tribes. Meanwhile he also sent secret orders to his engineer officer to begin "quietly" dismantling Fort Malden. The Canadian workmen had a unique conception of quiet because on the morning of September 13 they began ripping apart the fort's picket facing and tossing it violently into the surrounding ditch. The racket attracted a stunned Tecumseh. Confronting Lt. Col. August Warburton, the acting commander of the 41st Regiment, atop the vanishing ramparts of Fort Malden, Tecumseh demanded an explanation of what looked like British perfidy. Warburton, however, had not been privy to Procter's secret instructions; he could only shrug and direct the workmen to stop while he sought clarification. Seething, Tecumseh tracked down Matthew Elliott, Tenskwatawa, and his fellow chiefs and told them what he had seen.[2]

Tecumseh's outrage was contagious. Tenskwatawa suggested that the Indians should cut the wampum belt uniting them with the Great Father and present Procter with the British half—a sign of eternal separation. The belt was a powerful symbol, but the chiefs were more direct in their menace. Regretting that they had not grasped Harrison's hand when given a chance by Between-the-Logs, they vowed to murder Elliott and his deputy William Caldwell, Sr., if Procter retreated one step. Caldwell, who had fought with the Indians at Fallen Timbers, was so frightened that he sent his family out of the district. At the same time, he tried to reason with his volatile Indian friends: with the fleet destroyed and provisions exhausted, the British had no choice but retreat. But from the chiefs' perspective, matters were taking on the aspect of the British betrayals of 1783 and 1794. They refused to be deceived again.[3]

By the time Captain Hall reached Elliott and Tecumseh with Procter's call to council, the damage had been done. Tecumseh agreed to take part but hardly in the manner Procter expected. Acknowledging his continuing supremacy, the chiefs agreed that Tecumseh would deliver their ultimatum to the British general. More than three thousand Indian men put their faith in Tecumseh's persuasive power to compel the Great Father to honor his promises or suffer the consequences of their wrath.

Tecumseh had to deliver a speech that was both vital and persuasive. He would not compose it; for all his oratorical prowess, he sometimes stumbled when speaking words of his own creation. Occasionally he could be pedestrian, tedious, and even circumlocutory. The future governor of the Michigan Territory Lewis Cass, then aide-de-camp to Harrison and a fixture in Ohio politics, thought Tecumseh deficient in "those powers of imagination to which we have been indebted for the boldest flights of Indian eloquence." So too apparently did the Wyandot chiefs, and three of them helped Tecumseh prepare his address. Ironically, given his own secret duplicitous intent, Walk-in-the-Water took the lead in crafting the speech, while Tecumseh prepared the wampum belts he would use as mnemonic devices when he delivered it.[4]

On September 15, Tecumseh and Procter squared off at the Indian Department council house just beyond the gates of Fort Malden. It was a large, lofty building with a vaulted roof, off which bounced the boisterous speculation of the British officers, Indian chiefs, warriors, and assorted onlookers who crowded together expectantly. To the Indians, Procter articulated his strategy of survival. The British were nearly out of supplies, with no way of getting more now that the Americans controlled Lake Erie. He must destroy Forts Detroit and Malden and retreat to the Niagara frontier, where he would join forces with the British Center Division. Would the Indians accompany him? A few chiefs grunted their assent. Then, grasping his mnemonic wampum, Tecumseh arose. Beside him stood Billy Caldwell and several other interpreters to render the chief's words not only in English but also in multiple Indian languages.

The room fell silent. All eyes were on Tecumseh; the Prophet faded into the background of expectant chiefs and warriors. Tecumseh wore his customary close-fitting buckskin jacket and leggings that "admirably delineated" his athletic frame, noted the young Canadian ensign John Richardson. In a rare bit of sartorial self-indulgence appropriate to the august moment, Tecumseh had adorned his red turban with a huge plume of white ostrich feathers. They cast a shadow over his brow, contrasting sharply with the "brilliancy of his black and piercing eyes." Before speaking, Tecumseh scowled. Shuddering at the chief's "wild and terrific expression," Ensign Richardson said, "It was clear he could be terrible"[5]

Tecumseh opened with a hard history lesson. He reminded Procter that Great Britain had abandoned the Indians after the Revolutionary War: "Our father was thrown on his back by the Americans, and our father took them by the hand without our knowledge, and we are afraid our father will do so again at this time." Despite their sorry record, the Indians had agreed to bring their families to Michigan and take up the war hatchet again on behalf of the British. Tecumseh recognized his share of culpability in recent reverses, and he apologized for Indian timidity before the gates of Forts Meigs and Stephenson "It is hard," he said by way of mitigation, "to fight people who live like groundhogs." Then Tecumseh warmed to the issue at hand. Hopeful Barclay's flotilla might yet materialize, he declaimed, "Our ships have gone one way, and we are much astonished to see our father tying up everything and preparing to run away the other without letting his red children know what his intentions are. You always told us to remain here and take care of our lands; it made our hearts glad to hear that [that] was your wish." And then Tecumseh administered a startling rebuke. Procter had promised never to surrender British soil. "But now, father, we see you are drawing back ... without seeing the enemy. We must compare our father's conduct to a fat animal that carries its tail upon its back, but when affrighted, it drops it between its leg and runs off."

When the interpreters rendered Tecumseh's insult, the council room erupted in laughter. Weary redcoats, anxious Canadians, and angry Indians alike enjoyed the jab at Procter. After order was restored, Tecumseh cogently declared his purpose,

> Listen, father! The Americans have not yet defeated us by land; neither are we sure that they have done so by water. We therefore wish to remain here and fight our enemy should they make their appearance. If they defeat us, we will then retreat with our father....
> Father! You have got the arms and ammunition which our

great father sent for his red children. If you have any idea of going away, give them to us, and you may go in welcome for us. Our lives are in the hands of the Great Spirit. We are determined to defend our lands, and if it is his will, we wish to leave our bones upon them.[6]

With that assurance, Tecumseh ended his address. "The effect of his speech was instantaneous," Ensign Richardson observed. "No sooner had his last words died out than the various chieftains started up to a man and, brandishing their tomahawks in the most menacing manner, vociferated their approbation of his sentiments." An aggravated Procter promised an answer to Tecumseh's "contumelious" speech in two days. With that the council closed. Tecumseh walked out with Tenskwatawa.[7]

William Caldwell, Sr., of the Indian Department blocked their path. Perhaps unaware that Tecumseh was estranged from his wife, Caldwell promised that if the chief were killed on the retreat, his widow would receive a $700 annual pension; the widow of the next most senior chief (the Ottawa Naiwash) would get $600 a year; and those of any other chiefs or warriors who died—and Tenskwatawa fell into this subordinate category—would receive $500 annually. It was a lovely prospect for the Shawnee brothers to ponder.[8]

Before scuttling back to Sandwich, Procter charged Colonel Warburton and Matthew Elliott with winning over Tecumseh and defusing Indian dissension. Nothing, however, had improved when Procter returned on September 18; on the contrary, the Indians were determined to cut the Great Wampum Belt, cleave the skulls of Elliott and Caldwell, and rampage indiscriminately. Clearly another open council would be futile so long as Tecumseh remained hostile. Consequently, Procter asked Tecumseh to meet him privately.

An officer spread a map of the region on a table, and with Elliott interpreting, General Procter carefully explained the tactical situation to Tecumseh: how American gunboats could sail up the Detroit River and sever communications between Amherstburg and the Indians on the Michigan side, or negotiate the Thames River, intercept supplies, and cut off the line of retreat. He assured Tecumseh that, if the Indians went with them, the British would not withdraw beyond the Thames River. Together they would "mix their bones" and repel the Americans, should they be foolish enough to pursue. Tecumseh's spirit sagged beneath the weight of broken dreams, but he clutched at the thread of hope that Procter tendered him. He asked only for time to consult with Tenskwatawa and the chiefs before agreeing. Considering what we know of his duplicitous character, the Wyandot chief Walk-in-the-Water must have delighted in Tecumseh's dilemma—to trust the British and perhaps salvage a victory on Canadian soil, or to abandon the redcoats and face the Americans alone.

Chief Naiwash deferred to Tecumseh, as did Tenskwatawa. Two hours after excusing himself, Tecumseh returned to Procter. Not only had Tecumseh apparently prevailed on the Indians to cleave no British skulls, but Procter's aide also later swore that the chiefs "appeared to be overjoyed" with British assurances of an armed stand.

Where that stand would occur, however, was unclear. Tecumseh understood that Procter would dig entrenchments and emplace artillery at the forks of the Thames River and McGregor's Creek, above a hamlet known as Chatham. Elliott and Warburton both had the same impression. Billy Caldwell, however, could recall no such promise. Captain Hall thought the destination was Dolsen's Landing, five miles short of Chatham. Procter, who had never examined the terrain along the Thames River, assumed the Indians understood that he would fortify the forks only if his engineers reported the site defensible.[9]

Unaware of the apparent misunderstanding, much less that it would have serious consequences, General Procter shared his aide's optimism about the Indian mood. He also exulted in Tecumseh's sway over the Indians: "It was only necessary to persuade the reason of Tecumseh to ensure his consent [to retreat], and he undertook to prevail on the tribes to embrace the measure which he now saw to be unavoidable. It was one more example of his talent and influence that, despite all their prejudices and natural affection for the seat of their habitations...he had determined a large portion of his nation to give their cooperation to the step which they had most violently opposed."[10]

Procter overestimated Tecumseh's influence. Ever his own man, Main Poc refused to budge from his village on the River Rouge. Six hundred warriors and their families, predominantly but not exclusively Potawatomis, chose to remain with him on familiar ground rather than follow Tecumseh into the unknown wilds of Upper Canada. Main Poc planned for two contingencies: if the Americans invaded and won, he would flee into the forested recesses of the Michigan Territory; if the British prevailed, he would fall on the retreating Americans and garner a share of the glory.[11]

Main Poc's defection represented but a chink in the crumbling wall of the Shawnee brothers' confederacy. More than half of the Ojibwas and Ottawas also refused to follow Tecumseh, preferring to sue for peace when the Americans reached Detroit. The Miamis, the Munsee Delawares, and a few score Wyandots—less Walk-in-the-Water, who continued to bide his time with Tecumseh—also held back, intending to switch sides; or, as they would express it when they greeted the Americans, "to take hold of the same tomahawk with us and to strike all who are enemies to the United States."[12]

Tecumseh was partly at fault for the dissolution. His fiery speech at the September 15 council had shaken Indian confidence in the British irreparably. Many of those who chose to go with him were inclined to desert at the slightest setback. The old Indian maximum that every man was his own chief was coming home to roost.

As his Indian allies looked increasingly to their own interests, so too did Tecumseh. Perhaps he thought of his estranged wife Wabelegunequa, who as his last legitimate spouse under Indian custom would be well provided for should he die, and his beloved sister Tecumpease, now over fifty years old. Like all Shawnee women, she would bear the brunt of the hard journey ahead, from the dismantling of their present village to the erecting of a new one. Her husband Wahsikegaboe would stand beside Tecumseh in any forthcoming battle with the Long Knives, as would Tecumseh's seventeen-year-old son Paukeesa, whom she had raised as her own. Tecumseh's peripatetic ways and higher calling had left him little time for parenting. Nor had Tecumseh shown him any real affection. Paukeesa's unusually light complexion so annoyed Tecumseh that he enjoined his Shawnee followers not to elect Paukeesa chief should he, Tecumseh, fall in battle.[13]

The countdown to retreat continued. On September 22 the British torched the Amherstburg dockyard and pushed the remaining heavy ordnance into the Detroit River while the last of the Indians crossed to the Canadian shore. The next day Procter watched wagons rumble east from Sandwich over the King's Road along the southern shore of Lake St. Clair bearing the army's dependents—among them his wife and seriously ill eldest daughter—and more than one hundred

MAP 12 RETREAT ON THE THAMES RIVER, OCTOBER 1813

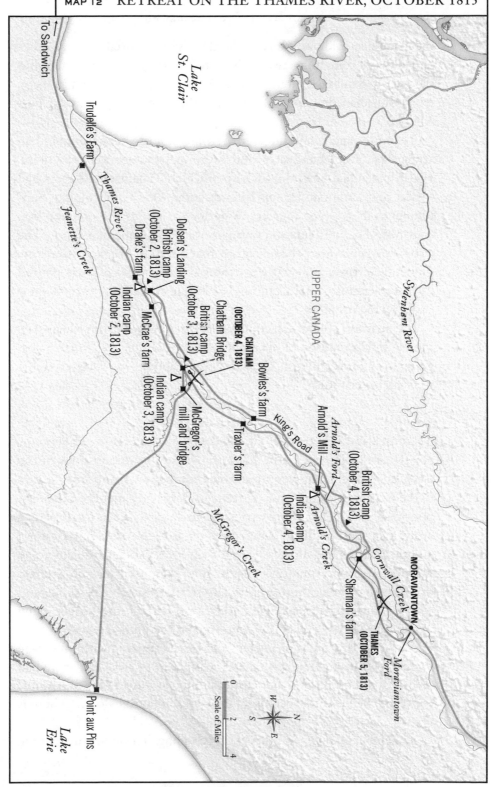

Lake
St. Clair

To Sandwich

Trudelle's farm

Thames River

Jeanette's Creek

Dolsen's Landing
British camp
(October 2, 1813)
Drake's farm

Indian camp
(October 2, 1813)

McCrae's farm

British camp
(October 3, 1813)

Chatham Bridge

CHATHAM
(OCTOBER 4, 1813)

Indian camp
(October 3, 1813)

McGregor's
mill and bridge

Bowles's farm

Traxler's farm

King's Road

UPPER CANADA

McGregor's Creek

Sydenham River

Arnold's Ford
Arnold's Mill

Arnold's Creek

Arnold's Creek

British camp
(October 4, 1813)

Indian camp
(October 4, 1813)

Sherman's farm

Cornwall Creek

MORAVIANTOWN

Moraviantown
Ford

THAMES
(OCTOBER 5, 1813)

Point aux Pins

Lake
Erie

Scale of Miles
0 2 4

W N E S

incapacitated soldiers. Meanwhile, the eight hundred redcoat rank-and-file and remaining twelve hundred warriors and their families trudged to Sandwich, there to await notice of the American invasion from Canadian dragoons posted near the smoldering ruins of Fort Malden.

Tecumseh and Elliott lingered at Amherstburg, shepherding Indian stragglers toward Sandwich. Both were loath to abandon the place. Fort Malden had been the rock upon which Tecumseh's dreams had rested, and Amherstburg was Elliott's home. On the morning of September 27 they espied fourteen American warships and one hundred transports bearing Harrison's army toward the Canadian shore. The two tarried even after the Canadian rear guard fell back. At four p.m. General Harrison and nearly five thousand American soldiers poured into Amherstburg. Reluctantly, Tecumseh and Elliott turned their backs on the invaders.[14]

At Sandwich, Tecumseh confided a deep disquiet to Jim Bluejacket, the youthful grandson of his mentor Chief Blue Jacket. "We are now going to follow the British," he whispered, "and I feel well assured that we shall never return."[15]

Tecumseh and Elliott rode into Sandwich on the evening of September 28, 1813, beneath a warm, hard rain. There were no troops in the town, and few civilians ventured from their homes. Continuing a mile to the elegant brick mansion of François Baby, they met the Canadian politician and militia officer packing his bags to leave for Procter's army, then presumably encamped ten miles to the east. Tenskwatawa and the Indians had already passed Baby's residence earlier that day with the same destination in view. But Tecumseh had no interest in overtaking them; there were likely stragglers to hurry along, and before going farther, he wanted a last look at the Long Knives. Baby would have to delay his own departure and accommodate two house-guests. Later that night, a courier from Procter arrived with a message for Elliott. The general apologized; while he was away, the army had bivouacked ten miles farther east than he had intended. After Elliott conveyed the news to Tecumseh, the chief pondered aloud, "There is no place for us."[16]

September 29 dawned gray and foreboding. Through a deepening

mist, Tecumseh got his look at the Long Knives. They were an imposing force. After detaching part of his army to garrison Detroit, William
Henry Harrison commanded 2,720 Kentuckians and 130 regulars, with
130 Shawnee and Wyandot warriors under the immediate leadership
of Chiefs Black Hoof and Tarhe scouting for the army. Twenty Delaware warriors also served with Harrison.[17]

Turning his black pony, Tecumseh set off along the rutted and tree-
lined King's Road with Elliott and Baby. A heavy rain fell, churning the path into paste. That night the three men made camp under
leaden skies at the mouth of Belle River. They were alone; the redcoats had fumbled again. Instead of waiting for the Indians to catch up
as intended, Procter's second-in-command, Colonel Warburton, had
marched the army fifteen miserable miles to the Trudelle farm, three
miles beyond the mouth of the Thames River. Seemingly uncon-
cerned at the mishap, Procter sloshed into camp in his carriage, then
continued upriver to examine possible defensive positions. Warburton
idled away September 30 in camp to allow the Indians to catch up. Fortunately for the unraveling British and Indian allies, supply problems
detained Harrison in Sandwich, and he did not begin his pursuit until
October 2.

Tecumseh spent September 30 in the saddle. Near the River Ruscom, well short of the Thames, he found Tenskwatawa and the Indians, the women collecting drenched brush and tree limbs to erect
wigwams for the night. At François Baby's suggestion, Tecumseh and
Elliott pushed the Indians onward lest the Long Knives overtake them.
Abandoning their incomplete shelters, the Indians trudged deep into
the night before finding the British at the Trudelle farm. The next
morning a false rumor reached Colonel Warburton that scouts had
spotted American ships near the mouth of the Thames. Breaking
camp in the unceasing rain, the redcoats filed eight miles along the
south bank and then crossed the river on scows near the hardscrabble
farms of Matthew and John Dolsen. Tecumseh followed the redcoats
despite his displeasure with Warburton's decision to quit the Trudelle
campsite without a fight. It was a case of contrary impulses. Warburton wanted to put as much distance as possible between his men and
their putative pursuers; Tecumseh deplored every mile that took him
deeper into the Canadian wilderness. Nevertheless, he was guardedly
optimistic. Together the allies numbered a respectable 1,750 warriors

and soldiers. Five miles farther upriver lay Chatham, which Tecumseh supposed Procter had fortified. Behind earthworks, the British and Indians would have a solid chance of repelling the Long Knives.[18]

Procter appeared briefly on the morning of October 2. Then he started downriver to reconnoiter the rumored American ships personally, in a plain effort to impress the Indians with his courage. Not only were they unimpressed, but Procter's native allies began to doubt his competence, if not his very sanity. "What is taking this other man [Procter] away?" Tecumseh asked Elliott. The old man could merely shrug and say, "We do not know what he is gone for." Reading Procter's peregrinations as proof of pure imbecility, Tenskwatawa growled that he "had a great mind to take the epaulettes of his shoulders, for he was not worthy to wear them."[19]

Procter returned, having disproven the unlikely presence of American warships on the Thames. But his stay in camp was fleeting. At dawn on October 3 he rattled off in his carriage to examine the defensive potential of the Moravian Christian Delaware village of Fairfield, known colloquially as Moraviantown; or, as some redcoat wags guessed, to see to his wife and daughters, who had settled into quarters there, twenty-six miles upriver. Neither Tecumseh nor Warburton knew anything of the general's designs.[20]

Moments after the general left, a Canadian dragoon galloped into camp to report that the Americans were approaching fast. Screened by friendly Indians, Col. Richard Mentor Johnson's 960-man regiment of mounted Kentucky riflemen, clad in red-fringed black hunting jackets and sporting black top hats tipped with red and white feathers, was pounding through the mucky King's Road on the south bank of the Thames. The métis Anthony Shane rode beside Colonel Johnson as guide. Behind the mounted riflemen marched Maj. Gen. Isaac Shelby's five Kentucky infantry brigades, 1,760 strong, and the small contingent of regulars. "Remember the Raisin" was the watchword of the vengeance-seeking Kentuckians.

Colonel Warburton formed a line of battle beside the Dolsen farm on the north side of the river with the three hundred redcoats available to him and anxiously awaited support from Tecumseh. Instead his voice arose from dense timber across the Thames, "haranguing the Indians in a loud and violent manner." Warburton's wonderment at Tecumseh's anger was answered when a tearful Matthew Elliott buttonholed the colonel. Tecumseh had reconnoitered Chatham and the adjacent forks of the Thames River and McGregor's Creek. There was no evidence of Procter's promised fortifications, only three or four dismounted cannons and a thousand boxed muskets stacked unguarded in a house a half-mile farther on. Now the Shawnee's rage knew no bounds. Tecumseh had been so confident that Procter would wage a decisive battle at Chatham that he had told Elliott, "Here General Harrison or I shall lay our bones." Elliott, who had never seen the Shawnee chief in such a state, wanted nothing further to do with him. "I will not by God sacrifice myself," stammered the snowy-haired Indian superintendent. Elliott regained his composure enough to tell Warburton that Tecumseh expected the British to fight beside the Indians on the south bank. But Warburton declined. Having sent the army's boats upriver, he had no way to cross the Thames. Neither had he heard from Procter. Mustering his last vestiges of courage, Elliott whipped his horse around to deliver the bad news to Tecumseh.[21]

The ire of Tecumseh and unease of Elliott amused Chief Walk-in-the-Water immensely. He had sent a messenger through the lines to General Harrison with word that he intended to surrender his people as soon as he could break away from Tecumseh. Meanwhile he had a laugh at Elliott's expense, telling the harried old man that he should make for the Niagara frontier with their absent father, General Procter.[22]

While Walk-in-the-Water chuckled, Colonel Warburton agonized. The Americans had not advanced, but neither had Procter returned. "Colonel Warburton did not appear to know how to act," recalled a sympathetic staff officer, "the general not having left any directions." Tecumseh had no quarrel with the colonel, but he had good reason to despise Procter. The general's behavior certainly appeared like that of an affrighted fat animal. But with the Americans closing fast, Tecumseh felt he had no choice but to follow him.

Tecumseh's subordinates thought otherwise. On the evening of October 3, Tecumseh and his war chiefs gathered in the dripping timber on the south bank of the Thames River for an informal but contentious council that marked the nadir of the Indian confederacy. Chief Naiwash stood by Tecumseh, but half the other chiefs deserted him, together with their warriors. Taking roundabout forest trails westward, some eventually surrendered to the Americans; others returned to their home villages. Slipping away with sixty-five Wyandot warriors and their families, Walk-in-the-Water hid out in the woods to await Harrison's call. He had played Tecumseh for a fool.[23]

The British were up before dawn on October 4. They were hungry, soaked to the skin, and surly. Some wanted to shoot Procter, a sentiment with which Colonel Warburton undoubtedly sympathized. He still had no instructions from the general, who dithered at Moraviantown. At ten a.m., Warburton started his soggy column. The rain subsided. Frost had formed overnight, hardening the road. That should have made for rapid marching, but Indian women and children, sent over the Thames on makeshift rafts by the warriors, clogged the way. Clinging fast to his carriage, Procter made a brief appearance to assure Warburton that he intended to fight at Moraviantown, then bounced away before nightfall to his marital bed in the village. At eight p.m. the famished and exhausted redcoats bivouacked at the Lemuel Sherman farm, just five miles short of their destination.[24]

The Indian warriors did more that day than merely march. Matthew Elliott encouraged Tecumseh and Naiwash to put up a fight at the forks of the Thames. Although Procter had reneged on his pledge to defend Chatham, the Indian chiefs reckoned themselves able to at least slow the Long Knives.

The ground was admirably suited to a delaying action. The Thames River flowed to the northeast, and McGregor's Creek entered the Thames from the southeast, creating a peninsula-like section of wooded land into which the chiefs ushered their warriors. Both watercourses were running high from recent rains. Neither was fordable. Two bridges spanned McGregor's Creek: one where the King's Road crossed the watercourse near the east bank of the Thames, the other a few hundred yards upstream, near the site of three mills and several outbuildings bulging with grain belonging to John McGregor.[25]

Tecumseh directed the warriors to prepare for the approaching Long Knives. They burned the small upper bridge and—contrary to Tecumseh's order—also McGregor's grain-filled mills. When the rain-soaked lower bridge resisted the torch, they ripped up the planks and cast them into the creek. Fashioning a raft, a handful of warriors negotiated the Thames and occupied a small house on the north bank from which to harass the Americans with a flanking fire.

Tecumseh's dispositions were sound, but a disloyal Canadian woman warned Harrison of the intended ambuscade, and he deployed Johnson's mounted Kentuckians in line of battle well short of McGregor's Creek. For two miles the horsemen wove through a morass checkered with fallen trees and thick underbrush until a musket volley halted them at the creek bank. Delivered from behind densely packed trees, the Indian fire came so fast and steady that Harrison believed he confronted both Procter's soldiers and Tecumseh's warriors. He deployed the five Kentucky infantry brigades into line of battle behind Johnson's dismounted riflemen. When the ensuing "warm skirmish" did not dislodge the Indians, Harrison brought up two cannons to blast the timberline opposite the partially wrecked lower bridge. Under cover of the artillery fire a detachment of dismounted riflemen made their way over the naked sills, then delivered a withering fire from the sheltered north bank. Others fished planks from the creek and began to rebuild the expanse. The musketry intensified. A bullet creased Tecumseh's arm. Blood flowed warm, but it was only a flesh wound. Tecumseh bound the grazed skin with a handkerchief and fought on. As the pressure mounted, the few hundred warriors gradually broke contact and sought cover in the forest. Tecumseh ordered them to fall back ten miles to Arnold's Creek, the last natural barrier of consequence between the Long Knives and Moraviantown.

The skirmish had lasted less than an hour. After all their years of verbal sparring, Tecumseh and Harrison had fought their first armed conflict. It had cost the lives of two Kentuckians—another six or seven were wounded—and a small but indeterminate number of casualties among the Indians. One hundred more warriors deserted afterward, and those who stood by Tecumseh were ill tempered. Approaching the Shawnee chief and Matthew Elliott that evening, a Sauk leveled his musket at the careworn Englishman: "I have a great mind to shoot you. We have lost a great number of our young children from [the British] just running away from us." As Elliott prepared to die, the warrior lowered his weapon and rode on.[26]

Tecumseh made camp below Arnold's Mill with his diminished force. Harrison bivouacked six miles to the southwest. Tenskwatawa had not taken part in the action, but he was with his brother that night. So too were their brother-in-law (Tecumpease's husband) Wahsikegaboe and Tecumseh's teenage son Paukeesa, bearing muskets and ready for the next clash with the Long Knives. Paukeesa had been a lifetime disappointment to his absentee father through no fault of the boy's own; perhaps, Paukeesa could impress his father on the morrow.[27]

Another teenager caught up in the conflict, sixteen-year-old Abraham Holmes spent the afternoon of October 4 watching Indians traipse past his family's farm above McGregor's Creek. Hoping to catch a glimpse of Tecumseh, he rose early on October 5 and hurried up the road to Arnold's Mill. There he found brush shelters and twisting spirals of smoke from smoldering but untended campfires. Picking his way through the forest in search of the famed Shawnee chief, Holmes instead met only a few loitering warriors.

Tecumseh had had a bad night. Nursing his stinging arm wound, he hunched over a campfire with Tenskwatawa, Billy Caldwell, Shabbona, and a few other trusted friends until a premonition struck him with the force of a musket ball. Conversation had eluded the men. All was still. Suddenly Tecumseh uttered a startled yell and, clutching his chest, declared a Long Knife had shot him. His friends remonstrated with him, but Tecumseh was certain that the next sunset would find him dead. Dropping his head with an expression of profound sadness, he muttered, "The [coming] battle will be the last scalping I ever do on earth."[28]

Young Abraham Holmes finally found Tecumseh. He was standing in front of Christopher Arnold's wood-plank mill, its large water wheel spinning lazily in the morning sunlight. Arnold's neighbor Joe Johnston, who had once lived among the Shawnees, was speaking earnestly with the chief in Shawnee. Afterward Johnston repeated the gist of their conversation to Holmes. Tecumseh had been sorry that his warriors had burned McGregor's mills; he had not authorized the depredation. Nor would he allow a reoccurrence at the mill of Christopher Arnold, who was a Canadian militia captain and had fought with Tecumseh at Fort Meigs. Tecumseh had slept beside the mill and was chivying the last Indian stragglers past when Holmes saw him. Having observed the great Shawnee for whom he would one day name a son, Holmes returned home to find General Harrison and Colonel Johnson breakfasting with his father. Kentucky mounted riflemen lounged around the farm feeding their horses. Only two miles separated Tecumseh and Harrison.[29]

Joe Johnston headed home shortly after Abraham Holmes. Tecumseh, however, tarried to consult with a grateful Christopher Arnold, who described for Tecumseh the terrain between his place and Moraviantown. Concluding their conversation, Tecumseh and Arnold separated to watch for the approaching Americans. Tecumseh took up a post under a large tree on the road, and Arnold climbed atop the milldam. Arnold was to throw a shovelful of earth in the air if he saw them first. The minutes dragged. His gaze fixed on the dark forest, Arnold at last spotted several black-jacketed horsemen emerging from the shadows. He shoveled dirt into the air and then looked over at Tecumseh, who galloped away to a gravel-bottomed ford across the Thames.[30]

Early in the afternoon, the youth David Sherman stepped outdoors to round up cattle in the fields of his father Lemuel Sherman's farm, on the King's Road five miles short of Moraviantown. Famished redcoats had shot several heads of the family stock but hurried on before they were able to carve them up. As David and his brothers gathered in the surviving creatures, Tecumseh pulled rein beside them. David Sherman never forgot Tecumseh's appearance. The Shawnee had daubed red and black war paint on his face. He wore deerskin leggings and a hunting shirt. A ring hung from his nose and the silver King George medal from his neck. Dried blood caked the handkerchief wrapped around his wounded arm. Tecumseh had tucked two flintlock pistols and a pipe tomahawk into his red silk waist sash. A single ostrich feather rose from the turban wrapped around his head. Tecumseh asked the boys a few questions and then told them to gather their stock and clear out: "Go back and stay home, for there will be a fight soon."[31]

It would be sooner than Tecumseh expected. Riding up the execrable King's Road from the Sherman farm, Tecumseh chanced upon the redcoats, their scarlet uniforms faded and grimy, clutching their single-shot smoothbore muskets in a ragged line of battle in open forest two miles short of Moraviantown. Tecumseh was perplexed; hadn't Procter posted his troops in the village?

That had been the general's intention. He had arrayed his artillery on an open ridge overlooking the settlement, then ridden forward at noon to hurry along the infantry. The Indians also expected to fight on the Moraviantown ridge and had left their families two miles farther upstream. They were about to occupy the high ground when word reached Naiwash and the chiefs that their British Father instead wanted to give battle in the tangled forests downstream. The warriors set off in search of their capricious allies.[32]

Procter's change of heart stemmed from scouts reporting the rapid approach of the American mounted infantry. Now that the mud had dried, Procter not unreasonably feared that they might overtake his foot soldiers strung out on the road. The redcoats were relieved when the order to halt came at one p.m. Weary of marching on empty stomachs, they preferred to fight and have done with it. Procter, on horseback now, and his staff galloped forward beyond the resting infantry to have a look for themselves, then returned and reshuffled the men sixty paces nearer the unseen but oncoming foe. Troops grumbled at the general's fidgeting. A lieutenant overheard his men grouse that "they were ready and willing to fight for their knapsacks [and] wished to meet the enemy but did not like to be knocked about in that manner, doing neither one thing nor the other." He silenced them, only to have others in the ranks grumble that they were about to be "cut to pieces and sacrificed."[33]

The young ensign John Richardson thought the entire arrangement preposterous. "The troops were ordered to defile into the heart of a thick and almost impervious wood," through which they could scarcely see twenty yards, much less "discover objects bearing so close a resemblance to the bark and foliage of the trees and bushes as the costume of the Americans." By contrast, the "glaring red of the [British] troops formed a point of relief on which the eye could not fail to dwell."[34]

As Procter finally formed it, the British line extended three hundred yards from the north bank of the Thames to the edge of a long and narrow swamp. The forest of which Richardson complained was a mix of large beech, maple, and walnut trees with only scattered underbrush. The British right flank rested on a small but treacherous and fetid swamp dotted with deep muddy pools and rotting vegetation. Just north of the swamp stretched a huge mire called Backmetack Marsh. Between the two morasses a strip of tangled high ground ran west the length of the smaller swamp, widening as it went from 100 to 450 yards.

When Tecumseh appeared, the Indians were filing into line behind moss-covered trees, twisted trunks, and fallen logs along the southern edge of Backmetack Marsh. Some warriors stood knee-deep in muck.

Procter envisioned the ground between the marsh and the river as a forest killing zone into which the Americans would have to march. By occupying the margin of Backmetack Marsh, the Indians were well placed to fall on the American flank.

Tecumseh agreed with Procter's dispositions. It was good ground for the Indian style of combat, and as he rode the line with the general and Elliott, Tecumseh's natural optimism and eagerness for a fight stifled his nocturnal premonition of death. He objected only to the compactness, by Indian standards, of the British line. Like Ensign Richardson, Tecumseh feared that their scarlet coats would make the troops easy targets for Kentucky marksmen. At the Shawnee's suggestion, Procter withdrew eighty men from his front line and formed a reserve one hundred yards to the rear. Tecumseh also thought the single British cannon, a small six-pounder posted on the road, was vulnerable to a cavalry charge, but Procter lacked men to protect it.

Aware of their vulnerability, the redcoats sought cover behind trees. Gaps appeared in the line, and a single tree trunk sometimes sheltered two or three soldiers. As one alarmed officer saw it, Procter lost "the advantages of close order without acquiring those of the extended, the most proper for such a situation." Procter also should have realized that the greater security from sniper fire that the open order afforded also invited a mounted onslaught. Procter might have mitigated the threat by instructing the men to build breastworks and makeshift abatis from the abundant felled trees, but he took no such action. Neither did such a rudimentary precaution occur to Tecumseh.

Tecumseh exuded confidence, as every British officer who saw him testified. His "good spirits" may not have been infectious, but the Shawnee did all he could to bolster the British. He walked their front, encouraging soldiers and greeting friends among the officers. Ensign Richardson watched him admiringly. Tecumseh "passed along our line, pleased with the [way] his left was supported and seemingly sanguine of success. He was dressed in his usual deerskin, which admirably displayed his sinewy figure, and in his handkerchief, rolled as a turban over his brow, was placed a handsome white ostrich feather.... He pressed the hand of each officer as he passed, made some remark in Shawnee appropriate to the occasion, which was sufficiently understood by the expressive signs accompanying them, and then passed from our view." Before leaving Procter, Tecumseh said, "Father, tell your men to be firm, and all will be well." And then, knowing well that

Procter lacked the late General Brock's moxie, he declared, "Father! Have a big heart!"[35]

Wheeling their mounts, Tecumseh and Elliott picked their way through the timber to Backmetack Marsh. Elliott continued to the center of the Indian line to help Chief Naiwash. He took Tecumseh's son Paukeesa with him. Tecumseh dismounted on the left, the better to communicate with the British. Surrounding him were the diehards: his devoted brother-in-law Wahsikegaboe, the robust Ottawa Shabbona, the reliable Billy Caldwell, the French-Canadian François Baby, and a worshipful white interpreter named Andrew Clark. The Shawnee and Munsee Delaware contingents also formed near Tecumseh. In all, five hundred warriors crouched in the damp, heavy air of Backmetack Marsh. Tenskwatawa, for his part, edged as near the firing line as a holy man dared.[36]

Three hours passed. Tecumseh splashed through the puddles and muck along the line of warriors, counseling them to "Be brave," "Stand firm," and "Shoot certain." At four p.m. the shrill notes of American bugles split the air. Although thickets and timber blinded him, Tecumseh heard scattered rifle fire signal the approach of the American sharpshooters against the British lines. Well in front of the sharpshooters, bolting from tree to tree and taking careful aim where most shot randomly, was his old foe Simon Kenton. Understanding the average frontiersman's propensity to overshoot his target, Tecumseh counseled those around him that the Long Knives, when they eventually came up against the Indians, would fire too high, at which point the warriors should aim deliberately and then spring forward with tomahawks. The warriors waited.[37]

Soon the rhythmic beating of horse hooves drowned the sporadic reports of sharpshooters' rifles. Weaving among the trees in four columns, the First Battalion of Col. Richard M. Johnson's Mounted Riflemen, 480 strong, galloped handily through the gaps in the British front line, cutting and slicing with sabers and tomahawks. Most of the redcoats squeezed off just one shot before breaking; a stalwart few stood long enough to fire a second round. The reserve fared no better. With yelling Kentuckians sweeping madly around their flanks and behind them, and eighteen men already dead, the British grounded their arms

MAP 13   BATTLE OF THE THAMES, OCTOBER 5, 1813

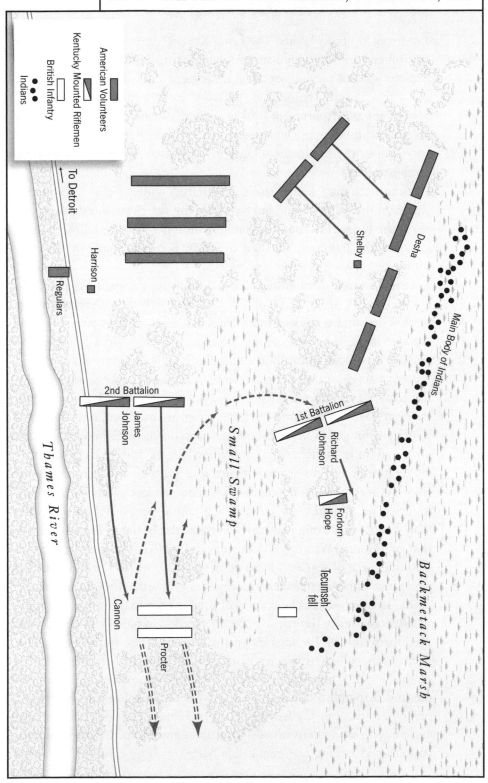

and threw up their hands. The Long Knives' dragnet ensnared all but one officer and fifty men in an affair lasting less than ten minutes. Procter was not present for the denouement. After making an ephemeral effort to rally the men, he galloped away with his escort toward Moraviantown. Apart from Ensign Richardson and two or three dozen men from his company who had attached themselves to the Indian left and escaped the Kentucky onslaught, Tecumseh and his warriors were on their own.[38]

Tecumseh had heard the brief British volleys and subsequent cheers of the Kentuckians, but he would not retreat without a fight. All along the Indian line, painted warriors hunched in eerie stillness, pulling back the hammers on their muskets, peering from behind trees, squinting through the thickets, waiting.

One hundred dismounted Kentuckians crept toward the marsh in open skirmish order, firing blindly into the web of undergrowth and trees. The Indians ignored them, intending to save their first volley for the inevitable mounted charge. Then a lone rider on a large, bright bay horse showed himself on a hillock directly in front of Tecumseh. He was a singular character; an old man dressed unlike anyone else in the army. Clad in Kentucky jeans and hunting shirt, with an old Revolutionary War–style three-cocked hat on his head and a white wampum belt slung over his left shoulder, to which he attached his powder horn and bullet pouch, the man made a bizarre and inviting target.

Tecumseh and those nearest him leveled their muskets and fired, riddling both horse and rider. Had Tecumseh known the dead man's identity, he undoubtedly would have taken special delight that this man was the first Long Knife to fall before the Indians. The corpse was that of William Whitley, whom some fellow Kentuckians had called "Colonel" out of respect for his fighting spirit, which bordered on the psychotic. Others had found him repellent, "a bitter Indian hater and a crank, so much so that he was never mustered into military service."[39]

Nineteen more Kentucky horsemen galloped past Whitley's crumpled form toward Tecumseh's part of the line. The Indians reloaded. Tecumseh yelled to the warriors nearest him to seize the bridles of the horses when they entered the Indian lines, knock the riders off, and dispatch them with tomahawks. But the Kentuckians never came near enough. Called the "Forlorn Hope," Colonel Johnson had assembled—and then joined—the detachment to draw Indian fire from the remaining 460 men of his battalion. The colonel succeeded handsomely in his purpose. Nearing the marsh, the Forlorn Hope's horses grew unmanageable in the maze of twisted timber. Hit five times, Colonel Johnson somehow managed to shoot a warrior who had darted out of the underbrush to claim Whitley's scalp. Only two members of the Forlorn Hope survived unscathed. One of those, Samuel Theobald, the regimental judge advocate, was hurled to the ground when his horse slammed into a tree. Staggering to his feet, Theobald met the blood-soaked Colonel Johnson tottering on his own exsanguinating horse. "I am severely wounded, which way shall I go," stammered Johnson. "Follow me," Theobald replied. Johnson slumped in the saddle, faint from loss of blood. Theobald left him with the regimental surgeon. In the first minutes of grappling with the Kentuckians, the advantage rested with Tecumseh.[40]

General Harrison had seen Johnson's second battalion off with the cry, "Charge them my brave Kentuckians." It was a stirring command, but the Forlorn Hope had proven the folly of a mounted charge into Backmetack Marsh. Capt. James Coleman, who assumed command after Johnson quit the field, prudently ordered his men to dismount and, as one grateful Kentuckian put it, "fight from behind trees and logs in the Indian way."[41]

The combat grew dark and desperate. Moist marsh air and overhanging tree limbs cradled the growing cloud of blue-white gun smoke close to the earth. The opposing lines advanced and receded over large swaths of forest. Maj. Gen. James Desha, commander of the left flank division of Kentucky foot soldiers, was startled to see 150 of Johnson's men stumble toward his neatly arrayed ranks with Indians under Naiwash in pursuit. Riding forward, Desha bellowed at Johnson's men to face about and drive away the Indians, which, to his surprise, they did.[42]

Meanwhile the fighting on Tecumseh's front became hand to hand. Ensign Richardson had an opportunity to witness "the cruel dexterity and dispatch" with which Indians used the tomahawk and scalping knife. Three Munsee Delaware Indians near him fired at a Kentucky rifleman. Their bullets hit home. "Though faint and tottering from loss of blood, he made every exertion to save himself," recalled Richardson, who watched the warriors give chase.

The foremost of his pursuers was a tall powerful man. When arrived within fifteen paces of his victim...he threw his tomahawk with such force and precision that it immediately opened the skull and extended him motionless on the earth. Laying down his rifle, he drew forth his knife, and after having removed the hatchet from the brain, proceeded to make a circular incision throughout the scalp. This done, he grasped the bloody instrument between his teeth, and placing his knees on the back of his victim, while at the same time he fastened his hands in the hair, the scalp was torn off without much apparent difficulty and thrust still bleeding into his bosom. The warrior then arose, and after having wiped his knife on the clothes of the unhappy man, returned it to its sheath, grasping at the same time the arms he had abandoned and hastening to rejoin his comrades. All this was the work of a minute.[43]

Richardson had seen a small triumph; the battle, in fact, was turning against Tecumseh. Indian casualties mounted. A Potawatomi warrior named Kichekemit fell dead beside the Shawnee chief. Riddled with fifteen buckshot, the interpreter Andrew Clark leaned against a tree. He drew his blanket about him and awaited death. Wahsikegaboe collapsed with half his head blasted off; in that instant, Tecumpease lost her husband to her younger brother's dying dream.

Crouched together behind a large fallen tree, Tecumseh confided to Billy Caldwell, "We must leave here; they are advancing on us." Caldwell ran. That was the last he saw of Tecumseh. Perhaps Tecumseh had no intention of running but wanted Caldwell to get away safely. In any event, the Shawnee chief stood up and started forward.[44]

And then in the swirling, smoke-choked melee, a Kentuckian lifted his musket loaded with buck and ball. He trained it on an Indian wearing a turban topped with a single ostrich feather and squeezed the trigger.

The musket ball struck Tecumseh in the chest, lodging in his heart. Two or three buckshot perforated his body. The impact threw the chief onto his back. Tecumseh likely was dead before he hit the ground.[45]

News of Tecumseh's fall crackled the length of the Indian line. Fifty-five minutes after the opening shot, the Kentucky mounted riflemen heard an unearthly howling arise from Backmetack Marsh. It was the Indian shout for retreat. "They gave," averred one volunteer, "the loudest yells I ever heard from human beings, and that ended the fight." Harrison shunned a pursuit; he was content to consolidate his position, count the cost, and tally the spoils. He had suffered at least fifteen men killed or mortally wounded, all in action against the Indians, who lost at least as many dead. Harrison had more than four hundred British prisoners in hand, together with the single cannon parked on the King's Road. It had not fired a single shot during the battle.[46]

Through bog and forest the beaten warriors fled into the night. No one took charge. Tenskwatawa's contribution consisted of leading several surviving Shawnee warriors off the field. Billy Caldwell ran into Elliott and Tecumseh's son. He told Paukeesa of his father's death. The young warrior made no reply, but as Paukeesa loaded his musket, Caldwell noticed the young Shawnee's hands trembling.[47]

Before retiring for the night, William Henry Harrison penned a summary of the Battle of the Thames for Brig. Gen. Duncan McArthur, who he had left at Detroit with a brigade to keep Main Poc in check. In his missive Harrison boasted of having destroyed Procter's army and slain Tecumseh. He based his claim that Tecumseh had fallen on camp rumors while Johnson's Kentuckians—few if any of whom had ever set eyes on the Shawnee—debated whether old man Whitley, their colonel, or a mere soldier in the ranks had dispatched the great chief.[48]

The next morning Harrison decided he had best examine Tecumseh's corpse for himself because, he later insisted, "I will venture my head if any American soldiers had ever seen Tecumseh in their lives, myself only excepted." Before Harrison set off, a staff officer cautioned him that he might not approve of the sight. The man was right. "I found the situation [as] described and was very much mortified and irritated," said Harrison. Souvenir-hunting Kentuckians had desecrated the Indian dead. Likely without knowing whose corpse they defiled, several Kentucky ghouls had sliced long strips of skin from Tecumseh's back and thighs to fashion into razor straps. Another Kentuckian scalped him and staved in his skull with a tomahawk. Still others had yanked out tufts of hair until his head was almost bald. Dried blood caked Tecumseh's body, and his face was badly swollen. Nevertheless Harrison was certain he had seen the dead man before, but he could not say whether it was Tecumseh or a Potawatomi who often had been at his side, so he made no mention of Tecumseh's demise in his official report of the battle. "I was, however," Harrison later wrote, "morally certain that he was killed."[49]

Samuel Theobald of the Forlorn Hope knew someone who would be able to recognize Tecumseh, if indeed his corpse remained recognizable—Anthony Shane. Conducted by a man who had just seen the body, Theobald and Shane trekked into Backmetack Marsh. Theobald "felt no little disappointment" when Shane hesitated to identify the mutilated corpse. "It is about Tecumseh's size and somewhat like him" was all Shane could say with certainty.

Another of the battlefield ghouls enjoyed greater success. A Kentucky company commander chanced upon Andrew Clark, still propped against the tree clinging to life. Yes, Clark gasped, Tecumseh was dead, but, the dying interpreter added with a dissembling flourish, Indian warriors had dragged the body away.[50]

Harrison's unwillingness to confirm Tecumseh's death in his official report did not prevent the American public from learning of his demise. Commodore Oliver H. Perry, the hero at Lake Erie, served as a volunteer aide to Harrison at the Battle of the Thames and was with him when he visited the corpse. In early November, Perry told a hometown correspondent that "beyond all question" the body was that of Tecumseh. Later that month, headlines nationwide proclaimed, DEATH OF TECUMSEH! The supposed proof was a letter from Thomas Rowlands, a Regular Army major who had served at the Thames and claimed to have been present when Tecumseh fell. This was impossible because his regiment was on the other end of the battlefield, but Rowlands's fiction made for stirring press: "Tecumseh is certainly killed—I saw him with my own eyes. It was the first time I had seen the celebrated chief. There was something so majestic, so dignified, and yet so mild in his countenance, as he lay stretched on his back on the ground, where a few minutes before he had rallied his men in the fight, that while gazing on him with admiration and pity, I forgot he was a savage.... He had such a countenance as I shall never forget.... The British say he compelled them to fight."[51]

Rowlands's tribute to a noble enemy was not the first to appear that month. On November 6, 1813, the day after Tecumseh died and before news of his death had passed beyond McArthur's Detroit headquarters, the Lexington, Kentucky, *Reporter* published in full the Shawnee chief's stirring "Our Lives Are in the Hands of the Great Spirit" speech, precisely as delivered to Procter in Amherstburg (a transcript of the address had been discovered in captured British papers). Families of the Kentucky volunteers in Harrison's army could read the very words of the ennobled spirit whom their kin had killed.[52]

Twilight of the Prophet

TECUMSEH most emphatically was dead. "With deep concern I mention the death of the Chief Tecumthée [*sic*], who was shot on the fifth," General Procter wrote General de Rottenburg two days after the battle of Moraviantown.[1] Procter had ample cause for deep concern. His Right Division had all but ceased to exist. The first troop returns submitted after the fiasco on the Thames showed twelve men dead and 601 missing, lost either during or incident to the battle, and only 250 men present. A court-martial convicted the general on two counts—failure to fortify the forks of the Thames near Chatham and quitting the field at Moraviantown without trying to rally his men to support the Indians—both of which would have been of some comfort to Tecumseh had he lived. Although the Crown rescinded the tribunal's sentence of a six-month forfeiture of rank and pay, Procter's reputation was ruined. He never again held a command.[2]

Despite all his missteps that had precipitated the disaster, Sir George Prévost at least appreciated the contribution of the Shawnee brothers in the late campaign. "Tecumseh at the head of 1,200 Indian warriors accompanied our little army in its retreat from Sandwich," the governor-general of the Canadas informed Lord Henry Bathurst, minister for war and the colonies, "and the Prophet, as well as his brother Tecumseh, were of most essential service in preserving it from annihilation."[3]

These were warm words, but Tenskwatawa, at forty, had to pick up the pieces of an Indian confederation that had been shattered as spectacularly as Procter's army. In late October 1813 the bedraggled Indian survivors gathered in the hamlet of Dundas, on the western shore of Lake Ontario, hundreds of miles from their homelands. They numbered 1,062, two-thirds of whom were women and children. More would straggle in. But on October 20 only 374 warriors, of the 3,500 who just four months earlier had pledged their allegiance to Tecumseh, answered an Indian Department roll call; of this number, just seventeen were Shawnees. The capable Ottawa chief Naiwash stood with Tenskwatawa. But the Prophet, devastated by his brother's death, was unable to muster even a thread of Tecumseh's steadying leadership. He couldn't even feed or clothe his followers. Crops in Upper Canada were scant that season. The Indian Department bought pork and flour but lacked the funds to provision all the refugees or to clothe more than a third of the Indians. The country was rich in elk, deer, and assorted small game, but the warriors had little ammunition with which to hunt. The Indians passed a miserable winter in the cold coniferous forests on the alien shore of Lake Ontario, the men occasionally reduced to robbing local farms to save their families from starvation.[4]

At least the Americans let them alone. The Kentucky militiamen mustered out, and the War Department transferred most of Harrison's regulars to the strategically critical Niagara frontier. Left with neither the necessary troops nor the desire to penetrate more deeply into Upper Canada, Harrison dedicated himself to governing the conquered Amherstburg District and concluding terms with Indians who flocked to Detroit to surrender and beg food for the winter. By the end of October, the newly appointed governor of the Michigan Territory, Lewis Cass, was rationing 3,419 former members of Tecumseh's confederacy.[5]

Main Poc, who had abandoned Tecumseh when the British quit Amherstburg, signed an armistice, only to vanish into the forests of central Michigan. Eventually he returned to the Illinois River, where in March 1816 Indian trader Thomas Forsyth met the former scourge of the western settlements—drunk, sick, and almost deaf. "I think," speculated Forsyth, "if he can procure any more spiritous liquor, the white people as well as the Indians will get rid of a very troublesome character." A few weeks after Forsyth's cold calculation, Main Poc died, an angry addition to Tecumseh and Roundhead on the rolls of deceased Indian confederacy leaders.[6]

As the winter of 1813–14 deepened, the British recognized the need for a strong Indian leader to rally the remnants of Tecumseh's confederacy and help the redcoats repel a probable American spring offensive on the Niagara frontier. Accordingly, Governor-General Prévost ordered the new British commander in Upper Canada, Maj. Gen. George Drummond, to assemble a delegation of native notables—a single man from each tribe—to visit him in Quebec. In a stunning snub, Prévost passed over Tenskwatawa in favor of Tecumseh's teenage son Paukeesa. Prévost also personally invited the widowed Tecumpease to accompany the delegates.

Matthew Elliott wanted nothing to do with the matter. He had no objection to Tecumpease participating; it was up to her to decide if traveling was consistent with her obligation to mourn her husband's death for a year. The inclusion of Paukeesa, however, he considered unacceptable, and he told Drummond as much: "It is my opinion that at present it would not be proper for me to meddle with young [Paukeesa]. He is very young, and it might disgust his nation. He has got time to show his nation whether they would like him as their chief." Orders were orders, however, and with Elliott as their reluctant escort, the delegation set out for Quebec in mid-February attended by twenty-six warriors, whom the British dared not prevent from making the journey.[7]

Braving bad weather and heavy snows, Elliott's party reached the Canadian capital a month later. Sir George received them regally in the great hall of the Old Castle of Quebec, the walls echoing the martial strains of a regimental band. The majesty of the moment so unnerved Chief Naiwash that he asked to postpone serious business until the next morning, and the Indians adjourned to a room replete with rich foods and hearty beverages. After indulging their sharp appetites, the warriors concluded the affair with an energetic calumet dance that delighted white attendees.

On March 17, Naiwash delivered an impassioned address to Prévost that, while lacking in eloquence, did Tecumseh's memory proud in terms of its content. Shorn of its circumlocutions, Naiwash's message was that the Indians had borne the brunt of Great Britain's battles against the Long Knives in the interest of their "old boundary lines" and expected their Great Father to provide them with the clothing and ammunition they needed to continue the conflict. Naiwash presented Sir George with black wampum and a bloodred war belt and awaited his reply.

Rising solemnly, Prévost expressed sadness at the death of the "great warrior" Tecumseh. When his words were interpreted, Tecumpease broke down in tears. After a suitable interval, Prévost assured the chiefs that their Great Father the prince regent considered the Indians his children and would well remember their interests at any peace council with the Americans, but "to preserve what we hold and recover from the enemy what belongs to us we must make great exertions." Prévost relied on the "undaunted courage" of the Indians to help their Great Father drive the Long Knives "off all our lands the ensuing summer." With Napoleon near final defeat, the Great Father would dispatch "more warriors from the other side of the Great Water who will join in attacking the enemy and will open the great road to your country." To symbolize the continuance of the British and Indian pact, Prévost returned the war belt to Naiwash, who paced about the room, chanting his determination to confront their common enemy. "Under the clouds I stand, with this belt I go; By this, my heart is strong; I shall have courage to die by the foe."

The ceremony concluded, Lady Prévost shook Tecumpease's hand and presented her with a basket of mourning ornaments and other gifts. Paukeesa came away with an officer's coat, buckles, and earrings.[8]

In his chill winter wigwam on the shores of Lake Ontario, Tenskwatawa plotted to restore his influence, even if it meant rending the weak shreds of the Indian alliance. With Tecumseh no longer alive to check his younger brother's tendency toward grandiosity, Tenskwatawa's ego led him badly astray. In early April 1814 he and his hardcore supporters announced to local Indian Department officials that the refugee Shawnees had elected him as their war chief—a ludicrous proposition given Tenskwatawa's combat ineptitude. A week later, in a meeting with Procter's successor, Maj. Gen. Phineas Riall, Tenskwatawa proclaimed himself the "principal chief of all the Western nations." Taking the Prophet at his word, Riall gave him a fine brace of pistols and a sword on behalf of the Prince Regent of England. For his part,

Tenskwatawa "promised the most cordial cooperation and says their smallest boys capable of bearing arms shall be ready to march at a moment's notice."

Inopportunely for the best interests of both the British and the Indians, Matthew Elliott, the one white man capable of exposing such nonsense for what it was, fell grievously ill. Seeing that his "nature is so much worn out as to be unable to bear the struggle both of mind and body," attending physicians gave up hope. A friend from the Indian Department blamed his decline on the Prophet's shenanigans; dealing with the Indians was simply more than Elliott's constitution could bear. On May 7, 1814, he died.[9]

Tenskwatawa's performance at Elliott's funeral was scandalous. After mourners tossed the last shovelfuls of dirt on the casket of one who had given his life to the thankless task of balancing British and Indian interests, the Prophet gathered Indian funeral-goers about himself and harangued Indian Department representatives. Accusing the deputy Indian superintendent William Claus of shorting Indian provisions during the past winter, Tenskwatawa demanded that the Indian Department summon Capt. Thomas McKee—the alcoholic son of the late Matthew Elliott's aged contemporary Alexander McKee—to Dundas because the Indians trusted only him to "attend to the wants of their women and children." Tenskwatawa also requested an immediate augmentation of rations because the "children were starving." And in a startling break with the bedrock of his religious doctrine, the Prophet asked that the department deliver four barrels of rum to him at once. There is no evidence that Tenskwatawa himself backslid, but he no longer objected to his warriors besotting themselves. When the request for rum was denied, Tenskwatawa took "great offense" and left. "It appears to me he is much inclined to be very troublesome," an Indian Department agent told Claus. "I am afraid he is put up to this."[10]

That was hardly news to Claus. The Indian Department was in turmoil. John Norton, a flamboyant Scotsman and adopted Mohawk who rose to dominate the pro-British Iroquois of Upper Canada, had wrangled from Prévost a captain's commission and appointment as "Leader of the Grand River Indians." With that title also came independent authority to dispense presents, of which Prévost gave him a generous supply. Locking horns with William Claus over control of the British Indians on the Niagara frontier, Norton opened his stores to entice western tribesmen who were in acute want to his Grand River settlements.

Tenskwatawa had no compunction about attaching himself to Norton's camp. He knew and respected the Scotsman, who had led a small contingent of Iroquois at Tippecanoe. The Shawnee holy man also was peeved that the British had ignored his wish and replaced the deceased Elliott with Col. William Caldwell, whom he disliked. Together Norton and Tenskwatawa induced the refugee Shawnees, Kickapoos, and Wyandots—581 persons in all—to resettle on the Grand River, sixty miles west of modern Toronto. Reaction from the Indian Department was swift and condemnatory. Colonel Caldwell (Billy's father) accused Norton of "debauching" the Prophet and seducing his followers to gratify his own ambition. Claus echoed his subordinates' conviction that Tenskwatawa was "much inclined to be troublesome" and had become a dupe for Norton's plan to foment discord among the western tribes.[11]

Tenskwatawa's defection mortified Chief Naiwash, who enjoyed the loyalty of 1,332 Indians (Ottawas, Ojibwas, Delawares, Sauks, and Foxes). "You are white, and we are red people, but we are now not one," he lamented to Colonel Caldwell. "We must express our sorrow that the Shawnees have parted with us. Our Elder Brothers have made me ashamed."[12]

The schism Tenskwatawa begat should have come as no surprise to those who knew him well. It was clear that the Shawnee holy man had lost his way. He no longer prophesied. Neither did he speak of the nativist revitalization that he had been spiritually reborn to lead a mere decade earlier. In Tenskwatawa's calculus, the pan-Indian unity for which his brother had given his life was secondary to his own survival and that of his adherents. He would compromise and connive, beg and badger—whatever it took to keep going. He and his people might yet find a permanent home far from the whites. In the meantime, they must live.

Of paramount concern to the British, on the other hand, was whether Tenskwatawa and his warriors would fight. On July 3, 1814, the Americans crossed the Niagara River and opened their expected invasion of the eastern reaches of Upper Canada. Their immediate aim was to capture the British Fort George at the junction of Lake

Ontario and the Niagara River. Outnumbered two to one, General Riall assumed a blocking position below Fort George on the Chippewa River and awaited the arrival of his Indian allies to help even the odds. Captain Norton and an Iroquois contingent rendezvoused with Riall as planned. Chief Naiwash marched to the British camp leading a hundred western warriors with the promise of more to follow. But from Tenskwatawa, in his first test as an elected war chief, came only equivocation and excuses.

Tenskwatawa finally set out from Grand River on June 30 at the head of 112 warriors, only to return to his village the next day, assigning as a reason General Riall's failure to return some wampum that Tenskwatawa had sent him. The general's flummoxed aide-de-camp appealed to Colonel Caldwell to intervene. "If any offense should have been given from his not having returned the wampum, the Prophet must be assured that it arose solely from the general not being sufficiently acquainted with the usual forms and ceremonies necessary on such occasion," he wrote. [The general] hopes that the Prophet should place the fullest reliance on the truth of this assurance and convince him that he is satisfied by coming again here and taking him by the hand." Evidently mollified, Tenskwatawa recommenced his march to the front.[13]

He was too late for the first clash of arms. On July 5 the Americans defeated Riall at the Battle of Chippewa. Riall held his line behind the Chippewa River, however, and was preparing to fall back and take up a new position at Lundy's Lane when Tenskwatawa arrived on the afternoon of July 6. Captain Norton, whose Iroquois had fumbled their assigned duties in the battle, cheered the Prophet's arrival, only to be "greatly disappointed" the next evening when he hastily decamped. Tenskwatawa and his warriors scarpered because they had seen British artillerymen roll an unserviceable cannon into the river, which Tenskwatawa construed as a preliminary to flight. Worse yet, many of the Prophet's departing warriors, together with those of Naiwash and Norton who stayed with the British, had become hopelessly drunk on a large store of rum that the redcoats had busted open.[14]

The bacchanalia on the Chippewa River marked the end of meaningful Indian participation in the war for Upper Canada. Nor could the Indians cooperate among themselves. It took every effort on the part of the Indian Department simply to bring the chiefs together to talk.

Invoking the memory of Tecumseh, an anguished Naiwash appealed to Tenskwatawa and other fractious leaders for unity in words that poignantly encapsulated the sorry state of the western Indian tribes:

> We Indians who are from the westward [*sic*], perhaps the Master of Life would give us more luck if we would stick together as we formerly did ... and we might go back and tread again upon our own lands.
>
> Chiefs and warriors—Since our great chief Tecumseh has been killed, we do not listen to one another, we do not rise together, we hurt ourselves by it, it is our own fault, it is not our Father's fault. We do not when we go to war rise together, but we go one or two, and the rest say they will go tomorrow.[15]

Stirring words, but the Prophet had a ready reply—his warriors could not fight because they were barefoot; promised supplies of moccasins had not materialized. In their impoverished state, the men had dispersed to hunt deer for leather to make replacement footwear and, more urgently, to feed their hungry wives and children, an "excuse [that] had some truth," confessed an Indian Department official. Tenskwatawa looked to the Grand River Iroquois for help, but Norton was disgusted with the Prophet and no longer welcomed him. The Pekowi Shawnees and most of the Kickapoos refused to follow Tenskwatawa and stayed at Dundas. His nephew Paukeesa not only defected but also relinquished the village chieftainship. Availing himself of the discord, William Claus threatened to cut off all provisions for the Kispoko Shawnees unless they too renounced the Prophet and helped repel an expedition of mounted Long Knives then rampaging through the country.[16]

Tenskwatawa relented. In mid-November he made camp with Naiwash, but in exchange for his fealty, the Prophet expected the British to fulfill their promises. "Father listen," he exhorted Colonel Caldwell. "When our Father [General Procter] spoke to us at Amherstburg he told us that if we followed him to the head of the lake [Erie], we should not want for anything; in doing so we have lost my brother, the great dependence of your children [who] are now very poor. Your breasts are very large and full of milk, and your children are very thirsty."[17]

Tenskwatawa spoke the truth, but he no longer had any leverage over the British because on December 24, 1814, the War of 1812 officially ended. The British had entered negotiations with the Americans at Ghent, Belgium, believing that the defeat of Napoleon gave them the diplomatic advantage. Assuming that the prospect of veteran redcoat regiments landing on the Atlantic coast would intimidate the Americans, Britain demanded, as a sine qua non for peace, the creation of an inalienable Indian buffer state in the Northwest based on the 1795 Greenville Treaty line. It was an attempt to honor the pledges the Crown had made to Tecumseh.

American negotiators refused the terms. Weary after two decades of warfare in Europe, Britain relented, and the resultant Treaty of Ghent simply restored the rights and territories that the British Indians had occupied before the war, with no guarantee of their future inviolability. The British Father had failed his Indian children yet again.

On April 24, 1815, William Claus assembled the refugee tribes at a grand council to "wipe the tears from the eyes" of Tenskwatawa, Tecumpease, and other Indians who had lost loved ones fighting the Long Knives and to assure them that, despite rampant rumors to the contrary, their British Father had not forgotten his children at Ghent. They could return to their antebellum tribal homelands whenever they and the Americans came to terms (for Tenskwatawa, this would mean yielding to the noxious Fort Wayne Treaty of 1809 that had precipitated war with the Americans in the first place), and they would always be welcome at Amherstburg, where the British would continue "to hold [them] fast by the hand and treat [them] with all kindness and generosity which obedient children have a right to expect." The Crown likewise would compensate widows and orphans of warriors fallen in the British cause. Tenskwatawa said nothing at the council. Tecumpease and Tecumseh's widow made their marks on a receipt for a mere fifty dollars each—a fraction of what William Caldwell had assured the Shawnee brothers a year earlier that the Crown would pay in survivor benefits. British duplicity knew no bounds.[18]

The reverse exodus of the Indian refugees began in the late spring. In mid-June, Tenskwatawa with six hundred followers plodded into the outskirts of Sandwich. Naiwash's people settled nearby and at once set about planting corn. Tenskwatawa's band, however, refused to till the soil; what was the point, the Prophet argued, when they would be home in the Indiana Territory before the corn matured. No sooner had the Shawnees arrived at Sandwich than a handful of warriors slipped across the Detroit River and stole some horses. Tenskwatawa condemned the act and helped the British restore the animals to their owners, but the theft deepened American misgivings about the Prophet.[19]

The distrust was mutual. Eager to conclude a formal peace with the British Indians, the U.S. government called a grand council in August at Spring Wells, the small riverside settlement near Detroit where Tecumseh had stepped ashore with Brock three years earlier to challenge Hull. That the lead commissioner was William Henry Harrison sufficed to give Tenskwatawa pause. The Prophet grew outright fearful when an Ottawa warrior brought news from Black Hoof—always ready to subvert Tenskwatawa—that the council was merely a ploy to murder the attendees. "Now Brother," Black Hoof warned his credulous rival, "I advise you to keep your war clubs in hand.... You are going to be attacked for they are marching their troops under the cloak that they are going to hold a council."

The British Indian Department took Harrison's part. Feeding the Indian refugees was expensive, and their presence in Upper Canada had become a source of friction with the United States. Moreover, by his earlier cozy relationship with John Norton, the Prophet had alienated Deputy Superintendent Claus. Eager to see the troublesome Shawnee go home, Claus dismissed Tenskwatawa's protestations that the Americans intended treachery at Spring Wells, remarking that "his usual character and conduct render it almost impossible to confide in anything he may say." After much wheedling, British agents persuaded Tenskwatawa to meet with the commissioners.[20]

The council had been in session two weeks when the Prophet crossed the Detroit River to address Harrison. Chief Naiwash had succumbed to the general's blandishments, as had representatives of every formerly belligerent tribe except Tenskwatawa's Shawnee and Kickapoo contingent. Harrison reported the Prophet's speech, delivered on September 4, as pacific in both "tenor and subject." Tenskwatawa did profess a desire to resettle peaceably in the United States, but he also peppered his remarks with sardonic humor that escaped Harrison. By making peace with the Americans, the British had "taken the tomahawk out of the [Indians'] hands," the Prophet quipped. "They had now come over to this side, and here also the tomahawk was taken out of their hands, so that they were now so completely deprived of tomahawks that...their old women could hardly cut wood enough to make a fire." Shaking hands with Harrison, Tenskwatawa pointedly addressed him as brother, not father. "Tell my sentiments to the President," Tenskwatawa instructed Harrison. "He is my father."

Loathing of Harrison aside, Tenskwatawa could not bring himself to accept the peace terms, which compelled his band to live with Black Hoof's people at Wapakoneta. Remarkably, he cherished the hope of rebuilding Prophetstown and rekindling his own council fire. Wary and disappointed, Tenskwatawa decamped to the British side, taking his Shawnee delegates and the Kickapoos with him. A surprised Harrison forbade the Prophet to again set foot on American soil. Five days later Tenskwatawa's wartime allies—the Wyandots, Winnebagos, Sauks, Ottawas, Miamis, Potawatomis, and Delawares—all signed the treaty. The Prophet's isolation from other Indians was near complete.[21]

On returning to Amherstburg, Tenskwatawa endured a chilly reception from the British. The Prophet offered a rambling rationale for having rejected peace. He insisted that the "artful and insinuating" Harrison had "told them all lies [and] was unworthy of credit." The unprovoked killing of a Kickapoo warrior by American settlers bolstered his defense, but British patience and resources were finite. As autumn deepened, the Prophet became a magnet for dissidents. Straggling Sauks and Winnebagos attached themselves to his camp; all depended on British provisions to survive. Tenskwatawa, who had once preached Indian self-reliance on inviolate homelands, had become a pauper to white charity in an alien country.

To prod Tenskwatawa into leaving Canada, the British reduced Indian rations. Indian Department officials exhorted the Prophet and his two hundred warriors to return to the woods and hunt rather than loiter about Amherstburg for handouts—notwithstanding that the British had promised to provision the Indians.[22]

British parsimony infuriated Tenskwatawa. Game was scarce, and his people were starving. "Yesterday was the ration day, and we received our allowance for ten days, which is so very small that one man might eat the whole of the allowance for a family in one day. In my own family counting of nine persons, our ten days' allowance is but a scanty allowance for two days," he told William Claus in council in February 1816. When that did not register, Tenskwatawa returned five days later with the women of his village so that Claus could see their "pitiful" condition firsthand. "The women look to me as their chief instead of my late brother, and I am to transmit their business according to ancient usage," he declared. "I am now put in the place of my brother Tecumseh, who is gone from us, and it is expected I will be listened to as he was." Tenskwatawa reminded Claus of past British guarantees always to care for their Indian allies. With a vehemence uncommon in an Indian leader supplicating his white "father," Tenskwatawa continued, "What was promised has not yet been done. Now, Father, I expect that our women, children, and young men will get satisfaction. We have suffered greatly."[23]

No longer the divinely empowered mystic commanding the loyalty of thousands of believers, Tenskwatawa had fallen mightily in the fragmented Indian world that he and Tecumseh had striven to unite. Increasingly, too, the British scorned him as an irritant. A lesser man might have buckled; as a recovered alcoholic fallen on hard times, he might have taken solitary solace in drink. But Tenskwatawa instead looked soberly outward, advocating for the worldly wants of his diminished following.

When appeals to honor did not move the British, Tenskwatawa resorted to subterfuge: he would bargain with Governor Lewis Cass of the Michigan Territory for a home in the unoccupied country south of Detroit. A former general in the Ohio militia and Harrison's aide-de-camp at the Battle of the Thames, the thirty-three-year-old New Hampshire native was an ardent expansionist who nonetheless lamented—and sometimes exaggerated—the debasement of the Indians living north of the Ohio River. "I have frequently conversed with them about their situation and prospects and have found them deeply sensible of their forlorn condition and anxiously desirous of ameliorating it," he told the secretary of war. "I doubt whether the eye of humanity in a survey of the world could discover a race of men more helpless and wretched." Both President Madison and his successor, James Monroe, trusted Cass implicitly in all matters relating to Indian affairs.[24]

Tenskwatawa orchestrated a compelling performance for the governor. In April 1816 he brought to the old two-story brick Indian Department council house that now served as the Michigan territorial capitol not only his warriors but also the women of the village so that Cass might behold their poverty. Presenting himself as a war chief determined to bury the hatchet, Tenskwatawa bore a demeanor that evoked mixed emotions in white onlookers. Reflecting on the Prophet's reputation for divine intercourse, Michigander James Witherell recorded, "Truly his whole body might be full of light for his eye is really single, having lost the right one." As for his external aspect, Tenskwatawa struck Witherell as "not far from forty years old, of about middling size, and rather sour and morose in countenance. He speaks fluently and with great energy." The Prophet had dressed in a manner he thought appropriate for a council of great import. "He wore a silver sash, brown suitcoat over a calico frock, a silver clasp on each arm and two silver rings round each ear with a bunch of painted horse hair on the right arm, a large silver gorget hanging to his neck, large ornaments hanging to his ears, and a bunch of painted feathers on his head."[25]

Although he had little leverage, Tenskwatawa was too proud to resist articulating his grievances to Cass. "You want me to return to my brethren the Shawnees. They live among the whites. They tend their fields. I cannot do so. I cannot live there. I wish to select my hunting ground and live upon them. What have you against me? Who began the war? Did not Governor Harrison come to my village? I gave him ground to encamp upon. The Winnebagos with me at Tippecanoe it is true struck your people. I was opposed to it but could not prevent it. If we had come to you, then you might have blamed us, but you came to my village. For this you are angry at me."

Turning to his larger purpose, Tenskwatawa asked Cass to select for them a place to settle where they might "forever procure game which the Great Spirit above has made for our support." He would prefer the River Raisin but acknowledged Cass's right to refuse him: "The land is yours; I know it." Whatever spot the governor might grant would only be temporary. Tenskwatawa truly wished to return to Indiana. "My eye is now upon the place where the sun sets. It is the place which my old chiefs have pointed out, the Wabash. It is there I wish to go with my young men, my women and children, where we may raise corn and hunt." Concluding a speech far too prolix even for Indians accustomed to the lengthy and redundant, Tenskwatawa declared his intention to return to Canada "and await in pity and distress the President's answer."[26]

Cass grudgingly admired Tenskwatawa: "The Prophet has collected from different nations a band of about two hundred warriors, who have adhered to him under all vicissitudes with unshaken fidelity." But he had no intention of obliging a man whose manner he adjudged "indicative of determined hostility to the United States." Not only did Cass peremptorily refuse the Prophet's request to settle on the River Raisin, but he also advised the Madison administration that Tenskwatawa's request to return to Indiana reflected a sinister British plan to rebuild a confederacy of disaffected Indians. The governor gave Tenskwatawa an ultimatum—dissolve the remnants of his intertribal alliance and take his Shawnees to Wapakoneta or continue in Canadian exile indefinitely. President Madison endorsed Cass's rebuff.[27]

It was a hard blow for Tenskwatawa. Desperate to reingratiate himself with the British, the Shawnee holy man instead compounded his troubles with both sides. In June he crossed the Detroit River with several warriors, seized an apparent British deserter, threw him bound and gagged into a canoe, and whisked him away to Fort Malden. Unfortunately for Tenskwatawa, the soldier had been in Michigan on legitimate business. A furious Governor Cass issued a warrant for Tenskwatawa's arrest on charges of forcible abduction. The Prophet was now a fugitive from territorial justice.[28]

Tenskwatawa's fortunes spiraled downward—he was unable to set foot in Michigan without risking incarceration in a Detroit prison. But his disciples faced no such impediment. In August sixty Kickapoos set out for the Wabash River. Two months later several dozen Shawnee and Sauk warriors and their families followed them. Rumors that the Prophet himself intended to return to the Indiana Territory and "incite the Indians to hostilities" caused the Miamis and pro-American Potawatomis to evict the intruders. The notion was absurd, and Cass knew it. With the War of 1812 over and Tecumseh a heroic memory, settlers crowded the roads west. The population of the Indiana Territory soared to nearly one hundred thousand. In December 1816 it became a state. Tenskwatawa knew none of this. Far from contemplating an uprising on the Wabash as Cass suggested, however,

Tenskwatawa spent the winter of 1816–17 on the frigid banks of Lake Erie, scraping by on British largesse.[29]

The years passed. The Western District of Upper Canada boomed. In 1813 its population had barely touched forty thousand; by 1820 that number had grown at least fourfold thanks to generous land grants to British settlers. Chatham, a backwoods hamlet of fifty inhabitants in 1813 when Tecumseh had hoped to make a fortified stand there, had become a thriving farm and shipping community of a thousand people, spreading into the forests beyond the Thames River. And there was much to ship. The Western District was a net exporter of wheat, its production doubling annually.[30]

There was little room left for the 6,121 Indians—mostly Ojibwas and Potawatomis—who coexisted uneasily with the prosperous and populous whites. Slow but steady attrition had reduced Tenskwatawa's core following to 233 Shawnee and 133 Kickapoo, Miami, Sauk, and Fox refugees, of whom seventeen were chiefs and 121 warriors. Two-hundred seventy-three displaced Michigan Wyandots also affiliated themselves with the Shawnee Prophet.[31]

Tenskwatawa might have been approaching political irrelevance, but in councils at Amherstburg he bellowed as loudly as had his brother during the halcyon days when Britain's hold on Upper Canada depended on the strength and loyalty of Tecumseh and his warriors. Tecumseh's thunderous demands of Procter were but a distant memory, however, and Tenskwatawa's words bore no menacing undertone. "We have been so bothered by the white people that we now wait on the King's officers to tell them our minds," Tenskwatawa told Crown representatives in June 1820. Indian Department officials were robbing them; the best of the goods were pilfered, and only the worst were issued to the Indians. Nothing changed. Nor did the British Great Father listen. The Prophet had worn out his welcome.[32]

Governor Cass, on the other hand, had begun to see real utility in extending a welcome to the irksome Shawnee. As the 1820s progressed, popular sentiment grew in Ohio for the expulsion of all Indians within its borders to the west of the Mississippi. In the state's crosshairs was Black Hoof's village of Wapakoneta and two outlying Shawnee settlements. The octogenarian chief had secured a measure of federal protection for them, which the state legislature resented. "It is becoming a matter of much importance to the local authorities that these Indians be removed at an early period," the Shawnee Indian agent John Johnston advised Cass. "They are becoming a complete bar in the way of our internal regulations and improvements."

Both Johnston and Cass maintained that it was in the Indians' best interest to emigrate because encroaching whites—many of whom made a living peddling rotgut whiskey to the reservation Indians—endangered their very survival. They murdered drunken warriors with impunity, stole horses and cattle, and robbed hunting camps. Cass told the Monroe administration that the Shawnees "should be protected in all their just rights and secured from their own improvidence, as well as from the avarices of the whites." Their just rights, however, did not include the freedom to keep their homes.[33]

With Black Hoof obdurate, Cass came to believe he could make common cause with Tenskwatawa. The governor thought the attraction of a new western reservation, rich in game and fine farmland and well removed from American settlements and the ruinous lure of liquor, might appeal to the Prophet. Hopeful that he could convert Tenskwatawa into becoming a catalyst for Shawnee removal, Cass invited him and Paukeesa, who had returned to his uncle's wigwam, to Detroit in December 1824.

Detroit had changed much since Tenskwatawa last visited the city eight years earlier. No longer was it a lightly peopled, French-Canadian-flavored foothold on the edge of the American frontier. The population had reached two thousand, making it the largest American community in which the Shawnee Prophet had ever set foot. Little Turtle, Black Hoof, and Main Poc had visited the populous and bustling cities of Baltimore and Philadelphia and the boisterous young capital Washington, D.C. They had seen firsthand something of the millions of whites who thronged the Atlantic Coast. But the latent power of the Americans had remained a mystery to the Shawnee brothers. The Long Knives of their world inhabited a hive of lonely farms, tiny settlements, and small towns hardly larger than Indian villages.

Now Tenskwatawa was getting a belated first taste of American urban enterprise. He wandered streets on which stood nearly two hundred homes—some of them brick structures as elegant as any found on the East Coast—and nearly 150 businesses. The old fort for which his brother and General Brock had contended had been razed, and the land donated to the community. Three "elegant" brick general stores and two large and lively hotels graced the city. Two hundred students crammed into the two-story, fifty-foot-long whitewashed structure that served as the University of Michigania. The bustle must have been dizzying to the Shawnee holy man. Crowds thronged the snow-crunched streets. Dozens of signs unintelligible to Tenskwatawa rocked in the breeze or lay splashed in paint on the sides of buildings. They advertised the services of a dozen blacksmiths, ten gunsmiths, twenty-three masons, twenty-four dry-goods stores, sixty carpenters, seven watchmakers, and five harness makers—all the trappings of the civilization that the Prophet had tried but failed to repudiate. Withal, there were still Indians in Detroit—"friendly" Indians who enjoyed privileges denied Tenskwatawa's band. Potawatomis and Wyandots primarily, they would beach their canoes bottom side up on the bank of the Detroit River. Along the shore road out of town they set out goods for sale. Baskets, canoe paddles, hand-woven mats, bows and arrows, embroidered moccasins—all were on display for passersby to buy or barter for. Indians mingled easily with the Americans. There was not a single soldier within five hundred miles. Times indeed had changed.

Tenskwatawa and his nephew lodged in the spacious brick mansion of Governor Cass. As befit the yuletide season and his desire to win over the Shawnee Prophet, Cass presented Tenskwatawa with one hundred dollars; a fine horse, saddle, and bridle; and many other presents. While in Detroit, Tenskwatawa posed for his first known portrait, done in watercolor by local artist James Otto Lewis. Cass, the Prophet, and Paukeesa spent long hours in the governor's enclosed garden study, reminiscing about past glories and present difficulties. Addressing a growing debate over who shot Tecumseh, Tenskwatawa laughed at the notion that anyone in the smoke-enveloped melee could have been certain who pulled the fateful trigger. Cass agreed.

On making Tenskwatawa's acquaintance, the governor's aide, Charles C. Trowbridge, found the "undersize and thin" Shawnee "demure, somewhat reserved, and suspicious, but very frank [regarding] Tecumseh." Through an interpreter, Tenskwatawa gave Trowbridge a full history—long since lost—of both his life and that of his brother. Warming to his new role as chronicler of his people, in later visits to Detroit he offered Trowbridge a wealth of information on Shawnee culture. More important from the governor's perspective, Tenskwatawa also embraced the emigration scheme. A home far from the corrupting influence of whites, where the Indians could practice the traditional way of life the Prophet had once espoused, appealed both to his vanity and to his genuine concern for the welfare of the Shawnees. In the early summer of 1825, he and his followers turned their backs on the British and journeyed to Wapakoneta.[34]

Governor Cass saw no risk that they might recant their newfound loyalty to the United States: "They have left Canada and removed to the Shawnee reservation in Ohio, radically cured, if we may credit their own declaration, of their Anglo-Mania. We are less apprehensive of being ourselves led into error on this topic as the Prophet and [Tecumseh's] son is sitting with us while we are writing these remarks, and as they have freely disclosed to us their history and present situation." They apparently also spoke ill of Britain to strangers. Tenskwatawa's traducing of the Crown trickled back to Amherstburg, where an infuriated Indian Department official informed Claus that the Prophet "has abused our government to Governor Cass, saying that the British had deceived him and all the Indians, and that he detested them and looked upon them like the dust under his feet— that not the Americans but the British killed his brother." The agent recommended Tenskwatawa be "excluded from His Majesty's bounty should he again call here."[35]

Tenskwatawa had no intention of ever returning to Canada. At Wapakoneta, he proved an able advocate of emigration. Tenskwatawa and Black Hoof sparred vigorously on the subject, or at least with such vigor as the eighty-five-year-old Mekoche chief was able to muster against a tenacious opponent thirty-plus years his junior. Overcoming the deeply held Mekoche distaste both for himself and his teachings, Tenskwatawa eventually pried one hundred tribesmen from the old chief's grasp. Among those he won over was the young chief Cornstalk, grandson of the martyred Shawnee hero. While Tenskwatawa recruited Indians for removal, the federal government opened a new Shawnee reservation bordering the Kansas River, to which the western

Shawnees agreed to move together with their Ohio kinsmen. Tenskwatawa and the other Ohio Shawnees knew nothing of the place except what Agent John Johnston told them: that no white men occupied the land, game abounded, and the soil was fertile. It would suffice.

On September 30, 1826, Tenskwatawa, Paukeesa, Cornstalk, and 269 other Shawnees started west from an emigration camp near Wapakoneta toward an unknown country. Johnston gave the sojourners, who left their corn crops, orchards, and most of their larger possessions behind, ten barrels of flour and enough salt pork for forty days. He also issued the Shawnees twenty horses, forty saddles and bridles, twenty-one rifles, powder and lead, and clothing for men, women, and children. And he hired two subagents on a per diem basis to escort them to the Mississippi River, at which point they would become the responsibility of the superintendent of Indian Affairs at St. Louis, the famed explorer William Clark.[36]

The journey began inauspiciously. Instead of leading the Shawnees due west across the level prairies of northern Indiana, their escorts took them southwest through the broken and forested White River Valley. Heavy rains drenched the travelers, and dysentery depleted them. Horses weakened for lack of grain and grew gaunt. Their Indian Bureau guides deserted them, forcing the Shawnees to plod on alone, selling their clothes for food. The anguished and disillusioned emigrants looked to the Prophet for magic to ease their plight, but he had none to offer. The Mekoches quarreled with the Kispokos and Pekowis and nearly turned back. But the Indian agent at the former Illinois territorial capital of Kaskaskia intervened, provisioning the Shawnees sufficiently to see them through a miserable winter in bark huts along the Mississippi River bottomlands outside town.

On the outskirts of Kaskaskia, Tenskwatawa and the Shawnees beheld a sight that must have filled them with wonder. Below their makeshift village, enormous smoke-belching, water-churning steamboats passed up and down the Mississippi River. Carrying passengers and cargo from distant ports, the steamboats were the lifeblood of the river trade. Apart from awing the Shawnees, the steamboats had the more practical effect of worsening their winter because ax-bearing crew members had denuded the riverbanks of trees in order to provide fuel for them.

With spring, prospects improved. William Clark proved as capable and sympathetic a governor and Indian superintendent as he had been a brilliant explorer of the uncharted Northwest. Not the Old Northwest of Tenskwatawa's time, but the vast reaches between the Missouri River and the Pacific Ocean. The American Republic was rolling westward faster than the Shawnees could imagine.

Having expected the Shawnees in St. Louis, Clark sent Indian agent Richard Graham to learn what had detained them. In a two-day council at Kaskaskia dominated by Tenskwatawa, the Shawnees cataloged the government's promises and rightly blamed John Johnston's poor planning for their misfortunes. But they retained faith in the American Great Father's munificence. "You see us here now before you, in great want," Tenskwatawa concluded his speech. "We ask you to take pity on us."[37]

Graham and Clark obliged them with rations and supplies. Tenskwatawa organized an exploratory party composed of both western and Ohio Shawnees to visit the promised reservation. The vast Kansas prairies perplexed the Ohio tribesmen, but Tenskwatawa and his companions found the soil as good as promised. Returning to Kaskaskia, they ushered their people to St. Louis in August 1827.

Here was another fast-growing frontier metropolis for Tenskwatawa's wonderment. The gateway to the West, St. Louis boasted a population of more than six thousand, three times that of Detroit. The city hosted a veritable carnival of nations. French-Canadian and Spanish mestizo residents shared in the commerce of the prairies. Black slaves trudged behind their American masters. Delegations of Indian tribes that were unknown to the Shawnees visited St. Louis from the upper Missouri River and the Great Plains to trade furs. Countless steamboats lined the great levee. At the St. Louis Arsenal complex of two dozen brick and wooden workshops, civilian workers assembled weapons and artillery in quantities beyond the Shawnees' reckoning.

William Clark eased the culture shock and material shortages of the Shawnees, opening both his storerooms and the council house to them. Tenskwatawa tried to take it all in stride. Papering over lingering friction among the emigrants, the Prophet proclaimed the Shawnees united and willing to "take the road we are told to go." Demonstrating that he still had a certain deftness when negotiating, Tenskwatawa convinced Clark to increase an offer of $750 from his general funds to a thousand dollars to enable the emigrants to buy needed supplies and farming implements, saying, "We are well pleased. We intend to leave this money with you for you to make the purchases for us, for we might be imposed upon by persons from whom we purchase. We know you have more sense than us and may be able to get the goods cheaper."[38]

The sojourn resumed in September. The Shawnees trekked along the south bank of the Missouri River to the mouth of the Osage. There they made a comfortable winter camp in a hunter's paradise well beyond the westernmost American settlements. In May 1828, after eighteen months of torturous travel, Tenskwatawa and the Shawnees arrived in Kansas.[39]

The land indeed was good, government provisions adequate. By October the Shawnees had harvested their first corn crop and erected snug bark wigwams. A year later they replaced them with hewed log cabins. Cattle, hogs, and work oxen became common, and many families owned plows, wagons, and carts. Gradually the Shawnee settlements became almost indistinguishable from those of frontier whites.[40]

Tenskwatawa's personal fortunes fared inversely with those of the larger Shawnee community. Clark declined to recognize him as the legitimate leader of the emigrants, and federal officials funneled rations and annuities through the young Cornstalk and other "government chiefs." Then came Christian missionaries, Baptists and Methodists, who brought the Bible on one hand and worldly "improvements" like plows, mills, and oxen in the other. These enticements chipped away at the traditional Shawnee aversion to Christianity. Children attending mission schools received good clothing and nourishing meals. The Baptists brought in a printing press, and a Shawnee-language newspaper soon appeared. In 1831 Black Hoof died at Wapakoneta, and late the following year his remaining adherents arrived on the Kansas reservation. Surrounded by former tribal foes, excluded from deputations to St. Louis, and nonplussed by the specter of Shawnee assimilation, Tenskwatawa withdrew with his family of nine (his son, four women, and four children) to a natural spring in a small wooded ravine close to the Shawnee Mission school. There at White Feather Spring he proclaimed the new Prophetstown—four lonely cabins that he and his relatives inhabited. Paukeesa was not among the residents, having again deserted his uncle, this time to set up household with a Shawnee band in Missouri. Few visited, and Tenskwatawa seldom strayed from the leafy swale except to stand in the mission church doorway and harangue the Shawnee congregation on the evils of Christianity.[41]

A tribal curiosity at fifty-nine, Tenskwatawa botched a final chance to prove his once vaunted healing powers. Friends with faith in the Prophet's medicine pestered a Christian Shawnee father into sending for Tenskwatawa to administer to his two sick children. The Prophet consented. But first he must dream. Accordingly, after a nap in which he communed with the Master of Life, Tenskwatawa hastened to the family's cabin to deliver the prescription the deity had dictated to him, leaving them with assurances of its infallibility. But the children died. With them, the parents buried their faith in the Prophet.[42]

In the autumn of 1832 Tenskwatawa received an invitation that stirred the aging holy man's soul. A young portrait painter from Philadelphia named George Catlin wondered if the Prophet might make the thirty-mile journey to Fort Leavenworth, a formidable army post on the Missouri River, to pose. On the first leg of a four-year western pilgrimage with paint, brush, and easel, Catlin hoped to "lend a hand to a dying nation [and] portray with fidelity their native looks and history, thus snatching [them] from a hasty oblivion ... for the benefit of posterity."

Tenskwatawa sensed Catlin's purpose because he brought with him the regalia of his better days. When he sat for his portrait in Detroit nine years earlier, Tenskwatawa had projected an acculturated image, wearing American garments and minimizing his native custom. But for Catlin he resurrected the Prophet in all his glory. Tenskwatawa sat bare-chested, an animal skin thrown over his shoulders. Around his head he wrapped a colorful cloth turban of the sort Tecumseh also had favored. Through his left ear lobe, he thrust two small arrows and a feather. He wore the same earbobs, gorgets, and bracelets that he had for his earlier portrait but added his former badges of office. In his right hand the Prophet clutched his "medicine fire," a short rod decorated with feathers and wampum. In his left hand he gripped the sacred string of beans, the mystical amulet with which disciples "shook hands with the Prophet" when converted to his faith.

Catlin's portrait captured more than Tenskwatawa likely wished. He had grown paunchy. His flesh sagged. Dark circles rimmed his eyes. Studying his subject, Catlin concluded, "This has been a very shrewd and influential man, but circumstances have destroyed him,

as they have many other great men before him, and he now lives...
silent and melancholy in his tribe." Catlin talked with Tenskwatawa a
great deal about Tecumseh, "of whom he spoke frankly and seemingly
with great pleasure." Of his own history, however, the Prophet would
say nothing. "He told me that Tecumseh's plans were to embody all
the Indian tribes in a grand confederacy... to unite their forces in an
army that would be able to meet and drive back the white people,
who were continually advancing on the Indian tribes and forcing them
from their lands—that Tecumseh was a great general, and that nothing but his premature death defeated his grand plan."[43]

Dr. J. Andrew Chute of Westport, Missouri, treated both the physical and spiritual needs of reservation Indian converts. An "excellent Christian gentleman" and graduate of Yale University medical
school, Chute also delighted in attending Indian church services. So
it came as no surprise to him that a fellow gentleman connected with
the Baptist Shawnee Mission would ask him one day in November
1835 to visit a desperately ill Indian. Only the identity of the patient
gave Chute pause—it was the famed Shawnee Prophet, who disdained
both Christianity and the white man's medicine. Good Christian that
he was, Chute went with an interpreter across the Kansas River to
attend to Tenskwatawa.

Walking a winding, wooded path, Chute descended a ridge to a
quadrangle of ramshackle cabins "secluded from all the world." It
was the new Prophetstown. The interpreter pointed out the Prophet's dwelling. Stooping beneath a low bark-covered portico, Chute
entered. A half-starved mongrel growled its greeting. The open door
cast a dim light on the grimy interior. Two or three platforms covered
with blankets and skins stood low beside the walls. A few ears of corn
and some dried pumpkins hung from the ceiling. Wooden ladles, trays,
pipes, bowls, and knives lay scattered about the dirt floor. "One corner
of the room, close to the apology for a fireplace, contained a platform
of split logs elevated about a foot from the floor and covered with a
blanket. This was the bed of the Prophet."

Chute recoiled momentarily, contemplating "the spectacle of a
man whose word was law to numerous tribes, now lying on a miserable
pallet, dying in poverty and neglect." As Chute came closer, Tenskwa-

tawa revealed himself. His body was wasted, his face sunken and haggard. Chute asked Tenskwatawa his symptoms. The Shawnee frowned
but related them freely. He wanted to try the white man's medicine,
but not just then. Tenskwatawa was meditating—"in a study," as the
interpreter explained it—and feared Chute's ministrations might disrupt his train of divine thought. Tenskwatawa asked that Chute return
in three days.

Chute meditated a bit himself as he retraced his steps to Westport. Why should Tenskwatawa seek the aid of a white physician, then
abruptly recoil from it? "Perhaps his spirit quailed at the approach
of death, and pride...gave way to fear, but further reflection on his
weakness induced him to discard the assistance tendered by one of a
race [that] he so heartily detested."

Dr. Chute nevertheless returned. "I went to his cabin punctually in
three days, but it was too late. He was speechless and evidently beyond
the reach of human aid." Tenskwatawa died the same day. Chute did
not record either the cause of death or the precise date the Prophet
expired. In the doctor's mind, Tenskwatawa had been merely an impi-
ous Indian.[44]

Appendix

Shawnees: The Shawnees consisted of five patrilineal descent groups most aptly labeled divisions. They might once have been separate tribes that coalesced to form the Shawnees. Whatever their origin, the divisions had well-defined responsibilities that, among a people long dispersed, were more theoretical than real. Even when the tribe coalesced, divisions remained semiautonomous. Shawnee villages took their names from the dominant resident division, and divisions sometimes maintained their own relations with other tribes. The spelling of division names varies. Listed below are the five divisions, their most common alternate spellings, and their traditional prerogatives:

Chillicothe (Chalahgawtha): One of the two principal divisions. Together with the Thawekila, they managed Shawnee political affairs, normally by furnishing the principal tribal chiefs.

Thawekila (Thawegila): The second of the two principal divisions.

Mekoche (Maykujay): Provided healers and saw to tribal health and medicine.

Pekowi (Peckuwe, Pequa): Managed matters of religion and ritual.

Kispoko (Kispugo): Responsible for war preparations and training and supplied tribal war chiefs.

Cherokees: A Southeastern Woodland people of the Iroquoian language group. Before contact with English colonists, the Cherokees were concentrated in what is today southwestern North Carolina, western South Carolina, eastern Tennessee, and northeastern Georgia.

Chickamaugas: A group of Cherokees who broke away from the greater Cherokee nation during the American Revolution and resettled along the Tennessee River near what is today Chattanooga. The Chickamaugas were the last of the Cherokees to surrender to U.S. authority.

Chickasaws: A Southeastern Woodland people of the Muskogean language group. The Chickasaw homeland included northern Mississippi and parts of modern southwestern Kentucky, western Tennessee, and northwestern Alabama.

Choctaws: A Southeastern Woodland people of the Muskogean language group. The Choctaw homeland included what is today southern Mississippi and part of southwestern Alabama.

Creeks: The largest of the Southeastern Woodland nations, the Creeks occupied most of modern Alabama and western Georgia. The Creeks were predominantly a Muskogee-speaking people but also included the affiliated remnants of non-Muskogee speaking tribes. It was the British who collectively referred to these people as Creeks, a named derived from a group of Muskogees who resided near early white settlements in Georgia. Those living along the Chattahoochee River became known as Lower Creeks; the others were labeled Upper Creeks because their towns were farther up the British trading path from the Atlantic Coast.

Delawares (Lenni Lenape): An Algonquian-speaking people originally located in modern New Jersey, eastern Pennsylvania, and the lower Hudson River Valley. Like the Shawnees, they migrated into the Ohio country in the eighteenth century. The Shawnees referred to the Delawares as their "grandfathers." The Shawnee and Delaware languages were similar enough for them to communicate with each other in ordinary discourse. Interpreters were needed for complex subjects or formal councils.

Hurons (see also *Wyandots*): Once an Iroquoian-speaking confederacy of several tribes calling themselves the Wendat with ancestral lands in southern Ontario, the Hurons were decimated by epidemics and dispersed by the Iroquois in the mid-seventeenth century.

Iroquois or *Six Nations:* Sometime foes of the Shawnees, they were of the Iroquoian-language group and called themselves the Haudenosaunee. The Shawnees referred to the Iroquois as their "cousins." The Iroquois confederacy stretched across upstate New York and consisted of the Mohawk, Oneida, Onondaga, Cayuga, Seneca, and Tuscarora tribes.

Kickapoos: An Algonquian-speaking people located between the Wabash and Illinois rivers in what is today westernmost Indiana and central Illinois. The Shawnees called them their "first brothers."

Menominees: An Algonquian-speaking people whose homeland lay along Green Bay in what is today northeastern Wisconsin. Menominee culture was quite similar to that of the Ojibwas; their language bore a close affinity to those of the Fox and Kickapoo tribes.

Miamis: An Algonquian-speaking people located in the Wabash River Valley of Indiana who also claimed the Ohio River Valley as their ancient tribal homeland. The Shawnees referred to the Miamis as their "younger brothers." The Shawnee and Miami languages were similar enough for them to communicate with each other in ordinary discourse. Interpreters were needed for complex subjects or formal councils.

Mingoes: A small Iroquoian band comprised principally of Senecas and Cayugas who took up residence in the Ohio country in the eighteenth century and affiliated themselves closely with the Shawnees.

Munsees: A subtribe, or division, of the Delawares, often known as the Wolf Tribe of the Delaware nation. They had a reputation as the most warlike Delaware people.

Nanticokes: An Algonquian-speaking people who migrated from Chesapeake Bay and southern Delaware in the mid-eighteenth century. Some eventually settled near the Delawares and Shawnees in Ohio.

Ojibwas (Chippewas): An Algonquian-speaking people native to the Great Lakes region, with most villages concentrated in Ontario and Michigan. Together with the Potawatomis and Ottawas, they constituted the Three Fires Confederacy. The Shawnees generally were unable to communicate with any of the Three Fires tribes without the aid of interpreters. The Shawnees referred to the Ojibwas as their "youngest brothers."

Ottawas: An Algonquian-speaking people who resided principally in Michigan. Together with the Potawatomis and Ojibwas, they constituted the Three Fires Confederacy. The Shawnees called them their "younger brothers."

Piankeshaws: An Algonquian-speaking people, the Piankeshaws were members of the Miami nation but lived apart from the Miamis in modern central and southern Indiana and southeastern Illinois. The Piankeshaws were closely affiliated with the Weas, oftentimes sharing the same villages.

Potawatomis: An Algonquian-speaking people who occupied a wide arc of land bordering Lake Michigan from what is today southern Michigan, through northeastern Illinois and far up into eastern Wisconsin. The Potawatomis were considered the "youngest brothers" of the Three Fires Confederacy (Potawatomis, Ojibwas, and Ottawas). The Shawnees called them their "youngest brothers."

Sauks (Sacs) and *Foxes* (Meskwakis): The Sauks and Foxes were Algonquian-speaking peoples who confederated in the early eighteenth century and resided on the upper Mississippi River in what is today northwestern Illinois and western Wisconsin. The Shawnees referred to the Sauks as their "younger brothers" and the Foxes as their "second brothers."

Weas: An Algonquian-speaking people, the Weas were members of the Miami nation, although they lived apart from the Miamis. The United States referred to the Weas as a separate tribe in the Treaty of Greenville (1795). The Weas inhabited much of what is today western Indiana and were closely affiliated with the Piankeshaws.

Winnebagos (Ho-chunk): A Siouan-speaking people who inhabited much of modern central Wisconsin.

Wyandots: A band of Hurons who migrated into southern Michigan and northern Ohio after the Iroquois destroyed the Huron confederacy. The Shawnees referred to them as their "elder brothers" or "uncles."

Acknowledgments

I would like to express my deep gratitude to my friends and fellow historians S. C. Gwyne, Bob Drury, and Colin G. Calloway for their careful reading of the manuscript and their invaluable suggestions for improving it. I am particularly indebted to Professor Calloway, not only for his comments and criticism, but also for his many fine books on the Eastern Woodland Indians and their clashes with the early American Republic, which informed much of my research.

I also wish to thank John Macleod, a collections specialist with Parks Canada, for his gracious help during my visit to the Fort Malden Historic Site in Amherstburg, Canada.

I'd also like to thank my dear friend artist Keith Rocco, Tradition Studios, for permitting me to reproduce his marvelous portrait of Tecumseh. (I am proud to own the original, which watched over me—approvingly I hope—as I toiled on the manuscript.) I am deeply grateful to artist Doug Hall (Doug Hall's Log Cabin Art Gallery and Studio) for permitting me to reproduce three evocative paintings of Shawnees. Once again, I am profoundly grateful to my literary agent, Deborah Grosenvor, for her continued support of my work, for her ideas and critiques, and for her friendship. It is also my singular good fortune to again work with Andrew Miller, my editor at Knopf. As was the case with *The Earth Is Weeping*, he has made this a much better book than it otherwise would have been. I am grateful to copy editor Janet Biehl for her diligent work to improve the manuscript. My sincere thanks also go to editorial assistant Maris Dyer, production editor Kathleen Fridella, and interior designer Maggie Hinders.

My deepest debt is and will always be to my wife, Antonia. She gave me the emotional support and encouragement I needed to persevere during the three years I spent working on this book. Lastly, the contributions of my canine companion, Jake (as fine a Yellow Labrador as there ever was) cannot be overstated. Day in and day out, he lay patiently at my side, never doubting me and asking only for occasional walks.

Notes

ABBREVIATIONS

AC: Edward E. Ayer Collection

ASP-IA [United States]: *American State Papers: Indian Affairs*

BHC: Bentley Historical Collection

DC: Lyman C. Draper Collection

DCFF: Daniel Claus Family and Fonds

DPL: Detroit Public Library

DRIC: E. A. Cruikshank, ed. *Documents Relating to the Invasion of Canada and the Surrender of Detroit 1812.* Ottawa: Government Printing Bureau, 1912.

FMNHS: Fort Malden National Historic Site, Amherstburg, Canada

IHS: Indiana Historical Society (Indianapolis)

IU: Indiana University (Bloomington)

LC: Library of Congress (Washington, D.C.)

LCSIB: Ferdinand B. Tupper. *The Life and Correspondence of Major-General Sir Isaac Brock, K. B.* London: Simpkin, Marshall & Co., 1847.

MHS: Missouri Historical Society (St. Louis)

MLWHH: Logan Esarey, ed. *Messages and Letters of William Henry Harrison.* 2 vols. Indianapolis: Indiana Historical Commission, 1922.

MPHC: Michigan Pioneer Historical Society, *Michigan Historical Collections.* Lansing: Wynkoop, Hallenbeck, Crawford, 1874–1916.

NA: National Archives and Records Administration (Washington, D.C.)

NAC: National Archives of Canada (Toronto)

NL: Newberry Library (Chicago)

OHC: Ohio History Center (Columbus)

PCM: Court-Martial of Maj. Gen. Henry Procter

SBD: William Wood, ed. *Select British Documents of the Canadian War of 1812.* 3 vols. Toronto: Champlain Society, 1923–28.

TCHA: Tippecanoe County Historical Association (Indiana)

UM: University of Michigan (Ann Arbor)

WHS: Wisconsin Historical Society (Madison)

WRHS: Western Reserve Historical Society (Cleveland)

EPIGRAPHS

1. Sass, *Hear Me, My Chiefs*, 31.
2. Klinck, *Tecumseh*, 70–72

PREFACE

1. "American Indian Historian Alvin Josephy Jr. Dies," *Washington Post*, October 18, 2005.
2. Josephy, *Patriot Chiefs*, 161–62, 173.
3. *Publisher's Weekly*, February 3, 1992.
4. Eckert, *Sorrow in Our Heart*, xvii.
5. *Kirkus Reviews*, December 15, 1991.

PROLOGUE

1. "Speech of the Shawanese to Alex. McKee, 1774," in Hazard, *Pennsylvania Archives*, 4:497–98; "Sketch of Cornstalk," 3D18, Border Forays Papers, and "Report of Lord Dunmore," 15J7, George Rogers Clark Papers, DC, WHS; Butterfield, *Washington-Crawford Letters*, 25.
2. Downes, *Council Fires*, 159–74; "Logan, the Mingo Chief," 189; Jefferson, *Notes on the State of Virginia*, 252–53, 262–65; Arthur Campbell to William Preston, October 12, 1774, 3QQ118, Preston Papers, and Michael Cresap, Jr., to Lyman C. Draper, 2SS5, Shepherd Papers, DC, WHS.
3. Downes, *Council Fires*, 176; G. E. Williams, *Dunmore's War*, 237–66; Stephen D. Ruddell narrative, January 1822, 2YY120, Tecumseh Papers, DC, WHS; *Western Sun*, January 11, 1812.
4. Randall, "Dunmore War," 171.
5. Winkler, *Point Pleasant 1774*, 54; William Christian to William Preston, October 15, 1774, in Thwaite, *Dunmore's War*, 264.
6. Lewis, *Point Pleasant*, 52; William Fleming to William Bowyer, n. d., 2ZZ7, Virginia Papers, William Ingles to William Preston, October 14, 1774, 3QQ121, and William Preston to Patrick Henry, October 31, 1774, 3QQ128, Preston Papers, DC, WHS.
7. Draper, "Battle of Point Pleasant," 382; William Christian to William Preston, October 15, 1774, in Thwaite, *Dunmore's War*, 264; *Pennsylvania Gazette*, November 16, 1774.
8. G. E. Williams, *Dunmore's War*, 281.
9. Stephen D. Ruddell narrative, January 1822, 2YY120–21, Tecumseh Papers, DC, WHS; Edmunds, *Tecumseh*, 23; Schoolcraft, *Travels*, 138; Randall, "Tecumseh," 429–30; Sugden, *Tecumseh*, 19; Schutz, "Shawnee Myth," 436.

I: THE GREAT AWAKENING

1. Lakomäki, *Gathering Together,* 24–26; McKenney and Hall, *Indian Tribes,* 1:49–50; *Georgia Gazette,* July 19, 1764; Weir, *Paradise of Blood,* 16–17; William R. Ruddell to Lyman C. Draper, November 16, 1884, 8YY86, Tecumseh Papers, DC, WHS; Wheeler-Voegelin, "Noted Shawnee Leaders," 1.

2. Warren, *Worlds,* 206–7.

3. Hill, *John Johnston,* 1; H. H. Tanner, *Atlas,* 44–47; White, *Middle Ground,* 223, 240–45, 255–56; Downes, *Council Fires,* 76–80; Pouchot, *Memoir,* 2:261.

4. Kenny, "Journal," 172; Hanna, *Wilderness Trail,* 2:367; White, *Middle Ground,* 261, 341; Goltz, "Tecumseh," 23–24; Banta, *Ohio,* 229; Downes, *Council Fires,* 114–16; Doddridge, *Notes,* 92–93.

5. Dowd, *Spirited Resistance,* 33; Burton, *Journal of Pontiac's Conspiracy,* 28–29.

6. Schoolcraft, *Algic Researches,* 242–48; Dowd, *Spirited Resistance,* 19, 27, 33–34; White, *Middle Ground,* 279–83; Kenny, "Journal," 171–72, 175; Loudon, *Interesting Narratives,* 1:272–76.

7. Burton, *Pontiac's Conspiracy,* 29–40; H. H. Tanner, *Atlas,* 48–53; White, *Middle Ground,* 313.

8. White, *Middle Ground,* 351–53; Flick, *Johnson Papers,* 12:629. For a superb analysis of the Fort Stanwix treaty conference, see Billington, "Fort Stanwix Treaty."

9. Calloway, *Shawnees,* 44–48.

10. Calloway, *Shawnees,* 48; Faragher, *Daniel Boone,* 77–81; Metcalf, *Interesting Narratives,* 2–9.

11. H. H. Tanner, *Atlas,* 58–59, 66; *Historical Account of the Expedition against the Ohio Indians,* 97–98; Greene, *American Population,* 205; Galloway, *Old Chillicothe,* 54.

12. Stephen D. Ruddell narrative, January 1822, 2YY120, Tecumseh Papers, DC, WHS; *Cincinnati Liberty Hall,* December 25, 1811; Ellet, *Pioneer Women,* 156.

13. Ellet, *Pioneer Women,* 157; George W. Sevier interview, 30S297, Lyman C. Draper's Notes, DC, WHS; Sugden, *Tecumseh,* 19–20.

14. Galloway, *Old Chillicothe,* 54, 164; Stephen D. Ruddell narrative, January 1822, 2YY120, Tecumseh Papers, DC, WHS. Thomas Wildcat Alford (1860–1938), the great-grandson of Tecumseh, was born in Oklahoma. While attending the Hampton Institute, he converted to Christianity, forfeiting his right to a tribal chieftainship. He lived much of his adult life straddling two cultures, and—as the late Shawnee ethnologist Erminie Voegelin noted—his knowledge of Shawnee ethnography and his own heritage was somewhat limited. In September 1928 he assisted the Daughters of American Revolution in locating the site of Tecumseh's birth as just outside "Old Chillicothe," near present-day Xenia, Ohio. The state of Ohio has since erected a marker based on Alford's designation. Voegelin, "Book Reviews: *Civilization,*" 536–37, and "Book Reviews: *Old Chillicothe,*" 536; "Birthplace of Tecumseh," https://www.hmdb.org/marker.asp?marker=14064. Alford, however, confused the Chillicothe village near Xenia with an earlier Shawnee village of the same name located some fifty miles to the southeast on the Scioto River. It was there that Tecumseh was born. The residents of the first Chillicothe—170 families in all—did

not relocate to the location on the Little Miami River near Xenia until after the Battle of Point Pleasant in 1774. H. H. Tanner, *Atlas*, 79, 81; Flick, *Johnson Papers*, 12:1052.

15. Stephen D. Ruddell narrative, January 1822, 2YY120, and Stephen D. Ruddell to Lyman C. Draper, August 6, 1884, 8YY29, Tecumseh Papers, DC, WHS; Gatschet and Hodge, "Tecumseh's Name," 91–92. Another philologist gave the meaning of Tecumseh's name as "One who passes across intervening space from one point to another . . . the name indicates that the owner belongs to the gens of the Great Medicine Panther, or Meteor, hence the interpretations Crouching Panther and Shooting Star." Galbreath, "Tecumseh and His Descendants," 148.

16. Voegelin and Voegelin, "Shawnee Name Groups," 622–25; Alford, *Absentee Shawnees*, 4; Harrington, "Shawnee Indian Notes," 18–21, Erminie Wheeler-Voegelin Papers, AC, NL; Mooney, *Ghost Dance*, 682–83. Occasionally the naming-ceremony was delayed until the sixth month. See Kinietz and Voegelin, *Shawnese Traditions*, 26–27.

17. Harrington, "Shawnee Indian Notes,"29, Erminie Wheeler-Voegelin Papers, AC, NL; Alford, *Absentee Shawnees*, 21; Kinietz and Voegelin, *Shawnese Traditions*, 29.

18. Alford, *Absentee Shawnees*, 20–22, 46; Harrington, "Shawnee Indian Notes," 30; J. Smith, *Account*, 141.

19. Wickliffe, "Tecumseh and the Thames," 48; McKenney and Hall, *Indian Tribes*, 1:50. Edmunds, *Tecumseh and Quest*, 19, incorrectly calls Nehaaseemo a girl, repeating a mistake first made in Tucker, *Tecumseh*. Voegelin and Voegelin, "Shawnee Name Groups," 618. A second, less devastating smallpox epidemic struck Shawnee villages in 1776. Howerton, "Logan," 325.

20. Anthony Shane statement, 12YY6–8, C. C. Trowbridge to Lyman C. Draper, July 12, 1882, 5YY1, and Stephen D. Ruddell to Lyman C. Draper, August 6, 1884, 8YY29, Tecumseh Papers, DC, WHS; Wheeler-Voegelin, "Noted Shawnee Leaders," 1.

21. Sugden, *Blue Jacket*, 21, 52; Gilbert, *"God Gave Us,"* 71–72; Edmunds, *Shawnee Prophet*, 18–19; Galloway, *Old Chillicothe*, 114.

22. White, *Middle Ground*, 201, 364–65; Calloway, "We Have Always Been the Frontier," 42; "Conference with Kayaghshota [January 5–15, 1774]," Flick, *Johnson Papers*, 12:1052.

23. *Olden Time* 2, no. 1 (January 1847), 6–7.

24. Heckewelder, *History, Manners, and Customs*, 130.

25. Calloway, "'We Have Always Been the Frontier,'" 40–41; Thwaites, "Cornstalk," 253–61; W. D. Brown, "Delayed Response," 147.

26. Galloway, *Old Chillicothe*, 13–14, 61–62; D. A. Jones, *Journal*, 41.

27. Hulbert and Schwarze, "Zeisberger's History," 59–60.

28. Alford, *Absentee Shawnees*, 23–25; Anthony Shane statement, 12YY30, and John Ruddell to Lyman C. Draper, September 5, 1884, 8YY40, both in Tecumseh Papers, DC, WHS; J. Spencer, "Shawnee Indians," 391; Wheeler-Voegelin, "Noted Shawnee Leaders," 30.

29. Heckewelder, *History, Manners, and Customs*, 195–96; D. A. Jones, *Journal*, 38; Quaife, *Indian Captivity*, 125–26; Ridout, "My Capture," 20; Alford, *Absentee Shawnees*, 38–40; Nelson, *Jonathan Alder*, 74–75, 79.

30. Hulbert and Schwarze, "Zeisberger's History," 12–15, D. A. Jones, *Journal*, 53; Heck-

ewelder, *History, Manners, and Customs*, 202–7; Harrington, "Shawnee Indian Notes," 41, 93–94.

31. Quaife, *Indian Captivity*, 88; Hulbert and Schwarze, "Zeisberger's History," 12–15; Harrington, "Shawnee Indian Notes," 93.

32. Schutz, "Shawnee Myth," 215–32, 481.

2: A RESTLESS PEOPLE

1. Callender, "Shawnee," 630; H. H. Tanner, *Atlas*, maps 2, 3, and 9; Trowbridge, *Mee-armeear Traditions*, 8–9.

2. White, *Middle Ground*, 11, 35–49; H. H. Tanner, *Atlas*, 29–35, 169–73, and map 19.

3. Gilbert, "*God Gave Us*," 43; Calloway, *Shawnees*, 2–12; Downes, *Council Fires*, 9, 17–23; Callender, "Shawnee," 630–31.

4. Hazard, *Pennsylvania Archives*, 4:737–38.

5. Callender, "Shawnee," 631; Calloway, *Shawnees*, 13.

6. Kinietz and Voegelin, *Shawnese Traditions*, xiii–xiv; Galloway, *Old Chillicothe*, 181; Callender, "Shawnee," 623–24; D. A. Jones, *Journal*, 54; Calloway, *Shawnees*, 5; Voegelin and Voegelin, "Shawnee Name Groups," 630. Myriad spellings exist for each Shawnee division, stemming in part from the difficulty in capturing English renditions of words from a language with no orthography. I have chosen to follow those given in Calloway, *Shawnees*, as they are the simplest, and as accurate as any other.

7. Voegelin and Voegelin, "Shawnee Name Groups," 628; Kinietz and Voegelin, *Shawnese Traditions*, xvi–xvii; Gilbert, "*God Gave Us*," 9; Alford, *Absentee Shawnees*, 4; Harrington, "Shawnee Indian Notes," 20, Erminie Wheeler-Voegelin Papers, AC, NL.

8. Nelson, *Jonathan Alder*, 55; J. Spencer, "Shawnee Indians," 393–94; D. A. Jones, *Journal*, 52–53; Klinck and Talman, *John Norton*, 188–89.

9. Kinietz and Voegelin, *Shawnese Traditions*, 3, 10; Downes, *Council Fires*, 4–5.

10. Nelson, *Jonathan Alder*, 48; J. Smith, *Account*, 13–17; Heckewelder, *History, Manners, and Customs*, 221; Quaife, *Indian Captivity*, 100–1.

11. McClure, *Diary*, 87–88.

12. Dowd, *Spirited Resistance*, 15–16; Knowles, "Torture of Captives," 151–52, 177–79; Kinietz and Voegelin, *Shawnese Traditions*, 21; Ridout, "My Capture," 24–25; Banta, *Ohio*, 230–31; *London Chronicle*, September 8, 1757; Loudon, *Interesting Narratives*, 1:99–100.

13. Hamilton, *Adventures in Wilderness*, 134; D. A. Jones, *Journal*, 55; Alford, *Absentee Shawnees*, 45; Kinietz and Voegelin, *Shawnese Traditions*, 11, 13.

14. Voegelin, "Shawnee Laws," 36–37, 39–43; John Johnston interview, 11YY11, Tecumseh Papers, DC, WHS.

15. Dowd, *Spirited Resistance*, 3–7; Schutz, "Shawnee Myth," 215, 217–33, 499; Kinietz and Voegelin, *Shawnese Traditions*, 43.

16. Downes, *Council Fires*, 7–8; Blair, *Indian Tribes*, 2:187; White, *Middle Ground*, 16, 21; Kinietz and Voegelin, *Shawnese Traditions*, 9; Heckewelder, *History, Manners, and Customs*, 109–10.

17. Hildreth, *Pioneer History*, 484–86; Hulbert, *Course of Empire*, 71–72,76; Quaife, *Indian Captivity*, 80–83; Callender, "Shawnee," 625; H. H. Tanner, *Atlas*, 5; Alford, *Absentee Shawnees*, 14–15.

18. Harvey, *Shawnees*, 146–51; Callender, "Shawnee," 624; Alford, *Absentee Shawnees*, 56–59; Nelson, *Jonathan Alder*, 71–73; Ridout, "My Capture," 20; J. Spencer, "Shawnee Indians," 392–93; Quaife, *Indian Captivity*, 103–5; Harrington, "Shawnee Indian Notes," 63.

3: A TURBULENT YOUTH

1. Faragher, *Daniel Boone*, 156–64; Hammon, *My Father Daniel Boone*, 55–60; Thomas S. Hinde diary, 39YY225, Thomas S. Hinde Papers, DC, WHS; "Hinde's Letter, May 6, 1842," 326; "Hinde's Letter, May 30, 1842," 374; Metcalf, *Collection*, 20–21.

2. Miriani, "Against the Wind," 34; Schutz, "Shawnee Myth," 371; Warren, *Shawnees*, 74–75; Calloway, "'We Have Always Been the Frontier,'" 42; Alford, *Absentee Shawnees*, 201.

3. Anthony Shane statement, 12YY8, Tecumseh Papers, DC, WHS; Edmunds, *Shawnee Prophet*, 29–30; Sugden, *Tecumseh*, 23. Gilbert, *"God Gave Us,"* 101, asserts that there was nothing unusual in Methoataske's abandonment of her children, nor that it would have had any emotional impact on them. Offering no evidence, Gilbert contends that "as the Shawnee looked at things, if Methoataske thought it wise to migrate…there was no practical reason for her to feel guilty about doing so or for her children to think that they had been cruelly abandoned and rejected." This absurd suggestion ignores the vast contemporaneous literature that demonstrates that the Shawnees loved their offspring, whether biological or adopted, no less than did any other people. Methoataske clearly was the exception to the rule.

4. Greene, *American Population*, 192; Butterfield, *Expedition Against Sandusky*, 65–66; Lafferty, "Destruction of Ruddle's and Martin's Forts," 300; "Bowman's Expedition," 449, 452, 454; Gilbert, *"God Gave Us,"* 102–3; "Bowman's Campaign," 503–4; Talbert, "Kentucky Invades Ohio—1779," 230–31.

5. "Bowman's Campaign," 504–506; "Bowman's Expedition," 455–57; Talbert, "Kentucky Invades Ohio—1779," 231–34; "Speech of the Delawares and Shawnees Assembled at the Upper Shawnee Village to Their Father Major De Peyster," August 22, 1780, H–1446:383, Haldimand Papers, NAC.

6. Calloway, "'We Have Always Been the Frontier,'" 42–48.

7. Wheeler-Voegelin, "Noted Shawnee Leaders," 1; Kinietz and Voegelin, *Shawnese Traditions*, 29.

8. Alexander McKee to Arent S. De Peyster, July 8, 1780, H–1446:413–15, Haldimand Papers, NAC; Lafferty, "Destruction of Ruddle's and Martin's Forts," 297–98; John Duncan statement, 29J25, George Rogers Clark Papers, Stephen D. Ruddell narrative, January 1822, 2YY121, Tecumseh Papers, DC, WHS.

9. Lafferty, "Destruction of Ruddle's and Martin's Forts," 297–99, 301, 303, 310–12, 320, 322, 325–26; *Kentucky Gazette*, October 20, 1826; Collins and Collins, *Kentucky*, 327–28; John Russell interview, 22S42–43, 58, Lyman C. Draper's Notes, DC, WHS.

10. *Springfield Republican*, June 17, 1880; White, *Middle Ground*, 368; Arent S. De Peyster to Lieutenant Colonel Boldon, August 6, 1780, H-1446:445, Haldimand Papers, NAC; Randall, "Tecumseh," 427–28; Galloway, *Old Chillicothe*, 77–78; H. H. Tanner, *Atlas*, 85; Sugden, *Blue Jacket*, 62–63.

11. Randall, "Tecumseh," 434; Draper, "Notes on Tecumseh," 1YY10, Tecumseh Papers, DC, WHS; B. Drake, *Life of Tecumseh*, 68–69; Cass, "Indian Biography," 435; *Springfield Republican*, August 12, 1880.

12. Stephen D. Ruddell narrative, January 1822, 2YY122, and John Ruddell to Lyman C. Draper, September 5, 1884, 8YY40, both in Tecumseh Papers, DC, WHS; Peter Navarre interview, 17S148, and John Ruddell interview, 22S42–43, 58, both in Lyman C. Draper's Notes, DC, WHS; Smelser, "Tecumseh, Harrison, and War of 1812," 33; Galloway, *Old Chillicothe*, 122–23.

4: A NATION DIVIDED

1. Nelson, *Jonathan Alder*, 95; James Galloway to Benjamin Drake, January 12, 1839, 8J256, George Rogers Clark Papers, and Stephen D. Ruddell narrative, January 1822, 2YY122, Tecumseh Papers, both in DC, WHS.

2. Heckewelder, *History, Manners, and Customs*, 245–46.

3. Kinietz and Voegelin, *Shawnese Traditions*, 21–22; Dowd, *Spirited Resistance*, 10–11.

4. Quoted in Schutz, "Shawnee Myth," 254.

5. Kinietz and Voegelin, *Shawnese Traditions*, 22.

6. Downing, "Narrow Escapes," 371–72.

7. W. H. Harrison, "Discourse on Aborigines," 257; J. Smith, *Account*, 11–12; Eid, "Their Rules of War," 16; Heckewelder, *History, Manners, and Customs*, 215–16; Knowles, "Torture of Captives," 216; Lewis Bond Journal, 197, LC.

8. Gipson, *Moravian Indian Mission*, 2–6; *True History of the Massacre*, 1–8; Mutterly, "Colonel David Williamson," 425–31.

9. Downes, *Council Fires*, 272–74; P. B. Brown, "Fate of Crawford Volunteers," 324–31.

10. Draper, "Notes on Tecumseh," 1YY10, Tecumseh Papers, DC, WHS; Faragher, *Boone*, 217–21; Metcalf, *Collection*, 28–31; "Battle of Blue Licks," 247–49.

11. Thomas H. Waters interview, 18S201, Lyman C. Draper's Notes, DC, WHS.

12. Talbert, "Kentucky Invades Ohio—1782," 289–95; White, *Middle Ground*, 403; Frederic Haldimand to Thomas Townsend, October 23, 1782, *MPHC*, 10:663; Alexander McKee to Arent S. De Peyster, November 15, 1782, H-1451:1672–73, and De Peyster to Frederick Haldimand, November 21, 1782, H-1451:1674–76, both in Frederick Haldimand Papers; Metcalf, *Collection*, 32.

13. Quoted in Calloway, "We Have Always Been the Frontier," 47.

14. Calloway, "Suspicion and Self-Interest," 59. For evolving British and American Indian polices, see Horsman, "American Indian Policy"; Allen, "His Majesty's Indian Allies"; and Calloway, "Suspicion and Self Interest."

15. White, *Middle Ground*, 418–19; Heckewelder, *History, Manners, and Customs*, 104.

16. Stephen D. Ruddell narrative, January 1882, 1YY125–26, Tecumseh Papers, DC, WHS; Hulbert, *Ohio River*, 139; Thatcher, *Indian Biography*, 2:186; Gilbert, *"God Gave Us,"*

III. Sugden, *Tecumseh*, 48–51, posits that the flatboat attack occurred five years later, basing his assumption on Kentucky newspaper accounts that speak of particularly violent attacks that occurred in the spring of 1788, and the account of an Englishman, Thomas Ridout, seized by the Shawnees in a flatboat ambuscade that year. But Ridout never mentioned Tecumseh in his account, which he certainly would have, as Ridout was surveyor general of Canada at the times of Tecumseh's exploits there. Also, Ruddell insisted that Tecumseh was fifteen years old when the flatboat raid occurred, which would have placed it in 1783. Ridout, "My Capture," 3–11.

17. Kinietz and Voegelin, *Shawnese Traditions*, 29; John Ruddell to Lyman C. Draper, September 5 and November 1, 1884, 8YY40, Tecumseh Papers, DC, WHS.

18. John Ruddell interview, 22S44–46, Lyman C. Draper's Notes, DC, WHS; Sugden, *Blue Jacket*, 25–27.

19. Calloway, *Victory with No Name*, 101; Quaife, *Indian Captivity*, 89–90.

20. The Treaty of Fort Finney was also known as the Treaty at the Mouth of the Great Miami. Hurt, *Ohio Frontier*, 95–97; Sugden, *Blue Jacket*, 69–71; Denny, *Military Journal*, 73–76.

21. Sugden, *Blue Jacket*, 72; White, *Middle Ground*, 440; Talbert, "Kentucky Invades Ohio—1786," 203–4.

22. Henry Lee interview, 9BB60, Simon Kenton Papers, DC, WHS; Denny, *Military Journal*, 94; Nelson, *Jonathan Alder*, 77–78; Galloway, *Old Chillicothe*, 91–92; Hurt, *Ohio Frontier*, 99; Talbert, "Kentucky Invades Ohio—1786."

23. Hurt, *Ohio Frontier*, 98–100; Dowd, *Spirited Resistance*, 95; "Speech of the United Indian Nations, at Their Confederate Council . . . 28th November and 18th December 1786," in *ASP-IA*, 1:8–9.

24. Horsman, "American Indian Policy," 40; White, *Middle Ground*, 418.

5: WAR AND WANDERINGS

1. H. H. Tanner, *Atlas*, 87, 92; Gilbert, *"God Gave Us,"* 124; Denny, *Military Journal*, 105; Thornbrough, *Outpost*, 120, 166.

2. Sugden, *Blue Jacket*, 76–84, and *Tecumseh*, 48–51; Stephen D. Ruddell narrative, January 1822, 2YY123, Tecumseh Papers, DC, WHS, "My Capture," 3–11; B. Drake, *Life of Tecumseh*, 69.

3. Kinietz and Voegelin, *Shawnese Traditions*, 28–29; "Memorandum of Conversation with Simon Kenton, February 13, 1833," 5BB109, Simon Kenton Papers, DC, WHS; Joseph McCormick interview, 3YY109, Stephen D. Ruddell narrative, January 1822, 2YY132, Anthony Shane statement, 12YY6, 31, and John Johnston to Benjamin Drake, November 14, 1821, 11YY17, both in Tecumseh Papers, DC, WHS; *Phoenix Civilian*, December 22, 1838; Johnston, *Recollections*, 12; Voegelin, "Shawnee Laws," 37.

4. Sugden, *Tecumseh*, 52–53; Gilbert, *"God Gave Us,"* 125; Anthony Shane statement, 12YY6, and Stephen D. Ruddell narrative, January 1822, 2YY126, both in Tecumseh Papers, DC, WHS.

5. Thornbrough, *Outpost*, 167; H. H. Tanner, *Atlas*, 14–15; Stephen D. Ruddell narra-

tive, January 1822, 2YY126, and Anthony Shane statement, 12YY36, both in Tecumseh Papers, DC, WHS; Wickliffe, "Tecumseh and the Thames," 48; Randall, "Tecumseh," 435; William Walker interview, 11U74, Frontier War Papers, DC, WHS; B. Drake, *Life of Tecumseh*, 69.

6. Houck, *Spanish Regime*, 1:316–18; *Louisiana Gazette*, June 30, 1811; Stephen D. Ruddell narrative, January 1822, 2YY126, Tecumseh Papers, DC, WHS; Sugden, *Tecumseh*, 55–56. Cheeseekau is called the Shawnee Warrior in contemporaneous accounts of his activities among the Chickamaugas. For a convincing argument that Cheeseekau and the Shawnee Warrior were the same man, which I accept, see Sugden, *Tecumseh*, 421–22n. I also accept Sugden's conclusion that Tecumseh accompanied his elder brother, which would have been culturally correct behavior on his part. The narrative of Tecumseh's adventures in Tennessee that follows is predicated on this surmise.

7. Pate, "Chickamauga," ii–iv, 52–53, 70–81.

8. Dowd, *Spirited Resistance*, 47–48, 51, 92–94; Arent S. De Peyster to Allan Maclean, March 5, 1783, *MPHC*, 20:96.

9. Pate, "Chickamauga," 2, 8, 10–11, 20–21, 129–31, 159–64, 176; "Description of Five Cherokee Towns Lying Northwest of Chatanuga [sic] Mountain," in *ASP-IA*, 1:264; D. Smith, *Short Description of Tennessee*, 1–2; Goodpasture, "Indian Wars," 161; Connelly, "Indian Warfare," 14.

10. John Douty to Josiah Harmar, 2W201, Josiah Harmar Papers, DC, WHS; W. H. Smith, *Arthur St. Clair*, 2:148; *Providence Gazette*, June 5, 1790; *Minutes of Debates*, 11–12; "Statement of Causes of the Indian War," in C. E. Carter, *Territorial Papers*, 2:364; Henry Knox to Mr. Doughty, June 16, 1790, Henry Knox Papers, Gilder Lehrman Institute.

11. Caughey, *McGillivray*, 258–59; Sugden, *Tecumseh*, 60.

12. John Ruddell interview, 22S53–54, Lyman C. Draper's Notes, DC, WHS.

13. Stephen D. Ruddell narrative, January 1822, 2YY124, and Anthony Shane statement, 12YY31, both in Tecumseh Papers, DC, WHS.

14. B. Drake, *Life of Tecumseh*, 71; Anthony Shane statement, 12YY36, Tecumseh Papers, DC, WHS.

15. White, *Middle Ground*, 448, 453–55; "Statement of Causes of the Indian War," in C. E. Carter, *Territorial Papers*, 2:362–63; George Washington to the Senate, May 25, 1789, in *ASP-IA*, 1:5–7.

16. Arthur St. Clair to the Secretary of War, September 28, 1788, in C. E. Carter, *Territorial Papers*, 2:89.

17. Whittlesey, "White Men as Scalpers," 5–6.

18. George Washington to the Senate, May 25, 1789, in *ASP-IA*, 2:7.

19. Downes, *Council Fires*, 314; Thornbrough, *Outpost*, 268–69; Goltz, "Tecumseh," 35.

20. Horsman, "American Indian Policy," 44; Calloway, *Victory*, 161.

21. Quaife, "First United States Army," 43; Denny, *Military Journal*, 153.

22. Kinnan, *True Narrative*, 5–8; Hildreth, *Pioneer History*, 300–4; Draper, "Notes on Tecumseh," 1YY10, and John Ruddell to Lyman C. Draper, November 15, 1884, 8YY43, both in Tecumseh Papers, DC, WHS; Randall, "Tecumseh," 434.

23. Anthony Shane statement, 12YY36–37, Tecumseh Papers, DC, WHS.

24. Calloway, *Victory*, 85–92, 109–13; Quaife, "First United States Army," 69, 71; Winkler, *Wabash 1791*, 49.

25. Anthony Shane statement, 12YY37–38, and Stephen D. Ruddell narrative, January 1822, 2YY127, both in Tecumseh Papers, DC, WHS; Denny, *Military Journal*, 162–68; Winkler, *Wabash 1791*, 55, 83; Calloway, *Victory*, 127–28.

26. Brickell, "Narrative of Captivity," 50.

27. Cass, "Indian Biography," 436; Stephen D. Ruddell narrative, January 1822, 2YY124, Tecumseh Papers, DC, WHS.

28. James Galloway to Benjamin Drake, January 12, 1839, George Rogers Clark Papers, DC, WHS.

6: OUT FROM THE SHADOWS

1. Horsman, "American Indian Policy," 44–45, and *Frontier in Formative Years*, 41–43; Calloway, *Indian World*, 328–40; "XIII. Population of the Northwest Territory, 31 January 1791," *Founders Online*, National Archives, https://founders.archives.gov/documents/Jefferson/01-18-02-0110-0026.

2. Downes, *Council Fires*, 320; Hogeland, *Autumn of Black Snake*, 183–84; Sugden, *Blue Jacket*, 129–33; "Indian Council at the Glaize," in Cruikshank, *Simcoe Correspondence*, 1:220.

3. B. Drake, *Life of Tecumseh*, 71–72; Anthony Shane statement, 12YY25, 38–39, and John Ruddell to Lyman C. Draper, November 15, 1884, 8YY43, both in Tecumseh Papers, DC, WHS.

4. B. Drake, *Life of Tecumseh*, 72; "Memorandum of Conversation with Simon Kenton, February 13, 1833," 5BB109, and "Muster Roll of Captain Simon Kenton's Company of Militia Ordered into Service to Repel the Invasion of the Indians, April 7, 1792," 6BB98, both in Simon Kenton Papers, DC, WHS.

5. McFarland, "Simon Kenton," 5–32; McClung, *Sketches*, 199; Collins and Collins, *Kentucky*, 572–73; Kenton, *Simon Kenton*, xxii–xxiii, 216–18; Benjamin Whiteman interview, 5BB1, Simon Kenton Papers, DC, WHS; *Highland Weekly News*, December 13, 1866.

6. Kenton, *Simon Kenton*, 219–20; Benjamin Whiteman interview, 5BB1, and "Memorandum of Conversation with Simon Kenton, February 13, 1833," 5BB109, both in Simon Kenton Papers, DC, WHS; Jahns, *Violent Years*, 237. Tecumseh's camp rested near the confluence of the East Fork of the Little Miami River and Dodson's Creek, about two miles south of present-day Lynchburg, Ohio.

7. Stephen D. Ruddell narrative, January 1822, 2YY129-31, and John Ruddell interview, 8YY48, both in Tecumseh Papers, DC, WHS; "Muster Roll of Captain Simon Kenton's Company of Militia Ordered into Service to Repel the Invasion of the Indians, April 7, 1792," 6BB98, Simon Kenton Papers, DC, WHS; Collins and Collins, *Kentucky*, 574; B. Drake, *Life of Tecumseh*, 75; *Highland Weekly News*, December 13, 1866; Kenton, *Simon Kenton*, 222.

8. William Blount to Henry Knox, September 26, 1792, in *ASP-IA*, 1:290; Lyman C.

Draper, "Notes on Tecumseh," 1YY14, Tecumseh Papers, DC, WHS; Connelly, "Indian Warfare," 15; Goodpasture, "Indian Wars," 181, 185–86.

9. *Philadelphia General Advertiser*, October 4, 1792; Goodpasture, "Indian Wars," 182–83; William Blount to Henry Knox, September 11, 1792, and "Miro District casualties," in *ASP-IA*, 1:276, 330; Ramsey, *Annals of Tennessee*, 563.

10. Red Bird statement, September 15, 1792, and William Blount to the Henry Knox, September 26, 1792, in *ASP-IA*, 1:282, 290–91. When war with the Tennesseans became inevitable, Fool Charley changed sides and led a contingent of Chickamauga warriors under John Watts in his September 1792 invasion of Middle Tennessee.

11. Stephen D. Ruddell narrative, January 1822, 2Y122, Tecumseh Papers, DC, WHS.

12. William Blount to Henry Knox, September 26 and November 8, 1792, in *ASP-IA*, 1:290, 328.

13. William Blount to Henry Knox, September 26, 1792, in *ASP-IA*, 1:290.

14. Goodpasture, "Indian Wars," 190–91; William Blount to Henry Knox, October 10, 1792, in *ASP-IA*, 1:294.

15. Goodpasture, "Indian Wars," 192–93; Connelly, "Indian Warfare," 15.

16. William Blount to Henry Knox, September 26, 1792, in *ASP-IA*, 1:290; Connelly, "Indian Warfare," 16.

17. Connelly, "Indian Warfare," 16; Stephen D. Ruddell narrative, January 1822, 2YY126-27, Tecumseh Papers, DC, WHS; Carr, "Early History," 79.

18. William Blount to Henry Knox, October 10, 1792, and "Account of the attack on Buchanan's Station," in *ASP-IA*, 1:294–95; James Robertson to William Blount, November 7, 1792, 4XX14, and John Buchanan Todd interview, 6XX64, both in Tennessee Papers, DC, WHS; Lyman C. Draper, "Notes on Tecumseh," 1YY13, in Tecumseh Papers, DC, WHS; Goodpasture, "Indian Wars," 1:194–95; T. Washington, "Attack on Buchanan's Station," 378, 381, 426; Sugden, *Tecumseh*, 74–76; *Illinois Weekly State Journal*, March 15, 1834; S. L. Knapp, *Lectures*, 211; *Philadelphia General Advertiser*, November 29, 1792.

19. William Blount to Henry Knox, October 10, 1792, in *ASP-IA*, 1:294.

20. "The Indian Council at the Glaize," in Cruikshank, *Simcoe Correspondence*, 1:220, 227; H. H. Tanner, "Glaize," 15–17; Dowd, *Spirited Resistance*, 103–4. The military posts that Red Pole wanted the Americans to destroy were Forts Hamilton and Jefferson, constructed north of Cincinnati in 1791.

21. H. H. Tanner, "Glaize," 17–20; Quaife, *Indian Captivity*, 90–92; Hutton, "William Wells," 184, 186.

22. H. H. Tanner, "Glaize," 17; "Daily Journal of Wayne's Campaign," 316–17; Brickell, "Narrative of Captivity," 52.

23. H. H. Tanner, "Glaize," 21–23, and "Coocoochee," 23–33.

24. *Kentucky Gazette*, April 20, 1793, "Examination of two Shawanese warriors, taken prisoner on the Miami of the Lake … on the 22d instant, June [1794]," in *ASP-IA*, 1:489.

25. Kenton, *Simon Kenton*, 226–29; *Kentucky Gazette*, April 20, 1793; Stephen D. Ruddell narrative, January 22, 1822, 2YY131, Tecumseh Papers, DC, WHS; "Memorandum of Conversation with Simon Kenton, February 13, 1833, 5BB109, Simon Kenton Papers,

DC, WHS; Collins and Collins, *Kentucky*, 374–75; B. Drake, *Life of Tecumseh*, 76–79. Shane said that Tecumseh had women and children with him. Ruddell made no such claim, and it seems highly improbable. Anthony Shane statement, 12YY40, Tecumseh Papers.

26. Onderdonk, "Tecumseh," 8, LC.

27. Pension Application of John Waggoner S7824, RG 93, M804, NA; S. G. Drake, *Aboriginal Races*, 616; Onderdonk, "Tecumseh," 7, LC; Withers, *Border Warfare*, 408–10; James Woods to Governor of Virginia, May 10, 1793, in McRae, *Calendar*, 366.

28. Nelson, *Jonathan Alder*, 88; James Woods to Governor of Virginia, May 10, 1793, in McRae, *Calendar*, 366.

29. "Examination of two Shawanese warriors, taken prisoner on the Miami of the Lake … on the 22d instant, June [1794]," in *ASP-IA*, 1:489; Stephen D. Ruddell narrative, January 1822, 2YY131, Tecumseh Papers, DC, WHS; B. Drake, *Life of Tecumseh*, 79.

30. Quoted in Calloway, *Indian World*, 416.

31. Calloway, *Indian World*, 420–21; Downes, *Council Fires*, 323–24.

32. Hogeland, *Autumn of the Black Snake*, 323–24; Nelson, "Never Have They Done So Little," 44–46.

7: THE MAKING OF A CHIEF

1. Hogeland, *Autumn of Black Snake*, 326–27; "Extract of a Letter from Lieutenant Pilkington, July 7, 1794," in Cruikshank, *Simcoe Correspondence*, 5:309; John Johnston interview, 11Y11, Tecumseh Papers, DC, WHS.

2. "Examination of Two Pattawattamies [*sic*], captured … on the north side of the Miami of the Lake, on the 5th of June 1794," in *ASP-IA*, 1:489–90; Matthew Elliott to Alexander McKee, June 20, 1794, and "Diary of an Officer," in Cruikshank, *Simcoe Correspondence*, 5:90–91; Sugden, *Blue Jacket*, 159–64.

3. "Diary of an Officer," in Cruikshank, *Simcoe Correspondence*, 5:91–92; Nelson, *Jonathan Alder*, 108–9; Sugden, *Blue Jacket*, 164; H. L. Carter, *Little Turtle*, 130–31; Klinck and Talman, *John Norton*, 181–83.

4. Nelson, *Jonathan Alder*, 109, and Nelson, "Never Have They Done So Little," 48–50; Alexander McKee to Joseph Chew, July 7, 1794, in Cruikshank, *Simcoe Correspondence*, 5:310; Anthony Wayne to Henry Knox, July 7, 1794, in *ASP-IA*, 1:487–88.

5. Nelson, *Jonathan Alder*, 109–10.

6. "Diary of an Officer," and Alexander McKee to Joseph Chew, July 7, 1794, in Cruikshank, *Simcoe Correspondence*, 5:94, 310; Sugden, *Blue Jacket*, 167–68.

7. R. G. England to John Simcoe, July 22, 1794, in Cruikshank, *Simcoe Correspondence*, 5:334; H. L. Carter, *Little Turtle*, 131–32.

8. S. G. Drake, *Aboriginal Races*, 572; H. L. Carter, *Little Turtle*, 134.

9. Brickell, "Narrative of Captivity," 52; Nelson, *Jonathan Alder*, 113.

10. Winkler, *Fallen Timbers*, 29, 69; Sword, *President Washington's War*, 297–98; "Examination of a Shawnee Prisoner, August 11, 1794," in *ASP-IA*, 1:494.

11. John Ruddell interview, 22S54, Lyman C. Draper's Notes, DC, WHS; John Ruddell to

Lyman C. Draper, September 5, 1884, 8YY40, Tecumseh Papers, DC, WHS; B. Drake, *Life of Tecumseh*, 81; Edmunds, *Shawnee Prophet*, 31; *Cincinnati Liberty Hall*, December 25, 1811.

12. Nelson, *Jonathan Alder*, 113–14; H. L. Carter, *Little Turtle*, 135.

13. John Ruddell to Lyman C. Draper, September 5, 1884, 8YY40, and Anthony Shane statement, 12YY40, both in Tecumseh Papers, DC, WHS; Winkler, *Fallen Timbers*, 69, 74; Sugden, *Blue Jacket*, 176–78; Anthony Wayne to Henry Knox, August 28, 1794, in *ASP-IA*, 1:491.

14. Anthony Shane statement, 12YY41–42, Tecumseh Papers, DC, WHS; B. Drake, *Life of Tecumseh*, 81–82; Winkler, *Fallen Timbers*, 75, 79.

15. Sugden, *Tecumseh*, 90; Nelson, *Jonathan Alder*, 115.

16. Alexander McKee to Joseph Chew, September 20, 1794, in *MPHC*, 20:372.

17. H. L. Carter, *Little Turtle*, 136; Sugden, *Blue Jacket*, 181; Brickell, "Narrative of Captivity," 53.

18. Lyman C. Draper, "Notes on Tecumseh," 1YY18, Tecumseh Papers, DC, WHS.

19. "Treaty of Greenville," in *ASP-IA*, 1:561–63; Owens, "Jeffersonian Benevolence," 408–9; Dowd, *Spirited Resistance*, 113–14.

20. "Return of Numbers of Indians Present at Greenville," in *ASP-IA*, 1:582; Heath, *William Wells*, 219–28; Thomas Forsyth to William Clark, December 23, 1812, 9T49, Thomas Forsyth Papers, DC, WHS. A total of 1,130 Indians were present at the Greenville council. The Delawares were dominant numerically, with 381 in attendance, followed by the Potawatomis with 240, the Wyandots with 180, the Shawnees with 143, and the Miamis with 73.

21. H. L. Carter, *Little Turtle*, 147; Bottiger, *Borderland of Fear*, 38–41; Calloway, *Indian World*, 443; "Treaty of Greenville," in *ASP-IA*, 1:568, 583; B. Drake, *Life of Tecumseh*, 39–42; Sugden, *Blue Jacket*, 206–10; Warren, *Worlds*, 15.

22. Edmunds, "Heron Who Waits," 256.

23. Anthony Shane statement, 12YY43, and Lyman C. Draper, "Notes on Tecumseh," 1YY19, both in Tecumseh Papers, DC, WHS; Lankford, "Losing the Past," 217; *Boston Gazette*, July 13, 1795.

24. B. Drake, *Life of Tecumseh*, 43–44; Anthony Shane statement, 12YY44, Tecumseh Papers, DC, WHS; Warren, *Worlds*, 24.

25. Stephen D. Ruddell narrative, January 1822, 2YY133, Tecumseh Papers, DC, WHS.

26. Cass, "Indian Biography," 435; B. Drake, *Life of Tecumseh*, 83, 84, 224; Anthony Shane statement, 12YY44, Tecumseh Papers, DC; Kinietz and Voegelin, *Shawnese Traditions*, 27.

27. Anthony Shane statement, 12YY44, Tecumseh Papers, DC, WHS; Hill, *John Johnston*, 24; B. Drake, *Life of Tecumseh*, 225.

28. Anthony Shane statement, 12YY32–33, and John Johnston to Benjamin Drake, November 13, 1821, 11YY17, both in Tecumseh Papers, DC, WHS; D. A. Jones, *Journal*, 55–56; Heckewelder, *History, Manners, and Customs*, 154.

29. Brown, *History of Madison County*, 286–87.

30. Galloway, *Old Chillicothe*, 121–23, 166–67; Simon Kenton interview, 5BB10, Simon Kenton Papers, DC, WHS; Lyman C. Draper, "Notes on Tecumseh," 1YY20, Tecumseh

Papers, DC, WHS; James Galloway to Benjamin Drake, January 12, 1839, 8J245, George Rogers Clark Papers, DC, WHS.

31. Sugden, *Tecumseh*, 100–1.

32. John Johnston interview, 11YY11, Tecumseh Papers, DC, WHS.

33. James Galloway to Benjamin Drake, January 12, 1839, 8J245–46, George Rogers Clark Papers, DC, WHS; *Cincinnati Western Spy and Hamilton Gazette*, August 27, 1799.

34. Michigan governor Lewis Cass penned the words criticizing Tecumseh's oratorical skills more than a decade after Tecumseh's death. But Cass had known Tecumseh well. More important, Tenskwatawa was with Cass when he composed the article in which the critical assessment of Tecumseh as speechmaker appeared. Tenskwatawa had become an informant of Cass on Indian traditions and Tecumseh's life, and it is reasonable to assume that Cass was echoing Lalawethika's views. Cass, "Indians of North America," 99.

35. *Philadelphia Gazette*, September 6, 1799.

8: A CULTURE IN CRISIS

1. Gunderson, "Harrison: Apprentice in Arms," 3, 6, 8–15, 18–19; Skaggs, *William Henry Harrison*, 5–7; "General Wayne's Orderly Book," in *MPHC*, 34:396–97, 461; Johnston, *Recollections*, 28.

2. Dawson, *Harrison*, 3–4; Barnhart, "Harrison-Worthington Letters," 56–57, 59, 60, 65; William Henry Harrison to his Constituents, May 14, 1800, in *MLWHH*, 1:13–14; Cayton, *Frontier Indiana*, 174–76; Horsman, *Frontier in Formative Years*, 73.

3. Dawson, *Harrison*, 5; Greene, *American Population*, 190; MacLean, "Kentucky Revival," 242; Bottiger, *Borderland of Fear*, 74, and "Stabbed in the Back," 92; Ogg, *Old Northwest*, 115–16; Hover, *Memoirs of the Miami Valley*, 265–66; Bird, "Adventures," 122; William Henry Harrison to James Findlay, October 15, 1801, in *MLWHH*, 1:34–35; *Chicago Tribune*, March 6, 1886.

4. C. C. Trowbridge to Lyman C. Draper, July 12, 1882, 5YY1; John Ruddell to Lyman C. Draper, September 5, 1884 8YY40; and J. M. Finch to Lyman C. Draper, June 8, 1890, 8YY18, both in Tecumseh Papers, DC, WHS.

5. Gipson, *Moravian Indian Mission*, 67, 96, 121–22, 156–57, 164–67, 184, 364; White, *Middle Ground*, 497; Mills, "'It Is the Cause,'" 6–7.

6. *New York American*, November 17, 1826; Warren, *Shawnees*, 74–76.

7. H. L. Carter, *Little Turtle*, 159–62, 164; Hill, *Johnston*, 17; "Summary Account," 16–17.

8. Woehrmann, *Headwaters of Maumee*, 84–85, 142–43.

9. Cayton, *Frontier Indiana*, 202–3; Hill, *Johnston*, 24.

10. Volney, *View*, 352–54.

11. William Henry Harrison to Henry Dearborn, July 13, 1801, in *MLWHH*, 1:24–29.

12. Cayton, *Frontier Indiana*, 200; White, *Middle Ground*, 489–91; Lincoln, "Journal," 152–53; Hulbert and Schwarze, "Zeisberger's History," 14.

13. "Proclamation Forbidding Traders from Selling Liquor to Indians in and around Vincennes," July 20, 1801, and William Henry Harrison to Henry Dearborn, Febru-

ary 26, 1802, in *MLWHH*, 1:31–32, 41; Henry Dearborn to William Henry Harrison, February 23, 1802, in C. E. Carter, *Territorial Papers*, 7:49.

14. John Johnston, "Tecumseh Notes," 11YY11, 18, Tecumseh Papers, DC, WHS; Johnston, *Recollections*, 11; McKenney and Hall, *Indian Tribes*, 326–32; White, *Middle Ground*, 494–95; Bacon, "Unsuccessful Mission," 34–36.

15. Edmunds, "Evil Men," 2–3; Miriani, "Against the Wind," 38; Lakomäki, "'Our Line,'" 607–8.

16. Wallace, *Jefferson and Indians*, 224–26; Owens, "Jeffersonian Benevolence," 405–6; Horsman, "Indian Policy," 47; Wood, *Empire of Liberty*, 357.

17. Quoted in Wood, *Empire of Liberty*, 358.

18. Thomas Jefferson to William Henry Harrison, February 27, 1803, in *MLWHH*, 1:69–71.

19. White, *Middle Ground*, 496; Wallace, *Jefferson and Indians*, 227–34; Bottiger, *Borderland of Fear*, 42; Owens, "Jeffersonian Benevolence," 414–25; William Henry Harrison to Henry Dearborn, August 26, 1805, in *MLWHH*, 1:163–64; Dearborn to Thomas Jefferson, January 12, 1805, in C. E. Carter, *Territorial Papers*, 7:255–56.

20. Anthony Shane statement, 12YY34, Tecumseh Papers, DC, WHS; Procter and Procter, *Lucubrations*, 341; Schoolcraft, *Travels*, 139; Thatcher, *Indian Biography*, 2:185.

21. "Address of Thomas F. McGraw on the Anniversary of Clark's Attack on Piqua," unidentified newspaper clipping, 8J8, George Rogers Clark Papers, DC, WHS; *Virginia Argus*, June 8 and 22, 1803; B. Drake, *Life of Tecumseh*, 84–85.

22. B. Drake, *Life of Tecumseh*, 21–22; Lakomäki, "'Our Line,'" 610.

9: A PROPHET ARISES

1. Sugden, *Tecumseh*, 110.

2. Stocker, "Moravian Mission," 322–26.

3. McKenney and Hall, *Indian Tribes*, 1:66; C. C. Trowbridge to Lyman C. Draper, July 12, 1882, 5YY1, John Ruddell to Lyman C. Draper, September 4, 1884, 8YY40, Charles Tucker to Lyman C. Draper, June 26, 1887, 3YY112, J. M. Finch to Lyman C. Draper, June 8, 1890, 8YY18, and John Conner notes, 7YY21, all in Tecumseh Papers, DC, WHS; Cass, "Indians of North America," 99; Thomas Forsyth to William Clark, December 23, 1812, 9T50, Thomas Forsyth Papers, DC, WHS; Andrews, "Shaker Mission," 222; Radin, "Winnebago Tribe," 70–71.

4. Edmunds, *Shawnee Prophet*, 32; Kinietz and Voegelin, *Shawnese Traditions*, 35–36; Wheeler-Voegelin, "Noted Shawnee Leaders," 15, Erminie Wheeler-Voegelin Papers, AC, NL.

5. MacLean, "Shaker Mission," 223; Law, *Vincennes*, 100; Edmunds, *Shawnee Prophet*, 29–33; Eckert, *Sorrow in Our Heart*, 760n.

6. Dowd, *Spirited Resistance*, xvii–xviii, 23–39; Brainerd, *Life*, 233–334.

7. MacLean, "Shaker Mission," 222–23; Quaife, *Indian Captivity*, 126–27; Ogg, *Old Northwest*, 126–28; McNemar, *Kentucky Revival*, 20–28; White, *Middle Ground*, 504; Stocker, "Moravian Mission," 323.

8. Edmunds, *Shawnee Prophet*, 33; Cayton, *Frontier Indiana*, 206; Kinietz and Voegelin, *Shawnese Traditions*, 24–25.

9. Andrews, "Shaker Mission," 122–23; MacLean, "Shaker Mission," 223–24; Kinietz and Voegelin, *Shawnese Traditions*, 41; Stocker, "Moravian Mission," 333; Mooney, *Ghost Dance*, 673, 678.

10. Andrews, "Shaker Mission," 123; Thatcher, *Indian Biography*, 2:189; Cass, "Indian Biography," 446; J. M. Finch to Lyman C. Draper, June 8, 1890, 8YY18, Tecumseh Papers, DC, WHS; Thomas Forsyth, "Sketch of Tecumseh," 8T54, Thomas Forsyth Papers, DC, WHS; J. Spencer, "Shawnee Indians," 387; Cayton, *Frontier Indiana*, 206.

11. Lankford, "Losing the Past," 217; J. Spencer, "Shawnee Indians," 387; John Ruddell to Lyman C. Draper, November 15, 1884, 8YY40, and Stephen D. Ruddell to Lyman C. Draper, August 6, 1884, 8YY29, both in Tecumseh Papers, DC, WHS; John Ruddell interview, 22S46, Lyman C. Draper's Notes, DC, WHS. Anthony Shane asserted that Tecumseh disbelieved the dreams and prophecies of his brother but assented to them as a matter of policy, making use of Lalawethika "to further his own design." Anthony Shane statement, 12YY47, Tecumseh Papers. Shane's comments simply don't ring true, considering Tecumseh's subsequent missions undertaken on his brother's behalf, his own statements of belief, and their ongoing relationship, which might best be characterized as symbiotic.

12. Andrews, "Shaker Mission," 123; Kinietz and Voegelin, *Shawnese Traditions*, 41.

13. Andrews, "Shaker Mission," 118; B. Drake, *Life of Tecumseh*, 86; Bottiger, *Borderland of Fear*, 53–55; Andrews, "Shaker Mission," 123, 126; J. Spencer, "Shawnee Indians," 389–90.

14. Mooney, *Ghost Dance*, 672; Anthony Shane statement, 12YY10, Tecumseh Papers, DC, WHS.

15. Anthony Shane statement, 12YY4, Tecumseh Papers, DC, WHS; "Speech of Indian Chief [Le Maigouis] to Various Tribes," in *MPHC*, 40:127–28.

16. Edmunds, *Shawnee Prophet*, 36–37; Kinietz and Voegelin, *Shawnese Traditions*, 45–46; Gipson, *Moravian Indian Mission*, 392; Mooney, *Ghost Dance*, 671.

17. Anthony Shane statement, 12YY10–12, Tecumseh Papers, DC, WHS; Thomas Forsyth to William Clark, December 23, 1812, and January 15, 1827, 9T50-54, Thomas Forsyth Papers, DC, WHS; Thomas Worthington and Duncan McArthur to Thomas Kirker, September 22, 1807, 7BB49, Simon Kenton Papers, DC, WHS; Sass, *Hear Me, My Chiefs*, 31–32; Kinietz and Voegelin, *Shawnese Traditions*, 41–42; Gipson, *Moravian Indian Mission*, 392; Mooney, *Ghost Dance*, 671–72; MacLean, "Shaker Mission," 224; "Speech of Indian Chief [Le Maigouis] to Various Tribes," in *MPHC*, 40:127–28; Edmunds, *Shawnee Prophet*, 37–40; Schutz, "Shawnee Myth," 178–79; J. Tanner, *Narrative of Captivity*, 155–58.

18. Dawson, *Harrison*, 82; Gipson, *Moravian Indian Mission*, 402.

19. Gipson, *Moravian Indian Mission*, 403.

20. Brady, "Moravian Mission," 293; Thomas Moore to Edward Tiffin, February 16, 1806, 7BB22, Charles McConnell affidavit, February 16, 1806, 7BB23, and Tiffin to Moore, February 19, 1806, 7BB26, all in Simon Kenton Papers, DC, WHS; Tiffin to Thomas Worthington, February 20 and March 20, 1806, Thomas Worthington Papers, OHC; *Scioto Gazette*, April 17, 1806.

21. *Scioto Gazette*, April 17, 1806.

22. Miller, "1806 Purge," 248–53; Cave, "Prophet's Witch-Hunt," 454; Stocker, "Moravian Mission," 320.

23. Brady, "Moravian Mission," 293; Miller, "1806 Purge," 254; Gipson, *Moravian Indian Mission*, 407, 409, 411–13; Goltz, "Tecumseh," 75; B. Drake, *Life of Tecumseh*, 91.

24. Miller, "1806 Purge," 258–59; Gipson, *Moravian Indian Mission*, 111.

25. White, *Middle Ground*, 499; Miller, "1806 Purge," 257; Anthony Shane statement, 12YY12–13, Tecumseh Papers, DC, WHS; Gipson, *Moravian Indian Mission*, 412.

26. Anthony Shane statement, 12YY13, Tecumseh Papers, DC, WHS; Gipson, *Moravian Indian Mission*, 415, 558; Miller, "1806 Purge," 254–55.

27. White, *Middle Ground*, 499; Gipson, *Moravian Indian Mission*, 559; Anthony Shane statement, 12YY14, Tecumseh Papers, DC, WHS.

28. Gipson, *Moravian Indian Mission*, 416–17, 420–22, 428–29, 433; Anthony Shane statement, 12YY16–18, Tecumseh Papers, DC, WHS; Thatcher, *Indian Biography*, 2:198; Miller, "1806 Purge," 260–61; David Zeisberger to John Heckewelder, May 10, 1806, Northwest Territory Collection, IHS; Goltz, "Tecumseh," 79.

10: BLACK SUN

1. Badger, *Memoir*, 99–100, 114, 145; *Poulson's American Daily Advertiser*, October 22, 1806; Meek, "Tarhe—the Crane," 68–69.

2. William Henry Harrison to the Delawares, early in 1806, in *MLWHH*, 1:182–83.

3. *Connecticut Journal*, August 28, 1806; Goltz, "Tecumseh," 73; Horsman, *Matthew Elliott*, 168–69.

4. Kinietz and Voegelin, *Shawnese Traditions*, 37; *Connecticut Journal*, August 28, 1806; Badger, *Memoir*, 146.

5. Anthony Shane statement, 12YY20, 30, Tecumseh Papers, DC, WHS; Edmunds, *Shawnee Prophet*, 48–49; Sugden, *Blue Jacket*, 238.

6. *Connecticut Journal*, August 28, 1806; *Republican Star*, September 2, 1806.

7. Cass, "Discourse," 130; Sugden, *Blue Jacket*, 239–31; Edmunds, "Watchful Safeguard," 168–69; Dawson, *Harrison*, 84; *Otsego Herald*, September 18, 1806.

8. *Otsego Herald*, September 18, 1806; Goltz, "Tecumseh," 78.

9. Andrews, "Shaker Mission," 120–26; MacLean, "Shaker Mission," 220–26; McNemar, *Kentucky Revival*, 123–29; *Cincinnati Liberty Hall*, October 24, 1810.

10. Farmer, *History of Detroit*, 373, 489–90; Ross and Catlin, *Landmarks of Detroit*, 277; Council of Sauks, Foxes, Ottawas, and Potawatomis held at Amherstburg, June 8, 1805, RG 10, vol. 26:15578–82, NAC; White, *Middle Ground*, 512.

11. William Wells to Henry Dearborn, April 19 and 25, 1807, RG 107, M221, NA.

12. Cass, "Discourse," 103–4.

13. Radin, "Winnebago Tribe," 71–72.

14. "Speech of Indian Chief [Le Maigouis] to Various Tribes," in *MPHC*, 40:127–28; *Philadelphia Gazette*, January 24, 1812;

15. Heath, *William Wells*, 312–13; Anthony Shane narrative, 12YY47–51, Tecumseh Papers,

DC, WHS; H. L. Carter, *Little Turtle*, 187; Goltz, "Tecumseh," 83–84; Brice, *Fort Wayne*, 172; "Speech to the Shawnees Residing at Greenville, April 22," enclosed in William Wells to Henry Dearborn, April 25, 1807, RG 107, M221, NA.

16. Anthony Shane narrative, 12YY51–54, Tecumseh Papers, DC, WHS; Goltz, "Tecumseh," 84–85.

17. Heath, *William Wells*, 313–14.

18. *Chillicothe Freedonian*, May 28, 1807; James Vance to Benjamin Drake, 2YY110–13, Tecumseh Papers, DC, WHS; Benjamin Whiteman interview 1846, 9BB1, Simon Kenton Papers, DC, WHS.

19. Sugden, *Tecumseh*, 132–33.

20. "Roundhead's Address to Benjamin Whiteman on Murder of Boyer," 3YY72–73, Tecumseh Papers, DC, WHS.

21. William Dugan interview, 8J87, George Rogers Clark Papers, DC, WHS; "Memorandum of Conversation with Simon Kenton, February 13, 1833," 5BB106–109, DC, WHS; Benjamin Whiteman interview 1846, 9BB1, Simon Kenton Papers, DC, WHS; *Cincinnati Gazette*, November 4, 1841.

22. Black Hoof to Benjamin Whiteman, June 15, 1807, 5U181, Frontier War Papers, DC, WHS; "Proceedings of a Council Held with the Indians at Springfield June 24 and 24 Concerning the Murder of John Boyer," 5U183, Frontier War Papers, DC, WHS; Heckewelder, *History, Manners and Customs*, 104.

23. Kenton, *Simon Kenton*, 270–72; William Kirk to Henry Dearborn, July 20, 1807, RG 107, M221, NA; "Proceedings of a Council Held with the Indians at Springfield June 24 and 24 Concerning the Murder of John Boyer," 5U183, Frontier War Papers, DC, WHS; Richard Hunt account, August 24, 1840, 3YY134, and Thomas Forsyth, "Sketch of Tecumseh," 8YY54, both in Tecumseh Papers, DC, WHS; Sugden, *Tecumseh*, 133–34.

11: GREENVILLE INTERLUDE

1. Josiah Dunham to Henry Dearborn, May 20 and 24, 1807, Charles Reaume to Josiah Dunham, June 4, 1807, and William Hull to Dearborn, June 18 and 22, 1807, all in RG 107, M221, NA; "Speech of Indian Chief to Various Tribes," Dunham to Hull, June 22, 1807, and Hull to Dearborn, July 25, 1807, in *MPHC*, 40:142–43, 159–60.

2. William Wells to the Secretary of War, June 4, 1807, RG 107, M221, M221, NA.

3. Goltz, "Tecumseh," 76, 86–87; Black Hoof document dated August 14, 1807, 5U186–87, Frontier War Papers, DC, WHS.

4. William Henry Harrison to the Shawnee Chiefs, Prophet to Harrison, [August] 1807, and Harrison to Dearborn, July 11 and August 13, 1807, in *MLWHH*, 1:223–24, 229, 249–51; R. J. Conner notes, June 19, 1891, 7YY21, Tecumseh Papers, DC, WHS.

5. William Wells to Henry Dearborn, July 14, 1807, in C. E. Carter, *Territorial Papers*, 7:465–66; Wells to Dearborn, August 4 and 14, 1807, and Wells to William Henry Harrison, August 20, 1807, RG 107, M221, NA; Wells to Thomas Kirker, August 4, 1807, 7BB37, Simon Kenton Papers, DC, WHS.

6. William Wells to John Gerard, August 22, 1807, 7BB42, Simon Kenton Papers, DC, WHS.

7. *Staunton Eagle*, November 20, 1807; *Cincinnati Liberty Hall*, October 24, 1810.

8. William Creighton to Thomas Kirker, August 23, 1807, Samuel Williams Papers, IU.

9. Thomas Worthington to Jefferson, October 5, 1807, *Founders Online*, NA, http:// founders.archives.gov/documents/Jefferson/99-01-02-6506; Worthington and Duncan McArthur to Thomas Kirker, September 22, 1807, 7BB49, Simon Kenton Papers, DC, WHS; *Washington National Intelligencer*, October 9, 1807.

10. James T. Worthington to Benjamin Drake, April 7, 1840, 5U180, Frontier War Papers, DC, WHS.

11. John Johnston interview, 11YY11, Tecumseh Papers, DC, WHS; Galloway, *Old Chillicothe*, 213; Sugden, *Tecumseh*, 8; James T. Worthington to Benjamin Drake, April 7, 1840, 5U180, Frontier War Papers, DC, WHS.

12. Charles A. Stuart to Lyman C. Draper, February 17, 1846, 8CC59, Kentucky Papers, DC, WHS; *Chillicothe Freedonian*, September 25, 1807.

13. B. Drake, *Life of Tecumseh*, 97; Goltz, "Tecumseh," 93; Sugden, *Blue Jacket*, 248–50; McDonald, "Tragical Death of Wawillowa," 1; *Chillicothe Fredonian*, September 25, 1807; Thomas S. Hinde account, 16Y45–50, Thomas S. Hinde Papers, DC, WHS; Charles A. Stuart to Lyman Draper, February 17, 1846, Kentucky Papers, DC, WHS.

14. *Chillicothe Freedonian*, September 25, 1807; "General Orders from the Commander-in-chief, Ohio Militia, dated September 21, 1807," 7BB48, Simon Kenton Papers, DC, WHS; Thomas Kirker to Thomas Jefferson, October 8, 1807, *Founders Online*, NA, http://founders.archives.gov/documents/Jefferson/99-01-02-6528.

15. Alford, *Absentee Shawnees*, 214; John Johnston interview, 11YY11, Tecumseh Papers, DC, WHS.

16. John Johnston to Henry Dearborn, May 31, 1807, in M. L. Carter, "Johnston and Friends," 41; Shawnee Chiefs to the Secretary of War [1807], Jefferson to the Shawnee Chiefs, February 19, 1807, and Thomas Kirk to Henry Dearborn, May 28, 1807, all in RG 107, M221, NA; Miriani, "Against the Wind," 41; Woehrmann, *Headwaters of Maumee*, 123–27.

17. William Hull to Henry Dearborn, November 4 and 18, 1807, in *MPHC*, 40:213–14, 219; William Wells to Dearborn, December 21, 1807, and Speech of Five Medals to Benjamin F. Stickney, both in RG 107, M221, NA; Wallace, *Jefferson and Indians*, 236.

18. Charles Jouett to Henry Dearborn, December 7, 1807, and William Wells to Dearborn, January 23, 1808, both in RG 107, M221, NA; Finley, *Autobiography*, 440; Bontrager, "Nation of Drunkards," 611.

19. William Wells to Henry Dearborn, January 7, 1808, RG 107, M221, NA; Wells to Dearborn, April 20, 1808, in C. E. Carter, *Territorial Papers*, 7:566.

20. Thomas Forsyth, "Sketch of Tecumseh," 8YY54, and "Main Poque," 8YY50–52, both in Tecumseh Papers, DC, WHS; Edmunds, *Potawatomis*, 153–66, and Edmunds, "Main Poc," 259–62, 269.

21. Edmunds, "Main Poc," 262–63; Blair, *Indian Tribes*, 2:203; William Wells to Henry Dearborn, January 7, 1808, RG 107, M221, NA; Whicker, "Zachariah Cicot," 100–2.

22. William Wells to Henry Dearborn, December 5 and 21, 1807, and John Johnston to Dearborn, December 31, 1807, both in RG 107, M221, NA.

23. William Wells to Henry Dearborn, April 20, 1808, in C. E. Carter, *Territorial Papers*, 7:555–57.

12: A DOUBLE GAME

1. Anthony Shane narrative, 12YY34, Tecumseh Papers, DC, WHS; Sugden, *Blue Jacket*, 311n1; H. L. Carter, *Little Turtle*, 189; William Wells to Henry Dearborn, April 20, 1808, in C. E. Carter, *Territorial Papers*, 7:557–58; Wells to Dearborn, June 5, 1808, RG 107, M221, NA.

2. William Wells to Henry Dearborn, April 22 and 23, 1808, in C. E. Carter, *Territorial Papers*, 7:557–60; Dawson, *Harrison*, 106; H. L. Carter, *Little Turtle*, 189; John Johnston to Samuel Drake, December 14, 1831, 11YY18, Tecumseh Papers, DC, WHS.

3. Dawson, *Harrison*, 106; William Henry Harrison to Henry Dearborn, May 19, 1808, in Clanin, *Harrison Papers*, 3:156–57.

4. Bottiger, *Borderland of Fear*, 20; George Winter, "Tippecanoe Battle Ground, October 6, 1840," and "Prophet's Town and Tippecanoe Battle Ground 1840," both in George Winter Papers, TCHA; Turpie, *Sketches*, 171–72.

5. Charles C. Trowbridge, "Kickarpoo [*sic*] Indians," Charles C. Trowbridge Papers, University of Michigan.

6. Blair, *Indian Tribes*, 2:278–79.

7. Thomas Forsyth to William Clark, December 23, 1812, 9YY53–54, Tecumseh Papers, DC, WHS.

8. Calloway, *Crown and Calumet*, 206; James Craig to Francis Gore, December 28, 1807, in *MPHC*, 25:232–33; Byrd, "Northwest Indians," 44; Horsman, *Matthew Elliott*, 165.

9. Horsman, *Matthew Elliott*, 168; Edmunds, *Shawnee Prophet*, 70; *United States Gazette*, October 12, 1807; Francis Gore to James Craig, January 7, 1808, in Brymner, *Canadian Archives*, 37.

10. William Claus to Francis Gore, February 27, 1808, in *MPHC*, 23:44; Claus to Prideaux Selby, May 3, 1808, in *MPHC*, 14:49; Gore to Craig, April 8 and July 27, 1808, RG 10, vol. 2:842, 902–3, NAC; Claus to the Prophet, May 18, 1808, Claus to Gore, May 22, 1808, and William Claus Diary, 53–54 (entries of June 11, 13, 14, and 15, 1808), all in DCFF, NAC; William Wells to Henry Dearborn, June 5, 1808, RG 107, M221, NA; Horsman, *Matthew Elliott*, 170; R. J. Conner to Lyman Draper, June 19, 1891, 8YY21, Tecumseh Papers, DC, WSH.

11. Elizabeth Tooker, "Wyandot," in Sturtevant, *Handbook*, 15:398, 402; Sugden, *Tecumseh*, 290.

12. Francis Gore to James Craig, July 27, 1808, RG 10, vol. 2:903, NAC; William Claus diary, 57 (July 11, 1808), DCFF, and Matthew Elliott to William Halton, May 19, 1809, both in RG 10, vol. 3:990, NAC; Horsman, *Matthew Elliott*, 171.

13. John Conner statement, June 18, 1808, and William Wells to Henry Dearborn, June 5, 1808, RG 107, M221, NA; R. J. Conner to Lyman C. Draper, June 19, 1891. 8YY21, Tecumseh Papers, DC, WHS.

14. *Western Sun*, July 2, 1808; "Message to the Prophet," June 24, 1808, in Clanin, *Harrison Papers*, 3:176–80; William Henry Harrison to Henry Dearborn, July 12, 1808, RG 107, M221, NA.

15. Prophet to William Henry Harrison, August 1, 1808, and Harrison to Henry Dearborn, September 1, 1808, in *MLWHH*, 1:299–300, 302; Dawson, *Harrison*, 107–8; Goltz, "Tecumseh," 129; Edmunds, *Shawnee Prophet*, 74–75.

16. Harrison to the Secretary of War, November 9, 1808, Esarey, *MLWHH*, 1:321; Dowd, *Spirited Resistance*, 120; Edmunds, *Shawnee Prophet*, 75–76, and "Main Poc," 263; Warren, "History of the Ojibways," 321–22; Wells to the Secretary of War, March 31, 1809, RG 107, OSW/LR.

17. Anthony Shane statement, 12YY55–56, R. J. Conner notes, June 19, 1891, 7YY21, and R. J. Conner to Lyman Draper, June 19, 1891, 8YY21, all in Tecumseh Papers, DC, WHS.

18. Black Hoof and others to Thomas Jefferson, Spring 1808, Citizens of Ohio to the War Department, September 25, 1808, Shawnee Chiefs at Wapakoneta to the President, December 1, 1808, Statement of Francois Duchouquet, December 4, 1808, and Citizens of Champaign County to President James Madison, January 30, 1809, all in RG 107, M221, NA.

19. William Wells to William Eustis, March 31, 1809, and William Henry Harrison to Eustis, April 26, 1809, both in RG 107, M221, NA; John Johnston to the Prophet, May 3, 1809, in Thornbrough, *Letter Book*, 49.

20. William Henry Harrison to William Eustis, May 3, 1809, in *MLWHH*, 1:344–45.

21. Edmunds, "Main Poc," 263–65.

22. Edmunds, *Shawnee Prophet*, 77–78.

23. Matthew Elliott to William Halton, May 19, 1809, RG 10, vol. 3:990, NAC.

24. *Missouri Gazette and Advertiser*, April 5, 1809; Blair, *Indian Tribes*, 2:184; Sugden, "Tecumseh's Travels Revisited," 159–60; Black Hawk, *Autobiography*, 29; Keating, *Narrative*, 1:230–31.

25. Bottiger, *Borderland of Fear*, 93–96.

26. William Henry Harrison to William Eustis, April 18, 26, and 29, and May 3, 1809, in *MLWHH*, 1:340–45; John Johnston to the Prophet, May 3, 1809, in Thornbrough, *Letter Book*, 49–51.

27. John Johnston to William Eustis, July 1, 1809, and William Henry Harrison to William Eustis, May 16, 1809, both in RG 107, M221, NA; *Frankfort Argus*, June 7, 1809; *Vincennes Western Sun*, May 13, 1809.

28. William Hull to William Eustis, June 16, 1809, RG 107, M221, NA.

29. William Henry Harrison to William Eustis, July 5, 1809, RG 107, M221, NA.

13: ONE TREATY TOO MANY

1. Bottiger, *Borderland of Fear*, 74; William Henry Harrison to William Eustis, May 16, 1809, and Eustis to Harrison, June 5, 1809, in *MLWHH*, 1:346, 348; Eustis to Harrison, July 15, 1809, in *ASP-IA*, 1:761.

2. Owens, *Jefferson's Hammer*, 199–206; H. L. Carter, *Little Turtle*, 190–92; Dowd, "Thinking and Believing," 31–32; *National Intelligencer*, October 30, 1809; *Scioto Gazette*, November 6, 1809; William Henry Harrison to William Eustis, December 10, 1809, in *MLWHH*, 1:396; William Wells to Eustis, December 20, 1811, RG 107, M221, NA.

3. Matthew Elliott to William Claus, June 10, 1810, RG 10, vol. 27:16099–100, NAC.

4. Klinck and Talman, *John Norton*, 173.

5. Edmunds, "Watchful Safeguard," 172–73; Klinck and Talman, *John Norton*, 173–74;

Western Sun, July 11, 1810; John Johnston to William Henry Harrison, June 24, 1810, in *MLWHH*, 1:430–31; Johnston to William Eustis, July 3, 1810, RG 107, M221, NA.

6. B. Drake, *Life of Tecumseh*, 119–20; William Hull to William Eustis, July 6, 1810, RG 107, M221, NA; Edmunds, "Watchful Safeguard," 173; Thatcher, *Indian Biography*, 2:198–99; Nelson, *Jonathan Alder*, 101–2; O. Curry, "Doomed Wyandott [*sic*]," 45–46; W. L. Curry, "Leather Lips," 30–31; Schlup, "Tarhe—the Crane," 133.

7. William Henry Harrison to William Eustis, June 14, 1810, in *MLWHH*, 1:424.

8. William Henry Harrison to John Johnston, June 16, 1810, enclosed in William Hull to William Eustis, July 6, 1810, RG 107, M221, NA; Matthew Elliott to William Claus, June 10, 1810, RG 10, vol. 27:16100, NAC; Dawson, *Harrison*, 138.

9. William Henry Harrison to William Eustis, June 14, 1810, in *MLWHH*, 1:433–34; Harrison to Eustis, June 26, 1810, RG 107, M221, NA; Michel Brouillette Deposition, June 30, 1810, Albert Gallatin Papers, IHS.

10. Edmunds, "Main Poc," 265, and *Potawatomis*, 172–73; Thomas Forsyth, "Main Poc," 8YY57, Tecumseh Papers, DC, WHS.

11. Michel Brouillette Disposition, June 30, 1810, Albert Gallatin Papers, IHS; Dawson, *Harrison*, 142; *Western Sun*, June 30, 1810.

12. William Henry Harrison to William Eustis, April 25 and June 14, 1810, in *MLWHH*, 1:417–19, 425–27; Eustis to Harrison, May 10, 1810, in C. E. Carter, *Territorial Papers*, 8:26.

13. Thornbrough, *Badollet-Gallatin Correspondence*, 111, 151–54, 163, 195; Certificate of James Johnson [June 1810], in C. E. Carter, *Territorial Papers*, 8:27–29.

14. William Henry Harrison to William Eustis, July 1 and 4, 1810, in *MLWHH*, 1:439–40, 446–49n; Law, *Vincennes*, 101–2; Lossing, *Field Book*, 191; Charles Tucker to Lyman C. Draper, n.d. and John Ruddell to Lyman C. Draper, July 25, 1890, 3YY110–15, Tecumseh Papers, EC, MHS.

15. William Henry Harrison to William Eustis, July 1, 1810, and Harrison to the Prophet, July 19, 1810, in *MLWHH*, 1:447–48, 449n; William Hull to Eustis, July 20, 1810, and John Johnston to Eustis, July 25 and August 7, 1810, both in RG 107, M221, NA; Dawson, *Harrison*, 154–55.

16. William Henry Harrison to William Eustis, July 1, and August 6, 1810, in *MLWHH*, 1:454–56.

14: NO DIFFICULTIES DETER HIM

1. William Henry Harrison to William Eustis, August 6, 1810, in *MLWHH*, 1:456; *Philadelphia Gazette*, August 31, 1810.

2. William Henry Harrison to William Eustis, July 25, 1810, in *MLWHH*, 1:450.

3. B. Drake, *Life of Tecumseh*, 124–25; Dawson, *Harrison*, 156; Augustus Hones to Lyman C. Draper, 3YY107, and Joseph McCormick interview, 3YY109, Tecumseh Papers, DC, WHS; John Ruddell interview, 22S52–53, and James S. Whitaker interview, 18S139–40, Lyman C. Draper's Notes, DC, WHS; William Henry Harrison to William Eustis, August 28, 1810, in *MLWHH*, 1:470; *Western Sun*, August 25, 1810.

4. Dawson, *Harrison*, 156; William Henry Harrison to William Eustis, August 22, 1810, in *MLWHH*, 1:160–61; Gunn, *Ethnology and Empire*, 101–7.

5. B. Drake, *Life of Tecumseh*, 127.

6. Dawson, *Harrison*, 156–57; William Henry Harrison to William Eustis, August 22, 1810, in *MLWHH*, 1:167–68; James S. Whitaker interview, 18S140, Lyman C. Draper's Notes, DC, WHS; Badollet to Gallatin, September 25, 1810, in Thornbrough, *Badollet-Gallatin Correspondence*, 168.

7. William Henry Harrison to William Eustis, August 22, 1810, in *MLWHH*, 1:169; William Henry Harrison comments, 19S247, Lyman C. Draper's Notes, DC, WHS.

8. Dawson, *Harrison*, 159; W. H. Harrison, "Discourse on Aborigines," 257.

9. Matson, "Sketch of Shau-be-na," 416, and Matson, *Memories of Saubena*, 19; Biddle, "Recollections," 53–54.

10. Sugden, *Tecumseh*, 207–10.

11. Edmunds, *Shawnee Prophet*, 94; William Henry Harrison to William Eustis, October 17, 1810, in *MLWHH*, 2:40.

12. William Hull to John Johnston, September 27, 1810, Thornbrough, *Letter Book*, 83–90; Hull to William Eustis, October 4, 1810, RG 107, M221, NA; *Spirit of Seventy-Six*, December 7, 1810; *American Mercury*, December 27, 1810.

13. Horsman, *Matthew Elliott*, 179–80; Edmunds, *Shawnee Prophet*, 96–97.

14. John Johnston to William Henry Harrison, October 14, 1810, and Harrison to William Eustis, October 17, 1810, in *MLWHH*, 1:176–79; "Fort Wayne Indian Agency," in Thornbrough, *Letter Book*, 91; H. L. Carter, *Little Turtle*, 206–7.

15. Edmunds, *Shawnee Prophet*, 97.

16. "Speech of Tecumseh, the Shawnee Prophet's Brother, Delivered at Amherstburg, November 15, 1810," RG 10, vol. 27:16177–78, NAC; Goltz, "Tecumseh," 223; J. Witherell to Theophilus Harrington, November 15, 1810, and David Botsford to Jane Consolino, August 20, 1960, Tecumseh Information File, FMNHS; Allen, "His Majesty's Indian Allies," 10; Horsman, *Matthew Elliott*, 180.

17. Grignon, "Seventy-five Years' Recollections," 268; B. Drake, *Life of Tecumseh*, 131–32; William Henry Harrison to William Eustis, December 24, 1810, in *MLWHH*, 1:498–99, 507–8; John Johnston to Eustis, February 8, 1811, RG 107, M221, NA.

18. Benjamin Hough to Thomas Worthington, January 26, 1811, Thomas Worthington Diaries and Letter-books, LC.

19. William Henry Harrison to William Eustis, June 6, 1811, John Lalime to William Clark, May 26, 1811, and Clark to Eustis, July 3, 1811, in *MLWHH*, 1:511–13; Harrison to Jared Mansfield, July 15, 1811, in C. E. Carter, *Territorial Papers*, 8:127; Edmunds, "Main Poc," 265; William Irvine to Eustis, May 13, 1811, in *ASP-IA*, 1:800; Clark to Eustis, May 24, 1811, and "Ioway [*sic*] Chiefs' Speech (May 1811)," RG 107, M221, NA.

20. Dawson, *Harrison*, 178; John Johnston to William Eustis, August 18, 1811, RG 107, M221, NA; William Henry Harrison to Eustis, June 19, 1811, in *MLWHH*, 1:518–19.

21. Dawson, *Harrison*, 179–81; William Henry Harrison to William Eustis, June 25 and July 10, 1811, in *MLWHH*, 1:524; *Western Sun*, July 27, 1811.

22. *Western Sun*, July 27, 1811; William Henry Harrison to William Eustis, July 19, 1811, in *MLWHH*, 1: 533.

23. William Henry Harrison to William Eustis, August 6, 1811, in *MLWHH*, 1:545; Dawson, *Harrison*, 186; *Western Sun*, August 3, 1811; John Badollet to Albert Gallatin, August 6, 1811, in Thornbrough, *Badollet-Gallatin Correspondence*, 185.

24. Dawson, *Harrison*, 184–85; B. Drake, *Life of Tecumseh*, 142–43; *Western Sun*, April 18, 1812.

25. John Badollet to Albert Gallatin, August 6, 1811, in Thornbrough, *Badollet-Gallatin Correspondence*, 184–86; Wood, *Empire of Liberty*, 362–63.

26. William Henry Harrison to William Eustis, August 7 and 13, 1813, in *MLWHH*, 1:547–58; *Western Sun*, August 3, 1811.

27. William Eustis to William Henry Harrison, July 20, 1813, RG 75, M1, NA.

15: SOUTHERN ODYSSEY

1. Randall, "Tecumseh," 473; William Blount to William Eustis, September 16, 1811, RG 107, M221, NA; H. S. Halbert, "Seekaboo and Tecumseh," 12YY4, Anthony Shane narrative, 12YY58, and Charley Hoentubbee statement, October 5, 1882, 4YY79, all in Tecumseh Papers, DC, WHS; Halbert and Ball, *Creek War*, 40.

2. Burnham, *Great Comets*, 53; Crawford, "Bacon's Journal," 380.

3. Weir, *Paradise of Blood*, 53.

4. James Neelly to William Eustis, November 29, 1811, RG 107, M221, NA; W. G. Harris interview, 4YY60, Tecumseh Papers, DC, WHS; Halbert and Ball, *Creek War*, 40–41; Weir, *Paradise of Blood*, 60; Sugden, "Early Pan-Indianism," 279–81; Hudson, *Southeastern Indians*, 258–59.

5. H. S. Halbert, "Tecumseh's Visit to the Choctaws," 4YY75, and Charley Hoentubbee statement, October 5, 1882, 4YY79, both in Tecumseh Papers, DC, WHS; Halbert and Ball, *Creek War*, 44–45; James Neelly to William Eustis, November 29, 1811, RG 107, M221, NA; Whicker, "Tecumseh and Pushmataha," 319–20; Sugden, "Early Pan-Indianism," 282–83.

6. H. S. Halbert, "Tecumseh's Visit to the Choctaws," 4YY75, and Charley Hoentubbee statement, October 5, 1882, 4YY79, both in Tecumseh Papers, DC, WHS; Halbert, "Some Inaccuracies," 162–63.

7. Charley Hoentubbee statement, October 5, 1882, 4YY79, Tecumseh Papers, DC, WHS.

8. Halbert and Ball, *Creek War*, 49–52; H. S. Halbert, "Tecumseh's Visit to the Choctaws," 4YY75, and Charley Hoentubbee statement, October 5, 1882, 4YY79, both in Tecumseh Papers, DC, WHS; Sugden, "Early Pan-Indianism," 283.

9. Weir, *Paradise of Blood*, 69; Davis, "Remembering Fort Mims," 620–28; H. S. Halbert, "Seekaboo and Tecumseh," 12YY4, Tecumseh Papers, DC, WHS.

10. H. S. Halbert, "Tecumseh's Visit to the Choctaws," 4YY75, Tecumseh Papers, DC, WHS; Halbert and Ball, *Creek War*, 52–54.

11. *Savannah Republican*, October 17, 1811, and November 5, 1811; Weir, *Paradise of Blood*, 73–74; Woodward, *Reminiscences*, 84; Samuel Moniac [Manac] Deposition, Alabama Department of Archives and History; Benjamin Hawkins to Wade Hampton, Sep-

tember 21, 1811, RG 107, M221, NA; Sugden, "Early Pan-Indianism, 285; Monnette, *Valley*, 2:394–95; Vandiver, "Pioneer Talladega," 47.

12. Woodward, *Reminiscences*, 95; Return J. Meigs to William Eustis, December 4, 1811, RG 107, M221, NA; W. A. Duncan to Lyman C. Draper, January 12, 1882, 4YY71–72, Tecumseh Papers, DC, WHS.

13. J. T. Adair to Lyman C. Draper, May 1882, 4YY31, Judge Law interview, 4YY73–74, and Anthony Shane statement, 12YY57, all in Tecumseh Papers, DC, WHS; Weir, *Paradise of Blood*, 80–82; Sugden, "Tecumseh's Travels Revisited," 164.

14. Dowd, *Spirited Resistance*, 159–66.

16: THE PROPHET STUMBLES

1. William Henry Harrison to William Eustis, September 17, 1811, in *MLWHH*, 1:570–71; *New England Palladium*, October 22, 1811.

2. *Alexandria Gazette*, September 24, 1811; *Philadelphia Gazette*, September 27, 1811; Hill, *John Johnston*, 50–53; Beckwith, *Fort-Wayne Manuscript*, 65–78; John Johnston to William Eustis, August 27 and 29, 1811, RG 107, M221, NA.

3. Ninian Edwards to William Eustis, August 11, 1811, in *ASP-IA*, 1:801; William Henry Harrison to William Eustis, August 13, 1811, in *MLWHH*, 1:553.

4. Harrison to the Secretary of War, August 13, 1811, in *MLWHH*, 1:554.

5. Harrison to the Secretary of War, September 25, 1811, in *MLWHH*, 1:589–90; John Badollet to Albert Gallatin, October 15, 1811, in Thornbrough, *Badollet-Gallatin Correspondence*, 195–96; Edmunds, *Shawnee Prophet*, 105; Watts, "Larrabee's Account," 233.

6. "Field Report of Harrison's Army," October 12, 1811, in *MLWHH*, 1:598; Crawford, "Bacon's Journal," 380.

7. Whicker, "Shabonee's Account of Tippecanoe," 357; *Cincinnati Liberty Hall*, September 26, 1810; Matthew Elliott to Isaac Brock, January 12, 1812, C Series, vol. 728:62, NAC; John Johnston to William Eustis, November 28, 1811, RG 107, M221, NA; William Henry Harrison to Eustis, October 28, 1811, and Adam Walker journal, November 6, 1811, in *MLWHH*, 1:605, 700; *National Intelligencer*, December 7, 1811; Thomas Forsyth to William Clark, November 1, 1811, Thomas Forsyth Papers, MHS; *Cincinnati Liberty Hall*, December 25, 1811.

8. William Henry Harrison to William Eustis, October 28, 1811, in *MLWHH*, 1:605; Eustis to Harrison, September 18, 1811, in C. E. Carter, *Territorial Papers*, 8:133–34; Winkler, *Tippecanoe 1811*, 50–54.

9. James Miller to Ruth Miller, November 4, 1811, Benson J. Lossing Papers, BHC, DPL; William Henry Harrison to William Eustis, October 13, 1811, and Adam Walker journal, October 20, 1811, in *MLWHH*, 1:599, 699–700.

10. William Henry Harrison to William Eustis, October 13, 1811, in *MLWHH*, 1:599.

11. Whicker, "Shabonee's Account of Tippecanoe," 354.

12. Edmunds, *Shawnee Prophet*, 107; William Henry Harrison to William Eustis, October 28, 1811, in *MLWHH*, 1:605.

13. William Henry Harrison to William Eustis, November 26, 1811, in *MLWHH*, 1:649.

14. Whicker, "Shabonee's Account of Tippecanoe," 355; Edmunds, *Potawatomis*, 176; B. Drake, *Life of Tecumseh*, 221–22; *Cincinnati Liberty Hall*, December 25, 1811; "Speech of the Indians on the Wabash in Reply to Message of Colonel M. Elliott," June 8, 1812, in *DRIC*, 34; Speech of Tecumseh, enclosed in William Claus to Isaac Brock, June 16, 1812, in *MLWHH*, 2:63.

15. Adam Walker journal, November 6, 1811, in *MLWHH*, 1:700; Watts, "Larrabee's Account," 241; Edmunds, *Shawnee Prophet*, 109.

16. "Speech from the Shawnee Chief Yealabahcah and the Prophet in a Council with Lewis Cass, 1816," Lewis Cass Papers, UM.

17. William Henry Harrison to William Eustis, November 18, 1811, and Adam Walker Journal, November 6, 1811, in *MLWHH*, 1:620–21, 700–1; McAfee, *Late War*, 35; Matthew Elliott to Isaac Brock, January 12, 1812, C Series, vol. 728:62; Carlson, "Peters' Version of Tippecanoe," 40; Schoolcraft, *Travels*, 144.

18. "Speech from the Shawnee Chief Yealabahcah and the Prophet," Lewis Cass Papers, UM; John Lalime to Benjamin Howard, February 4, 1812, RG 107, M221, NA; Winkler, *Tippecanoe 1811*, 62–63; B. Drake, *Life of Tecumseh*, 221–22; McAfee, *Late War*, 41.

19. "Report of a Meeting Between P. B. Whiteman and the Shawnees," December 4, 1811, 5YY8, and Anthony Shane statement, 12YY29, both in Tecumseh Papers, DC, WHS; Whicker, "Shabonee's Account of Tippecanoe," 356, 358, 359; *Cincinnati Liberty Hall*, December 25, 1811; Smith, *Treatise*, 22.

20. Whicker, "Shabonee's Account of Tippecanoe," 358–59; Joseph Barron statement dated 1840, George Winter Papers, TCHA.

21. Matthew Elliott to Isaac Brock, January 12, 1812, C Series, vol. 728:62; Winkler, *Tippecanoe*, 63; Joseph Barron statement dated 1840, George Winter Papers, TCHA.

22. Harrison to the Secretary of War, November 18, 1811, in *MLWHH*, 1:621–22; Watts, "Larrabee's Account," 242; Carlson, "Peters' Version of Tippecanoe," 41.

23. Whicker, "Shabonee's Account of Tippecanoe," 356–57.

24. William Henry Harrison to William Claus, November 18, 1811, and Adam Walker journal, November 7, 1811, in *MLWHH*, 1:622–23, 701; Carlson, "Peters' Version of Tippecanoe," 42.

25. Winkler, *Tippecanoe*, 68–69, 72–73; Joseph Barron statement dated 1840, George Winter Papers; Whicker, "Shabonee's Account of Tippecanoe," 357, 359; John Lalime to Benjamin Howard, February 4, 1812, and Thomas Forsyth to Howard, February 18, 812, RG 107, M221, NA; Harrison to William Eustis, November 18, 1811, and Adam Walker journal, both in *MLWHH*, 1:623–25, 701; Watts, "Larrabee's Account of Tippecanoe," 243–45; Naylor, "Battle of Tippecanoe," 168.

26. Edmunds, *Shawnee Prophet*, 113–14; *Cincinnati Liberty Hall*, December 25, 1811; Dowd, "Thinking and Believing," 323.

27. Watts, "Larrabee's Account of Tippecanoe," 245; James Miller to Ruth Miller, November 10, 1811, James Miller Papers, OHC; *Cincinnati Liberty Hall*, December 25, 1811; John Johnston to William Eustis, November 28, 1811, John Lalime to Benjamin Howard, February 4, 1812, and Thomas Forsyth to Howard, February 18, 1812, RG 107, M221, NA; Matthew Elliott to Isaac Brock, January 12, 1812, C Series, vol. 728:62;

William Henry Harrison to Eustis, November 8 and 18, 1811, in *MLWHH*, 1:606, 626; Radin, "Winnebago Tribe," 72–73.

17: FROM THE ASHES OF PROPHETSTOWN

1. *New York Spectator*, February 19, 1812; *Cincinnati Liberty Hall*, December 12, 1811; Mortimer, "Ohio Frontier in 1812," 207; Kanon, "Scared from Their Sins," 21–22, 25, 26; Ross, "New Madrid Earthquake," 87–88, 89–90; John R. Stokes to Thomas Worthington, February 23, 1812, Thomas Worthington Diaries and Letter-books, LC.

2. Sugden, "Early Pan-Indianism," 290–92; Mortimer, "Ohio Frontier in 1812," 206; *Louisiana Gazette*, June 30, 1811; William Clark to William Eustis, March 22, 1812, RG 107, M221, NA; Hunter, *Memoirs*, 42; *Missouri Gazette and Public Advertiser*, March 21 and May 9, 1812.

3. William Clark to William Eustis, January 22, 1811, RG 107, M221, NA; *Louisiana Gazette*, June 30, 1811; McDermott, "Audubon's 'Journey,'" 159–60.

4. Hunter, *Memoirs*, 43–48; Sugden, "Early Pan-Indianism," 293–95.

5. Ninian Edwards to William Eustis, March 3, March 23, April 24, 1812, and William Clark to Eustis, January 12, 1812, both in RG 107, M221, NA.

6. Radin, "Winnebago Tribe," 73; Wyandot chiefs to the President, February 5, 1812, in *ASP-IA*, 1:795; William Henry Harrison to William Eustis, January 7, 1812, in *MLWHH*, 2:5–6; William Wells to John Johnston, December 3, 1811, Ninian Edwards to William Eustis, March 3, 1812, and Robert Forsyth to James Rhea, March 10, 1812, all in RG 107, M221, NA; Crawford, "Bacon's Journal," 384; *Cincinnati Liberty Hall*, December 25, 1811; Dowd, "Thinking and Believing," 324; Edmunds, *Potawatomis*, 177; Johnston to Daniel Drake, December 3, 1811, 11YY15, Tecumseh Papers, DCWHS; Johnston to Eustis, December 5, 1811, in Hill, *John Johnston*, 56; *Western Sun*, December 28, 1811; Niles, *Tippecanoe Text-Book*, 12.

7. William Eustis to William Henry Harrison, January 17, 1812, RG 75, M1, NA.

8. *Cincinnati Liberty Hall*, December 25, 1811, and February 19, 1812; Thomas Fish to Return J. Meigs, January 14, 1812, and Benjamin F. Stickney to William Eustis, May 7, 1812, both in RG 107, M221, NA; Matthew Elliott to Isaac Brock, January 12, 1812, C Series, vol. 728:62, NAC.

9. B. Drake, *Life of Tecumseh*, 56; Anthony Shane statement, 12YY46–47, 58, Tecumseh Papers, DC, WHS; Little Turtle to William Henry Harrison, January 25, 1812, William Claus to Isaac Brock, June 16, 1812, and William Wells to William Eustis, all in Esarey, *Messages and Letters*, 2:18, 27, 62; William Hull to Eustis, March 4, 1812, RG 107, M221, NA; Dowd, "Thinking and Believing," 325–27.

10. William Henry Harrison to William Eustis, February 19 and 26, 1812, in *MLWHH*, 2:25–26; Harrison to Eustis, March 4, 1812, RG 107, M221, NA; "Prophet's Speech," RG 10, vol. 32:18831, NAC.

11. *National Intelligencer*, April 4, 1812; Crawford, "Bacon's Journal," 385–86.

12. *National Intelligencer*, March 3, 1812; Maurice Blandon to William Wells, January 12, 1812, Nicholas Boilvion to Benjamin Howard, January 5, 1812, Nathan Heald to Wells,

February 7, 1812, Ninian Edwards to William Eustis, January 25, February 16, and March 3, 1812, and Howard to Eustis, January 13, 1812, all in RG 107, M221, NA; Cruikshank, "Hull's Invasion," 218.

13. William Wells to William Eustis, February 10, 1812, in *MLWHH*, 2:21–22; Robert Forsyth to James Rhea, March 10, 1812, and Thomas Forsyth to Benjamin Howard, February 18, 1812, both in RG 107, M221, NA.

14. William Wells to William Eustis, March 1, 1812, in *MLWHH*, 2:27; "Declaration of Melessello a Sac Indian to John Johnston at Fort Madison, July 3, 1812," in C. E. Carter, *Territorial Papers* 14:578–79; John Johnston to Thomas Worthington, January 23, 1812, Thomas Worthington Papers, OHC; Robert Forsyth to Ninian Edwards, June 8, 1812, Thomas Forsyth Papers, MHS; James Neelly to William Eustis, May 13, 1812, RG 107, M221, NA; Cass, "Discourse," 105; *Missouri Gazette and Public Advertiser*, March 21, 1812; *New York Literary World*, May 3, 1857; Sugden, *Tecumseh*, 272–73.

15. John Shaw to James Rhea, March 1, 1812, RG 107, M221, NA; *National Intelligencer*, February 29, 1812; William Wells to William Eustis, March 1, 1812, in *MLWHH*, 2:27; Horsman, "British Indian Policy," 63–64.

16. Edmunds, *Potawatomis*, 179, and *Shawnee Prophet*, 124; *Western Sun*, April 18 and 25, 1812; *New York Commercial Advertiser*, May 19, 1812; *Charleston City Gazette*, June 15, 1812; *Frankfort Argus*, May 21, 1812; William Henry Harrison to William Eustis, April 14, 1812, in *MLWHH*, 2:31.

17. John Badollet to Albert Gallatin, April 29, 1812, in Thornbrough, *Badollet-Gallatin Correspondence*, 226–27.

18. *Western Sun*, April 18 and 25, 1812; Adam Walker journal, April 11, 1812, and William Henry Harrison to William Eustis, May 13, 1812, in *MLWHH*, 1:708, 2:48–49; Edmund Munger to Return J. Meigs, Return Jonathan Meigs Papers, OHC; Thomas Forsyth to William Clark, Thomas Forsyth Papers, DC, WHS.

19. William Claus to Isaac Brock, June 16, 1812, in *MLWHH*, 2:61, 126; Benjamin Stickney to William Hull, May 25, 1812, in Thornbrough, *Letter Book*, 128–29; Reuben Atwater to William Eustis, January 21, 1812, RG 107, M221, NA; Clarke, *Wyandots*, 87–88.

20. "Speeches of Indians at Massassinway [*sic*]," May 15, 1812, in *MLWHH*, 2:50–53; Edmunds, *Shawnee Prophet*, 122–23; Benjamin Stickney to William Henry Harrison, April 18, 1812, RG 107, M221, NA.

21. Tecumseh to Matthew Elliott, June 8, 1812, in *MLWHH*, 2:60–61.

22. William Claus to Isaac Brock, June 16, 1812, and William Henry Harrison to William Eustis, July 7, 1812, in *MLWHH*, 2:61–62, 66; Benjamin Stickney to William Hull, May 25 and June 20, 1812, in Thornbrough, *Letter Book*, 128–29, 141–42; Edmunds, *Potawatomis*, 182.

18: INTO THE MAELSTROM

1. Hall, "Canadian Annexation Sentiment," 372–80.
2. Quoted in Hickey, *War of 1812*, 26.
3. "President Madison's War Message," June 1, 1812, https://edsitement.neh.gov /curriculum-unit/president-madisons-1812-war-message.

4. Adams, *War of 1812*, 3; S. R. Brown, *Campaigns*, 154; "Memorial to Congress by the Citizens of the Michigan Territory [1812]," in *MPHC*, 40:348–49; Cruikshank, "Hull's Invasion," 212–14.

5. William Hull to Charles Scott, May 12, 1812, War of 1812 Collection, Lily Library, IU; John Johnston, *Recollections*, 32–33; Trimble, "Autobiography and Correspondence," 37.

6. Trimble, "Autobiography and Correspondence," 37; S. Williams, *Two Western Campaigns*, 14–15; Cruikshank, "Hull's Invasion," 220; *Muskingham Messenger*, July 22, 1812; William Hull to E. Watson, May 31, 1812, War of 1812 Collection, Lily Library, IU; Hull to William Eustis, June 9, 1812, RG 107, M221, NA.

7. *Western Sun*, June 16, 1812; Sugden, *Tecumseh*, 274; Benjamin Stickney to William Hull, June 20, 1812, in Thornbrough, *Letter Book*, 141; Stephen Johnston to Lyman C. Draper, August 23, 1880, 11Y3, Tecumseh Papers, DC, WHS.

8. Benjamin Stickney to William Hull, June 20, 1812, and Stickney to John Johnston, June 22, 1812, in Thornbrough, *Letter Book*, 141–46; William Wells to William Henry Harrison, July 22, 1812, in *MLWHH*, 2:76–77; *American and Commercial Advertiser*, July 30, 1812; John B. Glegg to Edward Baynes, November 11, 1812, in *MPHC*, 15:181.

9. Carter-Edwards, "War of 1812," 25–27; Isaac Brock to George Prévost, December 3, 1811, in *MPHC*, 25:290–91.

10. George Prévost to Isaac Brock, July 7 and 10, 1812, in *LCSIB*, 199, 201; Carter-Edwards, "War of 1812," 28.

11. Wood, *Empire of Liberty*, 672–74; Adams, *War of 1812*, 2–4.

12. Parish, "Lucas Journal," 357, 359–61; Benjamin Stickney to William Eustis, June 7, 1812, in Thornbrough, *Letter Book*, 136.

13. Witherell, "Reminiscences," 302; Beall, "Journal," 793; Richardson, "Canadian Campaign—No. I," 543; Lewis Bond Journal, 183, LC; Douglas, *Uppermost Canada*, 31.

14. M. C. Dixon to R. H. Bruyeres, July 8, 1812, in *DRIC*, 49; Clarke, *Wyandotts*, 99; "Extract of a Letter from a Gentleman of Detroit to His Friend," July 7, 1812, RG 107, M221, NA; Thomas St. George to Isaac Brock, July 8, 1812, in *DRIC*, 43–44, and Matthew Elliott to William Claus, July 15, 1812, RG 10, vol. 28:16393–94, NAC; Forbes, *Trial of General Hull*, 101, 146.

15. Coffin, *1812: War and Its Moral*, 199; William H. Merritt, "Journal," in Wood, *Canadian War* 3, pt. 2, 549; Thomas St. George to Brock, July 8, 1812, *DRIC*, 44–46; Cruikshank, "Hull's Invasion," 234–35.

16. Antal, *Wampum Denied*, 40; Benjamin Stickney to William Eustis, July 19, 1812, RG 107, M221, NA; Cruikshank, "Hull's Invasion," 235.

17. Anthony Shane statement 12YY60–61, Tecumseh Papers, DC, WHS; 18S171, 23S173, Lyman C. Draper's Notes, DC, WHS; Martin Hardin to Henry Clay, December 2, 1812, Frontier War Papers, DC, WHS.

18. Blanchard, *Discovery and Conquests*, 310. Lewis Cass offered a similar explanation. Cass, who served under Hull, later became governor of the Michigan Territory. In that capacity he became well acquainted with Tenskwatawa, who related to him and his private secretary much of his brother's and his own lives and beliefs. "The arguments used to induce Indians to join in a war against the Americans were well calculated to produce the intended effect," Cass wrote. "They were told that the

Americans, who were intruders upon their lands, were to be driven back—that they would never terminate the war until the Americans were driven back over the Allegheny Mountains. That, after this event, the Indians should be put into possession of their ancient hunting grounds and placed under the protection of the British government, who would guarantee their independence." Cass, "Discourse," 105.

19. William Wells to William Henry Harrison, July 22, 1812, in *MLWHH*, 2:76–77.

20. Thomas St. George to Isaac Brock, July 15, 1812, in *DRIC*, 61–62; Matthew Elliott to William Claus, July 26, 1812, RG 10, vol. 28:16395–95, NAC.

21. Matthew Elliott to William Claus, July 15, 1812, in *DRIC*, 62.

22. Procter and Procter, *Lucubrations*, 343; Fairchild, *Journal*, 11; Coffin, *1812: War, and Its Moral*, 200; Edmunds, "Main Poc," 266; Quaife, *War on Detroit*, 248.

23. Quaife, *War on Detroit*, 251, 257–59; Parish, "Lucas Journal," 380–81, 390–92; *National Intelligencer*, August 6, 1812; Turney, "Correspondence of Denny," 289–90.

24. Isaac Brock to George Prévost, November 10, 1811, in *LCSIB*, 126; Lomax, *41st Regiment*, 48–49; George B. Catlin, *Story of Detroit*, 180; Antal, *Wampum Denied*, 68–69.

25. Henry Procter to Isaac Brock, July 26, 1812, in *MPHC*, 15:119–20; Procter and Procter, *Lucubrations*, 340, 342–43.

26. Porter Hanks to William Hull, August 4, 1812, RG 107, M221, NA; Clarke, *Wyandotts*, 88; Procter and Procter, *Lucubrations*, 335.

27. Cass, "Indian Treaties," 423; Cruikshank, "Hull's Invasion," 253; Clarke, *Wyandotts*, 90–97.

28. Henry Procter to Roger Sheaffe, November 20, 1812, RG 59, War of 1812 Papers, NA; Procter and Procter, *Lucubrations*, 342–43.

29. Henry Procter to Isaac Brock, August 11, 1812, in *SBD*, 1:455–56; Hull to the Secretary of War, July 29 and August 4, 1812, RG 107, M221, NA; Cass, "Indian Treaties," 424; Cruikshank, "Hull's Invasion," 254, 257; Matthew Elliott to William Claus, August 8, 1812, RG 10, vol. 28:16396, NAC.

30. Quaife, "Story of Brownstown," 68–69; Dalliba, *Battle of Brownstown*, 10; Parish, "Lucas Journal," 395–99; "General Order, Sandwich," August 7, 1812, in *DRIC*, 125–26; Cruikshank, "Hull's Invasion," 256–57; Antal, *Wampum Denied*, 87n.

31. Casselman, *Richardson's War*, 27–29; Quaife, *War on Detroit*, 91; Richardson, "Canadian Campaign—No. I," 543.

32. Hatch, *War of 1812 in Northwest*, 34, 36.

33. William Hull to William Eustis, August 7, 1812, RG 107, M221, NA; Bishop, "Battle of Monguagon," 466–67; Cruikshank, "Hull's Invasion," 258–63; Quaife, *War on Detroit*, 93–98; Dalliba, *Battle of Brownstown*, 18–25; Casselman, *Richardson's War*, 33–46; Lewis Peckham to his father, September 8, 1812, Lewis Peckham Letter, IHS; Edmunds, "Main Poc," 266–67; Matthew Elliott to William Claus, August 10, 1812, RG 10, vol. 28:16398, NAC; "Battle of Monguagon," 21S60, Lyman C. Draper's Notes, DC, WHS; *American Advocate*, September 17, 1812.

34. Henry Procter to Isaac Brock, August 11, 1812, in *DRIC*, 136; Calvin Austin to Return J. Meigs, August 11, 1812, Return Jonathan Meigs Papers, OHC; William H. Merritt, "Journal," in *SBD* 3, pt. 2, 553; Samuel Williams to Eliza Williams, August 12 and 14, 1812, Samuel Williams Papers, OHC.

35. Isaac Brock to George Prévost, *SBD*, 1:467.

19: KINDRED SPIRITS

1. Cruikshank, "Hull's Invasion," 265–71; Read, *Brock*, 152; Laxer, *Tecumseh and Brock*, 65–76; Hatch, *War of 1812 in Northwest*, 63; Casselman, *Richardson's War*, 204.

2. William Claus to Matthew Elliott, August 11, 1812, RG 10, vol. 28, NAC; *LCIB*, 243–44.

3. Isaac Brock to Lord Liverpool, August 29, 1812, in *SBD*, 1:508.

4. Edgar, *Brock*, 245–47; *LCIB*, 244–45, 262; Coffin, *1812: War and Its Moral*, 47.

5. Isaac Brock to George Prévost, September 28, 1812, RG 8, C Series, vol. 677:94, NAC; Brock to Lord Liverpool, August 29, 1812, in *SBD*, 1:508; Cruikshank, "Hull's Invasion," 274–75.

6. Isaac Brock to William Hull, August 15, 1813, in *SBD*, 1:461; John Askin to Charles Askin, September 16, 1812, in Quaife, *Askin Papers* 2:731; Cruikshank, "Hull's Invasion," 276, 282.

7. Quaife, *War on Detroit*, 107–8; Rauch, "Stain upon Nation," 148.

8. Coffin, *1812: War and Its Moral*, 47; Casselman, *Richardson's War*, 51–54; William H. Merritt, "Journal," in *SBD*, 3, pt. 2, 545; Cruikshank, "Hull's Invasion," 279–81; Byfield, *Narrative*, 65; William Hull to William Eustis, August 26, 1812, RG 107, M221, NA.

9. Antal, *Wampum Denied*, 97; Charles Askin journal, August 15–16, 1812, in Quaife, *Askin Papers*, 2:717; Parish, "Lucas Journal," 415; Hatch, *War of 1812 in Northwest*, 30–31; Witherell, "Reminiscences," 305–6.

10. Charles Askin journal, August 17–18, 1812, in Quaife, *Askin Papers*, 2:720; James, *Military Occurrences*, 1:290; B. Drake, *Life of Tecumseh*, 165.

11. *Montreal Gazette*, September 3, 1812; S. R. Brown, *Campaigns*, 155–56.

12. Hatch, *War of 1812 in Old Northwest*, 114–15.

13. Tupper, *Family Records*, 25.

14. Heath, *William Wells*, 358–60; Edmunds, *Potawatomis*, 185–86, and "Main Poc," 267; *National Intelligencer*, November 3, 1812.

15. Charles Askin journal, August 19, 1812, in Quaife, *Askin Papers*, 2:721–24; Peter Chambers to Henry Procter, August 24, 1812, RG 8, C Series, vol. 688A:229–31, NAC; B. Drake, *Life of Tecumseh*, 226–27; Forbes, *Trial of General Hull*, 33; Horsman, *Matthew Elliott*, 196.

16. H. S. Knapp, *Maumee Valley*, 204–5; Witherell, "Reminiscences," 315–16.

17. Antal, *Wampum Denied*, 113; Lewis Bond to Henry Procter, December 27, 1812, in *MPHC*, 8:637–38; *War*, October 17, 1812.

18. Edward Dewar to Henry Procter, August 28, 1812, RG 8, C Series, vol. 688A:222, NAC; Edward Baynes to Isaac Brock, September 10, 1812, in *LCIB*, 290; Stewart, "Recollections," 327; Horsman, *Matthew Elliott*, 196–97; William Foster to William Eustis, September 22, 1812, RG 107, M221, NA.

19. Antal, *Wampum Denied*, 103; Adams, *War of 1812*, 23.

20: A MAN OF MERCY

1. Benjamin Stickney to William Eustis, July 19, 1812, RG 107, M221, NA; *Federal Gazette*, August 25, 1812.

2. Declaration of Mellessello, July 2, 1812, and Ninian Edwards to William Eustis, July 21, 1812, in C. E. Carter, *Territorial Papers*, 14:578–79, 16:244.

3. William Wells to the Secretary of War, July 22, 1812, in *DRIC*, 79; Edwards to the Secretary of War, July 21, 1812, in C. E. Carter, *Territorial Papers*, 16:247.

4. William Wells to the Secretary of War, July 22, 1812, in *DRIC*, 79–80; *Federal Republican*, August 10, 1812; William Henry Harrison to the Secretary of War, August 10, 1812, RG 107, M221, NA.

5. William Wells to William Henry Harrison and Ninian Edwards, July 22, 1812, in *MLWHH*, 2:76–78; Edwards to William Eustis, August 8, 1812, RG 107, M221, NA; *Weekly Register*, August 29, 1812.

6. Zachary Taylor to William Henry Harrison, September 10, 1812, in *MLWHH*, 2:125, 126; Hamilton, *Zachary Taylor*, 21, 40; Skaggs, *William Henry Harrison*, 74.

7. Beckwith, *Illinois and Indiana Indians*, 133–35; Zachary Taylor to William Henry Harrison, September 10, 1812, in *MLWHH*, 2:126–27; Hamilton, *Zachary Taylor*, 42; *War*, October 10, 1812; T. M. Hopkins, *John Ketchum*, 13; Edmunds, *Shawnee Prophet*, 130–31.

8. Edmunds, *Potawatomis*, 188–89; Isaac Brock to George Prévost, September 18, 1812, in *SBD*, 1:592–94; Brock to Prévost, September 28, 1812, in *LCIB*, 320.

9. William Claus to John Johnston, October 8, 1812, DCFF, NAC; Henry Procter to Roger Sheaffe, October 30, 1812, RG 8, C Series, vol. 677:163, NAC; *National Intelligencer*, October 15, 1812; S. C. Hugunin to Lyman C. Draper, 8YY56, Tecumseh Papers, DC, WHS; *Pittsfield Sun*, October 8, 1812; Benjamin Stickney to William Henry Harrison, September 29, 1812, in Thornbrough, *Letter Book*, 174.

10. Peckham, "Recent Documentary Acquisitions," 416–17; Hedges, "Early Recollections," 171; Darnell, *Journal*, 17; Edmunds, "Main Poc," 267; Byfield, *Narrative*, 67; Adam Muir to Henry Procter, September 30, 1812, and Henry Procter to Roger Sheaffe, October 30, 1812, in *MPHC*, 15:151–54, 174; Procter to Isaac Brock, October 3, 1812, RG 8, C Series, vol. 677:102, NAC.

11. Sugden, *Tecumseh*, 316–17; Edward W. Tupper to Return J. Meigs, February 16, 1813, Return Jonathan Meigs Papers, OHC; William Eustis to William Henry Harrison, September 17, 1812, and Harrison to Isaac Shelby, September 1812, in *MLWHH*, 2:136–37; Skaggs, *William Henry Harrison*, 109; Antal, *Wampum Denied*, 131; Isaac Brock to Henry Procter, n.d., in *LCIB*, 326–27.

12. George Prévost to Earl Bathurst, October 5, 1812, in *MPHC*, 25:258–60.

13. Cruikshank, "Harrison and Proctor [*sic*]," 130–38; John Johnston to William Eustis, October 14, 1812, RG 107, M221, NA; William Henry Harrison to John Campbell, November 25, 1812, in *MLWHH*, 2:231; Edward W. Tupper to Return J. Meigs, January 26, 1813, Return Jonathan Meigs Papers, OHC; *Ohio Centinel*, December 23, 1812.

14. Samuel Hopkins to Isaac Shelby, November 27, 1812, in *MLWHH*, 2: 232–34; Matson, "Shau-be-na," 418; Poulson's *American Daily Advertiser*, December 21, 1812; Sugden, *Tecumseh*, 318; Anthony Shane statement, 12YY4, Tecumseh Papers, DC, WHS.

15. Kinietz and Voegelin, *Shawnese Traditions*, 20–21.

16. Cruikshank, "Harrison and Proctor [*sic*]," 138–39; Matthew Elliott to William Claus, October 28, 1812, and Elliott to Thomas St. George, November 11, 1812, in *MPHC*, 15:173, 182–83; Nye, "Tupper," 4, WRHS; Edward W. Tupper to Return J. Meigs, November 9,

1812, and Nathan Newsom, "Summary of a Journey," 33–37, both in Return Jonathan Meigs Papers, OHC.

17. Edward Munger to Return J. Meigs, December 30, 1812, Return Jonathan Meigs Papers, OHC; Matson, "Shau-be-na," 418; Edmunds, "Main Poc," 267; William Henry Harrison to William Eustis, December 21, 1812, James Morrison to Henry Clay, December 24, 1812, and Richard M. Johnson to Harrison, December 26, 1812, all in RG 107, M221, NA.

18. Skaggs, *William Henry Harrison*, 140–46; Procter and Procter, "Campaigns," 422, and *Lucubrations*, 339; Henry Procter to Roger Sheaffe, January 13, 1813, in *SBD*, 2:3; John Johnston to William Henry Harrison, February 4, 1813, William Henry Harrison Papers, LC.

19. *Poulson's American Daily Advertiser*, February 26, 1813.

20. Thomas Forsyth to William Clark, December 23, 1812, 9T54, Thomas Forsyth Papers, DC, WHS; "Report of August LaRoche and Louis Chevalier, St. Louis," April 4, 1813, RG 107, M221, NA.

21. G. Procter, *Tales of Chivalry*, 78–79; Procter and Procter, "Campaigns," 422, and *Lucubrations*, 339, 341–42; George Prévost to Earl Bathurst, February 27, 1813, in *MPHC*, 25:431; Henry Procter to Roger Sheaffe, April 3, 1813, RG 8, C Series, vol. 678:228, NAC.

22. R. Spencer, "Gibraltar of the Maumee," i–ii, 98–99; John Armstrong to William Henry Harrison, March 5, 1813, in *War*, March 15, 1813; Harrison to James Monroe, March 17, 1813, in *MPHC*, 15:387; Harrison to Armstrong, April 21, 1813, RG 107, M221, NA.

23. James Morrison to Duncan McArthur, April 12, 1813, and William Henry Harrison to John Armstrong, April 17 and 21, 1813, RG 107, M221, NA.

24. Nelson, "Dudley's Defeat," 20; Peter Chambers to Noah Freer, May 13, 1813, and Henry Procter to George Prévost, May 14, 1813, in *MPHC*, 15:290, 294; Lindley, *Captain Cushing*, 102–3; Procter and Procter, *Lucubrations*, 343–44; McAfee, *Late War*, 281–82.

25. R. Spencer, "Gibraltar of the Maumee," 101–2; Henry Procter to George Prévost, May 14, 1812, in *MPHC*, 15:294.

26. Peter Chambers to Noah Freer, May 13, 1813, in *MPHC*, 15:290; Casselman, *Richardson's War*, 148–49; Salsich, "Siege of Fort Meigs," 40–41; McAfee, *Late War*, 285; Lindley, *Captain Cushing*, 103; Nelson, "Dudley's Defeat," 24.

27. Nelson, "Dudley's Defeat," 14, 25, 27–28; McAfee, *Late War*, 288–89; Joseph R. Underwood, "Col. Dudley's Defeat – May 5, 1813," 6YY23, Tecumseh Papers, DC, WHS.

28. McAfee, *Late War*, 290–91; Klinck and Talman, *John Norton*, 321; Nelson, "Dudley's Defeat," 28.

29. Joseph R. Underwood, "Col. Dudley's Defeat," 6YY23, Tecumseh Papers, DC, WRS; Isaac Shelby to Green Clay, June 18, 1813, War of 1812 Miscellaneous Collection, WRHS; Asa Green to Green Clay, June 9, 1813, AC, NL; Combs, "Dudley's Defeat," 4–6; Christian, "Campaign of 1813," 5; Nelson, Dudley's Defeat," 32–34.

30. G. Ewing to J. H. James, May 2, 1818, 2YY180, Tecumseh Papers, DC, WHS; Combs, "Dudley's Defeat," 7–8; Christian, "Campaign of 1813," 5; Joseph R. Underwood, "Col. Dudley's Defeat," 6YY23, Tecumseh Papers, DC, WHS; Asa Green to Green Clay, June 9, 1813; Byfield, *Narrative*, 70; *Ohio Fredonian*, May 27, 1813; Statement of Black

Hoof, et. al., May 19, 1813, enclosed in John Wingate to William Henry Harrison, June 10, 1813, William Henry Harrison Papers, LC.

31. Joseph R. Underwood, "Col. Dudley's Defeat," 6YY23, Tecumseh Papers, DC, WHS; Christian, "Campaign of 1813," 6; Klinck and Talman, *John Norton*, 321–22; Casselman, *Richardson's War*, 153–54; Billy Caldwell interview, 17S212, and Samuel Stivers interview, 19S122, in Lyman C. Draper's Notes, DC, WRHS.

32. Casselman, *Richardson's War*, 154.

33. Combs, "Dudley's Defeat," 11; "Border History and Biography," 17S219–220, and Joseph Markle interview, 19S248, in Lyman C. Draper's Notes, DC, WHS; Joseph R. Underwood, "Col. Dudley's Defeat," 6YY23, Leslie Combs to George McLaughlin, February 18, 1863, 6YY22, and Combs to Lyman C. Draper, 6YY21, all in Tecumseh Papers, DC, WHS; Samuel Finley to Thomas Worthington, June 1, 1813, Thomas Worthington Papers, OHC.

34. John Hunt interview, 21S65–66, Lyman C. Draper's Notes, DC, WHS; Nancy Wright to Lyman C. Draper, February 18, 1879, 6YY18, and Joseph Underwood, "Col. Dudley's Defeat," 6YY23, Tecumseh Papers, DC, WHS; Nelson, "Dudley's Defeat," 39; *Ohio Fredonian*, May 27, 1813.

35. Statement of Black Hoof, et. al., May 19, 1813, enclosed in John Wingate to William Henry Harrison, June 10, 1813, William Henry Harrison Papers, LC.

36. Peter Chambers to Noah Freer, May 13, 1813, and Henry Procter to George Prévost, May 14, 1813, in *MPHC*, 15:291, 295–96; Edmunds, *Shawnee Prophet*, 135; Procter and Procter, *Lucubrations*, 346.

37. Antal, *Wampum Denied*, 230–31; Lomax, *41st Regiment*, 73; Procter and Procter, *Lucubrations*, 346.

21: AN ADEQUATE SACRIFICE TO INDIAN OPINION

1. Henry Procter to Robert McDouall, May 14, 1813, in *MPHC*, 15:297; Sugden, *Tecumseh*, 355; Edmunds, *Shawnee Prophet*, 135.

2. Henry Procter to Robert McDouall, June 19, 1813, Procter to John Sherbrooke, June 15, 1813, Procter to McDouall, June 28, 1813, and Procter to George Prévost, July 13, 1813, all in RG 8, C Series, vol. 679:107, 110, 155, NAC; Antal, *Wampum Denied*, 236–46.

3. Wright, *John Hunt Memoirs*, 25.

4. Robert Dickson to Noah Freer, June 23, 1813, in *MPHC*, 15:321–23; Henry Procter to George Prévost, July 13, 1813, RG 8, C Series, vol. 679:86, NAC; Procter to Robert McDouall, July 4, 1813, in *SBD*; Procter and Procter, *Lucubrations*, 348–49, and "Campaigns," 426.

5. Casselman, *Richardson's War*, 177; Coffin, *1812: War and Its Moral*, 210–11; Procter and Procter, "Campaigns," 426; Edmunds, *Shawnee Prophet*, 135.

6. Antal, *Wampum Denied*, 269n; *Philadelphia Democratic Press*, July 10, 1813; Lossing, *Pictorial Field-Book*, 496.

7. *National Intelligencer*, August 28, 1813; Lindley, *Captain Cushing*, 119–21; Casselman, *Richardson's War*, 177; *Kentucky Argus*, September 9, 1813; John Hunt interview, 21S67,

Lyman C. Draper's Notes, and William Gaines to Lyman C. Draper, December 4, 1881, 5YY147, both in Tecumseh Papers, in DC, WHS; Casselman, *Richardson's War*, 177; Lossing, *Pictorial Field-Book*, 498.

8. Lindley, *Captain Cushing*, 121–22; William Gaines to Lyman C. Draper, December 4, 1881, 5YY147, Tecumseh Papers, DC, WHS; Casselman, *Richardson's War*, 178; *Kentucky Argus*, September 9, 1813; Henry Clay to William Henry Harrison, July 26, 1813, in *MLWHH*, 2:499–500; *National Intelligencer*, August 28, 1813.

9. William Henry Harrison to John Armstrong, August 4, 1813, and George Croghan to Harrison, August 5, 1813, in *MLWHH*, 2:512–14; Lossing, *Pictorial Field-Book*, 501; Klinck and Talman, *John Norton*, 340; Henry Procter to George Prévost, August 9, 1813, in *SBD*, 2:44; Procter and Procter, "Campaigns," 426–27.

10. Lossing, *Pictorial Field-Book*, 502–4; Black Hawk, *Autobiography*, 36; George Croghan to William Henry Harrison, August 5, 1813, in *MLWHH*, 2:514–15; Lomax, *41st Regiment*, 75–76; Casselman, *Richardson's War*, 178–81; Edward Baynes to the Adjutant General's Office, September 13, 1813, in *SBD*, 2:50; Byfield, *Narrative*, 77–78.

11. Black Hawk, *Autobiography*, 36; Procter and Procter, "Campaigns," 427; Henry Procter to George Prévost, August 9, 1813, in *SBD*, 2:45.

12. John Norris to A. S. Goodman, April 7, 1869, War of 1812 Miscellaneous Collection, WRHS; Henry Procter to George Prévost, August 9, 1813, in *SBD*, 2:45.

13. B. Drake, *Life of Tecumseh*, 186; Cass, "Indian Treaties," 385–86; Procter and Procter, "Campaigns," 427–28; Antal, *Wampum Denied*, 282; Henry Procter to Edward Baynes, August 19, 1813, Procter to Noah Freer, September 6, 1813, and Robert Barclay to James Yeo, September 1, 1813, in *SBD*, 2:262–63, 267–68.

14. Matthew Elliott to William Claus, August 29, 1813, RG 10, vol. 28:16551, NAC; Cass, "Indian Treaties," 385; Antal, *Wampum Denied*, 280–81.

15. B. Drake, *Life of Tecumseh*, 186–87; Billy Caldwell testimony, in *PCM*, 161, NAC; *New York Gazette*, September 24, 1813.

16. H. H. Tanner, *Atlas*, 116–17.

17. *National Intelligencer*, September 1, 1813; Billy Caldwell testimony, in *PCM*, 158, NAC; Harrison to the Secretary of War, September 8, 1813, in *MLWHH*, 2:537–38.

18. Cass, "Indian Treaties," 425–27; Thatcher, *Indian Biography*, 2:217–19; Billy Caldwell testimony, in *PCM*, 158, and "August 23, 10:00 P. M.—Minutes of an Indian Council at Brownstown," RG 8, C Series, vol. 679:279, NAC.

19. Cass, "Indian Treaties," 428; Finley, *Autobiography*, 441; Bontrager, "Nation of Drunkards," 611; Edmunds, *Shawnee Prophet*, 137.

20. Henry Procter to Francis de Rottenburg, October 23, 1813, in *SBD*, 2:323; Sugden, *Tecumseh*, 357.

21. B. Drake, *Life of Tecumseh*, 187; Procter and Procter, "Campaigns," 429.

22. "Description of Tecumsch as he appeared at a banquet given by the Honorable Jacque Baby, Sept. 1813," Tecumseh Information File, FMNHS.

23. Altoff, "Oliver Hazard Perry," 41; Henry Procter to Francis de Rottenburg, September 12, 1813, RG 8, C Series, vol. 680:71, NAC; Sugden, *Tecumseh*, 356.

24. Henry Procter to Francis de Rottenburg, September 12, 1813, RG 8, C Series, vol. 680:71; Antal, *Wampum Denied*, 288, 293.

22: DEATH ON THE THAMES

1. Coffin, *1812: War and Its Moral*, 219–20; Lomax, *41st Regiment*, 82–83.

2. Henry Procter to Francis de Rottenburg, September 12, 1813, RG 8, C Series, vol. 680:74, NAC; *Defence of Procter*, 10; Augustus Warburton, Billy Caldwell, William Jones, and John Hall testimonies, in *PCM*, 8–9, 156, 179, 236, NAC; Antal, *Wampum Denied*, 300–1.

3. François Baby testimony, and Billy and William Caldwell testimonies, in *PCM*, 151, 163–64, 175–76, NAC; Matthew Elliott to William Claus, October 24, 1813, RG 10, vol. 28:16551, NAC; *Defence of Procter*, 10, 32.

4. John Hall testimony, in *PCM*, 237, NAC; Cass, "Indians of North America," 99; Procter and Procter, *Lucubrations*, 354.

5. Richardson, "Canadian Campaigns," 252.

6. Hickling, "Caldwell and Shabonee," 30; Casselman, *Richardson's War*, 205–7; *War*, November 16, 1813; Peter Navarre interview, 17S208, Lyman C. Draper's Notes, DC, WHS.

7. Richardson, "Canadian Campaigns," 252; William Jones testimony, *PCM*, 180–81; *Defence of Procter*, 10; Procter and Procter, *Lucubrations*, 354–55.

8. "Speech of the Shawnee Prophet to Colonel [William] Caldwell, November 20, 1814," RG 10, vol. 29:17331, NAC.

9. Augustus Warburton, Billy Caldwell, William Jones, and John Hall testimonies, in *PCM*, 20, 159, 181, 237–38, NAC; Matthew Elliott to William Claus, October 24, 1813, RG 10, vol. 28:16551, NAC; *Defence of Procter*, 10–11; Antal, *Wampum Denied*, 304–5; Sugden, *Tecumseh's Last Stand*, 66, 85.

10. Procter and Procter, *Lucubrations*, 356; Henry Procter to Thomas Talbot, September 23, 1813, in Coyne, *Talbot Papers*, 193.

11. Peter Trisler, Jr., to his father, October 8, 1813, Durrett Manuscripts, Chicago History Museum; Edmunds, "Main Poc," 268.

12. William Henry Harrison to John Armstrong, September 30, 1813, in *MLWHH*, 2:555; Matthew Elliott to William Claus, October 24, 1813, RG 10, vol. 28:16552–53, NAC; *Vermont Mirror*, October 27, 1813.

13. Sugden, *Tecumseh*, 362; Procter and Procter, *Lucubrations*, 342; Anthony Shane statement, 11YY8, Tecumseh Papers, DC, WHS.

14. Augustus Warburton testimony, *PCM*, 9, NAC; Sugden, *Tecumseh*, 363; Antal, *Wampum Denied*, 307; Isaac Shelby to Susan Shelby, Isaac Shelby Papers, LC; William Henry Harrison to John Armstrong, September 30, 1813, in *MLWHH*, 2:555; Matthew Elliott to William Claus, October 24, 1813, RG 10, vol. 28:16553, NAC.

15. B. Drake, *Life of Tecumseh*, 191.

16. François Baby and Billy Caldwell testimonies, in *PCM*, 146, 150, 159, NAC.

17. Winkler, *Thames 1813*, 25; Edmunds, "Watchful Safeguard," 192. Black Hoof's age and infirmities compelled him to turn over active leadership of the pro-American Shawnees to the younger Blacksnake and Captain Lewis.

18. Augustus Warburton, François Baby, Allan McLean, and John Hall testimonies, in *PCM*, 10, 146, 150, 221–22, 249; William Henry Harrison to John Armstrong, October 9, 1813, in *MLWHH*, 2:558; Henry Procter to Francis de Rottenburg, October 23, 1813, in

SBD, 2:324; Thomas McRae diary, September 30, 1813, in Cruikshank, *Campaign upon Niagara Frontier*, 3:180; Antal, *Wampum Denied*, 318; Sugden, *Tecumseh*, 364, and *Tecumseh's Last Stand*, 75–77.

19. Sugden, *Tecumseh's Last Stand*, 77; Billy Caldwell and John Hall testimonies, in *PCM*, 138, 245, NAC; Casselman, *Richardson's War*, 226.

20. Henry Procter to Francis de Rottenburg, October 23, 1813, in *SBD*, 2:324–25; Augustus Warburton and William Evans testimonies, in *PCM*, 10, 50, NAC.

21. Augustus Warburton, Peter Chambers, Thomas Coleman, Billy Caldwell, and William Evans testimonies, in *PCM*, 11, 50, 83, 122, 138, 288, NAC; McAfee, *Late War*, 409, 416; Casselman, *Richardson's War*, 231; William Henry Harrison to John Tipton, May 2, 1834, in *MLWHH*, 2:753.

22. William Henry Harrison, October 10, 1813, in *MLWHH*, 2:573; François Baby and Billy Caldwell testimonies, in *PCM*, 138, 147, 162, NAC.

23. Casselman, *Richardson's War*, 225, 231; William Evans, Peter Chambers, and Billy Caldwell testimonies, in *PCM*, 51, 84, 160, NAC; Sugden, *Tecumseh's Last Stand*, 86; Matthew Elliott to William Claus, October 24, 1813, RG 10, vol. 28:16553, NAC.

24. William Evans and Peter Chambers testimonies, in *PCM*, 50–51, 84, NAC; Casselman, *Richardson's War*, 225, 231–32; Coffin, *1812: War and Its Moral*, 225–26.

25. Matthew Elliott to William Claus, October 24, 1813, RG 10, vol. 28:16554; Billy Caldwell testimony, in *PCM*, 160, NAC; Stott, *Greater Evils*, 53, 65.

26. William Henry Harrison to John Armstrong, October 9, 1813, in *MLWHH*, 2:559–60; McAfee, *Late War*, 415–17; Sugden, *Tecumseh's Last Stand*, 86–87, 239n; Stott, *Greater Evils*, 65; *Columbian Gazette*, November 30, 1813; Billy Caldwell testimony, in *PCM*, 163, NAC.

27. Stott, *Greater Evils*, 55; Edmunds, *Shawnee Prophet*, 141.

28. David R. Botsford to Mrs. Teeter, January 6, 1945, Tecumseh Information File, FMNHS; Shabbona interview, 23S185, Lyman C. Draper's Notes, and D. K. Foster to Lyman C. Draper, December 30, 1884, 7YY20, all in Tecumseh Papers, in DC, WHS.

29. Tecumseh K. Holmes to Lyman C. Draper, April 20, 1882, 7YY67, Tecumseh Papers, DC, WHS; Arnold, "Battle of Thames," 30.

30. Arnold, "Battle of Thames," 33–34; Stott, *Greater Evils*, 62, 93.

31. Lossing, *Pictorial Field-Book*, 560; Casselman, *Richardson's War*, 232; Benjamin Drake memoranda, 1YY162, and William Gaines to Lyman C. Draper, November 25, 1881, 5YY46, Tecumseh Papers, DC, WHS; Hedges, "Early Recollections," 172.

32. Augustus Warburton testimony, in *PCM*, 32–33, NAC; Richardson, "Canadian Campaign—III," 253; *London Free Press*, November 6, 1948; Sugden, *Tecumseh's Last Stand*, 105–7; Matthew Elliott to William Claus, RG 10, vol. 28:16555, NAC.

33. Richard Bullock to Richard Friend, December 6, 1813, in Casselman, *Richardson's War*, 232; Lomax, *41st Regiment*, 84; Matthew Dixon testimony, in *PCM*, 103, NAC.

34. Richardson, "Canadian Campaign—III," 253.

35. Coffin, *1812: War and Its Moral*, 227–28; Casselman, *Richardson's War*, 208–9; Augustus Warburton, Peter Chambers, François Baby, Billy Caldwell, Allan McLean, and John Hall testimonies, in *PCM*, 13, 84, 149, 153, 154–55, 161, 227, 256, NAC; Procter and Procter, *Lucubrations*, 357.

36. François Baby and Billy Caldwell testimonies, in *PCM*, 151, 161, NAC; Sugden, *Tecum-

seh, 370, 372; Procter and Procter, *Lucubrations*, 342; C. C. Trowbridge to Lyman C. Draper, July 12, 1882, 5YY1, Tecumseh Papers, DC, WHS; Clifton, "Merchant, Soldier, Broker, Chief," 196.

37. Shabbona interview, 23S186, Lyman C. Draper's Notes, and Simon Kenton interview, 8J59–60, George Rogers Clark manuscript, all in DC, WHS; Hatch, *War of 1812 in Northwest*, 156; Kenton, *Simon Kenton*, 285.

38. Lomax, *41st Regiment*, 85; Byfield, *Narrative*, 80; Bullock to Friend, December 6, 1813, in Casselman, *Richardson's War*, 233; William Evans and Peter Chambers testimonies, in *PCM*, 53, 85, 89, NAC; Procter and Procter, *Lucubrations*, 357.

39. Brunson, *Western Pioneer*, 140–41, and "Death of Tecumseh," 370–71; Fredericksen, "Kentucky at Thames 1813," 104; R. J. Conner notes, June 19, 1891, 7YY21, Tecumseh Papers, DC, WHS; Lossing, *American Historical Record*, 1:285.

40. Wickliffe, "Tecumseh and Thames," 48–49; Thomas Forsyth to Ninian Edwards, March 31, 1816, in Thwaite, "Letter-Book of Thomas Forsyth," 347; Peter Trisler to his father, October 8, 1813, Durrett Manuscript, Chicago Historical Museum; Davidson, "Who Killed Tecumseh," 205; Samuel Theobald to Benson Lossing, January 16, 1861, 7YY36–37, Tecumseh Papers, and Lyman C. Draper's Notes, 18S184–85, in DC, WHS; B. Drake, *Life of Tecumseh*, 62, 197.

41. McAfee diary, October 5, 1813, in McAfee, "McAfee Papers," 127–28.

42. Joseph Desha to A. Mitchell, October 5, 1840, in Padgett, "Joseph Desha," 302–3; Matthew Elliott to William Claus, RG 10, vol. 28:16557, NAC.

43. Richardson, "Canadian Campaign—III," 254.

44. S. C. Hugunin to Lyman C. Draper, April 17, 1874, 8YY56, and Samuel Theobald to Benson Lossing, January 16, 1861, 7YY44, Tecumseh Papers, DC, WHS; Thomas Forsyth to Ninian Edwards, March 31, 1815, in Thwaite, "Letter-Book of Thomas Forsyth," 346–47.

45. Hedges, "Early Recollections," 172; B. Drake, *Life of Tecumseh*, 206; Peter Trisler to his father, October 8, 1813, Durrett Manuscript, Chicago Historical Museum; R. J. Conner notes, June 19, 1891, 7YY21, Tecumseh Papers, DC, WHS; Woodward, *Reminiscences*, 85.

46. Winkler, *Battle of Thames*, 79; Sugden, *Tecumseh's Last Stand*, 133; Chalou, "Red Pawns," 287; Wickliffe, "Tecumseh and Thames," 47; Byfield, *Narrative*, 80.

47. Edmunds, "Watchful Safeguard," 163.

48. Duncan McArthur to Thomas Worthington, October 6, 1813, Thomas Worthington Papers, OHC; McAfee diary, October 5, 1813, in McAfee, "McAfee Papers," 128; R. J. Conner to Lyman C. Draper, June 19, 1891, 8YY21, Tecumseh Papers, DC, WHS; Fredericksen, "Kentucky at Thames 1813," 104; William Henry Harrison to John Tipton, May 2, 1834, in *MLWHH*, 2:749.

49. William Henry Harrison to John Tipton, May 2, 1834, in *MLWHH*, 2:751–52; Harrison to John O'Fallon, April 9, 1834, David Ives Busnell, Jr., Papers, College of William and Mary; Alfred Brunson to Lyman C. Draper, April 26 and May 1, 1882, 7YY30, Samuel Theobald to Draper, January 16, 1861, 7YY38, and William Gaines to Draper, November 25, 1881, 5YY46–47, all in Tecumseh Papers, DC, WHS.

50. Samuel Theobald to Lyman C. Draper, January 16, 1861, 7YY40, Tecumseh Papers,

DC, WHS. No one knows what became of Tecumseh's corpse. For speculation on its possible fate, see St. Denis, *Tecumseh's Bones*.

51. *New York Commercial Advertiser*, November 10, 1813; *War*, November 16, 1813; *American and Commercial Daily Advertiser*, November 19, 1813; *Columbian Gazette*, November 30, 1813.

52. *Lexington Reporter*, November 6, 1813.

23: TWILIGHT OF THE PROPHET

1. Henry Procter to Francis de Rottenburg, October 23, 1813, in *SBD*, 2:327.
2. Sugden, *Tecumseh's Last Stand*, 183–86.
3. George Prévost to Henry Bathurst, RG 8, C Series, vol. 1219:127, NAC.
4. Charles Blue Jacket statement, Lyman C. Draper's Notes, 23S168–69, DC, WHS; "Return of the Western Indians who have arrived at Dundas, as near as can be ascertained, 20 October 1813," RG 10, vol. 28:16519, NAC; William Claus to Edward McMahon, November 4, 1813, RG 8, C Series, vol. 257:176–77, NAC; Martin, *Upper and Lower Canada*, 238–39; Cruikshank, *Battle of Lundy's Lane*, 7.
5. Skaggs, *William Henry Harrison*, 218–22; Young, *General Lewis Cass*, 88–89; *Mercantile Advertiser*, November 8, 1813.
6. Edmunds, "Main Poc," 268.
7. Noah Freer to George Drummond, January 29, 1814, RG 8, C Series, vol. 1222:27, Matthew Elliott to J. B. Glegg, January 31, 1814, RG 8, C Series, vol. 682:101, and Drummond to Freer, February 5, 1814, RG 8, C Series, vol. 257:211–12, all in NAC; Drummond to Freer, February 16, 1814, in *MPHC*, 15:492–93.
8. *Quebec Gazette*, March 24, 1814.
9. George Drummond to George Prévost, RG 8, C Series, vol. 683:33, NAC; Drummond to Prévost, in *MPHC*, 15:534; Edmunds, *Shawnee Prophet*, 144–45; Horsman, *Matthew Elliott*, 218–19.
10. James Givins to William Claus, May 11, 1814, RG 10, vol. 28:16862, NAC.
11. Johnston, "Claus and Norton," 101–4; William Claus to George Drummond, June 22, 1814, and William Caldwell to William Claus, June 22, 1813, in RG 10, vol. 28:17028, 17037–38, NAC.
12. "Speech of Naiwash," RG 10, vol. 28:16889–90, NAC.
13. Charles Blue Jacket statement, Lyman C. Draper's Notes, 23S169, DC, WHS; Adams, *War of 1812*, 174–75; George Drummond to Henry Prévost, July 10, 1814, in Cruikshank, *Campaign upon Niagara Frontier*, 1:35–36; J. A. Clegg to William Caldwell, July 1, 1814—4 p.m., and Caldwell to William Claus, July 2, 1814, in RG 10, vol. 29:17082, 17083, NAC.
14. Klinck and Talman, *John Norton*, 352; Lossing, *Pictorial Field-Book*, 811–12.
15. "Speech of Naiwash," October 6, 1814, RG 10, vol. 29:1751–52, NAC.
16. Matthew Elliott to William Claus, October 14, 1814, George Ironside to Duncan Cameron, October 28, 1814, and "General Return of the Western Indians, 1 November 1814," in RG 10, vol. 29:17271–72, 17316, 17328, NAC; Edmunds, *Shawnee Prophet*, 147–50.

17. "Speech of the Shawnee Prophet to Colonel Caldwell, November 20, 1814," and "Speech of the Shawnee Prophet, [Winter] 1814," in RG 10, vol. 29:17381–82, 17518–20, NAC.

18. Record of the Indian council at Burlington, April 24–27, 1815, RG 10, vol. 30:17857–66, NAC; Sugden, *Tecumseh*, 386.

19. Edmunds, *Shawnee Prophet*, 152.

20. "Speech of the Prophet, August 4, 1815," William Caldwell to William Claus, August 4, 1815, Claus to Caldwell, August 15, 1815, and George Ironside to Caldwell, August 26, 1815, in RG 10, vol. 31:18268–69, 18273, 18309–10, 18342, NAC.

21. "Journal of the proceedings of the commissioners appointed to treat with the Northwest Indians at Detroit," in *ASP-IA*, 2:17–25; *Canton Repository*, September 28, 1815.

22. William James to Frederick Robinson, RG 8, C Series, vol. 258:370–71, NAC; James to Robinson, October 15, 1815, "Speech of the Shawnee Prophet Delivered in Council, November 8, 1815," and John Wilson to Duncan Cameron, December 24, 1815, in RG 10, vol. 31:18548–50, 18742–46, 18758–59, NAC, and William Claus to Francis Gore, RG 10, vol. 4:1927, NAC.

23. Speeches of the Prophet, February 8, 13, and 20, 1816, RG 10, vol. 32:18828–29, 18831–33, NAC.

24. Stockwell, *Other Trail of Tears*, 74.

25. James Witherell to Amy Witherell, April 20, 1816, Benjamin F. Witherell Collection, BHC, DPL; Farmer, *History of Detroit*, 472–73.

26. "Speech from the Shawnee Chief Yealabahcah and the Prophet in Council with Lewis Cass," Lewis Cass Papers, UM; James to Amy Witherell, April 20, 1816, Benjamin F. Witherell Papers, BHC, DPL; *Christian Mirror*, October 20, 1836.

27. Lewis Cass to William H. Crawford, April 24, 1816, and the Crawford to Cass, May 22, 1816, in C. E. Carter, *Territorial Papers*, 10:629–30, 637; Gabriel Godfrey to William Caldwell, July 5, 1815, RG 10, vol. 12:10809, NAC.

28. William Caldwell to Gabriel Godfrey, July 1, 1816, and Godfrey to Caldwell, July 5, 1816, in RG 10, vol. 12:10809–12, NAC.

29. William Caldwell to William Claus, September 2, 1816, RG 10, vol. 12:10818, NAC; John Whistler to Lewis Cass, September 2, 1816, and Lewis Stickney to Cass, December 1, 1816, and January 1, 1817, in RG 75, M1, NA.

30. Martin, *Upper and Lower Canada*, 233, 266, 320, 325.

31. "Return of Indians, Amherstburg," June 24, 1824, RG 10, vol. 42:22527, NAC.

32. "Indian Speeches, June 15, 1820," in *MPHC*, 13:101–3; George Ironside to William Claus, July 25, 1824, RG 10, vol. 42:22507, NAC.

33. John Johnston to Lewis Cass, January 11 and 25, 1826, RG 75, M1, NA; Stockwell, *Other Trail of Tears*, 74; Johnston to Cass, May 30, 1825, in *Niles' Register*, June 25, 1825.

34. George Ironside to William Claus, RG 10, vol. 42:22708, NAC; Charles Trowbridge to Lyman C. Draper, December 12, 1882, 5YY1, Tecumseh Papers, DC, WHS; Kinietz and Voegelin, *Shawnese Traditions*, ix–x, 1–59; Edmunds, *Shawnee Prophet*, 165–68; Farmer, *History of Detroit*, 373, 457, 480, 729, 731, 768–70.

35. Cass, "Indians of North America," 98; "Extract of a Letter from George Ironside, Superintendent of Indians Affairs at the Post of Amherstburg and date December 1825

and Addressed to the Deputy Superintendent of Indians, Fort George," in *MPHC*, 23:128–29.

36. Edmunds, *Shawnee Prophet*, 172–74; William Clark to James Barbour, March 8, 1827, and "Speech of the Shawnee Prophet," April 2, 1827, in RG 75, M234, NA.

37. Edmunds, *Shawnee Prophet*, 174–75; Pierre Menard to William Clark, February 22, 1827, "Speech of the Shawnee Prophet, April 3, 1827," Shawnee Chiefs to the Secretary of War, April 3, 1827, and Graham to Clark, April 4, 1827, all in RG 75, M234, NA.

38. Primm, *Lion of Valley*, 143, 147; T. Spencer, *Old St. Louis*, 110, 116–17; Barry, "William Clark's Diary," 27–33, "Speech of the Prophet to General Clark, August 29 and 30, 1827," and Clark to the Secretary of War, November 23, 1827," all in RG 75, M234, NA.

39. Edmunds, *Shawnee Prophet*, 183.

40. Barnes, "Journal of Isaac McCoy, 1828," 260; Lutz, "Methodist Missions," 164.

41. Johnston, "Account of the Present State," 274; Lutz, "Methodist Missions," 164–65, 168, 169, 170; Warren, "Baptists, Methodists, and Shawnees," 150, 152, 155, 159; "Talk of a Deputation of Shawnees from White River to the President of the United States, July 20, 1832, and An Examination of the Shawnees Who Have Emigrated West of the Mississippi … April 8, 1830," in RG 75, M234, NA.

42. "The Far West, Westport, September 15, 1836," *Christian Mirror*, October 20, 1836.

43. Sarton, "Indian-Loving Catlin," 78; George Catlin, *Letters and Notes*, 2:117–18; Edmunds, *Shawnee Prophet*, 186–87.

44. "The Far West, Westport, September 15, 1836," *Christian Mirror*, October 20, 1836.

Bibliography

BOOKS

Adams, Henry. *The War of 1812.* New York: Cooper Square Press, 1999.

Alford, Thomas W. *Civilization and the Story of the Absentee Shawnees.* Norman: University of Oklahoma Press, 1936; reprint 1979.

American State Papers, Documents, Legislative and Executive, of the Congress of the United States. 38 vols. Washington, D.C.: Gales & Seaton, 1832–61.

Antal, Sandy. *A Wampum Denied: Procter's War of 1812.* Ottawa: Carleton University Press, 1997.

Badger, Joseph. *A Memoir of Rev. Joseph Badger.* Hudson, Ohio: Sawyer, Ingersoll & Co., 1851.

Banta, R. E. *The Ohio.* New York: Rinehart & Co., 1949.

Beard, Reed. *The Battle of Tippecanoe . . . Lives of the Prophet and Tecumseh . . . The Campaign of 1888.* Chicago: Donohue and Henneberry, 1889.

Beckwith, Hiram W., ed. *The Fort-Wayne Manuscript: An Old Writing (Lately Found) Containing Indian Speeches and a Treatise on the Western Tribes.* Chicago: Fergus, 1879.
_____. *The Illinois and Indiana Indians.* Chicago: Fergus, 1884.

[Black Hawk]. *Autobiography of Ma-Ka-Tai-Me-She-Kia-Kiak, or Black Hawk.* Oquawka, Ill.: J. B. Patterson, 1882; reprint 1916.

Blackbird, A. J. *History of the Ottawa and Chippewa Indians of Michigan.* Ypsilanti, Mich.: Job Printing House, 1887.

Blair, Emma H., ed. *The Indian Tribes of the Upper Mississippi Valley and Region of the Great Lakes.* 2 vols. Cleveland: Arthur H. Clark Co., 1912.

Blanchard, Rufus. *Discovery and Conquests of the North-West, with the History of Chicago.* Wheaton, Ill.: R. Blanchard & Co., 1881.

Bottiger, Patrick. *The Borderland of Fear: Vincennes, Prophetstown, and the Invasion of the Miami Homeland.* Lincoln: University of Nebraska Press, 2016.

Brice, Wallace A. *History of Fort Wayne.* Fort Wayne: D. W. Jones & Son, 1868.

Brown, Robert C. *The History of Madison County, Ohio.* Chicago: W. H. Beers, 1883.

Brown, Samuel R. *Views of the Campaigns of the North-Western Army.* Troy, N.Y.: Francis Adancourt, 1814.

Brunson, Alfred. *A Western Pioneer: Or, Incidents of the Life and Times of Rev. Alfred Brunson.* 2 vols. Cincinnati: Hitchcock & Walden, 1872.

Brymner, Douglas, ed. *Report on Canadian Archives 1896.* Ottawa: S. E. Dawson, 1897.

Burnham, Robert. *Great Comets.* Cambridge, U.K.: Cambridge University Press, 2000.

Burton, Agnes. *Journal of Pontiac's Conspiracy*. Detroit: Michigan Society of the Colonial Wars, 1912.

Butterfield, C. W. *An Historical Account of the Expedition against Sandusky Under Col. William Crawford in 1782*. Cincinnati: Robert Clarke & Co., 1873.

_____. *The Washington-Crawford Letters: Being the Correspondence Between George Washington and William Crawford, from 1767 to 1781, Concerning Western Lands*. Cincinnati: Robert Clarke & Co., 1877.

Byfield, Shadrach. *A Narrative of a Light Company Soldier's Service in the Forty-First Regiment of Foot (1807–1814)*. Bradford (U.K.): John Bubb, 1840; reprint 1910.

Calloway, Colin G. *Crown and Calumet: British-Indian Relations, 1783–1815*. Norman: University of Oklahoma Press, 1986.

_____. *The Indian World of George Washington*. New York: Oxford University Press, 2018.

_____. *The Shawnees and the War for America*. New York: Penguin, 2007.

_____. *The Victory with No Name: The Native American Defeat of the First American Army*. Oxford: Oxford University Press, 2015.

Carter, Clarence E., ed. *The Territorial Papers of the United States*. 28 vols. Washington, D.C.: Government Printing Office, 1934–75.

Carter, Harvey L. *The Life and Times of Little Turtle, First Sagamore of the Wabash*. Urbana: University of Illinois Press, 1987.

Casselman, Alexander C. *Richardson's War of 1812*. Toronto: Historical Publishing Co., 1902.

Catlin, George. *Letters and Notes on the Manner, Customs, and Conditions of the North American Indians*. 2 vols. New York: Wiley & Putnam, 1844.

Catlin, George B. *The Story of Detroit*. Detroit: Detroit News, 1926.

Caughey, John W. *McGillivray of the Creeks*. Norman: University of Oklahoma Press, 1938.

Cave, Alfred A. *Prophets of the Great Spirit: Native American Revitalization Movements in Eastern North America*. Lincoln: University of Nebraska Press, 2006.

Cayton, Andrew R. I. *Frontier Indiana*. Bloomington: Indiana University Press, 1978.

Claiborne, James F. H. *Mississippi, as a Province, Territory and State*. 2 vols. Jackson, Miss.: Power & Barksdale, 1880.

Clanin, Douglas E., ed. *The Papers of William Henry Harrison, 1800–1815*. Indianapolis: Indiana Historical Society, 1993 [microform.]

Clarke, Peter D. *Origin and Traditional History of the Wyandotts, and Sketches of Other Indian Tribes of North America. True Traditional Stories of Tecumseh and His League in the Years 1811 and 1812*. Toronto: Hunter, Rose, 1870.

Cleaves, Freeman. *Old Tippecanoe: William Henry Harrison and His Time*. New York: Charles Scribner's Sons, 1937.

Coffin, William F. *1812: The War, and Its Moral: A Canadian Chronicle*. Montreal: John Lovell, 1864.

Collins, Lewis, and Richard H. Collins. *History of Kentucky*. 2 vols. Covington, Ky.: Collins & Co., 1878.

Combs, Leslie. *Col. Wm. Dudley's Defeat Opposite Fort Meigs, May 5th, 1813. Official Reports from Captain Leslie Combs to General Green Clay*. Cincinnati: Spiller & Gates, 1869.

_____. *Narrative of the Life of General Leslie Combs*. Washington, D.C.: J. T. & Lem Towers, 1855.

Coyne, James H. *The Talbot Papers*. Ottawa: Transactions of the Royal Society of Canada, 1909.

Cruikshank, E. A. *The Battle of Lundy's Lane, 25th July 1814*. Welland, Ont.: Tribune Office, 1893.

Cruikshank, E. A., ed. *The Correspondence of Lieut. Governor John Graves Simcoe. 5* vols. Toronto: Ontario Historical Society, 1931.

_____. *The Documentary History of the Campaign upon the Niagara Frontier in the Year 1813*. Part 3, *August to October 1813*. Welland, Ontario: Tribune Office, 1905.

Dalliba, James. *A Narrative of the Battle of Brownstown*. New York: David Longworth, 1816.

Darnell, Elias. *A Journal Containing an Accurate and Interesting Account of the Hardships, Sufferings, Battles, Defeat, and Captivity of Those Heroic Kentucky Volunteers and Regulars Commanded by General Winchester in the Years, 1812–1813*. Philadelphia: Lippincott, Grambo & Co., 1854.

Dawson, Moses. *Historical Narrative of the Civil and Military Services of Major-General William H. Harrison*. Cincinnati: M. Dawson, 1824.

Defence of Major General Proctor [sic], *Tried at Montreal by a General Court Martial, Upon Charges Affecting His Character as a Soldier*. Montreal: John Lovell, 1842.

Denny, Ebenezer. *Military Journal of Major Ebenezer Denny, an Officer in the Revolutionary and Indian Wars*. Philadelphia: J. B. Lippincott & Co., 1859.

Doddridge, Joseph. *Notes on the Settlement and Indian Wars*. Pittsburgh: N. p., 1912.

Douglas, R. Alan. *Uppermost Canada: The Western District and the Detroit Frontier, 1800–1850*. Detroit: Wayne State University Press, 2001.

Dowd, Gregory E. *A Spirited Resistance: The North American Indian Struggle for Unity, 1745–1815*. Baltimore, Md.: Johns Hopkins University Press, 1992.

Downes, Randolph C. *Council Fires on the Upper Ohio*. Pittsburgh: University of Pittsburgh Press, 1977.

Drake, Benjamin. *Life of Tecumseh and of his Brother the Prophet; with a Historical Sketch of the Shawanoe Indians*. Cincinnati: R. M. Rullison, 1856.

Drake, Samuel G. *The Aboriginal Races of North America*. Philadelphia: Charles Desilver, 1860.

Eckert, Allan W. *A Sorrow in Our Heart: The Life of Tecumseh*. New York: Bantam, 1992.

Edgar, Matlia. *The Makers of Canada, General Brock*. Toronto: Morang & Co., 1904.

_____. *Ten Years of Upper Canada in Peace and War, 1805–1815; being the Ridout Letters with Annotations*. Toronto: William Briggs, 1890.

Edmunds, R. David. *The Potawatomis: Keepers of the Fire*. Norman: University of Oklahoma Press, 1978.

_____. *The Shawnee Prophet*. Lincoln: University of Nebraska Press, 1983.

_____. *Tecumseh and the Quest for Indian Leadership*. New York: HarperCollins, 1984.

Edwards, Ninian W. *History of Illinois, from 1778 to 1833; and Life and Times of Ninian Edwards*. Springfield: Illinois State Journal Co., 1870.

Ellet, Elizabeth F. *Pioneer Women of the West*. New York: Charles Scribner, 1856.

Esarey, Logan, ed. *Messages and Letters of William Henry Harrison*. 2 vols. Indianapolis: Indiana Historical Commission, 1922.

Fairfield, G. M. *Journal of an American Prisoner at Fort Malden and Quebec in the War of 1812*. Quebec: Frank Carrel, 1900.

Faragher, John M. *Daniel Boone: The Life and Legend of an American Pioneer*. New York: Henry Holt, 1992.

Farmer, Silas. *The History of Detroit and Michigan, or the Metropolis Illustrated.* Detroit: Silas Farmer & Co., 1884.

Finley, James B. *Autobiography of Rev. James B. Finley, or, Pioneer Life in the West.* Cincinnati: Cranston & Curtis, 1853.

Flick, Alexander C., et al., eds. *The Papers of Sir William Johnson.* 14 vols. Albany: State University of New York Press, 1921–65.

Forbes, John. *Report of the Trial of Brigadier General William Hull; Commanding the Northwestern Army of the United States.* New York: Eastburn, Kirk, & Co., 1814.

Galloway, William A. *Old Chillicothe: Shawnee and Pioneer History.* Xenia, Ohio: Buckeye Press, 1934; reprint 1990.

Gilbert, Bil. *"God Gave Us This Country": Tekamthi and the First American Civil War.* New York: Athenaeum, 1989.

Gilpin, Alec R. *The War of 1812 in the Old Northwest.* East Lansing: Michigan State University Press, 1958.

Gipson, Lawrence H., ed. *The Moravian Indian Mission on White River, Diaries and Letters, May 5, 1799, to November 12, 1806.* Indianapolis: Indiana Historical Bureau, 1938.

Greene, Evarts B. *American Population before the Federal Census of 1790.* New York: Columbia University Press, 1932.

Gunn, Robert L. *Ethnology and Empire: Languages, Literature, and the Making of North American Borderlands.* New York: New York University Press, 2015.

Halbert, H. S., and T. H. Ball. *The Creek War of 1813 and 1814.* Chicago: Donohue & Henneberry, 1895.

Hamilton, Edward P., ed. *Adventures in the Wilderness: The American Journals of Antoine de Bougainville.* Norman: University of Oklahoma Press, 1990.

Hamilton, Holman. *Zachary Taylor: Soldier of the Republic.* Indianapolis: Bobbs-Merrill, 1941.

Hammon, Neal O. *My Father, Daniel Boone: The Draper Interviews with Nathan Boone.* Lexington: University of Kentucky Press, 1999.

Hanna, Charles A. *The Wilderness Trail.* 2 vols. New York: G. P. Putnam's Sons, 1911.

Harvey, Henry. *History of the Shawnee Indians, from the Year 1681 to 1854 Inclusive.* Cincinnati: Ephraim Morgan & Sons, 1855.

Hatch, William S. *A Chapter of the History of the War of 1812 in the Northwest.* Cincinnati: Miami, 1872.

Hazard, Samuel. *Pennsylvania Archives. Selected and Arranged from Original Documents in the Offices of the Secretary of the Commonwealth, Conformably to Acts of the General Assembly, February 15, 1851, and March 1, 1852.* 12 vols. Philadelphia: Joseph Severns & Co., 1853.

Heath, William. *William Wells and the Struggle for the Old Northwest.* Norman: University of Oklahoma Press, 2015.

Heckewelder, John. *An Account of the History, Manners, and Customs of the Indian Nations Who Once Inhabited Pennsylvania and the Neighbouring States.* Philadelphia: Abraham Small, 1819.

———. *A Narrative of the Mission of the United Brethren among the Delaware and Mohegan Indians.* Philadelphia: M'Carty & Davis, 1820.

Hickey, Donald R. *The War of 1812: A Forgotten Conflict.* Champaign: University of Illinois Press, 1990, reprint 2012.

Hildreth, Samuel P. *Pioneer History: Being an Account of the First Examinations of the*

Ohio Valley, and the Early Settlement of the Northwest. Cincinnati: H. W. Derby & Co., 1848.

Hill, Leonard U. *John Johnston and the Indians in the Land of the Three Miamis*. Piqua, Ohio: Stoneman Press, 1957.

An Historical Account of the Expedition against the Ohio Indians in the Year MDCCLXIV, under the Command of Henry Bouquet, Esq. Dublin, Ireland: John Millikin, 1769.

Hodgson, Adam. *Letters from North America*. 2 vols. London: Hurst, Robinson, 1824.

Hogeland, William. *Autumn of the Black Snake: The Creation of the U.S. Army and the Invasion That Opened the West*. New York: Farrar, Straus, & Giroux, 2017.

Hopkins, Gerard T. A. *Mission to the Indians, from the Indian Committee of Baltimore Yearly Meeting, to Fort Wayne, in 1804*. Philadelphia: T. Ellwood Zell, 1862.

Hopkins, Thomas M. *Reminiscences of Col. John Ketcham, of Monroe County Indiana, by his Pastor, Rev. T. M. Hopkins of Bloomington, Indiana*. Bloomington: Whitaker & Walker, 1866.

Horsman, Reginald. *Expansion and American Indian Policy 1783–1812*. East Lansing: Michigan State University Press, 1967; reprint 1992.

_____. *The Frontier in the Formative Years, 1783–1815*. New York: Holt, Rinehart, & Winston, 1970.

_____. *Mathew Elliott, British Indian Agent*. Detroit: Wayne State University Press, 1964.

Houck, Louis. *The Spanish Regime in Missouri*. 2 vols. Chicago: R. R. Donnelley & Sons, 1909.

Hover, John C., ed. *Memoirs of the Miami Valley*. 3 vols. Chicago: Robert O. Law, 1919.

Howard, James H. *Shawnee! The Ceremonialism of a Native American Tribe and Its Cultural Background*. Athens: Ohio University Press, 1981.

Howe, Henry. *Historical Collections of Ohio, and Encyclopedia of the State*. 3 vols. Columbus, Ohio: Henry Howe & Son, 1891.

Howland, Eron. *Life, Letters, and Papers of William Dunbar*. Jackson: Mississippi Historical Society Press, 1930.

Hudson, Charles. *The Southeastern Indians*. Knoxville: University of Tennessee Press, 1976.

Hulbert, Archer B. *The Ohio River: A Course of Empire*. New York: Knickerbocker Press, 1906.

Hunter, John D. *Memoirs of a Captivity Among the Indians of North America*. London: Longman, Hurst, Bees, Orme, Brown, & Greene, 1824.

Hurt, R. Douglas. *The Ohio Frontier: Crucible of the Old Northwest, 1720–1830*. Bloomington: Indiana University Press, 1997.

Incidents of Border Life. Lancaster, Pa.: G. Hills, 1841.

Jahns, Patricia. *The Violent Years: Simon Kenton and the Ohio-Kentucky Frontier*. New York: Hastings House, 1962.

James, James A., ed. *George Rogers Clark Papers, 1771–1781, Virginia Series*. Springfield: Illinois State Historical Library, 1912.

James, William. *A Full and Correct Account of the Military Occurrences of the Late War between Great Britain and the United States of America*. 2 vols. London: For the author, 1818.

Jefferson, Thomas. *Notes of the State of Virginia, a New Edition*. Richmond: J. W. Randolph, 1853.

Johnston, John. *Recollections of Sixty Years*. N. p., 1915.

Jones, David. *A Journal of Two Visits Made to Some Nations of Indians on the West Side of the River Ohio in the Years 1772 and 1773*. Burlington, Vt.: Isaac Collins, 1774.

[Jones, Peter.] *Journal of the Proceedings, Indian Treaty, Fort Wayne, September 30th, 1809.* Connersville, Ind.: N.p., 1910.

Jortner, Adam. *The Gods of Prophetstown: The Battle of Tippecanoe and the Holy War for the American Frontier.* New York: Oxford University Press, 2012.

Keating, William H. *Narrative of an Expedition to the Source of St. Peter's River.* 2 vols. Philadelphia: H. C. Carey & I. Lea, 1824.

Kenton, Edna. *Simon Kenton, His Life and Period 1755–1836.* New York: Doubleday, Doran & Co., 1930.

Kinietz, Vernon, and Ermine W. Voegelin, eds. *Shawnese Traditions, C. C. Trowbridge's Account. Occasional Contributions from the Museum of Anthropology of the University of Michigan, No. 9.* Ann Arbor: University of Michigan Press, 1939.

Kinnan, Mary L. *A True Narrative of the Sufferings of Mary Kinnan, Who was Taken Prisoner by the Shawanee Nation of Indians.* Elizabethtown, N.J.: Shepard Kollock, 1795.

Klinck, Carl F., ed. *Tecumseh: Fact and Fiction in Early Records, a Book of Primary Source Materials.* Englewood Cliffs, N.J.: Prentice-Hall, 1961.

Klinck, Carl F., and James J. Talman, eds. *The Journal of Major John Norton 1816.* Toronto: Champlain Society, 1970.

Knapp, H. S. *History of the Maumee Valley.* Toledo: Slade Mammoth, 1872.

Knapp, Samuel L. *Lectures on American Literature, with Remarks on Some Passages of American History.* New York: Elam Bliss, 1829.

Knopf, Richard C., ed. *Document Transcriptions of the War of 1812 in the Northwest, Vol. VI: Letters to the Secretary of War 1812, Relating to the War of 1812 in the Northwest.* Columbus: Ohio Historical Society, 1959.

Kuron, Frank E. *"Thus Fell Tecumseh."* N.p.: Kuron, 2011.

Lakomäki, Sami. *Gathering Together: The Shawnee People though Diaspora and Nationhood, 1600–1870.* New Haven, Conn.: Yale University Press, 2014.

Landmann, George T. *Adventures and Recollections of Colonel Landmann.* 2 vols. London: Colburn, 1852.

Langguth, A. J. *Union 1812.* New York: Simon & Schuster, 2006.

Law, Judge. *The Colonial History of Vincennes under the French, British and American Governments.* Vincennes, Ind.: Harvey, Mason & Co., 1858.

Laxer, James. *Tecumseh and Brock: The War of 1812.* Toronto: Anansi, 2012.

Lewis, Virgil A. *History of the Battle of Point Pleasant.* Charleston, W.V.: Tribune, 1909.

Lincecum, Gideon. *Pushmataha: A Choctaw Leader and His People.* Tuscaloosa: University of Alabama Press, 2004.

Lindley, Harlow, ed. *Captain Cushing in the War of 1812.* Columbus: Ohio State Archaeological and Historical Society, 1944.

Lomax, D. A. N. *A History of the Services of the 41st (the Welch) Regiment.* Davenport, U.K.: Hiorns & Miller, 1899.

Lossing, Benson J. *Hull's Surrender of Detroit.* Philadelphia: John E. Potter, 1875.

———. *The Pictorial Field-Book of the War of 1812.* New York: Harper & Brothers, 1869.

Lossing, Benson J., ed. *The American Historical Record, and Repertory of Notes and Queries.* 3 vols. Philadelphia: Chase & Town, 1872.

Loudon, Archibald. *A Selection, of Some of the Most Interesting Narratives, of the Outrages, Committed by the Indians, in Their Wars, with the White People.* 2 vols. Carlisle, Pa.: A. Loudon, 1808.

MacLean, J. P. *Shakers of Ohio: Fugitive Papers Concerning the Shakers of Ohio, with Unpublished Manuscripts.* Columbus, Ohio: F. J. Heer, 1907.

Manning, William R., ed. *Diplomatic Correspondence of the United States: Canadian Relations, 1784–1860.* 2 vols. Washington, D.C.: Carnegie Endowment for International Peace, 1940.

Marszalek, John F. *Sherman: A Soldier's Passion for Order.* New York: Free Press, 1992.

Martin, Robert M. *History of Upper and Lower Canada.* London: John Mortimer, 1836.

Mason, Philip P., ed. *After Tippecanoe: Some Aspects of the War of 1812.* East Lansing: Michigan State University Press, 1963.

Matson, N. *Memories of Saubena.* Chicago: D. B. Cooke, 1878.

McAfee, Robert B. *History of the Late War in the Western Country.* Lexington, Ky.: Worsley & Smith, 1816; reprint 1919.

McClung, John A. *Sketches of Western Adventure.* Covington, Ky.: Richard H. Collins, 1872.

McClure, David. *Diary of David McClure, Doctor of Divinity, 1748–1820.* New York: Knickerbocker Press, 1899.

McCoy, Isaac. *History of Baptist Indian Missions.* New York: H. & S. Raynor, 1840.

McDonald, John. *Biographical Sketches of General Nathaniel Massie, General Duncan McArthur, Captain William Wells, and General Simon Kenton, Who were Early Settlers in the Western Country.* Dayton, Ohio: D. Osborn & Son, 1852.

McKenney, Thomas L., and James Hall. *History of the Indian Tribes of North America, with Biographical Sketches and Anecdotes of the Principal Chiefs.* 3 vols. Philadelphia: D. Rice, 1836–44.

McNemar, Richard. *The Kentucky Revival; or, a Short History of the Late Extraordinary Outpouring of the Spirit of God in the Western States of America.* New York: Edward O. Jenkins, 1846.

McRae, Sherwin, ed. *Calendar of Virginia State Papers and Other Manuscripts.* 11 vols. Richmond: A. R. Micou, 1875–96.

Metcalf, Samuel L. *A Collection of Some of the Most Interesting Narratives of Indian Warfare in the West, Containing an Account of the Adventures of Colonel Daniel Boone.* Lexington, Ky.: William G. Hunt, 1821.

Michigan Pioneer and Historical Society Historical Collections. 40 vols. Lansing, Mich.: [various publishers], 1877–29.

Minutes of Debates in Council on the Banks of the Ottawa River, November 1791. Philadelphia: William Young, 1792.

Monnette, John W. *History of the Discovery and Settlement of the Valley of the Mississippi.* 2 vols. New York: Harper & Brothers, 1846.

Mooney, James. *The Ghost Dance Religion and the Sioux Outbreak of 1890. Fourteenth Annual Report of the Bureau of Ethnology to the Secretary of the Smithsonian Institution 1892–93. Part 2.* Washington, D.C.: Government Printing Office, 1896.

Nelson, Larry L. *Men of Patriotism, Courage, and Enterprise! Fort Meigs in the War of 1812.* Bowie, Md.: Heritage Books, 1985.

Nelson, Larry L., ed. *A History of Jonathan Alder: His Captivity and Life with the Indians.* Akron, Ohio: University of Akron Press, 2002.

Niles, William O. *The Tippecanoe Text-Book, Compiled from Niles' Register and Other Authentic Sources.* Baltimore: Hogan & Thompson, 1840.

Noe, Randolph. *The Shawnee Indians: An Annotated Bibliography.* Lanham, Md.: Scarecrow Press, 2011.

Oberg, Barbara B., and J. Jefferson Looney, eds. *The Papers of Thomas Jefferson. Digital Edition.* Charlottesville: University of Virginia Press, 2008.

Ogg, Frederic A. *The Old Northwest: A Chronicle of the Ohio Valley and Beyond.* New Haven, Conn.: Yale University Press, 1921.

O'Kenney, Thomas L. *Memoirs, Official and Personal; Sketches of Travels among the Northern and Indians.* 2 vols. New York: Paine & Burgess, 1846.

Oskison, John M. *Tecumseh and His Times.* New York: G. P. Putnam's, 1938.

Owens, Robert M. *Mr. Jefferson's Hammer: William Henry Harrison and the Origins of American Indian Policy.* Norman: University of Oklahoma Press, 2007.

Pickett, Albert J. *History of Alabama, and Incidentally of Georgia and Mississippi.* 2 vols. Charleston, S.C.: Walker & James, 1851.

Pouchot, Pierre. *Memoir upon the Late War in North America between the French and English, 1755–60.* 2 vols. Roxbury, Mass.: W. E. Woodward, 1866.

Pound, Merritt B. *Benjamin Hawkins - Indian Agent.* Athens: University of Georgia Press, 1951.

Primm, James Neal. *Lion of the Valley: St. Louis, Missouri, 1764–1980.* St. Louis: Missouri Historical Society Press, 1998.

[Procter, George]. *Tales of Chivalry and Romance.* Edinburgh: James Robertson, 1826.

[Procter, George, and Henry Procter]. *The Lucubrations of Humphrey Ravelin, Esq.* London: G. & W. B. Whitaker, 1823.

Prucha, Francis Paul. *The Great Father: The United States Government and the American Indian.* Lincoln: University of Nebraska Press, 1984.

Quaife, Milo M. *Chicago and the Old Northwest, 1673–1835.* Chicago: University of Chicago Press, 1913.

Quaife, Milo M., ed. *The Indian Captivity of O. M. Spencer.* Chicago: Lakeside Press, 1917.

———. *The John Askin Papers.* 2 vols. Detroit: Detroit Library Commission, 1931.

———. *War on the Detroit: The Chronicles of Thomas Vercheres de Boucherville and the Capitulation of an Ohio Volunteer.* Chicago: Lakeside Press, 1940.

Ramsey, James G. M. *Annals of Tennessee to the End of the Eighteenth Century.* Philadelphia: J. B. Lippincott, 1853.

Read, D. N. *Life and Times of Major-General Sir Isaac Brock, K. B.* Toronto: William Briggs, 1894.

Rohrbough, Malcolm J. *Trans-Appalachian Frontier: People, Societies, and Institutions, 1775–1850.* Bloomington: Indiana University Press, 2008.

Ross, Robert B., and George B. Catlin. *Landmarks of Detroit: A History of the City.* Detroit: Evening News Association, 1898.

Rowland, Dunbar. *Official Letter Books of W. C. C. Claiborne, 1801–1816.* 11 vols. Jackson, Miss.: State Department of Archives and History, 1917.

St.-Denis, Guy. *Tecumseh's Bones.* Montreal: McGill-Queen's University Press, 2005.

Sass, Herbert R. *Hear Me, My Chiefs.* New York: William Morrow, 1940.

Schoolcraft, Henry R. *Algic Researches, Comprising Inquiries Respecting the Mental Characteristics of the North American Indians.* 2 vols. New York: Harper & Brothers, 1839.

———. *Information Respecting the History, Condition and Prospects of the Indian Tribes of the United States.* 5 vols. Philadelphia: Lippincott, Grambo, 1853–56.

———. *Travels in the Central Portions of the Mississippi Valley.* New York: Collins & Hanna, 1825.

[Sewell, Stephen]. *The Letters of Veritas, Re-Published from the Montreal Herald; Containing a Succinct Narrative of the Military Administration of Sir George Prévost.* Montreal: W. Gray, 1815.

Siberell, Lloyd E. *Tecumseh: His Career, the Man, His Chillicothe Portrait.* Chillicothe, Ohio: Ross County Historical Society, 1944.

Skaggs, David C. *William Henry Harrison and the Conquest of the Ohio Country: Frontier Fighting in the War of 1812.* Baltimore, Md.: Johns Hopkins University Press, 2014.

Slocum, Charles E. *History of the Maumee River Basin.* 3 vols. Indianapolis: Bowen & Slocum, 1905.

Smith, Daniel. *A Short Description of the State of Tennessee, Lately Called the Territory of the United States, South of the Ohio River.* Philadelphia: Lang & Ustick, 1796.

Smith, James. *An Account of the Remarkable Occurrences in the Life and Travels of Col. James Smith during His Captivity with the Indians in the Years, 1755, '56, '57, '58, & '59.* Lexington, Ky.: John Bradford, 1799.

_____. *A Treatise, on the Mode and Manner of Indian War.* Paris, Ky.: Joel R. Lyle, 1812.

Smith, William H. *The Life and Public Services of Arthur St. Clair.* 2 vols. Cincinnati: Robert Clarke, 1882.

Spencer, Thomas Edwin. *The Story of Old St. Louis.* St. Louis: 1914.

Stockwell, Mary. *The Other Trail of Tears: The Removal of the Ohio Indians.* Yardley, Pa.: Westholme, 2014.

Stoddard, Amos. *Sketches, Historical and Descriptive, of Louisiana.* Philadelphia: Mathew Carey, 1812.

Stott, Glenn. *Greater Evils: The War of 1812 in Southwestern Ontario.* Milton, Ont.: By the author, 2012.

Sugden, John. *Blue Jacket: Warrior of the Shawnees.* Lincoln: University of Nebraska Press, 2000.

_____. *Tecumseh: A Life.* New York: Henry Holt, 1997.

_____. *Tecumseh's Last Stand.* Norman: University of Oklahoma Press, 1985.

Sullivan, James. *The Papers of Sir William Johnson.* 14 vols. Albany: State of New York University Press, 1921–65.

Sword, Wiley. *President Washington's Indian War: The Struggle for the Old Northwest, 1790–1795.* Norman: University of Oklahoma Press, 1985.

Tanner, Helen H., ed. *Atlas of Great Lakes Indian History.* Norman: University of Oklahoma Press, 1987.

Tanner, John. *Narrative of the Captivity and Adventures of John Tanner, During Thirty Years Residence among the Indians in the Interior of North America.* New York: G. & C. &. H. Carvill, 1830.

Taylor, Alan. *The Civil War of 1812.* New York: Random House, 2010.

Thatcher, Benjamin B. *Indian Biography, or, an Historical Account of Those Individuals Who Have Been Distinguished among the North American Natives.* 2 vols. New York: Harper & Brothers, 1841.

Thornbrough, Gayle, ed. *The Correspondence of John Badollet and Albert Gallatin 1804–1836.* Indianapolis: Indiana Historical Society, 1963.

_____. *Journals of the General Assembly of Indian Territory 1805–1815.* Indianapolis: Indiana Historical Bureau, 1950.

_____. *Letter Book of the Indian Agency at Fort Wayne, 1809–1815.* Indianapolis: Indiana Historical Society, 1961.

_____. *Outpost on the Wabash, 1787–1791.* Indianapolis: Indiana Historical Society, 1957.

Thwaite, Reuben G. *Documentary History of Dunmore's War 1774.* Madison: Wisconsin Historical Society, 1905.

Trowbridge, Charles C. *Meearmeear Traditions. Occasional Contributions from the Museum of Anthropology of the University of Michigan, No. 9.* Ann Arbor: University of Michigan Press, 1938.

A True History of the Massacre of Ninety-six Christian Indians at Gnadenhutten, Ohio, March 8, 1782. New Philadelphia: Lutheran Standard Office, 1844.

Tucker, Glenn. *Tecumseh: Vision of Glory.* Indianapolis: Bobbs-Merrill, 1956.

Tupper, Ferdinand B. *Family Records: Containing Memoirs of Major-General Sir Isaac Brock, K. B.* Guernsey, U.K.: Stephen Barbet, 1835.

_____. *The Life and Correspondence of Major-General Sir Isaac Brock, K. B.* London: Simpkin, Marshall, 1847.

Turpie, David. *Sketches of My Own Times.* Indianapolis: Bobbs-Merrill, 1903.

Van Hoose, William H. *Tecumseh, an Indian Moses.* Canton, Ohio: Daring Books, 1984.

Volney, C. F. *A View of the Soil and Climate of the United States of America.* Philadelphia: J. Conrad, 1804.

Walker, Adam. *A Journal of Two Campaigns of the Fourth Regiment of U. S. Infantry, in the Michigan and Indiana Territories.* Keene, N.H.: By the author, 1816.

Walker, Mary R. *On to Oregon: The Diaries of Mary Walker and Myra Ells.* Lincoln: University of Nebraska Press, 1998.

Wallace, Anthony F. C. *The Death and Rebirth of the Seneca.* New York: Knopf, 1970.

_____. *Jefferson and the Indians: The Tragic Fate of the First Americans.* Cambridge, Mass.: Harvard University Press, 2001.

Warren, Stephen. *The Shawnees and Their Neighbors 1795–1870.* Urbana: University of Illinois Press, 2005.

_____. *The Worlds the Shawnees Made: Migration and Violence in Early America.* Chapel Hill: University of North Carolina Press, 2014.

Washington, H. A. *The Writings of Thomas Jefferson.* 9 vols. Washington, D.C.: Taylor & Maury, 1854.

Weir, Howard T. III. *A Paradise of Blood: The Creek War of 1813–14.* Yardley, Pa.: Westholme, 2016.

Wheeler-Voegelin, Erminie, and David B. Stout. *Indians of Illinois and Northwestern Indiana.* New York: Garland, 1974.

White, Richard. *The Middle Ground: Indians, Empires, and Republics in the Great Lakes Region, 1650–1815.* Cambridge, U.K.: Cambridge University Press, 1991.

Williams, Glenn E. *Dunmore's War: The Last Conflict of America's Colonial Era.* Yardley, Pa.: Westholme, 2017.

Williams, Samuel. *Two Western Campaigns in the War of 1812.* Cincinnati: Robert Clarke, 1870.

Winkler, John F. *Fallen Timbers 1794: The U. S. Army's First Victory.* New York: Osprey, 2013.

_____. *Point Pleasant 1774: Prelude to the American Revolution.* New York: Osprey, 2014.

_____. *The Thames 1813: The War of 1812 on the Northwest Frontier.* New York: Osprey, 2016.

_____. *Tippecanoe 1811: The Prophet's Battle.* New York: Osprey, 2015.

_____. *Wabash 1791: St. Clair's Defeat.* New York: Osprey, 2011.

Withers, Alexander S. *Chronicles of Border Warfare . . . a New Edition Edited and Annotated by Reuben Gold Thwaites.* Cincinnati: Robert Clarke, 1895.

Woehrmann, Paul. *At the Headwaters of the Maumee: A History of the Forts of Fort Wayne.* Indianapolis: Indiana Historical Society, 1971.

Wood, Gordon S. *Empire of Liberty: A History of the Early Republic, 1789–1815.* New York: Oxford University Press, 2009.

Wood, William, ed. *Select British Documents of the Canadian War of 1812.* 3 vols. Toronto: Champlain Society, 1923–28.

Woodward, Thomas S. *Woodward's Reminiscences of the Creek, or Muscogee Indians.* Montgomery: Barrett & Wimbish, 1859.

Wright, Richard J., ed. *The John Hunt Memoirs*. Maumee, Ohio: Maumee Valley Historical Association, 1977.

Young, William T. *Sketch of the Life and Public Services of General Lewis Cass*. Detroit:
Markham & Elwood, 1852.

Zaslow, Morris, ed. *The Defended Border: Upper Canada and the War of 1812*. Toronto:
Macmillan, 1964.

ARTICLES, ADDRESSES, AND ESSAYS

Allen, Robert S. "His Majesty's Indian Allies: Native Peoples, the British Crown and the
War of 1812." *Michigan Historical Review* 14, no. 2 (Fall 1988).

Altoff, Gerry T. "Oliver Hazard Perry and the Battle of Lake Erie." *Michigan Historical
Review* 14, no. 2 (Fall 1988).

Andrews, Edward D. "The Shaker Mission to the Shawnee Indians." *Winterthur Portfolio*
7 (1972).

Arnold, T. S. "Battle of the Thames and Death of Tecumseh." *The United Empire Loyalists' Association of Ontario: Annual Transactions for the Years Ending March 1901 and
March 1902*. Toronto: Graham & Harrap, 1903.

Bacon, David. "An Unsuccessful Mission to the Shawanese, 1802." *Northwest Ohio Quarterly* 16, no. 1 (January 1944).

Bald, F. Clever. "Colonel John Francis Hamtramck." *Indiana Magazine of History* 44, no.
4 (December 1948).

*Barbarities of the Enemy; Exposed in a Report of the Committee of the House of Representa-
tives of the United States, Appointed to Enquire into the Spirit and Manner in which
the War Has Been Waged by the Enemy*. Troy, N.Y.: Francis Adancourt, 1813.

Barce, Elmore. "Tecumseh's Confederacy." *Indiana Magazine of History* 13, no. 1 (March
1917).

Barnard, Susan K., and Grace M. Schwartzman. "Tecumseh and the Creek Indian War of
1813–1814." *Georgia Historical Quarterly* 82, no. 3 (Fall 1998).

Barnes, Lela, ed. "Journal of Isaac McCoy for the Exploring Expedition of 1828." *Kansas
Historical Quarterly* 5, no. 3 (August 1936).

_____. "Journal of Isaac McCoy for the Exploring Expedition of 1830." *Kansas Historical
Quarterly* 5, no. 4 (November 1936).

Barnhart, John D. "Letters of William Henry Harrison to Thomas Worthington." *Indiana
Magazine of History* 47, no. 1 (March 1951).

Barry, Louise, ed. "William Clark's Diary, May 1826–February 1831." *Kansas Historical
Quarterly* 16 (February 1948).

"Battle of Blue Licks." *Register of the Kentucky Historical Society* 47, no. 160 (July 1949).

Beall, William K. "Journal of William K. Beall, July–August 1812." *American Historical
Review* 17, no. 4 (July 1912).

Biddle, James W. "Recollections of Green Bay in 1816–17." *Collections of the State Historical
Society of Wisconsin* 1. Madison: By the society, 1903.

Billington, Ray A. "The Fort Stanwix Treaty of 1768." *New York History* 25, no. 2 (April
1944).

Bird, Henry. "The Adventures of Henry Bird." *Analectic Magazine* 6 (1815).

Bishop, Levi. "The Battle of Monguagon." *Collections of the Pioneer Society of the State
of Michigan* 6 (1907).

Blount, Willie. "Letter on Indian Affairs." *American Historical Magazine* 2 (1896).

Bontrager, Shannon. "'From a Nation of Drunkards, We Have Become a Sober People': The Wyandot Experience in the Ohio Valley during the Early Republic." *Journal of the Early Republic* 32, no. 4 (Winter 2012).

Bottiger, Patrick. "Prophetstown for Their Own Purposes: The French, Miamis, and Cultural Identities in the Wabash-Maumee Valley." *Journal of the Early Republic* 33, no. 1 (Spring 2013).

———. "Stabbed in the Back: Vincennes, Slavery, and the Indian 'Threat.'" *Indiana Magazine of History* 107 (June 2011).

"Bowman's Campaign of 1779." *Ohio Archaeological and Historical Quarterly* 22, no. 4 (October 1913).

"Bowman's Expedition against Chillicothe, May–June 1779." *Ohio Archaeological and Historical Publications* 19 (1910).

Brady, Arthur W. "The Moravian Mission in Indiana." *Proceedings of the Mississippi Valley Historical Association* 10, pt. 2 (1919–20).

Brickell, John. "Narrative of John Brickell's Captivity among the Delaware Indians." *American Pioneer* 1, no. 2 (February 1842).

Brown, Parker B. "The Fate of Crawford Volunteers Captured by Indians Following the Battle of Sandusky in 1782." *Western Pennsylvania Historical Magazine* 65, no. 4 (October 1982).

Brown, William D. "Delayed Response: Col. John Bowman and the Kentucky Expedition of 1777." *Register of the Kentucky Historical Society* 97, no. 2 (Spring 1999).

Brunson, Alfred. "Death of Tecumseh." *Collections of the State Historical Society of Wisconsin* 4 (1906).

Buff, Rachel. "Tecumseh and Tenskwatawa: Myth, Historiography and Popular Memory." *Historical Reflections* 21, no. 2 (Spring 1995).

Byrd, Cecil K. "The Northwest Indians and the British Preceding the War of 1812." *Indiana Magazine of History* 38, no. 1 (March 1942).

Callender, Charles. "Shawnee." In William C. Sturtevant, ed., *Handbook of North American Indians*. Volume 15: *Northeast*. (Washington D.C.: Smithsonian Institution, 1978).

Calloway, Collin G. "Suspicion and Self-Interest: The British-Indian Alliance and the Peace of Paris." *Historian* 48, no. 1 (November 1985).

———. "We Have Always Been the Frontier": The American Revolution in Shawnee Country." *American Indian Quarterly* 16, no. 1 (Winter 1992).

Campbell, James V. "Biographical Sketch of Charles C. Trowbridge." *Pioneer Collections: Report of the Pioneer Society of the State of Michigan* 6 (1884).

Carlson, Richard G., ed. "George P. Peters' Version of the Battle of Tippecanoe (November 7, 1811)." *Vermont History* 45, no. 1 (Winter 1977).

Carr, John. "Early History of the South-West." *South-Western Monthly* 2, no. 2 (1852).

Carter, Max L. "John Johnston and the Friends: A Midwestern Indian Agent's Relationship with Quakers in the Early 1800s." *Quaker History* 78, no. 1 (Spring 1989).

Carter-Edwards, Dennis. "The War of 1812 Along the Detroit Frontier: A Canadian Perspective." *Michigan Historical Review* 13, no. 2 (Fall 1987).

Cass, Lewis. "Discourse Delivered Before the Historical Society of Michigan." *Historic and Scientific Sketches of Michigan*. Detroit: Stephen Wells and George L. Whitney, 1834.

———. "Indian Biography." *North American Review* 34, no. 75 (April 1832).

——— "Indian Treaties, and Laws and Regulations." *North American Review* 24, no. 55 (April 1827).

_____. "Indians of North America." *North American Review* 22, no. 50 (January 1826).

Cave, Alfred A. "The Failure of the Shawnee Prophet's Witch-Hunt." *Ethnohistory* 42, no. 3 (Summer 1995).

_____. "The Shawnee Prophet, Tecumseh, and Tippecanoe: A Case Study of Historical Myth-Making." *Journal of the Early Republic* 22, no. 4 (Winter 2002).

Christian, Thomas. "Campaign of 1813 on the Ohio River: Sortie at Fort Meigs, May 1813." *Western Reserve Historical Society Publication* 23 (1874).

Chute, J. Andrew. "A Common Season Among the Weas." *Foreign Missionary Chronicle* 5, no. 5 (May 1837).

Clifton, James A. "Merchant, Soldier, Broker, Chief: A Corrected Obituary of Captain Billy Caldwell." *Journal of the Illinois State Historical Society* 71, no. 3 (August 1978).

Connelly, Thomas L. "Indian Warfare on the Tennessee Frontier, 1776–1794: Strategy and Tactics." *East Tennessee Historical Society's Publications* 36 (1964).

"Correspondence between Governor Isaac Shelby and Gen. William Henry Harrison." *Register of the Kentucky State Historical Society* 20, no. 59 (May 1922).

Coyne, James H. "The Talbot Papers, Part I." *Proceedings and Transactions of the Royal Society of Canada*, 3rd ser., vol. 1, *Meeting of May 1907*. Ottawa: James Jope & Son, 1907.

Crawford, Mary M. "Mrs. Lydia B. Bacon's Journal, 1811–1812." *Indiana Magazine of History* 40, no. 4 (December 1944).

Cruikshank, Ernest A. "General Hull's Invasion of Canada in 1812." *Publications of the Royal Society of Canada*, 3rd ser. 1, sec. 2 (1908).

_____. "Harrison and Proctor [*sic*]: The River Raisin." *Transactions of the Royal Society of Canada*, 3rd ser. 4, sec. 2 (1910).

Curry, Otway. "The Doomed Wyandott [*sic*]." *Hesperian, or, Western Monthly Magazine* 1 (May 1838)

Curry, William L. "The Wyandot Chief, Leather Lips." *Ohio Archaeological and Historical Publications* 12 (1903).

"Daily Journal of Wayne's Campaign." *American Pioneer* 1, no. 9 (September 1842).

Davidson, James. "Who Killed Tecumseh?" *Historical Magazine, and Notes and Queries* 10, no. 7 (July 1866).

Davis, Karl. "Remembering Fort Mims: Reinterpreting the Origins of the Creek War." *Journal of the Early Republic* 22 (Winter 2002).

"Documents Relating to the War of 1812: The Letter-Book of Gen. Sir Roger Hale Sheaffe." *Publications of the Buffalo Historical Society* 17 (1913).

Donalson, Israel. "Captivity of Israel Donalson." *American Pioneer* 1, no. 12 (December 1842).

Dowd, Gregory E. "Thinking and Believing: Nativism and Unity in the Ages of Pontiac and Tecumseh." *American Indian Quarterly* 16, no. 3 (Summer 1992).

_____. "Thinking Outside the Circle: Tecumseh's 1811 Mission." In Kathryn E. Holland Braund, ed., *Tohopeka: Rethinking the Creek War and the War of 1812*. Auburn, Ala.: Pebble Hill, 2012.

Downes, Randolph C. "Dunmore's War: An Interpretation." *Mississippi Valley Historical Review* 21, no. 3 (December 1934).

Downing, Francis. "Narrow Escapes from Destruction by the Indians." *Western Review and Miscellaneous Magazine* 2 (February–July 1820).

Draper, Lyman C. "The Battle of Point Pleasant." *American Pioneer* 1, no. 11 (November 1842).

Dudley, Thomas P. "Battle and Massacre at Frenchtown, Michigan, January 1813." *Historical and Archaeological Tracts* 1 (1870).

Edmunds, R. David. "'Evil Men Who Add to Our Difficulties': Shawnees, Quakers, and William Wells, 1807–1808." *American Culture and Research Journal* 14, no. 4 (1990).

_____. "Heron Who Waits at the Speleawee-thepee: The Ohio River and the Shawnee World." *Register of the Kentucky Historical Society* 91, no. 3 (Summer 1993).

_____. "Main Poc, Potawatomi Wabeno." *American Indian Quarterly* 9, no. 3 (Summer 1985).

_____. "Tecumseh, The Shawnee Prophet, and American History: A Reassessment." *Western Historical Quarterly* 14, no. 3 (July 1983).

_____. "The Thin Red Line: Tecumseh, the Prophet and Shawnee Resistance." *Timeline* 4, no. 6 (December 1987).

_____. "'A Watchful Safeguard to Our Habitations': Black Hoof and the Loyal Shawnees." In Frederick E. Hoxie, ed., *Native Americans and the Early Republic.* Charlottesville: University of Virginia Press, 1999.

Eid, Leroy V. "'Their Rules of War': The Validity of James Smith's Summary of Indian Woodland War." *Register of the Kentucky Historical Society* 86, no. 1 (Winter 1988).

Ermatinger, Charles O. "The Retreat of Procter and Tecumseh." *Papers and Records of the Ontario Historical Society* 17 (1919).

Fear, Jacqueline. "The 'Civilization' of Thomas Wildcat Alford." *Revue française d'études américaines* 17 (May 1983).

"Fort Harmar, the First Permanent Settlement in Ohio." *American Pioneer* 1, no. 1 (January 1842).

Franz, William. "'To Live by Depredations': Main Poc's Strategic Use of Violence." *Journal of the Illinois State Historical Society* 102, no. 3/4 (Fall–Winter 2009).

Fredericksen, John C. "Kentucky at the Thames, 1813: A Rediscovered Narrative by William Greathouse." *Register of the Kentucky Historical Society* 83, no. 2 (Spring 1985).

Friedrichs, Michael. "Tecumseh's Forty-one Names in the English Language: Some Remarks About Their Genesis." *Native American Studies* 8, no. 2 (1994).

Galbreath, C. B. "Tecumseh and His Descendants." *Ohio Archeological and Historical Society Publications* 34 (1925).

Gatschet, A. S., and F. W. Hodge. "Tecumseh's Name." *American Anthropologist* 8, no. 1 (January 1895).

Goodpasture, Albert V. "Indian Wars and Warriors of the Old Southwest." *Tennessee Historical Magazine* 4, no. 3 (September 1918).

Green, James A., ed. "Journal of Ensign William Schillinger, a Soldier of the War of 1812." *Ohio Archaeological and Historical Quarterly* 41, no. 1 (January 1932).

Grignon, Auguste. "Seventy-five Years' Recollections of Wisconsin." *Collections of the Wisconsin State Historical Society* 3 (1856).

Gunderson, Robert G. "Chief Tomah's Reply: A Pacific Footnote on the Folklore of Tecumseh." *Indiana Magazine of History* 86 (September 1990).

_____. "William Henry Harrison: Apprentice in Arms." *Northwest Ohio Quarterly* 65, no. 1 (Winter 1993).

Halbert, Henry S. "Some Inaccuracies in Claiborne's History in Regard to Tecumseh." *Publications of the Mississippi Historical Society* 1 (1898).

_____. "Tecumseh at Tukabatchi 1811." *Arrow Points* 4, no. 3 (March 5, 1872).

Hall, Ellery L. "Canadian Annexation Sentiment in Kentucky Prior to the War of 1812." *Register of the Kentucky State Historical Society* 28, no. 85 (October 1930).

Hamilton, Robert. "The Expedition of Major-General Samuel Hopkins up the Wabash, 1812: The Letters of Captain Robert Hamilton." *Indiana Magazine of History* 43, no. 4 (December 1947.)

Harrison, Lowell H. "Nat Crain and the Battle of the Thames." *Filson Club History Quarterly* 64, no. 3 (July 1990).

Harrison, William Henry. "A Discourse on the Aborigines of the Valley of the Ohio." *Transactions of the Historical and Philosophical Society of Ohio*, pt. 2, vol. 1 (1839).

Heath, William. "Re-evaluating the 'Fort Wayne Manuscript': William Wells and the Manners and Customs of the Miami Nation." *Indiana Magazine of History* 106, no. 2 (June 2010).

Hedges, John P. "Early Recollections of John P. Hedges." *Indiana Quarterly Magazine of History* 8, no. 4 (December 1912).

Hickling, William. "Sketches of Billy Caldwell and Shabonee." In *Addresses Delivered at the Annual Meeting, Chicago Historical Society, November 19, 1868*. Chicago: Fergus, 1877.

"Historical Sketch of the Siege of Fort Meigs." *Analectic Magazine* 13 (Philadelphia, 1819).

Horsman, Reginald. "American Indian Policy in the Old Northwest, 1783–1812." *William and Mary Quarterly* 18, no. 1 (January 1961).

———. "British Indian Policy in the Northwest, 1807–1812." *Journal of American History* 45, no. 1 (June 1958).

———. "The Indian Policy of an 'Empire for Liberty.'" In Frederick E. Hoxie, ed., *Native Americans and the Early Republic*. Charlottesville: University of Virginia Press, 1999.

———. "William Henry Harrison: Virginia Gentleman in the Old Northwest." *Indiana Magazine of History* 96, no. (June 2000).

Houchens, Mariam S. "The Great Revival of 1800." *Register of the Kentucky Historical Society* 69, no. 3 (July 1971).

Howerton, Ernest H. "Logan, the Shawnee Indian Capital of West Virginia, 1760–1780." *West Virginia History* 16 (July 1955).

Hulbert, Archer B., and William N. Schwarze, eds. "David Zeisberger's History of the Northern American Indians." *Ohio Archaeological and Historical Publications* 19 (1910).

Hutton, Paul A. "William Wells: Frontier Scout and Indian Agent." *Indiana Magazine of History* 74, no. 3 (September 1978).

Johnston, John. "Account of the Present State of the Indian Tribes Inhabiting Ohio." *Transactions and Collections of the American Antiquarian Society* (1820).

Kanon, Tom. "'Scared from Their Sins for a Season': The Religious Ramifications of the New Madrid Earthquakes, 1811–1812." *Ohio Valley History* 5, no. 2 (Summer 2005).

Kenny, James. "Journal of James Kenny, 1761–1763." *Pennsylvania Magazine of History and Biography* 37, no. 2 (1913).

King, Charles R. "'Physician to Body and Soul,' Jonathan Meeker—Kansas Missionary." *Kansas History* 17, no. 4 (Winter 1994–95).

Kingston, John T. "Death of Tecumseh: Letter by the Hon. John T. Kingston, of Necedah." *Collections of the State Historical Society of Wisconsin* 4 (1906).

Klopfenstein, Carl G. "Westward Ho: Removal of Ohio Shawnees, 1832–1833." *Bulletin of the Historical and Philosophical Society of Ohio* 15, no. 1 (January 1957).

Knowles, Nathaniel. "The Torture of Captives by the Indians of Eastern North America." *Proceedings of the American Philosophical Society* 82, no. 2 (March 22, 1940).

Lafferty, Maude W. "Destruction of Ruddle's and Martin's Forts in the Revolutionary War." *Register of the Kentucky Historical Society* 54, no. 189 (October 1956).

Lakomäki, Sami. "'Our Line': The Shawnees, the United States, and Competing Borders on the Great Lakes Borderlands." *Journal of the Early Republic* 34, no. 4 (Winter 2014).

Lankford, George E. "Losing the Past: Draper and the Ruddell Indian Captivity." *Arkansas Historical Quarterly* 49, no. 3 (Autumn 1990).

Lincoln, Benjamin. "Journal of a Treaty Held in 1793, with the Indian Tribes North-West of the Ohio, by Commissioners of the United States." *Collections of the Massachusetts Historical Society* 5, 3rd ser. (1836).

"Logan, the Mingo Chief." *American Pioneer* 1, no. 1 (January 1842).

"Logan—the Mingo Chief, 1710–1780." *Ohio Archaeological and Historical Publications* 20 (1911).

"Lord Dunmore's War." *Olden Time* 2, no. 1 (January 1847).

Lutz, J. J. "The Methodist Missions among the Indian Tribes in Kansas. *Transactions of the Kansas State Historical Society* 9 (1905–6).

MacLean, J. P. "The Kentucky Revival and Its Influence on the Miami Valley." *Ohio Archaeological and Historical Publications* 12 (1904).

———. "Shaker Mission to the Shawnee Indians." *Ohio Archaeological and Historical Publications* 11 (1903).

Mancall, Peter C. "Men, Women, and Alcohol in Indian Villages in the Great Lakes Region in the Early Republic." *Journal of the Early Republic* 15, no. 3 (Autumn 1995).

Matson, N. "Sketch of Shau-be-na, a Pottawattamie Chief." *Report and Collections of the State Historical Society of Wisconsin* 7 (1876).

McAfee, Robert B. "The McAfee Papers: Book and Journal of Robt. B. McAfee's Mounted Company, in Col. Richard M. Johnson's Regiment." *Register of the Kentucky State Historical Society* 26, no. 77 (May 1928).

McAllister, J. T. "The Battle of Point Pleasant (Continued)." *Virginia Historical Magazine* 10, no. 1 (July 1902).

McDermott, John F. "Audubon's 'Journey up the Mississippi.'" *Journal of the Illinois State Historical Society* 35, no. 2 (June 1942).

McDonald, John. "The Tragical Death of Wawillowa, a Chief of the Shawnee Tribe." *Western Christian Advocate* (April 22, 1836).

McFarland, R. W. "Simon Kenton." *Ohio Archaeological and Historical Publications* 13 (1904).

McGowan, William. "The McGowan Murder at Hindostan." *Indiana Magazine of History* 18, no. 2 (1922).

McHenry, Francis. "The Indian Prophet." *Halcyon Luminary and Theological Repository* 1, no. 6 (June 1812).

[Meek, Basil.] "Tarhe—The Crane." *Ohio Archaeological and Historical Publications* 20 (1911).

Miller, Jay. "The 1806 Purge among the Indiana Delaware: Sorcery, Gender, Boundaries, and Legitimacy." *Ethnohistory* 41, no. 2 (Spring 1994).

Mills, Randy J. "'It Is the Cause of All Mischief Which the Indians Suffer': Native Americans and Alcohol Abuse in the Old Northwest." *Ohio Valley History* 3, no. 3 (Fall 2003).

Miriani, Ronald. "Against the Wind: The Shawnee at Wapakoneta." *Queen City Heritage* (Spring 1990).

Mortimer, Benjamin. "The Ohio Frontier in 1812." *Ohio Archaeological and Historical Publications* 22 (1913).

Mutterly, Charles. "Colonel David Williamson, and the Massacre of the Moravian Indians, 1782." *American Pioneer* 2, no. 9 (September 1839).

Naylor, Isaac. "The Battle of Tippecanoe, as Described by Judge Isaac Naylor, a Participant." *Indiana Magazine of History* 2, no. 4 (December 1906).

Nelson, Larry L. "Dudley's Defeat and the Relief of Fort Meigs During the War of 1812." *Register of the Kentucky Historical Society* 104, no. 1 (Winter 2006).

_____. "'Never Have They Done So Little:' The Battle of Fort Recovery and the Collapse of the Miami Confederacy." *Northwest Ohio Quarterly* 64, no. 2 (Spring 1992).

93d Anniversary of the Battle of Fort Stephenson. Reinternment of Remains of Major Geo. Croghan, beneath the Monument Erected in His Honor on Fort Stephenson, Fremont, Ohio, Thursday, August 2, 1906. Columbus: Ohio State Archaeological and Historical Society, 1907.

"Ohio in the War of 1812." *Ohio Archaeological and Historical Publications* 28 (1919).

Owens, Robert M. "Jeffersonian Benevolence on the Ground: The Indian Land Cession Treaties of William Henry Harrison." *Journal of the Early Republic* 22, no. 3 (Autumn 2002).

Padgett, James A. "Joseph Desha, Letters and Papers." *Register of the Kentucky Historical Society* 51, no. 177 (October 1953).

Parish, John C., ed. "The Robert Lucas Journal." *Iowa Journal of History and Politics* 4, no. 3 (July 1906).

Peckham, Howard H. "Recent Documentary Acquisitions to the Indiana Historical Library Relating to Fort Wayne." *Indiana Magazine of History* 44, no. 4 (December 1948).

Pirtle, Alfred. "The Battle of Tippecanoe, Read before the Filson Club, November 1, 1897." *Filson Club Publications*, no. 15. Louisville: John P. Morton, 1900.

[Procter, George, and Henry] "Campaigns in the Canadas." *Quarterly Review* 27 (April–July 1822).

Quaife, Milo M., ed. "The Ohio Campaign of 1782." *Mississippi Valley Historical Review* 12, no. 4 (March 1931).

_____. "A Picture of the First United States Army: The Journal of Captain Samuel Newman." *Wisconsin Magazine of History* 2, no. 1 (September 1918).

_____. "The Story of Brownstown." *Burton Historical Collection Leaflet* 4, no. 5 (May 1926).

Radin, Paul. "The Winnebago Tribe." In *Thirty-seventh Annual Report of the Bureau of American Ethnology 1915–1916.* Washington, D.C.: Government Printing Office, 1923.

Randall, E. O. "The Dunmore War." *Ohio Archaeological Publications* 11 (1903).

_____. "Tecumseh, the Shawanee Chief." *Ohio Archaeological Publications* 15 (1906).

Rauch, Steven J. "A Stain upon the Nation? A Review of the Detroit Campaign of 1812 in United States Military History." *Michigan Historical Review* 38, no. 1 (Spring 2012).

Richardson, John. "A Canadian Campaign, by a British Officer—No. I." *New Monthly Magazine and Literary Journal* 19, no. 72 (December 1826).

_____. "A Canadian Campaign, by a British Officer—No. II." *New Monthly Magazine and Literary Journal* 19, no. 74 (February 1827).

_____. "A Canadian Campaign, by a British Officer—No. III." *New Monthly Magazine and Literary Journal* 19, no. 75 (March 1827).

Ridout, Thomas. "An Account of My Capture by the Shawanese Indians." *Western Pennsylvania Historical Magazine* 12, no. 1 (January 1929).

Ross, Margaret. "The New Madrid Earthquake." *Arkansas Historical Quarterly* 27, no. 2 (Summer 1968).

Rugeley, Terry. "Savage and Statesman: Changing Historical Interpretations of Tecumseh." *Indiana Magazine of History* 85, no. 4 (December 1989).

Salsich, Neil E., ed. "The Siege of Fort Meigs Year 1813: An Eye-Witness Account by Colonel Alexander Bourne." *Northwest Ohio Quarterly* 17, no. 4 (October 1945) and 18, no. 1 (January 1946).

Sarton, George. "Indian-Loving Catlin." *Isis* 22, no. 1 (December 1934).

Schlup, Emil. "Tarhe—The Crane." *Ohio Archaeological and Historical Publications* 14 (1905).

Shelby, John. "Letter of Dr. Shelby." *South-Western Monthly* 2, no. 3 (September 1852).

Smelser, Marshall. "Tecumseh, Harrison, and the War of 1812." *Indiana Magazine of History* 65, no. 1 (Spring 1969).

"Speech of Te-cum-seh." *Canadian Antiquarian and Numismatic Journal* 7, no. 1 (July 1878).

Spencer, Joab. "The Shawnee Indians: Their Customs, Traditions and Folk-Lore." *Transactions of the Kansas State Historical Society* 10 (1908).

Stanley, George F. G. "The Indians in the War of 1812," in Morris Zaslow, ed., *The Defended Border: Upper Canada and the War of 1812*. Toronto: Macmillan, 1964.

Stewart, Aura P. "Recollections of Aura P. Stewart of St. Clair County." *Report of the Pioneer Society of the State of Michigan* 4 (1883).

Stocker, Harry E. "A History of the Moravian Mission Among the Indians on the White River in Indiana." *Transactions of the Moravian Historical Society* 10, pts. 1–4 (1915–17).

Sugden, John. "Early Pan-Indianism: Tecumseh's Tour of the Indian Country, 1811–1812." *American Indian Quarterly* 10, no. 4 (Autumn 1986).

———. "Tecumseh's Travels Revisited." *Indiana Magazine of History* 96, no. (June 2000).

"A Summary Account of the Means Used after the Treaty of Greenville in 1795, to Promote the Civilization of the Indians, in Some Parts of North America." *Belfast Monthly Magazine* 8, no. 42 (January 31, 1812).

"T. S. Hinde's Letter, May 6, 1842." *American Pioneer* 1, no. 9 (September 1842).

"T. S. Hinde's Letter, May 30, 1842." *American Pioneer* 1, no. 11 (November 1842).

Talbert, Charles G. "Kentucky Invades Ohio—1779." *Register of the Kentucky Historical Society* 51, no. 176 (July 1953).

———. "Kentucky Invades Ohio—1782." *Register of the Kentucky Historical Society* 53, no. 185 (October 1955).

———. "Kentucky Invades Ohio—1786." *Register of the Kentucky Historical Society* 54, no. 188 (July 1956).

Tanner, Helen H. "Coocoochee: Mohawk Medicine Woman." *American Indian Culture and Research Journal* 3, no. 3 (1979).

———. "The Glaze in 1792: A Composite Indian Community." *Ethnohistory* 25, no. 1 (Winter 1978).

Thwaites, Reuben G. "Cornstalk." *Ohio Archaeological and Historical Publications* 21 (1912).

Thwaites, Reuben G., ed. "Letter Book of Thomas Forsyth, 1814–1818." *Collections of the State Historical Society of Wisconsin* 2 (1888).

"Trade and Prospect of Trade on the Ohio and Mississippi, Seventy-Six Years Ago." *Olden Time* 2, no. 1 (January 1847).

Trimble, Allen. "Autobiography and Correspondence of Allen Trimble." *Old Northwest Genealogical Quarterly* 10 (1907).

Turney, Henry D., ed. "Correspondence of Col. James Denny, of Circleville, Ohio, 1812–1815." *Old Northwest Genealogical Quarterly* 10, no. 3 (July 1907).

Vandiver, Wellington. "Pioneer Talladega." *Alabama Historical Quarterly* 16, no. 1 (Spring 1954).

Voegelin, C. F. "Shawnee Laws: Perceptual Statement for the Language and for the Content." In Harry Hoijer, ed. *Language in Culture, Conference on the Interrelations of Language and Other Aspects of Culture*. Chicago: University of Chicago Press, 1954.

Voegelin, C. F., and E. W. Voegelin. "Shawnee Name Groups." *American Anthropologist* 37, no. 4, pt. 1 (October–December 1935).

Voegelin, Erminie W. "Book Review: *Civilization*." *American Anthropologist* 39, no. 3 (July–September 1937).

_____. "Book Review: *Old Chillicothe*." *American Anthropologist* 37, no. 4, pt. 1 (October–December 1935).

Warren, Stephen A. "The Baptists, the Methodists, and the Shawnees." *Kansas History* 17, no. 3 (Autumn 1994).

Warren, William W. "History of the Ojibways, Based upon Traditions and Oral Statements." *Collections of the Minnesota Historical Society* 5 (1885).

[Washington, Thomas]. "The Attack on Buchanan's Station." In Edwin L. Drake, ed., *The Annals of the Army of Tennessee and Early Western History*. Nashville: A. D. Haynes, 1878.

Watson, O. K. "Moraviantown." *Ohio Historical Society Papers and Records* 28 (1932).

Watts, Florence G. "Lieutenant Charles Larrabee's Account of the Battle of Tippecanoe, 1811." *Indiana Magazine of History* 57, no. 3. (September 1961).

Weekes, William M. "The War of 1812: Civil Authority and Martial Law in Upper Canada." In Morris Zaslow, ed., *The Defended Border: Upper Canada and the War of 1812*. Toronto: Macmillan of Canada, 1964.

Weight, Donovan. "Begging for an Irremediable Evil: Slavery, Petitioning, and Territorial Advancement in the Indiana Territory, 1787–1807." *Journal of the Illinois State Historical Society* 103, no. 3/4 (Fall–Winter 2010).

Wentworth, John. *Early Chicago, Fort Dearborn. An Address*. Chicago: Fergus, 1881.

West, Elliott. "Tecumseh's Last Stand." *American History* 47, no. 5 (December 2012).

Whicker, J. Wesley. "Shabonee's Account of Tippecanoe." *Indiana Magazine of History* 17, no. 4 (December 1921).

_____. "Tecumseh and Pushmataha." *Indiana Magazine of History* 18, no. 4 (December 1922).

_____. "Zachariah Cicot." *Indiana Magazine of History* 21, no. 1 (March 1925).

Whittlesey, Charles. "White Men as Scalpers." *Western Reserve and Northern Ohio Historical Society* 22 (August 1874).

Whittley, Trevor. "William Whitley, Pioneer and Indian Fighter." *North Irish Roots* 11, no. 2 (2000).

Wickliffe, Charles A. "Tecumseh and the Battle of the Thames." *Register of the Kentucky Historical Society* 60, no. 1 (January 1962).

Willig, Timothy D. "Prophetstown on the Wabash: The Native Spiritual Defense of the Old Northwest." *Michigan Historical Review* 23, no. 2 (Fall 1997).

Wilson, Samuel M. "Shawnee Warriors at the Blue Licks." *Register of Kentucky State Historical Society* 32, no. 99 (April 1934).

Witherell, B. F. H. "Reminiscences of the Northwest." *Collections of the State Historical Society of Wisconsin* 3 (1904).

MANUSCRIPTS

Alabama Department of Archives and History, Montgomery
Samuel Moniac [Manac] Deposition

College of William and Mary, Swem Library, Williamsburg, Va.
David Ives Busnell, Jr., Papers

Detroit Public Library, Burton Historical Collection
Lewis Cass Papers
Orderly Book of Colonel John P. Boyd, 1811–1812
Benson J. Lossing Papers
Charles C. Trowbridge Papers
Benjamin F. Witherell Papers

Fort Malden National Historic Site, Amherstburg, Ontario
Battle of the Thames Information File
Fort Meigs Information File
Tecumseh Information File

Gilder Lehrman Institute of American History, New York
Henry Knox Papers

Historical Society of Pennsylvania, Philadelphia
Daniel Parker Papers

Indiana Historical Society, Indianapolis
Albert Gallatin Papers
Lewis Peckham Letter
Northwest Territory Collection

Indiana University, Eli Lilly Library, Bloomington
War of 1812 Manuscripts
Samuel Williams Papers

Library of Congress, Washington, D.C.
Lewis Bond Journal
William Henry Harrison Papers
Henry Onderonk, Jr., "Life and Times of Tecumseh"
Isaac Shelby Papers
Thomas Diaries and Letter-books

Missouri Historical Society, St. Louis
Thomas Forsyth Papers

National Archives and Records Administration, Washington, D.C.
Record Group 59: General Records of the Department of State:
"War of 1812 Papers of the Department of State, 1789–1815":
Miscellaneous Intercepted Correspondence, 1789–1814 (Microcopy 588)
Record Group 75: Bureau of Indian Affairs, 1793–1999:
Letters Received by the Office of Indian Affairs (Microcopy 234)
Letters Sent by the Secretary of War Relating to Indian Affairs, 1800–1824 (Microcopy 15)
Letters Received by the Secretary of War Relating to Indian Affairs, 1800–1824 (Micro-
    copy 271)
Records of the Michigan Superintendency (Microcopy 1)
Record Group 93: Revolutionary War Pension and Bounty Land Warrant Applications
    (Microcopy 804)

Record Group 107: Records of the Office of the Secretary of War:
Letters Received, 1800–1889 (Microcopy 221)
Letters Received, Unregistered Series (Microcopy 222)

National Archives of Canada, Toronto
Daniel Claus Family Fonds
Frederick Haldimand Papers
Henry Procter Court Martial Proceedings (MG13-WO71, Volume 243)
Record Group 8, C Series: British Military and Naval Records
Record Group 10: Indian Affairs Papers

Newberry Library, Chicago
Edward E. Ayer Collection:
Asa Lewis Letter
Erminie Wheeler-Voegelin Papers
Erminie Wheeler-Voegelin, "Noted Shawnee Leaders"
Mark R. Harrington, "Shawnee Indian Notes"

Ohio History Center, Columbus
John Johnston Papers
Return Jonathan Meigs Papers
James Miller Papers
Nathan Newsom, "A Short Summary of a Journey, Taken by Volunteers from Gallia
    County for the Purpose of Destroying Indians and the Invasion of Canada"
Samuel Williams Papers
Thomas Worthington Papers

Tippecanoe County Historical Association, Lafayette
George Winter Papers

University of Chicago Library
Durrett Miscellaneous Manuscripts and Codices:
Peter Trisler, Jr., Letters

University of Michigan, Bentley Historical Library, Ann Arbor
Charles C. Trowbridge Papers

University of Michigan, Clements Library, Ann Arbor
Lewis Cass Papers

Western Reserve Historical Society, Cleveland
A. T. Nye, "General Edward White Tupper"
War of 1812 Miscellaneous Collection

Wisconsin Historical Society, Madison
Lyman C. Draper Manuscript Collection:
    Daniel Boone Papers (C)
    Border Forays Papers (D)
    George Rogers Clark Papers (J)
    Daniel Drake Papers (O)
    Lyman C. Draper's Notes (S)

Thomas Forsyth Papers (T)
Frontier War Papers (U)
Josiah Harmar Papers (W)
Thomas S. Hinde Papers (Y)
Simon Kenton Papers (BB)
Kentucky Papers (CC)
William Preston Papers (QQ)
Shepherd Papers (SS)
Tennessee Papers (XX)
Tecumseh Papers (YY)
Virginia Papers (ZZ)

NEWSPAPERS

Alexandria (Va.) *Gazette*
American Advocate (Hallowell, Me.)
American and Commercial Daily Advertiser (Baltimore, Md.)
American Mercury (Hartford, Conn.)
Army and Navy Chronicle
Canton Repository (Ohio)
Centinel of Freedom (Newark, N.J.)
Charleston (S.C.) *City Gazette*
Christian Mirror (Portland, Me.)
Cincinnati Gazette
Columbian Gazette (Utica, N.Y.)
Columbus Ohio Monitor
Connecticut Journal (New Haven)
Dayton Republican
District of Columbia Courier
Federal Gazette (Baltimore, Md.)
Frankfurt Argus (Kentucky)
Fredonian (Chillicothe, Ohio)
General Advertiser (Philadelphia)
Georgia Gazette (Savannah)
Green-Mountain Farmer (Bennington, Vt.)
Highland County Weekly News (Hillsboro, Ohio)
Illinois State Journal (Springfield)
Kentucky Gazette (Lexington)
Liberty Hall (Cincinnati)
Liberty Star and Union Banner (Liberty, In.)
London Chronicle
London Free Press (Ontario)
Long-Island Star (Brooklyn)
Louisiana Gazette (St. Louis)
Missouri Gazette and Public Advertiser (St. Louis)
Montreal Gazette
National Intelligencer (Washington, D.C.)

New England Palladium (Boston)
New Hampshire Sentinel
New York American
New York Commercial Advertiser
New York Gazette
New York Herald
New York Literary World
New York Mercantile Advertiser
New York Spectator
Niles' Weekly Register (Baltimore)
Ohio Centinel (Dayton)
Orange County Patriot (Goshen, N.Y.)
Otsego Herald (Cooperstown, N.Y.)
Pennsylvania Gazette (Philadelphia)
Philadelphia Democrat Press
Philadelphia General Advertiser
Philadelphia Weekly Aurora
Phoenix Civilian (Cumberland, Md.)
Pittsburg Gazette
Pittsfield Sun (Mass.)
Poulson's American Daily Advertiser (Philadelphia)
Providence Gazette
Republican Star (Easton, Md.)
Richmond Enquirer
Savannah Republican
Scioto Gazette (Ohio)
Spirit of 'Seventy-Six (Washington, D.C.)
Spooner's Vermont Journal (Windsor)
Springfield Republican (Ohio)
Staunton Eagle (Va.)
Telegraph and Daily Advertiser (Baltimore)
Topeka Weekly Capital
Trump of Fame (Warren, Ohio)
United States Gazette (Philadelphia)
Vermont Mirror (Middlebury)
Virginia Argus (Richmond)
War (New York, N.Y.)
War Journal (Portsmouth)
Weekly Aurora (Philadelphia)
Weekly Register (Baltimore)
Western Spy (Cincinnati)
Western Spy and Hamilton Gazette (Cincinnati)
Western Sun (Vincennes)

DISSERTATIONS

Chalou, George C. "The Red Pawns Go to War: British-American Indian Relations, 1810–1815." Indiana University, 1971.

Goltz, Herbert C. "Tecumseh, the Prophet, and the Rise of the Northwest Indian Confederation." Western University, 1973.

Pate, James P. "The Chickamauga: A Forgotten Segment of Indian Resistance on the Southern Frontier." Mississippi State University, 1969.

Schutz, Neal W. "The Study of Shawnee Myth in an Ethnographic and Ethnohistorical Perspective." Indiana University, 1975.

Spencer, Rex L. "The Gibraltar of the Maumee: Fort Meigs in the War of 1812." Ball State University, 1988.

ONLINE SOURCES

Founders Online, National Archives, http://founders.archives.gov.

Index

Page numbers in *italics* refer to maps.

Adams, John, 119, 131

Alabama, 11, 33, 76, 263, 269, 272, 438

Alabama River, *265*

Albany, *19*

alcohol, 14, 30, 34, 96, 98, 105, 134–35, 111,
134–40, 149, 154, 159, 166, 169–71, 177,
205, 218–19, 223–24, 228, 247, 338, 344,
413, 416, 418, 427

Alder, Jonathan, 112–13, 141
adoption of, 37, 107
horse trading with Tecumseh and,
124–25, 134
Leather Lips and, 231
on preparing for battle, 116

Alexandria, *66*

Alford, Thomas Wildcat (Tecumseh's
great-grandson), 20, 445n14

Algonquian language, 32, 222, 438–40

Algonquins, 12–15, 17, *19*, 21–33, 52–53, 65, 71,
79, 180

Allegheny River, *24*, 34, *66*

Amherstburg, 170, 178–79, 213, 214, 216, 226,
233, 301–2. *See also* Fort Malden
American capture of, 394, 413
council at, after Treaty of Ghent, 420
retreat of October 1813, 386–87, 392–93,
394
Tecumseh at, 357–58
Tecumseh's speech to Procter and,
411
Tenskwatawa and, post-1815, 422–23,
426, 429

wampum belt and, 230
War of 1812 and, *315*, 316, 318–20, 322, 325,
331, 333, 335–37, 341–42, 344–45, 351–53,
355, 371, 385

annuities, 119, 120, 137, 144, 228–29, 233–34,
248–49, 252–54, 256–57, 269, 273

Appalachians, xiv

Arnold, Benedict, 129

Arnold, Christopher, 400–401

Arnold's Creek, *393*, 399–400

Askin, Charles, 342, 343

Audubon, John James, 292

Auglaize River, *24*, 81–82, 103, 122, 141, 157,
360

Baby, François, *315*, 394–95, 404

Backmetack Marsh, 402–8, *405*, 410

Bacon, Lydia, 299

Bad Creek, *360*

Badger, Rev. Joseph, 170–71, 173

Badollet, John, 235–36, 244, 258–60, 277,
302–3

Baker, Joshua, 106

Baltimore Society of Friends, 136–37

Baptiste's Creek, *315*

Baptist missionaries, 231, 432

Baptist Shawnee Mission, 434

Barclay, Robert, 384–86, 389

Barnes, cattle drover, 83

Barr, Samuel, 93

Barrett, Abner, 125–26

Barron, Joseph, 237–41, 244, 258, 282, 287

Bathurst, Lord Henry, 356, 412

Baton Rouge, *265*

Bay Settlement, *315, 360*

Beata, Delaware mystic, 150–51, 154, 164–67

Belle River, *315*, 395

Between-the-Logs, Wyandot chief, 203, 381–83, 387

Bird, Henry, 48–50

Blackfish, Chillicothe chief, 23, 44–45
    death of, 46–48
    as foster father of Tecumseh, 44

Black Hawk, Sauk warrior, 223, 377–78

Black Hoof, Shawnee chief, 50, 115, 120–22, 126, 478n17
    aligned with Little Turtle and Tarhe, 203
    annuities and, 248–49
    Blue Jacket and, 174
    Boyer murder and, 184–87
    Brownstown council of 1810 and, 247
    death of, 432
    Fort Wayne Treaty and, 146, 230–31, 248–49
    Greenville and, 179–80, 182–83, 192–93, 196
    Harrison and, 141–42, 146, 302, 395
    Indian removal of 1820s and, 426–27, 429
    Jefferson and, 142, 201–2, 220
    shot by Harrison's soldier, 354
    Spring Wells council of 1815 and, 421–22
    Tecumseh and, 174, 178, 183–87, 199–201
    Tenskwatawa vs., 158, 163, 174, 178–80, 182, 200–201, 209, 296, 298, 429
    Vincennes council of 1802 and, 141–42
    Wapakoneta land title and, 142, 201–2
    War of 1812 and, 313, 320, 349, 395
    Wells and, 182–83

blacks, 95–96, 132, 227, 270, 431

Blacksnake, Shawnee chief, 478n17

Black Turkey, 90–91

Black Warrior River, *265*

Blanchard River, *360*

Blount, William, 76, 95–98, 100–101

Bluejacket, George (son of chief), 174, 176–77

Bluejacket, Jim (grandson of chief), 262, 394

Blue Jacket, Logan, 330, 338

Blue Jacket, Pekowi Shawnee chief, xiv, 37, 301, 361, 381
    appearance and personality of, 63–64, 103
    Black Hoof vs., 174
    British and, 111
    Chillicothe council of 1807 and, 197–98, 200
    Chillicothe meeting with Kirker and, 174–75
    common land ownership and, 144
    Coocoochee and, 105
    death of, 208
    Fallen Timbers battle and, 115–18, 317
    Fort Finney Treaty and, 63–64
    Fort Harmar Treaty and, 79–81
    Fort Recovery attack and, 112–14
    Glaize council of 1792 and, 102, 103
    Glaize town of, 104
    Greenville and, 174–75, 182
    Greenville council of 1807 and, 195–97
    Greenville Treaty and, 120–21
    moves north of Ohio River, 68–69
    Northwestern Confederacy and, 77–82, 90, 110–18, 317
    retirement of, 141
    Shakers and, 177
    St. Clair's defeat and, 85–87
    Tecumseh as youth and, 62
    Tecumseh joins confederacy of, 78–79
    Tenskwatawa and, 203
    town of, *315*
    treaties and, 144

Blue Licks, ambush at, *24*, 58–59, 64–65

Bockongahelas, Delaware chief, 102

Bois Blanc Island, *315*, 318–20, 335–36, 339, 384

Boone, Daniel, 16, 44–45, 51, 54, 58, 60, 64, 91

Boonesborough, *24*
    siege of, 45

Boswell, *362*

Bourne, Alexander, 363

Bowman, John, 46–48

Boyer, John, murder of, 184–88

Braddock, Edward, 12

Brant, Joseph, Mohawk chief, 65, 71, 230

Bread Dance, 42

Brickell, John, 86, 103–4

British Center Division, 388

British fleet, 385

British Indian Department, 36, 49, 58, 110, 172, 178, 213–14, 216–17, 230, 302, 319, 372, 379, 382, 387–88, 390, 413, 415–19, 421, 426, 429

British Rangers, 58

British Royal Navy, impressment and, 192, 296, 304, 351

British traders, 143, 270

British West Florida, 23

Brock, Sir Isaac, 302–4, 316–17, 320, 322, 325–26, 328, 333–42, 345, 351, 353, 356, 358, 377, 404, 421, 428
    death of, 353–54

Brouillette, Michel, 234, 237, 247

Brown, Dee, xii

Brownstown, 24, 170–71, 215–16, 255
    council of 1786, 65
    council of 1810, 247–48
    council of 1812, 313, 320–21
    council of 1813, 382–83
    Tecumseh's negotiations at, 216, 222
    War of 1812 and, 315, 318, 320, 326, 329–31

Brownstown, Battle of, 329–32, 342

Brownstown Creek, 329

Buchanan, John, 99

Buchanan's Station raid, 98–101, 103

Buckongahelas, Delaware chief, 102, 110–11, 115, 118, 120
    death of, 150–51, 165, 167
    old ways and, 150
    treaties and, 144

buffalo, 62, 73, 140

Buffalo *umsoma*, 35

Bullskin Creek, 91–92

Bureau of Indian Affairs, 430

Bury My Heart at Wounded Knee (Brown), xii

Caldwell, Billy (son of Colonel), 328, 332, 352, 388, 391, 400, 404, 408–9, 417

Caldwell, Col. William, Sr., 58, 387, 390, 417–20

Canard River, Battle of, 315, 322–24

Cape Girardeau, Missouri, 45, 68

Captain John Logan, Mingo chief, 4

Captain Johnny, Mekoche chief, 61, 68

Captain Lewis, Shawnee chief, 478n17

Captain Pipe, Delaware chief, 56, 57

Captain Will, Shawnee chief, 16, 44, 51

Carleton, Guy, 110

Carpenter, Nicholas, 83–84

Cass, Lewis, 388, 413, 456n34, 456n35, 471n18
    Shawnee removal to west of Mississippi, 427
    on Tecumseh, 86
    Tenskwatawa and, 151, 423–29, 471n18

Catlin, George, 433–34

Cayugas, 439

Chaine, Isadore, Wyandot chief, 304–7, 313–14

Chambers, Peter, 342–43

Charity, Ann, 167

Charleston, 66

Chatham, Upper Canada, 391, 396–98, 426

Chattahoochee River, 265, 438

Chattanooga, 75, 438

Cheeseekau (brother of Tecumseh and Tenskwatawa), 57, 69, 246, 383, 451n6
    birth of, 17
    Blue Licks ambush and, 58
    Clark attack on new Piqua and, 59
    death of, at Buchanan's Station, 100–101, 124
    death of father and, 6–7
    Doughty peace mission and, 76–77, 80
    Fort Finney Treaty and, 63
    joins Chickamaugas on Tennessee River, 74–79, 94–96
    as surrogate parent for brothers, 22–23, 46, 51
    travels with Tecumseh to Spanish Louisiana, 71–74
    war vs. settlers and, 61–62, 67
    Watts's call to war and, 97–101
    wounded in Piqua battle, 50
    Ziegler's Station attack and, 95–96, 444n9

Cherokees, xiii, 64, 74–75, 89, 95, 98, 173, 250, 252, 253, 263–64, 265, 272–74, 291, 437–38

Chesapeake Bay, 101, 439

Chesapeake-Leopard affair, 191–93, 212, 296

Chicago River, 204, 245, 299

Chickamaugas, xiii, 64, 68–69, 74–79, 82, 94–101, 235, 264, 273, 438, 453n10

Chickasaws, 76, 96, 127, 250, 252, *253*, 263–67, *265*, 438

Chillicothe (Ohio town), 145, 164–65, 174–75, 194, *255*
    council of 1807, with Blue Jacket, 196–200, 202, 210

Chillicothe (old Shawnee village), *18*, 20, 23, *24*, 26–27, 106, *133*, 445n14
    attacks on, 46–48, 50–51, 125
    burial mound at, 197
    population falls, 45
    Tecumseh's birthplace in, 197

Chillicothe Shawnee division, 23, 25, 35, 46, 63–64, 201, 437

Chippewa, Battle of, 418

Chippewa River, 418

Chippewas. *See* Ojibwas

Choctaws, 96, 250, 252, *253*, 263–69, *265*, 438

Christian, Thomas, 367–68

Christianity, 164, 170, 432–33

Chunky Town, *265*, 268

Chute, Dr. J. Andrew, 434–35

Cicero, 130

Cicot, Zachariah, 206

Cincinnati, 34, 80, 88–89, 91, 126, 131, *133*, 251, *253*, *255*

Cincinnati Land Office, 131

Cincinnati Western Spy, 127

Clark, Andrew, 404, 408, 410

Clark, George Rogers, 49–50, 58–59, 377

Claus, William, 213–16, 233, 251, 416–17, 419–21, 423, 429–32

Clay, Green, *362*, 363–64, 374–77

Clay, Henry, 187, 311, 312

Cleveland, 57, 375

Colbert, George, Chickasaw chief, 266

Coleman, James, 407

Columbus, Ohio, 20, 85

Combs, Leslie, *362*, 368–69

Connecticut, *66*, *253*

Conner, John, 151–52, 193, 217
    on Tecumseh, 220

Conner, William, on Shawnee brothers, 217, 220

Continental Army, 57

Continental Congress, 25

Coocoochee, Mohawk prophetess, 104–5, 153

Coosa River, *265*

Corn Dance, 43

Cornstalk, Peter (son of chief), 125, 175–76

Cornstalk, Shawnee chief, 15, 23, 25–26, 50, 63, 64, 125
    American Revolution and, 25–26
    Fort Pitt council and murder of, 25–26, 44–45, 242
    Fort Pitt Treaty and, 25, 50
    Point Pleasant battle and Dunmore's War and, 3–7, 23, 85
    Pontiac's War and, 15
    torture and, 39

Cornstalk, young chief (grandson of chief), 429–30, 432

Cornstalk's town, *24*

Cornwall Creek, *393*

Council Fire, 216

Coweta, *265*

Craig, Sir James, 212–13, 216–17, 250

Crawford, William, 57

Crawford's Defeat, *24*, 57

Crazy Horse, xii

Creeks, 11–12, 23, 68, 76, 89, 94–96, 98, 100, 136, 250, 252, *253*, 262–64, *265*, 267, 269–73, 278, 300, 438
    Lower, 269–70, 272, 438
    Upper, 33, 269–70, 272, 291, 438

Croghan, George, 377

Cumberland Gap, 15–16

Cumberland River, 75–76, 98

Cuyahoga River, *24*, 63

Dakota Sioux, 300, 326, 373

Dance of the Lakes, 271

Darrow, David, 175

Deaf Chief, Potawatomi chief, 257–58

Dearborn, Henry, 140, 142, 184, 189, 191, 206, 218–19, 221, 317, 335, 351

Declaration of Independence, 129

deer, 140, 264

Deer Creek, Tecumseh village on, 121–22

Deer *umsoma*, 35

Delaware River, *19*

Delaware (state), *66*, 439

Delawares, xiv, 13, 16, *19*, 25, 33–34, 37, 41, 50, 55–57, 61, 63, 65, 72, 79–80, 101–4, 110–11, 114–18, 123, 135, 140–41, 149–51, 178, 209–10, 220, 228–30, 233, 248, 278–83, 286–87, 292, 306, *360*, 392, 395, 404, 407, 417, 422, 438–39, 455n20

  prophets and visionaries and, 150, 153–57

  witch hunts and executions, 65–69

Denny, Ebenezer, 82, 85–86

Denny, James, 324

Desha, James, *405*, 407

Detroit, *24*, 70, 170, 172, 179, 204, 213–14. *See also* Fort Detroit

  British Indian Department and, 371

  education of Blue Jacket's son at, 63

  fire of 1805, 179

  Tenskwatawa meeting with Cass at, 427–29

  War of 1812 and, 312–18, *315*, 320, 325, 329–30, 337–42, 344, 348, 355, 357–59, 379, 392

Detroit River, 120, 213–16, 222, 232, 249, 299–300, 312, *315*, 318, 322, 330, 333–34, 339, 344, 356, 371, 372, 387, 390, 392

Dickson, Robert, 326, 330, 352, 373, 376–78, 380–81

Dolsen, John, 395

Dolsen, Matthew, 395

Dolsen's Landing, 391, *393*

Doughty, John, 76–77, 80

Dragging Canoe, Chickamauga chief, 74–76, 95, 100

Drummond, George, 414

Dubois, Toussaint, 224, 236–37

Duchouquet, François, 126–27

Dudley, William, *362*, 364–66, 369–71

Dundas, Tenskwatawa's camp at, 413, 415–16, 419

Dunham, Josiah, 189–91

Dunmore, John Murray, Earl of, 4–5, 23, 91

East Sister Island, *360*

Eckert, Allan, xiii

Edmunds, R. David, xiv

Edwards, Ninian, 276, 299, 347–48

elk, 140

Elk *umsoma*, 35

Elliott, Alexander, 342

Elliott, Matthew

  Amherstburg council of 1808 and, 213–16

  Amherstburg council of 1810 and Great Wampum Belt, 230, 233, 248–50

  Amherstburg council of 1812 and promise to Tecumseh, *315*, 319, 321–22

  Brock council with Tecumseh and, 336–37

  Brock ruse with Shawnee brothers and, 304–6, 316

  Brownstown council of 1813 and, 382–83

  death of, 416–17

  delegation to Prévost in Quebec and, 414

  Detroit and Frenchtown captures and, 341–43

  Fallen Timbers battle and, 118

  food shortages and, 380

  Fort Meigs battle and, 368–69, 372, 374

  Fort Stephenson battle and, 377–78

  Fort Wayne attack and, 352–53

  Northwestern Confederacy and, 104, 110–11, 118

  Procter's retreat of 1813 and, 387–88, 390–91, 394–99

  Revolutionary War and, 58

  Tecumseh first meets, 49

  Tecumseh's appeal for aid, 301

  Thames battle and, 403–4, 409

  Tippecanoe and, 289

  War of 1812 and, 329, 355, 358

Ellis, cattle drover, 83

European trade goods, 14, 28

Eustis, William, 227–28, 235–37, 240, 251, 254, 256, 261, 277–79, 312, 347–48

Evil Spirit (Motshee Manitou), 155, 161

  Americans as children of, 190

  witchcraft and, 168

Fallen Timbers, Battle of, *24*, 115–18, 120–21, 131, 144, 153, 195, 202, 215, 238–39, 278, 323, 327, 361, 387

federal government. *See also specific presidents*

  civilization policy of, 225

  Indian agents and, 137, 225

  Indian trading stations or factories and, 137–38

Federal Road, *265*, 270–71
Fisher, Frederick, 172, 174, 194–95, 213, 249
Five Medals, Potawatomi chief, 201, 233, 304–6, 306
    village of, 224
Floyd, George, 240, 243
Folsom, David, 268–70
food shortages, 169, 229–30, 295–96, 301, 307, 422–23
    Prophetstown and, 217–19
    War of 1812 and, 347, 355, 372–73, 379–80, 385
Fool Charley, Chickamauga subchief, 96, 453n10
Forlorn Hope, *405*, 406–7, 410
Forsyth, Thomas, 205, 413
Fort Ancient culture, 32
Fort Avery, *360*
Fort Ball, *360*
Fort Dearborn, *133*, 204–5, 222, 245, *253*, 299
    capture of, 341–42, 347–48, 351, 355
Fort Defiance, *24*, *360*
Fort Detroit, 14, *18*, 25, 45, 48, 50, 56, 60, *66*, 110, 114, 189, *253*, *255*
    British retreat of 1813 from, 388
    capture of, 339–41
    Harrison recaptures, 353, 372, 395, 409
    razed, by 1824, 428
    siege of 1763, 14–15
    War of 1812 and, 312, *315*, 317, 336–41
Fort Fayette, *66*
Fort Findlay, *360*
Fort Franklin, *66*
Fort George, capture of, 417–18
Fort Greene Ville, *24*, 109, 112, 118, 158
Fort Hamilton, *24*, 453n20
Fort Hampton, *265*
Fort Harmar, *24*, 88
Fort Harrison, *255*, 278, 280, 295, 307
    attack on, 348–51, 358
Fort Hawkins, *265*
Fort Henry, *24*
Fort Jefferson, *24*, *66*, 453n20
Fort Jennings, *360*
Fort Knox, *66*, 72, 240–41
Fort Leavenworth, 433–34
Fort Madison, *133*, 222, *253*, 318

Fort Malden (Amherstburg), 206, 213, *253*, *255*, 300, 302, 346, 358, 425. *See also* Amherstburg
    British retreat of 1813 from, 394
    council of 1808, 214–18, 224
    council of 1812, 326–28
    council on retreat of 1813, 386–89, 392
    Great Lakes delegation to, 178–79
    war council of 1813, 373–74
    War of 1812 and, 312–19, *315*, 323, 326, 331–32, 353, 356, 359, 370–72, 380, 384–89
Fort Massac, *133*
Fort Meigs, Battle of, 358–70, *360*, *362*, 389, 400
    second attack on, 371–76
Fort Miamis, *18*, *24*, 110, 215
    British betrayal at, after Fallen Timbers, 118, 317, 338
    massacre of prisoners at, 367–68
    Northwestern Confederacy and, 111, 115, 117, 215
    ruins, 361, *362*, 374
Fort Michilimackinac (*later* Mackinac), *18*, 60, *66*, 110, *133*, 181, 189, *253*, *255*, 326–28, 338, 340, 352–53
Fort Niagara, 15, *19*, 25, *66*, 110
Fort Pitt, 15, *19*, *24*
Fort Recovery, 109
    attack on, 112–14
Fort Seneca, *360*
Fort Stanwix, *18*, *19*, 23
Fort Stephenson, Battle of, *360*, 375, 377–79, 389
Fort Stoddert, *265*
Fort Washington, *24*, *66*, 88–89, 109, 130
Fort Wayne, 68, 70, 120, *133*, 136, 201, 206–7, 211, 221–22, *253*, *255*, 295, 343. *See also* Treaty of Fort Wayne
    Brock's ruse and, 304–5
    Indian factory at, 138
    siege of, 351–54
    War of 1812 and, 322, 342, 346, 348–49, *360*
Foxes, 144, 205, 210, 221–23, *255*, 278–99, 300, 327, 373, 417, 426, 439–40
Fox River, 245, *255*, 355
Frank (slave boy), 82–84
French, xiv, 33, 34, 36, 39–40, 160, 190
    Napoleonic Wars and, 110, 142, 296

French and Indian (Seven Years') War,
11–12, 14, 34, 36, 153
French-Canadians, 312, 318, 325, 431
Frenchtown, *315*, 342–43, 356
Battle of, 356, *360*
French traders, 15, 72, 101, 136, 223, 268
fur trade, 32–34, 42, 68, 138, 219

Gallatin, Albert, 235, 244, 259–60, 303
Galloway, James, 125–27, 141, 145
Galloway, Rebecca, 125
game and hunting, 139–40, 150, 199, 208, 211, 219, 246
Gamlin, John, 234
gauntlet, 37, 91, 367
Geneseo, *19*
George III, King of England, 63
Georgia, 33, *66*, 74, 76, 89, *253*, 263, 269, 272–73, 437, 438
Gibson, John, 243
Gilbert, Bil, 448n3
Gimewane the "Queen" (wife of Tenskwatawa), 153, 237, 238, 245
Glaize, The, *24*, 81–82, 103–5, 108–10, 114–15
council of 1792, 101–3, 108
Northwestern Confederacy and, 111, 114–15
Gnadenhutten, *24*
massacre of Delawares at, 55–57, 135, 165, 242
Gore, Francis, 212–16
Graham, Richard, 431
Grand River, Tenskwatawa settles with Norton at, 417, 419
Great Black Swamp, *360*
Great Comet of 1811, 263, 272, 290
Great Council Fire, 304, 326
Great Kanawha River, 3
Great Miami River, *18, 24*, 90, 123, *133*, 164, *255*
Logan attacks on, 64, 68
skirmish with Kentuckians at, 185
Great Serpent, 30, 121, 162, 205, 217
Great Wampum Belt, 216, 222, 232, 249–50, 390
Green Bay, 190, 246, 439
green corn dance, 97
Greenville Creek, 158

Greenville (Indian village), *133, 255*, 297, 455n20. *See also* Fort Green Ville
Black Hoof vs., and Boyer murder, 184–88
Chillicothe council of 1807 on fate of, 197–200
council house built, 158, 169, 175
council of 1807 with Blue Jacket, 194–97
decision to vacate, for Wabash River, 196, 199–200, 205–9
Fisher as Indian trader at, 172
Harrison and, 172, 193–94
hunger and, 208, 210
Indian pilgrims in, 178–82, 194, 202–3
Kirker and, 174–75, 193–94
Main Poc and, 205–6
population of, 196, 201
Roundhead and, 185
Shakers and, 175–78, 194
solar eclipse and, 172–74
Tenskwatawa (Lalawethika) leads followers to, 157–58, 163–65, 169, 178–81
Wapakoneta and, 201
Wells's pressure to vacate, 174, 179, 182–84, 191–96, 199–203, 206–7
Greenville Treaty Line, 132, 139, 141, 188, 200, 205
Greenville town built on American side of, 164, 182–85, 195
Treaty of Ghent and, 420
Grosse Island, *315*

Hacker's Creek, raid on, 107
Half King, Wyandot chief, 56
Hall, John, 387–88, 391
Harmar, Josiah, *24*, 81–82, 85
Harrison, Anna Tuthill Symmes, 131
Harrison, Benjamin, V, 129
Harrison, Benjamin, VI, 130–31
Harrison, William Henry
antislavery sentiment and, 258–59
assigned to Fort Washington, 1791–93, 130
background and personality of, 129–31
Badollet and, 235–36, 244, 258–61, 277, 302–3
Black Hoof and, 230–31
British hated by, 129, 223–24, 303
Cass and, 388

Harrison, William Henry *(continued)*
  challenges Tenskwatawa to make sun
    stand still, 172–73
  chiefs bribed by, for land cessions,
    144–47
  Deaf Chief and, 257–58
  death of Tecumseh and, 409–11
  elected to Congress, 131–32
  Eustis letter on Shawnee brothers and,
    260–61
  Fallen Timbers battle and, 116, 131
  Fort Meigs battle and, 364–65, 369–70,
    374–76
  Fort Stephenson battle and, 377
  Fort Wayne Treaty land cessions and,
    227–29, 234–35, 242, 249–51, 303
  Greenville Treaty land cessions and,
    140–41
  Grouseland estate of, 134, 241
  heads Northwest Army, in War of 1812,
    353–55, 358–59, 372, 413
  Indiana Territory governor, xi, 132–34
  Indian decline into poverty and,
    138–40
  Indians under command of, 395
  Jefferson letter on dispossessing
    Indians, 143–44
  Johnston vs., 225–26
  Lake Erie battle and, 385–86
  Leopold-Chesapeake affair and, 192–94
  Little Turtle and, 144
  Madison and, 296–97
  marries Anna Tuthill Symmes, 131
  Mississinewa council of 1812 and, 307
  offensive of 1813 and, 379, 381–83
  Procter's retreat of 1813 and, 387, 394–97,
    399–400
  Prophetstown conflict vs. Tenskwatawa
    and, 209–10, 217–19, 224–26, 233–41,
    251–54
  Prophetstown march by, 275–84
  Prophetstown razed by, 288, 303, 354
  Public Land Law and, 132
  Spring Wells council of 1815 and,
    421–22
  St. Louis Treaty and, 222–24
  Tecumseh and, 191, 193, 198, 252, 276–77,
    298, 325, 328
  Tecumseh's council with, 1810 at
    Grouseland, xi, 240–45
  Tecumseh's council with, 1811 at
    Vincennes, 255–61
  Tecumseh's recruiting trips and, 254
  Tecumseh suspected of ties to British,
    302
  Tecumseh tribute by, xi–xii, 260–61
  Tenskwatawa forbidden to reenter U.S.
    by, 422
  Tetapachsit land treaties and, 166–67
  Thames battle and, 400, 403, *405*, 407,
    409–11
  Tippecanoe battle and, 284–89, *285*,
    296–99, 303, 311, 314, 346, 348, 424
  treaty councils and Shawnee
    resentment of, 146
  treaty lands hard line and, 257
  Walk-in-the-Water and, 397–98
  War of 1812 and, 347, 349
  Wells and, 137, 218, 225
Hatch, William, 341
Hawkins, Benjamin, 263, 269–71
Henry, Patrick, 4
Hoentubbee, Choctaw chief, 266, 268,
  270
Holmes, Abraham, 400–401
Hopkins, Samuel, 354–55
Howard, Benjamin, 276, 299
Hudson River, *19*, 438
Hughes, Jesse, 83
Hull, David, 343
Hull, William, 190–91, 202, 209, 222, 226,
  233, 247–49, 304
  War of 1812 and, 312–14, 317–18, 320, 322,
    324–26, 328–30, 333, 335–44, 348, 352,
    377, 384
Hunter, John D., 293
Huron confederacy, 17, 33, 215, 438, 440
Huron River, *360*, 371
Hutton family, murder of, 302

Illinois, xi, *18*, 295, 440
Illinois River, *24*, *133*, 203–5, 245–46, *255*,
  299, 413, 439
Illinois Territory, 33, 73, 132, *133*, 140, 144,
  227, 229, 245, 249, 251, *253*, *255*, 258, *265*,
  276, 300–301, 320, 341–42, 347

Indiana, state, 63, 118, 123, 132, 227, 425, 439, 440
Indiana legislature, 193
Indiana Territory, 38, 120, 132, *133*, 140–41, 144, 199, 206, 211, 227–29, 235, 250–51, *253*, 258–59, *265*, 273, 295–96, 302–3, 326, 329, 348–49, 353, *360*, 425–26
  Harrison appointed governor of, 132
  Land Office, 235
Indian factory system, 137–38, 142–44
Indian Land Cessions. *See also specific treaties*
  map of, *133*
Indian Territory, 15
influenza, 149–50, 152, 219, 230–31
Iowa Indians, 300
Iowa River, *133*
Ironside, George, 104–5, 177–78
Iroquoian language, 32, 74–75
Iroquois, 15–16, *19*, 32–34, 41, *53*, 65, 79, 102, 230, 247–48, 416, 417–18, 438–39

Jackson, Joseph, 87
Jay, John, 118
Jeanette's Creek, *393*
Jefferson, Thomas, 168
  Black Hoof and, 142, 201, 220
  civilizing mission and, 201
  desire for Indian land and, 142–44, 179
  Empire of Liberty and, 142, 179, 190
  Greenville and, 182–84, 199–200
  Harrison and, 132, 141–44
  Indian factory system and, 138
  Leopard-Chesapeake affair and, 192
  Little Turtle's plea to, 136
  Madison and, 227–28, 264
  meets Main Poc and Little Turtle, 219, 221
  Mingo massacre and, 4
  Ohio Valley battles and, 81–82, 108–9
Jennings, Jonathan, 259
Johnson, James, *405*
Johnson, Richard Mentor, 396, 399–400, 404–7, *405*, 409
Johnston, Joe, 400–401
Johnston, John
  death of brother and, 351
  food aid to Indians and, 296

as Fort Wayne factor and, 137–38, 206
Fort Wayne meeting with Tenskwatawa and, 224–26
Fort Wayne Treaty of 1809 and, 229, 248–49
Hull and, 313
promoted to Indian agent, 225
Prophetstown and, 277–78, 295–96
removal of Tenskwatawa to Kansas and, 427, 430–31
Tecumseh and, 70, 126, 137, 356
Tippecanoe and, 289
Jones, Rev. David, 35
Josephy, Alvin M., xii–xiii
Joshua, Delaware Christian, 167–68

Kanawha River, 3, *19*
Kansas River, removal of Shawnee to reservation on, 432–33
Kaskaskias, *24*, *133*, 144, 204
Kaskaskia town, 430
  council of 1827, 431
Kekionga, *18*, *24*, 68
Kelly, Benjamin, 59
Kelly's Island, *360*
Kennedy, John F., xiii
Kenton, Simon, 126, 246, 341, 452n6
  Black Hoof tensions, 184–86
  council with Tecumseh near Urbana of 1799, 126–27
  council with Tecumseh over Greenville, 194
  skirmish with Tecumseh (April 1792), 91–94
  skirmish with Tecumseh (March 1793), 106
  Thames battle and, 404
Kentucky, 3, 5, 11, 15–17, 23, 37, 44, 48–50, 55, 58, 62–65, *66*, 69, 73–74, 80, 89–91, 121–22, 125, *133*, *253*, *255*, 262, *265*, 349, 438, 311
Kentucky militia, 46–48, 58–60, 89–94, 349, 354, 359, 363–69, 371, 375–76, 379, 395–96, 399–400, 404–5, 413
Kentucky Mounted Riflemen, *405*, 406, 408–9, 411
Kentucky Revival of 1800–1, 154, 175. *See also* Shakers

Kentucky River, 24
Kichekemit, warrior, 408
Kickapoos, 18, 80, 205, 210–12, 220, 229, 234,
   247, 252, 255, 262, 275, 277, 281, 283–86,
   285, 289, 299, 306, 320, 347–49, 351, 355,
   417, 419, 421–22, 425–26, 439
Kickapoo Treaty (1809), 133
King's Road, 315, 386, 392, 393, 395–96, 398,
   401, 409
Kinzie, John, 245
Kirk, William, 201–2, 209, 220
Kirker, Thomas, 174–75, 193–200
   Tecumseh's speech at Chillicothe
      council and, 198–200
Kispoko Shawnee division, 17, 25, 35, 45, 121,
   141, 174, 430, 437
Kluge, Brother John, 164, 168, 169
Knox, Henry, 108–9, 130
Knoxville, 98, 265
Kumskaukau (twin of Tenskwatawa)
   birth of, 23
   Fallen Timbers battle, 115
   War of 1812 and, 354–55

Lafayette, Indiana, 211
Lafontaine, Peter, 224
Lake Erie, 19, 24, 25, 66, 133, 253, 312
   Battle of 1813, 360, 361, 384–85, 410
   British retreat of 1813, 393
   War of 1812 and, 315, 318, 325, 335, 359, 360,
      372, 379
Lake Huron, 19–20, 66, 133, 253, 255, 326
Lake Michigan, 18, 24, 66, 133, 224, 253, 255,
   440
Lake Ontario, 19, 66, 133, 253, 413, 418
Lake Peoria, 300
Lake St. Clair, 392, 393
Lake Superior, 66, 180, 253, 255
Lalawethika (formerly Laloeshiga, later
   Tenskwatawa). See also Tenskwatawa
   adultery and, 152
   affection for Tecumseh and, 134–35
   alcoholism of, 134–35, 145, 151, 152, 153
   appearance and dress of, 159
   Clark attack on new Piqua and, 59–60
   Conner friendship with, 151–52
   Coocoochee Mohawk woman's
      sermons and, 105
   divine revelation and, 152–58

eloquence of, 151
eye injury and, 53, 72–73, 134
failure of, in vision quest, 53–54
Fallen Timbers and, 115–17, 153
friendships with whites and, 151–52
at Glaize with Tecumseh, 104
Great Spirit snake and, 87
hunting and, 73, 122
marriages and children of, 151
marriage to Gimewane and, 153
Master of Life and, 157
mentored by Penagashea medicine
   man, 152
moves to Maumee River, 68
name changed from Laloeshiga, 46
name changed to Tenskwatawa, 159
Northwestern Confederacy and, 111,
   115–17
personality of, 151
"Rattler" nickname of, 72
St. Clair's defeat and, 85, 87
Tecumseh influenced by, 156–57
Tecumseh's hunting and, 122
Tecumseh's speech at council with
   whites of 1799 and, 127
Tecumseh's wife Mamata and, 123
traditional medicine and, 145, 151–52
travels and proselytizing and, 158
travels with Tecumseh to Spanish
   Louisiana, 72–74
Wapakoneta council of 1805 and,
   158–60
Laloeshiga (later Lalawethika;
   Tenskwatawa), 23, 30. See also
   Lalawethika; Tenskwatawa
   childhood and, 44–46
   humor and, 35
   Kentucky militia attack of 1779 and,
      47–48
   mother's migration to west of
      Mississippi, 45–46
   name changed to Lalawethika, 46
   personality of, 46
   shoots out own right eye, 46
   torture witnessed by, 38
land speculators, 16, 23–24, 132
L'Arbre Croche, Ottawa and Ojibwa
   community, 181, 189
Lavalle's farm, 315

Leather Lips, Wyandot subchief, 171,
    231–32, 258
Lee, Richard Henry, 129
Legion of the U.S.
    Fallen Timbers and, 116–17, 131
    Glaize strike and, 109
    Harrison serves in, 130–31
Legit, George, 83
Le Maigouis, Ottawa warrior, 181, 189–91
Lewis, Andrew, 5–6
Lewis, James Otto, 428
Lewis and Clark expedition, 251
Lexington, Kentucky, *66, 133*
Lexington, Kentucky, *Reporter*, 410–11
Licking River, 49–50, 58
Lincoln, Abraham, 223
Little Bighorn River, xii
Little Kanawha River Valley, 82
Little Miami River, *18*, 23, 26, 59, *133*
    Kenton raid near, 93–94, 452n6
Little Turtle, Miami chief
    American second wife of, 103
    Black Hoof and Tarhe vs., 203
    Brock's ruse and, 304
    Brownstown council of 1810 and, 247
    death of, 320
    Fallen Timbers and, 118
    Fort Harmar Treaty and, 79
    Fort Wayne Treaty of 1809 and, 228–29,
        249
    Greenville Treaty and, 120, 183
    Harrison and, 228–29, 302
    meets Jefferson, 219, 221
    Mississinewa council of May 1812, 306
    Northwestern Confederacy and, xiv,
        79–81, 85, 87, 90, 110–12, 114–15, 301, 381
    pan-Indianism and, 90
    pleads for end to whiskey trade, 136–37
    Shawnee brother at Prophetstown
        opposed by, 207, 209–10, 225, 276, 298,
        300
    Shawnee brothers vs., 137, 298
    son-in-law Wells and, 103, 120, 136–37,
        183, 201, 207
    St. Clair's defeat and, 85, 87
    Tecumseh and, 137, 183
    Tenskwatawa and, 225, 276, 296
    treaties and, 144
    War of 1812 and, 320

Little Turtle's Town, 103–4, *133*, 136, 201, *255*
Logan, Benjamin, 64, 68
Logan, Jim (son of chief), 125, 321
Logan Blue Jacket, Shawnee chief, 330, 338
Lookout Mountain, 75, 97
Loramie Creek skirmish, 90–91
Louisiana Purchase, 142–43, 207, 233, 251
Louisiana Territory, 12, *133*, 233, *253*, *255*, *265*,
    276, 290, 299
Louisville, 89, *133*, *253*, *255*
Luckenbach, Abraham, 164
Lundy's Land, 418

Madison, James, 227–28, 244, 259, 261, 264,
    279, 423, 425
    conciliatory policy of, 298–99
    Tippecanoe and, 296, 312
    War of 1812 and, 296–97, 304, 312–13
Mad River, 50, 84, 85, 126, 164–65, 174
    Boyer murder at, 184
Mahicans, 33
Maine, *253*
Main Poc, Potawatomi chief and *wabeno*
    alcoholism and, 205, 221, 413
    appearance and personality of, 203–6,
        219
    Canard River battle and, 323
    death of, 413
    Fort Dearborn and, 204–5, 356
    Fort Detroit capture and, 341
    Fort Wayne Treaty and, 228, 233, 251
    Maguaga battle and, 331–32
    meets Jefferson with Little Turtle, 219,
        221–22, 427
    Mississinewa council of 1812 and, 305–6
    Procter's retreat of 1813 and, 373, 391–92,
        409
    Prophetstown and, 205–7, 209–11, 219,
        221, 278
    settlers attacked by, 251, 257, 276
    Tecumseh's confederacy and, 226, 246,
        251, 300–303, 306–7
    Tenskwatawa and, 357
    town of, *133*, *255*
    Wabash River atrocities and, 302–3, 306
    War of 1812 and, 318, 320, 331–33, 336, 341,
        352–53, 355, 357, 373
    Wells and, 206–7, 219, 222
    wounded in Osage attack, 233–34, 245

malaria, 134, 152, 165–66, 386

Mamata (Tecumseh's first wife), 123

Marietta village, 79, 88–89

Martin's Station raid, 48–50

Maryland, 33, *66*

Massachusetts, *66, 253*

Master of Life (Great Spirit), xiii, 13, 14, 31, 36, 38, 42, 54, 87, 146, 190, 204–5, 231

    law given to Shawnees by, 40

    manitous given to earth by, 40

    name-giving ceremony, 21

    solar eclipse and, 173–74

    sun as fatherly presence of, 242

    Tenskwatawa's description of, 164

    Tenskwatawa's vision of, 153–59

Maumee Rapids, *24*, 110, 115, 117–18, 314, 342–44, 352, 355–56, 361

    Fort Meigs battle and, 358–59, 364–66, 374

Maumee River, *24, 66*, 68, 80–82, 101–5, *133, 255*, 345, 353

    War of 1812 and, *360, 362*

McArthur, Duncan, 194–97, 409–10

McGary, Hugh, 58, 64–65

McGregor, John, 398

McGregor's Creek, 391, *393*, 397–400

McIntyre, Alexander, 92, 94

McKee, Alexander, 49, 58, 86, 89–90, 104, 110, 118, 341–42, 352, 416

McKee, Thomas, 342, 416

McNemar, Richard, 175–76

measles, 364

medicine bags, 14, 162, 223

medicine men, 132

Mekoche Shawnee division, 25, 29–30, 35, 46, 57, 61, 63–64, 68, 102, 120, 122, 141–42, 158, 174, 201, 429–30, 437

Menominees, 195, 202, 246, 373, 439

Methoataske (mother of Tecumseh and Tenskwatawa), 11, 17, 25, 27, 246

    adopted white child Sparks and, 17–20

    background of, 11, 17, 25

    birth of Cheeseekau and, 17

    birth of Kumskaukau and Laloeshiga (*later* Tenskwatawa) and, 23

    birth of Nehaaseemo and, 22

    birth of Sauwauseekau, 17

    birth of Tecumpease, 17

    birth of Tecumseh and, 20–22, 197

    migrates west, 45–46, 448n3

    Tecumseh's trip of 1788–89 to visit, 72–74

    Tecumseh's trip of 1801 to visit, 136

Methodist missionaries, 432

Miamis, 12–13, 17, *18*, 33, 41, 68–69, 79–81, 101, 103, 110–11, 113–15, 118, 120, 136–37, 142, 149, 178, 201, 205, 209–10, 224, 228–29, 232–33, 243, 248–49, 252, *255*, 275–76, 278, 281–82, 300, 320, 342, 352, 354, 392, 422, 425–26, 439–40, 455n20

Michigan, xi, 17, 214–15, 330, 439, 440

Michigan Territory, *133*, 172–73, 181, 189–90, 202, 213, 247, *253*, 254, *255*, 278, 281, 300, 304, 312–13, *315*, 342–45, 358–59, *360*, 371, 389, 413, 423–26, 471n18

Mid Day, 250

Middle Bass Island, *360*

Mill Creek, 99

Miller, James, 330–33, *362*

Milwaukee, 300

Mingoes, 3–6, *19*, 25, 37, 48, 50, 64, 69, 101, 111, 115, 118, 165, 439

Minnesota, 132, 300

Missisauga, *18, 19*

Mississinewa River, *18, 133*, 209–10, *253*, 354

    peace conference of 1812, 305

Mississippi, 76, 263, 266, 268, 430–31, 438

Mississippi River, 23, 32, 33, 45, 68, 90, 119, 143, *255*, 440

Mississippi Territory, *253*, 264, *265*, 270

Mississippi Valley, 222

Missouri Shawnees, 72, 86

    New Madrid earthquake, 292

    Tecumseh and, 246–47, 292

Mobile, *265*

Mohawks, *65*, 79, *335*, 439

Mokalusha (Choctaw town), 267–68

Moluntha, Mekoche chief, 63–65

Monguagon (Maguaga), Battle of, *315*, 326, 329–33, 352

Monongahela River, *19*

Monroe, James, 143, 423, 427

Montgomery, Alabama, 270

Montreal, *66*

Moravian missionaries, 56, 124, 135, 151–52, 154, 156, 164, 166–67

Moraviantown (Fairfield), *393*, 396, 398–99, 401, 406

    Battle of (1813), 412

    Procter court-martial and, 412

Moraviantown Ford, *393*

Morrison, *362*

Muir, Adam, 322, 328, 331–33, 352–53

Muscle Shoals, *265*

Mushulatubbee, Choctaw chief, *265*, 266, 268

Muskingham River, 88, 132, *133*

Muskogee language, 438

Naiwash, Ottawa chief

    appeals for unity, after death of Tecumseh, 419

    delegation to Prévost in Quebec and, 414–15

    settlements of, post-1815, 420

    Spring Wells council of 1815 and, 421

    Tenskwatawa and, 417

    War of 1812 and, 383, 390–91, 397–98, 402, 404, 407, 413, 418

Nanitcokes, 101, 165, 439

Napoleon Bonaparte, 191, 212, 296, 304, 356, 415, 420

Nashville, 76, 95–96, *265*

    Watts and expedition against, 98–101

National Republican Party, 304, 311–12

Neal, James, 82

Nehaaseemo (brother of Tecumseh and Tenskwatawa), 22, 72, 74, 446n19

Neolin, Delaware mystic

    influence of, on Tenskwatawa, 153–54, 157–58, 163

    pan-Indianism of, xiv, 13–15, 71, 149–50

Nettle Creek, 85

New Hampshire, *66*, *253*

New Jersey, *66*, 438

New Madrid, Missouri, 73

    earthquake of 1811 and, 290–91

New Orleans, *66*

New York City, *19*, *66*, *253*

New York State, 32–33, *66*, *253*, 438

Niagara frontier, 328, 345, 353, 379, 388, 397, 413–14, 417

Niagara River, 335, 417–18

Nixon, Richard, xiii

North Bass Island, *315*, *360*

North Carolina, *66*, 74, *253*, 263, 437

Northwestern Confederacy, 77–90, 110–20, 359

    Fallen Timbers and, 115–18

    Fort Recovery attack and, 112–14

    Glaize abandoned by, 114–15

    Glaize council of 1792 and, 101–2, 108

    Greenville Treaty and, 119–20, 142

    St. Clair's defeat by, 81–90

Northwest Ordinance (1787), 65–67

Northwest Territory, xi, *24*, 65, *66*, 76, 80, 89, 108, 130–32

Norton, John, 230, 416–19, 421

Ohio, xi, 63, 132, 158, 174–75, 179, 251, *253*, *255*, 320, 326, 329–30, 353, 371–72, 387, 426–27, 438, 440

    statehood and, 146

    state legislature, 427

Ohio Company, 88, 89

Ohio militia, 145–46, 313, 323–25, 329–30, 359

Ohio River, 3–4, 15–16, *18*, 23–25, *24*, 34, 50, 58, 61, 65, *66*, 69–70, 76, 80, 82–84, 88–90, 108–9, 119, 130, *133*, *253*, *255*, *265*, 316, 337, 344, 370

Ohio Valley, 11, 13–17, *18–19*, 23–24, 32, 33, 41–42, 45, 55–56, 60–61, 68, 71–72, 79–80, 172, 234, 439

Ojibwas, *18*, *19*, 48, 102, 111, 113–15, 179, 181, 186, 189–91, 195, 202, 219–24, *255*, 281, 300, 314, 320, 326, 352–53, 367, 373, 381, 392, 417, 426, 439

Oneida, 439

Onondaga, 439

Ontario, 33, 438, 439

Orleans Territory, *253*

Osages, 72, 136, 205, 207, 233, 247, 257, 267, 291–95

Osage Treaty (1808), *133*

Ottawa River, *66*

Ottawas, xiv, 14–15, 17, *18*, *19*, 41, 102, 111, 114–15, 158, 179, 181, 189–91, 202, 214, 219–24, 254, 278, 300–301, 314, *315*, 318, 320, 326, 331–32, 352–53, *360*, 373, 392, 413, 417, 422, 439

Pacan, Miami chief, 248–50

Paint Creek, Kenton raid at, 106

Pakoisheecan, Kickapoo chief, 349–50

panther, 21, 27

Panther *umsoma*, 21, 35

Patriot Chiefs, The (Josephy), xii–xiii

Patterson, Billy, 168

Paukeesa (son of Tecumseh and Mamata), 208, 392, 399–400, 404
    birth of, 123
    death of Tecumseh and, 409
    defection of, after death of Tecumseh, 419
    delegation to Prévost in Quebec and, 414–15
    Detroit meeting with Tenskwatawa and Cass and, 427–29
    moves to Missouri, 432
    removal to Kansas River reservation and, 430

Paul, John, 83

Peace of Paris (1783), 118

Pekowi Shawnee division, 17, 25, 35, 42, 45, 62, 122, 419, 430, 437

Pelee Island, *315*, *360*

Penagashea, medicine man, 152

Penn, William, 34

Pennsylvania, 11–12, *24*, 33–34, 56–57, 438

Pensacola, 97, *265*

Perry, Oliver H., 379, 384–85, 410

Philadelphia, *19*, *66*, 89, 102, *253*

Piankeshaws, *18*, 138, 440

Piqua (Shawnee town), *18*, 26
    Clark attack on, 50–52
    Kentucky militia attack on, 47
    new, attacked by Clark, 59–60
    population dwindles, 45
    Tecumseh's final pilgrimage to, 122–23
    Tecumseh's panic at, 58

Pittsburgh, 25, 130, *253*, *254*
    battle of 1755 at (Braddock's Defeat), 12

Point au Pins, *393*

Point Pleasant, Battle of, 3–7, 22–23, *24*, 85, 91, 186

Pontiac, Ottawa chief, 71, 243, 381
    exile and death of, 15
    Harrison on Tecumseh vs., 256
    Neolin and, xiv, 14–15
    pan-Indianism and, 101–2, 149

    spiritual creed of, 153, 158
    war of 1763 and, 13–15, 17, 82

Portage River, *360*

Potawatomis, *18*, 33, 41, 48, 102, 111, 114–15, 120, 179, 187, 191, 195, 201–11, 221–29, 233–34, 242, 245, 248–54, 255, 275–78, 281, 284–87, *285*, 299–306, *315*, 318, 320, 323, 331–32, 341, 347–48, 351–54, *360*, 391, 408–9, 422, 425–26, 428, 440, 455n20

Presbyterian missionaries, 170

Presque Isle, 372, 374

Prévost, Lady, 415

Prévost, Sir George, 316–17, 334, 338, 351, 353–54, 358, 370–72, 374, 377, 379–80, 412, 414, 416

Procter, Henry, 325–28, 333–34, 336, 344–45, 351, 353, 355–61
    court-martial of, 412
    death of Roundhead and, 383–84
    death of Tecumseh and, 412
    Fort Malden (Amherstburg) council and Tecumseh speech of 1813, 387–92, 411, 419
    Fort Malden war council of 1813, 373–74
    Fort Meigs battle and, 363–64, 368–70
    Fort Meigs second battle and, 372–76
    Fort Stephenson battle and, 377–79
    Lake Erie battle and, 384–86
    Prévost refuses to aid, 379–80
    retreat after of October 1813 and, 386–99, 413
    Sandusky battle and, 379
    Tecumseh's falling-out with, 380–81, 384
    Thames battle and, 401–4, *405*, 406, 409, 412–13
    War of 1812 and desire to create Indian buffer state, 371–72

Prophetstown, *133*, 211–61, *253*, *255*
    council house, 211
    council of 1810 at, 232–34
    established, with move from Greenville, 207–13, 217–21
    food shortages and, 217–21
    Fort Wayne Treaty and, 229–34
    Harrison burns, after Tippecanoe, 288–89, 297–98, 303, 307
    Harrison council of 1810 on, 238–45
    Harrison council of 1811 on, 254–59

Harrison march and attack on, 275–89, 314

Harrison provides food aid for, 217–19

Harrison's suspicions and threats against, 224–25, 229–30, 235–45, 254–61

new, built by Tenskwatawa in Kansas, 432–35

razed, in 1812, 354–55

rebuilt, after Tippecanoe, 298–300, 302–4, 307

salt annuities and, 252–54

Tenskwatawa hopes to rebuild, after 1814, 422

Tippecanoe battle and, 284–89, *285*

War of 1812 and, 321, 342, 346–55

Protestant missionaries, 35, 174, 170

Public Land Law (1799), 132

Puckeshaw, Shawnee war leader, 120–21

Puckeshinwau (father of Tecumseh and Tenskwatawa)

birth of Tecumseh and, 20–22

Blackfish and, 23

Blue Jacket and, 62

children born, 17

death of, at Point Pleasant, xv, 5–7, 22

early life with Creeks, 11–12

Kispoko village of, 17

Ohio Valley and, 11–13, 34

Panther *umsoma* and, 35

second wife Methoataske and, 11

smallpox and, 12–13

town of, *24*

white adoptee Sparks and, 17–20

Pushmataha, Choctaw chief, 267–68

Put-in-Bay, *360*, 384

Quakers, 34, 56, 136–37, 153–54, 194, 201–2, 209, 221–22

Quebec, *66*, 316, 351

Paukeesa and Tecumpease's delegation to Prévost in, 414–15

Queenston Heights, Battle of, 353

Red Jacket, Iroquois chief, 247–48

Red Pole, Mekoche Shawnee chief, 102, 108, 453n20

Red River, 263

Renick, William, 188

Revolutionary War, 25–26, 48–50, 55, 57–59, 65, 74, 89, 107, 109, 131, 317, 389, 438

Rhode Island, *66, 253*

Riall, Phineas, 415–16, 418

Richardson, John, 388–90, 402–3, 406–8

Richmond, Virginia, *66*

Ridout, Thomas, 69–70, 450n16

Rivard, Mr., 343

River Raisin, *18, 315,* 329–30, 333, 343, 345, 356–57, 359, *360,* 424–25

Battle of, *360,* 396

massacre at, 364–65, 369

River Rouge, 214, *315,* 331, 391

Rock River Valley, 222, 246

Roman Catholics, 170, 178, 215

Rottenburg, Francis de, 384–85, 412

Roundhead, Wyandot chief

Black Sun miracle and, 173

Brock council and, 337

Brownstown council with Between-the-Logs and, 382–83

Chillicothe council with Blue Jacket and, 196–97

death of, 383–84, 413

Fort Meigs battle and, 365

Fort Wayne siege and, 351–53

Frenchtown battle and, 342–44

Harrison drive against Prophetstown and, 278, 281

Leather Lips killed by, 231–32

personality of, 185–86

Springfield council on Boyer murder and, 185–86

Tenskwatawa and, 173, 203

War of 1812 and, 320, 327, 336–37, 356, 363, 373, 382–83

Rowlands, Thomas, 410

Ruddell, Abraham, 49, 87

Ruddell, Elizabeth, 49

Ruddell, Isaac, 48–49

Ruddell, Stephen D., 454n25

adoption of, and boyhood with Tecumseh, *24,* 48–52, 61–62, 141, 450n16

as Baptist minister, 156, 231

on birth of Tecumseh, 20

Buchanan's Station and, 99

Chillicothe speech by Tecumseh and, 198–200

Ruddell, Stephen D. *(continued)*
  Fallen Timbers battle and, 115–17
  Fort Recovery attack and, 112
  Fort Wayne Treaty and, 231
  Greenville council with Blue Jacket
    and, 194–97
  Kenton attack and, 93–94
  on Lalawethika's wife Gimewane, 153
  Loramie Creek skirmish and, 90–91
  returns to white relations, 121
  Shawnee raids as youth and, 69–70
  on Tecumseh's belief in brother's
    conjuring, 156–57
  on Tecumseh's drinking and, 96
  on Tecumseh's generosity, 86–87
  on Tecumseh's raids and, 105
  on Tecumseh's relations with women,
    70, 78
  on Tecumseh's treatment of
    prisoners, 70
  Tenskwatawa and, 194
  Vincennes council and, 241, 243
  War of 1812 and, 322
Ruddell's Station raid, *24*, 48–49
Running Water village, 75, 96, *265*
Ruscom River, *315*
Russia, 356

Sandusky Bay, *360*, 375, 377
Sandusky River, *18*, *24*, 118, 170, 231, *255*, *360*,
    381
Sandusky villages, Crawford's Defeat at,
    56–57
Sandwich, 179, 319–20, 322, 339, 387, 390, 392,
    394
  Tenskwatawa settles near, 420–21
Sangamon River, *18*, 245
Sauks, *18*, 41, 144, 195, 205, 210, 221–23, 246,
    249, *255*, 278, 300, 320, 327, 373, 377, 417,
    422, 425–26, 440
Sauwauseekau (brother of Tecumseh and
    Tenskwatawa), 17
  death of, at Fallen Timbers, 117
  Northwestern Confederacy and, 111, 115
Savannah, *66*
Savannah River, 33
Scioto River, *18*, 20, 23, *24*, 34, 84, 106, 121,
    133, 231, *255*
Scioto Valley, 197

Scott, Winfield, 317
Seekaboo
  language skills of, 262
  Tecumseh's southern travels and, 262,
    267–68, 272
Senecas, 102, 158, 220, 439
Seven Years' War, 12
Shabbona, 245–46, 279–81, 283–87, 400, 404
Shakers, 154, 175–78, 194
Shane, Anthony, 454n25, 458n11
  death of Tecumseh and, 410
  on Tecumseh and women, 71, 78, 123–24
  on Tecumseh as hunter, 27, 122
  trading post of, *255*
  War of 1812 and, 396, 410
  Wells's demand to vacate Greenville
    and, 182–84, 191
Shaver, Michael, 95
Shawnees, 3. *See also specific battles; divisions;
    individuals; towns; and treaties*
  Algonquian language and, 32
  ancient roots of, 32
  character of, 35–36
  chiefs and, 35, 40–41
  clothing and adornments, 28–29
  culture and religion of, 35, 40–43
  defined, 437
  diet and, 27–28
  first encounters with whites, 29–30
  gauntlet run and, 37–38
  health and hygiene of, 28, 35
  hunting and, 42, 52
  individual rights and, 39–40
  intertribal council fire and, 41
  intratribal divisions and *umsomas* of,
    34–35, 447n6
  laws of, 40
  marriage and family and, 40, 52
  medicine bags and, 54
  men's roles and, 40–41
  neighboring tribes as family, 17, 41
  peace conferences and calumet
    ceremony, 41
  prisoners and slaves and, 96
  removal of, to reservation on Kansas
    River, 429–33
  sexuality and, 40–41, 43, 71, 78
  Shawnee language newspaper, 432
  storytelling and, 29–30

torture and, 38–39

tribal divisions of, 17, 34–35

umsomas of, 35

visionaries and, 153–54

vision quest and, 52–54

wampum and, 41

wanderings of 1600s, 33–34

war methods and tactics, 29, 33, 35, 52–55

white captives and adoptees and, 36–38

wigwams of, 42

witches and, 30–31

women's roles and, 29, 40–42

Shawnee Prophet, The (Edmunds), xiv

Sheaffe, Roger, 356

Shelby, Isaac, *362*, 396, *405*

Sherman, David, 401

Sherman, Lemuel, *393*, 398, 401

Simcoe, John, 110

Siouan language, 180, 440

Sitting Bull, xii

slavery, 125, 227, 235, 259, 264, 270, 273

smallpox, 12–13, 152, 446n19

Smith, James, 37

solar eclipse of 1806 (Black Sun), 172–74, 280

Sorrow in Our Heart, A (Eckert), xiii

South Carolina, *66*, 74, *253*, 437

southern tribes

matrilineal kinship and, 266

Tecumseh alliance and, 257

Tecumseh's travels to recruit, 262–74, *265*

Southwest Territory, *66*, 76, 95–98

Spain, 264

Spaniards, 142–43, 160, 190, 270

Spanish East Florida, *66*, *253*, 264

Spanish Louisiana, *66*, 68, 72–74

Spanish mestizos, 431

Spanish West Florida, *66*, 75, 95, 97, *253*, 264, *265*

Sparks, Richard (adoptee of Puckeshinwau), 17–20

Split Log, Ojibwa war leader, 367–69

Springfield, Ohio (*formerly* Piqua), 26, *255*

council on Boyer murder and, 185–88

Spring Wells grand council of 1815, 421

St. Clair, Arthur, 65, 80–87, 89–90, 92, 101–3, 105, 109, 115, 130–31, 283

St. George, Thomas, 317, 319–20, 322, 325

Stickney, Benjamin, 313–14, 320, 346–47

St. Joseph, *18*

St. Joseph's River, *255*, *360*

St. Lawrence River, *66*

St. Louis, *18*, *24*, *66*, *265*

Tenskwatawa at, 431

Stoney Creek enclave, 164–65

Stuart, William, 100

Sugden, John, xiii, 450n16, 451n6

Susquehanna River, *19*

Susquehanna Valley, 153

Swan Creek, *360*

Sydenham River, *393*

Symmes, John Cleves, 131–32

Talladega, *265*

Tallapoosa River, *265*, 269

Tarhe, Wyandot chief, 215

aligned with Little Turtle and Black Hoof, 203

Brownstown council of 1810 and, 247

Fallen Timbers battle and, 115, 118

Greenville Treaty and, 120

Presbyterian missionaries and, 170–71

Roundhead attempt to murder, 232

solar eclipse and, 173–74

Tecumseh visits, 220

Tenskwatawa vs., 171–72, 296

treaties and, 144

War of 1812 and, 313, 320, 349, 381–82, 395

witch hunt stopped by, 171–72

Tarhe's Town, *133*, 170–74, 231, *255*, *360*

Taylor, Zachary, 349–50

Tecumpease (sister of Tecumseh and Tenskwatawa)

adopts Tecumseh and Laloeshiga, 46, 152

adopts Tecumseh's son Paukeesa, 123, 208

birth of, 17

death of father, 22–23

death of husband, 408

delegation to Prévost in Quebec and, 414–15

Glaize and, 104–5

Greenville Treaty and, 121

marriage to Wahsikegaboe, 22–23

Prophetstown and, 217

resettled, after War of 1812, 420

Tecumseh and, 27, 392

Tecumseh, Shawnee chief, 57
  ailments of, broken thighbone and limp,
    73, 341
  ailments of, wounds and illness of 1813,
    333, 352, 356–57
  alcohol and, 96, 134–36
  Alder and, horse trade incident, 37,
    124–25, 134
  Amherstburg council of 1808, and
    meeting with Elliott, 214–18
  Amherstburg council of 1810, and
    speech on death of Fisher, 249–50
  appeal and popularity of, xii, 122, 188,
    251, 357
  appearance and dress of, 70, 126, 240–41,
    262–63, 318–19, 341, 388–89, 401
  Badollet on remarkable nature of,
    259–60
  birth and naming ceremony for, 20–21,
    445n16
  birth of brother Laloeshiga (*later*
    Lalawethika; Tenskwatawa), 23
  birth of brothers and sisters, 17
  birth site of, in old Chillicothe, 197,
    445–46n14
  Black Hoof and, 174, 182–83, 186–87, 199,
    203, 230–31
  Blue Jacket as mentor, 37, 62–63, 78–79,
    82–83, 90, 174–75, 182
  Blue Licks ambush and, 58–59
  Boyer murder and, 184–88
  Brant's United Indian Nations and,
    65–67
  British pledges to, and Treaty of
    Ghent, 420
  Brock and, 335–41, 345, 351, 353–54, 421
  Brock's death and, 354
  Brock's ruse vs. Americans and, 304–5
  brother Cheeseekau and, 7, 51, 67
  brother Cheeseekau in Tennessee and,
    74–79, 94–96
  brother Cheeseekau's death and, 99–101,
    103, 108, 124
  Brownstown council of 1810, with Hull,
    247–48
  Brownstown council of 1813, with
    Between-the-Logs, 382–83
  Buchanan's Station raid and, 99–100, 103

Caldwell and, 58
Carpenter raid of 1791 and slave boy
  hostage, 82–84
Chaine and, 313–14, 316
Chatham and, 426
Cherokees and, 273–74
childhood of, 21–23, 44
childhood of, and mother's migration
  west, 45–46, 51
childhood of, and warrior skills of,
  26–30, 51–53, 72
Chillicothe attacks of 1779 and, 47–48,
  51–52
Chillicothe council of 1807, and debut
  of pan-Indian vision, 200, 202
Chillicothe courthouse speech of 1807,
  194–200
Choctaws and, 266–69, 270
country of, 1774–94, 24
country of, 1811, 255
Creeks and, 269–73
cross-cultural diplomacy of, 126
Deaf Chief murder threat and, 257–58
death of, 408–19, 428, 481n50
death premonition of, 400
Deer Creek village erected by, after
  Fallen Timbers, 121–22
diet of, 27–28, 126
Doughty peace mission of 1790 and,
  76–77
Eckert biography of, xiii
Elliott and, 49, 58
English language skills and, 45, 51–52,
  59, 125
Fallen Timbers battle and, 115–17, 121, 131,
  215, 238–39
father's death and, xv, 6–7, 51
father's last wish and, 7
first great battle with whites and, 109
Fort Detroit capture and, 339–41
Fort Finney Treaty and, 63
Fort Malden (Amherstburg) council of
  1812, 326–28
Fort Malden council of 1813, and
  ultimatum to Proctor, 388–92, 411
Fort Malden gathering of 1813, and push
  for attack, 373–75
Fort Malden visits of, 224

Fort Meigs battle and, 359–70
Fort Meigs second battle and, 371–76
Fort Recovery battle and, 112
Fort Stephenson battle and, 378–81
Fort Wayne Treaty and, 230–32, 234–35, 240–45, 249, 252
Galloway and gift of ceremonial pipe, 125–26
Glaize and, 103–6, 108
Glaize council of 1792 and, 103
Greenville town and, 157–58, 164–65, 176–78, 182, 194–200
Greenville town and, Wells's demand to vacate, 182–84
Greenville Treaty and, 121–23, 183
Hacker's Creek attack of 1793 and, 107–8
Harrison and, xi, 193, 226, 236–39, 247, 252, 276–77, 298–99, 325
Harrison and, after Tippecanoe, 298–302
Harrison council of 1802 and, 141
Harrison council of 1810 and, 238–45
Harrison council of 1811 and, xi, 254–59
Harrison's razing of Prophetstown and, 354
Harrison's tribute to, xi, 260–61
Harrison vs. Tenskwatawa after Fort Wayne and Barron mission, 236–39
historical perception of, imbalances in, xiii–xiv
Hunter on speaking ability of, 293
hunting and, 27, 52–53, 62–63, 73, 87, 122
Indiana Territory, and desire to drive whites from, 303
Josephy biography on, xii–xiii
Kelly and, 45, 51
Kenton council of 1799, and speaking ability, 126–28
Kenton raid on Little Miami of 1792 and, 24, 91–94
Kenton raid on Paint Creek of 1793 and, 24, 106–7
Kentucky raids of 1780 and, 48
Kentucky raids of 1791–93, 90–91, 105
Kirker and, 174–75
Lake Erie Battle and, 384–85
leadership skills, 51
Little Turtle and, 90, 183, 203, 210

Logan and, 321
Mad River Valley and, 126
Main Poc and, 251
marriages and romances, Chickamauga paramour and possible child, 78–79
marriages and romances, first wife Mamata, 123
marriages and romances, second wife, 123–24
marriages and romances, third wife Wabelegunequa, 145, 208, 390
McKee and, 49, 58
Michigan (Detroit River) Wyandots and Great Wampum Belt, 215–16, 222
Michigan Territory and, desire to expel Americans, 344–45
Michigan Territory recruiting and, 254
Mississinewa council of 1812, 303–7
Monguagon battle and, 329–33
myths about, xii
name, meaning of, 446n15
New Madrid earthquake, 290–92, 294
Northwestern Confederacy and, 90, 111, 114–17, 119, 121
Ohio settlers ambushed by, 61–62, 68–70
Osages and, 292–95
pan-Indian confederacy and, after death of, 412–14
pan-Indian confederacy and, becomes primary spokesman, 183–84
pan-Indian confederacy and, co-architect with Tenskwatawa, xii, 199, 208, 210–11, 298
pan-Indian confederacy and, four earthly purposes injected by, 234–35
pan-Indian confederacy and, religious underpinnings, xiii–xiv
pan-Indian confederacy and, Tippecanoe facilitates recruitment, 298–302
pan-Indian confederacy of 1788 and, 71–72
panther as guardian, 27
Panther *umsoma* or clan and, 21
personality of, 27, 35, 51–52, 86–87, 91
Piqua battles and, 50–52, 59–60
Piqua pilgrimage of, 122–23
political skills of, xii, 27, 126, 182–84, 298

Tecumseh, Shawnee chief *(continued)*
  Prévost on, 412, 415
  Procter and, 325–28, 334, 345, 356–60,
    372–73, 380–81, 390–91, 396–97
  Procter's retreat of 1813, 386–400
  Prophetstown and, 207–12, 220, 307,
    346–48, 353
  Revolutionary War and, 58
  Ridout capture and, 69–70
  Roundhead and, 185, 383–84
  Ruddell and, 51–52, 156–57, 231
  Ruddell's return to whites and, 121–22
  Ruddell's Station raid and, 48–49
  sexuality of, 70–71, 78–79, 152, 211–12
  Shakers and, 176–78
  Shane and, 182–84, 191
  sister Tecumpease and, 27, 392
  smallpox and, 22
  solar eclipse of 1806 and, 173
  son Paukeesa and, 123, 392
  speaking ability of, 126–28, 187, 388, 411,
    456n34
  Springfield council on Boyer murder
    and, 184–88
  St. Clair attacks and, 84–87
  storytelling by elders and, 29–31
  Sugden's biography of, xiii
  Tarhe and, 203
  Tenskwatawa and, xiii–xv, 151, 183–84,
    358–59, 458n11
  Tenskwatawa and, council of 1810 on
    Fort Wayne Treaty, 232–34
  Tenskwatawa and, during War of 1812,
    381
  Tenskwatawa on, to Catlin in old age,
    434
  Tenskwatawa's alcoholism and, 105,
    134–35
  Tenskwatawa's family aided by, 152
  Tenskwatawa's vision and, 156–57,
    458n11
  Tenskwatawa's wager on hunting with,
    122
  Thames battle and, on British retreat of
    1813, 400–411, *405*
  Thames River council of October 3,
    1813, and, confederacy dissolves,
    397–98

  Tiffin and, 145–46, 165
  Tippecanoe and, 295–98
  torture opposed by, 38, 62–63, 70, 78
  as transformative figure, xiv
  travels to Canada after Mississinewa,
    307
  travels to Illinois Fox and Sauk, 222–23
  travels to Illinois Potawatomis and
    western Shawnees, recruiting, 245–47
  travels to recruit southern tribes of 1811,
    250, 252, 262–75, *265*, 290–95
  travels to visit mother in 1788, 72–74
  travels to visit mother in 1801, 136
  travels with Lalawethika preaching
    Indian renewal, 158
  vision quest of, 52–53
  Waggoners taken prisoner by, 107–8
  Wapakoneta council of 1805 and, 158,
    163
  Wapakoneta council of 1810 and, 230–32
  Wapicomekoke witch controversy and,
    166
  War of 1812 and, 304, 312–45, 346–48,
    351–53, 355–58. *See also specific battles;*
    generals; and councils
  Waters and, 59
  Watts council on war of 1792, 97–98
  Wayne strike vs. Glaize of 1793 and, 109
  Wells and, 103, 199–200
  Wells's demand to vacate Greensville
    and, 182–84
  white friends of, 45, 51–52, 59, 124–26
  White River and, 123–24, 151
  whites scalps and, 55
  whites settlers and, 145
  witches and witchcraft and, 30–31, 166
  Ziegler's Station attack and, 95–96
Tecumseh: A Life (Sugden), xiii
Tennessee, 74–76, 94–95, 262–64, *265*, 273,
  437, 453n10
Tennessee River, 68, 74–77, 98, *265*, 266, 438
Tenskwatawa, Shawnee Prophet (*formerly*
  Laloeshiga, Lalawethika)
  Amherstburg council of 1808 and, 213–15
  Amherstburg residence by, after 1814,
    422–23
  appeal and popularity of, xii, xiv–xv,
    202–3, 251, 357

appearance and dress of, xii, 177, 424, 428–29
Badollet defends, to Gallatin, 259–60
Between-the-Logs and, 203, 382–83
birth and childhood of, as Laloeshiga, 23, 30, 38, 44–48
Black Hoof vs., 174, 179, 182, 202–3
Blue Jacket and, 174, 203
Brock's ruse and, 304–5
Brownstown council of 1810 and, 247–48
Brownstown council of 1813 and, 382–83
Cass allows return of, to Michigan, 423–27
Cass and, 456n34, 471n18
Cass aids resettlement of, in west, 427–29
Cass warrant for arrest and, 425
Clark and, 251
country of, 1774–94, 24
country of, 1811, 255
death of, 434–35
demonization of, xii
disciples of, 163, 191, 425–26
disciples required to make confessions, 178
double game of, with British and Americans, 192, 206, 224
early adulthood of, as Lalawethika, 46, 53–54, 58–60, 68, 72–74, 87, 105, 115–17, 122–23, 134–35, 145, 151–59. *See also* Lalawethika
Eckert biography of Tecumseh and, xiii
Edmunds biography of, xiv
Elliott's death and, 416
failure of medicine of, in old age, 433
father's death and, xv
food shortages and, 219–20, 355
Fort Malden, 1813, 358
Fort Meigs battle and, 359, 361, 363, 370, 371
Fort Wayne meeting of 1812 and, 346–47
Fort Wayne Treaty and, 229–34, 249
Great Wampum Belt and, 249
Greenville and, 182–83, 191
Greenville pilgrims and mission of, 157–58, 163–65, 169, 175–81

Greenville vacated by, for Prophetstown, 196, 200, 207
Greenville visit by Shakers and, 175–78
Harrison's council at Vincennes and, 242–43
Harrison's march vs. Prophetstown provoked by, 275–89, 299
Harrison suspicions and threats vs., 172–74, 192–97, 217–19, 223–26, 229, 231, 235–39, 247–48, 251–54
Hull and, 247–48
Indiana Territory and, desire to drive whites from, 303
Johnston as agent at Fort Wayne and, 225–26
Josephy biography on, xiii
Lake Erie winter of 1816–17 and, 426
Leather Lips's death and, 231
Le Maigouis as apostle of, 189–91
Little Turtle and, 225
Main Poc and, 205–6, 251
marriage to Gimewane, 153, 237, 245
Master of Life described by, 164
McArthur mission and, 192–97
medicine men and, 162
Mississinewa council of 1812 and, 303–7
myths and misperceptions about, xii–xiv
Naiwash schism and, 417–19
name changed from Lalawethika to Tenskwatawa, 159
New Madrid earthquake, 291–92
nickname Shawnee Prophet and, 159
Norton's camp on Grand River, after War of 1812, 417–19
oral history of, narrated to Trowbridge and, 428–29
pan-Indianism of, and religious underpinnings, xii–xiv
personality of, xii
portrait by James Otto Lewis, 428
portrait of, by Caitlin, 433–34
Prévost on, 412
Procter's retreat of 1813 and, 387–88, 390–91, 394–95, 396, 399–400, 412
Prophetstown and, rebuilt, 297, 298–300, 302–4, 307

Tenskwatawa, Shawnee Prophet (*formerly* Laloeshiga, Lalawethika) (*continued*)
   Prophetstown council of 1810 and, 232–34
   Prophetstown razing of 1812 and, 354–55
   Prophetstown reestablished by, in Kansas, 432–35
   removal of to Kansas of 1826–28, 429–33
   resettlement of, post–War of 1812, 420–21
   Roundhead and, 185, 203
   salt annuities confiscated by, 252–54, 257
   Shane and, 182–83, 191
   sins of children seven years old, 177–78
   solar eclipse (Black Sun) of 1806 and, 172–74
   spiritual doctrine described by, at Wapakoneta, 159–65
   spiritual doctrine of, and Faustian story of Lalawethika, 180–81
   spiritual doctrine of, and pan-Indianism, xiii–xiv
   spiritual doctrine of, and proselytizing, 250
   Spring Wells grand council of 1815 and, 421–22
   Spring Wells Treaty rejected by, 422
   Sugden on, xiii–xiv
   talent for prevarication, 346
   Tecumseh becomes spokesman for, 183–84
   Tecumseh elevated at expense of, xiii
   Tecumseh farewell by, after Fort Meigs battle, 371
   Tecumseh handles politics for, after Tippecanoe, 298
   Tecumseh's death and, 412–16
   Tecumseh's death and, aftermath despair over broken British promises, 416–20
   Tecumseh's relationship with, xiii–xiv, 358, 458n11
   Tecumseh's resistance plan supported by, 208, 210–11
   Tecumseh vs., on fraternizing with whites, 188
   Thames battle and, 404, 409
   Tiffin's overture to, with white wampum belt, 165–66

Tippecanoe battle and, 275–89, 295, 297–98
as transformative figure, xiv
Wapakoneta and Kirk success at, 202–3
War of 1812 and, 304, 312–13, 316–17, 322, 342, 346–51, 353–55, 371, 381
warriors mustered and threat posed by, xii
Wells, 179, 182–84, 191, 217–19
Wells dismissal from Fort Wayne and, 224–25
whites and, xii, 188
witches and witch hunts and, 161–69, 171–72
Tetapachsit, Delaware chief, 166–69
Thames (town), *393*
Thames, British Retreat on (October 1813), *393*, 394–98
   Battle (October 5, 1813), 400–412, *405*, 423
   Procter's court-martial and, 412
   Tecumseh and (October 3, 1813) council and anger about, 397–98
Thames River, *19, 24, 315,* 379, 386, 390–91, *393*
Thawekila Shawnee division, 23, 35, 45, 437
Theobald, Samuel, 407, 410
Three Fires Confederacy, 102, 110–14, 118, 203–4, 217, 230, 233, 439, 440
Tiffin, Edward, 145–46, 191, 193
   Greenville and, 165, 176
   Kenton council with Tecumseh and, 184–86
   Tenskwatawa witch hunts and, 172
Tiffin River, *360*
Tippecanoe, Battle of, xiii, xiv, 275–89, *285,* 295–302, 305–6, 311, 312, 330, 346, 354, 358, 417, 424
   confederacy fueled by anger at, 299–302
Tippecanoe River, *255*
   Mississinewa council 1812 and, 305–6
   Shawnee brothers move to, 209, 211, 220
   Shawnee brothers offered land near, by Main Poc, 205
   War of 1812 and, 351
Toledo, 118, 359
Tombigbee River, *265,* 266, 268–69
   Tecumseh's battle vs. Creek horse thieves at, 270
Tometah, Menominee chief, 246
Tories, 48–49, 58

Toussaint Creek, *360*
Treaty of Detroit
  (1802), *133*
  (1807), 202
Treaty of 1809, 322
Treaty of Fort Finney (1786), 63, 65, 450n20
  Brant's call to abrogate, 65
Treaty of Fort Harmar (1789), 79–80, 88, 102
Treaty of Fort Industry (1804), *133*
Treaty of Fort Pitt (1775), 25–26, 50
Treaty of Fort Stanwix, 445n8
  (1761), 20, 23
  (1768), 15, 16, *18*, *19*, 23
Treaty of Fort Vincennes
  (1803), *133*
  (1804), *133*
Treaty of Fort Wayne (1803), *133*, 144, 146
Treaty of Fort Wayne (1809), *133*, 225–35,
    242–44, 257, 346, 348
  land concessions, 182–83, 247–52, 346,
    348, 420
Treaty of Ghent (1814), 420
Treaty of Greenville (1795), 119–22, 127,
    140–42, 182, 185, 198–99, 322, 440
  Harrison's council of 1802 and, 140–42
  Tenskwatawa's renunciation of, 157–158
Treaty of Grouseland (1805), *133*
Treaty of Kaskaskia (1804), *133*
Treaty of Piankeshaw
  (1804), *133*
  (1805), *133*
Treaty of Spring Wells (1815), 422
Treaty of St. Louis (1804), *133*, 144, 222
Trowbridge, Charles C., 428–29
Trudelle's farm, *393*, 395
tuberculosis, 152
Tuckabatchee, *265*, 269–71, 278
Turtle Creek, 175, 178, 324
Tuscaroras, 439

umsomas (Shawnee patrilineal units), 35
Underwood, Joseph, 367, 369
United Indian Nations, 65
University of Michigania, 428
U.S. Army, 81, 129–30, 190, 304
  St. Clair leads vs. Northwestern
    confederacy, 81–82, 84–87
  reconstituted, to fight Indians, 101, 108
  War of 1812 and, 317–18, 322, 396, 410

U.S. Army First Infantry Regiment, 130
U.S. Army Fourth Infantry Regiment, 254,
    261, 277–78, 284, 330
  Tippecanoe and, 286, 330
  War of 1812 and, 330
U.S. Congress, 129–30, 258, 259, 296
  Harrison as delegate to, 131–32
  Public Land Law and, 132
  War of 1812 and, 304, 311–12, 314, 317–18
U.S. government grand council of August
    1815, 421
U.S. House of Representatives, 311
U.S. Navy, 318
U.S. Senate, 193

Van Horne, Thomas, 329–31
venereal diseases, 152
Verchères de Boucherville, Thomas, 384
Vermilion River, *255*
Vermont, *66*, 253
Viceroyalty of New Spain, 253
Vincennes, *18*, *24*, 72, 103, *133*, 134, 138–39, 144,
    211, 217–18, 224–25, 234–36, 239, 252–54,
    253, *255*, 261, *265*, 302–3, 322, 348, 351
  Harrison's council of 1802 at, 141
  New Madrid earthquake and, 291
  Tecumseh visit to Harrison at, 239–45
  Tecumseh visit to Harrison of July 1811,
    254–57
  Tecumseh visit to Harrison of 1812,
    298–99
  Tenskwatawa delegation of 1811, 277
Vincennes Western Sun, 241, 299
Virginia, 4, 12, 15, *24*, 25, 34, 59, *66*, 80, 107,
    108, 129, *253*, 263
Virginia militiamen, 3–7
Virginia Regulars, 58
Voegelin, Erminie, 445n14

Wabash Indians, 235, 243
Wabash River, *18*, *24*, 72, 85, *133*, 134, 199,
    205–11, 227–28, *255*, 345, 348, 355, 358,
    424, 439
Wabash Valley, 138, 247, 302–3, 305, 348
Wabaunsee, Potawatomi chief, 281
Wabelegunequa (Tecumseh's third wife),
    145, 208, 392
wabenos (sorcerers), 203–5, 207
Waggoner, John, 107–8

Wahsikegaboe (husband of Tecumpease),
    22, 46, 121, 392, 399, 404, 408
  death of, 408
  moves to Wabash River, 207
Wakatomica (village), 14, *24*, 57, 122, 126
Walk-in-the-Water, Wyandot chief, 215,
    320, 326–28, 331, 336–37, 369, 373, 383, 388,
    391–92, 397–98
wampum belts, 41. *See also* Great Wampum
    Belt
  black, 14, 114, 164, 314, 342
  British-Indian, cut, 387
  white wampum, 346
Wangomend, Delaware prophet, 154
Wapakoneta (town), *133*, 157, 193, 194, 196,
    209, 220, 252, 321, 369–70, 422, 425
  Black Hoof requests title to lands,
    141–42, 201–2
  council of 1805, 158–66
  death of Black Hoof and, 432
  Fort Wayne Treaty and, 230–31
  Kirk teaches farming skills at, 201–2, 209
  resettlement west of Mississippi and,
    426–27, 432
  salt annuities and, 252
  Shawnee brothers vs., 163, 174–75,
    200–201
  Springfield council and Boyer murder,
    186–87
  Tenskwatawa returns to, and removal to
    Kansas River, 429–32
  War of 1812 and, *360*, 369
Wapicomekoke (town)
  mystics in council house and, 150–51
  witch-hunters and executions at,
    165–69
Warburton, August, 387, 390–91, 395–98
Ward, Charles, 106
Ward, James, 186
Ward, John, 106, 186
Ward, William, 126–27, 186–87, 194
War Department, 81, 193, 210, 220, 224–25,
    261, 276, 349, 359, 413
War Hawks, 296–97, 304, 311, 318
War of 1812, 296–97, 311–412. *See also specific
    battles; individuals; and locations*
  British retreat on Thames River,
    392–95

  theater of operations, *360*
  Treaty of Ghent ends, 420
  war for Upper Canada and, 417–19
War of Independence, xiv
Warrow, Wyandot chief, 320
Washington, D.C., *253*
Washington, George, 4, 57
  Doughty peace mission, 76, 80
  Greenville Treaty and, 119
  Indian trading stations and, 138
  Iroquois and, 102
  Northwestern Confederacy and, 80–81
  Northwest Ordinance and, 65, 89
  Red Pole council and, 108
Water, Philemon, 59
Watts, John, Chickamauga chief, 95–101,
    453n10
Wayne, Anthony "Mad Anthony," 108–9,
    359
  Fallen Timbers and, 111–12, 114–16, 118,
    131, 238, 278
  Greenville Treaty and, 120–21, 127
  Harrison and, 130–31
Weas, *18*, 138, 242, 250–52, 349, 440
Wells, William
  death of, at Fort Dearborn, 342
  death of Little Turtle and, 320
  Fort Wayne Treaty and, 228–29, 249,
    252
  Greenville Treaty and, 120
  Harrison and, 137, 217–18, 228–29
  as Indian agent at Fort Wayne, 120,
    136–38, 168, 203
  Jefferson visit and, 219, 221
  Johnston vs., 137–38, 225, 249
  Kirk and, 201
  as Little Turtle's adoptee, 103, 136
  Main Poc and, 203, 206–7, 221
  Mississinewa council and, 305–6
  ouster of, as Indian agent, 224–25, 229
  Tecumseh vs., 137, 199–203, 214, 252
  Tenskwatawa at Greenville and, 174, 179,
    182–84, 191, 193–96, 199–203, 206–7
  Tenskwatawa at Prophetstown and,
    209–10, 217–18, 221, 224–25
  War of 1812 and, 320, 322, 342, 347–48
Wennebea, Sauk warrior, 223
Western Shawnee, *265*

Wheeling, 58
Whiteman, Benjamin, 184–85, 187
White River, *18*, *24*, 123–24, *133*, 135, 140–41,
  149–51, 154–57, 164–69, 172, *255*, 430
  Tecumseh's village on, *133*, 135, 140, 145,
  151
Whitewater River, *18*, 123
Whitley, William, 406, 407, 409
whooping cough, 219
Wildcat Creek, Shawnee brothers' town
  on, 298
Williams, General, 185
Williamson, Peter, 39
Willow Island, *362*
Wilson, Joseph, 95
Wilson, Walter, 254–56
Winamac, Potawatomi chief, 207, 211, 228
  Mississinewa council of 1812 and,
  305–6
  Tecumseh's council with Harrison at
  Vincennes and, 242–43
  Tenskwatawa's council of 1810 and, 233
  town of, 211, 224
Winchester, James, 356–57
Winnebagos, *18*, 180–81, 189, 195, 202, 217,
  222–24, 247, 249, *255*, 262, 277, 281–88,
  285, 299–300, 322, 331–32, 348, 351, 373,
  422, 440

Wisconsin, xi, 132, 180, 295, 439–40
Wisconsin River, *133*, *255*
witches and witchcraft, 30–31, 150–51,
  161–62, 165–68, 230, 231–32, 247,
  264–65
Witherell, James, 424
Wolf Tribe, 439
wolves, 52
Worthington, James, 197
Worthington, Mrs. Thomas, 197, 200
Worthington, Thomas, 194–97, 200
Wyandots, 17, *19*, 41, 50, 56–58, 63, 65, 73,
  79–81, 102, 108, 111, 115, 118, 120, 141, 149,
  151, 158, 170–71, 173, 178, 185–86, 195, 202,
  214–16, 220, 222, 230–32, 249, *255*, 278,
  281, 286, 299–300, 303–6, 314, *315*, 318,
  320, 326–32, 341, 352, *360*, 369–70, 381–83,
  388, 391–92, 395, 417, 422, 426, 428, 440,
  455n20

Xenia, Ohio, 445–46n14

Yorktown, British surrender at, *55*, 58
Young, Benjamin, 175–77

Ziegler, Jacob, 95
Ziegler girls, 95–96
Ziegler's Station attack, 95–96

ILLUSTRATION CREDITS

Battle of Point Pleasant: Virgil Lewis, *History of West Virginia*. New York: American Book Co., 1904

Shawnee warrior: *Battle Ready* by Doug Hall, oil on canvas, Courtesy of Doug Hall's Log Cabin Art Gallery and Studio, Neosho, Missouri

Shawnee warrior in tree: *A Closer Look* by Doug Hall, oil on canvas, Courtesy of Doug Hall's Log Cabin Art Gallery and Studio, Neosho, Missouri

Shawnee village: *Reconstruction of a Shawnee Village*, photograph, c. 1860–1920, Miriam and Ira D. Wallach Division of Art, Prints and Photographs, New York Public Library, no. 92318

Flatboat: *Century Magazine*, 1916

Red Coat—Shawnee Chief Tecumseh, by Doug Hall, oil on canvas, 2012, Courtesy of Doug Hall's Log Cabin Art Gallery and Studio, Neosho, Missouri

Simon Kenton: nineteenth-century steel engraving in author's possession

Dragoon charge: *The Charge of the Dragoons*, by R. F. Zogbraum, 1895, in *Harper's New Monthly Magazine*, 1896

William Henry Harrison by Rembrandt Peale: National Portrait Gallery, Smithsonian Institution, gift of Mrs. Herbert Lee Pratt, Jr., no. NPG.75.27

An Indian with His Squaw, print, 1810, Library and Archives Canada, C-014488

Edward Tiffin: *Governors of the Northwest Territory*, c. 1923 image in author's possession

Chillicothe courthouse: *American Pioneer*, January 1842

Tenskwatawa: *Prophet, Shawanese—Brother of Tecumsi* by Charles Bird King, oil on canvas, 1829, Gilcrease Museum, Tulsa, Oklahoma, acc. no. 01.1197

Black Hoof: *Ca-Ta-He-Cas-Sa, Black Hoof, principal chief of the Shawanees*, by Charles Bird King, oil on canvas, c. 1831, lithographic reproduction in Thomas McKenney and James Hall, *Indian Tribes of North America*. Philadelphia: E. C. Biddle, 1836

Wampum strings: Fort Malden National Historic Site, Parks Canada

Tecumseh: undated print, Library and Archives Canada, acc. no. 1997-481-5

Fort Wayne: *Old Fort Wayne*, by Carol M. Highsmith, photo, 2016, Carol M. Highsmith Archive. Library of Congress Prints and Photographs Division, LC-DIG-highsm-41291

Grouseland: vintage postcard in author's possession

Vincennes council: *Council of Vincennes*, print, 1851, Miriam and Ira D. Wallach Division of Arts, Prints and Photographs, New York Public Library, no. 808896

Fort Harrison: *Fort Harrison in 1812*, lithograph, 1848, Library of Congress Prints and Photograph Division, LC-DIG-pga-07680

Tippecanoe: *Battle of Tippecanoe* by Alonzo Chappell, steel engraving, 1859, in author's possession

William Hull: *General William Hull* by Gilbert Stuart, oil on canvas, 1823, National Portrait Gallery, Smithsonian Institution, no. NPG.84.177

Henry Procter: by John Forster, oil on canvas, c. 1970, Fort Malden National Historic Site, Parks Canada

Elliott's homestead: *Ruins of Old Elliott Homestead*, postcard, 1910, Southwestern Ontario Digital Archive, University of Windsor

Isaac Brock: *Sir Isaac Brock*, by John W. L. Forster, oil on canvas, c. 1900, Library and Archives Canada, acc. no. 1991-30-1

Brock and Tecumseh: *The Meeting of Brock and Tecumseh*, by C. W. Jeffreys, color drawing, in Ethel T. Raymond, *Tecumseh: A Chronicle of the Last Leader of His People*. Toronto: Glasgow, Brook & Co., 1915

Tecumseh; *Tecumseh*, by Keith Rocco, oil on board, 2018, Courtesy of Traditions Studios, Woodstock, Va.

Amherstburg: *View of Amherstburg in 1813*, by Catherine Margaret Reynolds, watercolor, 1813, Fort Malden National Historic Site, Parks Canada

Fort Meigs: *Fort Meigs, 1813*, by S. H. Phillips, drawing, 1913, Library of Congress Prints and Photograph Division, LC-USZ62-22182

Johnson's mounted riflemen: *"Remember the Raisin!"* by Ken Riley, c. 1965, print, National Guard Heritage series, U. S. Government Printing Office, 1983

Battle of the Thames: *Battle of the Thames*, by William Emmons, lithograph, 1833, Library of Congress Prints and Photograph Division, LC-DIG-pga-03613

Tecumseh at the Thames: C. W. Jefferys, *The Picture Gallery of Canadian History*, vol. 2. Toronto: Ryerson Press, 1945

Life into legend: carte-de-visite, 1866, in author's possession.

Indian delegation: *Deputation of Indians from the Mississippi Tribes to the Governor-General of British North America, Sir George Prévost*, watercolor, 1814, Library and Archives Canada, acc. no. 1989-264-1

Lewis Cass: engraving by T. B. Welch, 1833, in author's possession

Tenskwatawa: *Tens-Qua-Ta-Wa, the One That Opens the Door*, by J. O. Lewis, oil on canvas, 1824, lithographic reproduction in Thomas McKenney and James Hall, *Indian Tribes of North America*. Philadelphia: E. C. Biddle, 1836. Copy courtesy of McCracken Library, Buffalo Bill Center of the American West

Tenskwatawa: by Henry Inman, oil on canvas, c. 1830–33, National Portrait Gallery, Smithsonian Institution, NPG.82.71

Tenskwatawa, preliminary study: *Ten-sqat-a-way [sic], the Open Door, "Shawnee Prophet,"* by George Catlin, watercolor on paper, c. 1832, Gilcrease Museum, Tulsa, Oklahoma, acc. no. 02.1570

Tenskwatawa, formal portrait: *Tens-squat-a-way, the Open Door, Known as the Prophet,* by George Catlin, oil on canvas, 1832, Smithsonian American Art Museum, gift of Mrs. Joseph Harrison, Jr., 1985.66.279

Tenskwatawa and Shawnee Indians: *Shawano. 96. Lay-law-she-kaw (He who Goes up the River), an aged man, and Chief of the tribe: the rims of his ears curiously separated and elongated; 97. Kay-te-qua (the Female Eagle), daughter of the Chief; 98. Pah-te-coo-saw (the Open Door)*, by George Catlin, drawing, 1850, in Catlin, Souvenir of the North American Indians, N. p., 1850. New York Public Library Digital Collections, no. 466069, https://digitalcollections.nypl.org/items/510d47da-da5b-a3d9-e040-e00a18064a99

Peter Cozzens is the author or editor of seventeen acclaimed books on the American Civil War and the Indian Wars of the American West. In 2002 he was awarded the American Foreign Service Association's highest honor, the William R. Rivkin Award, given annually to one Foreign Service Officer for exemplary moral courage, integrity, and creative dissent. He lives with his wife, Antonia Feldman, in Kensington, Maryland.

A NOTE ON THE TYPE

This book was set in Janson, a typeface thought to have been made by the Dutchman Anton Janson, a typefounder in Leipzig during the years 1668–1687. However, it has been conclusively demonstrated that these types are the work of Nicholas Kis (1650–1702) who probably learned his trade from the master Dutch typefounder Dirk Voskens. The type is an example of the Dutch types that prevailed in England up to the time William Caslon (1692–1766) developed his own designs from them.

Composed by North Market Street Graphics, Lancaster, Pennsylvania

Printed and bound by Berryville Graphics, Berryville, Virginia

Designed by Maggie Hinders